Perspectives in Politics and Discourse

Discourse Approaches to Politics, Society and Culture (DAPSAC)

The editors invite contributions that investigate political, social and cultural processes from a linguistic/discourse-analytic point of view. The aim is to publish monographs and edited volumes which combine language-based approaches with disciplines concerned essentially with human interaction – disciplines such as political science, international relations, social psychology, social anthropology, sociology, economics, and gender studies.

General Editors

Ruth Wodak and Greg Myers
University of Lancaster

Editorial address: Lancaster University, County College South, Department of Linguistics and English Language, Lancaster LA1 4YL, UK.
r.wodak@lancaster.ac.uk and g.myers@lancaster.ac.uk

Advisory Board

Volume 36

Perspectives in Politics and Discourse
Edited by Urszula Okulska and Piotr Cap

Perspectives in Politics and Discourse

Edited by

Urszula Okulska
University of Warsaw

Piotr Cap
University of Łódź

John Benjamins Publishing Company

Amsterdam / Philadelphia

The paper used in this publication meets the minimum requirements of
American National Standard for Information Sciences – Permanence of
Paper for Printed Library Materials, ANSI z39.48-1984.

Library of Congress Cataloging-in-Publication Data

Perspectives in politics and discourse / edited by Urszula Okulska and Piotr Cap.
    p.   cm. (Discourse Approaches to Politics, Society and Culture, ISSN 1569-9463 ; v. 36)
Includes bibliographical references and index.
1. Communication in politics. 2. Communication--Political aspects. 3. Political participa-
        tion. I. Okulska, Urszula. II. Cap, Piotr.
JA85.P47   2010
320.01'4--dc22   2010006947
ISBN 978 90 272 0627 5   (Hb ; alk. paper)
ISBN 978 90 272 8821 9   (Eb)

John Benjamins Publishing Co. · P.O. Box 36224 · 1020 ME Amsterdam · The Netherlands
John Benjamins North America · P.O. Box 27519 · Philadelphia PA 19118-0519 · USA

Table of contents

Acknowledgements

The editors wish to thank Dr. Joanna Nijakowska (University of Łódź) for her technical assistance in preparing the volume for publication.

PART I

Introduction

CHAPTER 1

Analysis of Political Discourse
Landmarks, challenges and prospects

Urszula Okulska and Piotr Cap

1. **From Political Linguistics to Analysis of Political Discourse**

The last couple of decades have seen Political Linguistics (PL) develop into a uniquely *heterogeneous* and *fragmented* domain. It is also, as of today, a rather 'magnetic' field, given how readily it gets informed by neighboring disciplines. This characterization applies equally to PL's conceptual groundwork, its methodology and the major themes and topics investigated. Some terminological liberalism is a factor here: while scholars contribute their own developments at the level of dialogue between PL and the related disciplines,[1] they tend to agree on the broad definition of PL as an area encompassing studies of language in mainly (but not exclusively) political settings (viz. 'language and[/in/of] politics') complemented by research on power positions and social perceptions of languages as means of struggle for cultural/communal superiority and dominance (viz. 'language politics' – see Blommaert 1997). This volume presents recent investigations in the vast and heterogeneous territory of PL, subsuming and structuring its theoretical concepts, thematic ranges, and methodological devices into combined and coherent Analysis of Political Discourse (APD).[2] The collection arises from a clear need to systematize the research stage and methods of investigation since, in its thematic and descriptive orientation, APD inherits from PL the underspecified meaning of virtually any practice of analyzing language and language matters in broadly understood political, official and institutional contexts. They all share their

---

1.   For instance, there are attempts to define – viz. Hodges and Nilep (2007) – how much of the territory of PL lends itself to 'critical' discourse analytic approaches and how much is rigidly a 'political' ground.

2.   We find the term Analysis of Political Discourse (APD) clearer and more scientifically objective than 'Political Discourse Analysis' (PDA), which has been used in the literature on several occasions (cf., e.g., Hodges and Nilep 2007). In contrast to PDA, APD entails no ambiguity resulting from its possible interpretation as an ideologically motivated enterprise. Furthermore, our term and its acronym make no collision with PDA standing for 'Positive Discourse Analysis' in works by Martin and others (cf., e.g., Martin and Rose 2003).

common characteristic of triggering power differential in social interaction, which forces individuals or groups to take competing or conflicting positions in linguistic communication. Thus, APD accommodates, indiscriminately, socially oriented studies of *polity* and/or *policies*, located at the intersection of political/public discourse and political/social institutions (cf., e.g., Hodge and Kress 1993; Watts [1996] 2005), and studies conducted within the Critical Discourse Analysis paradigm with emphasis on *politics*, i.e. strategies of running the political contest of gaining and maintaining power (cf., e.g., Fairclough 1995; van Dijk 1998; Chilton and Schäffner 2002). Furthermore, gathering, exploiting and expanding all PL's frameworks, APD integrates theory-driven approaches that draw on cognitive insights but remain fairly critical in data presentation (e.g., Lakoff 1996; Chilton 2004), with works that reflect, generally, a growing cross-fertilization of ideas from cognitive science, social communication and the evolution of language and the political mind-set (cf., e.g., Dirven at al. 2001). Regarding the topics, the plethora of choices for researchers is also quite extensive. Considered 'political' within APD are at the same time studies on violence and war, on social identity construction, on migration, racism, and nationalism. Moreover, the label also embraces investigations into state-governed procedures, such as elections and referenda, language planning and standardization, as well as research into operations within/among state-promoted/controlled systems, including public institutions, education, the media, and many more. As evidenced by this ultra-short sketch, there cannot possibly be a single theory or methodology suiting the range of APD.

As a result, it is often the case that contributions to the APD literature are, as has been mentioned before, not so much an attempt to redefine the basic concept(s) of political discourse, but to appropriate some extra theoretical tools to set up a methodological dialogue with the existing procedural resources within PL, so that new themes and topics could be analyzed from a more complex perspective. A classic example of such a dialogue is the relationship between PL and Critical Linguistics (CL, cf., e.g., Fowler et al. 1979), Systemic Functional Linguistics (SFL, cf., e.g., Halliday 1985) and, most recently, Critical Discourse Analysis (CDA, cf., e.g., Wodak and Chilton 2005). It can be said, in a nutshell, that critical scholarship (whether under the label of CL, SFL or CDA), provides PL/APD with important insights into the ways of analyzing, via discourse, the existing wrongs in a society, in an effort to contribute to social change (cf., e.g., Fairclough and Wodak 1997; Lassen, Strunck and Vestergaard 2006; etc.). In so doing, it not only echoes the Bakhtinian (1981, 1986) idea that language is never neutral as perceived from any *current* perspective, but also corroborates the status of APD as a bound set of PL approaches with a both *retrospective* and *prospective* focus of attention. APD, like discourse analysis in general, does more than merely reflect events which take place in the world; it interprets these events and formulates understandings, thus contributing to the constitution of a new reality.[3]

---

3.   This orientation has nothing to do with 'negative discourse analysis' or 'exclusionary criticism' of/in some political cultures (cf. Wodak and Chilton 2005: xvi). Critical scholarship, as a product

The consequences of placing political language under the lens of critical research are far-reaching. First of all, the implementation of critical approaches into APD means that the latter gets indirectly informed by the conceptual groundworks that critical scholarship has borrowed from yet other disciplines. For example the bi-directional, retrospective and prospective orientation of critical studies bridges APD with early developments in linguistic pragmatics, especially as far as the relationship between the 'word' (i.e. language) and the 'world' (i.e. reality) is concerned (cf., e.g., Searle 1979). Accordingly, APD receives some extra conceptual tools to assess the power of *speech acts*, which at the same time inscribe into the pre-existing reality and affect the course of affairs in a new reality, after a given act has been successfully performed. And since such considerations inevitably address the pragmatic phenomena of interpersonal distance, power, directness, indirectness, etc., then the micro-level concepts that can account for them (e.g., deixis, implicature, presupposition, etc.) join the APD apparatus as well.

Secondly, the APD adoption of the critical stance means subscribing to a careful analysis of empirical data coming from the world under study and, importantly enough, acknowledging the status of the analyst as an active part of this world. This, of course, raises the question of objectivity, selectivity and interpretation of data, so that the study remains methodologically sound and descriptively plausible. Chilton (2007) suggests two ways in which the analyst can handle this problem. One way is to overtly acknowledge a political or ethical bias in data selection, interpretation and critical assessment. In this way, the analyst seems to contribute one standpoint in relation to a widely discussed problem, and the 'objectivity' arises from comparison of the converging standpoints within a multitude of contributions. It seems, however, that such an approach detracts from the analyst's capacity to give the ultimate verdict, without resorting to peer analyses. The other way, Chilton argues, is to propose a methodological separation between two analytic phases, "one phase establishing data and describing textual features with minimal selectivity, a second phase acknowledging hermeneutic commitment on the part of the analyst" (2007: 298).

The latter approach, while definitely ascribing more weight to an individual analytic endeavor, falls still short of providing a recipe for the avoidance of subjectivity, which will characterize, essentially, any study where the analyst belongs to the discourse stage (cf. Langacker 2001) no less than the data s/he describes – of course, the natural presumption obtains that s/he possesses different degrees of expert knowledge and familiarity with different areas of the stage. In APD the whole problem is especially acute as broadly 'political' processes (not to mention wars and other manifestations of conflict) tend to affect large groups of people, who are often of different opinions and perspectives depending on where they live. Since, as Hodges and Nilep (2007)

---

of Western culture, is anchored in the idea of critique as 'rational judgment' and thus draws, more or less directly, from biblical criticism, the critical philosophy of Kant, the Frankfurt School of critical social theory, etc. Of course, in so doing, it addresses a number of social and political phenomena commonly perceived as 'negative': nationalism, xenophobia, racism, and so on.

admit, the majority of political discourse analysts live in urban, Western settings, the talk and practices of people in highly dissimilar settings may be even more opaque from the point of view of discourse analysis. Just take the hostile reactions to President Bush's misfortunate use of the word *crusade* during the announcement of the war-on-terror. Many APD analysts would consider it a plain word-choice mistake, but to the Arab population occupying exactly the part of the discourse stage which was referred to, the force of the expression was incomparably bigger (cf. Stoltz 2007).

Just as the bi-directionality of critical approaches (as well as their natural focus on issues such as manipulation, social inequality, power relations, etc.) causes that APD comes in contact with linguistic pragmatics, the problems with the objectivity of analysis invite a turn to ethnography. The APD tools can study the function of discourses produced at, e.g., institutional and media levels, yet for an ultimate verification of findings they still rely on the access to individual recipients of these discourses (cf. van Leeuwen 2005). An excellent argument in favor of ethnography as an accompaniment to APD approaches comes from Hodges and Nilep (2007):

> [Political] discourse analysis can analyze presidential speeches and examine the language circulated among the media, but what are the reactions of an undecided voter in Ohio before the 2004 US presidential election? What does a soccer mom shopping at Wal-Mart really think about 9/11? What effect – if any – do the pronouncements of a member of parliament in Berlin have on a college student in Munich? These are all questions that discourse analysis cannot answer alone and require ethnography to illuminate (Hodges and Nilep 2007: 10–11).

All the foregoing discussion points to a natural heterogeneity of APD as a collection of PL analytical devices, which continually attracts a number of neighboring approaches, thus implementing a wealth of research tools utilized by them. The central question that arises is whether, given the pace of such a 'snowball effect', there is still a room for considering what is stable in the APD apparatus and scope, and what kind of systematization *is* possible – for the benefit of publication projects such as this one. And, speaking of a dissemination of knowledge, a by-question follows: how does the APD eclecticism impact its explanatory power?

Regarding systematization, any attempt at framing similar theories, methodologies or themes, must respond to a conception of 'political discourse' that acknowledges its existing points of contact with other disciplines and their study fields, as evidenced above. Such a comprehensive view of political discourse involves not only its institutionalized aspects but virtually any kind of human communication whose objective is to pursue a variety of discourse goals in different (power-marked) social relations and configurations; or, to promote and govern language attitudes forming a basis for societal developments and changes. It is only from this standpoint that we can move to some further specifications of focus, which usually lead to the already mentioned distinction between research in the *language of politics*, originally understood (to rephrase it once more in Davies' words [1994: 3212]) as "the [...] rhetoric of political activities and of politicians acting in their political capacity," and the *politics of language* – understood as "policies and decisions about official and standard languages, language planning, language academies, and educational language policies" (cf. also Blommaert 1997). At a yet lower level, both language of politics and politics of language can be viewed as manifesting, in different discourses, different degrees of input of polity, policy and politics (see above and also Fairclough 2006b), all of which acquire from the vantage point of APD a much broader than strictly political sense, traditionally attached to them (also in PL). They can, for instance, be analyzed in ontological terms, involving questions, such as, e.g., what concepts, labels, etiquettes are available to broadly 'political' (viz. socially competing or unequal) actors to handle a broadly 'political' (viz. power-infused/snatched) interaction, as well as in performative terms, involving problems such as, e.g., how and through what channels can 'political' actors communicate meanings salient in these concepts, for the maximum of their 'political' (viz. socially or institutionally beneficial) interests.

The above breakdown, largely thematic as such, entails the use of different theories and methodologies at different levels of description, but it can also serve as a structural basis for illustration of those theoretical models which could be applied at more than one level, thus extracting the concepts and terminologies whose explanatory power in APD is the greatest. For instance, while corpus analysis, with all its conceptual apparatus, seems confined to any pre-set stage (a pilot analysis, verification, illustration, etc.) of a quantitatively oriented study, the explanatory power of some cognitive and pragmatic concepts is much broader. One can imagine, e.g., the contemporary theory of metaphor (cf. Chilton 1996; Chilton and Lakoff 1995, etc.) as a viable tool to study political discourse at the levels of conceptual labeling, lexical constructs, their manipulative force, etc., but also at the uppermost level of framing entire discourses, be them the ones enacting the 'language of politics' or the 'politics of language' (see the final chapter in this volume). As a result, APD suffers from an unequal input of explanatory power provided by different concepts in the study of different discourses. The analyses of some discourses, like those involving metaphorization, can be blends of different approaches (e.g., pragmalinguistic, cognitive, lexical, etc.) collectively generating a multitude of observations from different angles of description, while in the case of other discourses (viz. Bastow's study of binomials in this volume or virtually any study focusing on individual language forms), conclusions are drawn from much narrower descriptions. This of course raises questions about maintaining a sound balance between the analytic coherence and evidentiality, an aspiration which often simply has to be surrendered, given a specific discourse type.

2.   The aims of this book

In view of the thematic and descriptive diversity of Political Linguistics and the resulting methodological heterogeneity of APD, our collection does not aspire to offer one single controlling parameter or a dominant theme of analysis. Instead, the volume responds to several most important characteristics of PL by subsuming, organizing, testing and developing them in the practice of APD. Given what has been said about APD and its relations to PL in the preceding section, the content and arrangement of the articles aim to reconcile the goal to give a structured, state-of-the-art thematic and methodological picture of the field, with the endeavor to provide an organized account of relativities and gaps, thus favoring (and proposing, in some chapters) further research in specific directions (a thematic direction promising the most in theoretical and methodological terms will be proposed in the chapter concluding the collection). From a more detailed perspective, the most important features and sub-traits of the present volume come under the following three headings:

Comprehesiveness. In general, none of the chapters loses sight of the assumption that language, daily social behavior and institutionalized (political) actions are closely intertwined, though, of course, different texts show different degrees of this micro-macro relationship. As a collection, they reflect the diversity of APD approaches making up the scene of contemporary PL. They involve the top-down and bottom-up procedures (viz., e.g., Janoschka vs. Moir), quantitative (Bastow) and qualitative (El-Hussari) methods, synchronic and diachronic accounts (Magistro vs. Okulska), critical and theoretical standpoints (Fraser vs. Cap), all applied against a wealth of empirical material drawn from both contemporary and historical discourses (reaching as far back as the Middle Ages, e.g., in Musolff's and Okulska's chapters) occurring in diverse geographical and geopolitical locations (America, EU countries, the Middle East, Eastern Europe, the Caribbean). As can be guessed from the above pairings, sometimes the chapters which share common thematic properties, apply different methodologies. The idea of having them, as if, 'compete' against each other, is that the reader receives insight in how similar data lend themselves to different (often conflicting) theoretical accounts. An example of such a competition is the argument in the first three chapters of the volume (Musolff, Skinner and Squillacote, Chovanec), which invites the reader to judge explanatory power of cognitive versus pragmatic/critical approaches to the analysis of political metaphor. Furthermore, responding to the characterization of PL as a 'magnetic' field of investigation, one which continually attracts contributions from the neighboring disciplines, chapters such as those by Cap or by El-Hussari show the points of contact between APD and CDA as well as other critical approaches. How APD gets informed by advances in ethnography can in turn be seen from the chapter by Bilewicz and Bocheńska. This of course is just a sample description of where and how the volume points to the methodological, theoretical and thematic heterogeneity of APD (with all the good and bad sides to it), a richer account being the overview of the consecutive texts, which follows towards the end of this introduction.

Structural rigor... While recognizing the plurality of approaches contributing to the PL (and thus also APD) scene as described earlier, the book aims to show that there *are* ways in which studies in political discourse can be systematized and that such a systematization is not only a reader-friendly characteristic of an edited collection, but it can effectively stimulate more organized research, both within and across the areas distinguished. Thus, within the following four parts of the book, Parts II-IV document research in the *language of politics*, and Part V includes texts concerning the *politics of language* – vide the earlier observations on (the prospects for) the systematization of the PL scene. Further in line with these observations, the three parts dealing with the language of politics differ in focus on what has been referred to as the ontological vs. performative ingredients of political discourse. The consecutive chapters take on the conceptual aspects of PL first, before the focus moves over to the social and institutional settings. Such an arrangement can be read as a link between what the current PL scene offers in terms of its (unrealized) potential for systematization and how the present book intends to exploit it. In a nutshell, it can be said that all the texts in the language of politics tradition in this volume discuss, from the multicultural and multilinguistic perspectives, the recent as well as historical communicative phenomena that evidence the rise and functioning of viable gambits in political rhetoric. More specifically, Part II focuses on their cognitive grounding vis-à-vis diversified realizations at the text macro- and micro-structural levels, Part III critically inspects their persuasive and manipulative forces, and Part IV investigates the media channels of their transmission. In other words, Parts II-IV reconcile the various avenues of research in discourse labeling, power and mediatization, by raising three basic questions which stimulate *a continual extension of the PL/APD scope* (see also the discussion of hierarchization in the concluding chapter). The questions are: i) what conceptualizations take place on the stage of political discourse which could be utilized as cognitive triggers for accomplishing discourse goals; ii) how to assist the accomplishment of these goals with the corresponding pragmalinguistic input reflecting the conceptualizations; iii) how to communicate the thus-arising rhetoric through channels that would ensure the maximum range of acceptance of the discourse goals by the audience.

    ... and economy of argument. The research in the *politics of language* has been captured in one part of the book only (Part V), and there are reasons. First of all, looking at the PL publication market, there are currently fewer works following this tradition than those dealing with a linguistic enactment of political goals – even though such a trend might change in the future (cf. Joseph 2004). Second, the focus of the subfield is essentially broad as what is often addressed is *institutional policies* which usually affect large social groups or even entire nations. From a methodological standpoint, this means the analyst's adoption of specific tools to account for the implementation and effects of institutional policies, and it seems to be the case (cf. Joseph 2004) that these tools are relatively set as regards their conceptual origin. Unlike the analysis of the language of politics, which evinces observable degrees of dialogue between, e.g., cognitive and pragmalinguistic strands, the analysis of the politics of language often maintains the same ratio of contributions from discourse research, sociolinguistics, culture studies, ethnography and other disciplines. In fact, the papers in Part V all respond to the overarching question of the politics of language choice, in the era of global multilingualism and multiculturalism on the one hand (cf. Duszak and Okulska

2004; Fairclough 2006a; Monaghan and Goodman 2007), and in contexts of linguistic imperialism and hegemony on the other (cf. Skutnabb-Kangas 1988; Phillipson 1992). Attention is consistently drawn to some specific multiglossic situations where institutional measures are being taken, first, to reduce a status imbalance between official and minority languages, and, second, to regularize (and hence also raise social consciousness of) the usage of individual languages that can be a source of prejudice and discrimination. In terms of the former, the chapters in Part V contend against the monolingual norm in education (cf. Skutnabb-Kangas 1988; Phillipson and Skutnabb-Kangas 1994) by discussing alternative policies and innovative programs of bilingual schooling for minority speakers. In terms of the latter, they uncover socio-cognitive and communicative mechanisms of racial prejudice, which may, in turn, explain regulatory processes underlying the choice of strategies of political correctness. On a more programmatic note, all chapters in Part V encourage further research in language policies as a way to contribute to shaping social relations. This opens up interesting – and yet to be explored – vistas for reconciling the *language of politics* and *politics of language* traditions under a common, critical umbrella. Last but not least, the content of Part V makes a direct, one-to-one contact with the complex issue of mediatization, which characterizes Part IV. So, while the relation holding between Part V and all preceding parts might suggest some unbalance notwithstanding the reasons given, the relation between Part V (dealing with the politics of language in potentially mediatized contexts) and Part IV (essentializing the potential of the language of politics when mediatized), is clearly balanced and this kind of balance is nothing but intentional. Namely, as will be pointed out in the final chapter, the mediatization perspective could eventually add to the coherence of the PL field as a whole. Thus far, the 'coherence' has been often defined (and searched for) through little more than the analytic consistency in duly representing the diversity of themes and theoretical standpoints.

3.   Overview of the chapters

In this section we shall take a closer look at the particular chapters in **Parts II–V** of the book. In addition to describing their thematic focus as well as theoretical orientation, we shall also point to how they inscribe in the existing body of research within the respective domains. As has been mentioned before, the texts in **Part II** concentrate upon the cognitive groundwork of political discourse and its macro-textual and micro-structural manifestations. They explore the conceptualizing and ordering powers of selected stylistic tools for naming and classifying political standpoints, problems and behaviors (cf. Edelman 1977). Focusing on traditional figures of political rhetoric, they present discourse-historical as well as current approaches to rhetorical tropes (e.g., Reisigl 2006), by which they contribute to classical and more recent research into metaphor (e.g., Howe 1988; Denton and Woodward 1990; Lakoff 1991, 1992; Chilton and Ilyin 1993; Chilton and Lakoff 1995; Schäffner 1995; Chilton 1996; Semino and

Masci 1996; Böke 1997; Musolff 2000, 2004; Taverniers [2002] 2005; El Refaie 2001; Panagl and Stürmer 2002; Goatly 2007; Scheithauer 2007; Falkowska 2008; etc.) and naming/labeling conventions in political discourse (e.g., Lee and Lee 1939; Wilson 1990; Zernicke 1990; Pratkanis and Aronson 2001; Fritz, Keefer and Nyhan 2004; Pisarek 2007). Accordingly, in the opening chapter **Andreas Musolff** illustrates the way political thought and expression have teemed for centuries with *body politic* metaphors (cf. also Chilton 1994), and the way body-related source concepts have productively served in the perception and metaphorical conceptualization of socio-political realities since the Middle Ages until today. Starting from John of Salisbury's body-state analogies in his portrayal of social hierarchy, and proceeding through Niccolò Machiavelli's and Thomas Hobbes' early modern notions of *body illness* (and *therapy*), encapsulating state and political crises (and their solutions), the chapter reaches its culminating point with 20th-century theoretical explorations of the classical body-state image by German political philosophers. In this light it discusses the pseudo-scientific interpretation of the concept by the Nazis, who made it a blueprint for their genocide and 'race hygiene' ideology. Similar conceptualizations of political problems by body-related metaphors, though this time in 21st-century political rhetoric, are referred to by **Dan Skinner and Rosa Squillacote** in their text on the metaphorical framing of the War-on-Terror. It is argued that these metaphors are enabled and sustained by a problematic conceptualization of the body (dating back to the 'scientific revolution' of the 17th century) that snatches the image of the world with such binary qualities as, for instance, 'cleanliness/dirtiness' and 'sickness/health'. The problem of the new concepts emerging from the original trope is that they themselves evoke new metaphors which convey a picture of a boundary-delineated (viz. anti-democratic) state with a body-constrained vision of its politics. The authors thus suggest retooling the primary metaphor or abandoning it completely for the sake of developing democratic rhetoric and implementing it into public debate. In so doing, they step beyond the traditional approaches to metaphor, encouraging a reconciliation of the cognitive-pragmatic research, with CDA and ethical mindsets.

Strategies of metaphorical framing in political rhetoric are also undertaken by **Jan Chovanec**, who demonstrates how an image of a political actor can be negatively skewed in media discourse through the use of referential and predicative markers. It turns out that the 'dehumanizing/animalizing' meaning of the stereotype-laden descriptive label *le worm*, used in reference to Jacques Chirac, was not only well able to underline the French president's adversarial position with respect to the 2003 military intervention in Iraq, but it also managed to present the French (as a group) as outside players in the political game. The polarization effect that the device helped to achieve corroborates strong manipulative force and rhetorical efficiency of negative labeling in political discourse. Finally, the rhetorical tropes of naming are tackled from a more general perspective by **Katarzyna Molek-Kozakowska**, who demonstrates their classifying and persuasive functions in a wide range of web-based media sources. Official government statements, mainstream political reports and popular political editorials studied in the chapter reveal how labels can effectively mask offensive meanings with euphemisms, legitimize official policies by simplifying complex and equivocal issues, and function as insults discrediting political opponents.

In **Part III**, the focus moves from the upper level of conceptualizations and framing, down to their actual realizations in language forms which are supposed to bring about concrete persuasive and manipulative effects in political-institutional communication. Thus, in line with the earlier remark about the natural relationship holding between PL/APD and critical scholarship (viz. discussion of *the PL scene*), the contributions often connect with previous work within the CL, SFL and CDA fields (cf., e.g., Fairclough 1989, 1995; Caldas-Coulthard and Coulthard 1996; Fairclough and Wodak 1997; Chouliaraki and Fairclough 1999; Wodak and Ludwig 1999; Wodak and Meyer 2001; Weiss and Wodak 2003; Wodak and Chilton 2005, etc.). They additionally show how critical theory and methodology can be extended to synchronic and diachronic, qualitative and quantitative corpus studies of public communication. With their focus on the discursive expression of the US policy in Iraq, the first two chapters make a bridge with the volume's previous part in that they screen, by means of the CDA approach, the use of manipulative techniques by politicians at the moment of a political crisis (cf. also Triandafyllidou, Wodak and Krzyżanowski eds. 2009). In the introductory text, which explores President Bush's address to the nation (and thus contributes to research on political speeches – cf., e.g., Schäffner 1997; Sauer 2002; Fairclough 2000; Muntigl 2002; Graham, Keenan and Dowd 2004; Dedaić 2006, etc.), **Ibrahim A. El-Hussari** shows how the politician adroitly constructs and imposes a version of reality that favors his own (hidden) plans in the eyes of different addressee groups. It is argued that Bush does it by 'manufacturing consent' with the public on the one hand, and with the state's lawmakers on the other. This helps him, first, take away much of his responsibility, and, second, sustain his positive self-image, both effects enabling him to proceed smoothly according to his agendas. In the second chapter, **Piotr Cap** implements his critically oriented *proximization* model to the American interventionist discourse, in order to trace legitimization effects in the US rhetoric in the Iraq war. By discussing spatial, temporal and axiological aspects of the proximization framework, he demonstrates how a gradual loss of the material premise for the military intervention (i.e. the alleged possession of weapons of mass destruction by the Iraqi regime) has necessitated a rhetorical switch to a more universal, ideological rationale.

The qualitative stance of the two introductory chapters is complemented by a corpus-based variationist perspective of the third text. **Tony Bastow's** study of a one-million-word corpus of the US Department of Defense speeches discusses stylistic trimmings of political oratory and of the US defense rhetoric alike, in terms of the use of binomial phrases. Aside the rhetorical value of binomials' modifying structures and of their semantic blurring capacity, the research demonstrates how context-driven findings within CDA (which largely rely on intuitive judgments) can effectively be verified, and thus placed on a firmer footing, by quantitative analytical methods. The remaining two chapters in the section shift the focus of the critical inspection to selected contemporary as well as historical aspects of institutional communication. From the synchronic perspective, **Elena Magistro** studies the phenomenon of the *marketization* of the EU discourse on the example of EU-authored employment policy documents, thus extending research into the EU (un)employment discourses and policy-making (cf. Muntigl, Weiss and Wodak 2000; Muntigl 2002). As is shown, the texts adopt a business-typical stance in institution/employer–job applicants communication, which is a consequence of equating the status of the citizen with that of the consumer. The abundance of promotional and advertising traits in the discourse of the EU recruit-ment procedures and career descriptions points to language change in progress to-wards the *conversationalization* of the EU genres and their general divergence from the institutionally accepted professional style. From the diachronic perspective, which draws upon earlier (critical) discourse-historical studies (e.g., Maas 1984; Ehlich 1989; Wodak et al. 1990, 1994, 1999; Martin and Wodak 2003; Wodak and Weiss 2004; Heer et al. 2008), **Urszula Okulska** explores the process of constructing the world of politics in Late Middle and Early Modern England through the social practice of letter writing in 15–17th-century institutions. Analyzing official correspondence from a wide range of politically oriented public domains, she uncovers (on the basis of data from the *Helsinki Corpus of English Texts* and *Corpus of Early English Correspondence*) discourse strategies of building networks of social relations in institutional fields that arranged forms of early English political life, and thus made the country's history in the period under scrutiny.

Part IV sketches processes of political communication through the lens of the 'mediatized politics' of the printed and broadcast media (cf., e.g., Fairclough 1995; Fetzer and Lauerbach 2007; Triandafyllidou, Wodak and Krzyżanowski eds. 2009), and demonstrates how the general order of political discourse is globally constructed through developments of specific generic links in chains of mediatized interactive en-counters. In the opening chapter **Bruce Fraser** concentrates on various acts of hedging in diversified media events of the US politics. A closer insight into speeches, conversa-tions and press conferences of the Bush administration allows to explain reasons for employing and avoiding particular types of hedges by American politicians. It addi-tionally reveals that the kind of facework associated with hedging and applied by poli-ticians in their discourse plays, ironically, little or no role in political rhetoric. The next text, by **Anja Janoschka**, continues the topic of building self-images by politicians, directing the discussion's focal point to the electronic channel of public communica-tion. Presenting the political blog as an effective means of circulating propaganda mes-sages, the study locates the genre among most potent interactive tools of contempo-rary political e-advertising and persuasion.

The 'top-down' perspective of the two chapters above (which takes politicians as a party initiating the communication process) is reverted to the 'bottom-up' stance (cf. Wodak and de Cillia 2006) in the next contribution, by **James Moir**, which departs from voters' reactions to politicians' undertakings to scrutinize their discursive echoing in the media. The mediatized discourse of public opinion – it is argued – is in itself ideological, since it presents a defaced image of people, who 'do think' and are 'concerned' about political matters, and thus crave for information on what others think about these issues. As a consequence, the weight of political facts can be reduced to individual opinionation only, which in turn may straightjacket the way people approach such matters in terms of short-term reactions to political problems. The last two chapters in the section, by **Christina Schäffner** and **Natalia Kovalyova**, underline the informative role of the mass media in 'mediating' politics cross-culturally – respectively – through translation, which recontextualizes original textual renditions of political events to adjust them to new cultural settings, and through journalistic practices, which (re)construct political reality textually, filtering it through the prism of carefully devised generic frames. Accordingly, Schäffner discusses examples of text transformations that occur as a result of journalistic translations of media reports. The questions posed relate to the values of news journalism that may guide the choice of translation procedures, and to institutional profiles of news agencies that may impose or determine the selection of specific recontextualization strategies. Kovalyova, in turn, demonstrates how a journalistic genre can assign a media-desirable status to a political event to make it a culturally universal newsworthy product, easily sellable to the international public. Taking on the case of the 2004 Orange Revolution in the Ukraine and its coverage by the Western press, she shows how the generic frame of the news report textually transforms a pre-election unrest into a political revolution (this is where the text also makes a point of reference to the topics of political crises in Part II), adjusting its scenario to the expectations of media recipients. The medial agitation around the events demonstrates the longing for accounts of spectacular revolutions and social transformations that are textually conveyed through the frame of a new grand narrative.

Finally, the chapters in **Part V**, which fall into the 'politics of language' branch of PL research, cater to the often neglected areas of the field that confront cases of discursive and political violation of 'linguistic human rights' (cf. Skutnabb-Kangas and Phillipson 1989, 1995; Anthonissen and Blommaert 2007). They shed new light on policies of language planning in contexts of societal multilingualism, propose systemic solutions to problems of discriminating minority languages and cultures in educational settings, and investigate processes of accommodating social prejudice through language. The first three contributions report on institutional endeavors in Europe and America to ensure ethnic minorities educational attainment and social integration through the reinforcement of their mother tongues in bilingual schooling. **Adrian Blackledge** concentrates on attitudes that students, parents, administrators, and teachers in English complementary schools have towards the use and visibility of minority languages. He probes specifically Bengali schools in Birmingham to observe how students' and teachers' linguistic practices work to negotiate young people's multilingual and multicultural identities. In the next chapter, **Carol Pfaff** provides an example of Germany, where aside the policy of speaking the official language as a requirement for naturalization and continued residence, provisions are made (as a response to the country's growing linguistic diversity, due to immigration from Eastern Europe) for education in languages other than German. Similarly, **Bruce Johnson-Beykont and Zeynep Beykont** pronounce the need for enriching a bilingual Spanish-English preschool program for Puerto Rican children in the US, so as to ensure the speakers full cognitive and social development, and prepare them for academic challenges of American schools. By indicating positive effects of plurilingual education on the symbiosis between linguistic communities, both these contributions are voices against policies of *linguicism* (cf. Skutnabb-Kangas 1988; Canagarajah 1999, etc.) and, what follows, against the subtractive approach to minority languages that these policies promote within the monolingual norm (cf., e.g., Lambert 1975). The last chapter in Part V, by **Michał Bilewicz and Agnieszka Bocheńska**, touches upon another aspect of violating linguistic human rights, namely discrimination practices, which – as Reisigl and Wodak (2001: 1) claim – "are prepared, promulgated and legitimized" by means of discourse. The core issue of the study, racial prejudice (see also van Dijk 1991, 1992, 1993, 2005), is tested in the Polish-French bilingual groups, against its cognitive and affective components. The implications that the research conveys, that people accommodate more the affective component of prejudice (emotions) than the cognitive one (beliefs), allow a better understanding of mechanisms of discursive discrimination, and may provide cues for a future course of action against discriminatory behaviors in social interaction.

The concluding chapter in **Part VI** of the collection reflects on the language of politics/politics of language distinction, assuming the reader's familiarity with (and the possible ways of reacting to) the content as well as the structure and aims of the volume. It finds the distinction eventually productive, as long as it can generate ways to take definition and systematization of PL and its scope further. One such avenue, the mediatization perspective, is explored in more detail.

✴✴✴

Like most studies of political discourse, especially those stressing the prominent role of language in understanding as well as shaping the power relations in the world, the present book is naturally raising questions about its possible social impact. These questions arise from more general doubts concerning the efficacy of discourse studies which aspire to function as instruments of social justice (cf., e.g., Chilton 2005; Cap 2008, etc.). Do academic analyses of 'politics' (in its broad sense) and language really provide any tangible benefits outside of their own scholarly settings? Do they play any role in restoring sanity and humanistic values which often fall victim to public discourse? While not even attempting to take a definitive position on these delicate issues, we shall nonetheless point to the following. If language partakes in processes of (political) persuasion, manipulation and discrimination, in legitimizing such phenomena as wars and acts of violence, in, oftentimes, spreading fear and dehumanizing (political) enemies, it should also possess the capacity of description which exposes the complexities of these practices to the public and thus pinpoints or prevents any potential *abuses of (political) power*. And although there have been many reasons to edit this book, the opportunity to collect, in many chapters, voices in line with the latter aspiration was certainly one of them.

References

Anthonissen, Christine and Blommaert, Jan (eds). 2007. *Discourse and Human Rights Violations.* Amsterdam: Benjamins.
Bakhtin, Mikhail. 1981. *The Dialogic Imagination: Four Essays.* Austin: University of Texas Press.
—. 1986. *Speech Genres and Other Late Essays.* Austin: University of Texas Press.
Blommaert, Jan. 1997. "Introduction: Language and politics, language politics and political linguistics." In *Political Linguistics,* Jan Blommaert and Chris Bulcaen (eds), 1–16. Amsterdam: Benjamins.
Böke, Karin. 1997. "Die 'Invasion' aus den 'Armenhäusern' Europas. Metaphern im Einwanderungsdiskurs." In *Die Sprache des Migrationsdiskurses. Das Reden über 'Ausländer' in Medien, Politik und Alltag,* Matthias Jung, Martin Wengeler and Karin Böke (eds), 164–193. Opladen: Westdeutcher.
Caldas-Coulthard, Carmen R. and Coulthard, Malcolm (eds). 1996. *Texts and Practices. Readings in Critical Discourse Analysis.* London: Routledge.
Canagarajah, Suresh. 1999. "On EFL teachers, awareness, and agency." *ELT Journal* 53: 207–214.
Cap, Piotr. 2008. *Legitimisation in Political Discourse: A Cross-Disciplinary Perspective on the Modern US War Rhetoric* [2nd revised ed.]. Newcastle: Cambridge Scholars Publishing.
Chilton, Paul. 1994. "Politics and language." In *The Encyclopedia of Language and Linguistics Vol. 6,* Ron E. Asher (ed.), 3215–3221. Oxford: Pergamon Press.
—. 1996. *Security Metaphors.* New York: Peter Lang.
—. 2004. *Analysing Political Discourse. Theory and Practice.* London: Routledge.
—. 2005. "Missing links in mainstream CDA: Modules, blends and the critical instinct." In *A New Agenda in (Critical) Discourse Analysis: Theory, Methodology and Interdisciplinarity,* Ruth Wodak and Paul Chilton (eds), 19–51. Amsterdam: Benjamins.
—. 2007. "Challenges in the study of language and politics, challenges for *JLP*." *Journal of Language and Politics* 6: 297–301.
Chilton, Paul and Ilyin, Mikhail. 1993. "Metaphor in political discourse: The case of the common 'European house.'" *Discourse and Society* 4: 7–31.
Chilton, Paul and Lakoff, George. 1995. "Foreign policy by metaphor." In *Language and Peace,* Christina Schäffner and Anita Wenden (eds), 37–60. Aldershot: Dartmouth.
Chilton, Paul and Schäffner, Christina (eds). 2002. *Politics as Text and Talk.* Amsterdam: Benjamins.
Chouliaraki, Lilie and Fairclough, Norman. 1999. *Discourse in Late Modernity. Rethinking Critical Discourse Analysis.* Edinburgh: Edinburgh University Press.
Davies, Alan. 1994. "Politicized language." In *The Encyclopedia of Language and Linguistics, Vol. 6,* Ron E. Asher (ed.), 3211–3214. Oxford: Pergamon Press.
Dedaić, Mirjana N. 2006. "Political speeches and persuasive argumentation." In *Encyclopedia of Language and Linguistics. Vol. 9,* Keith Brown (ed.), 700–707. Amsterdam: Elsevier.
Denton, Robert E. and Woodward, Gary C. 1990. *Political Communication in America.* New York: Praeger.

Dirven, Rene, Hawkins, Bruce and Sandikcioglu, Esra (eds). 2001. *Language and Ideology. Vol. I: Theoretical Cognitive Approaches*. Amsterdam: Benjamins.

Duszak, Anna and Okulska, Urszula (eds). 2004. *Speaking from the Margin. Global English from a European Perspective*. Frankfurt am Main: Peter Lang.

Edelman, Murray. 1977. *Political Language. Words that Succeed and Policies that Fail*. New York: Academic Press.

Ehlich, Konrad. 1989. "Über den Faschismus sprechen – Analyse und Diskurs." In *Sprache im Faschismus*, Konrad Ehlich (ed.), 7–34. Frankfurt am Main: Suhrkamp.

El Refaie, Elisabeth. 2001. "Metaphors we discriminate by: Naturalized themes in Austrian newspaper articles about asylum seekers." *Journal of Sociolinguistics* 5 (3): 352–371.

Fairclough, Norman. 1989. *Language and Power*. London: Longman.

—. 1995. *Critical Discourse Analysis: The Critical Study of Language*. London: Longman.

—. 1995. *Media Discourse*. London: Longman.

—. 2000. *Analysing Discourse: Textual Analysis for Social Research*. London: Routledge.

—. 2006a. *Language and Globalization*. London: Routledge.

—. 2006b. "Genres in political linguistics." In *Encyclopedia of Language and Linguistics, Vol. 5*, Keith Brown (ed.), 32–38. Amsterdam: Elsevier.

Fairclough, Norman and Wodak, Ruth. 1997. "Critical discourse analysis." In *Discourse as Social Interaction. Discourse Studies: A Multidisciplinary Introduction, Vol. 2*, Teun van Dijk (ed.), 20–45. London: Sage.

Falkowska, Marta. 2008. "'Global metaphors'? On metaphors of European integration in Polish, English and French." In *Discourse Variation across Communities, Cultures and Times*, Urszula Okulska and Grzegorz Kowalski (eds), 157–182. Warsaw: University of Warsaw.

Fetzer, Anita and Lauerbach, Gerda E. (eds). 2007. *Political Discourse in the Media*. Amsterdam: Benjamins.

Fowler, Roger. 1979. *Language and Control*. London: Routledge.

Fritz Ben, Keefer, Bryan and Nyhan, Brendan. 2004. *All the President's Spin*. New York: Simon and Schuster.

Goatly, Andrew. 2007. *Washing the Brain. Metaphor and Hidden Ideology*. Amsterdam/ Philadelphia: Benjamins.

Graham, Phil, Keenan, Thomas and Dowd, Anne M. 2004. "A call to arms at the end of history: A discourse-historical analysis of George W. Bush's declaration of war on terror." *Discourse and Society* 15 (2–3): 199–222.

Halliday, Michael A. K. 1985. *Spoken and Written Language*. Oxford: Oxford University Press.

Heer, Hannes, Manoschek, Walter, Pollak, Alexander and Wodak, Ruth (eds). 2008. *The Discursive Construction of History. Remembering the Wehrmacht's War of Annihilation*. Basingstoke: Palgrave Macmillan.

Hodge, Robert and Kress, Gunther. 1993. *Language and Ideology*. London: Routledge.

Hodges, Adam and Nilep, Chad (eds). 2007. *Discourse, War and Terrorism*. Amsterdam: Benjamins.

Joseph, John E. 2004. "Language and politics." In *The Handbook of Applied Linguistics*, Alan Davies and Catherine Elder (eds), 347–366. Oxford: Blackwell.

Lakoff, George. 1991. "Metaphor in politics. An open letter to the internet from George Lakoff." Retrieved July 15, 2009 from http://philosophy.uoregon.edu/metaphor/lakoff-1.html

—. 1992. "Metaphor and war: The metaphor system used to justify war in the gulf." In *Thirty Years of Linguistic Evolution*, Martin Pütz (ed.), 463–481. Philadelphia: Benjamins.

—. 1996. *Moral Politics*. Chicago: University of Chicago Press.

Lambert, Wallace. 1975. "Culture and language as factors in learning and education." In *Education of Immigrant Students*, Aaron Wolfgang (ed.), 55–83. Toronto: Ontario Institute for Studies in Education.

Langacker, Ronald. 2001. "Discourse in Cognitive Grammar." *Cognitive Linguistics* 12: 143–158.

Lassen, Inger, Strunck, Jeanne and Vestergaard, Torben (eds). 2006. *Mediating Ideology in Text and Image*. Amsterdam: Benjamins.

Lee McClung, Alfred and Lee, Elizabeth B. (eds). 1939. *The Fine Art of Propaganda: A Study of Father Coughlin's Speeches*. New York: Harcourt, Brace and Company.

Maas, Utz. 1984. *Als der Geist der Gemeinschaft eine Sprache fand. Sprache im Nazionalsozialismus*. Oplanden: Westdeutscher Verlag.

Martin, James and Rose, David. 2003. *Working with Discourse: Meaning beyond the Clause*. London: Continuum.

Martin, James and Wodak, Ruth (eds). 2003. *Re/reading the Past. Critical and Functional Perspectives on Time and Value*. Amsterdam: Benjamins.

Monaghan, Leila and Goodman, Jane (eds). 2007. *A Cultural Approach to Interpersonal Communication*. Oxford: Blackwell.

Muntigl, Peter. 2002. "Politicization and depolicization: Employment policy in the European Union." In *Politics as Text and Talk*, Paul Chilton and Christina Schäffner (eds), 45–79. Amsterdam: Benjamins.

Muntigl, Peter, Weiss, Gilbert and Wodak, Ruth (eds). 2000. *European Union Discourses on Unemployment: An Interdisciplinary Approach to Employment Policy-Making and Organizational Change*. Amsterdam: Benjamins.

Musolff, Andreas. 2000. "Metaphors and trains of thought: Spotting journey imagery in British and German political discourse." In *Language, Politics and Society: The New Languages Department*, Sue Wright, Linda Hantrais and Jolyon Howorth (eds), 100–109. Clevedon: Multilingual Matters.

—. 2004. *Metaphor and Political Discourse*. Basingstoke: Palgrave Macmillan.

Panagl, Oswald and Stürmer, Horst (eds). 2002. *Politische Konzepte und verbale Strategien – Brisante Wörter, Begrieffsfelder, Sprachbilder*. Frankfurt am Main: Peter Lang.

Phillipson, Robert. 1992. *Linguistic Imperialism*. Oxford: Oxford University Press.

Phillipson, Robert and Skutnabb-Kangas, Tove. 1994. "Discrimination and minority languages." In *The Encyclopedia of Language and Linguistics, Vol. 2*, Ron E. Asher (ed.), 993–995. Oxford: Pergamon Press.

Pisarek, Walery. 2007. *O mediach i języku [On Media and Language]*. Kraków: Universitas.

Pratkanis, Anthony and Aronson, Elliot. 2001. *Age of Propaganda: The Everyday Use and Abuse of Persuasion*. New York: W.H. Freeman.

Reisigl, Martin. 2006. "Rhetorical tropes in political discourse." In *Encyclopedia of Language and Linguistics, Vol. 10*, Keith Brown (ed.), 597–604. Amsterdam: Elsevier.

Reisigl, Martin and Wodak, Ruth. 2001. *Discourse and Discrimination*. London: Routledge.

Sauer, Christoph. 2002. "Ceremonial text and talk. A functional-pragmatic approach." In *Politics as Text and Talk*, Paul Chilton and Christina Schäffner (eds), 111–142. Amsterdam: Benjamins.

Schäffner, Christina. 1995. "The balance metaphor in relation to peace." In *Language and Peace*, Christina Schäffner and Anita Wenden (eds), 75–91. Aldershot: Dartmouth.

— (ed.). 1997. *Analysis of Political Speeches*. Clevedon: Multilingual Matters.

Scheithauer, Ruth. 2007. "Metaphors in election night television coverage in Britain, the United States and Germany." In *Political Discourse in the Media*, Anita Fetzer and Gerda E. Lauerbach (eds), 75–106. Amsterdam: Benjamins.

Searle, John. 1979. *Expression and Meaning*. Cambridge: Cambridge University Press.

Semino, Elena and Masci, Michela. 1996. "Politics is football: Metaphor in the discourse of Silvio Berlusconi." *Discourse and Society* 7: 243–269.

Skutnabb-Kangas, Tove. 1988. "Multilingualism and the education of minority children." In *Minority Education: From Shame to Struggle*, Tove Skutnabb-Kangas and Jim Cummins (eds), 30–48. Clevedon: Multilingual Matters.

Skutnabb-Kangas, Tove and Phillipson, Robert (eds). 1989. *Wanted! Linguistic Human Rights*. Roskilde: Roskilde Universitetscenter.

— (eds). 1995. *Linguistic Human Rights*. Cambridge: Cambridge University Press.

Stolz, Gregory. 2007. "Arabs in the morning paper: A case of shifting identity." In *Discourse, War and Terrorism*, Adam Hodges and Chad Nilep (eds), 105–121. Amsterdam: Benjamins.

Taverniers, Miriam. [2002] 2005. "Metaphor." *Handbook of Pragmatics Online*. John Benjamins Publishing Company. Retrieved August 24, 2009 from http://ipra.ua.ac.be/main.aspx?c=* HOME&n=1272&ct=1145&e=1461

Triandafyllidou, Anna, Wodak, Ruth and Krzyżanowski, Michał (eds). 2009. *The European Public Sphere and the Media. Europe in Crisis*. Basingstoke: Palgrave Macmillan.

van Dijk, Teun. 1991. *Racism and the Press*. London: Routledge.

—. 1992. "Discourse and the denial of racism." *Discourse and Society* 3: 87–118.

—. 1993. *Elite Discourse and Racism*. London: Sage.

—. 1998. *Ideology: An Interdisciplinary Approach*. London: Sage.

—. 2005. *Racism and Discourse in Spain and America*. Amsterdam: Benjamins.

van Leeuwen, Theo. 2005. "Three models of interdisciplinarity." In *A New Agenda in (Critical) Discourse Analysis: Theory, Methodology and Interdisciplinarity*, Ruth Wodak and Paul Chilton (eds), 3–18. Amsterdam: Benjamins.

Watts, Richard. [1996] 2005. "Social institutions." *Handbook of Pragmatics Online*. Amsterdam/ Philadelphia: Benjamins. Available at http://www.benjamins.com/online/hop/.

Weiss, Gilbert and Wodak, Ruth (eds). 2003. *Critical Discourse Analysis. Theory and Disciplinarity*. London: Palgrave Macmillan.

Wilson, John. 1990. *Politically Speaking: The Pragmatic Analysis of Political Language*. Oxford: Blackwell.

Wodak, Ruth. 2009. *The Discourse of Politics in Action – Politics as Usual*. Basingstoke: Palgrave Macmillan.

Wodak, Ruth and Chilton, Paul (eds). 2005. *A New Agenda in (Critical) Discourse Analysis: Theory, Methodology and Interdisciplinarity*. Amsterdam: Benjamins.

Wodak, Ruth and de Cillia, Rudolf. 2006. "Politics and language: Overview." In *Encyclopedia of Language and Linguistics, Vol. 9*, Keith Brown (ed.), 707–717. Amsterdam: Elsevier.

Wodak, Ruth and Ludwig, Christoph (eds). 1999. *Challenges in a Changing World: Issues in Critical Discourse Analysis*. Vienna: Passagen Verlag.

Wodak, Ruth and Meyer, Michael (eds). 2001. *Methods of Critical Discourse Analysis*. London: Sage.

Wodak, Ruth and Weiss, Gilbert. 2004. "Visions, ideologies and utopias in the discursive construction of European identities: Organizing, representing and legitimizing Europe." In *Communicating Ideologies: Language, Discourse and Social Practice*, Martin Pütz, JoAnne Neff-van Aertselaer and Teun van Dijk (eds), 225–252. Frankfurt am Main: Peter Lang.

Wodak, Ruth, de Cillia, Rudolf, Reisigl, Martin, and Liebhart, Karin. 1999. *The Discursive Construction of National Identity*. Edinburgh: Edinburgh University Press.

Wodak, Ruth, Menz, Florian, Mitten, Richard and Stern, Frank. 1994. *Die Sprachen der Vergangenheiten. Öffentliches Gedenken in österreichischen und deutschen Medien.* Frankfurt am Main: Suhrkamp.

Wodak, Ruth, Nowak, Peter, Pelikan, Johanna, Gruber, Helmut, de Cillia, Rudolf and Mitten, Richard. 1990. *Wir sind alle unschuldige Täter. Diskurshistorische Studien zum Nachkriegsantisemitismus.* Frankfurt am Main: Suhrkamp.

Zernicke, Paul H. 1990. "Presidential roles and rhetoric." *Political Communication and Persuasion* 7: 321–345.

PART II

Classification and naming in political rhetoric

CHAPTER 2

Political metaphor and *bodies politic*

Andreas Musolff

1. Introduction: Metaphor, history, and political discourse

According to Friedrich Nietzsche, the truths of everyday communication are nothing but an inventory of forgotten metaphors.[1] In principle, it should thus be possible to trace current patterns of language and thought back to images of the world as it was originally perceived by humans – not in the sense of objective, neutral impressions but as vivid, bodily based, metaphorical interpretations of experience. In a sense, the cognitively orientated approach of conceptual metaphor theory, especially the research on 'embodied cognition' and 'primary' metaphors grounded in experience-based metonymies,[2] can be seen as a late fulfillment of Nietzsche's program (though he was thinking more in terms of searching for traces of original creative imagination in the work of poets and artists).[3] But where does that leave the *historical* treatment of metaphor? Is it not an ahistorical and implausible perspective to assume that 'original' metaphors can be accessed directly, whether on the basis of artistic-philosophical speculation or through reconstruction of primary experiences? Are the current meanings of metaphors affected by the conceptual and argumentative 'baggage' that they have acquired through history?

The use of metaphor in political discourse may provide a test-case here, for it provides us with data that are sufficiently prominent to be well documented over longer periods of time and that are and were meant to make a strong emotional appeal to their audiences. One such metaphor that is employed frequently in public discourse today and seems to have been so for many centuries is the interpretation of the state in terms of the human body (see also Skinner and Squillacote this volume), which in British and American English is even manifested in a special lexicalized form, i.e., *body politic*. The term appears to be a loan translation from *corpus politicum*, synonymous with *corpus mysticum*, which was used in the fifteenth century to describe the state of England; by the early 16th century its Anglicized version can be found in the

---

1. Nietzsche (1976, vol. 3: 1022).
2. Cf. Johnson (1987), Lakoff and Johnson (1999), Grady and Johnson (2003).
3. Cf. Nietzsche (1976, vol. 3: 1027).

rhetoric of the Tudor kings.[4] A brief look at media texts shows that it is still employed ubiquitously today. In 1996, a reviewer of Noam Chomsky's political writings 'credited' him with having "disembowel[ed] the body politic,"[5] in 2005, Will Hutton, in the *Observer*, called for members of "the body politic" to "articulate a more sophisticated debate than that between criticism of obscene profit and calls to rejoice on the other,"[6] in 2005, the Tory politician Boris Johnson, mockingly described himself as "a mere toenail in the body politic,"[7] and in 2006, *Aljazeera International* accused US and British leaders of "Dismembering the body politic in Iraq."[8]

As Johnson's *toenail* example shows, parts of the body can be employed to denote different 'members' of political entities; in this sense, we still speak of *heads of government* or *of state*, of the military *arm* or *wing* and of the *organ* or *mouthpiece* of political groups.[9] In the 1990s, British public debates about EU policies focused on the question of whether Britain could and should work "at the very heart of Europe" (as promised by Prime Minister John Major in 1991 and later reiterated by his successor, Tony Blair),[10] or whether that *heart* (i.e., the centre of EU policy in the EU commission) was "diseased," "rotten" or "split."[11] Other body parts that appeared in British and German Euro-debates included *head, liver, gall-bladder* and *muscles*; and the *illnesses* of the European Union's *body* ranged from *Euro-sclerosis* and *-neurosis* to *infections, paralysis* and *tumours*; individual member states were depicted as *sick men of Europe* respectively.[12]

Whilst these data, as well as those of the well-documented evidence of body-related source concepts in metaphoric idioms,[13] demonstrate that the human body still serves as a highly 'productive' source domain in the perception and conceptualisation of socio-political reality, it has been claimed that in comparison with the heyday of the political body metaphor in the Middle Ages and the Renaissance, the image subsequently "lost most of its validity" and its later uses "were brief, unoriginal, and void of any implications,"[14] and that it had become a "dead metaphor – or at least one whose

---

4.   Cf. Hale (1971: 43–50), Dhorn-van-Rossum and Böckenförde (1978: 548), cf. also *Shorter Oxford English Dictionary* (2002, vol. 1: 258).

5.   *The Times Higher Education Supplement*, 22 November 1996.

6.   *The Observer*, 6 February 2005.

7.   *The Independent on Sunday*, 20 November 2005.

8.   Al-Jazeera, English, 27 June 2006.

9.   Cf. Deignan (1995: 2); *Brewer's Dictionary of Phrase and Fable* (1999: 149, 713).

10.   *The Guardian*, 12 March 1991 and 1 December 1997, *The Times*, 23 March 1998.

11.   Examples from *The Guardian*, 10 October 1996, *The SUN*, 17 March 1999, *The Guardian,* 16 December 2003. For a detailed analysis of the British "heart-of-Europe" debate cf. Musolff 2004b.

12.   Cf. Musolff (2004a: 83–114).

13.   For the use of body metaphors in idioms and proverbs cf. Johnson (1987), Pauwels and Vandenbergen (1995), Boers (1999), Niemeier (2000), Kövecses (2000).

14.   Hale (1971: 131).

descriptive power has become severely attenuated."[15] These characterizations seem to presuppose that the history of a metaphor can be conceived of and told as the narrative of a "life cycle" (which is, of course, itself a bio-metaphor), with the metaphor 'organism' going through phases of youth, maturity and old age.[16] However, even the few examples mentioned above show that current use of the state-body metaphor is not at all 'devoid of implications'. At the very least, the notion of the *body politic* implies a) the assumption that the *body* must be complex, as it can be taken apart (*dismembered, disemboweled*), b) a hierarchy of members: a *mere toenail* is not of the same importance/centrality as the *heart*, and c) a differentiation of states of *health* and *sickness*: in the latter case, a follow-up scenario of *diagnosis* and *therapy* (and/or *death*) is invoked.

Contrary to the pessimistic pronouncements on the metaphor's current status as almost dead, we could repeat what George Lakoff and Mark Turner (1989) have asserted about the (closely related) metaphor complex of the so-called *Great Chain of Being*, i.e., that it is commonly "taught [...] as if it somehow died out in the industrial age," but that on "the contrary a highly articulated version of it still exists as a contemporary unconscious cultural model indispensable to our understanding of ourselves, our world, and our language."[17] We thus seem to be confronted with almost diametrically opposed interpretations: one emphatically asserting the historical significance of the metaphor but tinged with "nostalgia" and "wistfulness" on account of its alleged decline;[18] the other claiming a universal and ahistoric access to body concepts as experience-based source inputs for the conceptualization of abstract entities. In the remainder of this paper I will argue that the cognitive and historical approaches need not oppose but can in fact complement each other. Cognitive analysis can establish the semantic elements and argumentative arrangements that provide the source inputs for the metaphor. Conceptual history and critical text studies provide complementary planks for reconstructing the conceptual and discursive traditions that can plausibly be assumed to have a representation in the socio-cultural memory of language users. Of course, it is not likely that, except for historians, today's speakers will remember a conceptual or terminological tradition reaching back centuries in every detail, but as we shall see, certain uses of the body-state metaphor have indeed become so famous, or infamous, that they have shaped semantic contours and are referred to in empirically observable meta-discursive comments.

---

15.   Harris (1998: 1).

16.   For the affirmative use of such imagery in historical linguistics cf. Croft and Cruse (2004: 204–206); for critical reflection cf. Frank (2009).

17.   Lakoff and Turner (1989: 166). For the classic account of the *Great Chain of Being* metaphor cf. Lovejoy (1936), for the positioning of the *body politic* at the interface of "micro"- and "macrocosm," Tillyard (1982), Harris (1998).

18.   Cf. Harris (1998: 2).

2.   The *body politic* tradition

Historical overviews of the *body politic* metaphor locate the origins of this conceptual tradition in pre-Socratic thinking and highlight a first flourishing in the writings of Plato and Aristotle (with *The Republic* and *Timaios, Politics* and *De motu animalium* as the respective key-texts).[19] They are followed by Hellenistic and Classical Roman historians and philosophers, the Stoics, Neo-Platonists and Biblical traditions (especially St. Paul's *Epistles to the Romans and Corinthians*), the Church Fathers and most political philosophies in the Middle Ages up until the Enlightenment in most if not all European national cultures and languages, with further important contributions to the present day.[20] A distinct but closely connected strand is constituted by the 'fable of the belly' (i.e., of the revolt of body members against the monarchical belly), which begins in Aesopian traditions dating back to the fifth century BC and reaches at least into Renaissance literature, with Shakespeare's version of it in *Coriolanus* (I, 1, 101–169) as arguably its most famous formulation.[21] In addition to these philosophical and poetic strands, there is a third tradition of politico-corporeal theory in juristic thought which includes, for instance, the development of the legal fiction of "the King's two bodies" as well as the rise of "corporationalism" in civic and international law.[22]

   In view of such a vast material, any attempt at providing a list, let alone a comprehensive discussion, of relevant texts in this chapter would be futile. It seems more promising to review the main historical hypotheses concerning the conceptual career of the metaphor, and test such hypotheses against available data. Three such hypotheses stand out in the research literature: they concern the epistemological, (scientific-) conceptual and argumentative status of the metaphor, respectively. The first of these, formulated by E.M.W. Tillyard in *The Elizabethan world-picture*, suggests that the system of ontological correspondences of micro-, macrocosm and body politic, which in the Middle Ages had been a coherent world-view that could be believed in a literal sense, was transformed into an inventory of metaphors: "on the one hand [the Elizabethans] made it express the idea of that order they so longed for [...] But they no longer allowed the details to take the form of minute mathematical equivalences: they

---

19.   Cf. Hale (1971: 18–23), Dhorn van Rossum and Böckenförde (1978: 521–525), Koschorke et al. (2007: 10, 19–54, 64).

20.   For an excellent analysis of nineteenth and twentieth century political/organizational theory based on body- and organism-concepts cf. the recent PhD. dissertation by Nicolaas Moton (2009).

21.   Shakespeare uses the background notion of a hierarchy of body members to ridicule the presumption of 'lower' parts to rebel against their 'superiors' by having senator Menenius insult the citizen's leader: "You, the great toe of this assembly? [...] For that, being one o' the lowest, basest, poorest, Of this most wise rebellion, thou go'st foremost." For the overall tradition of the "fable of the belly" cf. Hale (1971: 26–9), Peil (1985), Koschorke et al. (2007: 15–26).

22.   Cf. Coker (1967), Kantorowicz (1997), Koschorke et al. (2007: 103–141, 319–382).

made the imagination use these for its own ends."[23] According to this hypothesis, the conceptual complexes of the *Great Chain of Being* and the *Body Politic* only became 'metaphors' in the sense of conceptual and rhetorical figures in the course of the Renaissance: what had been an integral part of a fixed belief system was turned into a set of images, terminologies and arguments that were freely available for poets, rhetoricians and politicians.

The second hypothesis links the new metaphorical meaning to paradigm shifts that affected the body-state metaphor's conceptual source, i.e., the traditional knowledge of body and health as defined by the relationship of the 'four humours', which for a millennium and more had been based on writings of Hippocrates, Plato, Aristotle and Galen. Over the course of the 16th and into the 17th century, this knowledge system underwent a profound crisis: successive innovations, e.g., anti-Galenic Paracelsianism, the understanding of science as an evidence- and experiment-based enterprise (Galileo, Bacon) and the rise of a mechanistic views of blood-circulation and the senso-motoric system (Harvey, Descartes) shattered the humoral theory. These changing (proto-)scientific source-concepts of body, health and illness thus affected the scope and nature of metaphorical applications in political discourse.[24]

A further, related hypothesis was put forward by Susan Sontag in the essay *Illness and metaphor*, where she distinguished between 'classical' and 'modern' uses of illness imagery in political thought and discourse. She maintained that the "classical formulations which analogize a political disorder to an illness – from Plato to, say, Hobbes – presuppose the classical medical (and political) idea of balance"; hence the "treatment is aimed at restoring the right balance–in political terms, the right hierarchy," and the "prognosis is always, in principle, optimistic."[25] On the other hand, modern illness imagery, sourced from supposedly incurable "master illnesses" such as TB or cancer, are "specifically polemical" and serve "to propose new, critical standards of individual health, and to express a sense of dissatisfaction with society as such [...] Now, to liken a political event or situation to an illness is to impute guilt, to prescribe punishment."[26] Examples for this 'modern' use can be found from the time of the French Revolution up until the present, with the totalitarian ideologies of the 20th century providing the most infamous specimens.

We thus have three strong historical hypotheses that all point to a massive change in the epistemological, conceptual and argumentative-rhetorical status of the body-state metaphor during and/or after the Renaissance. Such a strong empirical claim is amenable to being tested against the evidence of historical data. However, even this specific task goes beyond the limits of a single chapter; the following discussion can

---

23. Tillyard (1982: 107).

24. Cf. Hale (1971: 110–114), Harris (1998: 19–47), Klibansky, Panofsky and Saxl (1964), Guldin (2000: 89–91).

25. Sontag (1978: 75).

26. Sontag (1978: 72, 80).

only aim to elucidate some of the methodological implications of such an analysis rather than presenting a comprehensive evaluation. We shall therefore provide three case-studies on medieval, Renaissance and 20th century uses that serve to illustrate the above-mentioned discontinuities in the tradition and provide data to review the latter's validity.

2.1   The *body politic* in the Middle Ages:
From John of Salisbury to Christine de Pizan

One of the earliest and most famous uses of the *body-state* imagery in the history of English political thought can be found in the treatise *Policraticus* (c. 1159), written by the cleric and philosopher John of Salisbury (c. 1115–1180) and dedicated to his friend Thomas Becket. In the treatise, John, who survived his friend's 'murder in the cathedral' and later became Bishop of Chartres, analyzed medieval society in analogy with the human body. He combined a hierarchical view of the *body* from the *head* 'down' to the *feet* with a strong emphasis on the church's role as the *soul* that rules the whole organism including the *head*, i.e., the prince, and on the *mutual duty of care* among all *body parts*.[27] The *feet*, which owe the rest of the *body* obedience, also have a right to be cared for by the other *body members*: "Remove from the fittest body the aid of the feet; it does not proceed under its own power, but either crawls shamefully, uselessly and offensively on its hands or else is moved with the assistance of brute animals."[28] John's concern for the *feet*, which forms part of the principle of mutual co-operation and solidarity among all body members, has been related to the innovative influence of his teachers in Paris and Chartres as well as to reformist 'medieval humanism.'[29] Nonetheless, it seems to fit well within the schema of the 'medieval-as-pre-modern' world-view that presented a stable perspective of society as part of the system of correspondences between 'micro' and 'macrocosm'. Tillyard, therefore, saw no problem in praising John's treatise as "one of the most elaborate medieval statements" of the *body-state* analogy.[30]

However, what of the *illnesses* in this well-balanced body, and the *treatments* they necessitate? John's position on the relative susceptibility and competence of different body members is ambivalent. On the one hand, he holds "negligence or dissimulation on the part of the ruler" responsible for "illness and blemishes" of the *body politic*,[31] and he quotes Plato as having warned of an oppressive magistrate being equal to a "swollen head" that makes it "impossible for the members of the body to endure it

---

27.   John of Salisbury (1990: 66–67); for the Latin original of these and further quotations from *Policraticus* cf. John of Salisbury (1909), Webb ed. (1909).

28.   John of Salisbury (1990: 67).

29.   Cf. Bass (1997: 203–210), Guldin (2000: 57–58).

30.   Tillyard (1982: 103).

31.   John of Salisbury (1990: 63).

either at all or without difficulty."[32] On the other hand, John leaves no doubt about the Prince's obligation to save, if "palliatives and gentle medicines" do not help, *body* and *soul* by way of *amputation* of any *afflicted* rebellious members, on the authority of the Bible (Matthew 18: 9): "That the members are [...] to be removed is clear from that which is written: 'If your eye or your foot offend you, root it out and cast it away from you.' [...] Indeed, neither the ears nor the tongue nor whatever else subsists within the body of the republic is safe if it revolts against the soul for whose sake the eyes themselves are gouged out."[33]

John's warning of *diseases* that can *ruin the whole body* and his justification of *amputation* put in question Sontag's hypothesis that in classical formulations the "prognosis is always, in principle, optimistic."[34] In defence of her analysis (which did not include John of Salisbury), one can point out that the purpose of the analogy in the *Policraticus* was to warn leaders of State and Church against *diseases* so as to avoid or manage them. Such a reading might still be squared with Sontag's overall assessment that in "political philosophy's great tradition, the analogy between disease and civil disorder is proposed to encourage rulers to pursue a more rational policy."[35] Nonetheless, John's zealous plea in favour of *amputation* if a member revolts against the *soul*, i.e., Christ's church, is still quite remote from Sontag's notion of benign pre-modern *illness* metaphors.

Neither does John apply a truly coherent schema of correspondences based on pre-scientific medicine: the humoral theory is hardly referred to and the *head* is not in fact sovereign; rather, it is ruled by the *soul/church*. Besides the 'head-to-feet' schema, John uses the 'fable of the belly' in an account of a conversation with the reigning Pope Adrian IV. John, after having reported complaints against the church concerning corruption and simony, claims to have even challenged the pontiff directly: "If you are father, therefore, why do you accept presents and payments from your children?" The pope's response consists in telling the fable and deducing from it the 'obvious' conclusion: "Measure neither our harshness nor that of secular princes, but attend to the utility of all."[36] John's version of the medieval *body politic* was in line with the papal self-perception as the supreme authority of Christianity's *corpus mysticum,* which was upheld and reconfirmed in corporeal terminology throughout the 12–14th centuries.[37]

By the end of the Middle Ages, however, neither the pope's nor the belly's authority was sacrosanct any longer. In her *Book of the Body Politic* (1406), Christine de Pizan, for instance, leaves the Church hierarchy out of her *body* schema altogether: she only

---

32.   John of Salisbury (1990: 76).

33.   John of Salisbury (1990: 140–141).

34.   Sontag (1978: 75).

35.   Sontag (1978: 76).

36.   John of Salisbury (1990: 135–136).

37.   For instance in Boniface VIIIth bull *Unam sanctam* of 1302; cf. Hale (1971: 36), Kantorowicz (1997: 194).

discusses the *head* (= the prince); the *hands/arms* (= knights and nobles); the *belly, feet* and *legs* (= the 'common' people).[38] She also tells the 'fable of the belly' in a new way: instead of blaming only the rebellious members, her version has the trouble in the body start with the belly complaining that the limbs "did not take care of it and feed as well as they should," in reaction, "the limbs said they were all exhausted from work, and yet despite all their labor [...] the belly wanted to have everything and was never satisfied": the ensuing mutual non-cooperation leads to the catastrophe.[39] Whilst the moral lesson thus still follows the line of an exhortation for solidarity among the members (in the tradition of St. Paul's Epistles), the allocation of responsibility for the crisis is clearly no longer a one-sided affair: the belly is depicted as responsible and as biased in his own favor as the other limbs. Again, neither humoral theory nor *Great Chain* cosmology come into this presentation of the *body politic*. Such corporeal/medical-political correspondences can indeed be found in medieval writings, especially in scholastic literature,[40] but they were less *de rigueur* than would seem from Tillyard's and Sontag's pronouncements.

2.2   The pathology of the *body politic*: Machiavelli and Hobbes

The most famous – and to some, notorious – author in the early 16th century to use the notion of *illness in the body politic* is Niccolò Machiavelli. In *The Prince*, published in 1532, he analogizes tuberculosis and its therapy with political "corruption" and its solution: just as "consumptive illnesses" are in the beginning "easy to cure but difficult to diagnose" but if not recognized or treated at the outset, become "easy to diagnose but difficult to cure," so also political "evils" that are foreseen "in advance (a gift granted only to the prudent ruler), they can be cured quickly; but when they are [...] left to grow to such an extent that everyone recognizes them, there is no longer any remedy."[41] Sontag interprets this as "an illness metaphor that is not so much about society as about statecraft (conceived as a therapeutic art): as prudence is needed to control serious diseases, so foresight is needed to control social crises."[42] However, Machiavelli's "call to foresight"[43] leaves out any concrete description of the necessary therapy: it claims that in an early phase the cure is "easy" but gives no specification of how drastic it may have to be. In the last chapter of the *Discorsi*, on the other hand, Machiavelli discusses possible *remedies* for *maladies* of the state: they include "judicial sentence of

---

38.   Christine de Pizan (1994: 4)

39.   Christine de Pizan (1994: 91).

40.   E.g., Albertus Magnus, Thomas Aquinas, Giles of Rome, Remigio dei Girolami; cf. Nederman and Forhan (1993), Kempshall (1999).

41.   Machiavelli (2005: 12).

42.   Sontag (1978: 76).

43.   Sontag (1978: 76).

death on a whole legion at a time, or on a city," mass-banishments and decimation as well as prudent constitutional changes that prevent further "corruption" of the *body politic*.[44] With the exception of the last, these cures are far from benign. According to Quentin Skinner, Machiavelli expected "men of the highest virtù" (i.e., the only competent healers of the political body) "to be capable, when the situation requires it, of behaving in a completely vicious way."[45] It is also important to note that the analogy in the *Prince does* include the worst-case scenario of the (too) late diagnosis when "there is no longer any remedy." There is precious little 'optimism' in this diagnosis – instead, it is more of a cool calculation of the chances of success. Machiavelli's analogy, therefore, allows for both optimistic and fatalistic/cynical interpretations.

After Machiavelli, the last in Sontag's list of 'classical' thinkers is Thomas Hobbes.[46] For David Hale, Hobbes also marked the end for the classical tradition to convey the idea of the state,[47] whereas Jonathan Gil Harris regards him as heralding *new* trends in the application of body-state imagery, i.e., the "tendency to regard disease as having its origin in alien invaders; and second, the recurrent assumption that poison possesses a medicinal potential."[48] Hobbes's use of the body image in conjunction with the mechanistic interpretation of the body and the allegory of *Leviathan* was certainly radically innovative at the target level, in justifying the idea that the Common-wealth's structure – just like that of a mechanically working body – was artificially construed, as a 'covenant' between ruler and the ruled.[49] In contrast, the traditional head-to-feet account of the *body politic* mattered little to him: in the text of *Leviathan*, neither *head* nor *feet* are mentioned. Instead it is mainly the functional body aspects that are listed and interpreted, e.g., *joynts, nerves, hands, eyes, eares, bloud, muscles, voice, memory.*[50]

As regards the *health* of the *body politic*, Hobbes devotes a special chapter to *The things that Weaken, or tend to the Dissolution of a Common-wealth.* He begins by discussing *Defectuous Procreation,* i.e., 'Imperfect Institution' of states, which he equates with the lack of power and resources of the sovereign.[51] In second place, he considers "*Diseases* of a Common-wealth, that proceed from the poison of seditious doctrines."[52] Here, *illness* imagery plays a significant role. The first cause of sedition that he highlights

---

44. Cf. Machiavelli (2003: 526–528); comp. also Pocock (2003: 204–211).

45. Cf. Skinner (1978, vol. 1: 138).

46. Sontag (1978: 76).

47. Hale (1971: 128–129).

48. Harris (1998: 142).

49. For the introductory exposition of this triple metaphor/allegory of the state as *body-machine-Leviathan* cf. Hobbes (1996: 9–10); for the impact on political philosophy cf. Johnston (1986), Prokhovnik (1991), Skinner (1996: 2002).

50. Cf. Hobbes (1996: 9–10).

51. Hobbes (1996: 222).

52. Hobbes (1996: 223).

is the 'Example of different Government' in other nations, which he deems to be so seductive that people cannot leave it be and "though they be grieved with the continuance of disorder; like hot blouds, that having gotten the itch, tear themselves with their own nayles, till they can endure the smart no longer."[53] This focus on graphic symptoms is also prominent in the discussion of the second main cause of political *poisoning*, i.e., "Reading of the books of Policy, and Histories of the antient Greeks, and Romans," because such books incite "young men and all others that are unprovided of the Antidote of solid Reason" to emulate the ancient revolts, leading to "frequent Seditions, and Civill warres."[54] Ancient republicanism appears to justify regicide (or, as its supporters euphemistically call it, 'Tyrannicide'): this "Venime" Hobbes "will not doubt to compare to the biting of a mad Dogge, which is a disease the Physicians call *Hydrophobia*, or *fear of Water*": "he that is so bitten, has a continuall torment of thirst, and yet abhorreth water; and is in such an estate, as if the poison endeavoureth to convert him into a Dogge: So when a Monarchy is once bitten to the quick, by those Democraticall writers, that continually snarle at that estate; it wanteth nothing more than a strong Monarch, which [...] when they have him, they abhorre."[55] Even more than the previous examples of grave illnesses of the body politic, this terrifying scenario of "Democraticall writers" that can "bite" a state "to the quick" seems to put into question Sontag's inclusion of Hobbes in the list of thinkers who employed illness metaphors benignly to encourage "rulers to pursue a more rational policy."[56] By comparing his ideological adversaries to *mad dogs*, whose *venom* can *kill* a state, Hobbes comes rather close to suggesting that such dangerous *beasts must be put down*, lest they ruin the *body politic*.

Hobbes's discussion of the third type of serious political *diseases* appears to hark back to ancient medical speculation: as there "have been Doctors, that hold there be three Soules in a man: so there be also that think there may be more Soules."[57] The first target of this comparison is the Church that claims supremacy over the state, which Hobbes sees as the chief cause of the fanaticism that can be compared "to the Epilepsie, or Falling-sicknesse": in both cases "an unnaturall spirit" causes "violent, and irregular motions" of the members, which puts the victim (person or state) in danger of falling (into fire/water or into "the Fire of Civill warre").[58] The implication of this analogy is that the sovereign must remain the sole *soul* of the state; any other rival authority is seen as a mortal danger to the *health* of the *body politic*. Hobbes recycles the notion of "three soules" in one (monstrous) body to consider the division of constitutional

---

53. Hobbes (1996: 225).

54. Hobbes (1996: 225–226).

55. Hobbes (1996: 226).

56. Sontag (1978: 75–76).

57. Hobbes (1996: 226).

58. Hobbes (1996: 228).

powers within the state, which are likened to *life-functions*, i.e., the powers of "levying mony, (which is the Nutritive faculty,)," "of conduct and command, (which is the Motive faculty,)" and "of making Lawes, (which is Rationall Faculty)."[59] As with the 'State vs. Church' rivalry, Hobbes dismisses any such arrangement as an "irregularity of Common-wealth" resembling the organic anomaly of conjoined twins, or – if this existed – conjoined triplets.[60]

Hobbes's system of illnesses of the political bodies still extends further,[61] but the passages quoted above should already suffice to demonstrate that generalist assessments of his application of the metaphor as marking either the end-point of its traditional or 'classical' use (based on the theory of humoral/constitutional balance), or as the starting-point for innovative applications of life-scientific insights to the state do not give full justice to his creative use of the body-state analogy. What unites him and Machiavelli is an interest in the pathologies of the *body politic*, which is more ambivalent than Sontag makes it out to be: the illnesses of the political body are much for specifically described than in the Middle Ages; their cure is still considered to be possible in principle but by no means assured and may involve therapeutic measures that may be just as dangerous as the illnesses themselves. The implications of this pathological reading of the metaphor would reach into the 20th century.

2.3   Leviathan's *body politic* in the twentieth century

In 1936 and 1938, respectively, two interpretations of Hobbes's concept of the state, and in particular its metaphorical explication in *Leviathan*, were published by German political theorists. One of them was Carl Schmitt, professor of law in Berlin, member of the Nazi party, who, on account of his contribution to the constitutional dismantling of the Weimar Republic and his praise of Hitler's dictatorship, was dubbed 'crown jurist' of the new Reich.[62] The other was Leo Strauss, then an emigrant from Nazi Germany in Britain, whose work had to be laboriously translated into English. The

---

59. Hobbes (1996: 228).

60. Hobbes (1996: 228).

61. After discussing diseases "of the greatest and most present danger" to the body politic, Hobbes goes on to describe less dangerous but still important conditions. Of these he notes "difficulty of raising Mony" (= "*Ague*"), monopolies that hoard "the treasure of the Commonwealth" (= "*pleurisie*"), "Popularity of a potent Subject" (= "effects of *Witchcraft*"), immoderate growth of corporations and "liberty of Disputing" (= "*wormes* in the entryles"), expansionist policies (= "*Bulimia*"), which in their consequence, lead to "*Wounds* [...] received from the enemy," excessive "Ease" (= "*Lethargy*") and "Riot and Vain Expense" ("*Consumption*"). Hobbes rounds off the discussion of *health* problems of the political *body* with a description of defeat in war as its *dissolution*, when the sovereign, as its *soul*, loses command of its *members* and only leaves the "carcase" of the state (Hobbes 1996: 228–230).

62. Cf. Koenen (1995), Stirk (2005).

former adopted Hobbes's own book title, indicating in the subtitle, *Meaning and Failure of a Political Symbol*, a moderately critical perspective.[63] The latter offered to give a general account of the *Political Philosophy of Hobbes: Its Basis and Genesis*, in which he highlighted the lack of the traditional 'head = prince' equation in Hobbes's *body politic* concept: "The holder of the sovereign power is not the 'head', that is the capacity to deliberate and plan, but the 'soul', that is the capacity to command, in the State."[64] Such a reading of Hobbes was not far away from that of Schmitt, whose *Concept of the Political* Strauss had reviewed in detail.[65] Schmitt's *Leviathan* book, in turn, provided a kind of historical commentary on *The Concept of the Political*, in so far as Schmitt explicated his own definition of the *friend-foe* relationship as the basis of politics and the justification of decisionism by referring to the personalisation of the 'Common-wealth' in Hobbes's figure of the *Leviathan*. Schmitt goes on to tell the history of Hobbes's basic metaphor as one of a gradual 'deconstruction' in liberal political thought. His denunciation of liberal 'Jewish thinkers' such as Baruch de Spinoza, Moses Mendelssohn and Friedrich Julius Stahl[66] as having subverted the idea of the unified sovereign state cannot, however, disguise the fact that he identifies Hobbes as *the* thinker who, despite his unparalleled genius, had originally set in motion the process of undermining the pure, unitary idea of the state by choosing the figure of the *Leviathan*.[67]

Notwithstanding his scepticism as regards the eventual impact of Hobbes's construction, Schmitt himself was fascinated by the mythical figure of the *Leviathan* and devoted two chapters to its historical and exegetical explication, with extensive references to its links with what he regarded as cabbalistic traditions based on the figure of the *Leviathan* in the Old Testament (*Job*, 40–41).[68] Schmitt combines the *Leviathan* myth with that of the other monster-figure from the same biblical book, which Hobbes also used, i.e., *Behemoth* (= the title of Hobbes's account of the English Civil War),[69] to present the opposition: "the one monster, i.e., the 'state' as Leviathan is necessary to subdue permanently the other monster, Behemoth, i.e., revolution."[70] The main body feature of the *Leviathan* that is relevant for Schmitt's interpretation is its unsurpassable strength, which already features in the Biblical characterization that "upon earth there

---

63. Cf. Schmitt (1996), for the German original Schmitt (1995).

64. Cf. Strauss (1963: 160).

65. Cf. Strauss (1998).

66. Cf. Schmitt (2003: 86–110, 126). Some historians have attempted to motivate – and even excuse – these strong anti-Jewish statements some as defensive moves after Schmitt himself had been attacked by the SS in 1937 for not being sufficiently committed to National Socialism, cf. Maschke (2003: 181–191); for a more critical view compare Gross (2000).

67. Cf. Schmitt (2003: 130).

68. Cf. Schmitt (2003: 29–40); for a detailed critique cf. Gross (2000: 267–284).

69. Cf. *Job*, 40, 15–24, Hobbes (1680).

70. Schmitt (2003: 34).

is not his like," quoted in Latin on the frontispiece of Hobbes's book.[71] For Schmitt, this strength made the state/*Leviathan* absolutely invincible, thus rendering the idea of any resistance to it futile and even nonsensical.[72]

Diametrically opposed to Schmitt's NS-apologetic interpretation of Hobbes's theory is the use of the symbol of *Behemoth* by the emigrant lawyer and sociologist Franz L. Neumann (1900–1954) to characterize National Socialism as "a non-state, a chaos, a rule of lawlessness and anarchy, which has 'swallowed' the rights and dignity of man, and is out to transform the world into a chaos" in the 1942 book *Behemoth: The Structure and Practice of National Socialism*.[73] In the conclusion, Neumann insists that the "National Socialist state is no Leviathan," for the "Leviathan, although its swallows society, does not swallow all of it."[74] The power of the sovereign may be enormous but it is still "merely a part of the bargain in which the sovereign has to fulfill his obligations, that is preserve order and security [...] If the sovereign cannot fulfill his side of the bargain he forfeits his sovereignty."[75] In comparison with such a rational theory, based in principle on the 'consent of men',[76] National Socialism is wholly unprincipled.

It is intriguing that at a time when the Nazis were erecting and exercising their political *body* power, three of the foremost political theorists of their time use the *Leviathan* image to define their respective take on the decisionist aspect of Hobbes's political philosophy. Schmitt wistfully acknowledges the fact that the ancient myth was not strong enough to withstand the alleged onslaught of liberal-'Jewish' thinkers; Strauss exposes the contradiction between Hobbes's naturalist vindication of *Leviathan's* decision-taking power and the humanistic and moral basis of his thought;[77] Neumann points to the meta-power of the *Führer* as the personification of Germany's national *body*, which destroys even the last vestiges of a mediated, rational form of state.[78] The target of their writings (in Schmitt's case, perhaps even the desired addressee), i.e., Adolf Hitler, had formulated a decade earlier his own vision of the German people/race as a body that had been 'penetrated' by Jewish 'poison'. Hitler's use marks the extreme endpoint of what Harris (1998) identified as a "tendency to regard disease as having its origin in alien invaders" that started in the seventeenth century (with too great a

---

71. *Job* 41, 33, Hobbes (1996: xciii).

72. Schmitt (2003: 71).

73. Neumann (1942: 5). With this use Neumann follows in the footsteps of Hobbes's account of the *Behemoth*-like English civil as "a non-state, a chaos, a situation of lawlessness, disorder, and anarchy" (Neumann 1942: 5). Cf. also the chapters on the 'Totalitarian State' (1942: 41–72), the *Reich* idea (1942: 110–53), 'National Socialist Law and Terror' (1942: 359–347), as well as the conclusion (1942: 383).

74. Neumann (1942: 375).

75. Neumann (1942: 375).

76. Neumann (1942: 375).

77. Strauss (1963: 6–29, 168–170).

78. Neumann (1942: 383–384).

teleological emphasis in respect of the early stages).[79] In Nazi ideology, the collective entity 'the Jew'/*parasite* was *the* central alien body that was about to destroy the unity, health and existence of the national *body politic:* it therefore had to be exterminated completely.[80] The crucial difference of Nazi understanding to 'merely rhetorical' use of illness/parasite imagery was that the source concepts were employed at the same time as general metaphor sources, and as descriptions of social reality, and even as a pseudo-scientific prediction in the context of so-called 'race hygiene', thus building a closed system of mutually reinforcing analogies.[81]

On account of its catastrophic impact in world-history, this use of *body/illness* metaphor is still remembered today, and not just as a historical reference. In German public debate, the accusation that an individual or party-political group employs Nazi terminology and imagery can still lead to political isolation and even expulsion from mainstream public discourse.[82] As late as 1998, a conservative politician who had invoked the *nation-as-a-homogenous-body* image in the immigration debate was attacked: "Whoever uses the homogeneity of the 'German nation's body' as an argument, pours oil into the fire of disturbances in the ghettos."[83] There is thus evidence of a public medium-term memory of particularly famous, in this case infamous, metaphor versions.

3.   Conclusion

It would be pointless to give an overall narrative of the 'semantic career' of the *body-state* metaphor from the few snapshots that we have taken of famous, and infamous, political texts. Their chronological ordering might be suggestive of the metaphor's 'life-cycle' ending in disgrace; however, as the analyses have shown, the conceptual and epistemological status of the different uses and their respective socio-cultural contexts are so variable that a straightforward comparison is impossible. We can say that in each case, the *body-state* analogy, plus some of its main domain aspects and argumentative application patterns, have been used and that there are similarities at the level of the argumentative bias (i.e., 'pro-cure/therapy' and, if need be, even 'pro-amputation'). We have also seen that there are cases of prominent uses, such as in Nazi anti-Semitic

---

79. Harris (1998: 142).

80. Cf. Hitler (1933: 268, 334), (1992: 224, 277). This use of the *alien body/parasite* metaphor confirms the characterization of Nazi anti-Semitism as distinct from other forms of racism in terms of its "redemptive," "exterminatory" or "eliminatory" bias, as highlighted in recent Holocaust research; cf. Bauer (2001), Browning (1992), Goldhagen (1996), Friedländer (1998/2007).

81. For detailed analyses of this 'self-fulfilling' power of the body-state metaphor in Nazi thought cf. Hawkins (2001), Chilton (2005), Rash (2006: 115–181), Musolff (2007).

82. Cf. Keller-Bauer (1983); Eitz and Stötzel (2007: 76–100, 294–317, 489–504).

83. *Die Zeit*, 18 June 1998: "Wer die Homogenität eines 'deutschen Volkskörpers' ins Feld führt, der gießt Öl ins Feuer der Ghettos."

propaganda, that are "remembered" in public consciousness for more than half a century later, and that at the time of Nazi rule both its apologists and opponents referred to Hobbes's famous philosophical application of the *body-state* metaphor from the seventeenth century in order to redefine the phenomenon of a totalitarian political sphere in the twentieth century. It could be argued that this conceptual link was only established at the level of (academic) political theory and was not available to ordinary members of the public. However, the fact that more distant historical instances of a conceptual metaphor are not precisely remembered does not necessarily mean that non-expert users of such imagery have absolutely no awareness of the metaphor's historicity and the polemical baggage it carries from previous uses. In a study of body- and health-related source concepts that underlie present-day emotion metaphors, Geeraerts and Grondelaers (1995) have, for instance, shown that the source concepts of these metaphors are products of culture-specific traditions, e.g., the Western tradition of humor theories: "If cognitive models are cultural models, they are also cultural institutions, and as such, they carry their history along with them [...] only by investigating their historical origins and their gradual transformation can their contemporary form be properly understood."[84] Though these traditions are not usually consciously accessible to most speakers, their implications (e.g., the notion of an inner-body 'balance' between humors) may still be operative and cannot be discounted a priori in a semantic/pragmatic reconstruction.

The project of writing a history of the *body politic* metaphor that goes beyond the mere chronological listing of texts in which it appears can thus be written on the basis of a cooperation between cognitive semantics, conceptual history and critical discourse analysis.[85] Cognitive analysis can establish, through investigation of conceptual mappings, the semantic elements that provide the source inputs for the metaphor. Thanks to the ordinary language users' non-scientific access to body-based knowledge, the semantics of physiological and pathological body imagery, and even of innovative uses can usually be 'resuscitated' easily. Pragmatic analysis can identify the main argumentative patterns of the metaphor's uses. In their turn, conceptual history and critical discourse analysis reconstruct the inter-textual relationships among the relevant texts and establish conceptual traditions that can be shown to have some degree of representation in the socio-cultural memory of speakers. This memory may vary in relation to historical informedness, political interest, etc., but some degree of memory has been established and can be tested and augmented empirically. Cognitive, historical and critical discourse analyses thus do not contradict or exclude each other; rather, they complement each other, as indicated in Table 1.

---

84. Geeraerts and Grondelaars (1995: 177).

85. For inter- and transdisciplinarity in critical discourse analysis cf. Martin and Wodak (2003), van Leeuwen (2005) and Fairclough (2005).

Table 1. Complementation schema of conceptual, pragmatic, and critical discourse analysis

	Conceptual Analysis	Pragmatic Analysis	Critical Discourse Analysis
Structural dimension	Identification of domains and schemas that provide input into metaphoric blend	Reconstruction of scenic/narrative and evaluative implications	Identification of relevant contextual effects
Genetic dimension	Identification of underlying conceptual mechanisms (primary scenes, embodiment ...)	Reconstruction of scenic/narrative and evaluative presuppositions	Identification of pragmatic strategies (argument by analogy ...)
Historical dimension	Model of the evolution of cognitive-linguistic faculties	Reconstruction of the development of patterns/ trends in historical text corpora	Reconstruction of discourse traditions on the basis of inter-textual cross-referencing in historical corpora

Evidently, the proof of feasibility for such a multi-dimensional approach can only lie in conducting the outlined conceptual-discursive analyses for real – perhaps, this is more the outline of a whole research program rather than that of one project. Still, the prospect of an integrated approach that treats cognitive, discourse-orientated and historical analyses as complementary seems to me to be the most promising one.

References

Bass, Allen M. 1997. "The metaphor of the human body in the political theory of John of Salisbury: Context and innovation." In *Metaphor and Rational Discourse*, Bernhard Debatin, Timothy R. Jackson and Daniel Steuer (eds), 201–213. Tübingen: Niemeyer.

Bauer, Yehuda. 2001. *Rethinking the Holocaust.* New Haven/London: Yale University Press.

Boers, Frank. 1999. "When a bodily source domain becomes prominent." In *Metaphor in Cognitive Linguistics*, Raymond W. Gibbs and Gerard Steen (eds), 47–56. Amsterdam: Benjamins.

Browning, Christopher. 1992. *The Path to Genocide.* Cambridge: Cambridge University Press.

Chilton, Paul. 2005. "Manipulation, memes and metaphors: The case of *Mein Kampf.*" In *Manipulation and Ideologies in the Twentieth Century*, Louis de Saussure and Peter Schulz (eds), 5–45. Amsterdam: Benjamins.

Christine de Pizan. 1994. *The Book of the Body Politic.* Kate Langdon Forhan (ed. and trans.). Cambridge: Cambridge University Press.

Coker, Francis W. 1967 [1910]. *Organismic Theories of the State. Nineteenth-Century Interpretations of the State as Organism or Person.* New York: AMS Press.

Croft, William and Cruse, D. Alan. 2004. *Cognitive Linguistics.* Cambridge: Cambridge University Press.

Deignan, Alice. 1995. *Collins COBUILD English Guides 7. Metaphors.* London: HarperCollins.

Dhorn-van-Rossum, Gerhard and Böckenförde, Ernst-Wolfgang. 1978. "Organ, Organismus, Organisation, politischer Körper." In *Geschichtliche Grundbegriffe, Vol. 4*, Otto Brunner, Werner Conze and Reinhart Koselleck (eds), 519–622. Stuttgart: Klett-Cotta.

Eitz, Thorsten and Stötzel, Georg. 2007. *Wörterbuch der 'Vergangenheitsbewältigung': Die NS-Vergangenheit im öffentlichen Sprachgebrauch.* Hildesheim: Olms.

Fairclough, Norman. 2005. "Critical discourse analysis in transdisciplinary research." In *A New Agenda in (Critical) Discourse Analysis: Theory, Methodology and Interdisciplinarity*, Ruth Wodak and Paul Chilton (eds), 53–70. Amsterdam: Benjamins.

Frank, Roslyn. 2009. "Metaphors of discourse evolution." In *Metaphor and Discourse*, Andreas Musolff and Jörg Zinken (eds), 173–189. Basingstoke: Palgrave-Macmillan.

Friedländer, Saul. 1998/2007. *Nazi Germany & the Jews. Vol. 1: The Years of Persecution, 1933–1939. Vol. 2: The Years of Extermination, 1939–1945.* London: HarperCollins.

Geeraerts, Dirk and Grondelaers, Stefan. 1995. "Looking back at anger: Cultural traditions and metaphorical patterns." In *Language and the Cognitive Construal of the World*, John R. Taylor and Robert E. MacLaury (eds), 153–179. Berlin: de Gruyter.

Goldhagen, Daniel Jonah. 1996. *Hitler's Willing Executioners: Ordinary Germans and the Holocaust.* New York: Vintage.

Grady, Joseph and Johnson, Christopher. 2003. "Converging evidence for the notions of subscene and primary scene." In *Metaphor and Metonymy in Comparison and Contrast*, René Dirven and Ralf Pörings (eds), 533–554. Berlin: De Gruyter.

Gross, Raphael. 2000. *Carl Schmitt und die Juden. Eine deutsche Rechtslehre.* Frankfurt am Main: Suhrkamp.

Guldin, Rainer. 2000. *Körpermetaphern: Zum Verhältnis von Politik und Medizin.* Würzburg: Königshausen & Neumann.

Hale, David George. 1971. *The Body Politic. A Political Metaphor in Renaissance English Literature.* The Hague/Paris: Mouton.

Harris, Jonathan Gil. 1998. *Foreign Bodies and the Body Politic. Discourses of Social Pathology in Early Modern England.* Cambridge: Cambridge University Press.

Hawkins, Bruce. 2001. "Ideology, metaphor and iconographic reference." In *Language and Ideology, Vol. II: Descriptive Cognitive Approaches*, René Dirven, Roslyn Frank and Cornelia Ilie (eds), 27–50, Amsterdam: Benjamins.

Hitler, Adolf. 1933. *Mein Kampf* [23rd ed.]. München: Franz Eher Nachfolger.

—. 1992. *Mein Kampf* [with an introduction by D.C. Watt]. Ralph Manheim (trans.). London: Pimlico.

Hobbes, Thomas. 1680. *Behemoth. The History of the Civil Wars of England, from the Year 1640, to the Year 1660.* London: Crooke.

—. 1996. *Leviathan* [revised ed.]. Richard Tuck (ed.). Cambridge: Cambridge University Press.

John of Salisbury. 1909. *Policraticus sive De nugis Curialium et vestigiis philosophorum* [2 vols.]. Clemens C. I. Webb (ed.). Oxford: Clarendon Press.

—. 1990. *Policraticus. Of the Frivolities of Courtiers and the Footprints of Philosophers.* Carl J. Nederman (ed. and trans.). Cambridge: Cambridge University Press.

Johnson, Mark. 1987. *The Body in the Mind: The Bodily Basis of Meaning, Imagination, and Reason.* Chicago: University of Chicago Press.

Johnston, David. 1986. *The Rhetoric of Leviathan.* Princeton, NJ: Princeton University Press.

Kantorowicz, Ernst H. 1997 [1957]. *The King's Two Bodies: A Study in Mediaeval Political Theology* [with a new Preface by William Chester Jordan]. Princeton, N.J.: Princeton University Press.

Keller-Bauer, Friedrich. 1983. "Metaphorische Präzedenzen." *Sprache und Literatur in Wissenschaft und Unterricht* 51: 46–60.

Kempshall, Matthew S. 1999. *The Common Good in Late Medieval Political Thought*. Oxford: Oxford University Press.

Klibansky, Raymond, Panofsky, Erwin and Saxl, Fritz. 1964. *Saturn and Melancholy*. London/ New York: Nelson.

Koenen, Andreas. 1995. *Der Fall Carl Schmitt: sein Aufstieg zum "Kronjuristen des Dritten Reiches."* Darmstadt: Wissenschaftliche Buchgesellschaft.

Koschorke, Albrecht, Lüdemann, Susanne, Frank, Thomas and Matala de Mazza, Ethel. 2007. *Der fiktive Staat. Konstruktionen des politischen Körpers in der Geschichte Europas*. Frankfurt am Main: Fischer.

Kövecses, Zoltán. 2000. *Metaphor and Emotion: Language, Culture, and Body in Human Feeling*. Cambridge: Cambridge University Press.

Lakoff, George and Johnson, Mark. 1999. *Philosophy in the Flesh: The Embodied Mind and its Challenge to Western Thought*. New York: Basic Books.

Lakoff, George and Turner, Mark. 1989. *More than Cool Reason. A Field Guide to Poetic Metaphor*. Chicago/London: University of Chicago Press.

Lovejoy, Arthur O. 1936. *The Great Chain of Being*. Cambridge, MA: Harvard University Press.

Machiavelli, Niccolò. 2003. *The Discourses* [with an Introduction by Bernard Crick and revisions by Brian Richardson]. Bernard Crick (ed.). Leslie J. Walker (trans.). London: Penguin.

—. 2005. *The Prince* [with an Introduction by Maurizio Viroli]. Peter Bondanella (ed. and trans.). Oxford: Oxford University Press.

Martin, James R. and Wodak, Ruth (eds). 2003. *Re-reading the Past: Critical and Functional Perspectives on Time and Value*. Amsterdam: Benjamins.

Maschke, Günter. 2003. "Zum 'Leviathan' von Carl Schmitt." In *Der Leviathan in der Staatslehre des Thomas Hobbes. Sinn und Fehlschlag eines politischen Symbols*, Carl Schmitt (ed.), 179–244, Stuttgart: Klett-Cotta.

Meier, Heinrich. 1998. *Carl Schmitt, Leo Strauss und der 'Der Begriff des Politischen.' Zu einem Dialog unter Abwesenden*. Stuttgart/Weimar: Metzler.

Mouton, Nicolaas T. O. 2009. *On the Evolution of Social Scientific Metaphors*. PhD Dissertation. Copenhagen Business School.

Musolff, Andreas. 2004a. *Metaphor and Political Discourse. Analogical Reasoning in Debates about Europe*. Basingstoke: Palgrave-Macmillan.

—. 2004b. "The *heart* of the European *body politic*. British and German perspectives on Europe's central *organ*." *Multilingual & Multicultural Development* 25: 437–452.

—. 2007. "Which role do metaphors play in racial prejudice? – The function of anti-Semitic imagery in Hitler's 'Mein Kampf.'" *Patterns of Prejudice* 41: 21–44.

Nederman, Carl and Langdon Forhan, Kate (eds). 1993. *Readings in Medieval Political Theory 1100–1400*. Indianapolis/Cambridge: Hackett Publishing.

Neumann, Franz L. 1942. *Behemoth: the structure and practice of national socialism*. London: Gollancz.

Niemeier, Susanne. 2000. "Straight from the heart – Metonymic and metaphorical explorations." In *Metaphor and Metonymy at the Crossroads. A Cognitive Perspective*, Antonio Barcelona (ed.), 195–213. Berlin: Mouton de Gruyter.

Nietzsche, Friedrich. 1976. "Über Wahrheit und Lüge im außermoralischen Sinne." In *Werke III*, Karl Schlechta (ed.), 309–322. Berlin: Ullstein.

Pauwels, Paul and Simon-Vandenbergen, Anne-Marie. 1995. "Body parts in linguistic action: Underlying schemata and value judgements." In *By Word of Mouth: Metaphor, Metonymy and Linguistic Action in Cognitive Perspective*, Louis Goossens, Paul Pauwels, Brygida Rudzka-Ostyn, Anne-Marie Simon-Vandenbergen and Johan Vanparys (eds), 35–69. Amsterdam: Benjamins.

Peil, Dietmar. 1985. *Der Streit der Glieder mit dem Magen. Studien zur Überlieferung und Deutungsgeschichte der Fabel des Menenius Agrippa von der Antike bis ins 20. Jahrhundert.* Frankfurt am Main: Lang.

Pocock, John G. A. 2003. *The Machiavellian Moment. Florentine Political Thought and the Atlantic Republican Tradition.* Princeton: Princeton University Press.

Prokhovnik, Raia. 1991. *Rhetoric and Philosophy in Hobbes's Leviathan.* New York: Garland.

Rash, Felicity. 2006. *The Language of Violence. Adolf Hitler's Mein Kampf.* Frankfurt am Main: Peter Lang.

Room, Adrian (ed.). 1999. *Brewer's Dictionary of Phrase and Fable.* London: Cassell & Co.

Schmitt, Carl. 1996. *The Leviathan in the State Theory of Thomas Hobbes: Meaning and Failure of a Political Symbol.* George Schwab and Erna Hilfstein (trans.). Westport, Conn. and London: Greenwood.

—. 2003. *Der Leviathan in der Staatslehre des Thomas Hobbes. Sinn und Fehlschlag eines politischen Symbols.* Edited by Günter Maschke. Stuttgart: Klett-Cotta [Originally published in 1938, Hamburg: Hanseatische Verlagsanstalt AG].

Shakespeare, William. 1983. *Coriolanus.* In *The Complete Works of William Shakespeare* [with a glossary by William James Craig]. William James Craig (ed.), 758–797. London: Pordes.

Shorter Oxford English Dictionary [5th ed., 2 vols.]. 2002. Oxford/New York: Oxford University Press.

Skinner, Quentin. 1978. *The Foundations of Modern Political Thought* [2 vols.]. Cambridge: Cambridge University Press.

—. 1996. *Reason and Rhetoric in the Philosophy of Hobbes.* Cambridge: Cambridge University Press.

—. 2002. *Vision of Politics, Vol. 3: Hobbes and Civil Science.* Cambridge: Cambridge University Press.

Sontag, Susan. 1978. *Illness as Metaphor.* New York: Vintage Books.

Stirk, Peter M. R. 2005. *Carl Schmitt, Crown Jurist of the Third Reich: On Preemptive War, Military Occupation, and World Empire.* Lewiston, N.Y.: Edwin Mellen Press.

Strauss, Leo. 1963. *The Political Philosophy of Hobbes: Its Basis and its Genesis.* Elsa M. Sinclair (trans.). Chicago, IL: The University of Chicago Press [Originally published in 1936, Oxford: Clarendon Press].

—. 1998. "Anmerkungen zu Carl Schmitt, Der Begriff des Politischen." In *Carl Schmitt, Leo Strauss und 'der Begriff des Politischen.' Zu einem Dialog unter Abwesenden*, Heinrich Meier (ed.), 97–125. Stuttgart/Weimar: Metzler [Originally published in 1932, *Archiv für Sozialwissenschaft und Sozialpolitik* 67: 732–749].

Tillyard, Eustace M. W. 1982 [1943]. *The Elizabethan World Picture.* Harmondsworth: Penguin.

van Leeuwen, Theo. 2005. "Three models of interdisciplinarity." In *A New Agenda in (Critical) Discourse Analysis: Theory, Methodology and Interdisciplinarity*, Ruth Wodak and Paul Chilton (eds), 3–18. Amsterdam: Benjamins.

CHAPTER 3

New bodies

Beyond illness, dirt, vermin and other metaphors of terror

Daniel Skinner and Rosa Squillacote*

1. Introduction

This paper addresses the political implications of metaphors used to frame the US government's War on Terror. We argue that these metaphors are enabled and sustained by a problematic conceptualization of the 'body' (see also Musolff this volume) dating back to the 'scientific revolution' of the 17th century. These visions of the body frame the world in ways that carry with them anti-democratic tendencies, conceptualizing contemporary political struggles in terms of rigid binaries such as 'clean/dirty', 'healthy/ sick'. We suggest a two tiered approach for moving past these metaphors. First, we suggest a reconceptualization of the body itself. By recognizing that bodies are themselves understood metaphorically (for example, as 'machines'), we seek to retool that primary metaphor. Second, we suggest, if only provisionally, that a democratic politics may require that we abandon the 'body' metaphor altogether and attempt to see the world anew, through different lenses, new metaphors. We attempt to sketch a trajectory for undertaking this admittedly difficult project of political vision.

2. The politics of metaphor

In a now canonical essay, *The Epistemology of Metaphor*, Paul de Man identifies a central fallacy in the traditional view of language championed by John Locke (De Man 1978). According to De Man, Locke's desire to strip language of its 'abuses', the most important and common of which Locke identified as metaphor, and to lean instead on the 'literal', rested on a misunderstanding of the role of metaphor in language. For De

---

* An earlier draft was presented at Political Linguistics 2007 Conference, organized by Institute of Applied Linguistics, University of Warsaw, and Institute of English, University of Łódź, Poland, September 13–15, 2007. The authors would like to thank the anonymous reviewers at John Benjamins for helpful feedback.

Man, "The use and abuse of language cannot be separated from each other" (De Man 1978: 21). Accordingly, there is no transcendent phenomenon called language that can be adorned with metaphor, and there is no substratum of meaning lingering beneath eloquence. De Man holds that language itself is largely, if not completely, metaphorical, and that metaphor is the structural feature that makes language expressive, pliable and possible. De Man suggests that contemporary thinkers continue to replicate Locke's error. We identify this replication as a specifically political problem.

Using De Man to consider the metaphors that frame the US government's War on Terror, our central question is not whether metaphors should be deployed or not, but which metaphors best suit the political goals and values that we wish to advocate. We are interested in the qualitative and political effects of different metaphors and, specifically, finding metaphors that can support and frame democratic political projects. De Man's argument frees us from what Nietzsche called the 'optimistic metaphysics of logic' (Nietzsche 1979: 28), which envisions fixed, neutral structures in language, and opens the door to a constantly evolving political engagement over epistemological and discursive structures. We argue that some metaphors lend themselves to democratic projects while others encourage anti-democratic practices, including perpetual war.

Metaphors are usually deployed unconsciously, as claims about the world ('the state is a body') and not comparisons ('the state is like a body'). As these examples show, an important structural feature of the metaphor is that it does not call attention to itself. (That 'like' jumps out at us in ways that the 'is' does not.) This suggests that it is not only the case, as Nietzsche claimed, that "the drive toward the formation of metaphors is the fundamental human drive" (Bizzell and Herzberg 2001: 1177), but that there is a broader critique of language to be leveled here, namely that the very structure of the language that binds us depends upon shared, culturally-specific metaphors that are so basic to everyday life as to appear natural. Naturalized or not, by structuring images and rhetorical practices, metaphors shape political debates because, through their specific framing of political questions, they encourage definite outcomes. The apparent incontestability of the politics that metaphors entail is troubling to us, since a democratic politics requires the ability to see the world from several different angles and to challenge hegemonic framings of that world. This requires an epistemological diversity that can come only from a disruption of those metaphors that come to appear natural and necessary in contemporary political discourse.

The 'which metaphor' question is at a crossroads where political valuation and epistemological commitments converge in language. Settling upon a point in language that is thought to be non-metaphorical – the 'literal' or the 'proper' – is merely to settle upon a particular metaphor, and to not view that metaphor as metaphorical, to naturalize it as the locus of meaning. Such a move simultaneously seeks to depoliticize that metaphor and to establish it as the norm. De Man notices this move in Locke:

> The closer the description comes to that of metaphor, the more dependent
> Locke becomes on the use of the word 'properly'. Like the blind man who cannot

understand the idea of light, the child who cannot tell the figural from the proper keeps recurring throughout eighteenth-century epistemology as barely disguised figures of our universal predicament (De Man 1978: 18).

De Man (1978: 19) concludes that Locke's 'proper' language is "not a question of ontology, of things as they are, but of authority, of things as they are decreed to be." It is in Locke – and not language – that the attempt to naturalize occurs.

We maintain that the question of which metaphors come to structure a society's linguistic and epistemological life is closely correlated with a specifically political question: What are the political consequences, in terms of vision and epistemic organization, of deploying certain metaphors? Different metaphors do different things and do things differently. They interact with and stabilize ideological frameworks. We want in part to perform a conscious reconsideration of often-unconscious metaphorical framings to find conceptual structures that help stimulate and frame democratic visions.[1] We maintain that the 'body' metaphor, in its most common contemporary articulation, is among the most anti-democratic of metaphors.[2]

In his study of circumcision, Gollaher notes that "Every age has its own metaphors for the body" (Gollaher 2000: 79). The 'body' metaphor that we locate in today's War on Terror finds a parallel statement in Thomas Hobbes's seminal work of political theory, *Leviathan* (1688). The scientific revolution of the 17th century, including Harvey's discovery of the circulation of blood, deeply impacted Hobbes, who sought to do to political order what biologists were doing to the human body. Hobbes's solution to the unruliness and contingency of the 'nature of 'men', which he famously characterized as a 'war of all against all', was a distribution of power that would guarantee that states would function like self-propelling systems. They would function, that is, like the human body that his contemporaries had theorized (Hobbes 1994: 76). In *Leviathan*'s opening pages, Hobbes establishes the metaphors upon which the latter parts of his argument are to be built:

> For seeing life is but a motion of limbs, the beginning whereof is in some principal part within, why may we not say that all automata (engines that move themselves by springs and wheels as doth a watch) have an artificial life? For what is the heart, but a spring; and the nerves, but so many strings; and the joints, but so many wheels, giving motion to the whole body, such as was intended by the Artificer? Art goes yet further, imitating that rational and most excellent work of Nature,

---

1. Admittedly, this is not De Man's project, but an application of his theory. We are primarily interested not in contributing to the theory of metaphor, but in leveling a political challenge to actively engage metaphor on the level of its political effects.

2. This has permeated all domains of social knowledge as well. For example, we speak of 'bodies of work', refer to groups of organized bodies as a 'corps', and speak of embodiment and disembodiment in a host of senses, in art, literature, psychology, metaphysics and beyond. Profit-making entities are afforded the legal appellation 'corporation', a status that gives such entities 'rights' and 'responsibilities' identical to those reserved for individual people.

man. For by art is created that great LEVIATHAN called a COMMONWEALTH, or STATE...in which the sovereignty is an artificial soul, as giving life and motion to the whole body; the magistrates and other officers of judicature and execution, artificial joints; reward and punishment...are the nerves, that do the same in the body natural; the wealth and riches of all the particular members are the strength; salus populi (the people's safety) its business; counselors... are the memory; equity and laws, an artificial reason and will; concord, health; sedition, sickness; and civil war, death (Hobbes 1994: 3–4).

That the body is at the center of Hobbes's political theory is clear enough. What is interesting to note, however, is that Hobbes's body is itself metaphored as a machine and that this paragraph uses these metaphors to do important political work. Hobbes's body is a picture of a system concerned primarily with its own internal workings, hostile to the world outside. This body is insular, unable to draw upon the world outside to transcend or build upon its inborn resources. Hobbes's metaphors control from a basic level his famous anti-Aristotelian move: the state is concerned with life itself, and not the attainment of the 'good life' that Aristotle envisioned beyond bodily maintenance. Hobbes is concerned not with moving beyond the systems of the body, but extending the logic of those systems to guarantee social order, of applying body-machine logic more completely and systematically.[3] The product of this move, for Hobbes, is the evacuation of politics – with all of its contingency and potential for disruption – from the social order. Hobbes thus prescribes the cleansing of politics as a prerequisite for stability and peace.

More recently, in the 20th century, Hannah Arendt has argued that the condition of political life left in the wake of the modern period is analogous to housekeeping. Arendt argues that repetitive and quotidian activities have consumed 'the political' and turned political actors into managers of 'social questions' (Arendt 1990: 59–114). With the aim of resuscitating politics from these repetitive cycles, Arendt conceptualizes freedom as the transcendence of the 'necessary' logics imposed by bodily maintenance. 'Action', the condition in which Arendt says that humans can be rightly called free (and Arendt thought that freedom was at the heart of politics) "would be an unnecessary luxury ... if men were endlessly reproducible repetitions of the same model..." (Arendt 1958: 7–8). In her hope that mankind would recover its ability to act, Arendt pushes against the subordination of political life to necessary logics such as those imposed by a politics modeled after the modern body metaphor.[4] To conceptualize

---

3.   For an overview of this history of body-as-machine metaphors, see Martin (1994: 23–44).

4.   Arendt conceptualizes politics against those forces that preclude possibility: theses of inevitability and non-political guarantees of freedom are antithetical to her vision, and thus Hegel, Marx and other supposed determinists come in for criticism. They also come in for criticism for other bodily metaphors. Marx, for example, often wrote of each epoch's being 'pregnant' with the possibility of the next and, in *Capital* (1990: 916), argued that "Force is the midwife of every old society pregnant with a new one." Arendt (1970: 44–45) argues that 'force' should be

political life through 'body' metaphors is, for Arendt, to remove politics from that body. The problem with understanding political life as a body, for Arendt, was that it could not be transcended, and the modes of life it made possible were therefore limited and predetermined. Arendt thinks that politics, on the other hand, is open-ended and unlimited. It is, literally, the place where 'miracles' can happen and peoples can discover possibilities and potentials that they themselves may never have thought possible. Politics, that is, is a source and site of motion and not the conservation of existing conditions (such as that suggested by health) or boundaries (such as that suggested by border control). Politics, in short, is not security for Arendt.

Though Hobbes and Arendt deploy 'body' metaphors differently in their political theories, a common thread runs through them: these metaphors serve to constrain, and not to expand, political possibility. The body never becomes an engine of change. Where Hobbes wants to seize the capacity of bodies to reduce contingency in the name of order, Arendt wants to look (and move) past it to establish a politics of freedom and action. Both see in the 'body' metaphor of the modern era the suppression of freedom and the prevention of politics. The key difference is that Hobbes finds this useful, while Arendt finds it dangerous.

As indicated above, the body that we are concerned with is not the body in general, but the 'body' of a specific metaphorical framing, the systemic, closed body located in the modern era. It is a body that views the pursuit of health as a kind of war and licenses aggression in the attainment of health. In her important study of illness metaphors, Susan Sontag expresses concern about the proliferation of military metaphors in confronting disease because "it is not desirable for medicine, any more than war, to be 'total'" (Sontag 1990: 182–83). Anthropologist Emily Martin adds to this insight that

> ...media coverage of the immune system operates largely in terms of the image of the body at war. Even when the problem is not an external enemy like a microbe but an internal part of 'self', the military imagery is extended to notions of 'mutiny', 'self-destruction', and so on (Martin 1994: 62).

We want to suggest not only that these military metaphors stem from a certain application of militarism to a non-contingent body, but that the metaphors by which we currently conceptualize the body often lend themselves *to* military metaphors and, in fact, cannot be separated from the military metaphors that shape them. It is quite 'natural' within this metaphorical world that a war footing should appear as the logical response. Within the metaphor that gives shape to the modern body, it *is* logical. By reconsidering the body itself, and freeing it from the logics that make it a site of those fantastical binaries of the modern imagination – healthy/sick, dirty/clean – we hope to begin to think about health anew in a way that can free us from cycles of political violence.

---

reserved for usages such as 'force of nature' – those activities in which humans are thought to play passive roles.

Sontag helps us to see just how deep the metaphoring of disease runs, and how heavy the social baggage of being sick can be. Her work makes clear that the conceptualization of disease is closely related to the conceptualization of the body, if not simultaneous. Sickness is part of the conceptualization of this body. In our view, Sontag's most important contribution is her claim that metaphors play crucial roles in determining social approaches toward and judgments about those with diseases, and therefore serve at least a precondition for political questions. Yet, for all of her insight into the cultural framing of disease, Sontag envisions a future that we believe to be both impossible and inadvisable, where disease is unencumbered by metaphor. Her legitimate concern with the capacity for 'illness' metaphors to produce stigma leads her to argue that disease should not possess meaning. We want to take one step further and argue that political movements, education, de-stigmatization, and care may potentially benefit from the flexible and discursive nature of language. Metaphor can produce stigma, but it can also frame problems so that we may address them. In other words, where Sontag wants to "expose, criticize, belabor and use up" the metaphors she criticizes (Sontag 1990: 182), we want to reinvigorate and reinvent these metaphors, to engage with the political project of giving disease new meanings that allow us to address the question of health – both bodily and social – anew. We want to recast the question of the 'body' metaphor so that we may widen and redirect the scope of moral and political critique, to remove it from the often exclusive site of a fictive victim's body to include a broader social analysis. What we decidedly do not want to do is to pretend that we may evade meaning altogether. To notice the metaphorical 'face' of disease is to notice the terrain on which political struggles and efforts around social approaches toward disease must take place. Attempts to escape this terrain merely cede the terms of an important political question and to grant legitimacy to a way of thinking that is not necessarily legitimate.

3.   Clean bodies/healthy bodies

The political questions we are concerned with here stem from the fact that by conceptualizing the political world through 'body' metaphors – especially the particular body we describe above – a range of corollary metaphors are simultaneously licensed. This license stems from the extension of the body to narratives of cleanliness and disease, as well as other metaphorical appendages that this body evokes. Such narratives work together in terrorism rhetoric.

The classic Judeo-Christian formulation of cleanliness is found in the book of *Leviticus*. While the specific (if labyrinthine) logics of this book are not important for our purposes, the more basic observation to be made about the Law of the Levites is that which anyone who has ever lived with another human being knows already: cleanliness is the site of consistent conceptual contestation and difference, and not an a priori universal truth. The same, though perhaps on a different register, can be said for disease.

The notion of what constitutes a condition of disease is both historical and subject to constant change.[5] The period of modern politics with which we are identifying the problematic 'body' metaphor is marked by a series of key conceptual shifts, perhaps the most important of which was the modern state. At the same time that the modern nation-state was coming into being out of the multilayered and less rigid Italian landscape, notions such as sovereignty were coming into focus. As Pitkin argues in her important psychological study of Machiavelli and gender, during Machiavelli's time

> [t]he community and its laws, its *nomos*, were now understood as human artifacts, the products of choice, subject to further action. Individuals increasingly felt required to create order for themselves and take charge of their communities (Pitkin 1999: 11–12).

Freud, as well, understands modernity to be bound up with the idea of continence – the construction and maintenance of borders, and a perpetual struggle to retain and keep pure that which lies within them. Yet, for Freud, modern civilization is also marked by pervasive metaphors of 'cleanliness' and 'hygiene': in modernity "we expect to see the signs of cleanliness and order..." for "[d]irtiness of any kind seems to us incompatible with civilization. We extend our demand for cleanliness to the human body too" (Freud 1961: 46). In her classic text, *Purity and Danger* (1966), Mary Douglas deepened the anthropological study of the relationship between cleanliness and social categories of risk and danger, showing that the organization of political and social categories is bound to codes of hygiene.

'Public service' announcements and posters placed on New York City and New Jersey Transit trains following September 11, 2001 illustrate the convergence of cleanliness and the threat of terrorism against the state, understood as body. These announcements and posters seamlessly merge anti-litter and 'clean train' campaigns with anti-terrorist rhetoric, playing on the same imagery that establishes the notion of the clean state. Visions of health and cleanliness in the body politic, accessible precisely because the state is conceptualized as a body, give shape to terrorism rhetoric by unraveling corollaries established the 'body' metaphor. Posters for the "If You See Something, Say Something" advertising campaign on New York City subway trains, depict a pristine (and somehow empty) train sullied by a single (and, of course, black) bag, ominously tucked under a seat. New Jersey Transit ads were even more explicit. A poster campaign introduced in early 2002 depicted an empty train seat with a September 11, 2001 issue of *The New York Times* ("US Attacked"),[6] surrounded by crumbs and

---

5.   The spirit of this approach stems from the kind of genealogical work Foucault introduces in *Discipline and Punish*. Noting the movements of the terms of criminality and sickness over time calls into question the necessity of these social classifications (Foucault 1979).

6.   The use of the 9/11 edition of the *Times* is instructive, suggesting that time must be frozen in the minds of riders of mass transportation. This freezing of time seems intended to remind riders of 9/11, producing a kind of zen-like trance on that event to remind them to remain disciplined and vigilant. (An analogy might be the proliferation of Post-It notes Americans put in

garbage. Beside the seat, Uncle Sam, the symbol of American military recruitment, points his 'we want you' finger at the reader to call attention to the following announcement, each point bulleted with American flag clipart:

(1) a. Security is a Team Effort
     b. Keep America Moving
     c. Here's how you can help:
     d. Avoid bringing any food or beverages on trains so that no crumbs, powder or residue can be misinterpreted.
     e. Clean Up your area when you depart, so that powders are not mistaken for hazardous substances that can result in police or HAZMAT[7] response.
     f. Remove your trash, bags, and other materials such as newspapers from the trains and stations.
     g. Remember to take everything with you upon your departure.
     h. Do not leave your bags or packages unattended.
     i. A Clean Environment is a Safe Environment.
     j. NJ Transit. The Way to Go.[8]

Other ads depicted greasy, dripping brown-paper packages, ominous not only for fat content and the epidemic of American obesity, but now also for terrorist attack potential. This merging of civic-minded cleanliness equates terrorist threats to subway trash. Keeping New York clean is integral to keeping New York safe, and encouraging subway riders to not litter is presented as a way to make it easier to identify potential threats; in post-September 11 America, trains are clean and run on time, as 'clean train campaigns' aim to reduce the number of reported 'suspicious packages' and service interruptions. Win-win for New York and New Jersey, free from attack and trash.

Yet, is this not enabled by a larger metaphorical framing related to this question of the body, and is not this merging of anti-terrorism and cleanliness campaigns directly related to our theorization of the healthy body, simultaneously rendered as an impossibly clean body? A body which is no longer fixated on the possibility of attacks from outside, but from attacks injected into subway trains, airports and other public spaces?[9] The important shift that terrorism supposedly marks is that the old security model – of attacks from outside, against a sovereign, bounded territory – is no longer operative and, just as the possibility of terrorism stews within, internal vigilance is required to combat it, much like we must survey and monitor our bodies for signs of sickness, or

---

their homes to remind them to take sandwiches to work or to take the trash out. These ads are laundry lists for life during the War on Terror.)

7. 'Hazardous Materials'

8. New Jersey Transit public service advertisement. This ad is no longer available online, but hangs in the Center for Place, Culture and Politics at the CUNY Graduate Center in New York.

9. One might also ask what this means about the pre-September 11 filth of New York subway trains and stations. Was the dirt and disease of the system a dormant 'breeding ground' for terrorists?

our homes from the crumbs that invite rodent and insect invaders. Terrorism is marked by an 'army' of such metaphors: terrorists 'breed' in 'sleeper cells', waiting to be 'activated', cancer-like, to make their attack, perhaps by detonating a 'dirty bomb'. With these individuals the outward diagnoses of cleanliness and benignity is of no value: any cell may be 'radicalized', made malignant (which, again, raises a problem of interpretation; what one sees may not be what one thinks it is). These invaders, moreover, will no longer arrive in planes and uniforms, their difference marked and announced, but will arise from within and among us, our 'body politic'. The 'scourge' of terrorism constitutes an insidious turning of the body against itself. Terrorism, like dirty trains, is a product of our own making, a grim illustration of what happens when we let down our 'guard'.[10] The cause of this problem, moreover, is a constant source of debate; it might even lay in pluralism itself, in America being made vulnerable by immigration or the penetration of borders by 'illegals'.[11] Many of these immigrants – even documented, 'legal' immigrants – will live in the most famously disgusting of conditions – houses stacked with bunk beds, barrack-like, trash strewn about the floors.[12] These threats are recognizable, moreover, via another metaphorical framing commonly found in immunological discourses: these threats do not speak 'our' language, and so we struggle to understand and decode them. The immune system identifies bacteria as alien precisely because it speaks a different language than the healthy body; immuno-defense systems recognize them as 'foreign' and 'attack' to eliminate them. Speaking a language different than that of the system arouses suspicion.

---

10. Televangelist Jerry Falwell went further, blaming moral degradation for 9/11: "God continues to lift the curtain and allow the enemies of America to give us probably what we deserve... I really believe that the pagans, and the abortionists, and the feminists, and the gays and the lesbians who are actively trying to make that an alternative lifestyle, the ACLU, People for the American Way – all of them who have tried to secularize America – I point the finger in their face and say, 'You helped this happen'" (Harris 2001).

11. More recently, this has been transferred to an unlikely domain: an argument against national health care. An attempt to bomb the Glasgow airport by four doctors of Middle Eastern descent unleashed a fury of speculation on American television, beginning with Fox News's "Your World with Neil Cavuto," that government-run health care, with its focus away from profit, would send qualified American doctors elsewhere or into other occupations, creating the need to import doctors from elsewhere, including the Middle East. Thus, the 'unintended consequences of socialized medicine' posed a potential threat by directing Middle Eastern immigration directly into the healthcare system. See www.crooksandliars.com, July 6, 2007.

12. One need only read the news about the conditions the airplane hi-jackers lived in to get a sense of this characterization. More recently, however, a problematic report was issued by the NYPD indicating that attempts to profile terrorists were difficult indeed: among its key findings was the "There is no useful profile to assist law enforcement or intelligence to predict who will follow this trajectory of radicalization. Rather, the individuals who take this course begin as 'unremarkable' from various walks of life." The full report, "Radicalization in the West: The Homegrown Threat," is at http://www.nyc.gov/html/nypd.

September 11 brought with it a resurgence of rodent metaphors. When George W. Bush promised Americans that "We will find those who did it, we'll smoke them out of their holes," he was not innovating, but evoking a traditional framing of racist political imagery that dates back at least to Nazi Germany, but probably earlier to the discovery of germs themselves.[13] Bush promised Americans that "We'll get them running and we'll bring them to justice," but these efforts culminated not in the hills of Afghanistan with Osama bin Laden but, oddly, in Iraq, in the squalid 'spider hole' from which Saddam Hussein was said, according to Maj. Gen. Raymond Odierno, to have been "caught like a rat" ("Saddam 'Caught Like a Rat' in a Hole"). Meanwhile, back in the War on Terror, promises of capturing the originally stated enemy – bin Laden – had gone unmet, with bin Laden's name all but disappearing from major speeches. Bush made clear that his priorities had shifted when asked about Bin Laden at a March 13, 2002 press conference, "I don't know where he is. You know, I just don't spend that much time on him" (Bush 2002). Could bin Laden's elusiveness serve to postpone, even permanently, the attainment of hygienic desire promised by the dominant body metaphor, with the Bush administration open to the charge of poor or failed house-keeping? Was Iraq – the event which provided the Administration with its "Mission Accomplished" moment – supposed to reinstate the neat, state-based imaginations of traditional warfare that lent themselves toward completion where terrorism allowed only for perpetual *interruptus* of the nationalist imagination? The displacement of bin Laden with Hussein seems to mark an attempt at structural completion within the terms marked by the modern body; the shift marks an attempt to wage war in spaces where the clean body could be located in American terrorism rhetoric. So established, that body could then be referenced and allowed to function as evidence that the American 'homeland' had been secured. The only question was whether the substitution would work, whether Iraq would in fact serve as a legitimate stand in, and whether Americans would let Bush cast Iraq for that particular role.

4.   Reworking the body

Our question is twofold: first, what are the stakes of metaphoring politics through visions of the body? Second, what metaphors govern this body itself; or: what is the

---

13.   A study of disease from the perspective of social imagination and imagery reveals the importance of the metaphors through which societies conceptualize health and threats to health. Bruno Latour's study of Louis Pasteur shows the dramatic shift that occurred as France (and, soon thereafter, the world), changed from believing contagions to transfer through smells – 'miasmas' – to germs (Latour 1988). What these and other studies of diseases underscore is the thoroughly discursive nature of 'disease', and the constraining function that these discourses have on political options and strategies. For Hitler's use of this imagery, and the structural benefits it affords a nationalist binary, see Kenneth Burke's "The rhetoric of Hitler's battle," in Shapiro (1984: 61–80).

epistemological status of that body? New metaphors are required to escape the logic of total commitment to the binaries of 'sickness/health' and 'cleanliness/dirtiness' that we have suggested the modern 'body' metaphor instantiates. Yet, a more immediate, short-term political intervention could involve re-working and re-conceptualizing the body itself. Indeed, in attempting to think of a metaphor unrelated to the body, we encounter a problem that any attempt to introduce new metaphors poses: whether we talk about machines, or households, or bodily functions, the framing of politics tends to revert back to the body. This problem may be that because this body metaphor is constitutive of the epistemology of contemporary political life we cannot easily see the work that it does (Martin 1990: 417). We are caught in and dependent upon its imagery. But if it is the case, as we think it is, that 'body' metaphors are usually themselves metaphored, and often, in contemporary politics, metaphored through the language of war, then surrendering to this double-metaphored body, reducing political life to it, is akin to reducing politics to a war mentality and allowing two different metaphorical systems to fuse. Refusing this reduction, and fusion, may seem overly idealistic and even to constitute an attempt to meddling in processes that lie beyond political control. But this is an idealism that we refuse, politically, to go without and a meddling that is necessary to resist the naturalization of, and surrender to, a political problem. Our first task lies in reconfiguring the 'body' metaphor rather than seeking to supplant it altogether. This strategy, within the context of bodies at war requires reconceptualizing the nature of the war itself (Martin 1994: 99).

We hope that these shorter-term offerings will call attention to the fact that the 'body' is itself already the site and subject of metaphorical shaping, thus making it accessible discursively and politically. We want to remember what Nietzsche claims moderns often forget, namely that our "original perceptual metaphors are metaphors" that we take "to be the things themselves" (Bizzell 2001: 1176). After this the Nietzschean methodological precaution – illustrated well by Hobbes's 'body/machine'[14] – we can see that the body itself is both doubly open to revision and doubly difficult to rework.

Any effort to suggest new metaphors through which we can re-envision political life, metaphors that escape the logical and political pitfalls associated with the body, is likely to slip into silliness, if only because those metaphors frame our political life to such a degree that stepping outside of them is necessarily awkward. It may be the case that silliness may actually be necessary to epistemic disruption. It is with weariness, then, that we offer a few preliminary thoughts on directions that theorists might want to consider in challenging the modern 'body' metaphor.

---

14. Machines, of course, are also understood metaphorically. The machine that fixes Hobbes's body does not serve as a backstop into which metaphorical shifting may slide. Yet, Galileo and Harvey's work served as such a reference point for Hobbes that it does seem to give firm grounding to the particular qualities of Hobbes's 'machine' metaphor. This only serves to underscore the epistemological importance of technology; the technologies extant when we enter into the world will likely frame our understanding of that world – and they will be naturalized.

In defining health, the 'body' metaphor that we have identified simultaneously produces a corollary sick nation. What this latter nation represents, by structural necessity, is whatever constitutes its 'opposite' – perhaps democracy, civilization, or freedom. Driven by an a priori commitment to the pursuit of a pure state of health, country X is justified in trying to 'cure' nation Y since these nations cannot co-exist in a world comprised of increasingly porous boundaries more akin to the human epidermis than the walls separating, for example, Israel and Palestine. Unable to keep threats out, this construction offers eradication as its only option, licensing not only defensive, but offensive postures. Beyond this structural analysis, the political problem with the binary 'body' metaphor is not its fixation on the absolutist notion of a 'cure', but its license of violence, its prescriptive aggressiveness. Distinctions of good and bad may be tenable, but when this choice leads the way for oppression, imperialism, and domestic militarism, we must take notice and consider the political function of those metaphors that prefigure the perceived terrain of political and ethical intervention. If questioning boundaries constitutes a foundational political act (and we think that it does), then questioning metaphors – the frames that maintain and structure those boundaries – constitutes an even more fundamental ethical and political imperative.

'Friend/enemy' rhetoric both establishes and seizes differences such as the 'sick', the 'dirty', the 'healthy' and the 'clean'. But how can we determine the seriousness of the threat they present? In the modern framing, the threat is total – deadly and not merely weakening, for the modern machine metaphor requires that bodies stay in motion unless countered. Will the attack come from the outside, or from within? Either way, what is the proper response to this invasion? What is the cure? The modern body answers: expelling, eliminating, and destroying the sickness and its threats. Its responses are totalized schemes bent on attaining a fantastical purity. These 'sick body' and 'sick state' metaphors perversely suggest the possibility of annihilating a body in the name of preserving its health. So understood from a perspective of politics, and a democratic politics in particular, such a vision is akin to radiation treatments that kill cancer patients or lobotomies that produce catatonic victims of the patients they are intend to cure.[15] Attempts by larger, purportedly healthier states to cure less-developed, mostly formerly-colonized or so-called rogue states often produce worse conditions in those states. Health practices are often localized culturally and intervening states usually do

---

15. This is not to say that these treatments are not efficacious at times – even most of the time. The broader point, however, is to understand the problems associated with the narratives and promises that encumber these treatments. A more robust, non-binary notion of health forces us to think anew about our goals in the pursuit of health. Even when a cure is simple and effective – for example, cough medicine or Advil for headaches – there is not always an imperative to make use of it, especially if the patient perceives the cure to be disagreeable in some way. One may not take Advil, especially if headaches are frequent, to resist becoming acclimated too quickly to higher dosages. Cough syrups typically taste awful and are avoided if at all possible by the victim of a cold. The presumption of 'health at all costs' is patently not a natural one, but rather imposed in such a way as to favor a reactionary and violent political agenda.

not adequately learn about the people they invade. In other words, aside from the in-herent ethical problems they pose, totalizing schemes of paternalism and intervention do not often result in improving conditions in those states.[16] (If one considers 'democ-racy' – to be the gauge of a nation's health, and understands democracy as a practice emanating from the local practices and preferences of a people, the idea of 'importing democracy' appears incredibly odd.) Nevertheless, a nation that sees itself as the mod-el of certain health is in danger of perpetuating a vicious cycle, invading cancerous terror cells to attain the healthy body but always missing the mark of health because that body was from the beginning wrongly theorized.

5.   Beyond the body

Two moments in American politics can help us think past the metaphorical framings of the present 'body' metaphor and War on Terror. The first occurred during a high profile interview of President Bush by television host, Matt Lauer:

> (2)   Lauer: You said to me a second ago, one of the things you'll lay out in your vision for the next four years is how to go about winning the war on terror. That phrase strikes me a little bit. Do you really think we can win this war on terror in the next four years?
>
> President Bush: I have never said we can win it in four years.
>
> Lauer: So I'm just saying can we win it? Do you see that?
>
> President Bush: I don't think you can win it. But I think you can create condi-tions so that those who use terror as a tool are less acceptable in parts of the world – let's put it that way. I have a two-pronged strategy. On the one hand is to find them before they hurt us, and that's necessary. I'm telling you it's necessary. The country must never yield, must never show weakness and must continue to lead. To find Al-Qaeda affiliates who are hiding around the world and want to harm us and bring 'em to justice – we're doing a good job of it. I mean we are dismantling the Al Qaeda as we knew it. The longterm strategy is to spread free-dom and liberty, and that's really kind of an interesting debate.... (Bush 2004).

In this passage, Bush attempts to negotiate and alter the totalizing rhetoric that he in-augurated on September 11, 2001. Predictably, the attempt failed, since it called into

---

16.   The proverbial 'elephant' in the room where words like 'rogue state' are traded requires that we at least note the stronger critique that such healthy states – the superpowers and colonial nations – may have produced the very sickness that they seek to cure. This is, in part, Noam Chomsky's critique of US policies in the Middle East and Latin America, in which he suggests that U.S. benefits from instability because of the 'pretexts' these conditions afford U.S. when it wants to intervene. This certainly changes the political calculation and 'problem' of unhealthy states and regions. See Chomsky (2000).

question earlier framings and thus appeared only as backpeddling. The next day, the 'life/death' stakes that he had established in the War on Terror forced him to return to his previous position: "Make no mistake about it: We are winning and we will win" (Allen 2004). In an apparent attempt to lower expectations and turn the 'war' into something reasonable and more politically palatable, Bush realized the power of his own metaphor, and was forced to return to its fold. It was, in fact, the revenge of that metaphor and the return of the limitations that Bush had established earlier.

The second moment involves a revision of bodily health that sought to alter the rhetorical orientation of the body's relationship with disease. In 2007, then Democratic presidential candidate John Edwards, and his wife Elizabeth, announced publicly that Elizabeth had stage-four breast cancer – a very serious prognosis in any metaphorical framing. In their announcement, Elizabeth appeared relaxed and confident, claiming to take the news without perceiving it as a death sentence. According to Mrs. Edwards's doctor, Lisa Carey, "Metastatic breast cancer is considered incurable, but it is also considered treatable and controllable. We don't know what's going to happen with Mrs. Edwards, but we do know there are very effective therapies." Edwards and her doctor would focus on treating and containing the cancer rather than trying to cure it, with Carey noting that the medical profession has moved away from thinking about cancer – and not just cancer as dire as Mrs. Edwards's – in terms of cure. In her comments, Carey emphasized the 'heterogenous' nature of stage four breast cancer, disarming the press – and the Edwards' – from leaning on binary, catch-all diagnoses or prescriptions. John Edwards analogized his wife's disease to diabetes – "no longer curable, but it is completely treatable" (Edwards: Cancer 'No Longer Curable').

The Edwards' approach to cancer recasts the 'body' metaphor as it is currently applied in political life. The policy implications are clear for conceptualizing sickness not as an enemy, but rather something incorporated into life, even as it needs to be addressed. Lacking an enemy to destroy, it becomes possible to focus on the role the perceived enemy may actually play in the state, or the rhetorical basis of the enemy's grievances against the state. It becomes possible to theorize 'health' and 'sickness' together, to understand their interaction but also the ways in which this interaction challenges constructions that hold only insofar as that body is constructed against an external world. Beyond individual deaths and terrorist attacks, this view allows us to think about the terrain of bio and social power, to think about what we call 'sickness' today as part of life, but also of life as part of sickness, and not its antithesis. Indeed, as Martin notes in her evaluation of the work of the biologist Ludwik Fleck, sickness is very much bound up in the possibility of life, and both concepts coexist in close proximity. Fleck understood that

> ...any "invading" organism had to have been living in our vicinity, symbiotically, long enough to be able to stick to our cells. The ability to generate a biological process could only come about from previous encounters. Thus, a previously minor organ is could only rise to prominence within the body's life unit, not invade it as a foreign "other" (Martin 1990: 421).

Fleck was concerned about the prevalence of 'war' metaphors in popular and scientific immunology. Though Martin goes on to argue that such 'events' would be 'rare', it is also the case that, when analogized back to the world where global capital continues with increased ferocity to "batte[r] down all Chinese walls" (Marx and Engels 2002: 55) and borders become less and less tenable, they are becoming more common. This is one reason that 'realist' international relations scholars who once defended the centrality of sovereignty arguments because they conceptualized the state through the metaphor of the modern body, have to a large extent been forced to rethink their positions. Those anachronistic conceptualizations simply do not make sense in today's world (Legro and Moravcsik 1999; Krasner 2000).

The new model, on the other hand, allows us to see that we already cope with the continual degradation and renewal of the body politic/body, and that neither is guaranteed by any one prescription or solution. They are, as Foucault might say, extralegal, non-juridical forms (Foucault 1994). 'Bodies politic' – if we still want to call them this – are not comprised of organic matter, consigned to eventual decay and death, but are systems of power, perpetuated by bodies across time, re-establishing and re-affirming these bodies' constitution. There is no reason why we should need to ascribe to nations the limitations of individual bodies, for states, as political and not organic productions, are capable of historical transcendence. They do not 'die' by some inexorable, inevitable or other metaphysical logic. Recognizing this difference removes from the political imagination a fantasy of the sovereign body capable of being walled off from environmental factors and posits disease itself – and the management of disease – as part of an organic system, bound up inextricably with indicators of health such as exercise, diet, environment, stress and other factors that make bodies vulnerable. The view that health is not the opposite of sickness opens the way to new policy and developmental possibilities. It rescues the body from the binary construction that fetishize the avoidance of death and the violent justifications and total war practices that these metaphors license.

Lest we be accused of espousing a crass idealism, it is important to note that the justifications and practices of the binary body, and that body's political possibilities, are probably not mistakes. Seen from some (in our view, unimaginative and undesirable) perspectives, binary-driven, Manichaen politics are certainly useful, and the body we are criticizing is attractive to advocates of those usually undemocratic positions and politics. But even as it is uncertain whether our perspective could find traction, for example, in the present War on Terror, it is nonetheless important to call extant political concepts and assumptions into question. This is why these questions are properly the domain of political theory, which has historically been among the few academic disciplines willing to take up the task of re-envisioning, by expanding, political possibility. New metaphors are needed to accomplish this.

Nor are the constructions we advocate 'immune' to being perverted and appropriated for violent political ends. As in the Lauer interview, the Bush (or any future) administration may claim that 'this enemy is not one we can kill' in order to shift the focus from total to perpetual war. In changing the 'body' metaphor, we must ensure that this new understanding is not redeployed as a justification for more violence, but rather as a means of avoiding violence altogether, a body that has positive content (dynamism, life) and is not defined in terms of its so-called enemies. Similarly, ideals of contentment and complacency must be kept at bay. An exodus from binary thinking is not an excuse for inaction, but a call for more carefully considered and politically informed action.

The democratic body that we would like to emphasize, then, is precisely (and ironically) the one that Bush attempted and failed to instate.[17] The moment of its utterance was, for Bush, a moment of acute political realism. We want to suggest a move toward this body, not out of political expediency, but because this new body enables us to think through political problems, rather than their being determined through a closed, systemic metaphor that is both outdated and wrong. This new body is open to a new range of as yet unforeseen possibilities of manipulation and management. Health, insofar as it is still used to think about politics, would be achieved through perpetual activity and interaction and not ends secured only with reference to some outside. As Foucault (1990) shows, there are a number of ways in which one can conceptualize the body. And the nature of this conceptualization matters gravely as one attempts to care for oneself in a world that constantly seeks new ways to deploy bodies to maintain and strengthen power relations. The body of the democratic society, however much it may militate against modern desires for stability, lives and changes in ways that elude attempts to make it predictable, and in fact relishes in that unpredictability, confident in its capacity to endure change. What Hobbes thought to be sickness is recast, in this view, as political health. This nation is conducive to life, unframed and undetermined by an absolutist, existentialist narrative given meaning only by the possibility of death. This new metaphor frames politics with open, as opposed to closed, imagery, and opens systems so that they may consort with the world formerly thought to be 'outside'. In so advocating, we are not revolutionizing visions so much as updating them to more accurately represent the world in which we live today.

6.   Conclusion

The 'body' metaphor's role in political discourse cannot be overstated. The political imagination of the US during the War on Terror continues to be constrained and guided by the visions of the body that we have outlined above. Just as American self-identification is staked on the stability of the framings that this body offers, its politics are

---

17.   In fairness, his reframing was not intended for the purposes we are suggesting, but seemed to be an attempt at reframing a badly mismanaged war. By suggesting a reevaluation of metaphors, we want to make the old body and the old sick/healthy model rhetorically inaccessible, not something to be used during good times and jettisoned when the going gets rough.

governed by this frame's logic. It may seem odd to claim that polities create frameworks that then appear to function as external constraints. However, this interplay between metaphor and political action is exactly what gives the 'body' metaphor its power. As it becomes naturalized in public discourse, its contingency is easily forgotten. It becomes unproblematic even as it stands at the center of deeply problematic political questions. It is therefore important to examine and critique the body metaphor in order to gain critical distance from the social epistemology it enforces. Democratic politics requires that it be denaturalized.

As discussed above, the current conception of the body metaphor installs a binary logic that directs us toward violence in addressing political questions and 'threats'. This metaphor externalizes sickness from the body in ways that are unnecessary and politically dangerous. We envision a project wherein the health/sickness binary that controls so much of our political language, hence policy, is reconfigured and replaced with a metaphor that embraces an interrelationship of health and sickness. This metaphor will alter the relationship between the body and the world and provide a conceptual framework that is more conducive to democratic practices. The metaphors of this new body will allow for a range of responses and actions that binary logics foreclose.

When we understand that a person can be healthy and simultaneously have a cold, or that a person with cancer can still be considered healthy in ways that today's body disallows, we can begin to understand that a country that one disagrees with is not necessarily sick. At the same time, we can begin to think about those problems in relation to and not outside of some fictive, boundary-delineated state. Instead, it is possible that such disagreements, formally thought to be signs of disease and dysfunction, can register as the very substance of democratic political life. In this view, violence becomes not a disease to be eradicated with more violence, but a symptom that requires careful social analysis and systemic reflection.

References

Allen, Mike. 2004, September 1. "Bush backtracks on terrorism remark." *The Washington Post*: A21.

Arendt, Hannah. 1958. *The Human Condition*. Chicago: University of Chicago Press.

—. 1979. *On Violence* San Diego: Harcourt Brace and Company.

—. 1990. *On Revolution*. London: Penguin Books.

Aristotle. 1986. *The Politics*. Thomas A. Sinclair (trans.). London, New York: Penguin Books.

Bizzell, Patricia and Herzberg, Bruce (eds). 2001. *The Rhetorical Tradition: Readings from Classical Times to the* Present [2nd ed.]. Boston and New York: Bedford/St. Martins.

Bush, George W. "Press Conference." Retrieved March 13, 2002 from http://www.whitehouse.gov/news/releases/2002/03/20020313–8.html.

Bush, George W. and Lauer, Matt. "Bush: 'You cannot show weakness in this world." Retrieved September 2, 2004 from http://www.msnbc.msn.com/id/5866571.

Chomsky, Noam. 2000. *Rogue States: The Rule of Force in World Affairs*. Cambridge: MA: South End Press.

De Man, Paul. 1978. "The epistemology of metaphor." *Critical Inquiry* 5 (1): 13–30.

Douglas, Mary. 1966. *Purity and Danger: An Analysis of Concepts of Pollution and Taboo.* London: Routledge & Kegan Paul.

"Edwards: Cancer 'No Longer Curable.'" Retrieved March 22, 2007 from www.cnn.com/2007/health/03/22/cancer.edwards.

Foucault, Michel. 1979. *Discipline and Punish: The Birth of the Prison.* New York: Vintage Books.

—. 1990 [1984]. *The History of Sexuality Vol. 3: The Care of Self.* London: Penguin.

—. 1994. *Power.* James D. Faubion (ed.). New York: The New Press.

Freud, Sigmund. 1961. *Civilization and Its Discontents.* James Strachey (trans.). New York and London: W.W. Norton and Company.

Gollaher, David. 2000. *Circumcision: A History of the World's Most Controversial Surgery.* New York: Basic Books.

Harris, John F. 2001, September 14. "God gave U.S. 'what we deserve', Falwell says." *The Washington Post*: C03.

Hobbes, Thomas. 1994. *Leviathan: With Selected Variants from the Latin Edition of 1668*, Edwin M. Curley (ed.). Indianapolis: Hackett.

Hodges, Adam and Nilep, Chad (eds). 2007. *Discourse, War and Terrorism.* Amsterdam: Benjamins.

Krasner, Stephen D. 2000. *Sovereignty: Organized Hypocrisy.* Princeton: Princeton University Press.

Latour, Bruno. 1988. *The Pasteurization of France.* Alan Sheridan and John Law (trans.). Cambridge, MA: Harvard University Press.

Martin, Emily. 1990. "Toward and anthropology of immunology: The body as nation state." *Medical Anthropology Quarterly* 4 (4): 410–26.

—. 1994. *Flexible Bodies: Tracking Immunity in American Culture from the Days of Polio to the Age of AIDS.* Boston: Beacon Press.

Marx, Karl. 1990. *Capital: A Critique of Political Economy, Vol. I.* Ben Fowkes (trans.). London: Penguin Classics.

Marx, Karl and Engels, Friedrich. 2002. *The Communist Manifesto.* London, New York: Penguin Books.

Merton, Robert K. and Trenn, Thaddeus J. (eds) 1979 [1935]. *Genesis and Development of a Scientific Fact.* Chicago: University of Chicago Press.

Moravcsik, Andrew and Legro, Jeffrey W. 1999. "Is anybody still a realist?" *International Security* 24 (2): 5–55.

Nietzsche, Friedrich. 1979. *Philosophy and Truth: Selections from Nietzsche's Notebooks of the Early 1870s.* Daniel Breazeale (trans.). New Jersey: Humanities Press.

Pitkin, Hanna Fenichel. 1999. *Fortune Is a Woman: Gender and Politics in the Thought of Niccolò Machiavelli.* Chicago, IL: University of Chicago Press.

Plato. 2003. *The Republic* [2nd ed., Penguin Classics]. Henry Desmond Pritchard Lee (trans.). London; New York: Penguin Books.

"Saddam 'Caught Like a Rat' in a Hole." Retrieved December 15, 2003 from www.cnn.com/2003/world/meast/12/14/sprj.irq.saddam.operation.

Shapiro, Michael. 1984. *Language and Politics.* New York: New York University Press.

Sontag, Susan. 1990. *Illness as Metaphor; AIDS and Its Metaphors.* New York: Doubleday.

CHAPTER 4

Legitimation through differentiation

Discursive construction of Jacques *Le Worm* Chirac as an opponent to military action

Jan Chovanec

1. Introduction

The legitimation of military action in public discourse tends to be accompanied by various linguistic strategies on all levels of analysis, including such techniques as hyperbolic rhetoric on the textual level, the skilful use of presuppositions on the pragmatic level, the manipulation of transitivity on the syntactic level, and the choices of naming and collocation on the lexical level. These all call for an interdisciplinary approach to analysis (cf. Wodak and Chilton 2005). The interplay between these factors results in the creation of in-group consensus on political issues with a typically international dimension, while contributing to the polarization of different opinions and the exacerbation of divisions between various national/political/religious groups, based on stereotypical perceptions.

Not surprisingly, the military intervention in Iraq in 2003, as one of the phases of the recent 'war on terror', was preceded by similar discursive practices in the media (cf., e.g., Lule 2004 on the use of metaphors). International opinion on the necessity and grounds for the intervention was divided – the official policy of the USA and its allies (most notably Great Britain) on the one hand versus the views of various opponents represented by the UN (most notably France) on the other.

One of the clear indicators of the growing polarization of opinion and tension was the negative presentation of 'others', namely opponents to unified action by western countries. Based on material from the British tabloid daily *The Sun* – one of the staunchest supporters of US-led military action – this analysis describes recurrent patterns of lexical choices used when referring to French opposition to US intervention, represented by the French president, Jacques Chirac. It documents the gradual development of the 'le worm' nickname in *The Sun* from an ad-hoc attribute and a quasi-title to an independently used form of reference. The form is interpreted in the context of the negative stereotyping of the French and the role of animalistic metaphors applied to members of 'out-groups'.

2. Legitimation, categorization and discursive construction of groups

Various social actions performed in the public context are sanctioned by a consensus held by the public on the reasons for such events. Legitimation, as the "widespread acknowledgement of the legitimacy of explanations and justifications for how things are done" (Fairclough 2003: 219), concerns not only the tacit presupposition of common knowledge and the existence of shared assumptions, but also a great deal of – often purposeful – discursive activity manufacturing such implicit and shared agreement between individual members of the public. The construction of the mass consensus may rely on positing a contrast between positive and negative legitimating values (cf. Fowler 1991; Caldas-Coulthard 2002), and allowing for a discursive formation of a simplified dichotomy: the mutually opposed groups of 'us' vs. 'them'.

In discourse, legitimation – as an overarching goal of discourse on the macro-level – is achieved through the use of several broad discursive strategies, realized by particular textual forms and structures as manifestations of the micro-level of discourse. Van Leeuwen (2007), for instance, describes the following four discursive strategies:

- authorization, i.e. legitimation by reference to the authority of tradition, custom and law, and persons with institutional authority, typically in the form of verbal process clauses and assertions;
- moral evaluation, i.e. legitimation based on moral values, typically hinged on evaluative adjectives triggering moral concepts and inviting value-based moral interpretations;
- rationalization, i.e. legitimation by references to the various goals, uses and effects of social practices, usually realized by generalized actions, goal-orientations, means-orientations, and effect orientations, as well as theoretical rationalizations referring to 'the way things are';
- mythopoesis, i.e. legitimation through narrative and storytelling, taking the form of either moral tales, where characters are "rewarded for engaging in legitimate social practices, or restoring the legitimate order," or cautionary tales, whose "protagonists engage in deviant activities that lead to unhappy endings" (van Leeuwen 2007: 105–6).

Analysts in the area of political linguistics also operate with a similar concept – legitimization, which is described in terms of "a linguistic enactment of the speaker's right to be obeyed" (Cap 2008: 22). It is connected with the speaker's authority, rationality and 'rightness', and is manifested by various strategies for listing reasons to be obeyed, such as "the awareness and/or assertion of the addressee's wants and needs, reinforcement of global and indisputable ideological principles, charismatic leadership projection, boasting about one's performance, positive self-presentation and many more" (Cap 2008: 22).

The audience or the adversary is, by contrast, typically subject to 'delegitimization', i.e. direct or indirect negative other-presentation, serving the purpose of explicating why the others should not be obeyed. As Chilton (2004: 47) notes, delegitimization includes "acts of blaming, scape-goating, marginalizing, excluding, attacking the moral character of some individual or group, attacking the communicative cooperation of the other, attacking the rationality and sanity of the other. The extreme is to deny the humanness of the other."

Legitimization in political discourse is connected with the need to promote certain representations (Chilton 2004: 23). As far as social actors are concerned, their representations lead to social categorization, i.e. the articulation of social identity in relation to group memberships. As Hausendorf and Kesselheim (2002) note, one's in-group is defined, to a considerable degree, on the basis of the image which the in-group has of other groups, as well as the perceived difference between them. Representation thus relies on the discursive expression of comparison and contrast between social groups.

From a cognitive perspective, categorization in linguistic communication concerns the processing of information and creating a mental picture of other people as a way of coping with the complexity of the outside world (Skarżyńska 2002: 252). The perception of others by categorization, i.e. their representation in terms of social types and groups rather than individuals, is a gross simplification because the individual features of a particular member are excluded. Categorization typically accompanies ideological thinking, suffering from underestimating similarities and overestimating differences between groups and categories (Skarżyńska 2002: 253). Where individuality yields to group presentation, stereotypes may prevail (Fowler 1991: 17).

In terms of linguistic resources, categorization of individuals is realized through various referential and predicative strategies (Reisigl and Wodak 2001; Richardson 2007). The former are naming options which can contribute towards the individualization or collectivization of social actors (cf. van Leeuwen 1996). The latter, as strategies whereby qualities are linguistically assigned to persons, events, entities etc., are expressed through attributes, predicates, collocations, comparisons, metaphors, allusions, presuppositions, implications, etc. It is through these referential and predicative strategies that authors of texts are able to "project meaning and social values on the referents" (Richardson 2007: 50).

Categorization in terms of the binary opposition of 'us' vs. 'them' is typically connected with what van Dijk (1992a, 2002) calls the 'ideological square'. This concerns the positive self-presentation and negative other-presentation, where negative characteristics and actions of the out-group are emphasized while any positive traits are downplayed and overlooked. The referential and predicative strategies of categorization with respect to the discursive construction of such mutually opposed groups have been subject to numerous studies in the area of discourse analysis. These studies have focused on racism (Reisigl and Wodak 2001; van Dijk 1992b, 2000), immigration (van Dijk 1987; Santa Ana 1999; El Refaie 2001), tabloids (Clark 1998; Conboy 2006), media (Caldas-Coulthard 2002; Chovanec 2007, 2009), politics (Duszak 2002), the Iraq war (van Dijk 2007; Becker 2007), etc.

The analytical part of this article will describe one specific referential strategy used for constituting an out-group and ultimately serving the purpose of discursive legitimation: the choice of a metaphorical category label as an extreme instance of negative other-presentation realized through dehumanization/animalization of one's opponent. This referential strategy is seen not merely as the result of a particular lexical choice. On the contrary, it is explained as a dynamic process gradually developing in time and modified by the particular newspaper to suit its momentary needs. It is understood as a part of tabloid rhetoric and a bottom-level technique of persuasion.

3.   Constructing opponents: Axis of evil and axis of weasels

The escalating international crisis at the beginning of 2003 gave hints of an impending military intervention in Iraq. The US-led international coalition sought authorization for its military action from the UN, which never came, as well as a justification for the intervention by various claims, some of which eventually turned out to be unfounded (e.g. the claim about weapons of mass destruction). This situation was marked by the emergence on the international scene of the dichotomy of 'us' vs. 'them', i.e. those involved in what came to be known as the 'War on Terror'. The opponents were clear – they were constituted by 'them', i.e. terrorists and their supporters, metaphorically labeled as 'the Axis of Evil', a famous phrase coined by the US President George W. Bush in his State of the Union Address on 29th January 2002. After the events of 2001 and the build-up to the military action in 2003, what was indisputable was that legitimization of actions in various media and discourses depended on the key discursive strategy construing "the 'international community' around the age-old cultural and political division between 'us', the civilized west, and 'them', the Islamic threat" (Chouliaraki 2007: 5). These group constructs – where "*We* represent[ed] the western democracies that fight against terrorism or 'rogue states', and *They* ... the terrorists or states that threaten us" (van Dijk 2007: 63) – became subject to the effects of semantic polarization, both positive self-presentation and negative other-presentation.

However, the definition of the in-group (i.e. 'us') was not so easy. From the very beginning, there were doubts about the support and active participation of some of the Western countries in the US-led coalition forces, i.e. countries traditionally classified among 'allies'. In other words, the notion of the 'international community' needed to be discursively affirmed with respect to *who is a part of it* and *who is outside of it*. On the international level, the 'troublemakers' were quite clear: those countries blocking the UN sanction for war. The strongest opponents were France and Germany, their opposition earning them the negative label of 'axis of weasels', coined on the basis of a punning allusion to 'axis of evil'.

The simple dichotomy of 'us' vs. 'them' thus eventually split into a set of three subgroups: the trichotomy of 'us' (countries willing to support military action) vs. 'them 1' (countries unwilling to support such action) vs. 'them 2' (countries seen as supporting terrorism). In metaphorical terms, these groups came to be occasionally referred to as 'the axis (or coalition) of the willing' vs. 'the axis of weasels' vs. 'the axis of evil'. Not surprisingly, the newly constructed division within what had previously been assumed to constitute the single group of 'us' (cf. Figure 1) was likely to become subject to discursive characterization in terms of bipolar categorization and the ideological square mentioned above: i.e. the negative other-presentation and affective polarization connected with the need of the first group ('us') to differentiate itself from and denigrate the second group ('them 1' – 'axis of weasels'), as set against the background of the third group ('them 2' – 'axis of evil').

Such a fragmentation of groups is not uncommon. Hausendorf and Kesselheim (2002), for instance, note how a social group is divided into two sub-groups, which are then related to each other. Under this mechanism of social categorization, the relevant groups are subject to three superior tasks: they are introduced, then compared/contrasted and eventually evaluated. They conclude that social categorization in discourse is "not a static and pre-fixed social given but a dynamic and open process," in which participants actualize and modify social categories available to them (Hausendorf and Kesselheim 2002: 280).

At this politically sensitive time, the British media largely took a partisan approach to the coverage of current international issues. While some media channels, such as the *Daily Mirror* stood in opposition to the official position of the British government, as vocalized by Prime Minister Tony Blair (cf. Figure 2, which uses the strategy of dehumanization by labelling Blair 'a monster'), others, most notably *The Sun*, firmly supported the government position on the necessity of taking military action in Iraq together with the US-led coalition forces. The example from the *Daily Mirror*, a paper with a different political agenda, show how the same strategy of differentiation by dehumanization is used to construct a different out-group: namely, one composed of those eager to go to the war as represented by Blair. Further delegitimization of Blair is achieved through the use of allusive word play, which strips away his seriousness to the point that the becomes ridiculous, denying and twisting his official title of 'Prime Minister'.

Not surprisingly, it was on the pages of *The Sun* that legitimation of the official position was played out to a significant degree. Since one of the legitimation strategies concerns the construction of mutually opposed groups and their polar categorization in affective terms, *The Sun* applied various techniques of negative other-presentation, most notably in the construction and negative characterization of the French as opponents to military intervention unsanctioned by the UN.

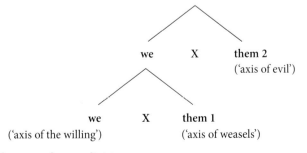

Figure 1. Trichotomy of group divisions

Figure 2. *Prime Monster? Drag us into this war without the U.N. Tony and that's how history will judge you. For God's sake man, DON'T DO IT*: Front page of the *Daily Mirror* (14 March 2003)

3.1   Foreignisms and social categorization

Discourse representation is not a static process; it dynamically changes and develops in correspondence with the changing circumstances (context) of the speech event. This was also the case with the gradual delimitation of the out-group, constituted by the French, as can be traced in the reporting of *The Sun*. The discursive strategy of affective polarization, connected with the delegitimation of the actions of the out-group (i.e. not supporting military action), became more pronounced once the French took a definite firm stand in opposition to the official British and American policies.

Initially, i.e. at the very beginning of 2003, the French position was not yet clearly determined. Since there were indications that the French might support the official Anglo-American position, there were no grounds for a negative other-presentation of a potential ally in the 'war on terror'. In other words, the French were still more or less perceived as a part of the 'we' group opposed to the 'axis of evil' constituted by 'them'.

Thus, for instance, the front page headline in *The Sun* of 5 February 2003 declared *French say oui to war*, without any trace of negative stereotyping. The text of the relevant article ran as follows:

(1)   Chirac hint he will bow to pressure from Blair and join attack on Iraq. French leader Jacques Chirac showed signs of caving in over a war in Iraq ...

At this moment, importantly, Chirac was still referred to by his full name and his official title (*French leader*), in contrast to the later developments in *The Sun*'s rhetoric.

As noted above, however, these developments were gradual. A few days later, *The Sun* ran a story under the headline *Shame on you Chirac*, in which the negativism towards the French was escalating, although the terms of reference still retained Chirac's full name and title:

(2)   Shame on you Chirac
       French repay WW2 Allies with *betrayal.* FRENCH president Jacques Chirac
       was denounced last night for *scuppering* NATO's central policy of pledging ...
       (*The Sun*, 11 February 2003).

The text includes highly negative lexical items; *betrayal* of the WW2 allies, for instance, is an example of moral evaluation (cf. van Leeuwen 2007 above), inviting a moral interpretation in terms of shared cultural context and the readers' expectations of what is right and wrong. A similar effect is achieved by the metaphorical verb *scuppering* (literally defined as 'the deliberate sinking of one's ship'), which connotes cowardice and dishonesty. The condensation of complex ideas ('Chirac refusing to support an unsanctioned war') into simplistic propositions ('French ingratitude and betrayal') is typical of tabloid rhetoric, in which the situation is redefined as a moral failure of the French – as the newly constructed out-group – towards their WW2 Allies, i.e. the British and the Americans ('us'). It is symptomatic that such a simplification is based on the use of classic figures of speech – metaphor (*scuppering*), metonymy and synecdoche (both *pars pro toto*, where 'Chirac' stands for 'the French' in general, and *totum pro parte*, where 'the French betrayal' stands for the reaction of one individual, i.e. the French president). The presentation of the French and of Chirac as semantic agents of the process verbs 'betray' and 'scupper' helps to construct the in-group as victims – a well-known rhetorical move that can be resorted to when some legitimating or justifying action needs to be taken against the out-group.

Significantly, the first of the two above-mentioned examples from *The Sun* contains the French expression *oui*. Such an inclusion of a foreignism, usually fairly simple and fully comprehensible within the media's national group, is common particularly in tabloids. The Daily Mirror, for example, ran the story on the same day under the following headline: *Non! Chirac rebuffs Blair on Iraq...then his own MPs snub him over Lords* (*Daily Mirror*, 5 Feb 2003). Such borrowings are stereotypically used to localize a news story or identify the nationality of the relevant news actor. More generally, they stand as illustrations of the media's lighthearted attitude towards mediating information and evidence of their playfulness with linguistic forms, despite the fact that such a manner of presentation may have political implications, e.g. confirming shared common-sense values (cf. Chovanec 2008: 240).

However, apart from being connected with 'infotainment', foreign words may serve a more profound social and political purpose. As Duszak (2002: 213) notes, "... borrowings carry the default value of 'otherness.'" This means that foreign words potentially predicate the existence of groups that are mutually opposed on the basis of linguistic/national/ethnic boundaries. A light-hearted tone of presentation may also contribute to a more effective persuasion; as Chouliaraki (2007: 4) notes in passing, "[t]he most effective work of legitimization takes place through leisure and seemingly 'innocent' entertainment."

As will be shown in the next section, such use of foreign words constituted one of the strategies for constructing 'otherness' that were resorted to in *The Sun* when legitimating the official British position on the war in Iraq in 2003. In this way, the divide between 'us', i.e. the British (as readers of *The Sun* and supporters of the impending military action) and 'them', i.e. the French (as represented and personified by their president Jacques Chirac) was deepened.

3.2   Le Worm Chirac

A crucial step in the process of constructing opponents occurred on 20th February 2003, when *The Sun* coined a new nickname for the French president Jacques Chirac – *Le Worm*. What is significant about this referential strategy is the combination of the French definite article and an English common noun designating an animal, which, when capitalized, assumes the properties of a proper name.

The foreign element not only identifies the nationality of the individual referred to by the common noun but also indicates 'otherness', which is possible with out-group members of nationalities other than one's own. British opponents to the military action, obviously, do not fall within exactly the same out-group, although they may have been referred to in the British pro-war media at the time in rather strong and negative terms, too (cf. the then common phrases *Labour rebels; quitters* – also used attributively as in *quitter Cook; (war) wobblers*, and even the ironic *doves* in *Chirac, Schroeder and the other doves don't realize that their actions are more likely to cause a war, The Sun*, 4 March 2003). Clearly, since British opponents cannot be classified as 'others' because of belonging to a different linguistic and national community, what needs to be found are means of naming other than just a simple linguistic indicator of otherness, such as the French definite article. The lexical labeling of opponents on the national level is, thus, a strategy of naming and shaming (i.e. derogating and delegitimizing), while it simultaneously legitimizes the policies of the in-group. Once again, since one's political opposition could be criticized for not being with 'us' (as van Dijk 2007: 68 suggests was the case in Aznar's Spain, with the inference along the lines of 'who is not with us is against the international community'), the ground is laid for semantic polarization, i.e. negative other-presentation.

The foreign element in the newly coined label activates group divisions and contributes to a dichotomizing view of the world. As Duszak (2002: 213) observes, "... foreign words in native texts can considerably influence, if not construct by themselves, the perception of social identities of their users. ... the 'other' word seems a viable candidate for cueing in-group and out-group meanings in communication." The single use of the French definite article can thus be a powerful linguistic tool contributing towards characterizing individuals and groups of people in terms of social inclusion or exclusion.

A similar explanation can be offered within the framework of van Leeuwen's theory of social actors (1996: 52). This referential strategy concerns determination of the identity of an individual which can be best described as differentiation, i.e. pointing out the difference between the author of the text (or the in-group) and some other individual (or the out-group). At the same time, the lexical combination *Le Worm* is a strategy of categorization, i.e. the placement of an individual within a group constituted by certain shared features. Importantly, the categorization in this case concerns the placement of Jacques Chirac into a group constituted by animals rather than humans. His categorization is thus connected with dehumanization: the denial of his placement within some group constituted by humans (even where such human groups might be strongly negative cf. the potential category labels *rebels, quitters* and *wobblers* mentioned above). The denial of humanness is a discursive act of extreme delegitimization (cf. Chilton 2004: 47), indicating that the opponent represented is not perceived on equal terms. In the mixed mode phrase *le worm*, dehumanization thus combines with foreignization as two specific subtypes of differentiation, serving the purpose of negative other-presentation. It may be argued that dehumanization/animalization constitutes an argumentative topos on par with other rhetorical topoi such as criminalization, orietalization and (e)vilification (cf. Chouliaraki 2007: 6), which tend to be resorted to when one is discursively construing one's enemy (in Chouliaraki's case, the 'Islamic threat' was construed in this way before the Iraq War in 2003).

3.2.1 *Negative national stereotyping*
In addition to the linguistic and social context of its initial usage, the nickname category label *Le Worm* calls for an explanation not only in terms of the negative connotations of the label but also in the context of negative national stereotyping. This will be supplemented, in the next section, by a description of its actual usage in *The Sun* and the gradual penetration of the nickname into the shared cultural context.

The category label *Le Worm* was first used in the headline *Le worm meets the monster* (20 February 2003). The explanation for the designation is provided in the text of the article by means of an inserted relative clause:

(3)   President Jacques Chirac – *dubbed le worm because he is so spineless* – put up Mugabe and his wife Grace at a five-star hotel, courtesy of the French taxpayer.

The negativity resides in the adjective *spineless*, which becomes highly evaluative on account of its metaphorical usage. The negative tone is continued throughout the text, in which Chirac is referred to as being *slimy* for meeting the Zimbabwean president Robert Mugabe (i.e. *the monster*), who was in international isolation at the time. Clearly, the negative stereotyping draws on semantic fields connected with unpleasant sensory perception – a strategy that turned out to be used heavily by *The Sun* in its subsequent articles.

The pro-war campaigning by *The Sun* even took the form of a special edition of the newspaper that was distributed in France. The front page contained Chirac's photograph superimposed on the body of an earthworm crawling out of a picture of France and supplemented with the headline *CHIRAC EST UN VER* [*Chirac is a worm*] (see Figure 3).

The accompanying text was fully in French and was specifically addressed to French readers (*THE SUN, journal lu quotidiennement par dix millions de personnes, présente ses salutations aux parisiens*). The article provides an explanation for the use of the expression *le ver/worm*:

> (4)   Les citoyens du Royaume-Uni estiment que M. Chirac, qui au Royaume-Uni est surnommé le "Ver," se pavane avec arrogance sur la scène internationale avec pour seul objectif de donner à son pays une importance démesurée par rapport à la réalité.
>   [British people feel Mr. Chirac, who in the UK is nicknamed the 'worm', is arrogantly strutting about trying to make France seem more important in the world than it really is][1] (*The Sun*, 20 February 2003, French edition).

The expression *le ver* ('worm') is not used in the text itself as a direct designation for Chirac. It occurs only in the headline and in the fourth paragraph where it is used

Figure 3. Front page of *The Sun* – a special edition distributed in France, 20 February 2003

---

1.   Translation from http://www.robbernard.com/archives/2003_02.html; see also http://archives.tcm.ie/businesspost/2003/03/30/story98843049.asp.

predicatively as a complement of the copula verb *to be*. This, as will be made apparent later, is significant, since the category label is – in this initial phase – employed to establish the characteristics of Chirac on the basis of an equational sentence ('Chirac is X'). The co-referential chain that consists of expressions referring to Chirac throughout the article thus runs as follows:

(5)   Chirac → (*est un ver/is a worm*) → votre président, Jacques Chirac/your President, Jacques Chirac → (is a disgrace) → le president Chirac/President Chirac → M Chirac → (qui au Royaume-Uni *est surnommé le "Ver"*/who in the UK *is nicknamed the 'worm'*) → le président français/the French President → France/France and its leader → votre President/your president

In this sense, the text of the front page article differs significantly from the second article in the same issue of *The Sun*. In the headline *Le Worm meets the monster*, the category label is used independently, which may indicate the paper's assumption that the reference of such a category label is clear to members of a particular speech community (i.e. it forms a part of shared background knowledge or cultural context).

Needless to say, the use of a category label in a headline independently of the name of the relevant person may also be a part of the textual conventions of headlines, under which a descriptive noun in the headline becomes linked with the proper name only in the subsequent text (cf. the progression of the co-referential chain: *Le Worm* → *Jacques Chirac*). In such a case, the delayed introduction of the proper name operates as a strategy of headline rhetoric: it activates readers' involvement by withholding factual information from the headline and providing it only in the text of the article proper (typically in the lead, i.e. the first paragraph). Last but not least, the autonomous use of a common noun – as a category label referring to a person – may be subject to multi-modal analysis (where the identity of the individual may be established extra-linguistically, for example, on the basis of an accompanying photograph or some other visual clue).

The negative content of the newly developed label *le worm* stems from two sources: first, its verbal context (i.e. its collocations as well as notions predicated about the bearer of the label), and second, its cultural context (i.e. its connotations with respect to animal metaphors and the tradition of negative national stereotyping of the French).

The negative stereotype is co-constructed and reinforced by lexical items used in connection with *le worm* or Chirac. Some of the examples above indicate that the negativity is carried by highly evaluative verbs and adjectives, such as to *strut (arrogantly)*, which conveys pride and insolence, and to *wriggle,* metaphorically conveying one's unwillingness to commit oneself to a clear position. The appositional explanations of the nickname likewise contain evaluative adjectives with a similar meaning (... *Chirac – dubbed le worm because he is so **spineless**)*. The expression *spineless* was, moreover, intertextually connected with the political discourse of the time and potentially dependent on the notorious *backbone* declaration by the US president, George Bush:

> (6)   I'm optimistic that the U.N. Security Council will rise to its responsibilities, and this time ensure enforcement of what it told Saddam Hussein he must do. See, I believe when it's all said and done, free nations will not allow the United Nations to fade into history as an ineffective, irrelevant debating society. (Applause) I'm optimistic that *free nations will show backbone* and courage in the face of true threats to peace and freedom (13 February 2003).[2]

Since Chirac is metaphorically lexicalized as an animal, it is no wonder that many of these negative expressions derive from the semantic field of animal characteristics. However, while such expressions are descriptive when applied to real animals, they assume highly evaluative connotations when used metaphorically, as in **wriggling** *anti-war worm Jacques Chirac,* **slippery** *Jacques Chirac, Le Worm Jacques Chirac* **wriggled out of** *a new veto threat*, etc. Significantly, not only do such expressions evoke the animal metaphor even in the absence of the lexeme *the worm*, but they are also very easy to visualize, unlike some of their possible replacements (cf. *slippery* vs. its synonyms **evasive, *indecisive, *faltering, *unsteady*).

The negative content of the nickname is also supported by some of the propositions. As a semantic agent, Chirac – alias le worm – *turns to terror state; blasts; does dirty deals* and, in one headline, readers are even told that *Le worm sold out his nation*. As a semantic patient, Chirac suffers actions typically reserved for animals, cf. *Blair* **buries** *le worm; Tony Blair yesterday* **stamped** *on wriggling anti-war worm Jacques Chirac* (reformulated in the relevant headline as *Iraq rap for Chirac*), etc.

The dehumanization of one's opponent through the use of an animal metaphor is a common discursive technique which serves the purpose of legitimation. El Refaie (2001), for instance, notes that such metaphors may sanction the use of inhuman and violent behavior and justify various official measures against immigrants (cf. e.g. phrases such as *tightening up the security net*, where the animal metaphor applied to people is activated indirectly by the expression 'net').

There are numerous other examples of such dehumanization of opponents – achieved through their animalization – in the area of political and media discourse. In the context of the Iraq war, Saddam Hussein, for instance, was frequently lexicalized by the media in terms of the 'rat' and 'spider' metaphors at the time of his capture in December 2003, partly also because of the circumstances under which he was apprehended (cf. the headline *Saddam captured in underground* **lair**. *Ace in the Hole;* Daily Mirror, 15 December 2003). On 7th December 2006, the New York Post referred to Chirac and the German Chancellor Schroeder as *Surrender Monkeys* for advocating

---

2.   The comment was made at a time when the U.N. Security Council was highly reluctant to authorize any military involvement in Iraq. Full text of the president's speech is available at: http://www.whitehouse.gov/news/releases/2003/02/20030213–4.html.

the withdrawal of troops from Iraq (and even made a rather banal collage of their faces superimposed onto monkey bodies). Similarly, the Iraqi opponents were labeled as 'flies' – a metaphorical transformation allowing for military action against them to be referred to as *swatting*, as revealed by a quote from a transcript of the National Security Advisor, Condoleezza Rice, testifying before the September 11 Commission:

> (7)   We also moved to develop a new and comprehensive strategy to try and eliminate the al Qaeda network. President Bush understood the threat and he understood its importance. He made clear to us that he did not want to respond to al Qaeda one attack at a time. He told me he was tired of *swatting flies*.[3]

Since worms, spiders, rats, and flies (as well as snakes and other vermin) are 'low' animals, considered as bothersome and of no immediate benefit to humans, they are, when applied to one's opponents, particularly effective as a strategy of negative social categorization. In this case, certain representations about one domain ('low animals') are metaphorically mapped onto a target domain ('Chirac'/'our opponents') (cf. Chilton 2004: 52). Dehumanizing metaphors are commonly used to describe powerless groups, such as various ethnic and racial minorities and immigrants (cf. Santa Ana 1999; El Refaie 2001).

In the case of the 'worm' metaphor, the negative perception is underlined by certain symbolic connotations and cultural knowledge. Owing to certain physical characteristics of invertebrate animals (notably the absence of legs), worms are in common wisdom seen as deviant creatures – rather peripheral to the prototypical concept of an 'animal' – and rank among taboo and 'dirty' animals. They tend to be connected with disease and absence of hygiene, i.e. as a potential threat to humans. Together with snakes, they are often seen as evil and dangerous creatures (cf. the perception of the snake in Western cultures as a result, among other, of its Biblical connotations).

3.2.2   *National stereotyping and English-French hostility*

Moreover, the application of the *le worm* label to Chirac also capitalized on the traditionally negative national stereotyping of the French. While there are certain positive animal stereotypes which the French themselves are proud of (cf. the symbolism of the 'rooster'), the French are commonly described in derogatory terms as frogs or, with a more specific reference to their culinary habits, as frog-eaters. This stereotype has existed since the 19th century; prior to that, the English speaking community used the metaphor of 'frogs' to refer to the Dutch, while the French were presented as 'apes' (due to their enjoyment of fashion, perceived by the British as excessive). Interestingly enough, negative sensory perception of the French plays a role here, too – cf. the stereotypical perception of their love of garlic (this was subject to ridicule by British artists themselves, cf. e.g. the satirical prints by James Gillray (1757–1815), such as *French*

---

3.   The full transcript is available online at: http://www.globalsecurity.org/security/library/congress/9–11_commission/040408-transcript.htm.

Freedom – English Slavery). The evocation of negative sensory connotations – as also present in expressions collocating with Chirac's 'worm' metaphor (*squirming; wriggling; spineless; slippery*) – thus needs to be considered among other strategies concerned with affective polarization and the presentation of out-groups.

Negative stereotyping of the French is, of course, related to the fact that the French serve as the most prominent reference group for the British (or, the English, to be more specific). The English-French historical, political, social and cultural relations over the past one thousand years have been so intense that the French – disliked in some respects and admired in others – stand as an out-group against which the English act out their national identity. Thomas (2003: 230), for instance, convincingly shows how Englishness was formed in early Norman England of the 11–13th centuries and what role "the French Other" played in "strengthening and reinforcing existing English identity." Very early, the enmity between the Normans and the French underlined the developing English-French hostility, especially after the Normans became settled and identified with the English. The animosity (though at times offset by admiration and friendship) that many people nowadays stereotypically feel towards the French thus has been at the root of English national identity for a very long time.

Clearly, historical events such as the Battle of Hastings, the Norman Conquest of Britain, the Hundred Years' War, the French Revolution, the Napoleonic Wars, the Allied invasion of Normandy, etc., provide a common cultural foundation upon which the notion of English identity is built in terms of oppositional differences between the English and their closest neighbor on the Continent. The media can – and do – make intertextual links to such background knowledge in their coverage of various events. This is the case not only of news reporting on politics (as with the political rhetoric discussed in this article; cf. example (2) containing the formulation *French repay **WWII Allies** with betrayal*) but also in other domains, most notably in sports reporting. In media coverage of sports events, military metaphors and cultural references emphasizing the mutual divide are so commonplace that they are almost taken for granted. Cf., for instance, media reports on some recent major international sports encounters, such as the participation of the England team at the EURO 2004 football championship in France, which was hailed by *The Sun* on its front page as *B-Day*, in allusion to both D-Day in 1944 and the initial letter of the name of the England team's captain (David Beckham). For a discussion of nationality contrasts between the English and other national groups, see Alabarces et al. (2001), Bishop and Jaworski (2003).

3.2.3   *Worm Chirac – from attribute to titleness*
The stereotypical perception of the French provides the necessary context for appreciating the use of the *le worm* label analyzed in this text. Not only did this new form become quite frequent but it also came to be used in several distinct patterns. From its first appearance in March 2003, the nickname *worm*, used in reference to the French president as part of *The Sun*'s pro-war rhetoric, occurred 49 times in *The Sun* during a single year. Its use was dynamic: after the quick formation of the nickname and the

acquisition of its negative content, it came to be used in several ways, most notably as an appositional attribute replacing the official title of the president.

The most frequent use of the *worm* label was in headlines. As the following list from the first two months after the formation of the nickname indicates, there is a certain variability not only in the use of the determiner – sometimes *The Sun* uses the French definite article *le/Le*, at other times it does without it – but also in the spelling of the common noun *worm*. While the ordinary spelling of *worm* is indicative of its use as a descriptive label, the capitalized form of *Worm* points to a degree of lexicalization, where the common noun is used as an appellation – a real nickname or a quasi proper name:

(8) *Le worm* meets the monster (20 Feb)
Squirm, *worm*! (21 Feb)
Dirty deals by *worm* (24 Feb)
U.S. tells *worm*: stop squirming (26 Feb)
Le Worm turns to terror state (3 Mar)
Worm squirm (6 Mar)
Worm warfare blasts French (7 Mar)
Worm beats Pounds 1m probe (8 Mar)
Blair buries *le worm* (13 Mar)
Here's how *worm* turns (14 Mar)
Le worm sold out his nation (14 Mar)
Worm in bid for Iraq deal (1 Apr)
French turn on *Le Worm* (11 Apr)
Worm Chirac turning after Straw threat (17 Apr)

Since each of these references to Chirac starts a co-referential chain of expressions within each respective article, the 'le worm' category labels are typically substituted by proper name references in the subsequent text. Beyond headlines, readers are thus reminded of the identity of 'le worm' by extended nominal phrases combining Chirac's name, title, and occasionally some other descriptive forms (typically adjectives or present participles). However, the 'worm' nickname creeps into the descriptive noun phrases and gradually develops into several patterns, as the following examples indicate:

(9) a.   Cowardly *Jacques "Le Worm" Chirac* (3 Mar)
     b.   President *Jacques "Le Worm" Chirac* (22 Mar)
     c.   French President *Jacques "Le Worm" Chirac* (26 Mar)
     d.   *Jacques Le Worm Chirac* (1 Apr)
     e.   *Le Worm Jacques Chirac* (17 Apr)
     f.   wriggling anti-war *worm Jacques Chirac* (13 Mar)

The first three examples (9a-c) incorporate the animal metaphor in between Chirac's first and last names, as is common practice in the case of nicknames or 'aliases' under which famous people are known (cf. *Elvis "The Pelvis" Presley*, following exactly the same pattern, or *William "Buffalo Bill" Cody*, with a nickname consisting of a full noun phrase). The inverted commas may indicate the novelty of such a creation rather than the detachment of the paper from such a representation (cf. 'scare quotes' in Fairclough 1992: 119). The absence of inverted commas in the other examples (9d-f) may, by contrast, indicate that *The Sun* treats the description as a given matter-of-fact.

A significant shift occurs in the examples **Le Worm** *Jacques Chirac* and *wriggling anti-war* **worm** *Jacques Chirac*, where the nickname prefaces the president's full name. What was previously a typical nickname is used as a specifying attribute in front of the name. Grammatically speaking, the noun phrase is an apposition, defined as the grammatical relation between two elements (appositives), usually of the same rank (e.g. noun phrases), and characterized by an identity of reference and placement in postposition (Quirk et al. 1985). The examples above are instances of full and strict apposition (i.e. the appositives can be separated and the resultant sentences are acceptable; they have the same syntactic function; there is no difference between the original sentence and either of the resultant sentences in extralinguistic reference); moreover, on account of their close connection, they are restrictive (as opposed to non-restrictive apposition, where the appositives form separate information units separated by commas in writing or tone units in speech – cf. ... *Le Worm, France's Jacques Chirac, ... The Sun*, 24 November 2003).

Semantically, appositives express several relationships: equivalence, attribution and inclusion. The pattern of *le worm Jacques Chirac* is an instance of equivalence, as either order of appositives is possible. Typically, apposition consists of a name appositive and a descriptive appositive (Jucker 1992), and can be multiple, i.e. consisting of several nouns or noun phrases (cf. *President Jacques "Le Worm" Chirac*).

The sequence of a descriptive appositive and a name appositive may be subject to the interesting phenomenon of the deletion of the initial determiner. This deletion may constitute a sociolinguistic variable reflecting, for example, the anticipated segmentation of the audiences of various media (cf. Bell 1991: 104 on audience design in radio broadcasting; Jucker 1992 on the same phenomenon in the British print media). The deletion may also be a grammatical convention, as in official titles, cf. *President Bush*; *Judge Hiller Zobel*, etc. Similar to this is the phenomenon of titleness, where a descriptive appositive is used as a quasi-title (Quirk et al. 1985), cf. **forensic pathologist** *Professor Bernard Knight*.

In the case of *The Sun*'s appositions involving Chirac, the French definite article (typically capitalized when forming a part of the descriptive appositive) should, on account of its foreign character, be considered as a lexicalized part of the nickname rather than a grammatical marker of definiteness. The combination *Le Worm Jacques Chirac* (as well as the mere *Worm Chirac* in one of the headlines above) therefore conveys a degree of such titleness.

In other words, the category label is used here in the function of a quasi-title, importantly also in place of the regular title. It is precisely in this respect that the typical nickname combinations of the type *(President) Jacques "Le Worm" Chirac* differ from the pattern *(Le) Worm (Jacques) Chirac*. In the latter case, the official title is actually denied to Chirac and a descriptive apposition denoting his office is replaced by a negative, value-laden and metaphorical category label. This technique contributes to his further denigration, and is a part of *The Sun*'s skill at efficiently exploiting the politics of address terms at a time when the international situation was most critical.

3.2.4 *Post-crisis fate of Le Worm*

With the beginning of military action in Iraq on 20th March 2003, the focus of the media eventually shifted to other issues. Nevertheless, when Jacques Chirac was on an official visit to Britain in autumn 2003, *The Sun* returned to its pre-war rhetoric, albeit in a slightly different and muted form, since there was no further need to define Chirac as an opponent and a representative of an out-group opposed to 'our' interests. Rather, his nickname came to be used as a starting point for nationalist and chauvinist assertions.

In the two articles reporting the news of Chirac's visit, the *worm* label was neither used independently nor as a nickname or a quasi-title within appositions of the patterns identified above. The category label was used again as a complement in clauses with an essentially metalinguistic function, i.e. reminding the readers of the former appellation used to refer to him (in conjunction with the reason for such a name). This is revealed by an inspection of the complete co-referential chains of the two articles:

(10)   Chirac jets in to see PM (headline, 24 Nov)
       Chirac [headline] → French President Jacques Chirac → Mr. Chirac → *(dubbed)* "*The Worm*" → he → he → the two leaders → they

       The sheer Gaul of it (25 Nov)
       Gaul [pun in the headline]→ Jacque Chirac → the French President → Mr. Chirac → *(dubbed) The Worm* → Mr. Chirac → the French leader → the French president → Mr. Chirac → President Chirac

The full verbal context in which the 'worm' metaphor was used is provided in the following two examples. What is significant here is that the expression has been domesticated – the French definite article has been replaced by its English equivalent (while the capitalization has been retained) – and that the readers are reminded of its negative stereotype by the evaluative metaphorical expressions *slippery* and *wriggling*:

(11)   a.   Mr. Chirac was dubbed "The Worm" by *The* Sun for his *slippery campaign* to undermine Britain and America (24 Nov).
       b.   The band blasted out the French national anthem, La Marseillaise, as Mr. Chirac – dubbed The Worm for *wriggling* over UN action – carried out the review with Tony Blair at his side (25 Nov).

On the same days, however, *The Sun* ran two accompanying commentaries in its 'Sun Says' section, in which it once again resorted to its rhetoric of negative other-presentation from the spring. Characteristically, within its emotionally charged tirade at the expense of Chirac, the paper used the category label *Le Worm* on its own, as the list of items within the co-referential chain shows:

(12)   Sick Sight (headline of a commentary, 25 Nov)
        Le Worm → President Jacques Chirac → the man (who) → he → a man like him?
        → Chirac → *Le Worm* → Chirac

In both texts, a contrast is drawn between Jacques Chirac and George Bush, cf.:

(13)   WORM WELCOME. They're both called Mr. President, but *what different men they are.* Last week George Bush was in Downing Street. Today Le Worm, France's Jacques Chirac, ... (24 Nov).

The text of the second commentary (cited in an abridged form) shows many of the structures and forms commonly found in the genre of tabloid commentary (cf. Conboy 2006). Restraint is not a part of the genre, since it aims to form opinions rather than be objective (cf. van Dijk 1992b). As typical examples of the rhetorical move of negative other-presentation, or derogation, of Chirac, the forms include negative evaluative words, rhetorical questions, hyperbole and exaggeration, etc. The negative stereotype attached to the appellation *Le Worm* in the first sentence (cf. the negative sensory perception connected with such lowly animals discussed above) enhances the main proposition of the sentence: the highly evocative phrase *stomach-churning*:

(14)   THERE are few more *stomach-churning* sights than *Le Worm strutting brazenly* along a line of Grenadier Guards.
        President Jacques Chirac is the man who, through *arrogance, vanity and sheer bloody stupidity*, put the lives of 300,000 British and American troops at risk in Iraq.
        And yet there he is inspecting a guard of honour – *honour? A man like him?* – as Tony Blair rolls out the red carpet.
        It's a disgrace *after what France did to us* and the United Nations.
        Chirac *isn't fit to set foot on the same soil* that President Bush graced last week. (...)

Last but not least, a note should be made on the penetration of the label *le worm* into the cultural context. Since 2003, *The Sun* has occasionally used the expression independently of Chirac's name in its headlines. This indicates that the paper anticipates the recognition of the nickname by its readers, even though it substitutes the category label with Chirac's proper name further in the text (typically boasting its authorship of the nickname), cf. the following two recent examples:

(15)   Le Sun confronts *Le Worm*
        The Sun presented French sulky *Jacques Chirac* with an English phrasebook yesterday to help him at EU summits (25 June 2006).

(16)   France's *Le Worm* slides off
French president *Jacques Chirac – dubbed Le Worm by The Sun* for his slippery
diplomacy – announced his retirement last night (12 March 2007).

Significantly, the function of the label has changed, and is no longer the negative other-presentation of 2003. It is no longer a part of the media's discourse strategy to legitimate a particular political stance, but, rather, an articulation of *The Sun*'s humorous presentation of (sometimes trivial) information, capitalizing on the traditional British/French rivalry. This is in line with van Dijk's (2007: 77) finding about the dynamic nature of context and the need for contextual rather than textual analysis: "negative other-presentations in political discourse are not just a description of a bad guy, but rather a politically relevant selection of, and emphasis on, what the currently politically relevant 'bad' things that need to be highlighted in discourse are."

4.   Conclusion

As the data indicates, the use of the expression *le worm* for Jacques Chirac in *The Sun* was far from accidental – it was closely tied both to the international political situation of the time and *The Sun*'s discursive aims, its attempt to foster a public consensus on controversial issues. Contextual analysis reveals that the nickname was coined as a special referential strategy at a time when the public discourse preceding military action in 2003 was called upon to legitimate the actions of the in-group and to cement the imaginary unity of the community vis-à-vis the perceived threat of various 'others'. The particular naming option chosen served to split the group of 'us', broadly defined as 'non-terrorists', into two mutually opposed subgroups which were, in other contexts, even lexicalized into the descriptive phrases 'axis of the willing' and 'axis of weasels'.

The discursive construction of the two groups was thus based on the strategy of differentiation of social actors, drawing on negative other-presentation. This was achieved by two specific substrategies – 'foreignization', i.e. the indication of out-group membership through a foreign word, and 'dehumanization'/'animalization', i.e. the denial of human characteristics by selecting an animal metaphor with extended social and cultural connotations. The category label *le worm* was subject to various predicative strategies, most notably its use as a noun appositive inserted within Chirac's name as a nickname and prefacing his name as a quasi title replacing his official title of President. In *The Sun*'s discourse, President Chirac was thus eventually transformed into Le Worm Chirac.

The application of such stereotype-laden metaphorical labels at times of crisis not only denigrates opponents but also contributes to the development of a 'hysterical style' of reporting which replaces logical argumentation with emotional appeals to pre-existing and newly constructed stereotypes.

References

Alabarces, Pablo, Tomlinson, Alan and Young, Christopher. 2001. "Argentina versus England at the France '98 World Cup: Narratives of nation and the mythologizing of the popular." *Media, Culture and Society* 23: 547–66.

Becker, Annette. 2007. "Between 'us' and 'them': Two TV interviews with German chancellor Gerhard Schröder in the run-up to the Iraq war." In *Discourse, War and Terrorism*, Adam Hodges and Chad Nilep (eds), 161–183. Amsterdam: John Benjamins Publishing.

Bell, Allan. 1991. *The Language of News Media*. Oxford UK and Cambridge MA: Blackwell.

Bishop, Hywel and Jaworski, Adam. 2003. "'We beat 'em': Nationalism and the hegemony of homogeneity in the British press reportage of Germany versus England during EURO 2000." *Discourse & Society* 14 (3): 243–271.

Caldas-Coulthard, Carmen Rosa. 2002. "Cross-cultural representation of 'otherness' in media discourse." In Critical Discourse Analysis: Interdisciplinary Perspectives, Gilbert Weiss and Ruth Wodak (eds), 272–296. London: Macmillan.

Cap, Piotr. 2008. "Towards the proximization model of the analysis of legitimization in political discourse." *Journal of Pragmatics* 40: 17–41.

Chilton, Paul. 2004. *Analysing Political Discourse. Theory and Practice*. London: Routledge.

Chouliaraki, Lilie. 2007. "Introduction: The soft power of war: Legitimacy and community in Iraq war discourses." In *The Soft Power of War*, Lilie Chouliaraki (ed.), 1–10. Amsterdam: John Benjamins Publishing.

Chovanec, Jan. 2007. "The role of nationality contrasts in the discursive construction of an in-group member: The Woodward case in the Telegraph." *Brno Studies in English* 33: 27–44.

—. 2008. "Focus on form: Foregrounding devices in football reporting." *Discourse & Communication* 2 (3): 219–242.

—. 2009. "Reference to normality as a way of asserting ingroup membership: The Woodward case in the media." In *Studies in American Language, Culture and Literature*, Piotr P. Chruszczewski and Jacek Fisiak (eds), 131–150. Kraków: Tertium.

Clark, Kate. 1998. "The linguistics of blame: Representations of women in *the Sun*'s reporting of crimes of sexual violence." In *The Feminist Critique of Language. A Reader* [2nd ed.], Deborah Cameron (ed.), 183–197. London: Routledge.

Conboy, Martin. 2006. *Tabloid Britain: Constructing a Community through Language*. London: Routledge.

Duszak, Anna. 2002. "Words and social identities." In *Us and Others. Social Identities across Languages, Discourses and Cultures*, Anna Duszak (ed.), 213–231. Amsterdam: John Benjamins Publishing Company.

El Refaie, Elisabeth. 2001. "Metaphors we discriminate by: Naturalized themes in Austrian newspaper articles about asylum seekers." *Journal of Sociolinguistics* 5 (3): 352–371.

Fairclough, Norman. 1992. *Discourse and Social Change*. Cambridge: Polity Press.

—. 2003. *Analysing Discourse. Textual Analysis for Social Research*. London: Routledge.

Fowler, Roger. 1991. *Language in the News: Language and Ideology in the Press*. London: Routledge.

Hausendorf, Heiko and Kesselheim, Wolfgang. 2002. "The communicative construction of group relationships. A basic mechanism of social categorisation." In *Us and Others. Social*

Identities across Languages, Discourses and Cultures, Anna Duszak (ed.), 265–289. Amsterdam: John Benjamins Publishing Company.

Jucker, Andreas H. 1992. *Social Stylistics. Syntactic Variation in British Newspapers*. Berlin, New York: Mouton de Gruyter.

Lule, Jack. 2004. "War and its metaphors: News language and the prelude to war in Iraq, 2003." *Journalism Studies* 5 (2): 179–190.

Quirk, Randolph, Greenbaum, Sidney, Leech, Geoffrey and Svartvik, Jan. 1985. *A Comprehensive Grammar of the English Language*. London and New York: Longman.

Reisigl, Martin and Wodak, Ruth. 2001. *Discourse and Discrimination: Rhetorics of Racism and Antisemitism*. London: Routledge.

Richardson, John E. 2007. *Analysing Newspapers. An Approach from Critical Discourse Analysis*. Basingstoke: Palgrave Macmillan.

Santa Ana, Otto. 1999. "'Like an animal I was treated': Anti-immigrant metaphor in US public discourse." *Discourse and Society* 10 (2): 191–224.

Skarżyńska, Krystyna. 2002. "*We* and *They* in Polish political discourse." In *Us and Others. Social Identities across Languages, Discourses and Cultures*, Anna Duszak (ed.), 249–264. Amsterdam: John Benjamins Publishing Company.

Thomas, Hugh M. 2003. *The English and the Normans: Ethnic Hostility, Assimilation, and Identity 1066–c.1220*. New York: Oxford University Press.

van Dijk, Teun A. 1987. "Semantics of a press panic: The Tamil 'invasion.'" *European Journal of Communication* 3: 167–187.

—. 1992a. "Discourse and the denial of racism." *Discourse & Society* 3: 87–118.

—. 1992b. "Racism and argumentation: Race riot Rretoric in tabloid editorials." In *Argumentation Illuminated*, Frans H. van Eemeren, Rob Grootendorst, J. Anthony Blair and Charles A. Willard (eds), 242–259. Dordrecht: Foris.

—. 2000. "New(s) racism: A discourse analytical approach." In *Ethnic Minorities and the Media*, Simon Cottle (ed.), 33–49. Milton Keynes, UK: Open University Press.

—. 2002. "Discourse and racism." In *The Blackwell Companion to Racial and Ethnic Studies*, David Goldberg and John Solomos (eds), 145–159. Oxford: Blackwell.

—. 2007. "War rhetoric of a little ally: Political implicatures and Aznar's legitimatization of the war in Iraq." In *The Soft Power of War*, Lilie Chouliaraki (ed.), 61–84. Amsterdam: John Benjamins Publishing.

van Leeuwen, Theo. 1996. "The representation of social actors." In *Texts and Practices. Readings in Critical Discourse Analysis*, Carmen Rosa Caldas-Coulthard and Malcolm Coulthard (eds), 32–70. London and New York: Routledge.

—. 2007. "Legitimation in discourse and communication." *Discourse & Communication* 1: 91–112.

Wodak, Ruth and Chilton, Paul (eds). 2005. *A New Agenda in (Critical) Discourse Analysis: Theory, Methodology and Interdisciplinarity*. Amsterdam: John Benjamins Publishing.

CHAPTER 5

Labeling and mislabeling in American political discourse

A survey based on insights of independent media monitors

Katarzyna Molek-Kozakowska

1. Introduction: Monitoring the media

As noted by Jean Baudrillard (1998) in his discussion of complicity in consumption, most people tend to "consume" politics in much the same way as they make use of other products of mass culture. That is partly because mass-mediated political discourse has become increasingly one-directional (from the elites to the masses) and non-negotiable (with suppression of non-elite opinions). Paradoxically, even opinion polls and call-in programs may be used to prevent rather than foster public debates. Notably, corporate media's flair for infotainment, sensation and focus on celebrity has begun to prevail over reasoned analysis and thorough reporting. In the midst of information overload, few citizens have the time, energy or inclination to check the reliability of news reports they receive. At the same time, mainstream news outlets seem to have started paying more attention to their profits and popularity rankings than to their standards of objectivity (as noted recently by both media and discourse analysts, e.g. Płudowski 2006; Lassen, Struck and Vestergaard 2006). And nowhere has it drawn more concern than in the U.S. (cf. Altheide 2007). The question is if it is still possible for citizens to actively participate in political discourse, after it has been almost completely appropriated by media conglomerates.

Media monitors, which are mostly internet-based watchdog initiatives, attempt to help citizens to engage in, rather than only "consume", political discourse. They aim to alert citizens to more or less subtle distortions of information by scanning political coverage for distraction, fabrication or spin. Not only do monitors check the truthfulness of news reports with regard to available documents and releases, but also conduct independent surveys to expose hidden media bias and manipulation. Their conclusions are often based not on what is available to the public but on what is lost on the way to the evening news. For example, by comparing various versions of coverage of the same event, they are able to determine if any manipulative techniques have been used and what effects are intended. Also, media monitors aim to raise awareness of the "constructedness" of mass-mediated reality through critical attention to some insidious discourse strategies used by broadcasters.

This paper reviews the postings by selected web-based media monitors in order to illustrate three distinct applications of one manipulative discourse strategy – (mis)labeling – with regard to issues pertaining to American politics. The material for the study has been collected through continual examination of online alerts by *Fairness and Accuracy in Reporting (FAIR)*, *Media Matters for America*, or *Columbia Journalism Review (CJR)* over the course of several months in 2007.

2. Politics in the media age

Politics in democratic countries is largely predicated on the Enlightenment's assumptions that citizens are able to make informed choices thanks to the unrestricted circulation of ideas in the public domain, which is guaranteed by freedom of speech and transparency of political processes. Moreover, citizens are assumed to be sensible enough to distinguish true claims from falsehoods in order to decide which policies are in their own interests. However, closer study reveals entirely different foundations of human behavior: People's choices are often motivated by simple emotions rather than sound analyses of facts and arguments, information processing and memory are exceedingly selective, while social conduct is subject to conformity (cf. from Le Bon's ([1894]1986) crowd mentality, through Lasswell's (1949) attention aggregates, to Aronson's (2003) social conformity and compliance). Recent studies in psychology also show that people tend to act as "cognitive misers" who do not like to waste their cognitive resources on matters they do not perceive as highly relevant, and often disregard information that challenges their existing beliefs (Pratkanis and Aronson 2004: 38). In their "informed choices" citizens seem to rely on stereotypes, over-generalizations and recurring labels that reduce the complex domain of politics to simple categories or even dichotomies, such as "us vs. them", "conservative vs. liberal", "government vs. opposition", or "pro-life vs. pro-choice."

Modern media, in their competitive struggle for readers and viewers, contribute to the perpetuation of such a simplified and distorted vision of politics. The commercialization of the media, particularly the rise of the tabloid press, the popularity of cheaply produced talk shows, and the ubiquity of advertising, has changed the quality of political discourse. For example, corporate news outlets in the USA have increasingly been representing politics as an entertaining "spectacle" (Mrozowski 2006: 20), with broadcasters either sensationalizing or trivializing some aspects of politics through selective omission, various combinations of fact and speculation, or focus on celebrities. Soundbites and foregone conclusions have gradually substituted thorough analyses or productive discussions. Presentations of expert opinions have been replaced with interviews that amplify personal conflicts and ideological differences, often with reporters posing enemy questions to provoke a confrontation. For example, according to Deborah Tannen, in an "argument culture", such as America's, there is a socially endorsed, pre-patterned, unreflective use of fighting in public communication even with respect to goals that do not necessarily require it (2003: 19). All this is designed to add drama to the political spectacle, as consensus and co-operation are not as magnetizing as emotional tension and verbal escalation of a row.

As political discourse in leading American media tends to be framed as entertainment, the popularity of political coverage (in the age of 24/7 news networks) has been sustained thanks to commentators' constant pursuit of scandals and blunders. This tendency has resulted in citizens' cynicism at being excluded from political decision-making (Płudowski 2008: 31–33). That is also why the surge of political propaganda, rather than persuasion, is said to coincide with the expansion of mass media in the twentieth century (Pratkanis and Aronson 2004: 11). This, in turn, confirms Baudrillard's thesis that postmodern mass-mediated politics is an example of simulacrum – an invented spectacle in hyperreality – which blends fact with fiction and gradually eradicates informed judgment ([1981]2005: 7).

And yet the corporate media's self-interested framing of politics as infotainment can be to some extent rectified by the advent of new technologies, particularly the internet (e.g. alternative news outlets, the blogosphere, mailing lists and chat rooms of grass-roots communities). The so-called "virtual reality" may, paradoxically, constitute a more informative, balanced and rational political arena than the mass-mediated hyperreality. The web, unless it is dominated by consumerism or corporate interests, offers a new opportunity for citizens to revisit the Enlightenment's ideals of participatory democracy (Mrozowski 2006: 28). With an unrestricted access to primary sources and the ability to respond to available information, everyone may become a watchdog of democracy. Rather than continue to be merely manipulated or increasingly cynical, individuals and monitoring organizations can be empowered to expose corporate media's distortions and raise awareness of those discourse strategies that have made political manipulation so pervasive in the media age.

3.   (Mis)labeling

(Mis)labeling is a discursive strategy that encapsulates the negative aspects of corporate media's political coverage that were discussed above: it converges oversimplification, infotainment and the rhetoric of conflict in search of popularity instead of objectivity. It had long ago been identified as one of the key propaganda devices (Lee and Lee 1939), and was subsequently referred to as name-calling. It was shown that associating an idea, an event or a person with an unequivocally negative name frequently makes people reject it without considering its merits and probing its real value. In other words, a label is a tempting "cognitive shortcut", which saves "cognitive misers" the effort of processing the incoming information, examining its logic and remembering details. In this paper, (mis)labeling in political discourse is understood as a strategy of introducing and/or propagating terminology that is either inaccurate or derogatory (or both) to refer to a person, a group, or a policy in order to gain political advantage. As its aim is to misinform, (mis)labeling may well be manipulative when certain labels are coined, selected or applied due to their specific emotional appeal and connotation rather than their referential meaning (cf. van Dijk 2006 on other discursive aspects of manipulation).

In the 1930s the Institute of Propaganda Analysis expressed concern with the growing frequency of insults in political discourse by observing that the American public domain resounded with such names as *heretic, revolutionary, Hun,* or *Nazi,* and well as *moron, bully, tramp, unscientific* or *backward* (Lee and Lee 1939). Recent examples demonstrate that some depreciatory labels have had the power to ruin reputations (e.g. President Bill Clinton's media-magnified *womanizer* stigma, or 2004 presidential candidate John Kerry's *flip-flopper* tag that stemmed from his Congress voting record), to discredit people and policy initiatives (e.g. the failure of Michael Dukakis's probation program after the release of 1988 Willie Horton ad that also led to labeling him as *soft on crime*), and even to legitimize bloodshed (e.g. Saddam Hussein as *the Thug of Baghdad,* America as *the Great Satan*). Sometimes (mis)labeling is employed indirectly, by implicature, so that the target cannot seek legal action against a slander or libel (e.g. the conservative pundit Ann Coulter commenting on Democratic presidential candidate John Edwards: "you can't really talk about him because you have to go into rehab if you use the word faggot"). Additionally, misleading labels can be masked by euphemisms, presuppositions, over-generalizations, misattributions, irrelevant details and loose associations (cf. Fritz, Keefer and Nyhan 2004 for a review of some recent examples).

Linguistically, labels can be very specific proper nouns (e.g. *Dubya* – George W. Bush's derogatory nickname – a play on the Southern pronunciation of his middle name's initial), but mostly they are general terms, whose meanings have accrued strong negative overtones (e.g. *liberal, radical, leftist*). Alternatively, in self-presentation, labels may function as less pejorative – even euphemistic – substitutes for unfavorable or offensive terms (e.g. *intervention* for invasion, or *incomplete success* for failure). Colloquial words may make particularly provocative labels if they are skillfully used in the context of public discourse (e.g. *pinko, commie*). As a result, labels may take the form of nouns (e.g. an *autocrat*), adjectives (e.g. *partisan*), participles (e.g. *debriefing),* compounds (e.g. *tax-and-spender*), phrases (e.g. *soft on defense*), or even clauses (e.g. *It's the economy, stupid!),* but even then they are not to function as propositions – statements about reality – but rather as new names for fragments of reality. As such, they cannot be negated or verified for truth value. Just as is the case with slogans and headlines, labels function to (re)categorize experience and to bring some order into informational chaos. As a result of labeling, complex categories are simplified, sometimes through straightforward associations to what the majority finds loathsome or scary.[1]

Labels tend to have a "self-fulfilling" quality: In political persuasion, advertising or education, people are bound to respond to some invented negative labels in the way they are largely intended to (Pratkanis and Aronson 2004: 69–70). Also, as people tend to remember information that is engaging and emotional, a label's humor, wit or outrageousness increases the chance of its being recycled. It has also been observed that recurring political labels, even if inaccurate, become entrenched in memory (Płudowski 2008: 90–91). As a result, such labels become a part of shared knowledge, a common way of thinking about politics, and subsequently an element of the unreflective lexicon.[2] It can be concluded that, as in George Orwell's *Nineteen Eighty-Four*, (mis)labeling is one of the insidious discursive strategies that facilitate social engineering through linguistic means: It gradually prompts people to speak and think in a designed way.

4.   Recent examples of (mis)labeling in American political discourse

A systematic survey of alerts and studies by independent media monitors, which relentlessly trace factual errors and manipulative techniques in American political discourse, yields an extensive body of textual data, of which only a sample of the most representative examples can be discussed here. The analysis will focus on three identifiable types of sources that seem to be using labels in distinct ways: (1) official government statements, which feature labels to gradually redefine some concepts in public policy, often by masking offensive meanings with euphemisms; (2) mainstream media's political reports (predominantly in the press), which feature labels that legitimize official policies by misrepresenting or simplifying complex and equivocal issues; (3) popular media's political editorials (predominantly on talk radio and TV), which employ insulting labels in order to discredit political opponents.

---

1.   For example, in 1990 Republican candidates were sent a pamphlet entitled *Language: A Key Mechanism of Control* endorsed by Newt Gingrich. The booklet contained two lists of words the candidates were instructed to use: one set of negative labels to be used to describe the Democrats (e.g. *betray, coercion, collapse, corruption, crisis, decay, destroy, destructive, devour, endanger, failure, greed, hypocrisy, ideological, impose, incompetent, insecure, liberal, lie, limit(s), pathetic, permissive, radical, self-serving, sensationalists, shallow, sick, threaten, traitors, waste*), and the other set of "positive, governing words" when speaking about themselves (e.g. *active(ly), challenge, courage, duty, humane, incentive, principle(d), proud/pride, provide, reform, rights, unique, vision*).

2.   This process is evident as for the increased colloquial use of what was once strictly military terminology (e.g. *weapons of mass destruction* or *collateral damage*).

4.1   'Officialese' – labels and euphemisms

U.S. government's press releases and statements by high-ranking officials provide a corpus for a study of various manipulative techniques, including (mis)labeling. Timothy Lynch (2006) has conducted a survey of legal materials and releases to examine "the disturbing new vocabulary" that has emerged over the recent years with respect to the political legitimization of the so-called *war on terror*. Lynch argues that a number of labels and euphemisms has been devised by government administrators who "use doublespeak to expand, or at least maintain, their power" by promoting policies that are supposedly designed to eliminate the threats posed by terrorists (2006: 1).

For example, the label *enemy combatant* has been invented to designate people suspected of terrorism that have been arrested and imprisoned without a trial (according to the Bush administration, the constitutional writ of habeas corpus may be suspended in their cases). After the U.S. Supreme Court declared this practice illegal – announcing that even *enemy combatants* retain certain citizen rights, such as access to lawyers and court hearings – the government slapped a new label on its prisoners: *imperative security internees* (Lynch 2006: 6–7). Apparently, until this label is outlawed as well, the American government can incarcerate any person on a mere suspicion of terrorism.

Alternatively, American authorities may use the label *material witness* to arrest an individual, as there is a rarely used federal rule that states that if a witness is highly likely to ignore a summons and flee the jurisdiction, the police are allowed to "secure his testimony" (Lynch 2006: 5). As a result, law enforcement agents may mislabel a suspect as a *material witness* and imprison him even if they lack enough evidence to charge him with a crime. It also appears that search warrants issued by independent judges are no longer necessary to search a person's private property. The administration uses another document with a formal name, a *national security letter*, to waive the constitutional limits on the search and seize powers of government (Lynch 2006: 3–4).

Lynch (2006: 10) also notes that under a recently implemented PATRIOT Act, the meaning of terms *terrorism* and *terrorist* has been considerably extended. Innocent people are sometimes mislabeled as *potential terrorists* and entered into databases if they are reported to have taken part in anti-war demonstrations, or to have made large withdrawals of cash, which are registered as "unusual transactions" by financial institutions. Also, *anti-terrorism* laws have been effectively used against street gang members, reckless airplane travelers, or drug users, dealers and producers.

National security and *homeland security* have proved to be exceedingly useful labels to ensure that even dubious policies are financed; by contrast, some unpopular initiatives have been re-labeled and re-sold. As demonstrated by Lynch (2006: 7–9), even though Americans are reluctant to accept *national identification cards,* most legislators were persuaded to vote for what had been presented "only" as *security-enhanced state issued drivers' licenses* (that meet specified federal criteria). And although President Bush had promised *no draft,* he also issued a *stop-loss order* in order to sustain the U.S. military activities involved in the war on terror. According to this order, the armed forces cannot leave the service even if they have fulfilled the terms of their enlistment contract. Finally, the administration's intelligence and military agencies deny any use of torture. Instead, they admit to using modern techniques of *debriefing*, or interrogation in the third degree, which "is professional, is lawful, yields good results and is not torture," as put by the ex-director of CIA Porter Goss (quoted in Lynch 2006: 8).

It is also evident that many of Washington's controversial domestic and foreign policy proposals, together with their innocuously sounding official labels, encountered little challenge from the Fourth Estate (cf. MacArthur 2003; Umansky 2006). David L. Altheide (2007: 289) notes that in the period between 9/11 attacks and the 2003 Iraqi invasion, there was an enormous amount of press self-censorship. This consisted in journalists mostly repeating the official line about war on terror without questioning its legitimacy or tactics. From 2003 onwards, many reporters followed military spokespeople's labeling of Iraqi fighters first as *criminals* and *thugs,* later as *insurgents,* and throughout as *gunmen* (Altheide 2007: 288). Such labels were in tune with President Bush's often repeated claims of America's moral duty to eliminate extremism and enforce law and order (e.g. "Al Qaeda is to terror what the mafia is to crime", "the desperate tactics of a hateful few", "an axis of evil").

As a result, the official propaganda managed to represent Muslims and Arabs as enemies, dehumanize the Iraqis, label their fight tactics as *barbarism* and portray torture as an indispensable strategy of intelligence gathering. This was accompanied by restrictions on information about military activities (i.e. allowing only embedded reporters to selected sites), and a ban to photograph the caskets of the killed soldiers, allegedly in order to respect their families' privacy. Indeed, the government has strategically controlled the releases about military deaths with discursively engineered "hero scripts" (Altheide 2007: 290) and with such euphemisms as *fallen soldiers* to ensure the army's heroic stature, *friendly fire* to diminish accountability for troops killed by comrades, or *collateral damage* to minimize American complicity in civilian deaths that "accidentally" occur in military operations.

The above examples illustrate the U.S. government's tendency to resort to (mis) labeling to frame the way policies related to *war on terror* are received to deflect criticism and evade responsibility. Thus, the insidious usage of military euphemisms (e.g. *collateral damage*), of distracting catchphrases (e.g. *troop surge policy* to mean escalation or deployment), and of negative connotations superimposed on previously neutral political terms (e.g. *liberal, compromise, dissent*) deserve closer scrutiny from the perspective of its manipulative potential in official political discourse.

4.2   Corporate media and a narrowing range of debate

According to media monitors, (costly and risky) investigative journalism is no longer appreciated in corporate media, which are interested in maximizing their profits that mostly come from commercial advertisers. Moreover, media owners, managers and celebrity reporters share interests and views with political elites with whom they have to cooperate as regards broadcasting policies and coverage production. Thus, in spite of the pretense of an adversarial relationship between the government and the Fourth Estate, the American corporate media tend to follow Washington's official line. This is especially evident in the coverage of foreign policy, but even with internal affairs the scope of debate is usually restricted to the differences between the two dominant parties. What most media monitors find disturbing is the lack of truly critical coverage of official agendas, as well as journalists' self-censorship in controversial issues (cf. Altheide 2007; Antonissen 2003 on censorship).

Independent media monitors are trying to study and expose the instances when complex and equivocal political issues are simplified and then trivialized or sensationalized to produce a distorted picture of politics, which, to a large extent, fits in with the official agenda. As regards the U.S. foreign policy, for example, *FAIR*'s Steve Rendall (2006) demonstrates how the Venezuelan "socialist" president has been reviled by the American press. Since his election in 1998, Hugo Chávez has repeatedly been labeled a *populist demagogue* or an *authoritarian* by the *New York Times* (*NYT*) for example (par. 1–2). With the intensifying enmity between the Venezuelan and American governments in the years 2005–2006, Chávez's presidency has been characterized as *destructive populism*, *authoritarian tilt* (*Newsweek*), *anti-democratic turn* (*New Republic, Atlantic*), *assaulting democracy, stifling dissent, autocratic demagoguery* (*Washington Post*), *autocracy not democracy, communism in Venezuela, terrible human rights record* (Fox News) (quoted in Rendall 2006: par. 3–8). These pejorative labels clash with some independent findings. Notwithstanding Chávez's political oversights and populism, the Venezuelan election proceedings have been certified as democratic by outside observers. In addition, independent polls show the positive results of the Venezuelan government's increase in spending to remedy poverty, the fostering of "participatory democracy" (often mislabeled as *socialism* or *communism*), and the population's general perception of democracy and stability (par. 11, 20).

Also as regards domestic affairs, American media seem to follow the official line. "Can you hear us NOW?" (2007) is a *FAIR* journalist Frances Cerra Whittelsey's report of how the mainstream media decide to present grass-roots anti-war initiatives, particularly street demonstrations, on the example of January 27, 2007 march – the eighth since 2003 to have gathered more than 100 000 protesters. The author has found that some editors decide to routinely avoid mentioning such events, as "covering dissent is unpatriotic" (par. 6). Others move the news to later pages, or use dismissive headlines or tired images (e.g. of actress and long-time anti-war advocate Jane Fonda) to diminish the event's significance. The study also provides many examples of how reporters at *NYT*, *Washington Post*, AP, NBC, ABC, CBS chose to frame, contextualize or label the anti-war march, particularly as part of a *liberal agenda*, as just an *emotional outpouring* of military families against Iraq, as *crowd courage* to demand President Bush's impeachment (obviously not to be taken seriously), as *same old protest* with comparisons, images and sequencing similar to anti-Vietnam protests, and as smaller than it actually was.

Each presidential election, together with the campaigning that precedes it, makes up a significant part of American media's coverage, but, as it was demonstrated by Jon Whiten (2006), media have the power of suppressing information often by means of effective (mis)labeling strategies. Whiten's study concerns post-2004 election signals that the voting process was disrupted in Ohio. It was claimed then that the registration of late voters in Ohio was impeded by additional bureaucracy and that the voting machines were misallocated: there were plenty of them in wealthy conservative districts, while voters in predominantly African-American Democratic districts had to wait in lines for several hours to cast their votes. Mainstream media editors generally ignored the suspicious situation or ridiculed the idea of questioning the fairness of the election process and condemned "stirring up another Florida 2000." Others focused on attacking internet bloggers and independent news outlets for publicizing the Ohio story. Those who raised questions were subsequently labeled *conspiracy theorists, Bush-haters, die-hards,* or *Democratic Party loyalists.* The irrationality of such "conspiracy theories" was deliberately stressed by means of exaggerations and clichés that were not supposed to be taken seriously by readers (e.g. *stolen election, massive vote fraud, election hijacked from a to z*). The words *rumor, allegations, faulty analyses* were used to discredit independent reports from Ohio, which were attributed to organizations "hostile to the president." The mainstream media preferred to focus on Bush's winning strategy rather than to examine the irregularities, which, as Whiten argues, indicates that "investigative journalism and truth as a priority are virtually absent in the mainstream media" (2006: par. 1).

The 2008 presidential campaign is also likely to be dominated by media's quest for sensations and gaffes. Two spring 2007 *FAIR* studies have already shown how media tend to create distorted images of presidential candidates – a technique that induces initial misrepresentations that may not be easily changed by alternative coverage. Peter Hart has documented in his piece "Obamamania" (2007) that Democratic Senator Barack Obama has been characterized as a politician that "transcends race" (*Time*) and who has a "non-confrontational, 'post-racial' approach" (*Newsweek*), or that, despite his blackness, he "has never positioned himself as the black candidate" (NBC). In terms of his political leanings, Obama was labeled an African-American Democrat "who is mainstream (...) who didn't come from the civil rights movement" (NBC). Also he is "not an orthodox liberal" (*NYT*), or rather "a liberal, but not a screechy partisan, (...) eager to find common ground with conservatives" (*Time*). Yet, the columnists' propagation of sometimes contradictory labels has rarely gone hand in hand with a thorough analysis of the candidate's political program.

The media's penchant for celebrity cult has been also illustrated in the case of another candidate – Republican Rudolph Giuliani, as documented by Steve Rendall in "The media's mayor" (2007). The author details how, after the full scope of the tragedy of 9/11 attacks had been relayed to the American public, journalists turned to the NYC Mayor in the search of a "wartime leader", who, after making countless comforting statements on TV, was declared a *national hero* – the mayor who saved New York. The press's endlessly recycled label *the Mayor of America,* which later morphed into *America's mayor,* earned Giuliani the title of Time 2001 Person of the Year, and still persists despite ample evidence of the mayor's fatal decisions and failures of coordination during 9/11 crisis. However, contrary to official reports that call into question the Giuliani myth, most mainstream columnists continue to profile him as *America's mayor, the rock of 9/11, crime fighter* and *tax cutter* (Rendall 2007: par. 9), especially after he decided to run for president in 2008. The above examples testify to the fact that strategies of (mis) labeling in the press have been effectively used to background the complexities inherent in politics and present it in such a way as to induce popular support for an ideological stance that is intertwined with corporate media's economic interests.

4.3   Labels, lies and insults

Arguably, some of the most popular political TV talk-shows (e.g. Fox News Channel's *The O'Reilly Factor* or *Hannity & Colmes,* MSNBC's *Hardball*) and radio programs (e.g. Michael Savage's *The Savage Nation, The Rush Limbaugh Show* or *The Sean Hannity Show*)[3] seem to have been designed solely to discredit political opponents. Thus, media analysts and independent media monitors have been paying close attention to such broadcasts to expose distortions of facts and applications of manipulation (cf. Naureckas, Rendall and Cohen 1995; Hart 2003; Pratkanis and Aronson 2004).

For example, Rush Limbaugh's nationally syndicated radio show, which has an estimated audience of nearly 15 million weekly listeners, regularly broadcasts invective and insinuation in service of the conservative viewpoint. As *Media Matters* indicates, during his long reign over the airwaves, Limbaugh has called abortion rights activists *feminazis,* told an African-American caller to "take that bone out of your nose," referred to prisoner abuse at Abu Ghraib as "blow[ing] some steam off," and declared that "what's good for Al Qaeda is good for the Democratic Party." In August 2005, Limbaugh asserted that Cindy Sheehan (the mother of a soldier killed in Iraq), who staged an anti-war protest outside President Bush's ranch in Texas, was "exploiting death." He has repeatedly attacked the Clinton family alleging that Hillary Rodham Clinton is an accomplice to Vince Foster's[4] murder and that Bill Clinton is gay. Limbaugh's popularity is a result of his skillful blending of fact and fabrication, often presented in a quick, witty or jocular manner to discourage critical thinking (Pratkanis and Aronson 2004: 53–56). As demonstrated above, in his fiery monologues Limbaugh also makes use of a wide array of offensive labels that cater to racist, sexist and political prejudices.

The application of various (mis)labeling strategies is also emblematic of Michael Savage, a San Francisco-based right-wing author and radio personality. Savage's daily syndicated radio program *The Savage Nation* appears on approximately 350 stations,

---

3.   According to *Media Matters* ranking of 30 most viewed programs available at http://media-matters.org/issues_topics/shows_publications?num=30 (30 August 2007).

4.   A White House counsel in Clinton's administration who committed suicide.

reaching an estimated weekly audience of 8 million listeners, making it the third most-listened-to talk show in America. As *Media Matters* has noted recently,[5] Savage frequently compares progressives and Democrats to Nazis. For example, on the April 23, 2007 broadcast of his show, Savage called a speech by Senator Hillary Rodham Clinton *Hitler dialogue*. On May 2, Savage labeled Democratic Representative from New York Maurice Hinchey *chief National Socialist*, adding that Hinchey was seeking "the final solution for conservatives on talk radio" because he advocated a broadcasting policy reform that would guarantee more balanced political views on the air. On May 11, the commentator denounced Democratic Representative from Florida Robert Wexler's questioning of Attorney General Alberto Gonzales saying: "the last time I saw a politician scream at someone like that was in Nazi Germany in the kangaroo court trial against people who conspired to kill Hitler." Having labeled Wexler a *schmuck* and a *moron*, Savage went on to say that the Congressman "has more hatred for Gonzales than he does for Osama bin Laden and the Islamists." On June 12, Savage compared the progressive movement to the Nazi storm troopers who aided Hitler's rise to power, saying: "they are the brownshirts of today." Savage also said: "When I see a woman walking around with a burqa, I see a Nazi ... a hateful Nazi who would like to cut your throat and kill your children" (May 3, 2007). Finally, on the July 9 broadcast of his show, Savage referred to former Vice President Al Gore's efforts to raise awareness of global warming during Live Earth concerts in the following way: "Of all of the dictators in the past, you know the one Al Gore strikes me as [being] closest [to] is Mussolini – sort of a non-racist, benign demagogue using global warming in an attempt to take over the world's economy and put it in his own hands and the hands of his cronies."

In terms of popularity with TV viewers, Bill O'Reilly's prime time *The O'Reilly Factor* on Fox News trumps competitors.[6] Although the talk-show's subject is politics, political news is a pretext for a spectacle of abusive labels and verbal attacks on non-conservatives. A content analysis of O'Reilly's rhetorical excesses conducted recently by Indiana University researchers Mike Conway, Maria E. Grabe and Kevin Grieves (2007) revealed that the host is exceptionally quick to resort to insulting labels (he calls a person or a group a derogatory name on average once every 6.8 seconds during his editorials that open his program each night) and often injects fear and prejudice to his comments. According to O'Reilly, the most prominent evil-doers on the American political arena are left-leaning media, which are both *anti-American* and *anti-Bush*. Media, together with the political left, are often characterized as a *moral threat*, because of their hypocrisy, selfishness and greed. Democrats, in turn, are most often labeled as *incompetents* that "allow terrorism." According to the study, the most dangerous villains in O'Reilly's world are illegal aliens, terrorists, and foreigners because they are apparently a *physical and moral threat* to the United States (Conway et al. 2007: 197).

---

5.   Available at www.mediamatters.org/issues_topics/people/michaelsavage.

6.   Second in *Media Matters* ranking of 30 most viewed programs available at http://mediamatters.org/issues_topics/shows_publications?num=30 (30 August 2007).

In yet another attempt at "unspinning" O'Reilly's style, *FAIR*'s Peter Hart (2003) chronicles O'Reilly's history of derogatory comments about non-Americans and non-WASPs. For example, during an interview in November 2002, O'Reilly opined that "the most unattractive women in the world are probably in the Muslim countries." During a September 2000 program about black athletes, O'Reilly commented: "Most of these kids come out and they can't speak English." His mantra is "Will African-Americans break away from the pack thinking and reject immorality – because that's the reason the family's breaking apart – alcohol, drugs, infidelity?" Another frequent theme of O'Reilly's commentary concerns cultural clashes, in which the West's superiority is undeniable: "You can't bring Western reasoning into the [African] culture. The same way you can't bring it into fundamental Islam" (quoted in Hart 2003: par. 6–12). Given O'Reilly's increasing popularity, it can be concluded that the host's creative penchant for outrageous new labels for political opponents has outweighed his lack of professionalism in reporting.

To summarize, researchers at *FAIR, Media Matters* and other web-based media monitors aim to sensitize citizens to the abusive rhetoric used by prime time TV and radio talk show hosts in America. Both the frequency and the offensive character of (mis)labeling stratagems reported make it reasonable to express concerns about the state of American political discourse. Such incidents as Jimmy Carter being called a *waste of skin* by Glenn Beck, Hillary Clinton *that buck-tooth witch* and *Satan* by Don Imus, Al Gore a *total fag* by Ann Coulter, or Barack Obama a *pothead* and a *wuss* by Tucker Carlson (all celebrity TV/radio commentators) are indicative of the erosion of standards of political discourse in popular media.

5. Conclusions

The above analysis of samples of American political discourse has been devoted to illustrating some pervasive ways of applying (mis)labeling – here treated as a manipulative discourse strategy. Such instances of name-calling are a frequent subject of online alerts by independent media monitors. The prevalence of scandal and spectacle in corporate media and the falling demand for serious coverage lead one to surmise that, for a large segment of American citizens, it is the label- and conflict-driven political infotainment that constitutes the basis for their election choices (cf. Płudowski 2008 for a review of latest trends in American political communication). Meanwhile, those who critically read the mainstream press may have an impression that American domestic politics is simply a "fight in the kitchen" between the two dominant parties, a fight that intensifies before each election when celebrity commentators provide readers with little but foregone conclusions, biased judgments and increasingly racy labels for contenders. Outside election times, political commentary is often devoted to publicizing the official agenda, together with its convoluted or euphemistic terminology, as many political journalists choose to cite government's spokespeople and avoid the risk of addressing the controversial nature of some foreign and domestic policies. As a result, independent media monitors, which attempt to sensitize citizens to (mis)labeling and other manipulative discursive strategies in mainstream political coverage, are becoming new conduits for political discourse. The awareness of manipulation they foster will hopefully lead to more active public engagement in politics and will help restore a more participatory democracy both in and beyond the U.S.

References

Altheide, David L. 2007. "The mass media and terrorism." *Discourse & Communication* 1 (3): 287–308.

Anthonissen, Christine. 2003. "Challenging media censoring: Writing between the lines in the face of stringent restrictions." In *Re-reading the Past: Critical and Functional Perspectives on Time and Value*, James R. Martin and Ruth Wodak (eds), 91–112. Amsterdam: Benjamins.

Aronson, Elliot. 2003. *The Social Animal* [9th ed.]. New York: Worth Publishers.

Baudrillard, Jean. 1998. *The Consumer Society: Myths and Structures*. London: Sage.

—. 2005 [1981]. *Symulakry i symulacja [Simulacres et simulacion]*. Sławomir Królak (trans.). Warszawa: Wydawnictwo Sic!

Conway, Mike, Grabe, Maria E. and Grieves, Kevin. 2007. "Villains, victims and the virtuous in Bill O'Reilly's 'No Spin Zone': Revisiting world war propaganda techniques." *Journalism Studies* 8 (2): 197–223.

Fritz, Ben, Keefer, Bryan and Nyhan, Brendan. 2004. *All the President's Spin*. New York: Simon and Schuster.

Hart, Peter. 2003. *The Oh Really? Factor: Unspinning Fox News Channel's Bill O'Reilly*. New York: Seven Stories Press.

—. "O'Reilly's racist slurs – in context." *Extra!* (June 2003). Retrieved July 30, 2007 from www.fair.org?index.php?page=1147.

—. "Obamamania. How loving Barack Obama helps pundits love themselves." *Extra!* (March/April 2007). Retrieved July 30, 2007 from www.fair.org/index.php?page=3094.

"Language, A Key Mechanism of Control." A memorandum by GOP Action Committee, 1990. Retrieved July 23, 2007 from www.fair.org/index.php?page=1276.

Lassen, Inger, Strunck, Jeanne and Vestergaard, Torben (eds). 2006. *Mediating Ideology in Text and Image*. Amsterdam: Benjamins.

Lasswell, Harold, Leites, Nathan, Fadner, Raymond, Goldsen, Joseph M., Grey, Alan, Janis, Irving L., Kaplan, Abraham, Mintz, Alexander, Pool, I. De Sola, Yakobson, Sergius, Kaplan, David and Stewart, George W. 1949. *Language of Politics*. New York: Steward.

Le Bon, Gustave. 1986 [1894]. *Psychologia tłumu [La psychologie des foules]*. Bolesław Kaprocki (trans.). Warszawa: Wydawnictwo Naukowe PWN.

Lee, Alfred McClung and Briant Lee, Elizabeth (eds). 1939. *The Fine Art of Propaganda: A Study of Father Coughlin's Speeches*. New York: Harcourt, Brace and Company.

Lynch, Timothy. 2006. "Doublespeak and the war on terrorism." *Cato Briefing Papers no. 98*. Washington D.C.: Cato Institute.

MacArthur, John R. "The lies we bought: The unchallenged 'evidence' for war." *Columbia Journalism Review* (May/June 2003). Retrieved July 30, 2007 from www.cjrarchives.org/issues 2003/3/lies-macarthur.asp.

Mrozowski, Maciej. 2006 „Media masowe i polityka – niebezpieczne związki [Mass media and politics – dangerous connections]." *Dyskurs* 4: 4–30.

Naureckas, James, Rendall, Steven and Cohen, Jeff. 1995. *The Way Things Aren't: Rush Limbaugh's Reign of Error*. New York: The New Press.

Płudowski, Tomasz (ed.). 2006. *Terrorism, Media, Society*. Toruń: Collegium Civitas and Wydawnictwo Adam Marszałek.

—. 2008. *Komunikacja polityczna w amerykańskich kampaniach wyborczych [Political Communication in American Election Campaigns]*. Warszawa: Wydawnictwo Naukowe PWN.

Pratkanis, Anthony and Aronson, Elliot. 2004 [2001]. *Wiek propagandy: Używanie i nadużywanie perswazji na codzień [Age of Propaganda: The Everyday Use and Abuse of Persuasion]*. Józef Radzicki and Marcin Szuster (trans.). Warszawa: Wydawnictwo Naukowe PWN.

Rendall, Steve. "The repeatedly re-elected autocrat. Painting Chavez as a 'would-be dictator.'" *Extra!* (Nov/Dec 2006). Retrieved July 30, 2007 from www.fair.org/index.php?page=3009.

—. "The media's mayor. Mythologizing Giuliani and 9/11." *Extra!* (May/June 2007). Retrieved July 30, 2007 from www.fair.org/index.php?page=3117.

Tannen, Deborah. 2003 [1998]. *Cywilizacja kłótni [The Argument Culture: Stopping America's War of Words]*. Piotr Budkiewicz (trans.). Warszawa: Zysk i S-ka.

Umansky, Eric. "Failures of imagination: American journalists and the coverage of torture." *Columbia Journalism Review* (Sept/Oct 2006). Retrieved July 30, 2007 from www.cjrarchives.org/issues/2006/5/Umansky.asp.

van Dijk, Teun A. 2006. "Discourse and manipulation." *Discourse & Society* 12: 359–383.

Whiten, Jon. "Subverting not preserving democracy. Marginalizing vote fraud 'conspiracy theories.'" *Extra!* (July/Aug 2006). Retrieved July 30, 2007 from www.fair.org/index.php?page=2932.

Whittelsey, Frances Cerra. "Can you hear us NOW? Anti-war march gets more coverage – but the message is still muted." *Extra!* (March/April 2007). Retrieved July 30, 2007 from www.fair.org/index.php?page=3096.

PART III

Critical insights into political communication

CHAPTER 6

President Bush's address to the nation on U.S. policy in Iraq
A critical discourse analysis approach*

Ibrahim A. El-Hussari

1. Introduction

Political language is basically used as a powerful tool in winning the support as well as the consent of both the public and the nation lawmakers, more especially at moments of crisis over which the nation may clearly divide. Whether in office or in the opposition, political leaders who deliver public speeches within a national context often tend to manipulate language to best-suit the rhetorical mode or genre they choose to pass a message through in an effort to gain political advantage, maintain power, and shirk responsibility. Unable, and perhaps unwilling, to coerce, political leaders in the so-called democratic polities often need to 'manufacture consent' in order to undertake their agendas. Such a practice occurs through discourse and verbal representation. To this end, discourse can be seen as a cultural tradition that comprises the linguistic self-consciousness as well as the skills and methodologies brought into play to shape the convictions of a particular audience and sustain a positive image of the public speaker. Critical discourse analysis (CDA; cf. e.g. Wodak and Chilton 2005), on the other hand, takes another path to send a different message. It is a tool that helps a discourse analyst to illustrate how unmasking the written/spoken word (with overt and covert meaning) can bring about a different perspective and a deeper understanding of whose interest is being served. In short, CDA tries to illuminate ways in which the dominant forces in a society construct versions of reality that favor their often hidden agendas. As an effective tool used by scholars to decipher a text, CDA compels us to make a move from seeing words in the abstract to seeing them as loaded with meanings in a particular context. Politically speaking, no public speech is ever neutral.

---

* This paper was presented at the Political Linguistics Conference (PL2007, 13–15 September 2007), organized by Institute of Applied Linguistics, University of Warsaw, and Institute of English, University of Łódź.

This paper uses CDA as a tool to explore President George W. Bush's "Address to the Nation on U.S. Policy in Iraq," which was delivered on January 10, 2007. The speech was transcribed and published by *The New York Times* on January 11, 2007 (see Appendix). It is framed within a particular yet uneasy political context which causes several segments of the speech to be mediated by hidden ideological assumptions and power relationships.

The paper examines chunks of public discourse that intensify 'political correctness' through the overuse and repetition of key words, such as *combating terror/terrorist/al-Qaeda* for the purpose of maintaining troop security, home safety, and world peace, as well as expediting the global war on terror. The paper analyses such repetition for frequency, duration, intensity, and rhetorical effects cushioning the change of policy endorsed by the President. It also studies the effect of the association technique, whether explicit or implicit, whose use triggers intense emotions shaping the future, not only of the U.S. but also that of the world at large. The confessional and apologetic tone of the speech, admitting 'unidentified' failings of previous strategies and outlining a new 'more effective' strategy for Iraq betrays a desperate call for public support and understanding of the new plan carrying the prospective strategic change in policy. As the President's motion evokes many intertextual references beyond the linguistic features of the text, I use this framework to draw on crucial moments in the history of earlier American administrations which sought a change of policy/strategy when power relationships across the governmental institutions of the United States altered as political parties divided over a set of policies proposed by the administration to solve war-related problems. Thus, part of the text related to intertextuality is looked at in terms of how President Bush's argumentation pattern is re-contextualized and reformulated in a different context to produce a different effect. In looking at the institutional change of policy as a key issue framing the Presidential address, the analysis will examine discursive practices that include rhetorical composition of words and phrases, omissions, diversion, and confusion, to mention only a few. By showing this, the speech becomes more than just words in the text; it discloses how those words were used in that particular political context to win support of the nation for the new strategy outlined in the speech.

The paper concludes by identifying unresolved issues and challenges underlying the speech, for the speech brought up to the fore nothing more than an adjustment of the initial mission assigned to the American armed forces on the eve of invading Iraq but was hastily described by the President, soon after the fall of Baghdad, as 'Mission Accomplished'. Ironically, much of the substance that the speech contained was previously transmitted through earlier speeches delivered by President Bush in the U.S. Congress and elsewhere.

2.   Rationale for studying the text

The reasons for selecting this political speech are simple. Firstly, it was delivered in the wake of the latest U.S. Senate Elections of 2006, the result of which gave the Democrats a slim majority in the Congress for the first time since the Presidential Election of 2000. Secondly, the general situation in Iraq had been deteriorating drastically since the Fall of Baghdad on April 9, 2003. Besides trillions of dollars budgeted to spend on the invasion and meet the aftermath obligations, there have been heavy losses in life and property, not only on the part of the Iraqi civilians and military personnel but also on the part of the Coalition Forces, especially the American troops. Thirdly, the speech was also delivered in the wake of the issuance of the Iraq Study Group (ISG) Report, prepared over a significant span of time by a bipartisan panel led by former Secretary of State, James Baker, and former Congressman, Lee Hamilton, to advise the American Administration for a solution. And lastly, perhaps, the speech came to redress the rift increasingly widening between the U.S. Administration and its allies in the Coalition Forces due to the public pressures exerted on quite a number of governments that participated in the invasion of Iraq, some of which opted for a military withdrawal from Iraq, for there was no time-line drawn for a pullout of forces as their mandate was open-ended. All these reasons, together with other equally grave yet undeclared reasons, must have been influenced by the President's political discourse in the direction of 'a change of course in Iraq'. The point to be highlighted by means of CDA is whether the change outlined in the speech is the outcome of a real evaluation of the tragic consequences of the war on Iraq or a new strategy to combat 'terror' within the framework of a preventive global war on terror.

3.   An overview of the speech as text

This written text is transcribed from the televised public speech in which President Bush is addressing the American people on U.S. policy in Iraq over the past four years of the invasion. The timing of the speech is significant as it occurs in the wake of the Republicans losing majority in the new Senate and the Congress as a whole, thus campaigning to keep the President's agendas and maintain power relations with the Congress and beyond. The speech is also a response to the Baker-Hamilton Report, produced by the bipartisan panel making the Iraq Study Group. Further, the speech is a text in conflict-resolution strategy planned by the President and his advisors. The language-based process of constructing a version of reality most suitable to the Bush Administration is remarkably subtle and comprehensive. Discourse carries the ideological assumptions under which the issues alluded to are known and ordered in the context it is used. This means that the content of the political language used in the speech contains the very rationale by which it is to be framed, defined, understood and acted upon. In common parlance, this is likely to bring about the consent of the audience targeted. Looking at the text as a whole, Henry and Tator (2002) recommend checking out what sort of perspective is being presented – what angle or point of view.

The thirty one paragraphs making the structure of the speech vary in length but are tightly framed by the particular modes of linear rational thought, empiricism, and objectivity that often characterize formal public speeches. The political language thus used conveys both the linguistic meaning of what is said and the corpus, or a part of it, of the political beliefs underpinning almost each and every statement made (cf. Geis 1987). The corpus of the text boils down to one point: the President is endorsing a new strategy to change the American course in Iraq. This is stated in paragraph 1 of the speech: "The new strategy I outline tonight will change America's course in Iraq, and help us succeed in the fight against terror." The rest of the speech presents a contentious justification of the failings of earlier strategies, a sanguine defense of the new strategy endorsed, and an admonitory message about 'unacceptable' consequences if the new strategy fails.

4.   What Critical Discourse Analysis says about the text

The principal unit of analysis for CDA is the text. Texts, whether spoken or written, are often taken to be acted upon as their form and structure are not arbitrary. As such, they remain affiliated with particular conventionalized discourses. The formal public speech under study features discourses of power relations, conflicting ideologies, domestic and foreign policies, and broad national strategies. As a conventional form, then, it constrains and enables meanings on many levels between the speaker as encoder and the receiver as decoder. Although the term *discourse* is slippery, elusive, and difficult to define (Henry and Tator 2002), the analyst's attempt, using CDA, to 'debunk' the words of those in power (McGregor 2003) cannot simply go unnoticed. A linguistic analysis of various lexical and grammatical devices used in the text is an essential part of CDA, for "texts are meaningful only because they actualize the meaning potential of the linguistic system" (Halliday 2004: 658). CDA as a tool to explore and further understand the text as a set of discourses seeks to link the text (micro level) with the underlying power structures in society (macro level) through the discursive practices upon which the text is built (Thompson 2002). I drew on a variety of techniques deriving from various disciplinary fields, as CDA does not have a unitary theoretical framework or methodology because it is best viewed as a shared perspective encompassing a range of approaches instead of one school (cf. van Dijk 2000). Political discourse, then, can be interpreted differently by people whose backgrounds, knowledge and power positions are different. In other words, the CDA analyst may not claim to essentially possess the sole interpretation of text. Instead, s/he offers to produce a more or less plausible or adequate interpretation when the text is approached apart from political indifference (cf. Fairclough 2002; Wodak and Ludwig 1999).

As discourse, President Bush's speech/text is effective in practical terms and evidenced by its ability to organize and regulate relations of power. Such a discourse might be called a 'regime of truth' (Foucault 1980). It is this regime that takes hold of a political system that constrains and enables analysts engaged in CDA to do a revealing job as they study what is included in and what is excluded from the text.

The text is a formal public speech: the President of the United States addressing the nation. The text frames the message of changing the current American policy in Iraq, and so does the concept of topicalization at the sentence level. In choosing what to put in the topic position, the speaker/writer creates a perspective or a slant that influences the perception of the audience.

(1)   *The new strategy* I outline tonight will change America's course in Iraq, and help us succeed in the fight against terror. (para.1)

       This will require increasing American force levels. So I have committed more than 20,000 additional American troops to Iraq (para.10).

Thus, from the outset of the speech, the President sets a problem – solution model, presumed to be culturally ingrained. This pattern is reinforced by the sequence of the textual segments making the entirety of the text. The sequence (situation – problem – solution) is conditioned by words signposting the text. This is subtly done through the ways of drawing attention to the difficult situation in which *the Armed Forces of the United States are engaged in a struggle that will determine the direction of the global war on terror and our safety here at home* (para.1). This is done by addressing and choosing the degree of formality in accordance with the normal conventions of the Western mode of persuasive writing.

5.   Grammatical and lexical features of cohesion

The linguistic choices, both lexical and grammatical, seem to sustain the speaker's intention for changing course, which later in the text becomes a change of mission to be accomplished by sending more troops to Iraq. Key-words, such as *terror, failure, success, danger* and *safety*, for instance, being a vital part of the contextual framework through frequency, illuminate and serve the topical key-word *change* which is supported by the modal auxiliary *will* followed (63 times) by action words, such as *make, chase, capture, kill, deploy, expand, disrupt, interrupt, help, improve, gain, help*, to convey certainty that the change is a serious issue. Thanks to the discourse relations of cohesion and coherence (expressed, for instance, through variation in conjunctive markers), the constituent parts of the text hang together as a unity. Although linguistic features are not the most salient characteristics of political discourse, no text could ever have a material existence without them (Halliday 2004).

The discursive practices used to tidy up the president's address to the nation render the text dynamic. Various labels to identify the meaning relations between chunks of the text take the forms of stating the problem, marketing the solution, justifying previous failure and possible success of the new strategy, and showing a power position from which the tone of concession felt is rather clothed in an air of motivation and challenge. The problem stated implicitly throughout the text places the speaker in a Hamlet-like situation as the struggle the U.S. is engaged in

(2) a. will determine the direction of the global war on terror and home safety (para.1);
     b. the situation is unacceptable to the American people and it is unacceptable to me (para.4).

The solution to this problem is *the new strategy* (see e.g. 1 above), frequent references to which (see also 3 below) are significant clues to understanding the gravity of the problem.

(3) It is clear that we need to *change our strategy* in Iraq" (para.5).

In the same vein,

(4) So my national security team, military commanders and diplomats conducted a comprehensive review ... We consulted members of Congress from both parties, our allies abroad and distinguished outside experts. We benefited from the thoughtful recommendations of the Iraq Study Group ... In our discussions, we *all* agreed that there is no magic formula of success in Iraq. And one message came through loud and clear: failure in Iraq would be a disaster for the United States (para.5).

Example 4 implies that the whole nation represented by the military, the diplomats, members of the Congress, the Iraq Study Group, and experts should be involved in reaching a solution to their problem, so that the U.S. new strategy in Iraq would not fail. This is followed by a series of justifications showing failure of earlier strategies and manipulating language through a concessionary attitude that invites sharing in finding a way out. The conjunctive discourse markers (additive, adversative, temporal and causal), together with nominal and gerund phrases mark this swerve in register.

(5) *But* in 2006, the opposite happened ... *And* the result was a vicious cycle of violence that continues today (para.3).
(6) *The consequences of failure* are clear (para.6).
(7) *The challenge playing out* across the broader Middle East ... (para.22).
(8) *Succeeding* in Iraq also requires *defending* its territorial integrity and *stabilizing* the region in the face of extremist challenge (para.19).

and

(9) Victory will not look like the ones our fathers and grandfathers achieved. *There will be no surrender ceremony on the deck of a battleship* (para.25).

The swerve in register, as implied in the quotes above, betrays signs of failure in the strategic policy of the Bush Administration when it comes to comparing the declared objectives of the military invasion of Iraq and the ambivalence of the immediacy of the new security goals branching out from that invasion. This 'mission', which was called 'accomplished', thus resulting in a ceasefire that was not formally signed by any surrendering Iraqi authority then, has allowed for violent and bloody counter-attacks carried out by Iraqi and non-Iraqi resistance fighters (labeled insurgents or libeled terrorists and extremists), on the one hand, and equally violent reprisals by the coalition forces occupying Iraq, on the other. Iraq has become more challenging, and the challenge has extended beyond Iraq to the broader Middle East, which needs to be stabilized, for Iraq no longer stands, as claimed at the early stages of the invasion, the role model for a would-be democratic country in the region. The American troops are now commissioned to take another risky job: defending the *territorial integrity* of Iraq and *stabilizing the region in the face of extremist challenge*. Hence, the rhetorical phrase *no surrender ceremony on the deck of a battleship* assumes a metaphorical effect. Used as an intertext, the phrase brings up association with the formal surrender of Japan in the Pacific battle during World War II. On September 2, 1945, Japan formally surrendered after accepting the Allies terms in a less than half an hour long ceremony which took place on board of the battleship *USS Missouri*, anchored with other American and British warships in the Bay of Tokyo. That short ceremony marked the end of the war and generated many memorable images that entered the cultural history of the United States. As the conception of memory is the prerequisite for registering the cultural meaning and space of intertextuality (Iser in Lachmann 1997: xvii), President Bush, in quote (9) above, distances himself from that cultural space by suspending the possibility of putting an end to the ongoing war. As there is no formal surrender ceremony in Iraq, this implies that the war is perpetual. No exit!

The President's discourse therefore works from within a system of language in use, where linguistic features of the text seem to be in keeping with the context of situation within the framework of the communicative function of language. This explains the polite but firm attitude of the speaker addressing a grave national issue to his people, more emphatically his political opponents on the receiving end whose anticipated response to the speech is crucial. To this effect, discourse includes representations of how things are and have been as well as representations of how things might or should or could be (Fairclough 2002). The question that a CDA analyst should raise concerning President Bush's asking the Congress members to get directly involved in the Iraqi issue and come up with improvements on his new strategy may read as follows: Are the Congress members really part of the solution, or as Brown (1993) so uncomfortably alleged, part of the problem? The power relations and the position of power from which the President is speaking are clear enough in the following paragraph.

(10) In the days ahead, my national security team will fully brief Congress on our new strategy. *If – if* members have improvements that can be made, we will make them. *If* circumstances change, we will adjust. *Honorable* people have different views and they will voice their criticisms. It is fair *to hold our views up to scrutiny.* And *all involved* have a responsibility to explain how the path they propose would be more likely to succeed (para.27).

Note the three *ifs* in the construction of the President's proposition. The same also applies to the lexical and grammatical linguistic features where conditional clauses are evident – frequency being eight for explicit *if* clauses, three of which in one paragraph (para.27) and fifteen for embedded conditional clauses with *as* and *as a result of* phrases being part of the omitted *if* clause (see examples 11 and 12 below).

(11)   *As* we make these changes, we will continue to pursue al Qaeda... (para.17).

(12)   *As a result*, our commanders believe we have an opportunity to deal a serious blow to the terrorists (para.18).

These conditional relations imply that the degree of certainty to whether the President asks for real involvement of the Congress in the solution to the problem is weakened by the power relations he is in control of as President of the United States. The challenge underlying the proposition in paragraph 27 (see e.g. 10 above) is that the Iraqi 'legacy' will be handed down to the new Administration succeeding Mr. Bush's in November 2008.

Unmasking other grammatical features of the discourse, more especially the conjunctive discourse markers, furthers the effect of the lexical relations carrying the President's message to the nation. This is quite clear when we examine the causal and temporal conjunctive discourse relations expressed by the most frequent words. The causal relations (12 occurrences), appear in such expressions, as *the result was* (para.3), *the consequences of failure* (para.6), *for the safety of* (para.6), *for it* [the plan] *to succeed* (para.10), *so* (para.10, 14, 18), *why* (para.11), *in the long run* (para.22), *come after* (para.26, 26), or *and we concluded that* (para.26), and so forth. The President's message about the need to change strategy in Iraq implies promises for a safer future concerning the U.S. troops involved in combat and the U.S. national security. The temporal relations, in turn (26 occurrences), vary with the use of time articles shifting between past, present and future to affirm the interconnectedness of various dangerous events in the U.S. history and the need to see them in the same context, as in the following: *tonight* (para.1), *when* (para.2), *in 2006* (para.3), *on September the 11th, 2001* (para.6), *our past efforts* (para.8), *now* (para.9, 12, 30), *earlier* (para.11), *this time* (para.11), *last week* (para.12), *over time* (para.13), *by November* (para.15), *benchmarks* (para.16), *soon* (para.16), *recently* (para.20), *on Friday* (para.21), *in the days ahead* (para.27), *in these dangerous times* (para.29, *the year ahead* (para.30), *throughout our history* (para.30), and *these trying hours* (para.31).

The President's clear intent here is rather persuasive: America can always accept the challenge, as ever before, and can emerge victorious, regardless of the cost. Hence, the grave task undertaken in Iraq is no longer that of the Bush Administration alone but it is that of the American nation that cannot tolerate threat or concede defeat.

At the level of lexical cohesion used throughout the speech, the linguistic choices made signpost the ideological assumption underlying the text. Dale (1989) uses the term 'sense legitimation' to describe a strategy for manufacturing consent in a particular group, and thereby achieving hegemony of a discourse. The words and word phrases used by President Bush here to intensify the enormity of the situation that needs to be urgently redressed seem to serve the hegemony of the discourse strategy encompassing the speech. This strategy involves couching unpopular policy changes in words whose meanings are subtly elusive. In CDA, it is clear that particular wordings are clues to discursive relationships in the text. Arguably, the more frequently a particular wording is used in a text, the more likely it is that a particular discourse is enlarging the base of its subscribers. In the speech under study, the subscribers are not only the people directly addressed (i.e. the American nation and the Congress) but also a larger number of people across the globe, including partner countries in the coalition forces and the moderate countries in the Middle East. In this context, CDA uncovers how the speaker wants to be seen, not so much as a speculator of forthcoming events but as an outspoken truth-teller who calls a spade a spade. The occurrence of the following lexical features could not have been a matter of arbitrariness.

The thematic level of meaning is intensified through word and phrase repetitions, contrasting images, metaphors, and untraditional, newly-coined collocations. For example, by addressing the current situation in Iraq as *unacceptable* (para.4), *challenging* (para.22), and *dangerous* (para.29), the President employs repeatedly negative images of the enemy, such as *Al-Qaeda terrorists, Sunni insurgents, Shia death squads, radical Islamic extremists* [who are] *building radical Islamic Empire* in an atmosphere of *sectarian violence* and *suicide bombings* (see Appendix, para.13, 17, 18, 24, and 26). This abhorrent image of the enemy is explicitly painted by the most frequently used synonymous words and expressions that occur (37) times throughout the text: *terror/terrorists* (12), *sectarian violence* (10), *extremists* (5), and *Al-Qaeda* (10).

On the other hand, the positive image of the American troops operating in Iraq is presented as

(13) *brave, selfless, young men and women in uniform* (para.29),

who understand that

(14) *our cause* in Iraq is *noble* and necessary and that the *advance of freedom* is the calling of our time ... They serve far from their families, who make the quiet sacrifices of lonely holidays and empty chairs at the dinner table (para.29).

They [the American troops] are there

(15) to *kill, destroy, capture, strike, blow a deal, fight, struggle, clear* (para.10),

for the new strategy will assign to them

(16) *a well-defined mission*: to help Iraqis clear and secure neighborhoods, to help them protect the local population and to help ensure that the Iraqi forces left behind are capable of providing *the security that Baghdad needs* (para.10).

In the above quoted material, the images of the American troops in uniform and the outlaws/terrorists [uniformless] are sharply juxtaposed as virtue versus vice or good versus evil. Ironically, such words as *kill* and *destroy*, which modify the two belligerent parties in the battlefield, mean something different when used to describe what each party does and why. In keeping with the *noble* cause of the American troops is the *well-defined mission* assigned to them to bring security to Baghdad. Note the omission of the other big cities of vast Iraq which are also insecure and not any safer at all.

The assertive tone of the speech is worded in rather short and clear-cut sentences that show resolve, determination and commitment. Even when using passive and negative forms of action verbs, the speech sends a message that everything in Iraq is under control: *We will not allow them* (para.18); *Where mistakes have been made, the responsibility rests with me* (para.4); *This is a strong commitment* (para.10); *Now is time to act* (para.12); *For the safety of our people, America must succeed in Iraq* (para.6); *We can and we will prevail* (para.30); and *We go forward with* trust (para.31). As a matter of fact, the wording of the President's firm stand is also framed within an explicitly worded ideological struggle that goes beyond Iraq and the American interests in Iraq to engage the international community in a declared war on terror (see e.g. 17 and 18 below).

(17)   It is the decisive *ideological struggle of our time* ... to provide a hopeful alternative to the *hateful ideology of the enemy* (para.22).

and

(18)   Now America is engaged in *a new struggle that will set the course for a new century.* We can and we will prevail (para.30).

However, there is confusion when it comes to real reasons behind the vicious cycle of violence in Iraq. Time-lines, benchmarks, and promises to be met by the Iraqi government, which the speech advises and warns at the same time to do necessary reforms across the socio-economic and the socio-political structures of Iraq, betray uncertainty of the situation the President claims is under control. The following conclusive statements rehashed in the text send a doubtful message about the prospects of a peaceful settlement in Iraq.

(19)   a.   *Only Iraqis* can end the *sectarian violence* and secure their people (para.7).
       b.   I have made it clear to the prime minister and Iraq's other leaders that *America's commitment is not open-ended...* (para.12).
       c.   So America will hold the Iraqi government to the *benchmarks* it has announced (para.14).
       d.   *A democratic Iraq will not be perfect* (para.25).

The quotes (see e.g. 19 above) redefine the rules of engagement in Iraq against a backdrop of historical tension which has unleashed sectarian violence. The President does not imply or indicate if the said *sectarian violence* has been, in one way or another, the direct result of the military invasion in 2003. This is an evasion of the whole war situation the President clearly states (see e.g. 17 and 18 above) concerning the resolve made by the American Administration in the name of the international community to combat terror across the globe. The American commitment to combat terror is no more open-ended, for it is reduced to a short-term mission (e.g. 19b). The President is blaming it on the Iraqi government which should meet benchmarks (e.g. 19c), and that the Iraqi democracy envisioned by the President as a model to be copied [by other countries in the Middle East] turns out to be imperfect (e.g. 19d).

The speech closes with a preaching tone *that the Author of Liberty will guide us through these trying hours* (para.31), reaffirming the ideological conflict underlying the situation in Iraq and beyond:

(20)   *On one side* are those who believe in freedom and moderation.
       On the other side are the extremists who kill the innocent and have declared their intention to destroy our way of life (para.22).

The ideology permeating the speech consists of a "systematic network of beliefs which needs discourse as its medium of expression" (Hodge and Kress 1991: 6). It is from this 'politically correct' stance that the President is trying to deliver his own version of reality about the war on terror. By selecting a rhetorical language which serves his political discourse, the President is also eschewing a credulous evaluation of the past four years during which the policy of the American administration was consistently faltering and the image of the American combat troops in Iraq was constantly blemished. Excluding a major part from the speech, and this is done quite consciously on the part of the President, would simply prompt the CDA analyst to dig for the true reasons behind the President's addressing a strategic change of policy in Iraq.

6.   What is excluded from the text?

Excluded from the text are points related to the real reasons behind the invasion of Iraq and the intensity of the dark situation in the process of rebuilding the torn country. The reasons which were worded in a highly elaborate, rhetorical manner on the eve of the invasion have now totally disappeared from the text. Saddam Hussein's 'Weapons of Mass Destruction' (WMD), which on the eve of the invasion was the focal point behind the Bush Administration rallying support and mobilizing coalition forces, contrary to the UN Inspectors' reports about WMD, is totally absented from the speech. Another reason for the deterioration of the Iraqi situation, also excluded from the text, is related to the preservation of Iraq unity and its territorial integrity, both of which are threatened in the absence of the strong Iraqi army and police force which were dismantled after formal surrender, to be replaced by a new army and police force made up mostly of sectarian militia men. Thanks to the chaos created after the army was dissolved, the Kurds in northern Iraq have established their own autonomous state (Kurdistan), the Shia groups are on the way to build their own state in southern Iraq, and the Sunni groups are building their own militia force. Besides these reasons, and definitely much more saddening, is the corruption across the public sectors of the state as well as the money spent on thousands of security contractors, which the speech does not even allude to. Absent yet from the speech is the rising number of casualties claimed whether on the part of the Iraqi population (not to mention millions of the displaced Iraqis within and without the country) or the Coalition Forces. A new report released by the CNN (August 17, 2007) on the Iraq situation shows that the suicide rate among the American military personnel rose to 25% in the year 2006. Further exclusions, in form of omissions, are the democratization process of the broader Middle East, to be replaced by full cooperation with the non-democratic 'moderate' Gulf countries and with the Iraqi tribal and sectarian forces. The Iraqi 'young democracy' being the example set for the greater Middle East seems to have gone down the drain. Still other exclusions behind the tragic situation in Iraq include the indefinite mandate of the coalition forces in Iraq – some of these forces have already left and some others are about to leave, unidentified mistakes made in Iraq, and the job being accomplished by the troops. We do not know, exactly, what mistakes have been made in Iraq and who has made them (agent omitted), and why the President claims his responsibility to that, as in *Where mistakes have been made, the responsibility rests with me* (para.4), or in *They* [troops] *have done everything we have asked them to do* (para.4), which sounds vague and is subject to further query, as in the case of Abu-Ghraib prison torture images which were denounced world-wide. Another important omission, perhaps, is concerned with the unidentified 'benefits' from the Baker-Hamilton ISG Report. The President says he will form another bi-partisan committee for Iraq in order to redress the differences between the Republicans and the Democrats, but the mission assigned to this new ISG is left vague and unknown. Omission from the text, whether done consciously or unconsciously, is a key-guide to inform CDA.

7.   Conclusion

CDA, used in this paper as an approach to political discourse, can be an effective tool that enables us to view reality as textually mediated through language systems, and text as a site of power struggle used for both the "inculcation and the contestation of discourses" (Locke 2004: 2). It also views analysis and interpretation of text as potentially revealing of ways in which discourses summon power to manipulate public opinions through covert calls (Janks 1997). This paper has illustrated the ways CDA debunks the hidden ideological meanings behind President Bush's speech of January 10, 2007, by peeling the layers of the text, both lexical and grammatical, to expose the invisible power of the written/spoken word within the field, and to examine what language in use reflects about such a field. This does not mean that CDA provides an answer to the political problem situated in a specific context; rather, it enables the analyst and the critical reader to understand the conditions behind that problem or, as Palmquist (1999) put it, 'the deep ideological roots of the issue'. The paper has also illustrated how

CDA can be effective in unmasking the text discursive practices by paying attention to what, as van Dijk (1999) argues, 'politicians say and do'. In short, CDA can be used as an effective tool that uncovers the hidden meaning of the text so that we discover the relationship between power, position, and language in use.

References

Brown, Marjorie. 1993. *Philosophical Studies of Home Economics in the United States: Basic Ideas by which Home Economists Understand Themselves*. East Lansing, Michigan: Michigan State University Press.

Dale, Roger. 1989. *The State and Education Policy*. Milton Keynes: Open University Press.

Fairclough, Norman. 2000. *Language and Power* [2nd ed.]. New York: Longman.

—. "The dialectics of discourse." Retrieved May 22, 2002 from http://www.geogr.ku.dk/courses/phd/glob-loc/papers/phdfairclough2.pdf.

Foucault, Michel. 1980. *Power/Knowledge*. New York: Pantheon.

Geis, Michael. 1987. *The Language of Politics*. New York: Springer.

Halliday, Michael A. K. 2004. *An Introduction to Functional Grammar* [3rd ed.]. London: Arnold.

Henry, Frances and Tator, Carol. 2002. *Discourses of Domination*. Toronto: University of Toronto Press.

Hodge, Robert and Kress, Gunther. 1991. *Language as Ideology*. London: Routledge.

Iser, Wolfgang. 1997. "Forward." In *Memory and Literature: Intertextuality in Russian Modernism*, Renate Lachmann (ed.), 34–51. Minneapolis: University of Minnesota Press.

Janks, Hilary. 1997. "Critical Discourse Analysis as a research tool." *Discourse: Studies in the Cultural Politics of Education* 18 (3): 329–342.

Locke, Terry. 2004. *Critical Discourse Analysis*. London and New York: Continuum.

McGregor, Sue. *Critical Science Approach – A Primer*. Retrieved June 18, 2003 from http://www.kon.org/cfp/critical_science_primer.pdf.

Palmquist, Ruth. *Discourse Analysis*. Retrieved November 26, 1999 from http://www.gslis.utexas.edu/-palmquist/courses/discourse.htm.

Thompson, Mark. *ICT, Power, and Development Discourse: A Critical Analysis*. Retrieved April 12, 2002 from http://www.jims.cam.ac.uk/research/seminar/thompson_ ab.pdf.

van Dijk, Teun A. 1999. "Critical Discourse Analysis and Conversation Analysis." *Discourse and Society* 10 (4): 450–459.

—. *Critical Discourse Analysis*. Retrieved June 24, 2000 from http://www.discourse-in-society.org/oldArticles.pdf.

Wodak, Ruth and Chilton, Paul (eds). 2005. *A New Agenda in (Critical) Discourse Analysis: Theory, Methodology and Interdisciplinarity*. Amsterdam: Benjamins.

Wodak, Ruth and Ludwig, Christoph (eds). 1999. *Challenges in a Changing World: Issues in Critical Discourse Analysis*. Vienna: Passagenverlag.

Appendix

President Bush's Address to Nation on U.S. Policy in Iraq, January 11, 2007
Available at http://www.nytimes.com/2007/01/11/us/11ptext.html [DOA: September 2008]

1. Good evening. Tonight in Iraq, the Armed Forces of the United States are engaged in a struggle that will determine the direction of the global war on terror and our safety here at home. The new strategy I outline tonight will change America's course in Iraq, and help us succeed in the fight against terror.

2. When I addressed you just over a year ago, nearly 12 million Iraqis had cast their ballots for a unified and democratic nation. The elections of 2005 were a stunning achievement. We thought that these elections would bring the Iraqis together, and that as we trained Iraqi security forces, we could accomplish our mission with fewer American troops.

3. But in 2006, the opposite happened. The violence in Iraq – particularly in Baghdad – overwhelmed the political gains the Iraqis had made. Al Qaeda terrorists and Sunni insurgents recognized the mortal danger that Iraq's elections posed for their cause. And they responded with outrageous acts of murder aimed at innocent Iraqis. They blew up one of the holiest shrines in Shia Islam, the Golden Mosque of Samarra, in a calculated effort to provoke Iraq's Shia population to retaliate. Their strategy worked. Radical Shia elements, some supported by Iran, formed death squads. And the result was a vicious cycle of sectarian violence that continues today.

4. The situation in Iraq is unacceptable to the American people and it is unacceptable to me. Our troops in Iraq have fought bravely. They have done everything we have asked them to do. Where mistakes have been made, the responsibility rests with me.

5. It is clear that we need to change our strategy in Iraq. So my national security team, military commanders and diplomats conducted a comprehensive review. We consulted members of Congress from both parties, our allies abroad and distinguished outside experts. We benefited from the thoughtful recommendations of the Iraq Study Group – a bipartisan panel led by former Secretary of State James Baker and former Congressman Lee Hamilton. In our discussions, we all agreed that there is no magic formula for success in Iraq. And one message came through loud and clear: Failure in Iraq would be a disaster for the United States.

6. The consequences of failure are clear: Radical Islamic extremists would grow – would – would grow in strength and gain new recruits. They would be in a better position to topple moderate governments, create chaos in the region and use oil revenues to fund their ambitions. Iran would be emboldened in its pursuit of nuclear weapons. Our enemies would have a safe haven from which to plan and launch attacks on the American people. On Sept. 11, 2001, we saw what a refuge for extremists on the other side of the world could bring to the streets of our own cities. For the safety of our people, America must succeed in Iraq.

7. The most urgent priority for success in Iraq is security, especially in Baghdad. Eighty percent of Iraq's sectarian violence occurs within 30 miles of the capital. This violence is splitting Baghdad into sectarian enclaves and shaking the confidence of all Iraqis. Only Iraqis can end the sectarian violence and secure their people. And their government has put forward an aggressive plan to do it.

8. Our past efforts to secure Baghdad failed for two principal reasons: There were not enough Iraqi and American troops to secure neighborhoods that had been cleared of terrorists and insurgents. And there were too many restrictions on the troops we did have. Our military commanders reviewed the new Iraqi plan to ensure that it addressed these mistakes. They report that it does. They also report that this plan can work.

9. Now, let me explain the main elements of this effort: The Iraqi government will appoint a military commander and two deputy commanders for their capital. The Iraqi government will deploy Iraqi Army and National Police brigades across Baghdad's nine districts. When these forces are fully deployed, there will be 18 Iraqi Army and National Police brigades committed to this effort – along with local police. These Iraqi forces will operate from local police stations – conducting patrols and setting up checkpoints and going door-to-door to gain the trust of Baghdad residents.

10. This is a strong commitment. But for it to succeed, our commanders say the Iraqis will need our help. So America will change our strategy to help the Iraqis carry out their campaign to put down sectarian violence and bring security to the people of Baghdad. This will require increasing American force levels. So I have committed more than 20,000 additional American troops to Iraq. The vast majority of them, five brigades, will be deployed to Baghdad. These troops will work alongside Iraqi units and be embedded in their formations. Our troops will have a well-defined mission: to help Iraqis clear and secure neighborhoods, to help them protect the local population and to help ensure that the Iraqi forces left behind are capable of providing the security that Baghdad needs.

11. Many listening tonight will ask why this effort will succeed when previous operations to secure Baghdad did not. Well, here are the differences: In earlier operations, Iraqi and American forces cleared many neighborhoods of terrorists and insurgents, but when our forces moved on to other targets, the killers returned. This time, we will have the force levels we need to hold the areas that have been cleared. In earlier operations, political and sectarian interference prevented Iraqi and American forces from going into neighborhoods that are home to those fueling the sectarian violence. This time, Iraqi and American forces will have a green light to enter these neighborhoods, and Prime Minister Maliki has pledged that political or sectarian interference will not be tolerated.

12. I have made it clear to the prime minister and Iraq's other leaders that America's commitment is not open-ended. If the Iraqi government does not follow through on its promises, it will lose the support of the American people – and it will lose

the support of the Iraqi people. Now is the time to act. The prime minister under-stands this. Here is what he told his people just last week: "The Baghdad security plan will not provide a safe haven for any outlaws, regardless of sectarian or po-litical affiliation."

13. This new strategy will not yield an immediate end to suicide bombings, assassina-tions or I.E.D. [improvised explosive device] attacks. Our enemies in Iraq will make every effort to ensure that our television screens are filled with images of death and suffering. Yet over time, we can expect to see Iraqi troops chasing down murderers, fewer brazen acts of terror, and growing trust and cooperation from Baghdad's residents. When this happens, daily life will improve, Iraqis will gain confidence in their leaders and the government will have the breathing space it needs to make progress in other critical areas. Most of Iraq's Sunni and Shia want to live together in peace, and reducing the violence in Baghdad will help make reconciliation possible.

14. A successful strategy for Iraq goes beyond military operations. Ordinary Iraqi citizens must see that military operations are accompanied by visible improve-ments in their neighborhoods and communities. So America will hold the Iraqi government to the benchmarks it has announced.

15. To establish its authority, the Iraqi government plans to take responsibility for se-curity in all of Iraq's provinces by November. To give every Iraqi citizen a stake in the country's economy, Iraq will pass legislation to share oil revenues among all Iraqis. To show that it is committed to delivering a better life, the Iraqi govern-ment will spend 10 billion dollars of its own money on reconstruction and infra-structure projects that will create new jobs. To empower local leaders, Iraqis plan to hold provincial elections later this year. And to allow more Iraqis to re-enter their nation's political life, the government will reform de-Baathification laws and establish a fair process for considering amendments to Iraq's constitution.

16. America will change our approach to help the Iraqi government as it works to meet these benchmarks. In keeping with the recommendations of the Iraq Study Group, we will increase the embedding of American advisers in Iraqi Army units and partner a Coalition brigade with every Iraqi Army division. We'll help the Iraqis build a larger and better-equipped Army and we will accelerate the training of Iraqi forces, which remains the essential U.S. security mission in Iraq. We will give our commanders and civilians greater flexibility to spend funds for economic assistance. We will double the number of provincial reconstruction teams. These teams bring together military and civilian experts to help local Iraqi communities pursue reconciliation, strengthen the moderates and speed the transition to Iraqi self-reliance. And Secretary Rice will soon appoint a reconstruction coordinator in Baghdad to ensure better results for economic assistance being spent in Iraq.

17. As we make these changes, we will continue to pursue Al Qaeda and foreign fight-ers. Al Qaeda is still active in Iraq. Its home base is Anbar Province. Al Qaeda has helped make Anbar the most violent area of Iraq outside the capital. A captured Al

Qaeda document describes the terrorists' plan to infiltrate and seize control of the province. This would bring Al Qaeda closer to its goals of taking down Iraq's democracy, building a radical Islamic empire, and launching new attacks on the United States at home and abroad.

18. Our military forces in Anbar are killing and capturing Al Qaeda leaders, and they are protecting the local population. Recently, local tribal leaders have begun to show their willingness to take on Al Qaeda. And as a result, our commanders believe we have an opportunity to deal a serious blow to the terrorists. So I have given orders to increase American forces in Anbar Province by 4,000 troops. These troops will work with Iraqi and tribal forces to up the pressure on the terrorists. America's men and women in uniform took away Al Qaeda's safe haven in Afghanistan – and we will not allow them to re-establish it in Iraq.

19. Succeeding in Iraq also requires defending its territorial integrity and stabilizing the region in the face of extremist challenge. This begins with addressing Iran and Syria. These two regimes are allowing terrorists and insurgents to use their territory to move in and out of Iraq. Iran is providing material support for attacks on American troops. We will disrupt the attacks on our forces. We will interrupt the flow of support from Iran and Syria. And we will seek out and destroy the networks providing advanced weaponry and training to our enemies in Iraq.

20. We are also taking other steps to bolster the security of Iraq and protect American interests in the Middle East. I recently ordered the deployment of an additional carrier strike group to the region. We will expand intelligence sharing and deploy Patriot air defense systems to reassure our friends and allies. We will work with the governments of Turkey and Iraq to help them resolve problems along their border. And we will work with others to prevent Iran from gaining nuclear weapons and dominating the region.

21. We will use America's full diplomatic resources to rally support for Iraq from nations throughout the Middle East. Countries like Saudi Arabia, Egypt, Jordan and the gulf states need to understand that an American defeat in Iraq would create a new sanctuary for extremists and a strategic threat to their survival. These nations have a stake in a successful Iraq that is at peace with its neighbors, and they must step up their support for Iraq's unity government. We endorse the Iraqi government's call to finalize an International Compact that will bring new economic assistance in exchange for greater economic reform. And on Friday, Secretary Rice will leave for the region to build support for Iraq, and continue the urgent diplomacy required to help bring peace to the Middle East.

22. The challenge playing out across the broader Middle East is more than a military conflict. It is the decisive ideological struggle of our time. On one side are those who believe in freedom and moderation. On the other side are extremists who kill the innocent and have declared their intention to destroy our way of life. In the long run, the most realistic way to protect the American people is to provide a hopeful alternative to the hateful ideology of the enemy – by advancing liberty across a

troubled region. It is in the interests of the United States to stand with the brave men and women who are risking their lives to claim their freedom, and to help them as they work to raise up just and hopeful societies across the Middle East.

23. From Afghanistan to Lebanon to the Palestinian Territories, millions of ordinary people are sick of the violence, and want a future of peace and opportunity for their children. And they are looking at Iraq. They want to know: Will America withdraw and yield the future of that country to the extremists – or will we stand with the Iraqis who have made the choice for freedom?

24. The changes I have outlined tonight are aimed at ensuring the survival of a young democracy that is fighting for its life in a part of the world of enormous importance to American security. Let me be clear: The terrorists and insurgents in Iraq are without conscience, and they will make the year ahead bloody and violent. Even if our new strategy works exactly as planned, deadly acts of violence will continue, and we must expect more Iraqi and American casualties. The question is whether our new strategy will bring us closer to success. I believe that it will.

25. Victory will not look like the ones our fathers and grandfathers achieved. There will be no surrender ceremony on the deck of a battleship. But victory in Iraq will bring something new in the Arab world: a functioning democracy that polices its territory, upholds the rule of law, respects fundamental human liberties and answers to its people. A democratic Iraq will not be perfect. But it will be a country that fights terrorists instead of harboring them, and it will help bring a future of peace and security for our children and our grandchildren.

26. This new approach comes after consultations with Congress about the different courses we could take in Iraq. Many are concerned that the Iraqis are becoming too dependent on the United States and therefore, our policy should focus on protecting Iraq's borders and hunting down Al Qaeda. Their solution is to scale back America's efforts in Baghdad or announce the phased withdrawal of our combat forces. We carefully considered these proposals. And we concluded that to step back now would force a collapse of the Iraqi government, tear the country apart and result in mass killings on an unimaginable scale. Such a scenario would result in our troops being forced to stay in Iraq even longer and confront an enemy that is even more lethal. If we increase our support at this crucial moment, and help the Iraqis break the current cycle of violence, we can hasten the day our troops begin coming home.

27. In the days ahead, my national security team will fully brief Congress on our new strategy. If – if members have improvements that can be made, we will make them. If circumstances change, we will adjust. Honorable people have different views and they will voice their criticisms. It is fair to hold our views up to scrutiny. And all involved have a responsibility to explain how the path they propose would be more likely to succeed.

28. Acting on the good advice of Senator Joe Lieberman and other key members of Congress, we will form a new, bipartisan working group that will help us come

together across party lines to win the war on terror. This group will meet regularly with me and my administration. It will help strengthen our relationship with Congress. We can begin by working together to increase the size of the active Army and Marine Corps, so that America has the Armed Forces we need for the 21st century. We also need to examine ways to mobilize talented American civilians to deploy overseas – where they can help build democratic institutions in communities and nations recovering from war and tyranny.

29. In these dangerous times, the United States is blessed to have extraordinary and selfless men and women willing to step forward and defend us. These young Americans understand that our cause in Iraq is noble and necessary, and that the advance of freedom is the calling of our time. They serve far from their families, who make the quiet sacrifices of lonely holidays and empty chairs at the dinner table. They have watched their comrades give their lives to ensure our liberty. We mourn the loss of every fallen American; and we owe it to them to build a future worthy of their sacrifice.

30. Fellow citizens: The year ahead will demand more patience, sacrifice and resolve. It can be tempting to think that America can put aside the burdens of freedom. Yet times of testing reveal the character of a nation. And throughout our history, Americans have always defied the pessimists and seen our faith in freedom redeemed. Now America is engaged in a new struggle that will set the course for a new century. We can and we will prevail.

31. We go forward with trust that the Author of Liberty will guide us through these trying hours. Thank you and good night.

CHAPTER 7

Proximizing objects, proximizing values

Towards an axiological contribution to the discourse of legitimization

Piotr Cap

1. Introduction: The concept of proximization

This paper develops a model of analysis of political discourse, whose primary application is to the *interventionist discourse*, i.e. involving legitimization of actions which a political speaker/actor chooses to undertake in order to neutralize a threat to his or her geopolitical camp (cf. e.g. Chouliaraki 2007). The discussion draws on my ongoing work on *proximization* (cf. Cap 2006, 2008), which I take as one of the most effective strategies in accomplishing legitimization effects.[1] Proximization is a pragmatic-cognitive strategy that relies upon the speaker's ability to present events on the discourse stage as directly affecting the addressee, usually in a negative or a threatening way. In Cap (2006, 2008) I have defined three aspects of proximization which conceptually bind the entities localized inside the *deictic center* (cf. Chilton 2004, 2005a) of the stage (speaker, addressee, the so-called *IDCs*) with the alien, outside-the-deictic-center

---

1.   I take legitimization in the CDA-favored sense of linguistic enactment of the speaker's right to be obeyed (cf. Chilton 2004, 2005b; Fairclough 2000, 2006; Fairclough and Wodak 1997; Van Dijk 1998; Weiss and Wodak 2003; Wodak and Chilton 2005, etc.). The claim to rightness and the resulting enactment of legitimization mean that the speaker's rhetoric is grounded in his implicit claim to inhabit a particular social or political role, and to possess a particular authority (cf. van Dijk 1998, 2005; Martin and Wodak 2003). The possession of authority, usually accompanied by the asserted absence thereof in the audience or in the adversary, provides argumentative rationale (cf. van Eemeren and Grootendorst 2004; Dedaic 2006, etc.) for listing reasons to be obeyed. Listing such reasons usually involves a symbolic assignment of different ideological principles to different parties on the discourse stage (cf. Reisigl and Wodak 2001; Chilton 2004, etc.), assertion of the addressee's wants in the moment of crisis (cf. Graham, Keenan and Dowd 2004; Martin and Wodak 2003; Hodges and Nilep 2007; Lakoff 1996, etc.), and construal of charismatic leadership matched against an emerging threat (cf. Chilton 1996; Chilton and Lakoff 1995; Chouliaraki 2007; Hodges and Nilep 2007, etc.). All these goals and techniques are addressed in the present paper, which organizes them into a formal discussion of how cognitive and especially axiological aspects of legitimization could be studied through lemma patterns.

entities (*ODCs*). The spatial aspect of proximization involves the construal of the ODC-instigated events as physically endangering the IDCs i.e., the addressee and the speaker. The temporal aspect involves presenting the events as momentous and historic and thus of central significance to both the addressee and the speaker. The axiological aspect, which this paper will eventually focus on, involves a clash between the system of values adhered to by the speaker and the addressee on the one hand, and the antagonistic values characterizing the ODCs on the other. The cumulative effect of the three proximization strategies is legitimization – political discourse addressees are likely to legitimize the speaker's pre-emptive actions against the gathering threat if they construe it as personally consequential.[2]

2.   The STA proximization model: Preliminaries

The *spatial-temporal-axiological (STA)* model of proximization proposed in Cap (2006, 2008) presupposes the constancy of the macro function of the speaker's performance within a defined timeframe – if, as a result of external factors, one strategy of proximization is downplayed or abandoned, the overall balance is redressed by an increase in the salience of another strategy. This translates, upon a specific text analysis, into a much more complex regularity involving the use of lexical items which make up a given proximization strategy. Namely,

> if within a macro scale a legitimization text is followed by another text, produced by the same political speaker, in relation to the same issue and with the same overall goal, but against so different a contextual background that it has affected the selection of bottom-level lexical items in such a way that the new text differs with regard to the kind of key lemmas from the previous one, any ensuing decrease/ increase in manifestation of one type of proximization must mean, respectively, an increased/decreased salience of another type (cf. also Cap 2006: 8).

The functional redressability of proximization has been tentatively verified in Cap (2006, 2008), in pilot corpus studies on the language of the US administration during the Iraq war, between March 2003 (commencement of the allies' military operations in

---

2.   To put things in a less formal way, the IDC-ODC dichotomy mirrors (at least in the case of the American political scene) the traditional "Us vs. Them" divide (cf. e.g. Huntington 2004). In the process of proximization the ideological as well as physical distance between "Us" and "Them" is construed as shrinking, which eventually produces a clash. To prevent the clash, the speaker solicits legitimization of pre-emptive actions, which are thus in direct, personal interest of his audience ("Us," i.e. IDCs). The model of proximization addressed in this paper shows how the IDC ("Us") – ODC ("Them") distance is construed symbolically in spatial, temporal and, most notably, axiological terms. Furthermore, it explains how the construal of conflict between the two camps is maintained over time in the service of lasting legitimization of political and military actions of the "Us" camp.

Iraq) and June 2004 (delegation of select executive powers to the new Iraqi interim government). I have analyzed the total of 64 presidential addresses within the two functionally distinct phases of the period: "Phase One," March-November 2003, and "Phase Two," December 2003-June 2004.[3] The conclusions have been that while the former sees as the major premise for war the alleged possession of weapons of mass destruction (henceforth: WMD) by Saddam's regime, the latter is dominated by a "compensatory" rhetoric, aimed at keeping the legitimization of the Iraqi intervention in place despite the already substantiated failure of the WMD argument.[4] The changes in the extralinguistic reality i.e. in the geopolitical context of the conflict have shown to affect the proximization pattern applied throughout the entire involvement period.

It has been postulated that in Phase One texts there is a dominance of spatial-temporal proximization, which follows from the US administration's easy access to the WMD premise for legitimization of the pre-emptive strike in Iraq (cf. Silberstein 2004). The discourse stage is thus construed in predominantly spatial-temporal terms; for instance, the analogy to 9/11 events is built to invoke the aura of physical danger closing in to impact the IDC entities. However, the later loss of the main argument for going to war (i.e. the alleged possession of weapons of mass destruction by Hussein's regime) means a gradual but consistent redefinition of the pro-war rhetoric and hence a change in the overall proximization pattern. What happens in Phase Two is thus a decline in the spatial-temporal proximization, and a corresponding increase in the more universally appealing axiological proximization (cf. Pomeroy 2005). The latter's principal function is to broaden the geopolitical spectrum of the Iraqi conflict and to deepen its ideological anchoring (cf. Chang and Mehan 2006), thereby claiming legitimization on a more global scale. At the same time the collapse of the original argument is downplayed and the WMD intelligence failure is construed in terms of an isolated incident in a series of successful operations governed by irrefutable ideological tenets (cf. Cap 2006, 2008).

These conceptual shifts have thus far been only partly corroborated by corpus counts. In Cap (2008) there is a proposal for the framework of spatial-temporal (S/T) proximization which makes possible the abstraction of the key lemmas responsible for

---

3.   The 64 presidential speeches on the Iraq war, covering the period March 2003-June 2004, were downloaded, in July 2004, from the official White House site http://www.whitehouse.org. All the 64 speeches on Iraq available from the site in July 2004 are used in the present analysis, there are no left-out cases. Within the entire corpus, 34 presidential speeches belong to "Phase One" (March-November 2003) and 30 to "Phase Two" (December 2003-June 2004). The total number of words in the Phase One speeches is 17.524, the Phase Two total being almost identical, 17.233.

4.   Similar points are raised in a number of journalistic texts on the Iraq war. They indicate a gradual change of the rhetorical stance, from emphasizing the closeness and immediacy of physical threat, to ideological juxtapositions and boundary-making. The change is, however, attributed not only to the WMD factor, but also to Bush's attempts at softening his rhetoric in general, to save the dwindling approval ratings. See, for instance: USA Today, Nov. 23, 2003; Washington Post, Nov. 2, 2003; Boston Globe, Jan. 2, 2004.

the enactment of S/T proximization in both Phase One and Phase Two of the Iraq war. The particular categories of the framework seem to work fine in elucidating the phase differences in the lexical counts; they clearly indicate the dominance of S/T proximization in Phase One, as well as its diminishing value in Phase Two. They are, however, incapable of explaining in the same lexical terms the internal composition of the axiological proximization module which has been heuristically claimed to keep the overall legitimization pattern intact, notwithstanding the proven decrease in the salience of the S/T strategy. Thus, the current task is to formalize the description of the axiological aspect of proximization, in order to show i) how axiological proximization works as a result of the interaction of language forms captured in different categories of the axiological proximization framework, and ii) what kind of potential it exhibits for the redressability of the general function of legitimization, considering that there is an obviously diminishing contribution from another proximization strategy.

In what follows I first review the S/T framework (cf. Cap 2008) for its explanatory power as regards the reflection of the extralinguistic (geopolitical) changes in the type and degree of the proximization strategy applied over time. Then, using the same Phase One – Phase Two data of the 64 presidential texts, I provide an original postulate for the axiological framework whose categories encompass the language forms responsible collectively for not only the operation of axiological (A) proximization in its own right, but also for the functioning of the A strategy as a compensation for the absence of another strategy, specifically the spatial-temporal one. Altogether, the envisaged account of the S/T-A mutual redressability (bi-directional, as will be shown) is an attempt at refining the STA model of proximization in terms of the further formalization of the dialogue between the conceptual and lexical constituents of legitimization. At the same time, the application of the refined model in the present chapter not only makes the critical discussion of the rhetoric of the Iraq war more organized and precise, but, consequently, makes it the case that more prospects open up for other applications within the field of political (interventionist) discourse and beyond.

3.   The spatial-temporal (S/T) proximization framework

I argue in Cap (2008) for a six-category framework of spatial-temporal proximization which applies directly to the rhetoric of the Iraq war, but potentially, to any kind of discourse which seeks legitimization of a pre-emptive reaction to a seemingly imminent threat. The six categories of the framework, involving traditional syntactic units such as noun and verb phrases, express a variety of conceptualizations of the discourse stage elements which differ in their deictic status:

1.   Noun phrases (NPs) conceptualized as elements of the deictic center (IDCs);
2.   NPs conceptualized as elements outside the deictic center (ODCs);
3.   Verb phrases (VPs) of motion and directionality conceptualized together as indicators of movement of ODCs towards the deictic center and vice versa;

4. VPs of action conceptualized as indicators of contact between ODCs and IDCs;
5. NPs expressing abstract notions conceptualized as anticipations of potential contact between ODCs and IDCs;
6. NPs expressing abstract notions conceptualized as effects of actual contact between ODCs and IDCs.

Let us first identify these six categories in a sample text from the Iraqi corpus. Consider an excerpt from the US ultimatum urging Saddam Hussein to leave Iraq within 48 hours to avoid war. The ultimatum was issued on March 17, 2003:

> [...] The danger is clear: using chemical, biological or, one day, nuclear weapons, obtained with the help of Iraq, the terrorists could fulfill their stated ambitions and kill thousands or hundreds of thousands of innocent people in our country, or any other. [...] The United States and other nations did nothing to deserve or invite this threat. But we will do everything to defeat it. Instead of drifting along toward tragedy, we will set a course toward safety. Before the day of horror can come, before it is too late to act, this danger will be removed [...]

To start with categories (1) and (2), the IDC elements involve lexical items and phrases such as "United States," "other nations," "innocent people," "our country," "we," etc. The conceptualization of indefinite entities (cf. "other nations") as members of the deictic center occurs through the implication of mutual relation, or sameness, triggered by the conjunction "and." At the other end of the event stage are the ODCs: "Iraq," "terrorists" and "their ambitions." Again, a relation of shared identity is established between some of these elements. "Iraq" and "terrorists" are put on common ground through the presupposition of lasting cooperation (viz. "help"), and the sheer proximity of their lexical occurrence in the text. The relative distance between IDCs and ODCs is shrinking as a result of two processes: (a) the ODC elements are construed as aspiring to physically affect the IDC territory ("kill thousands or hundreds of thousands of innocent people in our country"), which invokes the aura of "catastrophe" or "tragedy" (not-yet explicitly stated as such); (b) the IDC elements are construed as partly inert and thus sooner or later exposed to contact with ODCs, a clash resulting in "tragedy" (stated explicitly to fit in with the previously invoked aura). These two processes involve lexical items from all the four remaining categories: (3) ("drifting toward"), (4) ("kill"), (5) ("danger," "threat"), and (6) ("tragedy," "horror"). The presence of elements representing, within a markedly short text sample such as above, all of the six categories distinguished, goes a long way towards proving the pervasiveness of spatial-temporal proximization in the Iraq war and, specifically, in its early stage ("Phase One") which sees a consistent attachment to the WMD premise for war. But there is perhaps more to the picture and the S/T framework might be in need of complementation from a less "tangible" module. Moving beyond the proposed category distinction and looking at the use of modality in the quoted excerpt, it can be postulated that the process of spatial-temporal proximization is heavily aided by the "zooming in" on the probability of the conflict. First, a relatively remote possibility is drafted ("could fulfill their stated ambitions"), only to be replaced by a more concrete prediction ("before the day of horror can come"). Such a strategy can hardly be accounted for in "spatial" or "temporal" terms alone for it relies on the construal of the initially *ideological* conflict which turns, over time, into a *physical* threat. Thus, it binds together the spatial-temporal and the ideological ingredients of proximization, leading to *axiological* considerations addressing the issue of the spatial/temporal-axiological dynamics (and fuzziness!) of the discourse stage. Arguably, there exist some entities (cf. *threat*) whose construal as evidently "spatial," "physical" or not (i.e. not yet) depends on how radical or physically consequential has been the development of events on the discourse stage before the conceptualization takes place. Thus the S/T parameter alone might be insufficient to explain some of the more temporally-extensive legitimization processes, characteristic of a growing likelihood of construal shifts occurring as a result of extralinguistic (viz. geopolitical) changes. I shall take these important observations as a starting point for the discussion of the relationship between the "S/T" and the "A" proximization strategies later in the chapter.

For now, the explanatory power of the S/T framework gets substantiated if we abstract the key lemmas and major phraseological concordances representing each of the six categories (some of the key lemmas can in fact be abstracted directly from the quoted text) and compare their frequency of occurrence in the 34-text corpus of Phase One, both among themselves and against the only slightly smaller, 30-text corpus of Phase Two. Since the difference in the overall number of words in both corpora is negligible, such a quantitative comparison provides a fertile ground for qualitative considerations.[5]

These corpus data yield important observations, drawn from both the "vertical" and the "horizontal" readings, where the former involve comparison of frequency hits of different lemmas within the exclusively Phase One domain and the latter involve comparison of identical lemmas across the two phases.

Naturally enough, the explanatory power of the S/T framework is most readily reflected in the "vertical" readings which illustrate the case for war construed as a response to a tangible, physical threat. Within the first category, there is a striking gap between the vast number of hits indicating the US, the central IDC (involving the major discourse parties such as the speaker and the direct audience), and the relatively limited number of hits indicating the other IDCs (e.g. some other democracies sharing the US principles of freedom, equality, etc.). This difference reflects the predominant rhetorical ploy of Phase One, the strategy of alerting the American addressee to the proximity of physical danger following from the alleged possession of WMD by the Iraqi regime and, consequently, terrorist organizations such as Al-Qaeda. Since

---

5.   The key lemmas and concordances captured in Table 1 (esp. the third category), and later in Table 4 (the third category again), invite further engagement with corpus tools. The rhetorical shift in the axiological dimension needs corroboration from the distribution of collocations (i.e. which lemmas go together in which of the two phases; cf. e.g. Baker et al. 2008 or Bastow's work, this volume). The current findings are thus, as the title of Section 5.1 will suggest, largely a hypothesis.

Table 1. Phase differences in the number of lemmas defining spatial-temporal framework of the Iraq war rhetoric

Category	Key Lemma/Concordance*		Phase One	Phase Two
1.	*United States* or *America*		426	613
	free and/or *democratic world* (inclusive of synonyms such as *people*)		194	415
2.	*Iraq*		330	165
	terrorists		255	112
3.	*head* (of IDCs, followed by preposition and ctg. 6 abstract NP, like in *head toward tragedy*, inclusive of multiple passive synonyms such as *drift*)		126	41
	expand (of ODCs)	with reference to *WMD*	88	6
		without reference to *WMD*	61	55
4.	*destroy* (of ODCs)		105	30
	confront	of ODCs	18	38
		of IDCs	47	31
5.	*threat*		127	52
	danger		96	51
6.	*tragedy*		60	55
	catastrophe		45	7

* Inclusive of pronouns where applicable.

the most desired, home-front success of this strategy depends on the US addressee's conceptualization of the threat as maximally realistic and thus demanding a quick and radical response, the primary scope is temporarily narrowed down to cover the principal IDCs. In other words, although the overall range of the threat may be worldwide, it is the temporary centralization of the anticipated impact that ensures the fastest legitimization effects regarding the response, involving the very commencement of military operations, the funding priorities, etc.

In contrast to the above, the difference in the number of hits indicating the major ODCs ("Iraq" and "terrorists") is rather insignificant. In fact, what we're dealing with here is a conflation of the two concepts, which results in the perception of the Iraqi regime in terms of a terrorist entity representing a major threat to countries conceptualized as IDC elements. The conflation process relies heavily on the textual proximity of the two lemmas and, while Table 1 does not give this information, it should be noted that most of the time "Iraq" and "terrorists" occur in sufficient syntactic closeness to swiftly generate a link of relationship. Furthermore, as can be seen from the ultimatum excerpt, they are often construed within one causative pattern. The overall proximization effect of such a conflation is that, with the 9/11 analogy constantly in operation, an Iraqi threat is virtually becoming a terrorist threat and vice versa.

The concept of "threat," involving the anticipated impact of ODCs on the IDC elements, brings us to considerations of the relative distance between the two domains, a coordinate defined by VPs constituting the third category of the S/T framework. Since the success of the proximization strategy depends on the construal of the eventual clash between the ODC and the IDC entities, the most salient lemmas are those which indicate a conflict-bound movement on the part of both ODCs and IDCs, though the latter can also be construed as passive or inert and thus easily "invadable." As can be seen from Table 1, the overall number of hits referring to both domains is largely comparable in terms of the VP occurrence, however, on the ODC side there is a remarkable role played by the "WMD" complementation, which will cease in importance as the war goes on. Furthermore, it is worth noting that the presence of the IDC-related lemmas indicating both activity (as in "head") and inertia (as in "drift") reflects two and apparently conflicting characteristics of the spatial-temporal proximization rhetoric. One is a desire to justify the extremely radical response to the threat, which entails measures such as adding the maximum of momentum to the picture of the event stage – and hence the lemmas such as "head" – while the other is an equally dire need to enhance the spirit of leadership of the US president and the administration, by portraying their determination and resolve in a stark contrast to the general aura of passivity (viz. "drift").

The fourth category, involving VPs of action conceptualized as indicators of contact between ODCs and IDCs, features lemmas directly responsible for the pragmatic impact of spatial-temporal proximization. The pervasiveness of "destroy" (which obviously occurs in phrases where an ODC element is the agent) is staggering, and so is the difference in the use of "confront," a lemma occurring 2.6 times more frequently with an IDC-related agent than with an ODC-related one. The fact that the ODC-governed "destroy" easily surpasses in number the IDC-governed "confront" corroborates the existence of two regularities. First, as the war begins the most dynamic element of the event stage is Iraq and its alleged terrorist allies, and it is their (anticipated) actions that serve as a basis for most of the spatial-temporal proximization rhetoric. Second, as the ODC elements threaten to invade the deictic center, the IDCs (and the US in particular) are construed as steering a middle course between the pursuit of defensive measures and the legitimization of a pre-emptive strike. The duality of the stance adopted by the IDCs is expressed precisely in the use of the lexical item "confront," which implies a weaker or a stronger response to the ODC threat. Thus, in a sense, the second regularity is in line with the conflicting characteristics of the spatial-temporal proximization rhetoric that have been postulated with regard to the occurrence of the VPs of motion and directionality. It is important to observe that while "confront" is a popular lexical choice in IDC-related phrases, its occurrence with ODC-related agents is minimal. This finding clearly contributes to the feasibility of the S/T module in bringing on a *causative* picture of the Iraq war. Apparently, it is the Iraqi side that is the instigator of the conflict and the US assumes a merely self-defensive role. The idealistic connotations of "confront" and its general tendency to combine with such lexical items as "poverty," "misery," "injustice" or "danger," some of the phrases indeed coming up in the corpus,[6] only add to the picture.

While we will eventually find the fifth and the sixth category of the S/T framework conducive to many axiological considerations and thus a borderline case deserving a complex theoretical account, let us acknowledge that the lexical items included in these two classes are primarily part and parcel of the spatial-temporal premise for war, at least in terms of the legitimization of the initial strike. This time the "vertical" differences in the number of the particular lemmas are of secondary importance; what matters, however, is their combined occurrence i.e. the total number of hits reflecting the key concepts of "threat," "danger," "tragedy" and "catastrophe." The number, 328, is massive by itself but consider that *all* these hard-hitting words occur, within a cause-and-effect pattern, in phrases involving the spatial coordinates of IDC and ODC, as well as the mobile coordinate, which altogether define the spatial arrangement of major forces of the Iraqi conflict. Thus, the main elements in the arrangement substantially profit from the appeal of "potential contact" and "actual effect" concepts – in the sense of enhancing their own status and pragmatic force. Still, the most convincing argument for the validity of the fifth and the sixth category members in the spatial-temporal proximization strategy is perhaps the dramatic decline in the occurrence of the four lemmas in Phase Two, where, as will be seen from the axiologically profiled analysis, the premise for war is no longer the narrowing of the physical distance between the ODC and the IDC entities.

In fact, the axiological aspect comes up already in many of the "horizontal" readings of Table 1, but we shall address these first from the perspective of their original scope, i.e. a contribution to the spatial-temporal matrix. Within the first two categories, there is a remarkable increase in the number of hits indicating IDCs, at the expense of the ODC-related lemmas. This proves, following the original function of the S/T module and without yet engaging in ideological considerations, that in Phase One of the Iraq war the event stage is indeed dominated by the (anticipated) activity of ODCs. Their construal as physically threatening to the members of the deictic center is the cornerstone of spatial-temporal proximization as well as the major premise for legitimization of the IDC response to the threat. The activity of the ODCs is salient in the relatively large number of VPs containing lemmas which involve the steady closing of the gap between the ODC and the IDC entities (viz. "expand," category three). This process is construed as momentous and inherently devastating, which can be seen from the 105:30 ratio characterizing the Phase One – Phase Two distribution of "destroy," within the fourth category. Finally, the picture of the proximity of the threat is made complete by the vast number of lemmas indicating (effects) of the potential impact of ODCs on the deictic center – the "horizontal" reading of hits within the fifth and the

---

6.   Further research in this direction (collocations) is important for supporting postulates voiced in the present chapter, viz. footnote 5.

sixth category shows, by comparison with the timeframe of Phase Two, how important these lemmas are for the complex strategy of spatial-temporal proximization.

4.   Limitations of the S/T framework and implications for an axiological study

It seems that the six categories of the spatial-temporal framework of proximization are largely capable of defining and measuring, in the very "bottom" lexical terms, the character and intensity of the "legitimization via proximization" strategy applied at the outset of the Iraq war, whose initial premise was the alleged possession of weapons of mass destruction by Saddam Hussein's regime. There is a good reason to believe that they could in fact account for many lexical groundworks of proximization that draw on the presence of a material entity which can be construed as IDC-threatening and thereby necessitating a pre-emptive response. Furthermore, the last two categories of the framework, as well as the lemmatic-numerical differences that the application of the framework yields with regard to a more temporally extensive development of the discourse stage (viz. the cross-phasal lexical readings above), appear to possess explanatory power that goes beyond a merely spatial-temporal analysis and entails a more complex, axiological study. Still, such a refined analysis, one that could explain conditions for the continuity of legitimization and, specifically, the essence of compensation for a loss of the material premise for proximization, cannot entirely rely on the interpretation of figures generated by the S/T module, even if some of them belong to the focal period of the elaborated study (like the Phase Two figures in Table 1). As has been mentioned before, the S/T parameter is insufficient to explain some of the more temporally-extensive legitimization processes since they are characteristic of a growing likelihood of construal shifts occurring as a result of extralinguistic (mainly geopolitical) changes which make the kind of construal of some entities (for instance, the construal of the *threat* concept in physical or non-physical terms) dependent on the prior development of events on the discourse stage. Thus, while we might want the spatial-temporal module to contribute to the description of complex legitimization processes, the *redressability* of legitimization which normally pertains to these processes can only be defined (and, above all, measured) if there is a complementary framework whose applicability is to the whole period under analysis but whose origins are in the question of *compensation* which underlies the time span following the loss of the initial legitimization premise. The latter condition is a prerequisite for the framework of *axiological proximization* which will be developed below. In constructing it, we will utilize, on the one hand, observations of the diminishing role of the S/T proximization rhetoric and, on the other, findings from a formal typological study of lexical items making up the "compensatory," ideologically-loaded stance. Our data will continue to be the "Phase One – Phase Two" corpus of the 64 presidential addresses, with "Phase One" (34 speeches) symbolizing the WMD-based argument pursued in the early stages of the Iraq war (March – November 2003), and "Phase Two" (30 speeches, December

2003 – June 2004) referring to an updated and refined rhetorical pattern showing little attachment to the initial argumentative premise.

4.1 The emergence of an axiological perspective on proximization

The apparent loss of the main argument for going to war in Iraq (i.e. the alleged possession of weapons of mass destruction by Saddam Hussein's regime) means a gradual yet consistent redefinition of the pro-war rhetoric. At the conceptual level of the STA model, this change is marked by the emergence of the two simultaneously occurring phenomena: a decline in the spatial-temporal proximization, and a corresponding increase in the slightly more "universal," axiological proximization. We shall start the analysis by looking at the former trend i.e. from some observations on the diminishing role of the S/T-based rhetoric, a tendency which can be sensed around November 2003. The presumption must be, however, that although the loss of the WMD premise for war is first admitted in Bush's Whitehall Palace address[7] of November 19 and thus all of the Phase Two figures relate to the time span following this speech, one cannot attempt to define any *exact* boundaries of the S/T-A transition period.

If we look at the lexical realizations of the Phase Two proximization strategies, the decline in the quantitative and functional significance of the S/T-related forms is indeed staggering. Let us recapitulate some of the Table 1 counts to elucidate how the loss of the WMD premise for war has affected virtually all of the categories of the spatial-temporal proximization framework.

Since the geopolitical context of Phase Two is such that there has been no evidence found of the Iraqi regime ever having a WMD capacity, the current situation sees a

Table 2. Phase One–Phase Two select numerical changes (drops) in lexical realizations of the spatial-temporal proximization framework

Key lemma or concordance	Phase One–Phase Two drop
Iraq	330 >>>>>>>>>>>>>>>>>>>>>>>>165
terrorists	255 >>>>>>>>>>>>>>>>>>>>>>>112
head (of IDCs, followed by preposition and ctg. 6 abstract NP, like in *head toward tragedy*, inclusive of multiple passive synonyms such as *drift*)	126 >>>>>>>>>>>>>>>>>>>>>>>>41
expand (of ODCs, with reference to *WMD*)	88>>>>>>>>>>>>>>>>>>>>>>>>>6
destroy (of ODCs)	105 >>>>>>>>>>>>>>>>>>>>>>>30
threat	127 >>>>>>>>>>>>>>>>>>>>>>52
danger	96>>>>>>>>>>>>>>>>>>>>>>>>51
catastrophe	45>>>>>>>>>>>>>>>>>>>>>>>>>7

---

7.   To be quoted extensively later in the chapter.

feeble rationale for maintaining the dominance of the discourse stage by the ODC entities. Hence, most of the quantitative drops involve the lexemes which either mark (the activity of) the principal ODC agents ("Iraq," "terrorists," "expand," "destroy"), or express (the evaluations of) the different stages of physical contact between IDCs and ODCs along the formerly established "spatial impact" axis ("head," "threat," "danger," "catastrophe"). The *WMD* concept is thus less frequently invoked not only because the distribution of the corresponding lexeme has been minimized (note the dramatic 88-to-6 fall), but also because the whole volume of the "traffic" along the spatial impact axis has shrunk – there is a much smaller representation of the ODC agents and, significantly, the projected effects of the IDC-ODC contact no longer bear a destruction stamp. The latter fact is best corroborated by the 45-to-7 drop in the distribution of "catastrophe," a lemma conceptually related to a specific act of annihilation which normally involves the use of weapons of mass murder.

Most of the figures in Table 1 and Table 2 not only define the framework of the spatial-temporal proximization as such, but also, as the importance of the latter diminishes, effectively initiate the description of all the "compensatory" regularities. It is interesting to see how the select numbers, notably the ones that are absent from Table 2 but originally present in the Table 1 compilation, elegantly mirror the Phase Two change of emphasis, from spatial-temporal to axiological proximization. Let us isolate a group of lemmas whose Phase One – Phase Two ratios invite a promising (though of course tentative before the axiological lexical framework is provided) explanation of this change.

How do we find these figures useful for axiological considerations? Recall the mechanism of axiological proximization the way it has been pre-postulated in 1. and 2. and add the later postulates about the temporal extensiveness and the ideological variability of legitimization processes involving proximization as a whole. The emerging perspective is that axiological proximization consists in the construal of alien ideological beliefs and values relative (spatially and temporally) to the axiological background of the self, or the dominant ideology of the whole deictic center. It is, essentially, neither a physical phenomenon nor a temporal one; rather, it involves the *continual* narrowing of the gap between two different and opposing ideologies (ODCs' vs IDCs') whose clash could prompt *physical* events construed within the S/T dimension.

Table 3. Phase One–Phase Two select ratios of lexical realizations of the spatial-temporal proximization framework: "prompts" for an axiological perspective

Key lemma or concordance	Phase One–Phase Two ratio
United States or *America*	426:613
free and/or *democratic world* (inclusive of synonyms such as *people*)	194:415
expand (of ODCs, without reference to *WMD*)	61:55
tragedy	60:55

While spatial-temporal proximization can be effected through a construal of intense activity of ODCs, with a relatively smaller share of agency on the part of IDCs (viz. Phase One of the war), axiological proximization needs a much stronger "IDC contribution." Otherwise, any account of the axiological composition of ODC parties remains insufficient for proximization purposes. By being naturally distant from the deictic center, the ODCs are initially less well defined and, usually, need to be juxtaposed against the IDCs, in order to become distinctive enough for the axiological proximization to work. Thus, if the government of a country such as Iraq is to be conceptualized as a "regime," and if a continuing solidification of this regime is to be construed as a threat to "all democratic world," the latter must first be described in due quantitative detail and in such a way that the addressee receives a broad spectrum of "antithesis triggers." These are, from the axiological perspective, all the ideological premises that the addressee identifies with and, consequently, whose conceptual oppositions he or she would find not only unacceptable but also plainly threatening.

All this explains why Phase Two sees a radical increase in the number of the IDC-related lemmas, especially the NPs indicating the discourse stage agents (cf. Table 1, ctg. 1, recapitulated in the first two lines of Table 3 above). Particularly striking is, obviously, the increase in those IDC lemmas which define the non-US deictic center entities (194 to 415, in the case of "free" and/or "democratic world" and the synonyms). Of course, such a broadening of the geopolitical spectrum of the Iraqi conflict (note that an extended representation of IDCs entails an extended representation of their activity fields) means that the war is no longer construed in terms of a clash of particularized interests held by a limited number of parties; instead, the reasons for the ongoing US involvement have, apparently, a deeper ideological anchoring. The latter gives a license, valid both prospectively and retrospectively, to pursue actions whose sheer range justifies a certain degree of fallibility; logically, if the IDC agents operate multidirectionally and on a global scale, one cannot expect unequivocally positive effects. Thus, as we shall see later and especially from the text of the Whitehall address, a crucial rhetorical ploy of Phase Two is treating the Iraqi operation in terms of "one of the many," which opens up a most comfortable possibility of construing select negative aspects of the (military) involvement as virtually unavoidable given the size of the issue at stake.

Most of the textual examples of the Phase Two axiological proximization, though not all, reveal the following regularity. First, there is a description of the ideological composition of the IDC parties. Then, a temporarily static juxtaposition is built against the rather vague category of ODCs–after all, with the WMD premise and the 9/11 analogy both missing from the argument, the invoked antagonistic values can only occasionally be ascribed to concrete countries or groups. Finally, in line with the essence of the concept of proximization as such, the ODC-related values are construed as dynamic, in the sense of potentially prompting actions which could involve a physical IDC-ODC clash. This is where the future-oriented argument ends. At the same time, however, a stance of legitimization of the IDCs' activity is maintained retrospectively through multiple references to the ideologically alien (if not just plain-ly abhorrent) past actions of the principal ODC (i.e. the Iraqi regime) in and before Phase One of the war:

> The work of building a new Iraq is hard, and it is right. And America has always been willing to do what it takes for what is right. But as democracy takes hold in Iraq, the enemies of freedom will do all in their power to spread violence and fear. [...] Let me repeat what I said on the afternoon of December the 14th: the capture of Saddam Hussein does not mean the end of violence in Iraq. We still face terror-ists who would rather go on killing the innocent than accept the rise of liberty in the heart of the Middle East. (January 20, 2004)
>
> America and all freedom-loving countries are fighting on the side of liberty – liberty in Iraq, liberty in the Middle East and beyond it. This objective serves the interests of the Middle East, of the United States and of the whole democratic world. As the greater Middle East increasingly becomes a place where freedom flourishes, the lives of millions in that region will be bettered, and the American people and the entire world will be more secure. [...] As the June 30th date for Iraqi sovereignty draws near, a small fraction is attempting to derail Iraqi de-mocracy and seize power. In some cities, Saddam supporters and terrorists have struck against coalition forces. In other areas, attacks were incited by a radical named Muqtada-al-Sadr, who is wanted for the murder of a respected Shiite cler-ic. Al-Sadr has called for violence against coalition troops, and his band of thugs have terrorized Iraqi police and ordinary citizens. These enemies of freedom want to dictate the course of events in Iraq and to prevent the Iraqi people from having a true voice in their future. They want America and our coalition to falter in our commitments before a watching world. In their aspirations, they are a threat to all democratic people and to the people in our own country (April 10, 2004).

In these two excerpts, the axiological composition of IDCs involves i) a full and unfalter-ing commitment to universally acceptable norms and values ("democracy," "freedom," "liberty," the economic well-being of the people salient in "the lives of millions in that region will be bettered," etc.), and ii) a commitment to steadfast, continual enactment of these values ("has always been willing to do what it takes for what is right," "are fighting on the side of," etc. – note the use of progressive forms). Antithetical to this groundwork is the ensuing description of the ODCs' ideology which involves the rule of dictatorship ("a small fraction [...] want to dictate the course of events in Iraq") giving rise to "vio-lence" and "fear." The ODCs are then construed as potentially invading the IDCs' (operational) territory ("will do all in their power to spread [violence and fear]," "is at-tempting to derail Iraqi democracy and seize power," "are a threat to all democratic peo-ple and to the people in our own country") in a manner analogous to the (anticipated) workings of Saddam Hussein's regime. Finally, throughout the entire account, painful memories of the latter ("would rather go on killing the innocent," etc.) are invoked (whether directly or, as above, by setting up a past-vs-present activity link), in order to strengthen the legitimization of the ongoing US involvement in Iraq as a whole.

5. The axiological (A) proximization framework

The goal of the axiological proximization framework is, analogically to the S/T framework presented in 3, to provide a set of criteria and categories whereby one can define the lexical components of axiological proximization, in order to measure the axiological proximization (balancing) effects between different phases of the entire legitimization process i.e., in our case, between Phase One and Phase Two (or perhaps reversely, Phase Two and Phase One, considering that the analysis of axiological proximization is anchored in the question of compensation for a legitimization premise whose loss marks the end of "Phase One"). The intensity of these effects can be partly foreseen from the qualitative considerations thus far and, while we want precise lexical data to complement the picture in a quantitative manner, it seems logical to start from what the functional analysis of the sample texts has shown. Thus the axiological proximization framework, apart from its obvious roots in foci missing from the S/T model, draws on the ingredients/stages of the IDC-ODC axiological conflict as described above: the conflicting ideological characteristics of IDCs and ODCs, and the possibility of the ODC-related antagonistic values materializing within the deictic center. Altogether, we arrive at the following four categories of the framework:

1. Noun phrases (NPs) expressing abstract notions conceptualized as values and/or value sets/ideologies of IDCs;
2. Noun phrases (NPs) expressing abstract notions conceptualized as values and/or value sets/ideologies of ODCs;
3. Verb-phrase(VP)-framed phrases, sentences or cross-sentential discourse chunks involving
   3a. Ctg. 2 NP, embedded in or elaborated on by a "departure VP" (VP1), to produce the *remote possibility* script,
   3b. NP expressing (effect of) IDC-ODC physical contact (conflict), embedded in or elaborated on by a "destination VP" (VP2), to produce the *actual occurrence* script,
   whose combination in a linear discourse sequence 3a-3b results in *realis enhancing modality* of the text whereby a value set/ideology of ODCs *materializes* in the form of IDC-ODC physical contact (conflict);
4. NPs expressing abstract notions conceptualized as effects of IDC-ODC physical contact (conflict), NOT embedded in or elaborated on by a "destination VP" (VP2).

Admittedly, the composition of some of the categories, esp. (3), is complex enough to require a thorough text explanation. The following excerpts come from Bush's Whitehall Palace address of November 19, 2003. As I have remarked before, this speech can be considered a manifesto of the Phase Two rhetoric in the Iraq war:

> [...] The greatest threat of our age is nuclear, chemical, or biological weapons in the hands of terrorists, and the dictators who aid them. This evil might not have reached us yet but it is in plain sight, as plain as the horror sight of the collapsing

towers. The danger only increases with denial. [...]By advancing freedom in the greater Middle East, we help end a cycle of dictatorship and radicalism that brings millions of people to misery and brings danger and, one day, tragedy, to our own people. By struggling for justice in Iraq, Burma, in Sudan, and in Zimbabwe, we give hope to suffering people and improve the chances for stability and progress. [...]The stakes in that region could not be higher. If the Middle East remains a place where freedom and democracy do not flourish, it will remain a place of stagnation and anger and violence for export. And as we saw in the ruins of the towers, no distance on the map will protect our lives and way of life [...]

The categories (1), (2) and (4) are, compared to (3), relatively straightforward and thus we shall illustrate them first. Category 1 involves lexical items whose collective function is to define, in terms of a set of value-positive abstract concepts, the ideological groundwork of the IDC agents. In the text above these are, chronologically, the lexemes such as "freedom," "justice," "stability," "progress" and "democracy." Opposing this groundwork are the ODC-related lexemes which make up a set of value-negative concepts captured in the second category – "threat," "evil," "danger," "dictatorship," "radicalism," "anger" and "violence." The last NP-based category, (4), involves items such as "horror," "misery" and "tragedy," which lexicalize conceptualizations of physical contact between IDCs and ODCs. Of course, there is a certain degree of simplification and fuzziness involved, as conceptualizations of e.g. "threat" and "danger" are at the same time construals of elements of the antagonistic ideologies as such and construals of potency these elements exhibit in terms of materialization (cf. Pomeroy 2005; Hartman 2002) within the IDC territory. Furthermore, the fourth category must include not only the concepts which come explicitly in the form of the corresponding lexical items, but also the ones that need to be worked out inferentially in a manner similar to recovering implicatures (cf. e.g. Levinson 2000). Take, for instance, the closing excerpt "no distance on the map will protect our lives and way of life" – while no lexicalization of the effect of the IDC-ODC physical contact occurs explicitly, we do get enough data to recover the *loss of life* implicature which adds to the count alongside all the other NP-based concepts that fill in the category. Finally, as could have been guessed from the earlier discussion of categories 5 and 6 of the S/T framework and, generally, as the intrinsic complementarity and dynamics of the S/T-A model would suggest, the current A framework must involve (a) few concepts whose corresponding lexicalizations (viz. "threat," "danger," "tragedy") have shown a considerable potential for enacting spatial-temporal proximization as well.

To account for the remaining third category with due precision coupled with an adequate body of data, we might want to break the text down into three separate excerpts (i, ii, iii), with each one offering a specific example of the VP-NP interface:

i.   The greatest threat of our age is nuclear, chemical, or biological weapons in the hands of terrorists, and the dictators who aid them. This evil might not have reached us yet but it is in plain sight, as plain as the horror sight of the collapsing towers. The danger only increases with denial.

ii.   By advancing freedom in the greater Middle East, we help end a cycle of dictator-
      ship and radicalism that brings millions of people to misery and brings danger
      and, one day, tragedy, to our own people. By struggling for justice in Iraq, Burma,
      in Sudan, and in Zimbabwe, we give hope to suffering people and improve the
      chances for stability and progress.
iii. The stakes in that region could not be higher. If the Middle East remains a place
      where freedom and democracy do not flourish, it will remain a place of stagnation
      and anger and violence for export. And as we saw in the ruins of the towers, no
      distance on the map will protect our lives and way of life.

In (i) the ctg. 2 NP is primarily "This evil," but one may in fact enrich it with concepts
such as "terrorism" and "dictatorship" since they get subsumed under the cover concept of "evil" via a clear anaphoric link. The NP is used to initiate the *remote possibility*
script which is further enacted by VP1 ("might not have reached us yet"). The modality of VP1 is such that it makes the addressee embark on merely the *departure stage* of
the IDC-ODC conflict scenario (hence naming the VP1 a "departure VP"), without
yet construing the antagonistic concepts in terms of tangible threats. Later, however,
the *destination stage* of the scenario has the conflict fully materialize within the IDC
territory (viz. analogy to "the collapsing towers"). The construed materialization of the
conflict comes in the *actual occurrence* script which involves, first, a "destination VP"
(VP2 – "is in plain sight") which enhances the probability of the conflict and, second,
the NP ("the horror sight") expressing its devastating effects. Thus, altogether, the (axiological) proximization of the ODC impact is dependent on the (ctg. 2 NP–VP1)–
(VP2–NP-of-effect) segments operating in a linear sequence involving a gradual shift
from an ideological conflict to a physical clash. In this very example the sequence
starts and finalizes within one complex sentence, but we shall see from (iii) that its segments could operate over two adjacent sentences as well.

Meanwhile, let us deal with (ii). Here, the remote possibility script is initiated by "a
cycle of dictatorship and radicalism" (ctg. 2 NP), which combines with "brings millions
of people to misery" (VP1) to encourage construal of the ODC values as breeding social
chaos, unrest and, conceivably, violence which might be spreading beyond the ODC
territory. Following this formula is again the ODC impact (actual occurrence) script
whereby the effect marker ("tragedy") is embedded in a verb phrase (VP2) which materializes (via the "danger"-to-"tragedy" route) the gathering threat. Compared to (i), the
current realis enhancement is not just the matter of a conceptual shift from "the abstract" to "the concrete," esp. at the superior level of the verbal framework. It also consists
in an act of geopolitical specification salient in a premeditated choice of nominal phrases – the remote possibility script involves reference to "millions of people," while the
actual occurrence script has this broad concept narrowed down to "our own people."

While example (iii) conforms to the design of the third category in the general
terms of its elements and their relations, it involves two interesting deviations from the
layouts in (i) and (ii). First, the sequence of the verb phrases (VP1 vs. VP2) develops

not within one sentence, but over two adjacent sentences; second, the actual occurrence script in the latter sentence involves an implicitly communicated NP of effect. The presence of these "irregularities," with all the distinctive features of the category otherwise met, counts as an incentive for a corpus search more extensive than the former examples would prompt.

Looking closer, the ctg. 2 NP is "a place of stagnation and anger and violence for export," a phrase possessing not only the expectable ideological load, but also a considerable potential for suggesting its impact (viz. "for export"). The construal of the impact is at this stage in hypothetical terms, though the verbal embedding – "it will remain [...]"(VP1) – makes its due contribution to seeing the threat as gathering. Thus the remote possibility script is concluded and the proximization mechanism continues in the next sentence. There, the actual occurrence script takes on an implicit form and the consequences of the ODC impact need to be worked out inferentially. Since, given the continuity of the threat leading to its final materialization within the IDC territory (the latter worked out from "the ruins of the towers"), there is "no distance" that could "protect our lives," the NP-of-effect is calculated from the conception that the ODC entities will be *crossing the distance* to annihilate the IDC entities. Thus, the NP-of-effect is *loss of life* on the part of the IDCs. Interestingly, this final inference relies on the former conceptualization of the ODC movement (*crossing the distance*) which is itself communicated indirectly. Altogether, what we deal with here is an (actual occurrence) script in which the verbal component (VP2) possesses a status comparable to an explicature (cf. e.g. Carston 2002) whose successful recovery ensures that the implicature (NP-of-effect) is worked out correctly.

The composition of the third category of the axiological proximization framework reflects the essence of axiological proximization as a conceptual mechanism. It accounts for the phenomenon of the continual narrowing of the distance between two different and opposing ideologies (ODCs' vs IDCs'), and treats the eventual axiological conflict in terms of a trigger for the actual occurrence of events construed within the spatial-temporal domain. In so doing, it integrates the proximization potential of entities classed in the other categories, esp. the 2nd category which holds lexicalizations of concepts constituting the ideological groundwork for the ODC impact.

By now we have been looking at axiological proximization as primarily a self-contained mechanism; except for a few comments on its relationship to the S/T framework, we have not made yet a systematic attempt at showing its potential for redressing the macro function of legitimization (of the Iraq war), in view of a vanishing contribution by another proximization strategy (i.e. spatial-temporal). This methodological aspiration entails that we approach the particular categories of the axiological framework in lexical terms, providing corpus counts for the most representative members of each category. Then, for a refined picture of the compensation, we shall analyse the cross-phasal (Phase Two vs. Phase One) occurrences of the particular lexemes (in the case of categories 1, 2, 4) as well as the lexicogrammatical sequences (in the case of 3). Of course, in accordance with the conceptual relation we have established for the S/T and A modules, the analysis must also relate the axiological counts to the formerly provided spatial-temporal counts. Specifically, we shall assume that as the war unfolds, at least some of the drops in the number of lexemes reflecting the S/T proximization are neutralized by a general increase in the number of lexical carriers of the A proximization. This makes us consider all the axiological figures in constant interaction with the counts generated by the S/T framework.

5.1   The axiological counts and the functional compensation hypothesis

The following table (Table 4) includes counts of the key lemmas representing categories 1, 2 and 4 of the A framework, as well as counts of syntactic forms which reflect the design of the third category. The same corpora have been used as in the case of the S/T framework – the 34-text Phase One corpus and the 30-text Phase Two corpus.

There are, apparently, two basic conditions under which these category counts corroborate the legitimization-redressing capacity of the A framework. First, the Phase Two counts should be generally higher than the Phase One counts, as the emerging axiological proximization must be given a lexical backup substantial enough to make up for the lexical losses incurred by the diminishing role of the spatial-temporal proximization. Second, within the first and the second category, the IDC counts in Phase Two should be higher than the ODC counts, as the rising role of the ideological aspect entails that IDCs are endowed with a multitude of values to broaden the source of comparison and contrast and thus increase the odds that the obviously antithetical values spotted in ODCs are automatically rejected (mark the concept of "antithesis triggers" in 4.1.). The accompanying rationale is, of course, that Phase Two sees a minimized contribution from the WMD premise, a concept originally associated with the activity of the ODC entities.

It doesn't take long to see that both conditions are largely met, though only a deeper look yields a number of interesting analytic observations, some of which have to do with the S/T-A conceptual and lexical borderline.

Starting with the more general first condition, the first thing to acknowledge is the staggering cross-phasal increase in the lexical realization of the realis enhancing formula. Its Phase Two occurrence is in fact seven times (!) higher than the Phase One occurrence, which obviously corroborates the cornerstone role of the third category in the general layout of the axiological proximization framework. The very count, (9:63) might not impress when compared with the total counts yielded by the other categories, but it certainly does if one allows for the internal complexity of the third category which poses ultra-high qualification requirements.

The dominance of axiological proximization in Phase Two is further substantiated by the Phase One – Phase Two ratios of the total counts in categories 1 and 4, while the 464-to-356 decrease in category 2 seems an exception, at least in bare quantitative terms. In actuality, it results from a twofold conceptual origin of the two member lemmas, "threat" and "danger." Much as they contribute to the ideological constitution of

Table 4. Phase differences in the number of lemmas and syntactic forms (ctg. 3) defining axiological framework of the Iraq war rhetoric

Category	Key Lemma or Syntactic Form (ctg. 3)		Phase One	Phase Two
1.	*freedom*		100	221
	democracy		76	150
	peace		31	50
	justice		12	19
	progress		7	34
	other IDC values		16	21
	TOTAL category 1		**242**	**495**
2.	*dictatorship*		44	71
	radicalism		27	71
	terrorism		154	90
	threat	with reference to *WMD* (marker of ODC-IDC impact)	95	12
		without reference to *WMD* (marker of ideology operating within the ODC camp)	32	40
			127 (cf. Table 1)	**52** (cf. Table 1)
	danger	with reference to *WMD* (marker of ODC-IDC impact)	70	13
		without reference to *WMD* (marker of ideology operating within the ODC camp)	32	40
			96 (cf. Table 1)	**51** (cf. Table 1)
	other ODC values		16	21
	TOTAL category 2		**464**	**356**
3.	realis enhancing syntactic or discourse form ((ctg. 2 NP–VP1$_{departure}$)–(VP2$_{destination}$–NP-of-effect))		9	63
	TOTAL category 3		**9**	**63**
4.*	*tragedy*		60 (cf. Table 1)	55 (cf. Table 1)
	misery		24	67
	horror		32	49
	murder		40	33
	other NPs-of-effect		11	18
	TOTAL category 4		**167**	**222**

*Although many of the fourth category lemmas are also part of the realis enhancing form captured in the third category, their frequency hits in the fourth category are "free hits" i.e. separate from those which contribute to the *actual occurrence* script.

the ODC camp as such, they are also exponents of the spatial impact which the ODCs might exert upon the IDC territory. The latter quality is in fact one that makes the two lemmas feasible for the S/T framework as well. Altogether then, the borderline status of "threat" and "danger" makes the second category of the A framework include both their physically and ideologically oriented readings since it is difficult to draw a clear boundary between the underlying concepts, especially considering the temporal extensiveness and geopolitical variability of the entire legitimization process. Hence, of course, the seemingly large Phase One total count in the second category and its resulting dominance over the Phase Two count, but mark the fact that no such relation would hold if we were to disregard the evidently "WMD-related" readings. With no reference to WMD, both "threat" and "danger" duly increase in Phase Two. And finally, even if the ODC Phase One count (464) is apparently higher than its Phase Two counterpart (356), it is still smaller than the IDC Phase Two count (495), which keeps evidencing the primacy of the ideological *self*-description in the process of axiological proximization.

Returning to the third category, let us note that the increase in the application of the realis enhancing form is only possible because of the increase in most of the lemmas carrying the ODC ideological load. Especially important are the growing occurrences of "dictatorship" (44:71) and "radicalism" (27:71) since these two lemmas are among the most frequent axiological constituents of the remote possibility script. In contrast, such a compositional contribution is much smaller in the case of "terrorism," a lemma which addresses the past rationale for war and thus only occasionally appears in the realis enhancing structure.

The realis enhancing form further benefits from the Phase One – Phase Two increase in many of the NPs-of-effect, with the exception of those few which, again, bring back the past legitimization stance (viz. "murder"). In fact, the lemmas making up the fourth category of the axiological framework show an interesting re-orientation of focus as compared to the sixth category of the S/T module: from a clear emphasis on the physically devastating effects of the ODC-IDC clash, to a vague indication of *some* kind of consequence, whether physical or not. Hence the phasing out of such items as "catastrophe" (viz. its obvious associations with the WMD impact), to replace them with lemmas which relate to physical impact only potentially and even if one does settle on the "physical" interpretation, the vagueness of "tragedy" or "misery" is such that the impact seems at least not necessarily WMD-related.

These observations prove the fulfillment of the first condition for the legitimization-redressing capacity of the A framework. That the less complex second condition is also met is evident from the comparison of the number of the IDC (category 1) and the ODC (category 2) hits in Phase Two of the war. The ratio, 495:356, is convincing enough but consider again the contribution to the latter figure from the "borderline lemmas," i.e. "threat" and "danger." Without this contribution, the picture gets even clearer.

Altogether, the readings from Table 4 seem to corroborate the complementarity of the spatial/temporal and the axiological accounts of proximization, inasmuch as they reveal an intriguing rhetorical regularity, which might be going beyond the scene of the

Iraq war and onto the field of the interventionist discourse as a whole. Namely, the interventionist solicitation of legitimization is firstly reliant on material premises since these are initially easier to obtain and possess a more direct appeal to the audience which can thus grant an immediate approval of the speaker's actions. Yet, the attachment to a material premise for intervention is, in the long run, disadvantaged by geopolitical changes and the resulting plasticity and evolution of the discourse stage, which often have the initial premise disappear. Then, a compensation from ideological premises is nothing but natural, considering that axiological groundworks are, first, much less vulnerable to the impact of geopolitical changes and, second, they contribute to setting up discourses which are essentially abstract and involve less specific interpretations (cf. Hartman 2002; Lemos 1995). This does not mean that arrangements of the discourse stage which are based on axiological construals are incapable of generating more material premises in the long run. As we have seen from the Iraqi case, a material threat which was initially construed as "standing in the IDC doorstep," was later temporarily set aside, but only to accumulate (and, possibly, reappear in a similar form) as a result of the growing axiological conflict.

6.   Concluding remarks

The contribution of the axiological parameter is thus not merely critical in nature; it also involves a solid methodological input in the functioning of the S/T-A model of legitimization. Apart from the issue of the functional redressability of legitimization, an important part of this input is the fact that axiological considerations prompt an analyst to engage in complementary spatial-temporal discussions no less than (the missing points in) the S/T framework presented in the opening parts of this chapter have prompted the axiological argument in the later parts.

What is it, then, about axiological proximization that allows the A-S/T chronology of analysis on a par with the original S/T-A track? The mechanism of axiological proximization involves a construal of a dynamic ideological antithesis made up of a conceptual frame encompassing conventionally "good" values (such as freedom, security, etc. – see our analysis in 5.) and a series of "evil" values and acts (such as calling for violence, spreading fear, etc.) targeted against the existence of this frame. The effectiveness of proximization depends on the addressee's assessment of the "evil" *acts* in terms of their capacity to impact the deictic center – how likely are the ensuing *actions* to (re)occur within the addressee's and the speaker's physical territory, and also, how capable is the antagonistic mind-set of prompting further actions that could threaten the deictic center elements. Crucial to such an assessment is a build-up of a spatial-temporal analogy whereby the current state of affairs is compared to all previous states of affairs of a similar causative structure, namely all situations where a series of micro-acts taking place apparently outside of the IDC space eventually culminated in a direct impact. Thus, the "action-promptability" of alien ideological concepts (e.g. dictatorship or violence) and the following acts (e.g. *calling* for violence) is construed relative to the number of events that *did* occur, within a specific timeframe prior to the current state of affairs. From a pragmatic-cognitive standpoint, such considerations are clearly space- and time-oriented, and the mechanism of the overall analysis comes to reflect the not only initiating but also the mediating role of the axiological parameter, which the latter, in a way, binds together the remaining parameters of (S)pace and (T)ime. It is as if we inserted an axiological analytic perspective into the well documented body of knowledge on spacetime. If the analyst holds it true that a (retrospective) series of events in spacetime creates an updated framework of values which in turn create a potential for new (prospective) events to occur,[8] temporal analogies seem heuristically feasible to consider and, possibly, measure, the ideological load of the particular lemmas in terms of the (range of) the spatial effects obtained.

References

Baker, Paul, Gabrielatos, Costas, Khosravinik, Majid, Krzyżanowski, Michał, McEnery, Tony and Wodak, Ruth. 2008. "A useful methodological synergy? Combining critical discourse analysis and corpus linguistics to examine discourses of refugees and asylum seekers in the UK press." *Discourse & Society* 19: 273–306.

Broder, David and Balz, Dan. 2003. "Nation once again split on Bush: Voters split on handling of Iraq and economy." *Washington Post*, Nov. 2, 2003.

Cap, Piotr. 2006. *Legitimization in Political Discourse: A Cross-Disciplinary Perspective on the Modern US War Rhetoric*. Newcastle: Cambridge Scholars Press.

—. 2008. "Towards the proximization model of the analysis of legitimization in political discourse." *Journal of Pragmatics* 40 (1): 17–41.

Carston, Robyn. 2002. *Thoughts and Utterances: The Pragmatics of Explicit Communication*. Oxford: Blackwell.

Chang, Gordon and Mehan, Hugh. 2006. "Discourse in a religious mode: The Bush administration's discourse in the War on Terrorism and its challenges." *Pragmatics* 16: 1–23.

Chilton, Paul. 1996. *Security Metaphors*. New York: Peter Lang.

—. 2004. *Analysing Political Discourse. Theory and Practice*. London: Routledge.

—. 2005a. "Discourse Space Theory: Geometry, brain and shifting viewpoints." *Annual Review of Cognitive Linguistics* 3: 78–116.

—. 2005b. "Missing links in mainstream CDA: Modules, blends and the critical instinct." In *A New Agenda in (Critical) Discourse Analysis*, Ruth Wodak and Paul Chilton (eds), 19–51. Amsterdam: Benjamins.

Chilton, Paul and Lakoff, George. 1995. "Foreign policy by metaphor." In *Language and Peace*, Christina Schäffner and Anita Wenden (eds), 37–60. Dartmouth: Aldershot.

Dedaić, Mirjana. 2006. "Political speeches and persuasive argumentation." In *Encyclopedia of Language and Linguistics, Vol. 9.*, Keith Brown (ed.), 700–707. Amsterdam: Elsevier.

Chouliaraki, Lilie (ed.). 2007. *The Soft Power of War*. Amsterdam: Benjamins.

---

8.   This is a largely tentative attempt at reformulation in linguistic terms of Hermann Minkowski's (1908) seminal account of Einstein's (1905) work on spacetime within the special relativity model; additionally, mark a much more explicit analogy to Langacker's (2001) theory of Current Discourse Space (CDS).

Einstein, Albert. 1905. "Zur Elektrodynamik bewegter Körper. " *Annalen der Physik* 17: 891–921.

Fairclough, Norman. 2000. *Analysing Discourse: Textual Analysis for Social Research*. London: Routledge.

—. 2006. "Genres in political linguistics." In *Encyclopedia of Language and Linguistics, Vol. 5.*, Keith Brown (ed.), 32–38. Amsterdam: Elsevier.

Fairclough, Norman and Wodak, Ruth. 1997. "Critical discourse analysis." In *Discourse as Social Interaction. Discourse Studies: A Multidisciplinary Introduction, Vol. 2.*, Teun van Dijk (ed.), 20–45. London: Sage.

Graham, Phil, Keenan, Thomas and Dowd, Anne. 2004. "A call to arms at the end of history: A discourse-historical analysis of George W. Bush's declaration of war on terror." *Discourse and Society* 15: 199–222.

Greenway, Henry. 2004. "Bush rides high as 2004 begins." *Boston Globe*, Jan. 2, 2004.

Hartman, Robert. 2002. *The Knowledge of Good: Critique of Axiological Reason*. Amsterdam: Rodopi.

Hodges, Adam and Nilep, Chad (eds). 2007. *Discourse, War and Terrorism*. Amsterdam: Benjamins.

Huntington, Samuel. 2004. *Who Are We: The Challenges to America's National Identity*. New York: Simon & Schuster.

Keen, Judy. 2003. "Bush makes surprise visit to Iraq for Thanksgiving holiday." *USA Today*, Nov. 23, 2003.

Lakoff, George. 1996. *Moral Politics*. Chicago: University of Chicago Press.

Langacker, Ronald. 2001. "Discourse in Cognitive Grammar." *Cognitive Linguistics* 12: 143–181.

Lemos, Ramon. 1995. *The Nature of Value: Axiological Investigations*. Gainesville, FL: The University of Florida Press.

Levinson, Stephen C. 2000. *Presumptive Meanings: The Theory of Generalized Conversational Implicature*. Cambridge, MA: The MIT Press.

Martin, James and Wodak, Ruth (eds). 2003. *Re/reading the Past. Critical and Functional Perspectives on Time and Value*. Amsterdam: Benjamins.

Minkowski, Hermann. 1908. Address delivered at the *80th Assembly of German Natural Scientists and Physicians*. Berlin.

Pomeroy, Leon. 2005. *The New Science of Axiological Psychology*. Amsterdam: Rodopi.

Reisigl, Martin and Wodak, Ruth. 2001. *Discourse and Discrimination*. London: Routledge.

Silberstein, Sandra. 2004. *War of Words*. London: Routledge.

van Dijk, Teun. 1998. *Ideology: An Interdisciplinary Approach*. London: Sage.

—. 2005. *Racism and Discourse in Spain and America*. Amsterdam: Benjamins.

van Eemeren, Frans and Grootendorst, Rob. 2004. *A Systematic Theory of Argumentation*. Cambridge: Cambridge University Press.

Weiss, Gilbert and Wodak, Ruth (eds). 2003. *Critical Discourse Analysis. Theory and Disciplinarity*. London: Palgrave.

Wodak, Ruth and Chilton, Paul (eds). 2005. *A New Agenda in (Critical) Discourse Analysis*. Amsterdam: Benjamins.

CHAPTER 8

Friends and allies

The rhetoric of binomial phrases
in a corpus of U.S. defense speeches

Tony Bastow

1.   Introduction

Methodologies associated with Corpus Linguistics (CL) and Critical Discourse Analysis (CDA) are increasingly being integrated as a means of exploring concepts such as
power, rhetoric, and discrimination in discourses. For example, Baker et al. (2008)
show how a synergy of the mainly qualitative methods of CDA can be combined with
the mainly quantitative methods of CL to explore how refugees, asylum seekers, immigrants and migrants are represented in British news articles.

One of the aims of this chapter is to show how corpus linguistic methodology may
be used to investigate the rhetorical difference underlying an identical grammatical
structure in a special corpus and a reference corpus. The structure in question is the
binomial phrase, and this study will look, in particular, at the phrase *men and women*,
as well as the reversible *friends and allies/allies and friends.* In its focus on the lexicogrammatical environment of these phrases, the research can thus be said to be mainly
qualitative in orientation, though taking an initial quantitative position as its starting-
point. In this respect, it falls within the area of what has been termed 'corpus-assisted
discourse studies' (Partington 2004).

Before proceeding to the main analysis, a few remarks should be made regarding
some of the acknowledged strengths of corpus methodology. Firstly, it is thought to
guard against some of the weaknesses theorists believe are inherent in much CDA research, including 'over-interpretation' (O'Halloran and Coffin 2004; O'Halloran 2007).
Over-interpretation is applied to instances where over-strong claims are felt to be
made by analysts who may have a vested interest in making such claims (see also Widdowson 1995, 2000, 2004). In other words, corpus methodology can be used to uncover recurrent language patterns over a range of similar texts, which a conventional
CDA analysis concentrating on a single or limited range of texts may over-privilege.
Thus, any claims that are made are made on the basis of quantitative evidence, and not
because they are merely *thought* to be representative, when, in actual fact, they might

be "quite unusual instances which have aroused the analyst's attention" (Koller and Mautner 2004: 218).

Secondly, corpus analysis facilitates comparison. It allows the chosen sample to be compared with language in everyday use, for example. Thus, a disproportionate use of certain items or phrases in a special corpus, such as those in US defense speeches, when compared to those in a reference corpus may be evidence of ideological bias, and may be a way in which particular values may be reinforced and sustained. As Stubbs (1996: 158) states, while "such recurrent ways of talking do not *determine* thought... they [do nevertheless] provide familiar and conventional representations of people and events, by filtering and crystallizing ideas, and by providing pre-fabricated means by which ideas can be easily conveyed and grasped" (emphasis added).

It is these recurrences, along with their collocational preferences, that may shed light on how an institution's values and beliefs are presented as taken-for-granted, routine and commonsensical.

2.   Corpora used in this study

The general (or reference) corpus used in this study was the Collins Cobuild 'Bank of English' (BoE), which contains over 500 million words of written and spoken English of various genres, divided into 11 sub-corpora, including British broadsheet newspapers, Australian newspapers, UK speech, and US books. This corpus, or a similar corpus such as the British National Corpus (BNC), can be used as a basis for comparison to show what is unusual or particular in respect of the special corpus. An example of a special corpus is the one used in this study, namely my own specially-created one-million word Department of Defense (DoD) corpus, comprising 269 geopolitical speeches between the years 1995–2001 given by senior defense officials (mostly secretaries of defense and chiefs of staff). These were downloaded from the Department's official website at www.defenselink.mil/speeches.

The next section presents the reasons for choosing binomial phrases for the present study.

3.   Binomial phrases

Hatzidaki (1999: 136), who carried out one of the first, large-scale, corpus-driven studies of binomial phrases, defines 'binomial' as follows: "The formula WORD1 *and* WORD2 is a binomial if its members are syntactically symmetrical, i.e. they belong to the same word class and have the same syntactic function." Examples include *hearts and minds*, *tough but necessary*, and *attract and retain*. The first of these is a nominal binomial, the second an adjectival binomial, and the third a verbal binomial.

Table 1. Three- and four-word clusters in the DoD corpus

Three-word clusters		Four-word clusters	
the United States	1539	weapons of mass destruction	335
the Cold War	501	the Department of Defense	229
we have to	445	the United States and	221
men and women	426	of the cold war	215
Secretary of Defense	365	of the United States	197
of mass destruction	352	in the United States	193
in the world	349	the end of the	193
one of the	348	at the same time	185
that we have	343	thank you very much	181
weapons of mass	337	*men and women* in	143
going to be	318	to be able to	143
we need to	304	I would like to	136
be able to	302	our *men and women*	129
the end of	297	and *women* in uniform	121
the Department of	295	the *men and women*	119

Before continuing, let us consider why binomials are of particularly interest in this case. Investigating 3- and 4-word n-grams (contiguous word sequences or 'clusters'; see Table 1), the analysis of the corpus revealed that amongst clusters foregrounding elite persons and places, such as *Secretary of Defense* and *the United States,* the sequence *men and women* was very frequent.

This evidence prompts a consideration of not only the possible reasons for the binomial's frequency, but the differences in its textual environments in the DoD corpus and the reference corpus, the BoE.

3.1   Men and women

As shown above, there are 426 examples (tokens) of the nominal binomial *men and women* in the DoD corpus. As Table 2 below also shows, the word *men* rarely coordinates with any other word in this corpus.

Table 2. Binomials with *men* in the DoD corpus

Types	Tokens
men and women	426
leaders and men	2
men and boys	1
men and material	1

The binomial *men and women* is also frequent in the Bank of English (Hatzidaki 1999: 391–99), for example, found it to be the most frequent binomial in both the BBC and British Books sub-corpora of the Bank of English), but it is the difference in *co-text* which is perhaps the most interesting.

If we consider the collocates of this binomial, first of all, we will note (see Table 3 below) the presence of *our* in 1st left, 2nd left and 2nd right position, as well as *uniform* in 2nd right position, with 75 instances of *our men and women* being followed by *in uniform*. The software used for this kind of analysis displays the collocates of the search term ranked in order of frequency. The collocation data produced by the collocate frequency data command is organized in four columns, where there is one column for each position surrounding the keyword: 2nd left, 1st left, 1st right and 2nd right. In other words, 1st left refers to the word before the search term and 1st right refers to the word following the search term (note that the table above cannot be read in linear, left-to-right fashion: the preposition *in* at 1st right position after *men and women* might govern a different noun phrase, such as *the Balkans*). The columns in Table 3 show the collocates in descending order of frequency.

A closer look at the corpus reveals that 75 instances of *our men and women* are followed by *in uniform*. As we will see from a representative sample of concordance lines below, the complete noun phrase *our men and women in uniform* is associated with a number of rhetorical items. Firstly, the determiner *our* may invite the listener to share in the actions, duties and responsibilities of the personnel concerned. *Our* here would seem to be maximally inclusive – it includes the American people. Secondly, *men and women* may be rhetorically resonant in a way, I would suggest, that a denotationally equivalent phrase (e.g. *US armed forces*) may not be. In being less abstract than *forces*, the phrase *men and women* is vivid and imaginable. The institution, in other words, is 'personalized'. This may be important to the spokesperson who seeks to involve and persuade his/her listeners. In using the phrase *men and women in uniform* the speaker is perhaps better able to appeal to the hearers' sense of indebtedness towards service personnel, while at the same time mitigating perceptions of the military world as a dehumanized (or dehumanizing) environment; they are, in other words, 'men and women' like us.

Table 3. Collocates of *men and women* in the DoD corpus

2nd left		1st left		1st right		2nd right	
58	of	107	*our*	120	in	101	*uniform*
33	to	99	the	86	who	44	the
22	the	23	*young*	59	of	36	are
19	*our*	16	military	7	to	17	*our*
15	for	10	of	5	have	15	*serve*
13	and	10	The	5	and	7	have

The rhetorical phrase *our men and women in uniform* is also surrounded by highly evaluative items – they are under *strain*, under *burden* for their *service and sacrifice* – therefore as civilians we must show our *commitment* and *support* for their *welfare* and *security*:

(1)
```
which help ease the burden on our men and women in uniform - Active,
his resolve and commitment to our men and women in uniform. A Chinese
job weighs heavily upon our men and women in uniform. All around the
safety and security of our men and women in uniform. America o are
managing the welfare of our men and women in uniform. And I mus very-
thing possible to support our men and women in uniform and their fety
and physical security of our men and women in uniform and their ob-
ligation we owe not only to our men and women in uniform, but to Am
he magnificent performance of our men and women in uniform. But this
the service and sacrifice of our men and women in uniform. Everyday,
gratitude on behalf of all of our men and women in uniform for all
th the biggest single strain on our men and women in uniform is the
```

It will be noted above that *our men and women in uniform* tends to be preceded by *of* and other noun phrases such as *magnificent performance (of)* and *service and sacrifice (of)*, and that it usually occurs in clause-final position (over half the lines), perhaps inviting applause (Atkinson 1984). On this latter point, only in a handful of cases does *men and women* occur in subject position, as in the following:

(2)
```
Our men and women in uniform put up with a lot of sacrifice. One of
the biggest sacrifices is constant...
Our men and women in uniform need the support of their leaders in
Washington - and they have it!
```

As far as the adjectival premodifiers of *men and women* are concerned, the most frequent is *young*, which is frequently preceded by other evaluative adjectives such as *bright*, *capable* and *outstanding*. It seems that if you are 'young' in this discourse you must also be 'superb' and 'impressive':

(3)
```
to continue recruiting bright young men and women of character from
to meet with the very capable young men and women that are serving.
G ountry, and for the dedicated young men and women who are serving
in men in uniform are the finest young men and women that our country
ca rld. It attracts high-quality young men and women, it trains them
to llenge. They're the finest of young men and women. I looked in their
ctivity, you find outstanding young men and women serving the nation
cial- gifted, serious- minded young men and women who were prepared
ing commitment to the superb young men and women who serve in its
excellent choice for talented young men and women. For fiscal year 1
s. And as impressive as those young men and women are, what is even
t produces fit, well-adjusted young men and women who have strong v
```

In contrast, in the Bank of English, statistically significant collocates of *men and women* include *between* and *both*. In a representative sample of lines from the BoE, *men and women*, as complement of the preposition *between*, are seen less as a composite body with a common objective than as discrete entities, in which contrasts of lifestyle, temperament and sexuality are emphasized:

(4)
```
and emotional differences between men and women which are ignored at
re were frequent disputes between men and women, between young and
ol the essential differences between men and women? Had Dr Lawrence
f the biggest differences between men and women. If you are used st
50 years the relations between men and women, and between races, h
ose days the relationship between men and women was very different
```

In summary, while the collocates of the binomial *men and women* in the Bank of English emphasize individualism and difference, *men and women* in the DoD corpus are construed as a cooperative entity. To underline this point, here are some examples in wider context from the Bank of English and the DoD corpus respectively. Firstly, the Bank of English:

(5)   "Each member state shall ensure and provide and maintain the application of the principle that men and women should receive equal pay for equal work."

(6)   Too slow progress is being made in achieving an equal balance of men and women MPs.

(7)   Friendships do seem to represent different things to men and women.

(8)   Many people believe that the Holy Spirit is leading the Church towards a fuller understanding of the relationship between men and women, and their relationship to God who created them, male and female in God's image.

In example (5), the fact that Article 119 of the EC Treaty makes provision for what states 'should' do suggests that, in many cases, men and women do *not* receive equal pay for equal work, while example (6) indicates that women are under-represented in certain jobs. Example (7) suggests that men and women relate to each other in different ways. This difference, in the context of one particular faith, the Church of England, has led to a radical reappraisal of the Church's traditional roles for men and women (Example 8).

Now let us look at what might be called the 'rhetorical conflation' of some of these differences in the DoD corpus:

(9)   I take great pride in the men and women in the military. And all of us should be very proud of the job they do for us in protecting us day in and day out.

(10) Our nation's men and women in uniform do amazing, difficult and frequently dangerous work, and they do it extraordinarily well in times of war and in times of peace.

(11) "Wanted: loyal and dedicated men and women willing to work for modest pay in austere conditions. Job entails enormous pressure with the future of the nation and the free world in your hands."

(12) We as Americans can give thanks that we live in a nation where men and women of all races and all faiths can serve side by side to defend a way of life that Abraham Lincoln correctly said "holds out a great promise to all people of the world for all time."

In example (9) the different jobs (plural) that men and women do in both civilian and military have been conflated to 'the job' (singular) of protecting 'us', while in example (10) there is no suggestion that it might be men *in particular* who do the 'frequently dangerous work' (such as frontline combat duty or mine clearance). Again, in example (11), it is the higher 'job' that 'loyal and dedicated men and women' are called on to do. This 'job' apparently entails 'modest pay' and 'austere conditions' which belies the fact that the military is a hierarchical organization, with clearly defined roles which attract different levels of pay and work conditions. Example (12), with its four-fold repetition of 'all' in 'all races...all faiths...all people...all time', merely reinforces the conflation of differences which clearly exist between races, faiths and people.

3.2   Friends and allies

Apart from the second most frequent binomial in the DoD corpus, i.e. *peace and stability* (which is not considerd this study), the next most frequent binomial in this corpus is *friends and allies*, with 67 instances. Unlike the majority of the other binomials in the DoD, this phrase also occurs in its reversed form *allies and friends*, with 47 instances. The question then arises as to the collocational differences between the two.

Both *allies* and *friends* refer to countries which accord with US policies; as such, the two coordinates of the binomial may incline us to categorizing the binomial as 'synonymous' (Gustafsson 1975). Rhetorically speaking, *friends and allies* may have an intensifying function, similar to 'echoic' binomials (where WORD1 is identical to WORD2), such as *more and more* and *stronger and stronger*.

Although *our* is the most frequent 1st left collocate in both *friends and allies* and *allies and friends*, proportionately this determiner collocates more frequently with *friends and allies* (66%) than with *allies and friends* (38%). It also tends to collocate with items such as *cooperation*, *interoperability*, and *engagement*:

(13)
```
ed States seeks cooperation with its friends and allies for political
ancing our interoperability with our friends and allies, maintaining
ay military engagement with our friends and allies through a of ac-
tive partnerships with our friends and allies. It means car Armaments
cooperation with our friends and allies will help us ve authority to
work closer with our friends and allies across a whol . y power;
```

```
working in concert with friends and allies; helps contri r greater
armaments cooperation with friends and allies. Deploying
```

Allies and friends, on the other hand, appear to be in a more asymmetrical relationship with respect to the US than *friends and allies*. Whereas the latter are construed as more or less cooperative partners in a joint enterprise of some kind, *allies and friends* are seen as discrete entities, of lower status, and frequently in need of *reassurance* and *support*:

(14)
```
eployment and use: assuring allies and friends of the United States;
ust be able to reassure our allies and friends – to work with the eme
to be able to reassure our allies and friends, and deter and defeat
nited States to support our allies and friends from NATO to Israel,
t is to be able to reassure allies and friends, and to deter and def
interests, and reassuring allies and friends. As stated in the NATO
```

The second significant difference is that *allies and friends* are frequently geographically specified as *European, German* or simply *regional*, which is not evident in *friends and allies*; i.e. *friends and allies* are thus vaguer, more indeterminate than *allies and friends*. The effect is to suggest that *our friends and allies* are so well known that the need to identify them overtly is unnecessary. *Allies and friends*, on the other hand, require qualification:

(15)
```
w the United States and our allies and friends in Europe are moving
t indeed all of our European allies and friends, is somewhat similar
chauble; and all our German allies and friends; ladies and gentlemen.
ns America and our regional allies and friends in recognizing the com
es, along with our regional allies and friends, has yielded results
relationships with regional allies and friends. For example, the
```

As noted, the binomial *friends and allies* occurs 67 times in the corpus, or 77% as a proportion of all binomials and coordinate structures with *friends* as WORD1. Other simple binomials with *friends* (such as *friends and colleagues*) accounted for only 7%, while other coordinate structures, which are strictly speaking non-binomial because of the presence of a premodifier before WORD2 (e.g. *friends and potential enemies*), accounted for another 7%. Compound binomials (*friends and coalition partners*) comprised 4%, while the remaining 12% consisted of phrases such as *our friends and our allies* (where a determiner, rather than a modifier, before WORD2 again excludes them from the category of binomial proper). In contrast, the simple binomial *allies and friends* only constituted 45% of the total. Other simple binomials with *allies* as WORD1 (*allies and partners, allies and forces*, and so forth) accounted for 7%, while compound binomials (*allies and coalition partners*) made up 24% of the total. Non-binomials constituted 24%. This information is illustrated in Table 4 and Table 5, shown below.

Table 4. Coordinate structures with *friends* as WORD1

Binomial	Percentage
friends and allies (binomial)	77%
Other binomials (e.g. *friends and foes*)	7%
Compound binomials (e.g. *friends and coalition partners*)	4%
Other coordinate structures (non-binomial) (e.g. *our friends and our allies*)	12%

Table 5. Coordinate structures with *allies* as WORD1

Binomial	Percentage
allies and friends (binomial)	45%
Other binomials (e.g. *allies and partners*)	7%
Compound binomials (e.g. *allies and US forces*)	24%
Other coordinate structures (non-binomial) (e.g. *our allies and the Russians*)	24%

Thus, not only does *friends and allies* simply occur more often than *allies and friends*, the former's rhetorical force, I would suggest, appears to be enhanced by the absence of other binomial types or coordinate structures in the discourse. Conversely, the relative frequency of *allies and* modified WORD2, in contrast to the simple binomial *allies and friends*, as well as the frequency of other simple and compound binomials with *allies* as WORD1, tends to 'mitigate' the taken-for-granted rhetoric of the simple binomial where it *does* occur. *Friends and allies* becomes a familiar but conveniently vague phrase, easily passing us by, if we do not stop to think who these 'friends and allies' might be.

A look at the wider context of *friends and allies* and *allies and friends* illustrates some of the discourse differences between the two. Below are four extended contexts in which *friends and allies* are to be found:

(16)   Our interests are threatened by regional aggression against our friends and allies. We're also threatened by the spread of weapons of mass destruction and by instability from ethnic hatreds.

(17)   What specific threats do the United States and our friends and allies see in the Asia-Pacific region? We are cooperating more and more closely with our neighbors at home and our friends and allies abroad.

(18)   The United States has no interest in deploying defenses that would separate us from our friends and allies. Indeed, we share similar threats. The U.S. has every interest in seeing that our friends and allies, as well as deployed forces, are defended from attack and are not vulnerable to threat or blackmail.

(19)   USEUCOM's fight to win strategy includes maintaining ready forces, enhancing our interoperability with our friends and allies, maintaining adequate infrastructure and basing, and supporting modernization.

In example (16) what happens to 'our friends and allies' affects 'our interests'. In the second sentence, the inclusive 'we' unites the United States and its 'friends and allies' against 'weapons of mass destruction' and 'instability from ethnic hatreds'. Example (17) shows the explicit conjoining of 'the United States' and 'our friends and allies' in their perception of threats in the Pacific, while example (18) argues against any 'separation' of the United States from its 'friends and allies'. In example (19), the key word is perhaps 'interoperability', in which the United States and its 'friends and allies' cooperate on issues concerning infrastructure, basing, and modernization. In all these examples, there is a merging of interests, fears, and actions with partners whose identity is implicit, assumed.

Although similar contexts can also be found with the reverse of this binomial doublet, namely *allies and friends*, there are a greater number of contexts where this sequence is modified compared to *friends and allies*:

(20)   We have major allies and friends like *Japan, the Republic of Korea, Australia, Thailand and the Philippines* who also want our presence in the region as a force for peace and stability.

(21)   Another critical pillar of the enduring Asian security architecture is our bilateral relationships with regional allies and friends. For example, the *U.S. and Japan Security Alliance* has been, and will remain, critical to the security of the region.

(22)   We must also reassure our allies and friends – to work with the emerging *countries in Central and Eastern Europe* and teach them about democracy and how important it is to have the military subordinate to a freely elected government.

(23)   Defenses from such attacks can therefore reinforce the commitment of the United States to support our allies and friends *from NATO* to Israel, to the Persian Gulf, to Northeast Asia, in the event they face a direct military threat from a rogue state.

In these examples, *allies and friends* are explicitly identified in terms of countries and regions, such as Japan, Australia, and Central and Eastern Europe. These countries frequently need 'reassurance' and 'support' (examples 22 and 23). In contrast, as we have already seen, *friends and allies* are generally not subject to pre- or post-modification in this way. The binomial *friends and allies* has become, to all intents and purposes, a fixed phrase, a monosemous 'unit of meaning', in a way that *allies and friends* has not.

4.   Conclusion

In a discussion of nominal binomials in quite a different genre, Shapiro (2005) draws attention to the fact that binomials may cause a blurring of distinctions. Commenting on the unusual number of binomial phrases in Shakespeare's *Hamlet* (Shapiro uses the classical term 'hendiadys'), he comments:

> Hendiadys literally means "one by means of two," a single idea conveyed through a pairing of nouns linked by "and." When conjoined in this way, the nouns begin to oscillate, seeming to qualify each other as much as the term each individually modifies...The more you think about hendiadys, the more they induce a kind of mental vertigo. Take for example Hamlet's description of "the book and volume of my brain." It's easy to get the gist of what he's saying and the phrase would pass unremarked in the course of a performance; but does he mean "the book-like volume" of my mind, or "the big book of my mind?" Part of the problem here is that words bleed into each other – "volume," of course, is another word for "book" but also means "space." The destabilizing effect of how these words play off each other is slightly and temporarily unnerving. It's only on reflection – which is, of course, Hamlet's problem – that we trip (Shapiro 2005: 321–2).

This blurring may, of course, be politically expedient in defence speeches that apparently downplay differences between 'men and women', and which equate 'friends' with 'allies'. If the single item *friends* is 'deeply misleading' in international relations, as Fairclough (2000: 153) suggests, how much more misleading might it be to conjoin *friends* with *allies*? Are all your 'allies' necessarily your 'friends'?

A particular strength of corpus methodology, as has been argued previously, is its ability to reveal the preferences an institution has for particular items and phrases, as well as the common patterns these items and phrases may enter into. Indeed, it is these oft-repeated linguistic routines that may precisely characterize the community under investigation, and be part of its rhetoric. While CDA's mainly qualitative analyses have provided interesting insights into the use of language on the part of institutions, corpus methodology can place these largely intuitive insights on a firmer footing.

In particular, this paper has considered a number of ways in which corpus methodology can be used to explore the lexico-grammar of a particular structure in a special corpus, namely the binomial phrase.

We have seen through an analysis of contiguous 3- and 4-word sequences, that the binomial phrase *men and women* is very common. While we have found that the same binomial is also frequent in the reference corpus, the textual environments are very different – the absence in the defense discourse of 'differences between' men and women, I would propose, leads to an assumption that no such difference exists. We have also seen that *friends and allies* is, to all intents and purposes, a single unit of meaning, 'friends' being rhetorically synonymous with 'allies'. Its reverse, on the other hand, *allies and friends*, on account of its different collocational preferences, is a binomial whose two lexical items are not yet fused into a single 'naturalized' unit of meaning.

In conclusion, corpus methodology, it is suggested, is a useful tool to reveal what is routine and ubiquitous in the discourse of an institution, though not necessarily in the world at large. As Sornig (1989: 95) maintains: "The selection and arrangement of stylistic resources and devices...may serve to bring a certain perspective to the fore, to 'talk' somebody over to one's own point of view." It has been the purpose of this paper to show how certain frequent binomial phrases in a special corpus may indeed be 'talking us over' to a particular point of view.

References

Atkinson, Max. 1984. *Our Master's Voices: The Language and Body Language of Politics*. London: Methuen.

Baker, Paul, Gabrielatos, Costas, Khosravinik, Majid, Krzyżanowski, Michał, McEnery, Tony and Wodak, Ruth. 2008. "A useful methodological synergy? Combining critical discourse analysis and corpus linguistics to examine discourses of refugees and asylum seekers in the UK press." *Discourse & Society* 19 (3): 273–306.

Fairclough, Norman. 2000. *New Labour, New Language?* London: Longman.

Gustafsson, Maria. 1975. *Binomial Expressions in Present-Day English*. Turku: Turun Yliopisto.

Hatzidaki, Ourania. 1999. *Part and Parcel: A Linguistic Analysis of Binomials and its Application to the Internal Characterisation of Corpora*. Unpublished PhD thesis: University of Birmingham.

Koller, Veronika and Mautner, Gerlinde. 2004. "Computer applications in Critical Discourse Analysis." In *Applying English Grammar: Corpus and Functional Approaches*, Caroline Coffin, Ann Hewings and Kieran O'Halloran (eds), 216–228. London: Arnold.

O'Halloran, Kieran. 2007. "Critical Discourse Analysis and the corpus-informed interpretation of metaphor at the register level." *Applied Linguistics* 28(1): 1–24.

O'Halloran, Kieran and Coffin, Caroline. 2004. "Checking overinterpretation and underinterpretation: Help from corpora in critical linguistics." In *Applying English Grammar: Functional and Corpus Approaches*, Caroline Coffin, Ann Hewings and Kieran O'Halloran (eds), 40–57. London: Arnold.

Partington, A. 2004. "Corpora and discourse, a most congruous beast." In *Corpora and Discourse*, Alan Partington, John Morley and Louann Haarman (eds), 11–20. Bern: Peter Lang.

Shapiro, James. 2005. *1599: A Year in the Life of William Shakespeare*. London: Penguin.

Sornig, Karl. 1989. "Some remarks on linguistic strategies of persuasion." In *Language, Power and Ideology*, Ruth Wodak (ed.), 20–35. Amsterdam: Benjamins.

Stubbs, Michael W. 1996. *Text and Corpus Analysis: Computer-assisted Studies of Language and Culture*. Oxford: Blackwell.

Widdowson, Henry G. 1995. "Discourse analysis: A critical view." *Language and Literature* 4 (3): 157–72.

—. 2000. "On the limitations of Linguistics Applied." *Applied Linguistics* 21 (1): 3–25.

—. 2004. *Text, Context, Pretext: Critical Issues in Discourse Analysis*. Oxford: Blackwell.

CHAPTER 9

The *marketization* of institutional discourse

The case of the European Union

Elena Magistro

1. Introduction

The new global order dominated by capitalist economies has witnessed the emergence and rapid mushrooming of service industries, as well as the enhancement of existing customer-care divisions (Cameron 2000). Cameron (2000: 16) notes that "it is often through its service that a company gains its competitive edge" and is able to offer an added value to its clients: competitiveness and efficient customer service ensure the client's satisfaction and fidelity, which in turn ensure a company high profits and a certain degree of market authority.

Because language and communication are fundamental components of the buyer/seller relationship, the spreading of customer-care culture had major repercussions on the communicative style of corporations. In corporate discourse there has been "a shift towards more *conversationalized* discursive practices" and towards a growing *informalization* of attitudes and approaches: companies make greater use of traits that are typically found in ordinary spoken language to simulate conversation, and they display greater informality and a more intimate and friendly approach towards their customers (Fairclough 1995: 101, 137; cf. Mautner 2008). This makes corporations appear more trustworthy and their language more appealing, thus more persuasive.

In these last few decades, 'consumer culture' (cf. Featherstone 1991) has spread from the private to the public sphere, resulting in the institutions' growing use of practices that are typical of the commercial sector. As Fairclough (1993: 143) highlights with reference to higher education in Britain, in the global age institutions "come increasingly to operate [...] as if they were ordinary businesses competing to sell their [public] products to consumers" (cf. Rutherford 2000). This redefinition of boundaries between the private and the public also had an effect on the language used in the public sector. Since businesses generally aim at selling services and commodities, the discursive genre the institutional context is drawing from is mostly marketing-oriented and promotional in nature. When institutions marry some of their traditional traits, by and large conservative and unemotional, to the appealing and informal style of the private sphere, they generate a new communicative blend, a hybrid form of communication that deviates from the style commonly attributed to institutional environments. Entailing greater informality and a person-to-person approach, the *conversationalization* of discourse at the institutional level is clearly in contrast with what is considered traditional institutional discourse, where impersonality and distance usually prevailed (Fairclough 1995: 101).

This discursive shift can be observed from two opposite perspectives. On the one hand, it seems that commercial-style communication has won and affected the language used in public settings, thereby revealing a real "colonization of the public domain by the practices of the private domain" (Fairclough 1993: 140; cf. Fairclough 2005ab; Chouliaraki and Fairclough 1999). Bhatia (2005: 223) expands on this and explains that texts that are "essentially informative and traditionally non-promotional in intent, are increasingly being influenced and even colonized by promotional concerns." On the other hand, Fairclough and Wodak (1997) claim that this alteration of traditional institution/individual interaction may conceal a strategic end.[1] Not necessarily are public institutions passively colonized by the style of the private sector: they may be intentionally embracing and appropriating managerial practices to achieve specific goals and obtain some sort of institutional profit, just as corporations pursue the company's profit (cf. Chouliaraki and Fairclough 1999; Fairclough 1995). On this topic, Bhatia (2005: 224) adds that the appropriation of resources from the language of corporate advertising "has offered a very attractive option because of its innovative character and creative use of language". According to the latter view, the discursive shift in the public milieu would be motivated by the fact that marketing-style communication makes language more attractive and persuasive and more capable of 'selling things' to the recipients (Markus and Cameron 2002). Besides, a more informal and dialogic approach allows "more democratic interaction" (Fairclough 1995: 101) or simply confers a democratic appearance, whether factual or not, to the relationship between the institution and its citizens.

When language is exploited for instrumental purposes and promotional goals, it is subject to instrumentalization or *marketization*: its meaning is subordinated to, and altered for, instrumental purposes (Fairclough 1993: 141; cf. Wodak and Weiss 2005). However, if the *marketization* of discourse in corporate settings does not particularly impress us given the commercial nature of corporations, the *marketization* of discourse in institutional settings is certainly a much more interesting phenomenon, as the public sector does not traditionally stage buyers and sellers and does not usually involve the sale of commodities. It follows from this that the process of *marketization* of discourse in the public field reveals a deeper trend of *commodification* of social life: an increasing number of public items and entities are seen as 'products',[2] and the

---

1.   On the notion of 'synthetic personalization' see Fairclough (1992), Fairclough (1995); cf. Cameron (2001).

2.   On the notion of 'public products' see Rutherford (2000).

recipients of these public items and entities have turned into 'customers'. In other words, there is a general reconstruction of social life on a market basis, and discourse has become an effective vehicle for selling public products, such as public services, public organizations, social relationships, ideologies, perspectives, people, and so forth (Fairclough 1993: 141). What is 'sold' will of course depend on the domain in which the institution operates.

In this work I look specifically at the discourse of the European Union and I examine linguistic and textual features contributing to the *informalization* and *conversationalization* of EU language. I will claim that the features discussed may be the manifestation of an underlying agenda on the part of the institution, a social intent that could be read in terms of 'institutional profit' or, rather, 'European profit'.

2. Theoretical assumptions and analytical model

Before presenting my findings in depth, I will briefly set out the main assumption and the analytical model followed in this work. This study relies on a social theory of language. The key assumption is that language is an instance of social practice (Wodak et al. 1999: 8; cf. Billig 2007): language is real social action (cf. van Dijk 1997) or, as Fairclough (1993: 134) defines it, a 'mode of action' which is socially and historically situated and which is always in a dialectical rapport with the social context (see also Okulska this volume). Hence, language is shaped by historical and societal dynamics, and at the same time it is capable of shaping society and affecting history: discourse does not only mirror society but can help produce social change and, in the long run, historical change (cf. Cameron 2001; Fairclough 1993, 1996, 2007; Fairclough and Wodak 1997). Wodak et al. (1999: 8) reiterate this point and declare that discourse is "largely responsible" for the occurrence and establishment of specific "social conditions." More precisely, language is constitutive of

- social identities
- social relations
- systems of knowledge and belief (Fairclough 1993: 134).

In this perspective, discourse becomes a powerful tool for influencing and controlling social dynamics, for redefining the *status quo* and for shaping power relations (cf. Bordieu 1991).

My analysis is based on the three-level model that Fairclough has developed to investigate discourse events and that he applied in his study on the discourse of British universities. Fairclough (1993: 136–138) defines a discourse event as an instance of language use, which stretches over three dimensions:

- it is an instance of textual practice, in that it consists of an oral or written text;

- it is an instance of discourse practice, in that it involves the production of a text on the part of the text producer and its consumption, or interpretation, on the part of the text recipient(s);
- it is an instance of social practice, in that it has repercussions in the real world.

Fairclough explains the tie underlying these dimensions as follows:

> the connection between text and social practice is seen as being mediated by discourse practice: on the one hand, processes of text production and interpretation are shaped by (and help shape) the nature of the social practice, and on the other hand the production process shapes (and leaves 'traces' in) the text, and the interpretative process operates upon 'cues' in the text (Fairclough 1993: 136).

The analysis of *textual practice* involves the study of the manifest features of a text so as to determine the meanings they carry ('form-and-meaning analysis'). In terms of form analysis, one can look at the formal and grammatical traits of a document, such as the general structure, graphic and visual elements, cohesive or dialogic transitions, vocabulary, and deeper grammatical features (i.e. tenses, mood, etc.). On meaning analysis, Fairclough argues that all these surface features normally convey meanings of different nature: they convey the author's perspective on the world, and the author's own experience of the world ('ideational meaning'); they establish or redefine identities and relationships between the participants in the interaction or the members of the social community ('interpersonal meaning'); they establish perspectives and convey knowledge through the way information is distributed in the text (i.e. theme/rheme, foregrounded/backgrounded information, etc.) ('textual meaning').

Discourse practice, the second dimension in the model, refers to "the socio-cognitive aspects of text production and text interpretation" (Fairclough 1993: 134). The focus lies on what the author is trying to communicate and what tools are used to convey the message, as well as on how the recipients of the text can interpret the author's message – this, of course, may lead to takes deviating from the author's intended meaning. Hence, the analysis of discourse practice consists in exploring the intentions and strategies of the text producer and, from an opposite perspective, the mechanisms for interpretation that are made available to the text recipients.

Amongst the most important elements to be taken into consideration are the genres drawn upon in a discourse event (see also Okulska this volume); in other words, whether and how interdiscursivity is exploited in the text. Interdiscursivity, or discursive hybridity, is described by Chouliaraki and Fairclough (1999: 49; cf. also Fairclough 2003, 2005b) as "the combination in discourse of different genres." A genre can be defined as "a conventionalized verbal form associated with conventionalized purpose or occasion," thus referring to a use of language that is specific of a type of social activity, or normally associated with it (Johnstone 2002: 156), also known as a "situated linguistic behaviour" in a given setting (Bhatia 2004: 22). Hence, the intertwining of different genres in the same text produces discursive hybridity, the borrowing of communicative attributes "from one genre of discourse to another" (Cameron 2001: 130). When techniques and features that belong to a particular domain and are designed for a particular purpose are reproduced in a different context, it can be assumed that they are 'alluded' to and 'echoed' in the new context to achieve some specific goals or to provoke some sort of reaction in the text recipients (Cameron 2000: 75; cf. Cameron 2001; Wodak and De Cillia 2006). After identifying the genres featured in a text on the basis of the genre conventions commonly acknowledged, we enter the third dimension of the analysis: the study of social practice.

Focusing on *social practice* means trying to determine what the author intends to affect or modify in the greater social environment; in other words, what social change is envisaged by the author through the exploitation of the socially constitutive force of language. The investigation of social practice may stretch over various levels of society: from the specific situational context where the text is produced and consumed to the greater institutional context, from the societal context to the cultural or historical contexts, and so on. This third dimension highlights therefore the crucial role that 'context' – in a broad sense – plays in language use (cf. Wodak and Weiss 2004).

In this work, the concern for social change follows the first orientation identified by Fairclough (1993: 137) in his study, which is primarily a synchronic orientation (for a diachronic analysis of parallel processes in social institutions see Okulska this volume): the specificity of a particular discursive event is seen as an attempt "to negotiate unstable and changing sociocultural circumstances in the medium of language, drawing upon [...] available discursive practices and orders of discourse." The starting point of my analysis is therefore the current state of language in the contemporary European scenario: it is a snapshot of contemporary institutional discourse in the EU context that can provide some insights on the communicative style and on any inferable underlying intentions of the institution. As it is clarified at the end of this paper, further research on EU discourse may help explore the second orientation described by Fairclough (1993: 137), in which a diachronic perspective is assumed: an orientation "towards orders of discourse in the longer term, towards shifting discursive practices within and across social domains and institutions as one facet of social change."

For the goals of this study, Fairclough's three-dimensional model has been applied to a sample of EU discourse relating to career opportunities at the European Union. More specifically, the discourse event I have analyzed as textual practice, discourse practice and social practice is the informative booklet that the European Personnel Selection Office (EPSO) made available on its website in 2005 to potential applicants for jobs at the EU institutions.[3] The text was called "Careers at the EU institutions" and consisted of 12 pages in PDF format outlining employment opportunities and recruitment procedures at the Union, and specifying the profiles of the ideal candidates and the duties they are expected to fulfill. As the text was intended for a broad audience

---

3.   I have analyzed the English version of the text; however, other versions in all the official languages were made available in the EUROPA website.

with varied personal and professional backgrounds, the language used was intuitive and not specialized. This topic (i.e. job opportunities and recruitment) was among the topics treated in Fairclough's corpus of texts; the choice of this EU publication was aimed to establish a parallel between the two studies. Looking at how the same subject is handled in two very different institutional contexts will help widen the array of institutions in which the phenomenon of *conversationalization* and *marketization* of language can be observed.

3.   Analysis: Textual practice, discourse practice and social practice

In this section, I will discuss some key examples of conversation-like language and some elements reducing the distance between the institution and its citizens. I will solely focus on traits deviating from the impersonal and detached style that is generally found in traditional institution-to-citizen communication.

3.1   Textual practice

3.1.1   *Personalization*
The personalization of both the institution and the citizen ('we' and 'you') simulates a dialogic exchange and establishes a peer-to-peer relationship between the parties, as opposed to impersonal forms of address (cf. Magistro 2007). It confers a 'human' component to the social actors involved in the discourse event (van Leeuwen 1996; cf. Caliendo and Magistro 2009).

(1)   What *we* do.
      Who *we* are.
      While preserving the overarching principle of selection on merit, *we* aim to establish appropriate geographical balance within the workforce and have policies in place to encourage better representation of women in more senior positions.
      If *you* are thinking of applying for graduate entry *you* might first like to consider spending time gaining valuable work experience on a traineeship with the EU institutions.
      There is really no limit to the sort of work *you* could be doing.
      The "Welcome offices" of each institution can help *you* settle in once you arrive in Brussels or Luxembourg and provide useful information on accommodation, schools, etc.

3.1.2   *Appropriation of the citizen's voice*
(2)   How will *my* career develop?
      How can *I* find out when competitions are being run?

These examples are simulations of self-questioning/self-interrogation. As noted in Magistro (2007: 58), by using the first person singular pronoun to embody the potential applicants, the author appropriates the readers' voice to temporarily modify their perspective. The use of the first person forces the readers to assume the role of askers: they are induced to think that the questions asked are their own questions. By implication, the readers are encouraged to believe that they are truly interested in applying for a job at the Union: the readers are pushed to take on the perspective that the author wants them to have, and consider the opportunity of applying for a job at the EU. We may venture that this strategy is an attempt to bring EU citizens closer to the European project and raise greater interest towards EU activity.

3.1.3 *Future*

The same alteration of perspective obtained through the use of the first person singular pronoun is achieved by means of the future.

(3) As a new staff member, *you will be given* a series of induction courses
In terms of the work *you will be doing* and in terms of the genuinely multicultural environment in which *you will find yourself.*
What sort of work *will you be doing*?

In these statements, the potential applicant has already taken up the role of employee: the citizen is already an EU official. This use of the future is a promotional move which forcefully projects the reader directly in the author's desired scenario (cf. Fairclough 1993: 147).

3.1.4 *Imperative mood*

(4) If, after reading this brochure, you think you would be well suited to the type of work you will find in the EU, then *do not just sit back*!
Competition is keen, and only the very best candidates will succeed. But *do not let this put you off*, if you think you may have what it takes.

The use of imperatives entails either a certain degree of familiarity between the parties or a power relation that confers more authority upon the person using this form than upon the addressee. Yet Fairclough (1989: 126) highlights that "there is not a one-to-one relationship between modes and the positioning of subjects." In these examples, imperatives mostly have an exhortative function, as they try to incite the reader to participate in the activities of the Union. By conferring an exhortative, not obligational, value to the message, the institution occupies a less authoritative position than the one an order would confer: this reduces the pressure on the reader to perform the action requested and the sense of imposition that a real command would convey. This use of imperatives is recurrent in advertising to simulate an informal and friendly attitude towards the consumer. Hence, in modern public discourse, imperatives seem to "accord with the new personalized institution-audience relationship" (Fairclough 1993: 148).

3.1.5   *Salience of coordination*

As noted by Fairclough, another discursive tool evoking conversational exchanges is the use of parataxis and its prevalence over hypotaxis. In many cases, sentences are simply juxtaposed and separated by periods. Moreover, the use of cohesive markers is limited; this means that the logical progression of the topic discussed is often left to the reader's discretion, without being clearly signaled by surface elements.

> (5)   An AD grade job at the EU will stretch you. You will need drive, initiative, and skills in managing resources and people from a wide range of backgrounds. You should be able to express yourself clearly on paper and in meetings. You will need to be able to plan your work to manage a busy schedule. But the rewards are good. As a new EU official you can look forward to a stimulating career.
>
> The selection procedure normally begins with preselection tests, which usually include multiple-choice papers covering verbal and, in some cases, numerical reasoning and knowledge of the European Union. There may also be a preselection test of specialist knowledge where appropriate. Pre-selection tests are followed by a written examination and the final stage of the competition is an oral examination. The structure of each competition and the types of tests are described in detail in the notice of competition. Sometimes some or all of these tests will be taken in the candidates' second language. Finally, groups of merit will be drawn up, and the highest-scoring candidates will be placed on a reserve list for consideration against specific vacancies.

3.1.6   *Salience of visuals*

Colors, images, the layout and overall structure of the booklet are certainly among the most striking superficial elements in this document. Semiotic elements are core in the exercise of social practice (Wodak et al. 1999; Fairclough 2005a, 2005b; Cook 2001) and play a major role in the advertising industry given that, as Blair (1994) notes, they represent authentic forms of 'visual argumentation.' The author makes consistent use of graphic and visual features and largely exploits colors and shades. Just as a traditional brochure, this document seems to be issued for promotional purposes rather than as a mere informative tool (cf. Fairclough 1993: 156). Visuals contribute to capture the readers' attention and graphically guide them through the information presented in the text. They also help foreground and background such information, according to the relevance attributed to it by the author.

3.2   Discourse practice

The focus of this second analytical stage lies on the types of genres used and merged by the author in the text. I will concentrate on those genres that differ or clearly deviate from the genre conventions characterizing traditional institutional discourse, as it is known, or, as Bhatia (2004) explains, that highlight "manipulations of established conventions" (xvi). The question is: considering the intents normally conveyed by these genres, how should the author's message be interpreted?

3.2.1 *Genre of commodity advertising: appealing and metaphorical language*
This text features traces of a variety of genres gravitating around advertising and promotional discourse, including self-promotion (cf. Chilton 2004; Cap 2005):

> (6) Who knows what part you could play in forming tomorrow's Europe?
>   Living and working in the heart of Europe.
>   A wide spectrum of career opportunities.
>   If you don't try, you will never know.

Catchy language and appealing formulae serve as attention-getting devices. Some of these promotional sentences are made even more captivating through the use of metaphors (for the functioning of metaphor in political discourse see also Musolff and Skinner and Squillacote this volume). Figurative language traditionally belongs to the literary domain. However, by virtue of the interdiscursive nature of modern communication, it is also widely employed in other sectors (Fairclough 1989).

The specificity of metaphorical PR ies in the fact that it "presents a particular view of reality by structuring the understanding of one idea in terms of something previously understood" (Gill and Whedbee 1997: 173; cf. Musolff 2001). Metaphors represent "an aspect of human experience in terms of another" (Fairclough 1989: 119), they exploit background knowledge, routines and established associations to create likeable evocative effects (cf. Condor and Antaki 1997). Hence, metaphorical language can be easily found in marketing texts, where its vivid power becomes a precious persuasive tool.

3.2.1.1 *Personalization.* As described above, the personalization of the reader and the institution is among the strategies commonly used in advertising to generate greater appeal and enhance the persuasive strength of a statement. In particular, the use of a personal form of address, unlike impersonal references, makes the reader feel more worthy of attention and more involved in the communicative exchange. At the same time, the institution is endowed with a 'human' side (cf. Caliendo and Magistro 2009).

3.2.1.2 *Visuals.* We remarked in section 3.1.6. that visuals are a prominent feature of the document. Fairclough (1993: 142) suggests that in advertising greater salience is given to semiotic modalities other than written language: advertising has shifted towards "greater dependence upon visual images at the [...] expense of verbal semiosis." Multimodality has become a key communicative approach in modern written discourse (e.g., Kress 2003; Horsbøl 2006; Cook 2001; Kress et al. 1997; Kress and van Leeuwen 1996; Kress 2000). Since the topic discussed in this text focuses on careers at the Union, what is mostly portrayed is a work setting where groups of professionals

Figure 1. © European Communities, 2005

are engaged in different office activities. The pictures featured in the document may remind one of an efficient and friendly work environment, with a strong 'team' component emphasizing the commonality of goals and ultimately conveying a notion of common profit and common wealth. The picture above (see Figure 1) is a clear example of the team-building intent of the EU as it portrays a group of employees at work in a seemingly relaxed and pleasant environment; this underlines the collective nature of the institution, based on mutual cooperation and constructive exchange.

3.2.2   Genre of service industry: FAQ section
In this booklet, a whole section is devoted to frequent questions and doubts on the Union. This part draws attention on the institution's efficiency in providing information to the potential 'customers'. The way in which such information is given (i.e. questions-answers) reproduces the many FAQ sections widely exploited in the service industry to maximize understanding and assure an intuitive and reader-friendly fruition of the information provided. Hence, it seems that the Union is particularly concerned with dispelling any doubts and fears that EU citizens may have.

3.2.2.1   Questions
(7)   What does the selection process for permanent staff involve?
        What sort of work will you be doing?
        How long does the whole selection process take?

Several questions appear throughout the text, not only in the FAQ section. Interrogative forms, unlike ordinary and inconspicuous declarative forms, grab the readers' attention and invite them to carry on reading the relevant answers. Questions also deliver the image of a considerate and sympathetic institution: by answering all potential questions, the Union shows involvement in and understanding of its citizens' interests, desires and reservations. Besides, the utter transparency of the institution's procedures and intentions is emphasized by the fact that the Union spontaneously provides such a large amount of information in an exhaustive way (cf. Magistro 2007).

3.2.3   *Genre of prestige advertising: Self-promotional claims*

(8)   The EU can offer exciting and varied careers in interpreting and translating. You will not find another organisation like it.
There is no job like it.
The European Union is built on an institutional system that is the only one of its kind in the world.
As a new EU official, you can look forward to a stimulating career.

Self-praising statements are used to make the Union appear as an exclusive and well-regarded environment. Belonging to the Union and taking part in its activities is portrayed as a unique opportunity for Europeans in terms of career boosting. This can contribute to appeal the readers and raise interest in the activity of the EU. Cap (2005: 5) lists "positive self-representation" while Chilton (2004: 47) mentions "self-praise" among the communicative strategies used to secure legitimation and consensus in public discourse.

3.2.3.1   *Logo*. The EU flag can be compared to a real corporate logo: just as the logo is the recognizable mark of a company's brand, so the EU flag is a recognizable symbol of EU-affiliation. The stars and the colors of the flag largely appear throughout the brochure to reproduce easily identifiable marks of belonging to Europe (Magistro 2007: 64–65). Wodak et al. (2009: 191) discuss the importance of national flags as a unifying symbol of national pride as well as a means to fortify national identity. Similarly, the European flag can also be viewed as a unifying symbol intended to establish a supranational membership and implicitly spread a sense of Europeanness (cf. Wodak et al. 2009: 237).

3.3   Social practice

The use of conversation-like, friendly and persuasive language, the appealing look of the booklet and the presence of genres that mostly belong to the field of advertising suggest that a redefinition of the role of Europeans is being prompted: the Union is relocating Europeans from the status of citizens to that of consumers, revealing a *commodification* of their role in EU building. One can wonder: if EU citizens are compared to consumers, what are they expected to buy?

Going back to the claims made in the introductory part of this paper, it was argued that institutions increasingly operate as commercial entities "competing to sell their products to consumers" (see Introduction). It was also pointed out that, as the result of the general reconstruction of social life on a market basis, discourse has become a crucial tool to sell public products, such as ideologies, public services, social perspectives, and even people. Now, looking specifically at the context of this study, discourse has also become a crucial tool to sell identities and negotiate consensus, or even to legitimate authority (Chilton 2004; Chilton and Schäffner 1997).

Let us consider the difficult path of EU building over the decades: the abundant literature on the EU reports on the hard-fought course of European integration, highlighting unimpressive participation on the part of Europeans. Numerous factors are mentioned to justify such mild interest: above all, the so-called European identity deficit and the lack of a sense of attachment to Europe, which are often ascribed to the vivid local identities of Europeans. Skepticism vis-à-vis EU matters has sometimes developed into open resistance to the EU project, especially when issues such as the loss of state autonomy, national sovereignty, traditional customs and local languages are raised (cf. Garcia 1993; Schäffner et al. 1996; Banchoff and Smith 1999; Gastelaars and de Ruijter 1999; Abélès 2000; Bellier and Wilson 2000; Phillipson 2003; Walters and Haar 2005; Fanelli 2006).

In this text, the author conveys closeness with its readers, portrays the Union as appealing and desirable, and suggests that being employed at the European institutions is a prestigious career option for Europeans. This is readable as an attempt to raise interest and appreciation, encourage popular participation, and promote a sense of European togetherness and willingness to cooperate. Teubert (1996: 129) writes that work is not only the drive of a nation's economy, but a real value in the contemporary world: "work is more than just occupation or activity. It certainly ranks among the top values upon which our societies are built." It follows from this that being employed or simply applying for a job at the Union represents a sign of active support to the EU project. If the Union is able to persuade its citizens to take part in the institution's activities, such can be getting a job at the EU, it will lead them to overtly espouse the EU project, it will lead them to get concretely involved in the building of the European Union, and it will lead them to cooperate with their fellow citizens for the sake of a common pan-European good. In the light of these considerations, I argue that the social change the institution seems to encourage in this document is greater involvement in European integration: this consists of both practical involvement in terms of active participation in EU activity and emotional involvement in terms of the spread of a European identity, a feeling of belonging to Europe.

Where is the institution's profit in involving EU citizens and building a European identity? What can reasonably appear as the Union's reward? Under many respects, the development of the Union could benefit from greater popular participation both at an emotional and practical level: diffidence and EU-related fears could be appeased, thus facilitating a solid long-term growth of the institution; greater consensus on the part of the population could be won, thus fortifying the democratic underpinnings of the Union and assuring its full legitimacy;[4] finally, greater involvement could open the doors to a brighter future of the European project, which can be translated into faster and easier decision-making at the EU level and, eventually, into further integration of the member states in various fields.

4. Final remarks

In line with Fairclough's intentions as stated in his work on British universities, I tried to show how the study of a sample of EU discourse as textual practice and discourse practice can shed light on the evolution of relationships and identities in the complex European context (i.e. social practice). What emerges in this booklet is a further example of the "investment of effort into the construction of [...] entrepreneurial institutional identities" (Fairclough 1993: 157). The new commercial stance that institutions seem to increasingly adopt results from a general reinterpretation of society from a market perspective and is strictly connected to a business-oriented redefinition of the role of all social actors.

The text examined in this study is not representative of the order of discourse of the European Union in all its manifestations. However, as I specified at the beginning of my work, it provides an interesting snapshot of contemporary EU language and can prompt valuable hints on the discourse practices of the European Union, as well as on any inferable agenda driving such practices. Moreover, this analysis can encourage further investigation on the phenomenon of *marketization* and *conversationalization* of EU discourse in a diachronic perspective.

Numerous issues need to be explored and questions answered on the language of the European Union. For instance, Fairclough (1993: 140) explains that the process of *informalization* of attitudes and discourse in the public setting began in the 1960s. Considering that the European Community was founded in the 1950s, and that it comprised goals, activities and domains of action that greatly differed from the ones of the contemporary Union, it would be interesting to observe whether the order of discourse of the institution has evolved over the decades, and has been subject to restructuring heading towards more marketing-like communication. It may well be that, because of the recent establishment of the institution, the discourse of the European Union has always featured traits of promotional discourse. In other words, the discursive approach of the EU may have been structured, since its origins, more on the model of market organizations than on that of conventional public institutions. In this latter perspective, the discursive approach of the Union may have always been a hybrid approach consisting of a combination of different genres and styles.

---

4.   On discourse as a tool to seek consensus and legitimacy, see Chilton (2004).

Conversely, in the event that the discourse of the European Union has evolved from a more impersonal style towards a marketing approach, another question arises on the rationales of such evolution. As highlighted, the traces of promotional discourse discussed in this work may be partly due to the natural course of globalization: the European Union, as many public institutions, may be 'colonized' by the practices of the private sector as part of the natural redefinition of borders between the public and the private occurring in the modern era (Fairclough 1992: 204; cf. Fairclough 1993; Fairclough and Wodak 1997; Rutherford 2000). However, if we consider the institutional profit attached to the support of greater emotional and practical involvement in the EU, it can be argued that the Union is deliberately appropriating features and elements of advertising and corporate communication to achieve specific social goals. Hence, on one hand, the *informalization/conversationalization* phenomena in the public sector could be due to the advance of 'consumer culture' and to the globalization-driven redefinition of roles and orders ('colonization'); on the other hand, these phenomena could result from the conscious appropriation of entrepreneurial practices on the part of institutions, for the purpose of attaining specific institutional goals ('appropriation'). In this second perspective, the Union would not simply or necessarily be affected by the naturally-spreading *marketization* of discourse, but would be intentionally prompting an instrumental use of language to favor EU-identity building (Millar 2007; Krzyżanowski 2005), to secure popular endorsement and to construct a prosperous future.

However we see it, it is a real prospect that the Union's reproduction of discourse practices conveying definite identities and relationships could affect the European social scenario. In other words, because of the constitutive nature of language, the discourse practices of the Union may eventually help produce some sort of social change in Europe, and some sort of identity shift in Europeans.

References

Abélès, Marc. 2000. "Virtual Europe." In *An Anthropology of the European Union: Building, Imaging and Experiencing the New Europe*, Irène Bellier and Thomas M. Wilson (eds), 31–52. Oxford: Berg.

Banchoff, Thomas and Smith, Mitchell P. 1999. "Conceptualizing legitimacy in a contested polity." In *Legitimacy and the European Union: The Contested Polity*, Thomas Banchoff and Mitchell P. Smith (eds), 1–23. London: Routledge.

Bellier, Irène and Wilson, Thomas M. 2000. "Building, imaging and experiencing Europe: Institutions and identities in the European Union." In *An Anthropology of the European Union: Building, Imaging and Experiencing the New Europe*, Irène Bellier and Thomas M. Wilson (eds), 1–27. Oxford: Berg.

Bhatia, Vijay K. 2004. *Worlds of Written Discourse*. London: Continuum.

—. 2005. "Generic patterns in promotional discourse." In *Persuasion across Genres: A Linguistic Approach*, Helena Halmani and Tuija Virtanen (eds), 213–225. Amsterdam: John Benjamins.

Billig, Michael. 2007. "Critical Discourse Analysis and the rhetoric of critique." In *Critical Discourse Analysis. Theory and Interdisciplinarity*, Gilbert Weiss and Ruth Wodak (eds), 35–46. London: Palgrave.

Blair, Anthony J. 1994. "The rhetoric of visual arguments." In *Defining Visual Rhetorics*, Charles A. Hill and Marguerite Helmers (eds), 41–62. Mahwah NJ: Lawrence Erlbaum.

Bourdieu, Pierre. 1991. *Language and Symbolic Power*. Cambridge: Polity Press.

Cameron, Deborah. 2000. *Good to Talk? Living and Working in a Communication Culture*. London: SAGE.

—. 2001. *Working with Spoken Discourse*. London: SAGE.

Caliendo, Giuditta and Magistro, Elena. 2009. "The human face of the European Union: A critical study." In *CADAAD* Journal 3(2): 176–202, http://www.cadaad.org/2009_volume_3_issue_2/55–44.

Cap, Piotr. 2005. "Language and legitimization: Developments in the proximization model of political discourse analysis." *Lodz Papers in Pragmatics* 1: 7–36.

Chilton, Paul. 2004. *Analysing Political Discourse: Theory and Practice*. London: Routledge.

Chouliaraki, Lilie and Fairclough, Norman. 1999. *Discourse in Late Modernity: Rethinking Critical Discourse Analysis*. Edinburgh: Edinburgh University Press.

Condor, Susan and Antaki, Charles. 1997. "Social cognition and discourse." In *Discourse as Structure and Process. Discourse Studies: A Multidisciplinary Introduction, Vol. 1*, Teun van Dijk (ed.), 320–347. London: SAGE.

Cook, Guy. 2001. *The Discourse of Advertising*. Second Edition. London: Routledge.

Fairclough, Norman. 1989. *Language and Power*. London: Longman.

—. 1992. *Discourse and Social Change*. Cambridge, UK: Polity Press.

—. 1993. "Critical discourse analysis and the marketization of public discourse: The universities." *Discourse and Society*, 4 (2): 133–168.

—. 1995. *Critical Discourse Analysis: The Critical Study of Language*. London: Longman.

—. 1996. "Technologisation of discourse." In *Texts and Practices: Readings in Critical Discourse Analysis*, Carmen Rosa Caldas-Coulthard and Malcom Coulthard (eds), 71–83. London: Routledge.

—. 2003. *Analysing Discourse: Textual Analysis for Social Research*, London: Routledge.

—. 2005a. "Critical discourse analysis." *Marges Linguistiques* 9: 76–94.

—. 2005b. "Critical discourse analysis in transdisciplinary research." In *A New Agenda in (Critical) Discourse Analysis: Theory, Methodology and Interdisciplinarity*, Ruth Wodak and Paul Chilton (eds), 53–70. Amsterdam: Benjamins.

—. 2007. "The contribution of discourse analysis to research on social change." In *Discourse in Contemporary Social Change*, Norman Fairclough, Giuseppina Cortese and Patrizia Ardizzone (eds), 25–48. Bern: Peter Lang.

Fairclough, Norman and Wodak, Ruth. 1997. "Critical discourse analysis." In *Discourse as Structure and Process. Discourse Studies: A Multidisciplinary Introduction, Vol. 2*, Teun van Dijk (ed.), 258–284. London: SAGE.

Fanelli Elisa. "Europei si, ma non troppo." BBL 1/2006. *Jean Monnet European Centre of Excellence*, Università degli Studi di Trento. Retrieved 20 October 2006, http://www4.soc.unitn.it:8080/poloeuropeo/content/e2611/index_ita.html.

Featherstone, Mike. 1991. *Consumer Culture and Postmodernism*. London: SAGE.

García, Soledad. 1993. "Europe's fragmented identities and the frontiers of citizenship." In *European Identity and the Search for Legitimacy*, Soledad García (ed.), 1–29. London: Pinter Publishers.

Gastelaars, Marja and de Ruijter, Arie. 1998. "Ambivalences and complexities in European identity formation." In *A United Europe: The Quest for a Multifaceted Identity*, Marja Gastelaars and Arie de Ruijter (eds), 1–12. Maastricht: Shaker.

Gill, Ann M. and Whedbee, Karen. 1997. "Rhetoric." In *Discourse as Structure and Process. Discourse Studies: A Multidisciplinary Introduction, Vol. 1*, Teun van Dijk (ed.), 157–184. London: SAGE.

Horsbøl, Anders. 2006. "From our plan to my promises: Multimodal shifts in political advertisements." In *Mediating Ideology in Text and Image*, Inger Lassen, Jeanne Strunck and Torben Vestergaard (eds), 149–172. Amsterdam: John Benjamins.

Johnstone, Barbara. 2002. *Discourse Analysis*. Malden, MA: Blackwell.

Kress, Gunther. 2000. "Text as punctuation of semiosis: Pulling at some threads." In *Intertextuality and the Media: From Genre to Every-day Life*, Ulrike H. Meinhof and Jonathon Smith (eds), 132–154. Manchester: Manchester University Press.

—. 2003. *Literacy in the New Media Age*. London: Routledge.

Kress, Gunther and van Leeuwen, Theo. 1996. *Reading Images: The Grammar of Visual Design*. London: Routledge.

Kress, Gunther, Leite-García, Regina and van Leeuwen, Theo. 1997. "Discourse semiotics." In *Discourse as Structure and Process. Discourse Studies: A Multidisciplinary Introduction, Vol. 1*, Teun van Dijk (ed.), 257–291. London: SAGE.

Krzyżanowski, Michał. 2005. "European identity wanted!: On discursive and communicative dimensions of the European Convention." In *A New Agenda in (Critical) Discourse Analysis: Theory, Methodology and Interdisciplinarity*, Ruth Wodak and Paul Chilton (eds), 137–163. Amsterdam: John Benjamins.

Magistro, Elena. 2007. "Promoting the European identity: Politeness strategies in the discourse of the European Union." *CADAAD Journal* 1 (1): 51–73. http://www.cadaad.org/ejournal/2007/1/magistro.

Markus, Thomas A. and Cameron, Deborah. 2002. *The Words between the Spaces: Buildings and Language*. London Routledge.

Mautner, Gerlinde. 2008. "Language and communication design in the marketplact". In *Handbook of Communication in the Public Sphere*, Ruth Wodak and Veronika Koller (eds), 131–154. Berlin: De Gruyter.

Millar, Sharon. 2007. "Rhetoricians at work: Constructing the European Union in Denmark." In *The Discourse of Europe*, John Wilson and Sharon Millar (eds), 113–130. Amsterdam: John Benjamins.

Musolff, Andreas. 2001. "The metaphorisation of European politics: Movement on the road to unification process." *In Attitudes towards Europe. Language in the Unification Process*, Andreas Musolff, Colin Good, Ruth Wittlinger and Petra Points (eds), 179–200. Aldershot: Ashgate.

Phillipson, Robert. 2003. *English-Only Europe? Challenging Language Policy*. London: Routledge.

Rutherford, Paul. 2003. *Endless Propaganda: The Advertising of Public Goods*. Toronto: University of Toronto Press.

Schäffner, Christina, Musolff, Andreas and Townson, Michale. 1996. "Diversity and unity in European debates." In *Conceiving of Europe: Diversity in Unity*, Christina Schäffner, Andreas Musolff and Michael Townson (eds), 1–14. Aldershot: Dartmouth.

Teubert, Wolfgang. 1996. "The concept of work in Europe." In *Conceiving of Europe: Diversity in Unity*, Christina Schäffner, Andreas Musolff and Michael Townson (eds), 129–145. Aldershot: Dartmouth.

van Dijk, Teun A. 1997. "The study of discourse." In *Discourse as Structure and Process. Discourse Studies: A Multidisciplinary Introduction, Vol. 1*, Teun van Dijk (ed.), 1–34. London: SAGE.

van Leeuwen, Theo. 1996. "The representation of social actors." In *Texts and Practices: Readings in Critical Discourse Analysis*, Carmen Rosa Caldas-Coulthard and Malcom Coulthard (eds), 32–70. London: Routledge.

Walters, William and Haahr, Jens Henrik. 2005. *Governing Europe: Discourse, Governmentality and European Integration*. Oxon: Routledge.

Wodak, Ruth and de Cillia, Rudolf. 2006. "Politics and language: Overview." In *Encyclopaedia of Language and Linguistics, Vol. 9* [2nd ed.], Keith Brown (ed.), 707–719. Oxford: Elsevier.

Wodak, Ruth and Weiss, Gilbert. 2004. "Visions, ideologies and utopias in the discursive construction of European identities: Organizing, representing and legitimizing Europe." In *Communicating Ideologies. Multidisciplinary Perspectives on Language, Discourse and Social Practice*, Martin Pütz, Joanne Neff-Van Aertselaer and Teun van Dijk (eds), 225–252. Frankfurt am Main: Peter Lang.

—. 2005. "Analyzing European Union discourses: Theories and applications." In *A New Agenda in (Critical) Discourse Analysis: Theory, Methodology and Interdisciplinarity*, Ruth Wodak and Paul Chilton (eds), 121–135. Amsterdam: John Benjamins.

Wodak, Ruth, de Cillia, Rudolf, Reisigl, Martin and Liebhart, Karin. 1999. *The Discursive Construction of National Identity*. Edinburgh: Edinburgh University Press.

—. 2009. *The Discursive Construction of National Identity* [2nd ed.]. Edinburgh: Edinburgh University Press.

CHAPTER 10

Performing the world of politics through the discourse of institutional correspondence in Late Middle and Early Modern England

Urszula Okulska

1. Introduction: Constituting early social institutions through the discourse of letter writing

Since time immemorial letter writing, as one of the world's oldest forms of communicative practice, has shaped social institutions (Watts [1996] 2005) in many domains of life. The institutional nature of correspondence, in all its modes and realizations, and in all the social milieus, both private and official, where it served as a channel mediating a wide range of long-distance interactions, is reflected in the highly conventionalized form of this kind of exchange, its huge generic productivity, and the broad scope of (especially public) fields that owe their rise and development to epistolary activities. In the course of history these practices have largely contributed to establishing and fostering interpersonal bonds, which in the long run arranged social communities, and perpetuated the growth of small- or large-scale social organizations, consolidated, maintained and reshaped to a great extent by the discourses that they evolved.

The role of letter writing in the emergence, constitution and reproduction of various spheres of public life, which is the focus of this investigation, at early stages of their growth in the history of human civilization goes back to the times of the ancient (Near) East (cf. White 1982). The earliest traces of cuneiform writing on clay tablets from this region indicate that official correspondence was a well developed communicative means in the field of diplomacy. Early written evidence from ancient Mesopotamia suggests that diplomatic letter writing was a fully-fledged form of information exchange in the political and administrative realms by two thousand years BC (Trolle-Larsen 1989). It enabled to maintain relations especially between rulers of ancient empires, of which records are preserved, for instance, in central Egypt. An archive of c. 360 clay tablets that has been found there, dating back to the 15–14th centuries BC, contains diplomatic correspondence of pharaohs of the 18th dynasty directed mainly to kings of neighboring states, especially of Assyria (Sutor 2004: 9). There is also copious evidence of political correspondence having been in wide circulation in ancient Greece (cf. Harris 1989). This was the time when letters acquired their long-lasting epistolary conventions, dictated to a great extent by early practices of delivering post by messengers, which resulted from the common in most history of political communication distrust in the written word. The original tradition of conveying epistolary communiqués orally, aside the written text that was usually enclosed, made authors adjust the format of their epistles to that typical of interaction in face-to-face encounters. This transformed letter writing into a highly ritualized form of linguistic exchange, and equipped it with indispensable generic conventions of (often formulaic) greetings, salutations, and closings (cf. Barton and Hall 2000: 5), whose choice was dictated by rules of courteous intercourse and professional gentility. Elements of the social drama associated with carrying and projecting the presence of the sender in front of the recipient (the so-called *parousia*; cf. Bazerman 2000: 18) as well as adopting by them suitable interactive positions appropriate for their status, relations and communicative goals are also discursively petrified in *inter alia* epistolary forms of address (cf., e.g., Nevalainen and Raumolin-Brunberg 1995; Nevala 2004), para- and hyper-textual rules (e.g., Austin 2004; Dossena 2004; Sutor 2004; Dury 2006), and the whole materiality of letter writing (e.g., Hall 2000; Sutor 2004), developed across the centuries to give voice to interactants' refinement, and to reflect their overall acquaintance with social etiquette.

The human need to communicate at a distance in the official sphere made correspondence pervade most of its layers in the old times, and, similar to what can be observed today, develop versatile interactive functions to enable and mediate a vast range of institutional contacts. The strong embedding of this mode in social contexts and its deep situatedness in cultural values and practices have imbued it with high generic flexibility, which in the course of history allowed other forms of expression to rise from letter writing. It is through correspondence that, as Barton and Hall (2000: 1) put it, "one can narrate experiences, dispute points, describe situations, offer explanations, give instructions and so on," all of which communicative acts may be enveloped in the form of letters. This diversity of interactive moves that letters have carried throughout history and the plethora of epistolary formats in which they could accommodate encoders' professional intentions have resulted in the rise of manifold letter-derived genres, which due to their official status and regular use have structured social institutions of public life linked with politics, for instance in the fields of business, economy, law, science, journalism, and church.

To begin with the business area, the traditional letter is referred to as a textual predecessor of, for instance, the contemporary memo, fax, corporate report, electronic dialogue, proposal, and e-mail (e.g., Yates and Orlikowski 1992; Orlikowski and Yates 1994; see also Niemeier, Campbell and Dirven 1998; Bargiela-Chiappini and Nickerson 1999; Geluykens and Pelsmaekers 1999; Gillaerts and Gotti 2005; Ramallo, Lorenzo and Rodriguez-Yáñez 2006; Geluykens and Kraft 2008). Such a broad letter-rooted repertoire of corporate texts has enabled the arrangement, management and functioning of early and modern companies. There is plenty of evidence that the discourse of business correspondence in its various generic shades fostered the rise and constitution of early business communities, for instance, in the 19th century (cf. Del Lungo Cami-ciotti 2005, 2006a, 2006b; Dossena 2006b), much the same as it also structured (vir-tual) professional groups in the 20th century (see esp. Orlikowski and Yates 1994). Also in the sphere of banking, trade and economy correspondence has its well-ground-ed position as a discourse practice that shaped forms and mechanisms of early finan-cial organizations. It is letter writing activities that have prompted the evolution of such financial instruments as, for instance, banknotes, bills of exchange, letters of credit, or money transfer authorizations (cf. Bazerman 2000: 21–23), which for centu-ries have established and mediated the world's systems of banking and finance. As Dossena (2006a, 2006b) observes in her corpus of 19th-century bank correspondence, epistolary tools of stance- and identity-marking were efficient discursive means of building interactants' institutional roles that enacted complex interpersonal ties in or-ganizational networks of the financial branch of this time.

Generic extensions of the letter can also be traced in some legal documents of medieval bureaucracy, including grants of immunities and privileges, contractual ar-rangements, deeds of transfer, and gifts (Murphy 1974: 200–202; Perelman 1991: 99), as well as in first patents (e.g., Bazerman 1997). Although the latter have recently been largely deprived of their originally epistolary format, they are still legally accompanied by extensive correspondence, in the form of the so-called 'file wrapper' (Bazerman 2000: 21). Through the performative function that such texts have had in social inter-action they would define individual and institutional subjects' mutual rights and obli-gations, by which they regularized and ordered social relations from the legal perspec-tive. Moreover, in the field of science and education correspondence, as a source of the early scientific article (e.g., Gotti 2006) and scientific journals (e.g., Rusnock 1999; Johns 2003; Gotti 2005), was a channel that, similar to its contemporary role (e.g., Mitra et al. 1999; Mulholland 1999; Warschauer 2002; Kowalski 2006; Sokół 2006, 2008), centuries ago brought together members of academic circles placed in different parts of the world. It was letters that lay at the basis of many international projects (Fris-inger 1999; Rusnock 1999), advanced scientific discoveries, promoted new methods and techniques, stimulated experiments, and disseminated news about inventions (see Gotti 2006). In this way they strengthened existing and promoted new profes-sional relationships, and also tightened bonds among learned people of aristocracy and culture, by which they consolidated both scholarly communities (e.g., Stocking 1983; Valle 2004) as well as intellectual elites (e.g., Sairio 2008).

With the advent of print culture, a growing need to convey information to ex-tended audiences with specialized interests caused the emergence of the profession of news correspondents, whose role was to provide epistolary reports from remote desti-nations and on different topics. Correspondence thus seems a transitional discourse on the way towards the rise of journalism, as well as a source of early newspapers (e.g., Fritz 2001), which first occurred in the form of political or commercial newsletters directed to the gentry in the provinces and to higher-ranking families (e.g., Andrews 1967; Raymond 1996; Somerville 1996). By adopting originally a personal style of expression, and directly addressing their readers, editors of these newsletters placed themselves in structured relations with their addressees, thus building readership bonds with the recipients. Reflexes of these networks are still preserved today discursively in meta-references to news reports as 'correspondence from...' and hyper-textually in by-lines or letters columns. Finally, trappings of the letter are also found in the written tradition of the early Christian church, which resorts to epistolary conventions, for instance, in the Books of the New Testament outside the gospels, as well as in such papal documents as, e.g., encyclicals, constitutions, bulls, briefs, rescripts, decrees, or personal autographs (Fremantle 1956: 23–25). The purpose of these epistolary forms, many of which are still in use today, aside reaffirming the church fellowship in faith, was to circulate doctrinal rulings, decisions of episcopal synods, as well as apostolic and pastoral messages, which bound church members together with uniform dogmatic, ethical and moral guidelines. Additionally, correspondence strengthened bonds of communion also among bishops and lower levels clergy, and as (Late) Middle and (Early and Late) Modern English evidence conveys (e.g., Tieken-Boon van Ostade 2003, 2005, 2006; Okulska 2006), it extended their social networks further into other rungs of the church hierarchy, as well as beyond them into lay terrains of state authorities and administration. In this context letter writing can be said to have functioned as an auxiliary social practice that established and mediated cross-disciplinary relations in the public domain.

What is more important from the point of view of the present study is that correspondence has always played a crucial role in the sphere of politics, in that it helped to monitor administrative and military affairs, and enabled to manage diplomatic business at the level of inter- and intra-national relations. As has already been signaled, the political significance of epistolary writing goes back to the ancient times, when, to put it in Bazerman's words (2000: 17), "early written commands along with other military, administrative, or political business of the state were cast in the form of letters." Deployed for similar communicative purposes in later epochs (see, e.g., Whigham 1981; Okulska 2008), epistolary conventions of the ancient rhetoric were in time adapted, for instance, to royal documents of legal and normative force. Traces of the letter can be found, for example, in such medieval documents as the Magna Charta (1215) and Letters Patent (1495), both these texts employing residual epistolary formulae (i.e. address, salutation, witness) and direct imperative style to assign interacting parties their institutional roles, and locate them in hierarchical positions with respect to each other (cf. Bazerman 2000: 20). Apart from its remnants in documents of state-internal policy, correspondence was often a vehicle for maintaining and uplifting the spirit of national identity, sentiment and patriotism in times of social discontent and political unrest. The tradition of writing the letter of petition, for example, as a way of expressing individual and group protest against authorities stretches back to the classical world (see, e.g., Kim 1972), and was continued in various epistolary forms both in the Middle and (Early) Modern times (e.g., Okulska 2008). Letters were also regularly used to stir up war-like attitudes, circulate information about outrages, and arrange acts of rebellion, an example of which can be, for instance, their use during the 1381 revolt of English peasants (see Justice 1994) or American Revolution (1775–1783) (cf. Bazerman 2000: 21). As Austin (2000: 48) shows in her small-scale study of 18th-century Cornish community, in times of war correspondence was a means that also allowed to sustain ties among family members, who through their letters to relatives and friends numbed the spirit of (usually) long-lasting separation.

Finally, on international arenas political correspondence, in its multifarious generic realizations – resulting from its diversified communicative roles (see, e.g., Sutor 2004), has to a great extent discursively configured countries' military and economic positions, thus constructing histories of their diplomatic relations. In the Middle Ages, for instance, epistolary exchange between Swedish authorities and the Hanseatic Councils (Tiisala 2004) as well as between the Finnish Bailiffs and the Council of Reval (Salminen 1997) largely established, shaped and recreated power structures in northern Baltic Europe. In the following periods, for instance in the Anglo-Saxon context, the diplomatic business carried out abroad by civil servants of King William's Foreign Office in the last decade of the 17th century (see Fitzmaurice 2006) indicates how diplomatic letters, aside fulfilling their institutional function of informing the English public policy at higher levels, themselves grew into communal discourse that constituted a social network of the Crown's diplomats. On the basis of Late Middle and Early Modern English material Okulska (2006, 2008) has demonstrated how professional activities of diplomatic and administrative letter writing led to the rise of specific epistolary genres of early English organizations. Overall, in all the domains and historical times discussed above letters, whether in their typically epistolary forms or in their different generic inflections, have served as a flexible medium that navigated many practices of the public sphere, thus enacting and reaffirming bonds of communality and fellowship in official milieus, by which they have for centuries built and consolidated institutions of social life.

2.   Early English political correspondence in the light of critical linguistics

The present investigation seeks to uncover the way Late Middle English (LME) and Early Modern English (EModE) epistolary discourse established, developed and reproduced, as well as was itself molded by, politically oriented public institutions of 15–17th-century England (for the role of discourse in arranging contemporary institutions see, e.g., Magistro this volume). The functioning of the early English social structures will be analyzed from the point of view of their reflections in the texture of one epistolary mode of LME and EModE written expression, i.e. the 'directive letter' (see Okulska 2008), which was a viable argumentative and persuasive tool in and across both secular and ecclesial institutions of Late Middle and Early Modern England. Such an approach to linguistic evidence invokes the social constructionist perspective (e.g., Berger and Luckman 1967; Burr 1995), in view of which discourse organizes,

controls, and modifies social institutions, and is itself shaped by their habitualized interactive practices, which in turn manage, govern, and perpetuate its growth (see also
Watts [1996] 2005). The framework thus presents the early English socio-cultural reality and political discourse as standing in dialectical relationship, where the processual
nature of the public world is reflected and constituted by discourse, which is itself a
socially constituted and socially constitutive factor (cf., e.g., Fairclough 1989, 1992,
1995). What follows from it is that discourse functions as an integral part of culture,
both as its natural medium as well as its shaping force, and as such it is a consequence,
carrier and motivator of interactive practices in socio-cultural space (e.g., Fairclough
1992, 1995; van Dijk 1997a, 1997b).

The diachronic perspective adopted in the project is a long time-span extension of
the (critical) discourse-historical approach established in reference to 20th-century
political communication, for instance, by Maas (1984), Ehlich (1989), Wodak et al.
(1990, 1994, 1999), Reisigl and Wodak 2001, Martin and Wodak (2003), Wodak and
Weiss (2004), Wodak and de Cillia (2006), Heer et al. (2008), or Triandafyllidou,
Wodak and Krzyżanowski (2009). It also responds to the long-articulated need in critical linguistics to employ the broadest historical/diachronic frame of reference, due to,
as Fowler (1996: 10) argues, "specific connections of aim and method with history." As
for aim, in his view, the critical linguist, like the historian

> aims to understand [synchronically] the values which underpin social, economic
> and political formations, and diachronically, changes in values and changes in
> formations. As for method, one aspect at any rate, the critical linguist, like the
> historian, treats texts as both types of discursive practice (charters, letters, proc-
> lamations, Acts of Parliament) and as documents (sources for the beliefs of in-
> stitutions, for example). Like the historiographer, the critical linguist is crucially
> concerned with the ideological relativity of representation (Fowler 1996: 10).

As Kress (1996) observes, representational resources in cultures, i.e. formal (viz. tex-
tual/discoursal) means and practices through which language-external structures,
processes and phenomena are transmitted, decoded and interpreted, "represent, realize, and embody ... rich social histories" (1996: 18), and, as van Leeuwen (1996) adds,
they are themselves "subject to historical change, sometimes even violent change"
(1996: 34). A sensitive barometer of their evolution, and a potent indicator of socio-
cultural transition are text heterogeneities (Fairclough 1995: 2). Similar to Fowler,
Kress and van Leeuwen, also Fairclough has made clear that "the place and role of
discourse in society and culture is a historical variable" (1995: 89). In his view, "discourse practice ensures attention to the historicity of discursive events by showing
both their continuity with the past (their dependence upon given orders of discourse)
and their involvement in making history (their remaking of orders of discourse)"
(1995: 11; see also Fairclough 1992). As our research shows, just as contemporary 'institutions of the state', which, according to Heer and Wodak (2008: 7–8), have an often
neglected significance (especially when they are in power, by means of legislation) in

implementing efficient policies of the so-called *Vergangenheitspolitik*, focused on coping with and solving problems with the (difficult) national past (for instance, by constructing unifying national narratives), the English political elites of the 15–17th centuries practised the so-called *Geschichtspolitik* (see Heer and Wodak 2008: 5–6). It involved re-making history by reformulating, manipulating, and thus functionalizing their nearest or more remote past for specific political ends, usually geared to promote their vested interests, and to gain public approval.

The critical stance employed in this study, in Fairclough's (1995: 97) words, "sets out to make visible through analysis, and to criticize, connections between properties of texts and social processes and relations (ideologies, power relations) which are generally not obvious to people who produce and interpret those texts, and whose effectiveness depends upon this opacity." It treats the discourse of the directive letter (after Miller 1984) as 'social/rhetorical action', which language users accomplish "when they communicate with each other in *social situations* and within *society* and *culture* at large [emphasis in the original]" (van Dijk 1997a: 14; cf. also van Dijk 1997b). This implies that the genre, as a carrier of social action, played a performative role in the LME and EModE periods in that it was a means by which writers recreated and changed the surrounding world by 'doing' things in their socio-cultural space. In this light directive letters represented one type from a myriad of social practices, or (in the Faircloughian sense) 'discourse practices', which altogether constituted the society's 'discourse order', as a network of formative and binding interactive strategies within the group of English gentry in the 15–17th-centuries. As recognizable and meaningful textual arrangements, they largely mediated social activities in Late Middle and Early Modern England, and became part of the community's share of knowledge, which in turn regulated their functioning as viable rhetorical acts of early English political communication (cf. also Okulska 2008).

When it comes to the sphere of politics as examined in this project, it is understood broadly as a heterogeneous macro-domain (see Okulska and Cap this volume) accommodating the life of various social institutions and organizations from a wide range of public fields. They include the crown, parliament, administration, church, and defense, all of which, through their dominant positions and struggles on the political stage, created the country's history in the periods under scrutiny. Epistolary activities in the LME and EModE directive letters studied embrace those forms of social interaction that shaped "the political sphere as a distinct and partially institutionalized area of social life [where] different social groups act[ed] in pursuance of their particular interests, needs, aspirations and values" (Fairclough 2006: 33). In this sense the discourse of the letters can be said to instantiate, produce, and reflect three constitutive dimensions of LME and EModE political culture, i.e. its polity, policy, and politics (cf., e.g., Hodge and Kress 1993; Fairclough 1995; van Dijk 1998; Reisigl 2006). In terms of the first, the research will uncover ways in which the epistolary messages constructed specific forms of LME and EModE public institutions together with their systems, and the way they also navigated mutual relations among them. In terms of the second, it will focus on discourse strategies employed by LME and EModE state officials with the purpose of identifying, managing and solving political problems. In terms of the third, it will discuss professional gambits of running the political contest, i.e. those focused on eliminating rivals and gaining power on the one hand, and those aimed at maintaining stable, mutually supportive relations with political allies on the other. Discursive means, or in Gumperzian terms (1982) 'contextualization cues', through which these aspects of the early English political reality are rendered will be tacked from the perspective of resources representing social action (see van Leeuwen 1995), which critically name, describe, explain and evaluate the social phenomena under discussion. In sum, the analysis of the material from the above-mentioned vantage points will show how directive epistolary exchange in the sphere of early English socio-political contacts developed (both within and across institutional and civil domains) its *cooperative* character, stabilizing the functioning of social structures and fostering the state–society dialectic, and also acquired its *conflictual* nature, accelerating – through imbalance of roles and differentiation of positions – the emergence, growth and fluctuation of political ideas and drives (cf., e.g., Chilton and Schaeffner 2002) in 15–17th-century England.

The sample studied involves altogether 134 letters from the *Helsinki Corpus of English Texts* (1991) and the *Corpus of Early English Correspondence Sampler* (1999), of which 33 (24.6%) represent LME documents, embracing the whole 15th century, and 101 (75.4%) EModE letters, covering the time span from the beginning of the 16th to the end of the 17th century.

3.   Constructing the early English political reality through directive epistolary discourse

The interactive nature of the LME and EModE directive letters under scrutiny encodes many institutional practices from the socio-political life of the time, which shaped the genre's structure across the periods, and which were themselves largely constituted by the discourse of letter writing. Discursive realizations of these actions are observable in rhetorical moves that compose body parts of the directive epistles. The stages include *enablement* (with internal orientation, facilitation and specification), assigning a general persuasive role to the message; *command*, representing a core directive that motivates the whole text (for directive speech acts see also Janoschka this volume); and *legitimization*, carrying positive and negative incentives behind letter writing (see Okulska 2008). The social practices that were transmitted and constituted by means of the letters' macro-structures involved building by the informants relations of similarity and/or difference with their addressees, in order to compel, often in manipulative ways, the recipients to perform desired activities. Constructing the relations of similarity consisted in demonstrating in-group solidarity with readers with an aim to attain particular objectives. Fostering the relations of difference, in turn, involved demonstrating positions of institutional (and social) hierarchy, which made it easier for the senders to dominate or influence the recipients, and coerce them into carrying out requested tasks. Speaking from these positions also legitimized the writers to implement specific rank-appropriate directives through which they could further and realize their communicative goals.

3.1   Building relations of similarity and difference

The gambit of structuring similarity bonds in the LME and EModE political life centers in the research material on implementing the 'us vs. others' approach (cf. the IDC-ODC divide in Cap this volume) to the interacting parties, mainly in the letter's orientation. It is deployed by the authors with an aim to build alliance with their interlocutors in struggles against their common political opponents. Example (1) below illustrates a directive issued by Edward IV to Thomas Stonor, where the King commands his recipient to support him in putting down the anti-royal rebellion of 1470 by the Duke of Warwick and the Earl of Clarence.

(1)   <Q STO 1470 EDWARD4>
   [\112. LETTERS OF PRIVY SEAL TO THOMAS STONOR\] }]
   ...*Letting you wit* +tat **our Traitours and Rebelles** +te Duc of Clarence and Therl of Warrewik, which daily labour +te weyes moyens at +**teir power of our final destruccion, and** +te subversion of this owre Realme and +te comon wele of +te same, been fledde westwardes: Whome **we wol folowe and pursue with our Ooste with al diligence possible, and let and represse** +**teir fals and traiteroux purpose** and entent **with Goddes grace**.

The function of the orientation move is to establish in-group solidarity between the interlocutors, who are portrayed as allies fighting against the same enemy. The author constructs the sense of community with the recipient through the inclusive indexicals *we* and *our*, and at the same time polarizes their positions with those of their adversaries by the contrasting *us–them* oppositions throughout the whole stage. This contrast is additionally emphasized in negatively marked evaluative comments, with a heavy load of pejoratively skewed third party-oriented attitudinal phrases, such as *Traitours and Rebelles; +teir power of our final destruccion; subversion of this owre Realme; +teir fals and traiteroux purpose...*, which are juxtaposed with positively marked interlocutors-directed formulae, such as *we wol folowe and pursue with our Ooste with al diligence possible, and let and represse....* The latter expression is a viable rhetorical device in the move due to fact that it, first, contains interactant-empowering boosters (i.e. *folowe; pursue ... with al diligence possible; represse*) and, second, a hope-imbuing invocation to God (i.e. *with Goddes grace*), both these tools equipping the stage with a strong persuasive force. The phrases' final position in the unit not only enhances the orientation's meaning, but also shifts some of its potential to the subsequent command, thus complementing its argumentative value. This generally provides evidence for the persuasive role of discourse schemata that are different from strictly logical argumentation (see also de Fina 2006: 367).

However, more than relations of similarity the directive letter constitutes (and is itself constituted by) relations of difference, which have always dominated public life. They are established by exposing (mainly in the stage of enablement) power inequalities and social distance between interlocutors, and by evaluating in contrastive ways (both in the letter's enablement and legitimization) writers' and readers' different situations or positions. The former strategy is particularly manifest in royal correspondence, and it is used by rulers as a medium to demonstrate superiority over their subjects. Example (2) below illustrates how a king exacts through the directive letter a delivery of provisions for the court by London citizens.

(2)   <N LET TO CITIZENS>
[} [\KING HENRY THE EIGHTH TO THE CITIZENS OF LONDON, ON THEIR NEGLECTING TO PROVIDE HORSES FOR THE CARRIAGE OF HIS WINES AND PROVISIONS.\] }]
...*Signifieng unto you* it is shewed unto **us** that albeit **our** welbiloved servant Edward Vaux, oon of the purveyors of **our** wynes, hath been with you sundry tymes **in our name to cause provision to be made for cariage of our wynes** from that **our** Citie of London, for th'expenses of **our** Household, into these parties: yet neverthelesse **ye have litle regarded the said provision**, as it is sayed, whereby **we** be destitute of suche wynes as **we** wold have here: of the which **your demeanor herin we cannot a litle mervaile**: wherfor we advertise you of the same, ...

In the orientation move, isolated from the surrounding co-text by the stage transition formulae *Signifieng unto you* and *we advertise you of the same* (cf. also, e.g., 1 above and 3, 4 below), Henry VIII constructs the position of superiority and distance through the 'I vs. you' approach to his recipients. It is realized, first, through the *we/us/our–ye/your* oppositions, which imply the addressees' out-group membership, and, second, through the discourse marker *in our name*, which invokes the sender's institutional rank, both enhancing the atmosphere of interpersonal distance. The sense of social hierarchy is dynamically produced through author-oriented discourse, with the prevalent 1st person plural indexicals, as well as through evaluative speech acts of power and dominance. They rebuke the readers for negligence of their duties with respect to the Crown (*ye have litle regarded the said provision*), and express the King's dissatisfaction with his subjects' approach to royal orders (*your demeanor herin we cannot a litle mervaile*). The seriousness of tone and the author's isolation are underlined by such contextualization cues as nominalizations (e.g., *provision, cariage*) and impersonal structures (e.g., *to cause provision to be made for cariage*), the passive constructions and infinitival phrases in the latter additionally emphasizing the message's formality.

The persuasive character of orientation and the hierarchical structure of social relations that it textually establishes are also transferred through the authors' references to institutional procedures, which manifest their authority, and license their overall directive stance. In her letter to Marquis of Northampton, Queen Jane (called also Nine Days' Queen) legitimizes her position as Queen of England by mentioning a number of institutional procedures, by which she tries to demonstrate that she performs her rank as a rightful ruler.[1] She additionally quotes her relations with prominent state officials, with respect to whom she figures herself as an empress:

(3) <Q OR2 1553 JGREY>

[} [\LETTER CLXXVII. THE LADY JANE GRAY, AS QUEEN, TO THE MARQUIS OF NORTHAMPTON, LIEUTENANT OF THE COUNTY OF SURREY.\] }]

...advertising the same that where **yt hath pleased Almighty God** *to call to his mercie out of this life our derest Cousen the King your late Sovereigne Lorde, by reason wherof ande suche Ordenances as the said late King did establishe in his lief tyme for the securitie and welthe of this Realme,* **we are enterid into our rightfull possession of this Kingdome, as by the last Will of our said derest Cousen,** *our late progenitor, and other severall instruments to that effect* **signed with his own hande and sealed with the grete Seale of this Realme in his own presence,** *wherunto the Nobles of this realme for the most parte and all our Counsaill and Judges, with the Mayor and Aldermen of our Cytie of London, and dyvers other grave personages of this our Realme of England, have also subscribed there names, as by the same Will and Instrument it maye more evidently and plainly apere;* **We therfore doo You to understand,** *that* **by th'ordenance and sufferaunce of the hevenly Lord and King, and by th'assent and consent of our said Nobles and Counsellors,** *and others before specifyed,* **We doo this daye make our enterye into our Towre of London as rightfull Quene of this realme;** *and* **have accordingly sett furthe our proclamacions to all our loving subjects gyvenge them therby to understande their duties and allegeaunce which they now of right owe unto us**

The passage accentuates the Queen's lawful (in her view) ascension to the throne through the explicit reference to her cousin's (Edward VI) last will, *signed,* as she reports, *with his own hande and sealed with the grete Seale of this Realme in his own presence,* and through the remark that she enters the Tower of London as *rightfull Quene of this realme.* This creates an impression of the author's power, which is additionally pronounced in the statement that she has obtained the authority by *th'ordenance and sufferaunce of the hevenly Lord and King, and by th'assent and consent of our said Nobles and Counsellors.*

---

1.   Lady Jane Grey's claim to the English throne is still a controversial matter among historians. It was raised as a consequence of the last will of her cousin, King Edward VI, the ruling son of Henry VIII (and a younger half-brother of Henry's two daughters, Mary I and Elizabeth I). On his deathbed, Edward issued a "Devise for the Succession" (1553), in which he indicated Jane as his heiress. He chose Jane in place of Mary, the presumed successor, in order to prevent England from returning to Catholicism under the latter. By naming Jane, Edward overruled Henry VIII's last will ("Third Succession Act", 1543), in which his father had re-established Mary and Elizabeth (previously declared by him illegitimate) in the line of succession behind Edward. In this way Edward deprived his sisters of the right to the throne, which upon his death became a bone of contention between Jane and her two cousins.

The occurrence of multiple invocations to God within the stage (including also the one at its beginning, i.e., *yt hath pleased Almighty God*) points to their role as relevant persuasive means in official correspondence at that time. In the enablement discourse of Jane's epistle these devices are additionally represented by emphatic verbal expressions (such as *We therfore doo You to understand...* and *We doo this daye make our enterye...*) as well as by imperative style, evident especially in the move-final account of the Monarch's proclamations, obliging the English subjects to loyalty to her as their queen.

Similar strategies are also deployed in 17th-century royal letters, which can be illustrated, for instance, by the correspondence of King Charles II. In his letter to the Earl of Essex (4 below), the King dynamically constructs his superior rank through discursive references to others in power and descriptions of historically sanctioned royal procedures, which enables him to perform a dominant position in hierarchical relations with state officials.

(4)   [} [\LXXVIII CHARLES R. TO THE EARL OF ESSEX 1673.\] }]
*<u>Whereas</u> **Wee were pleased** to referre the examination of the late difference arisen in the Corporae~on of Our City of Dublin in that Our Kingdome, about the Election of Com~on Councell men out of the severall Companies, to the Com~ittee of Our Privy Councill for the affaires of Ireland, and **they having reported their opinion thereupon to us**, and **Wee considered & approved of the same**, Wee have thought fit in pursuance thereof **to signify to you Our Pleasure** that **the last choice made by the Lord Mayor of that Our Citty** of the compleate number of Com~on Counsell men all at once, leaving out the ten or eleven Roman Catholiques that were chosen at the first choice, **shall stand and be confirmed**...*

In the letter's orientation the author wields his authority by depicting the work of governmental offices and his own role in the network of state administrative bodies. By evaluating positively the dealings of the Privy Council (in the attitudinal phrases *Wee were pleased* and *to signify to you Our Pleasure*), he presents the Council as an advisory unit (*they having reported their opinion thereupon to us*) which assists him in taking important decisions (*Wee considered & approved of the same; the last choice ... shall stand and be confirmed...*). In this way, he portrays himself as a sovereign who carries out the process of social action by forging through the discourse of his epistle a hierarchical structure of interpersonal ties in official life.

As the evidence shows, the practice of building relations of difference in the public domain is a factor structuring the directive letter also in the correspondence by gentry ranks other than royalty. Examples (5) and (6) below, representing letters of polite requests respectively in interaction–down and –up formats, demonstrate how the authors from the group of clergy produce the stage of the letter's orientation by evaluating contrastively their own and their readers' situations. The contrastive self-portrayals that the writers create respectively revert and highlight their traditional power roles. In (5), for instance, Cardinal Thomas Wolsey, who was in a downfall in his declining years, asks Secretary Stephen Gardener for help to improve his life conditions:

(5) <Q OR2 1520S? TWOLSEY>
     [} [\LETTER CIV. CARDINAL WOLSEY TO DR. STEPHEN GARDENER.\] }]
     *... **I can take no reste**; nat for any vayne fere, but onely for **the miserabli condy-**
     cion that I am presently yn, and lyclyhod to contynue in the same onles that ye,
     in whom ys myn assuryd truste, do help and releve me therein; for fyrst con-
     tynuyng here in thys moweste and corrupt eyer, beyng enteryd in to the passyon
     of the dropsy, (\cum prostratione appetitus, et continuo insompnus\), **I cannat**
     lyve; wherfor of necessyte **I muste be removyd** to summe other dryer eyer and
     place, wher I may have comodyte of Physycyans. Secondly havyng but Yorke,
     wych ys now decayd by viijC.=li= by the yeere **I can nat tell how to lyve and**
     kepe the poore nombyr of folks wych I nowe have; my howsys ther be in decay,
     and of every thyng mete for howsold onprovidyd and furnyshyd. **I have non ap-**
     parell for my howsys ther, nor money to bryng me thether, nor to lyve with tyl*
     the propysse tyme of the year shal come to remove thither.

     Thes thyngs consyderyd, M=r=. Secretary, **must nedys make me in agony**
     and hevynes; myn age therwith and sycknes consyderyd.

     Alas M=r=. Secretary, ye with other my lordys shewyd me that I shuld otherw-
     yse be furnyshyd, and seyn unto. Ye knowe in your lernyng and consyens
     whetherr I shuld forfit my spiritualties of Wynchester or no. Alas the qualytes
     *of myn offencys consyderyd, **with the gret punisshement and losse of goodes***
     ***that I have sustignyd**, owt to move petyfull hertys. And the moste nobyl Kyng, to*
     *whom yf yt wold please yow of **your cherytabli goodnes** to shew the premyses*
     *aftyr **your accustomable wysdom and dexteryte**, yt ys nat to be dowettyd but*
     hys Hyhnes wold have consyderacon and compassion, aggmentyng my lyvyng,
     and appoyntyng such thyngs as shuld be convenyent for my furniture;

     wych to do shalbe to the Kyngs high honer, **meryte, and discharge of consy-**
     ens; and **to yow gret praysse** for the bryngyng of the same to passe for your
     olde brynger up and lovyng frende. **Thys kyndnes exibite from the Kyngs**
     Hyghnes shal prolong my lyff for sum lytyl whyl, thow yt shall nat be long; **by**
     the meane wherof hys Grace shal take profygtt, and by my deth non.

In the letter's orientation (italicized), interwoven with a dipartite legitimization (standard font), the author contrasts his poor life situation with the powerful position of his
addressee. In the move's initial section he presents the reader with negative reasons
motivating the request, formulated in expressions such as, e.g., *I can take no reste; the*
miserabli condycion that I am presently yn; I cannat lyve; I muste be removyd; I can nat
tell how to lyve and kepe the poore nombyr of folks wych I nowe have; my howsys ther be
in decay; I have non apparell for my howsys ther, nor money. They altogether create a
picture of the Cardinal's tragic financial and health conditions, whose role is to coerce
Gardiner into following Wolsey's suggestions, and discussing his matters with the
King. The stage's second component complements the negative arguments with a flat-
tering account of the Secretary's merits and virtues (e.g., *ye with other my lordys shewyd*

me; *Ye knowe in your lernyng and consyens*; *your cherytabli goodness*; *your accustomable wysdom and dexteryte*), which are depicted as his qualifications as a competent negotiator. The move prepares the reader for the request proper (in the ensuing command) by providing additional details of Wolsey's downfall (e.g., *that I shuld otherwyse be furnyshyd, and seyn unto*; *whetherr I shuld forfit my spiritualties of Wynchester or no.*; *the gret punisshement and losse of goodes that I have sustignyd*), all strengthening the force of the writer's argumentation (*yt ys nat to be dowettyd but hys Hyhnes wold have consyderacon and compassion, aggmentyng my lyvyng, and appoyntyng such thyngs as shuld be convenyent for my furniture*). The Cardinal's humility is a trigger of discourse-mediated social action, which reconfigures the traditional order of superior–inferior interaction, leaving its traces in the letter's macro-structural composition.

A similar strategy of shaping relations of difference through contrasting discourse is exploited in (6) below, where a priest, who confesses guilt about having got married, uses orientation to provide reasons for his request to Lord Cromwell for mediation in the problem of his unlawful relationship with a woman:

(6)   <Q OR2 1530S? JFOSTER>
     [} [\LETTER CXLI. JOHN FOSTER TO LORD CROMWELL.\] }]
     ...nede compellythe me to wrytt. *Thys last Lentt I dyd no lesse then wrytt, and also to your presence I dyd approche, suyng for your lordschyppys gracious servyce; but now my sute ys muche other, for* **my dysfortune hathe byn to have conceyvyd untruly Goddys worde, and not only with yntellectyon to have thought yt, but exteryally and really I have fulfyllyd the same**; *for I, as then beyng a preste, have accompleschyd maryage*; **nothyng pretendyng but as an obedyentt subyect.**

     For yf the Kyngys Grace could have founde yt lawfull that prestys mught have byn maryd, **they wold have byn to the Crowne dubbyll and dubbyll faythefull**, furst **in love**, secondly **for fere** that the Bysshope of Rome schuld sette yn hys power unto ther desolacyon.

In the initial phase of the move he speaks critically about himself, and produces a guilt-ridden self-disclosure (*my dysfortune hathe byn to have conceyvyd untruly Goddys worde, and not only with yntellectyon to have thought yt, but exteryally and really I have fulfyllyd the same*), which in the stage closing is finally balanced by his positive self-evaluation (*nothyng pretendyng but as an obedyentt subyect*). Such a tactic justifies the author's decision to issue a request for intercession, locating him in a subordinate position with respect to the addressee. This is where the letter's discourse performs and itself becomes social action, recorded in the texture of the epistolary move. The self-blame stance that the encoder adopts invokes the peculiar capacity, observed by Goffman (1967: 21–22), to accomplish apology by verbalizing explicitly the fault committed. Naming overtly the act of offence, and assigning it to oneself as a third party is paradoxically an efficient manipulative strategy aimed to protect the social sinner against condemnation by averting the patron's negative emotions and arousing in him mercy or (even) charity (see also Whigham 1981: 872).

The coincidence of the contrasting rhetoric, evident in both (5) and (6) above, of self-depreciation and abnegation on the one hand, and of self-/other-praise and one's/ other's virtue on the other, instantiates the epideictic oratory of ceremonial display (see, e.g., Whigham 1981: 866), which generally characterized letters of supplication in Tudor times. A similar tone was often maintained in the move supporting orientation, i.e. legitimization, which additionally facilitated the senders' persuasive endeavors. It combined mosaics of positive and negative incentives that were used to motivate the addressees to carry out expected actions. In (5) above, for example, the first part of legitimization amplifies negative consequences of the author's poor life situation (*Thes thyngs consyderyd ... must nedys make me in agony and hevynes*), whereas its second element underlines benefits of fulfilling the request, first, to the King (*wych to do shalbe to the Kyngs high honer, meryte, and discharge of consyens; by the meane wherof hys Grace shal take profygtt, and by my deth non*), second, to the addressee (*to yow gret praysse*), and, third, to the writer himself (*Thys kyndnes exibite from the Kyngs Hyghnes shal prolong my lyff*). Similarly, the legitimization in (6) expresses both positive and negative incentives in an act of gratitude to the third party, i.e. the Crown (*they wold have byn to the Crowne dubbyll and dubbyll faythefull*), which additionally voices the subject's declaration of loyalty to the King, motivated by his love of the monarch on the one hand (positive incentive), and by fear of the Pope on the other (negative incentive).

As the research material shows, similar mechanisms work in legitimization stages of other gentry letters, both royal and non-royal, and in all formats of interactional exchange. They rest upon positive or negative remarks in reference to topics raised, and accentuate differences in power between the interacting parties, which makes them additional persuasive means that can influence readers' decisions. What follows from it is that the discourse of both enablement and legitimization encodes processes of building horizontal and vertical links in the social networks of 15–17th-century England. It is thus a bearer of social action, archived in the moves' semanto-pragmatic structures, motivated by the interlocutors' rhetorical purposes and communicative intentions in the context of specific cultural and situational conditions. The human attitudes, emotions and behaviors that the stages carry indicate that their shape is a textual corollary of social relations and interactive needs in the times under scrutiny.

3.2 Reconfiguring the political world through epistolary directives: The discourse of command as social action

As has already been suggested, more explicitly than in enablement and legitimization, the process of social action is reflected in the command stage, as the letter's pivotal move carrying the greatest weight of imposition of all the message's internal components. Its performative role can be observed in the effects that it brings for the interacting parties as well as for the surrounding world. The directive speech acts that command transmits modify the social order by changing people's ranks in the institutional milieu, and assigning them professional duties and tasks that affect the course of public life.

The process of social action as documented in the command move is most distinct in royal correspondence, which exposes the greatest power differential between the interacting parties. Its traces can be observed, for instance, in exercising by rulers their institutional right to nominate subjects for important positions in the state administration. Such a move is illustrated, for example, in (7) below, where King Richard III employs the command stage to appoint Bishop of St. David to a new position in the Church. To sanction this choice the King makes an explicit reference to his royal authority (*by auctoritie of oure licence royal*), and additionally supports his argumentation by enumerating a number of the Bishop's attributes (*laudable merites, highe vertues, and profounde cunnyng; his notable desertes, contynued trouthe, and feithful services to us*) which in his view make the clergyman the best candidate for the post.

> (7)   <Q RER 1484 RICHARD3>
> [} [\XXIX.\] }] [^TO THE DEAN AND CHAPTER OF SALISBURY^]
> We, havyng tendre regarde aswele unto the **laudable merites, highe vertues, and profounde cunnyng**, that the righte reverend fader in God ... is **notarily knowen to be of**, as unto othre **his notable desertes, contynued trouthe, and feithful services to us** in sundry wises doon to our singler pleasire, **desire and hertly pray** you that in your said eleccion ye wol have him to the said preemynence and pastoralle dignitie before alle othre especially recommended and preferred.

Similar administrative procedures are illustrated in (8), which documents the royal practice of assigning a state official the role of a monarch's supporter:

> (8)   <Q OR2 1553 JGREY>
> [} [\LETTER CLXXVII. THE LADY JANE GRAY, AS QUEEN, TO THE MARQUIS OF NORTHAMPTON, LIEUTENANT OF THE COUNTY OF SURREY.\] }]
> ...as more amplie by the same you shall briefly perceyve and understand; nothing doubting, right trustie and right welbeloued cosen, but **that you will indever yourself in all things to the uttermost of your powre, not only to defend our just title, but also assist us in our rightfull possession of this kingdome,** ...

In the command sent to the Marquis of Northampton, Queen Jane compels him *not only to defend*, as she argues, her *title*, but also to assist her in a *rightfull possession of this kingdome*. The act of the epistolary directive makes the Lieutenant of the County of Surrey Jane Grey's counselor and defender, thus affecting 16th-century English reality in that it exerts some influence directly on the course of the Queen's reign and, in some way, on the history of the country.

However, the majority of commands in the royal letters examined recreate the LME and EModE socio-political reality through direct orders issued to implement royal policies. Example (9) below shows how King Henry VII launches, through the discourse of the move, preparations for war against Margaret of Burgundy, who became his enemy by recognizing officially one of his rivals, Perkin Warbeck, as a pretender to the English throne.

(9) <Q OR1 1495? HENRY7>
     [LETTER XI. KING HENRY THE VII. TO SIR GILBERT TALBOT, KNIGHT]
     We therfor ... **wol and desire** you that preairing on horsbak, defensibly arraied, four score personnes, wherof we **desire** you to make asmany speres with their custrelles and di. lances wele horsed as ye can furnisshe, and the emaynder to bee archers and billes, **ye bee thoroughly appointed** and redy to comme upon a day warnyng for to do us service of warre in this caas. ... **We praye** you herein ye wol make suche delegens as that ye be redy with your said nombre to come unto us uppon any our sodein warnyng.

In the command of his letter, Henry compels the knight Gilbert Talbot to settle down to the military action against his political opponent. The multiple directives that he uses altogether produce a textual-experiential icon of the planned undertaking (cf. Okulska 2006: 62–68). On the one hand, the stage's imperative discourse (transmitted in the deontic modals *wol and desire*, the subjunctive *ye bee thoroughly appointed...*, and the volitional *We praye...*) encodes a cultural rut of historically grounded communication of an emperor (viz. social superior) with his subordinate, and on the other, it mediates a live process of constructing by the monarch relations of hierarchy and dominance with one of his subjects. In this way it amalgamates culturally sanctioned patterns of social behavior with situationally driven patterns of establishing specific interpersonal relations in the context of a particular interactive event.

The following excerpts (10–12) indicate that command was a relevant epistolary unit that enabled to carry out similar undertakings in the practice of social life in the LME and EModE times:

(10) <Q STO 1470 EDWARD4>
     [} [\112. LETTERS OF PRIVY SEAL TO THOMAS STONOR\] }]
     we wol and straitely charge you +tat immediatly after +te sight of +ties owre lettres ye arredie you, with such a fellasship on horssebak in defensible arraye as ye goodly can make, to come unto us...

(11) [} [\LXXVIII CHARLES R. TO THE EARL OF ESSEX, 1673.\] }]
     Wee doe hereby require and direct you to doe **all** things, and give **all** necessary Orders for the **speedy** settling of this affaire **accordingly**.

(12) <N LET TO CITIZENS>
     [} [\KING HENRY THE EIGHTH TO THE CITIZENS OF LONDON, ON THEIR NEGLECTING TO PROVIDE HORSES FOR THE CARRIAGE OF HIS WINES AND PROVISIONS.\] }]
     ye will **effectually** endevoir yourself for the **qwyk** expedicion therof...

Accordingly, in (10) the command is a textual carrier of Edward IV's order to support the King in stopping an anti-royal plot, in (11) it transmits Charles II's requirement to bring to an end elections for the Committee of the Privy Council, and in (12) it performs Henry VIII's directive to arrange the aforementioned (in 2 above) delivery of provisions to the royal court. The speech acts that the move conveys all reproduce the reality in that they, first, influence (and in certain cases change) the course of history (as, e.g., in 9 and 10), second, set new orders in socio-political space (as, e.g., in 11), and, third, verify old and facilitate new patterns of people's behavior in public life (as, e.g., in 12). By modifying the existing social relations and organizing new social arrangements they perform social action, which, as the evidence shows, is realized through the language of epistolary exchange, as a kind of discourse practice in the institutional (viz. political) world.

Finally, as the most persuasive stage in the structure of the directive letter, command plays a vital role also in non-royal epistolary texts of the LME and EModE periods. Their commands, apart from the speech acts of orders, which function in them in a similar way to those in royal correspondence, may be realized by various kinds of (direct or indirect) requests, assertions or suggestions. Their linguistic form depends on, *inter alia*, formats of interactional exchange, distance between interlocutors, their positions in social hierarchy, and topics raised. Examples (13–15) provide a sample of commands in directive letters by higher-ranking representatives of English gentry:

(13)   <Q OR2 1520S? TWOLSEY>
[} [\LETTER CIV. CARDINAL WOLSEY TO DR. STEPHEN GARDENER.\] }]
I pray you **at the reverens of God** to help, that exspedicion be usyd in my presents...
... do help and releve me therein;...
I beseche yow therfor, movyd with pity and compassyon, **soker me** in thys my calamyti, and **to your power, wych I do knowe ys gret, releve me**...

(14)   <Q OR2 1530S JROCHEFORD>
[} [\LETTER CXXIV. LADY ROCHEFORD TO SECRETARY CROMWELL.\] }]
...**prayng youe**, after your accustemyd gentyll maner to all them that be in suche lamentabull case as I ame in, to be meane to the Kyngs gracious Hyghnes for me for suche power stuffe and plate as my husbonde had, **whome God pardon**; that **of hys gracyous and mere lyberalyte I may have hyt to helpe me to my power lyvyng,**

(15)   [} [\XIX. THE EARL OF DANBY TO THE EARL OF ESSEX.\] }]
London 1st June 1675
I...concurre with you yt itt would be of great use to have yr Excellency here to conferr with his Ma=tie= upon those important matters mentioned therein.

The commands in (13) and (14) are rendered as requests for help in the up–down and down–up interaction formats, respectively, whereas the one in (15) is represented by a polite suggestion in the interaction–equal paradigm. They all perform social action by launching communicative processes aimed to change or improve the authors' situations. Hence, the requests in (13) and (14) are geared to better the writers' lot, the former corresponding to the already-mentioned (in 5 above) Cardinal Wolsey's downfall, and the latter illustrating a parallel situation of a noble woman caused by dubious dealings of her husband. In turn, the purpose of the suggestion in (15) is to encourage the Earl of Essex to take part in negotiations with the King. Due to the fact that the moves represent speech acts threatening the recipients' negative faces, they are often phrased in indirect style, which reduces their weight of imposition. This is especially noticeable in (15), where equality of the interlocutors' ranks and social distance between them are projected onto the hedge *I...concurre with you yt itt would be of great use to have yr Excellency here*, which in a polite way invites the reader to perform a desired activity (for hedging in contemporary political discourse see Fraser this volume).

However, more than on semantic implicitness, the discourse of commands (in forms of both requests and orders) rests on stylistic directness, which strengthens their overall illocutionary force. As examples (7–14) demonstrate, rhetorical devices that amplify the moves' argumentative meanings include volitional verb phrases, such as, e.g., *desire and **hertly** pray* (7), *we wol and **straitely** charge* (10), *wee **doe** hereby require and direct you* (11), *I beseche yow* (13), *prayng youe* (14), which are additionally emphasized by adverbial, adjectival, emphatic verbal, or clausal boosters (see esp. 9, 11, 12, 13). The devices moreover involve bold imperatives, such as, e.g., *soker me; releve me* (13), which can sometimes be accompanied by invocations to God, such as those in (13, 14) – *at the reverens of God; whome God pardon*, or maximizing expressions, such as those in (8) – *to the uttermost of your powre* or in (11) – *all*. The discourse-shaping role of such tools and the command's superordinate status in the letter's global structure make the text a directive macro-speech act (cf. van Dijk 1997a: 15), with its main communicative function gravitating to the dominant argumentative stage. In the final set of the examples quoted (13–15), the move's purpose, similar to the remaining cases, is to transmit the process of social action, which transforms, as in (13, 14), or reinforces, as in (15), the individuals' positions in the social world. This may speak in favor of the claim that the structure of command in particular, and of the directive letter in general, is a generic consequence of discourse-mediated practices of organizing the sphere of institutional life in LME and EModE times.

4.   Conclusions

The way 15–17th-century political correspondence carries mechanisms, and itself shapes the nature of interpersonal interaction in various professional domains of Late Middle and Early Modern England unveils the role of letter writing as discourse practice in the periods under investigation. As the research material shows, one of its modes is the directive letter, whose socially constitutive function can be observed both in the modifications that it introduced to the existing forms of the LME and EModE public life, and in the new arrangements that it established in the realm of social relations at that time. The discursive reproductions of the early English political world are enacted in the texts studied through the use of alliance-building and/or contrast-marking strategies, which are employed by the writers to construct most efficient interactive conditions for enforcing their own perspectives and furthering individual policies and aims. The new political installments are also created by discourse-mediated reformulations of people's professional activities, duties and tasks, causing changes in their ranks and positions, which in turn remodel structures of the early English institutions. The transitions that the directive epistolary genre generally brought to the LME and EModE extra-linguistic reality point to processes of social action that it transferred in these periods of English history. It has been demonstrated that the action's different aspects are managed by the letter's internal moves, whose recurrent linguistic patterns reflect culturally rooted codes of behavior, and whose contextually changing rhetorical structures dynamically realize situationally motivated authorial goals.

References

Akar, Didar and Louhiala-Salminen, Leena. 1999. "Towards a new genre: A comparative study of business faxes." In *Writing Business: Genres, Media and Discourses*, Francesca Bargiela-Chiappini and Catherine Nickerson (eds), 227–254. Harlow: Longman.

Andrews, Alexander. 1967. *The History of British Journalism*. London: Haskell House.

Austin, Frances. 2000. "Letter writing in a Cornish community in the 1790s." In *Letter Writing as a Social Practice*, David Barton and Nigel Hall (eds), 43–61. Amsterdam/Philadelphia: John Benjamins.

—. 2004. "Heaving this importunity: The survival of opening formulas in letters in the eighteenth and nineteenth centuries." *Historical Sociolinguistics and Sociohistorical Linguistics* 4. Retrieved July 31, 2009 from http://www.let.leidenuniv.nl/hsl_shl/heaving_this_importunity.htm

Bargiela-Chiappini, Francesca and Nickerson, Catherine (eds). 1999. *Writing Business: Genres, Media and Discourses*. Harlow: Longman.

Barton, David and Hall, Nigel. 2000. "Introduction." In *Writing Business: Genres, Media and Discourses*, David Barton and Nigel Hall (eds), 1–14. Harlow: Longman.

Bazerman, Charles. 1997. "Performatives constituting value: The case of patents." In *The Construction of Professional Discourse*, Britt-Louise Gunnarson, Per Linell and Bengt Nordberg (eds), 42–53. London: Longman.

—. 2000. "Letters and the social grounding of differentiated genres." In *Letter Writing as a Social Practice*, David Barton and Nigel Hall (eds), 15–29. Amsterdam/Philadelphia: John Benjamins.

Berger, Peter and Luckman, Thomas. 1967. *The Social Construction of Reality*. New York: Doubleday.

Bhatia, Vijay K. 1993. *Analysing Genre. Language Use in Professional Settings*. London: Longman.

—. 2005. "Interdiscursivity in business letters." In *Genre Variation in Business Letters*, Paul Gillaerts and Maurizio Gotti (eds), 31–54. Bern: Peter Lang.

Burr, Vivien. 1995. *An Introduction to Social Constructionism*. London: Routledge.

Chilton, Paul and Schaeffner, Christina (eds). 2002. *Politics as Text and Talk: Analytical Approaches to Political Discourse*. Amsterdam: John Benjamins.

de Fina, Anna. 2006. "Group identity, narrative and self-representations." In *Discourse and Identity*, Anna de Fina, Deborah Schiffrin and Michael Bamberg (eds), 351–375. Cambridge: Cambridge University Press.

del Lungo Camiciotti, Gabriela. 2005. "'I perceive, my dear friend, by your letter of the 20th inst. That you are decided on entering upon the career of commerce': Nineteenth century business correspondence." In *Genre Variation in Business Letters*, Paul Gillaerts and Maurizio Gotti (eds), 125–146. Bern: Peter Lang.

—. 2006a. "Conduct yourself towards all persons on every occasion with civility and in a wise and prudent manner; this will render you esteemed': Stance features in nineteenth-century business letters." In *Business and Official Correspondence: Historical Investigations*, Marina Dossena and Susan Fitzmaurice (eds), 153–151. Bern: Peter Lang.

—. 2006b. "'From 'Your obedient humble servants' to 'Yours faithfully': The negotiation of professional roles in the commercial correspondence of the secondhalf of the nineteenth century." In *Diachronic Perspectives on Domain-specific English*, Marina Dossena and Irma Taavitsainen (eds), 153–172. Bern: Peter Lang.

Dossena, Marina. 2006a. "Stance and authority in nineteenth-century bank correspondence – A case study." In *Business and Official Correspondence: Historical Investigations*, Marina Dossena and Susan Fitzmaurice (eds), 175–192. Bern: Peter Lang.

—. 2006b. "Forms of self-representation in nineteenth-century business letters." In *Diachronic Perspectives on Domain-specific English*, Marina Dossena and Irma Taavitsainen (eds), 173–190. Bern: Peter Lang.

Dury, Richard. 2006. „A Corpus of Nineteenth-century Business Correspondence: Methodology and transcription." In *Business and Official Correspondence: Historical Investigations*, Marina Dossena and Susan Fitzmaurice (eds), 193–205. Bern: Peter Lang.

Ehlich, Konrad. 1989. "Über den Faschismus sprechen – Analyse und Diskurs." In *Sprache im Faschismus*, Konrad Ehlich (ed.), 7–34. Frankfurt am Main: Suhrkamp.

Fairclough, Norman. 1989. *Language and Power*. London: Longman.

—. 1992. *Discourse and Social Change*. Malden, MA: Blackwell.

—. 1995. *Critical Discourse Analysis. The Critical Study of Language*. London: Longman.

—. 2006. "Genres in political linguistics." In *Encyclopedia of Language and Linguistics, Vol. 5*, Keith Brown (ed.), 32–38. Amsterdam: Elsevier.

Fitzmaurice, Susan M. 2006. "Diplomatic business: Information, power, and persuasion in Late Modern English diplomatic correspondence." In *Business and Official Correspondence: Historical Investigations*, Marina Dossena and Susan Fitzmaurice (eds), 77–106. Bern: Peter Lang.

Fowler, Roger. 1996. "On critical linguistics." In *Texts and Practice. Readings in Critical Discourse Analysis*, Carmen Rosa Caldas-Coulthard and Malcolm Coulthard (eds), 3–14. London and New York: Routledge.

Fremantle, Anne. 1956. *The Papal Encyclicals in their Historical Context*. New York: G.P. Putnam's.

Frisinger, Howard, H. 1977. *The History of Meteorology to 1800*. New York: Science History Publications.

Fritz, Gerd. 2001. "Text types in a new medium. The first newspapers (1609)." *Journal of Historical Pragmatics* 2 (1): 69–83.

Gillaerts, Paul and Gotti, Maurizio (eds). 2005. *Genre Variation in Business Letters*. Bern: Peter Lang.

Geluykens, Ronald and Kraft, Bettina (eds). 2008. *Institutional Discourse in Cross-cultural Contexts*. München: Lincom.

Geluykens, Ronald and Pelsmaekers, Katja (eds). 1999. *Discourse in Professional Contexts*. München: Lincom.

Goffman, Erving. 1967. *Interaction Ritual*. New York: Anchor Books.

Gotti, Maurizio. 2005. "Disseminating early modern science: Specialised news discourse in *The Philosophical Transactions*." In *News Discourse in Early Modern Britain*, Nicholas Brownlees (ed.), 41–70. Bern: Peter Lang.

—. 2006. "Communal correspondence in Early Modern English: The *Philosophical Transactions* Network." In *Business and Official Correspondence: Historical Investigations*, Marina Dossena and Susan Fitzmaurice (eds), 17–46. Bern: Peter Lang.

Gumperz, John, J. 1982. *Discourse Strategies*. Cambridge: CUP.

Hall, Nigel. 2000. "The materiality of letter writing: A nineteenth century perspective." In *Letter Writing as a Social Practice,* David Barton and Nigel Hall (eds), 83–108. Amsterdam/Philadelphia: John Benjamins.

Harris, William. 1989. *Ancient Literacy*. Cambridge, MA: Harvard University Press.

Heer, Hannes and Wodak, Ruth. 2008. "Introduction: Collective memory, national narratives and the politics of the past." In *The Discursive Construction of History. Remembering the Wehrmacht's War of Annihilation*, Heer, Hannes, Manoschek, Walter, Pollak, Alexander and Wodak, Ruth (eds), 1–13. Houndmills: Palgrave Macmillan.

Heer, Hannes, Manoschek, Walter, Pollak, Alexander and Wodak, Ruth (eds). 2008. *The Discursive Construction of History. Remembering the Wehrmacht's War of Annihilation*. Houndmills: Palgrave Macmillan.

Hodge, Robert and Kress, Gunther. 1993. *Language and Ideology*. London: Routledge.

Johns, Adrian. 2003. "Reading and experiment in the early Royal Society." In *Reading, Society and Politics in Early Modern England*, Kevin Sharpe and Zwicker, Steven (eds), 244–271. Cambridge: CUP.

Justice, Steven. 1994. *Writing and Rebellion: England in 1381*. Berkeley: University of California Press.

Kim, Chan-Hie. 1972. *The Form and Structure of the Familiar Greek Letter of Introduction*. Missoula, Montana: University of Montana Press.

Kowalski, Grzegorz. 2006. "Globalna 'konwersacjonalizacja' dyskursów a zmiany w stylu komunikacji akademickiej na przykładzie korespondencji e-mailowej między studentami i nauczycielami" ["Global 'conversationalization' of discourses and changes in the style of academic communication on the example of e-mail correspondence between students and teachers"]. In *Korpusy w angielsko-polskim językoznawstwie kontrastywnym: Teoria i praktyka [Corpora in English-Polish Contrastive Linguistics: Theory and Practice]*, Anna Duszak, Elżbieta Gajek and Urszula Okulska (eds), 287–304. Kraków: Universitas.

Kress, Gunther. 1996. "Representational resources and the production of subjectivity: Questions for the theoretical development of Critical Discourse Analysis in a multicultural society." In *Texts and Practice. Readings in Critical Discourse Analysis*, Carmen Rosa Caldas-Coulthard and Malcolm Coulthard (eds), 15–31. London and New York: Routledge.

Louhiala-Salminen, Leena. 1995. *'Drop me a fax, will you?' A Study of Written Business Communication*. Jyväskylä: University of Jyväskylä.

Louhiala-Salminen, Leena and Kankaanranta, Anne. 2005. "'Hello Monica, kindly change your arrangements': Business genres in a state of flux." In *Genre Variation in Business Letters*, Paul Gillaerts and Maurizio Gotti (eds), 55–84. Bern: Peter Lang.

Maas, Utz. 1984. *Als der Geist der Gemeinschaft eine Sprache fand. Sprache im Nazionalsozialis-mus.* Oplanden: Westdeutscher Verlag.

Martin, James and Wodak, Ruth (eds). 2003. *Re/reading the Past. Critical and Functional Per-spectives on Time and Value.* Amsterdam: Benjamins.

McCarthy, Michael and Carter, Ronald. 1994. *Language as Discourse: Perspectives for Language Teaching.* London and New York: Longman.

Miller, Carolyn. 1984. "Genre as social action." *Quarterly Journal of Speech* 70: 151–167.

Mitra, Ananda, Hazen, Michael D., LaFrance, Betty and Rogan, Randall G. 1999. "Faculty use and non-use of electronic mail: Attitudes, expectations and profiles." Retrieved September 30, 2009 from http://jcmc.indiana.edu/vol4/issue3/mitra.html.

Mulholland, Joan. 1999. "E-mail: Uses, issues and problems in an institutional setting." In *Writ-ing Business: Genres, Media and Discourses,* Francesca Bargiela-Chiappini and Catherine Nickerson (eds), 57–84. Harlow: Longman.

Murphy, James J. 1974. *Rhetoric in the Middle Ages.* Berkeley: University of California Press.

Niemeier, Susanne, Campbell, Charles P., Dirven, René (eds). 1998. *The Cultural Context in Business Communication.* Amsterdam/Philadelphia: John Benjamins.

Nevalainen, Terttu and Raumoling-Brunberg, Helena. 1995. "Constraints on politeness. The pragmatics of address formulae in Early Modern English correspondence." In *Historical Pragmatics,* Andreas H. Jucker (ed.), 541–601. Amsterdam: John Benjamins.

Nevala, Minna. 2004. "Inside and out: Forms of address in seventeenth- and eighteenth-century letters." *Journal of Historical Pragmatics* 5 (2): 271–296.

Okulska, Urszula. 2006. "Textual strategies in the diplomatic correspondence of the Middle and Early Modern English periods: The *narrative report letter* as a genre." In *Business and Offi-cial Correspondence: Historical Investigations,* Marina Dossena and Susan Fitzmaurice (eds), 47–76. Bern: Peter Lang.

—. 2008. "Early English professional correspondence as a socio-cultural practice. The case of the *directive letter.*" In *Discourse Variation across Communities, Cultures and Times,* Urszula Okulska and Grzegorz Kowalski (eds), 81–121. Warsaw: University of Warsaw.

Orlikowski, Wanda and Yates, JoAnna. 1994. "Genre repertoire: The structuring of communica-tive practices in organizations." *Administrative Science Quarterly* 39: 541–574.

Perelman, Les. 1991. "The medieval art of letter writing: Rhetoric as institutional expression." In *Textual Dynamics of the Professions,* Charles Bazerman and James Paradis (eds), 97–119. Madison: University of Wisconsin Press.

Ramallo, Fernando, Lorenzo, Anxo M. and Rodriguez-Yáñez, Xoán Paulo (eds). 2006. *Discourse and Enterprise. Communication, Business, Management and Other Professional Fields.* München: Lincom.

Raymond, Joad. 1996. *The Invention of the Newspaper: English Newsbooks, 1641–1649.* Oxford: Clarendon Press.

Reisigl, Martin. 2006. "Rhetorical tropes in political discourse." In *Encyclopedia of Language and Linguistics, Vol. 10,* Keith Brown (ed.), 597–604. Amsterdam: Elsevier.

Reisigl, Martin and Wodak, Ruth. 2001. *Discourse and Discrimination.* London: Routledge.

Rusnock, Andrea. 1999. "Correspondence networks and the Royal Society, 1700–1750." *British Journal for the History of Science* 32: 155–169.

Sairio, Anni. 2008. "A social network study of the eighteenth-century Bluestockings: The pro-gressive and preposition stranding in their letters." *Historical Sociolinguistics and Sociohis-torical Linguistics* 8. Retrieved September 30, 2009 from http://www.let.leidenuniv.nl/hsl_shl/Sairio.htm.

Salminen, Tapio. 1997. "Multilinguality and written correspondence in late medieval Northern Baltics – reflections of literacy and language in the communication between the Council of Reval and the Finnish Bailiffs." *Das Mittelalter. Perspektiven mediävistischer Forschung* 2 (1): 151–162.

Sokół, Małgorzata. 2006. "Genre analysis and digital communication: New approaches to genre theory." In *Bridges and Barriers in Metalinguistic Discourse*, Anna Duszak and Urszula Okulska (eds), 167–180. Frankfurt am Main: Peter Lang.

—. 2008. "Authorial voice through modality choices in academic e-discourse: A diachronic perspective." In *Discourse Variation across Communities, Cultures and Times*, Urszula Okulska and Grzegorz Kowalski (eds), 81–102. Warsaw: University of Warsaw.

Sommerville, C. John. 1996. *The News Revolution in England*. New York: Oxford University Press.

Stocking, George W. 1983. "The ethnographer's magic. Fieldwork in British anthropology from Tylor to Malinowski." In *Observers Observed. Essays on Ethnographic Fieldwork, Vol. 1. History of Anthropology*, George W. Stocking (ed.), 71–120. Madison: The University of Wisconsin Press.

Sutor, Julian. 2004. *Korespondencja dyplomatyczna [Diplomatic correspondence]*. Warszawa: Elipsa.

Tieken-Boon van Ostade, Ingrid. 2003. "Lowth's language." In *Insights into Late Modern English*, Marina Dossena and Charles Jones (eds), 241–264. Bern: Peter Lang.

—. 2004. "Of social networks and linguistic influence: The language of Robert Lowth and his correspondents." *International Journal of English Studies* 5 (1): 39–71.

—. 2006. "Edward Pearson Esqr.: The language of an eighteenth-century secretary." In *Business and Official Correspondence: Historical Investigations*, Marina Dossena and Susan Fitzmaurice (eds), 129–151. Bern: Peter Lang.

Tiisala, Seija. 2004. "Power and politeness: Language and salutation formulas in correspondence between Sweden and the German Hanse." *Journal of Historical Pragmatics* 5 (2): 193–206.

Triandafyllidou, Anna, Wodak, Ruth and Krzyżanowski, Michał (eds). 2009. *The European Public Sphere and the Media Europe in Crisis*. Houndmills: Palgrave Macmillan.

Trolle-Larsen, Mogens. 1989. "What they wrote on clay." In *Literacy and Society*, Karen Schoesbou and Mogens Trolle-Larsen (eds), 124–146. Copenhagen: Akademisk Forlag.

Valle, Ellen. 2004. "'The pleasure of receiving your favour': The colonial exchange in eighteenth-century natural history." *Journal of Historical Pragmatics* 5 (2): 313–336.

van Dijk, Teun. 1997a. "The study of discourse." In *Discourse as Structure and Process. Discourse Studies: A Multidisciplinary Introduction, Vol. 1*, Teun van Dijk (ed.), 1–34. London: SAGE.

—. 1997b. "Discourse as interaction in society." In *Discourse as Social Interaction. Discourse Studies: A Multidisciplinary Introduction, Vol. 2*, Teun van Dijk (ed.), 1–37. London: SAGE.

—. 1998. *Ideology: An Interdisciplinary Approach*. London: Sage.

van Leeuwen, Theo. 1995. "Representing social action.," *Discourse & Society* 6 (1): 81–106.

—. 1996. "The representation of social actors." In *Texts and Practice. Readings in Critical Discourse Analysis*, Carmen Rosa Caldas-Coulthard and Malcolm Coulthard (eds), 32–70. London and New York: Routledge.

van Nus, Miriam. 1999. "'Can we count on your bookings of potatoes to Madeira?' Corporate context and discourse practices in direct sales letters." In *Writing Business: Genres, Media and Discourses*. Francesca Bargiela-Chiappini and Catherine Nickerson (eds), 181–205. Harlow: Longman.

Warschauer, Mark. 2002. "Networking into academic discourse." *Journal of English for Academic Purposes* 1 (1): 45–58.

Watts, Richard. [1996] 2005. "Social institutions." *Handbook of Pragmatics Online*. Amsterdam/ Philadelphia: John Benjamins. Retrieved September 30, 2009 from http://www.benjamins. com/online/hop/.

Whigham, Mark. 1981. "The rhetoric of Elizabethan suitors' letters." *Publications of the Modern Language Association of America* (PMLA) 96 (5): 864–882.

White, John L. 1982. *Studies in Ancient Letter Writing*. Chico, CA: Scholars Press.

Wodak, Ruth, Nowak, Peter, Pelikan, Johanna, Gruber, Helmut, de Cillia, Rudolf and Mitten, Richard. 1990. *Wir sind alle unschuldige Täter. Diskurshistorische Studien zum Nachkriegsantisemitismus*. Frankfurt am Main: Suhrkamp.

Wodak, Ruth, Menz, Florian, Mitten, Richard and Stern, Frank. 1994. *Die Sprachen der Vergangenheiten. Öffentliches Gedenken in österreichischen und deutschen Medien*. Frankfurt am Main: Suhrkamp.

Wodak, Ruth, de Cillia, Rudolf, Reisigl, Martin, and Liebhart, Karin. 1999. *The Discursive Construction of National Identity*. Edinburgh: Edinburgh University Press.

Wodak, Ruth and de Cillia, Rudolf. 2006. "Politics and language: Overview." In *Encyclopedia of Language and Linguistics, Vol. 9*, Keith Brown (ed.), 707–717. Amsterdam: Elsevier.

Wodak, Ruth and Meyer, Michael (eds). 2001. *Methods of Critical Discourse Analysis*. London: Sage.

Wodak, Ruth and Weiss Gilbert. 2004. "Visions, ideologies and utopias in the discursive construction of European identities: Organizing, representing and legitimizing Europe." In *Communicating Ideologies: Language, Discourse and Social Practice*, Martin Pütz, JoAnne Neff-van Aertselaer and Teun A. van Dijk (eds), 225–252. Frankfurt am Main: Peter Lang.

Yates, JoAnna and Orlikowski, Wanda. 1992. "Genres of organizational communication: A structurational approach to studying to studying communication and media." *Academy of Management Review* 17: 299–326.

PART IV

Voices of mediatized politics

CHAPTER 11

Hedging in political discourse
The Bush 2007 press conferences*

Bruce Fraser

1. Introduction

A look at the research literature on Political Linguistics reveals that there has been considerable research on vagueness, evasion, equivocation, and deception in the speech of politicians, but with the exception of Partington (2003), almost nothing on hedging.[1] Given the nature of hedging and the image projected by President Bush, I was interested in the extent to which Bush would use hedging in response to challenging questions posed to him by reporters. I chose the 2007 Press Conferences as my source of data.

In Section 2 of this paper, I characterize hedging as it is thought of today, ignoring a detailed history of the topic, which will be found elsewhere (Fraser forthcoming). Then, in sections 3 and 4, I present the results of my analysis of the 2007 Press Conferences.[2]

2. What is hedging?

Hedging is a rhetorical strategy. By including a particular term, choosing a particular structure, or imposing a specific prosodic form on the utterance, the speaker signals a lack of a full commitment either to the full category membership of a term or expression in the utterance (content mitigation), or to the intended illocutionary force of the utterance (force mitigation). Simply put, it is attenuation of the full value which the utterance would have, absent the hedging.

---

* I am indebted to Polly Ulichny and Piotr Cap for constructive criticism on an earlier draft of this paper.

1. A recent paper by Fetzer (forthcoming) is an example.

2. The material for this analysis are scripts of 30 press conferences held by G. W. Bush between January 1 and December 31, 2007.

For example, in

> The pool has *sort of* an L-shaped design.
> Peter's house is *almost* 100 feet wide.

which are instances of content mitigation, there is an attenuation of the commitment to the pool having a true L-shaped design and to Peter's house being 100 feet in width. Analogously, in

> *I think* that I *must* ask you to leave now.
> *It seems* that no one wants to go.

which are instances of force mitigation, the speaker indicates that there is not a full commitment to requesting the hearer to leave, both by virtue of the *I think* as well as the modal *must*. Similarly, the speaker of the second sentence signals less than full endorsement to the declaration *No one wants to go*. Of course, this lack of commitment may truly reflect the extent of the speaker's knowledge, for example, when a researcher states that

> I find that the results *more or less* conform with those found by Johnson (1999)

where to make an explicit statement that the results conform is beyond what is justified by the data.

To the extent to which a speaker does not 'misspeak', either through mistake or misadventure, hedging must be considered an intentional action in that the speaker chooses a linguistic device over and above the propositional content of the message which will affect the interpretation of the utterance, either by modifying the content of the utterance or its force.[3]

Hedges are thus *linguistic* devices – lexical items, syntactic structures, prosodic features – which are used to bring about hedging, though almost none of these are used solely in this capacity. In the first example below, *kind of* is taken as a unit and used as a hedge while in the second, it is used as a Noun-Preposition sequence.

> He *kind of* missed the point.
> I like that *kind of* ice cream.
> *According to John*, there will be no class today.

In the second example, the expression *according to John* can be used to avoid responsibility (hedging) or simply to indicate the source of the information.

---

3.   In line with the initial writing on the topic when hedging was characterized as 'fuzziness' (cf. Lakoff 1972), there are some who would argue that the concept of hedging also embraces an emphasis in the membership category or force of an utterance, as in 'I *emphatically* state that she is here.' I find several reasons to reject this position: first, that the use of the term today in all areas of hedging research deals almost exclusively with the lack of commitment; second, the term 'reinforcement' has been adopted for this second use; and third, the sense of *reinforcement* does not imply more than class membership or force values. Thus, I will use 'hedging' in only the attenuation sense.

Hedges do not form a grammatical category, since they do not fall within a single syntactic form. Nor do they constitute a Functional Category, as Clemen (1997) writes:

> There is no limit to the linguistic expressions that can be considered as hedges... The difficulty with these functional definitions is that almost any linguistic item or expression can be interpreted as a hedge...no linguistic items are inherently hedges but can acquire this quality depending on the communicative context or the co-text. This also means that no clear-cut lists of hedging expressions are possible (Clemen 1997: 6).

In fact, a hedge can be an entire sentence, as in

> *I must ask you this*: why did you do such a foolish thing?
> *I think I can guarantee that* you will be awarded a full-tuition scholarship.

It seems best to treat them as an inventory of devices by which the speaker can qualify or attenuate commitment to either the meaning or the force which would be interpreted if the hedge were absent from the utterance.

Researchers have attempted to classify hedges into an array sub-categories, as the list below illustrates,[4]

> *adaptor, agent avoider, approximator, attenuator, attribution shield, bush, committer, compromiser, consultative device, deintensifier, diffuser, diminisher, downtoner, forewarner, hedge, indicator of degrees of reliability, minimizer, mitigator, plausibility shield, play-down, politeness marker, rounder, scope-stater, shield, understatement, understater, validity marker, vocal hesitator, weakener*

some researchers choosing the same term but for different groups of the hedges. I find the distinction between content and force hedging to be more than sufficient and have found no basis for any finer distinction, either descriptive or theoretical.

The focus of a hedge varies. It may be a word, a phrase, the entire sentence, or the intended illocutionary force of the utterance, or its perlocutionary effect, as shown below,

> That is a *kind of* [bird.]
> He has a *somewhat* [elevated temperature.]
> *As far as I can tell*, [you don't have anything to fear from him.]
> *I must* request that you stop talking while the music is playing. [Request]
> *I think* that she is *pretty much* guilty. [Perlocutionary Effect on hearer]

but the focus of a hedge is never an inference, entailment or a presupposition.

---

4. See, for example, Aijmer (1987), Blum-Kulka (1985), Clemen (1997), Holmes (1984), House and Kasper (1981), Hyland (1996), Loewenberg (1982) and Prince et al. (1982) for different treatments with differing terminology.

Propositional hedges include:

about, actually, almost, approximately, as it were, basically, can be viewed as, crypto-, especially, essentially, exceptionally, for the most part, generally, in a manner of speaking, in a real sense, in a sense, in a way, kind of, largely, literally, loosely speaking, more or less, mostly, often, occasionally, on the tall side, par excellence, particularly, pretty much, principally, pseudo-, quintessentially, rather, real, really, regular, relatively, roughly, so to say, somewhat, sort of, strictly speaking, technically, typically, very, virtually

though this list certainly does not exhaust the inventory. Illocutionary force hedges include:

Impersonal pronouns
　　One just doesn't do that.
Concessive conjunctions (*although, though, while, whereas, even though, even if, ...*)
　　Even though you dislike the beach, it's worth going for the view.
Hedged performative
　　I *must* ask you to sit down.
Indirect Speech Acts
　　Could you speak a little louder.
Introductory phrases – *I believe, to our knowledge, it is our view that, we feel that.*
　　I believe that he is here.
Modal adverbs *perhaps, possibly, probably, practically, presumably, apparently.*
　　I can *possibly* do that
Modal adjectives (*possible, probable, un/likely...*)
　　It is possible that there is no water in the well.
Modal noun (*assumption, claim, possibility, estimate, suggestion...*)
　　The *assumption* is that you are going to go.
Modal verbs (*might, can, would, could...*)
　　John *might* leave now.
Epistemic verbs (*seem, appear, believe, assume, suggest, think...*)
　　It seems that no one wants to go.
Negation
　　Didn't Harry leave? [I think Harry left]
　　I don't think I'm going. vs. I'm *not* going. [Former hedges the meaning of latter]
Reversal tag
　　He's coming, *isn't he*?
Parenthetic construction
　　The picnic is here, *I guess.*
If clause
　　If true, we're in deep trouble.

Agentless Passive
> Many of the troops were injured. (*by* Ø)

Conditional subordinators (*as long as, so long as, assuming that, given that...*)
> *Unless* the strike has been called off, there will be no trains tomorrow.

Progressive form
> I am *hoping* you will come.

Tentative Inference
> The mountains *should be* visible from here.

Conditional clause implying permission (*if you don't mind my saying so, if I may say so*)
> *If you don't mind me saying so*, your slip is showing.

Conditional clause as a metalinguistic comment (*if that's the right word...*)
> His style is florid, *if that's the right word.*

Conditional clause expressing uncertainty about the extralinguistic knowledge required for a correct interpretation of the utterance (*if I'm correct, in case you don't remember*)
> Chomsky views cannot be reconciled with Piaget, *if I understand him correctly.*

Metalinguistic comment such as (*strictly speaking, so to say, exactly, almost, just about, if you will*)
> He has an idea, a hypothesis, *if you will*, that you may find inter-esting.

In addition, Salager-Meyer (1995) indicates compound hedging devices which include

Modal with hedging verb
> It *would appear* that...

Hedging verb with hedging adverb/adjective
> It *seems reasonable* that...

Double hedges
> It *may suggest* that this *probably* indicates...

Treble hedges
> It *seems reasonable to assume* that...

Quadruple hedges
> It *would seem somewhat unlikely* that *it may appear somewhat speculative* that...

Here, again, there is no reason to believe that the above list captures all hedging devices in English nor that a given device is always used for hedging.

Finally, there have been a variety of discourse uses which hedging serves, some of which overlap: to accomplish politeness, both positive and negative; to mitigate; to provide some degree of self-protection; to avoid confrontation; to avoid responsibility for a fact or an act; to appear modest; to conceal the truth, to be apologetic, and to seem less powerful. However, I find these can be reduced to the following two general purposes:

hedging is used (1) to mitigate an undesirable effect on the hearer, thereby rendering the message (more) polite; and (2) to avoid providing the information which is expected or required in the speaker's contribution, thereby creating vagueness and/or evasion. It is the latter effect that will be relevant in the 2007 Bush Press Conferences.

3.   The framework of the Presidential press conference

The Presidential press conference (Davis 1992; Kernell 1986; Smith 1990) is a gathering of reporters in the same room with the President and perhaps another head of state, where the President initially makes some remarks followed by questions to him and his guest. The questions are not scripted, although his aides alert him to the likely content and the hot-button issues. The atmosphere is relatively informal and at times quite humorous.

The framework of the Presidential press conference involves an aspect which is important to this analysis. It is the fact that a small number of the reporters present who, at the moment, are in Bush's good graces, are typically permitted a single question and no follow-up. This means that reporters typically try to make the question as road and open ended as possible, and often link questions together – as evidenced below.

> Q. ...he [Putin] said – well, at least the quote said that. And he also said, quote, he "sees no evidence to suggest Iran wants to build a nuclear bomb." Were you disappointed with that message? And does that indicate possibly that international pressure is not as great as you once thought against Iran abandoning its nuclear program?
> Q. Mr. President, you mentioned that you see national reconciliation as a crucial goal there for your policy. Why then haven't you condemned the taunting that Saddam Hussein faced on the gallows from Shiite officials? And on a related subject, can you be more specific as to which day next week you'll be unveiling your Iraq policy?

Reasonably, the longer and more inquisitive the question sequences, the larger the number of hedges in the President's response.

In 2007 Bush held 30 press conferences: 20 with one or more guests, 10 where he was alone. In this paper, I am concerned only with his answers to questions posed by reporters and have not analyzed his prepared remarks at the start of the press conference. My initial hunches were that, there would be little opportunity to use hedging as a way of mitigating possible face threatening remarks, since Bush was answering questions and not debating with the reporters. The majority of Bush's remarks would be explanatory statements, and I was interested in whether under these circumstances he would use hedging as a strategy to evade responsibility for both facts presented and actions taken.[5]

---

5.   Partington (2003: 237–243) suggests that hedging is only one of the strategies for evading, others being bald on-record refusal to answer, claims of ignorance, referring the question, refusal to speculate, stating the answer is well-known, and claiming that the question has been answered already.

4. The findings

Contrary to the expectations of the use of hedging as a strategy to evade responsibility, I found, first of all, numerous cases of hedge-type expressions used in a non-hedging manner, as shown below.

(1) I appreciate that *kind of* commitment, Mr. Prime Minister.
(2) Newly elected President, Tony Blair came over, and he reached out; he was gracious – was able to converse *in a way* that – where our shared interests were the most important aspect of the relationship.

The terms *for the most part, honestly, in a sense, largely, literally, loosely speaking, mostly, to my knowledge, principally, roughly, so to say, strictly speaking, technically, typically, virtually* did not occur as hedges in Bush's answers to questions, though they might have been expected in his answers, given their potential for discourse attenuation. In addition, there were no cases of hedged performatives, very few cases of hedged felicity conditions or hedged Gricean maxims, and no cases of *I suggest that, I wonder if,* or *I suppose that,* all of which might have been anticipated to work as, again, attenuators of the President's commitment to the validity of the proposition following.

There were numerous cases of what I call *neutral hedging,* hedging which clearly had no impact on the issue being discussed. Specifically, in the context in which this hedging occurred, it was extremely difficult if not impossible to infer Bush's intention to create vagueness or to evade a more focused and specific answer to the question. In the examples below, I have not provided the context in which the utterance occurred, both for space considerations and because it would not change the general thrust of this point if one were to disagree with some of the examples.[6]

(3) We *don't believe* freedom is just confined to our neighborhood; we *believe* freedom is universal in its application.
(4) And as you know, we've been dealing with this issue ever since you've been covering me and *pretty much* ever since I've been the President.
(5) The bill *essentially* says that before any other reforms take place, certain benchmarks will be met when it comes to securing the border.
(6) ...there is an underground industry that has sprung up that I *think* is *essentially* anti-humanitarian. It is an industry based upon coyotes – those are smugglers.
(7) And that's why I find it *somewhat* astounding that people in Congress would start calling for withdrawal even before all the troops have made it to Baghdad.
(8) Since the tax cuts took full effect in 2003, our economy has added more than 8.3 million new jobs and *almost* 4 years of uninterrupted growth.

---

6. There were 64 instances of *kind of,* 41 of *actually,* 240 of *believe/not believe,* 258 of *think/ don't think,* 55 of *thought,* 25 of *we believe* and one instance of *we don't believe.*

(9)   What you're asking is whether or not Congress ought to be *basically* determining how troops are positioned or troop strength. And I just – *I don't think* that would be good for the country.

(10) He *kind of* got beaten up by people in the Democratic Party and by Mitt Romney in your party, Romney comparing him to Dr. Strangelove.

(11) I did have a good discussion with Prime Minister Maliki. It did *nearly* last for 2 hours.

(12) There really wasn't a serious debate until *pretty much* starting after the year 2000, *if my memory serves me well.*

(13) And the truth of the matter is, they *probably* didn't fully understand what they were signing up for.

(14) *As you probably are aware*, I've really never felt like the United States needs to get United Nations approval to make decisions necessary for our security.

(15) *As you probably know*, the public works committee is the largest committee – one of the largest committees in the House of Representatives.

(16) *I think* it's great to be able to say a good friend won reelection because…

(17) I cannot look a mother and father of a troop in the eye and say, "I'm sending your kid into combat, but *I don't think* we can achieve the objective."

(18) *I believe* we can succeed, and *I believe* we are making security progress that will enable the political tract to succeed as well.

Considered from the perspective of the general characteristics of President Bush's public address style (Silberstein 2004), the hedge-type expressions in (3–18) should be deemed examples of 'empty rhetoric' (often involving appeals to undeniable truths, as in 3), rather than instances purposefully aimed at exerting rhetorical impact (having the force of mitigation, responsibility shift, etc.).

Interestingly, such a rhetorical stance was often picked up by reporters (as in 19–21), who would join in an exchange of hedged expressions with no apparent performative rationale. As a result, the precision and directness of the interaction would dwindle, though it is rather unclear whether one could call it an effect truly intended by the President:

(19) Q. Mr. President, the Prime Minister has referred to terrorism as, quote, "a crime," and he's referred to it *in part* as a law enforcement issue. So for you, *I'm wondering*, does that underscore any *sort of* philosophical difference when your 2004 campaign took issue with *somewhat* similar descriptions from John Kerry?

(20) Q. Mr. President Bush, Hugo Chavez of Venezuela has been using his country's vast oil wealth to court a whole new generation of Latin Americans. You *pretty much* avoided using his name.

(21) Q. *I can't help but* read your body language this morning, Mr. President. You seem *somehow* dispirited – *somewhat* dispirited.

What I expected but did not find were examples of what I call *self-serving hedging*, hedging to evade answering the question in a straightforward and complete way. For example, none of the following occurred: *I believe that there are WMD still in Iraq., The plan to withdraw troops will **possibly** be revised., The ultimate decision will be decided (**by?**) by next month.*, though there were a couple of responses using *I think* to hedge (as in 22 below), which could be construed as evasion, and an occasional use of hedging used for mitigation (as in 23):

(22) Q. Is it all their [the Democrats'] fault that these bills aren't moving, that you've got these veto threats out?
      The President. I think it is their fault that bills aren't moving, yes. As I said, I'm not a part of the legislative branch. All I can do is ask them to move bills. It's up to the leaders to move the bills.

(23) Q. ...you weren't this circumspect when you were talking to reporters yesterday about the economy.
      The President. I think I *pretty much* said the same thing yesterday, *in all due respect.*

Rather than using hedging for purposes of evasion, I found numerous cases of clear, deliberate evasion: a failure to responsibly answer the question put to him. In what follows I present various Question-Answer sequences which reflect this evasion in different guises. Interestingly, there is no apparent difference which depends on the subject, for example, the war in Iraq, the state of the economy, or the President's ideological views.

In some cases, Bush seems to be at a loss for words (something attributed to him since he has been in office), as in (24):

(24) Q. Secretary Rice said that failure is not an option. You talked about substantial issues (sic.) need to be discussed. What is the minimum expectation from you that you will call this conference a success? And what you're (sic.) offering the Arab nations to encourage them to participate?
      The President. Right. Well, that's why Condi is making the trip she's making, is to explain to people in private, as well as in public, that, one, we're for comprehensive peace; two, that there is a – the meeting, the international meeting will be serious and substantive. In other words – as she said the other day, this isn't going to be just a photo opportunity. This is going to be a serious and substantive meeting.

but generally his clear evasion was polished albeit frustrating for those who expected an answer that was responsive to the question. The following Question-Answers (25–27) illustrate this:

(25) Q. But, Mr. President, there have been seven investigations and the Pentagon has not gotten to the bottom of it. Can you also tell us when you, personally, found out that it was not enemy fire, that it was friendly fire?

> **The President.** *I can't give you the precise moment.* But obviously, the minute I heard that the facts that people believed were true were not true, that I expect there to be a full investigation and get to the bottom of it.

(26) Q. Thank you, sir. You have spoken passionately about the consequences of failure in Iraq. Your critics say you failed to send enough troops there at the start, failed to keep Al Qaeda from stepping into the void created by the collapse of Saddam's army, failed to put enough pressure on Iraq's Government to make the political reconciliation necessary to keep the sectarian violence the country is suffering from now from occurring. So why should the American people feel you have the vision for victory in Iraq, sir?

> **The President.** Those are all legitimate questions that I'm sure historians will analyze. I mean, *one of the questions is, should we have sent more in the beginning?...*

(27) Q. Mr. President, thank you. Since General Pace made his comments that got a lot of attention about homosexuality, we haven't heard from you on that issue. Do you, sir, believe that homosexuality is immoral?

> **The President.** *I will not be rendering judgment about individual orientation.* I do believe the "don't ask, don't tell" policy is good policy.

The evasion strategies involve primarily outright refusals to answer (25, 27), but also a strategy to delegate the answer to another party (26), as well as self-reformulation and narrowing down the scope of the original question sequence (26), so that the answer detracts from the complexity of the issue at stake.

There were occasions where, rather than simply ignoring the question, Bush would use the evasive ploy of stating that the question had been asked and answered, as in (28) and (29):

(28) Q. ...you weren't this circumspect when you were talking to reporters yesterday about the economy.

> **The President.** *I think I pretty much* said the same thing yesterday, in all due respect.

(29) Q. Was it on your order, sir?

> **The President.** As I said, *this program is a necessary program that was constantly reviewed...*

When questioned about a general who had criticized the administration's actions, Bush again totally ignored the question:

(30) Q. I wonder if you felt blindsided by the very blistering criticism recently from retired General Ricardo Sanchez, who was one of your top commanders in Iraq. [who voiced strong criticism of incompetent strategic leadership on Iraq]

> **The President.** You know, look, I admire General Sanchez's service to the country. I appreciate his service to the country. The situation on the ground has changed quite dramatically since he left Iraq. The security situation is changing dramatically. The reconciliation that's taking place is changing. The

economy is getting better. And so I – I'm pleased with the progress we're making. And I admire the fact that he served. I appreciate his service.

A rare follow-up question by the same reporter who pursued the 'blindsiding' issue was met with a refusal to answer, another evasive technique, and another reporter was selected for a question, as in (31):

(31)   Q. Should the American people feel disturbed that a former top general says that?
       The President. Massimo. [Massimo Calabresi, *Time*]

Finally, Bush engages in downright lying, a form of evasion, although not hedging, as illustrated by the following (32), where his answer shows a marked disfluency, perhaps due to his dissembling:

(32)   Q. And he [Putin] said – well, at least the quote said that. And he also said, quote, he "sees no evidence to suggest Iran wants to build a nuclear bomb." Were you disappointed with that message? And does that indicate possibly that international pressure is not as great as you *once thought* against Iran abandoning its nuclear program?
       The President. I – as I say, I look forward to – if those are, in fact, his comments, I look forward to having him clarify those, because when I visited with him, he understands that it's in the world's interest to make sure that Iran does not have the capacity to make a nuclear weapon...I mean, if he wasn't concerned about it, Bret, then why did we have such good progress at the United Nations in round one and round two?
       The President. [continuing] And so I will visit with him about it. *I have not been briefed yet* by Condi or Bob Gates about, you know, their visit with Vladimir Putin.

It is common knowledge that the President is briefed immediately upon return home by administration officials. Another instance of downright lying follows below (in 33). When questioned about a report on torturing Iraqi captives, he denied having seen it, implying he had not been briefed on it:

(33)   Q. The New Yorker reports that the Red Cross has found the interrogation program in the CIA detention facilities used interrogation techniques that were tantamount to torture. I'm wondering if you have read that report, and what your reaction to it is.
       The President. I haven't seen it. We don't torture.

His rejection of waterboarding as a form of torture is as believable as Clinton's claim of "not having sex with that woman."

5.   Conclusion

As expected, I found numerous examples of neutral hedging, hedging where there was no indication that it was being used for evasion or politeness purposes but rather conveying a lack of precision. In addition, per my expectation, I did not find that hedging was used in the Press Conferences for mitigation purposes leading to polite effects. Lack of potential for adverse reaction would account for this.

Unexpectedly, I found only a few cases of hedging for purposes of evasion when the question was challenging, and Bush might be expected to avoid a direct, forthright answer on point. Rather I found that he moved directly to evading the issue, utilizing several of the techniques suggested by Partington (2003), including outright lying, often with sufficient dissonance that it made one wonder what question he was answering.

Press Conferences are one of the few venues where the President is confronted with challenging questions, and can be expected to answer them directly and completely. That Bush consistently does not conform to this expectation suggests that Press Conferences may be less of a forum for a President to explain views on tough policy issues and more of a change for the press to indirectly criticize an administration.

References

Aijmer, Karin. 1987. "Discourse variation and hedging." *Costerus* 57: 1–18.

Blum-Kulka, Shoshana. 1985. "Modifiers as indicating devices: The case of requests." *Theoretical Linguistics* 12 (2/3): 213–229.

Clemen, Gudrun. 1997. "The concept of hedging: Origins, approaches and definitions." In *Hedging and Discourse*, Hartmut Schroeder and Raija Markkanen (eds.), 80–97. Berlin: de Gruyter.

Davis, Richard. 1992. *The Press and American Politics: The New Mediator*. White Plains, New York: Longman.

Fetzer, Anita. Forthcoming. "Hedges in context: Form and function of *sort of* and *kind of.*" In *Vagueness in Language*, Stefan Schneider (ed.). Bingley: Emerald Publishing.

Fraser, Bruce. Forthcoming. "A brief history of hedging." In *Vagueness in Language*, Stefan Schneider (ed.). Bingley: Emerald Publishing.

Holmes, Janet. 1984. "Hedging your bets and sitting on the fence: Some evidence for hedges as support structures." *Te Reo* 27: 47–62.

House, Juliane and Kasper, Gabriele. 1981. "Politeness markers in English and in German." In *Conversational Routines*, Florian Coulmas (ed.), 157–185. The Hague: Mouton de Gruyter.

Hyland, Ken. 1996. "Writing without conviction? Hedging in science research articles." *Applied Linguistics* 17 (4): 433–454.

Kernell, Samuel. 1986. *Going Public: New Strategies of Presidential Leadership*. Washington, D.C.: Congressional Quarterly Press.

Lakoff, George. 1972. Hedges: A study in meaning criteria and the logic of fuzzy concepts. *CLS* 8: 183–228.

Loewenberg, Ina. 1982. "Labels and hedges: The metalinguistic turn." *Language and Style* 15 (3): 193–207.

Partington, Alan. 2003. *The Linguistics of Political Argument. The Spin-doctor and the Wolf-pack at the White House*. London: Routledge.

Prince, Ellen, Bosk, Charles and Frader, Joel. 1982. "On hedging in physician-physician discourse." In *Linguistics and the Professions*, Robert di Pietro (ed.), 83–97. Norwood/New Jersey: Ablex.

Salager-Meyer, Francoise. 1995. "I think that perhaps you should: A study of hedges in written scientific discourse." *The Journal of TESOL France* 2 (2): 127–143.

Silberstein, Sandra. 2004. *War of Words*. London: Routledge.

Smith, Carolyn. 1990. *Presidential Press Conferences: A Critical Approach*. New York: Praeger.

The 2007 Presidential Press Conferences (the total of 30). Retrieved April 30, 2008 from http://www.presidency.ucsb.edu/.

CHAPTER 12

Direct e-communication

Linguistic weapons in a political weblog

Anja Janoschka

1. Introduction

Politics is as old as rhetoric. It aims to persuade and change people's attitudes – much like advertising does. The emergence of the Internet, and especially the Web, has provided a new powerful tool in political campaigning. As evidenced in previous US presidential campaigns or by John McCain's, Hillary Clinton's and Barack Obama's present fundraising efforts, politicians have started actively and successfully to use the Web as an integral campaigning tool.

'Weblogs' (short 'blogs') are new Web-based social software tools. They are defined as frequently updated webpages, with posts arranged in reverse chronological order (Herring et al. 2004). In recent years, bloggers, i.e. blog authors, have become influential opinion makers in areas such as politics. American politicians were the first to fully appreciate the potential and the political power of blogging (cf. Sifry 2005). They began to invite bloggers to press conferences for election campaigns, and nowadays it is normal that politicians run their political blogs themselves. The 2004 US presidential election (George W. Bush vs. John F. Kerry) was the first campaign ever to use blogging as an integral device, facilitating communication with the electorate. In contrast to uni-directional, traditional mass communication tools, such as public speeches, interviews and TV talk shows, newspaper reports or party TV-commercials, blogs are two-directional (see also Łopacińska 2008). Similar to face-to-face communication, they offer the possibility to both contribute one's own opinion and to react to comments by blog participants. In other words, with this new powerful communication tool, political bloggers can exchange their propaganda messages with a wider audience of individuals, even on a one-to-one, personal level, allowing the politicians to monitor events at grass-roots level.

This analysis examines the political blog of an American Democratic representative in Illinois. The data comprises a wide range of regularly posted blog entries over a period of 12 months (March 2006 – February 2007). Due to various similarities between means of direct advertising, such as newsletters, and political weblogs,[1] it seems obvious that political blogs are also a means of direct advertising.[2] Taking this as a basic prerequisite, however, it does not necessarily mean that both types make use of similar linguistic devices. I have found some striking differences between them. This paper will investigate how and to what extent political blogs adopt the communication strategies of direct e-advertising. I am especially interested in the linguistic means politicians use in their posts to advertise political work.

The study will reflect the interactive nature of posts in political weblogs. It will start with a brief overview of direct e-advertising. In the second part, the exemplifying analysis of some linguistic strategies used in a newsletter serves as a basis for the study of the weblog. The main and last section, namely the quantitative and qualitative examination of posts, will concentrate on the use of linguistic weapons, i.e. personal and possessive pronouns, as well as different syntactic constructions.

2.   Direct e-advertising communication

2.1   Definition and scope

Direct marketing methods are interactive. In contrast to uni-directional mass advertising, such as print advertisements, they seek the addressees' feedback. Direct marketing or direct advertising can thus be defined as

> [a]n interactive system of marketing which uses one or more advertising media to effect a measurable response at any location, forming a basis for creating and further developing an ongoing direct relationship between an organization and its customers (Brassington and Pettitt 2005: 362).

The key terms in this definition are 'interactive system', 'effect a response' and 'ongoing direct relationship'. They describe the nature of direct advertising, viz. communication in terms of a continual, direct, two-directional message exchange between interactants. The scope of direct advertising communication is widespread and, with the emergence of the Internet, additional means of direct advertising have appeared (Figure 1). Yet, the definition above also applies to 'direct e-advertising', except that the Internet-based exchange provides substantial advantages as regards the fast and easy use of the feedback possibilities. The schema below (Figure 1) involves (mass) media carriers of both traditional mass media, such as printed media (grey boxes), and online media, such as the Internet and the World Wide Web (white boxes).

---

1.   There are parallels such as the mutual message exchange between sender and receiver, both promote a product or an idea and request for addressees' feedback.

2.   See, e.g., Horsbøl (2006) for the multimodal composition of political advertisements.

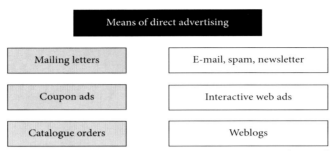

* For reasons of comparison with written weblogs, Figure 1 only considers written means of direct e-/advertising communication.

Figure 1. Selected means of written direct (e)-advertising

Non-electronic means such as mailing letters or direct mails are distributed by post to the receivers' home or business address. All means of direct advertising entail response elements, such as an answering card for addressee replies to make a response as easy and convenient as possible for them. Coupon advertisements are printed ads in magazines or newspapers. They are characterized by an integrated response element, i.e. often a demarcated section of the ad or just a fax and/or telephone number for immediate and fast feedback. The advantages of catalogue orders or home shopping are, for instance, that they utilize home delivery and the purchasing possibilities are unaffected by shopping hours. In short, they are time-saving features.

The differences between traditional mailings and e-mailings affect not only the transfer media but also the technical message realization. In e-mailings and newsletters, an interconnected website with additional information and/or immediate purchasing offers (e-commerce) can be activated via hyperlinks. In addition, e-mailings can be answered directly and immediately with a response via e-mail. With the rapidly growing market in commercial e-mail communication, the number of junk e-mails has increased. These unsolicited e-mails, or 'spam', are a special means of persuasive communication. In order to initiate a user response, they exploit various strategies, such as a very insistent language style (cf. Janoschka 2005). Not only spam, but all advertising messages that are irrelevant to their addressees fall under the heading of junk (e)-mail and thus are never answered, or in other words, they are unsuccessful in terms of an immediate reply.

Interactive web ads also seek interaction with users when they offer an individual information search which is based on the user's choice (Janoschka 2004: 59). This can be realized through pop-down menus or search engines integrated into the ad and/or a variety of additional information connected via links on the target website once the web ad is activated. As explained below, weblogs also distribute a message (=post), try to initiate a response and provide ongoing feedback possibilities.

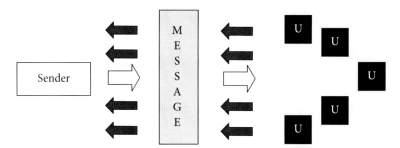

Figure 2. Process of written direct e-advertising communication

2.2   Process of communication in direct e-advertising

The process of communication in written direct e-advertising can be visualized as follows (Figure 2).

A company (=sender), for instance, distributes an e-mail or newsletter (=message) to individual users (=U 'single user') within a smaller or larger group. The advertising message is constructed in such a way as to generate receivers' feedback. This turns the uni-directional message flow originating from the sender into a two-directional one through the exchange of information between sender and receiver. Feedback triggers can be non-linguistic devices, such as special or customized offers which are only available for a certain time, and/or linguistic means and strategies that attract the user's attention and prompt a reaction, e.g., via the activation of hyperlinks.

2.3   Linguistic triggers in direct e-advertising

What determines the success of direct e-advertising? The obvious answer would be the appeal of, for instance, a newsletter, as this might also initiate a response. Since newsletters are potentially as interactive as face-to-face communication, one would expect to find similar principle features in them. In this heterogeneous advertising discourse with a mass and indeterminable audience, the personalization of the reader *you* and the institution or producer *we* seems to be important. Fairclough (2001: 168–9) calls this concept of advertising 'synthetic personalization'. It refers to the particular choice of linguistic constructions which presuppose an individual address within mass communication and, thus, simulates a conversational genre (Fairclough 1993: 146). Personal pronouns of address, questions and imperatives are, therefore, commonly used in direct advertising. They are designed to address conversation partners, give them the floor and encourage a reaction. Moreover, they could be useful in revealing the identities of participants and the social and personal relationship between them. On a more explicit level than personal pronouns, appealing key terms also have a teaser function. This is why direct e-mailings often try to address readers personally by their name. If there is no individual identification to hand, then generic terms of address such as *Dear readers* are chosen. Moreover, direct advertising habitually provides offers which are valid only in the short-term. More attractive deals are those tailored to customers' needs, based on previous transactions and gathered data.[3]

When constructing written direct e-advertising messages, however, additional aspects need to be considered. The message exchange via e-mails is usually time-shifted. Even though the reply in electronic communication could technically be realized on an almost synchronous basis,[4] there is usually no hurry to reply or activate offered links immediately. Thus, in order to initiate a prompt user reaction, authors need to anticipate what readers might want to know or, in advertising terms, what kind of artificial needs are to be satisfied through the offer.

In October 2007, I received a newsletter from *Swiss International Air Lines* in which they offered *international brands and quality Swiss products* that could be purchased in their *new online shop* (Figure 3).

At first sight, this newsletter (Figure 3) looks like a standard letter. It makes use of a formal, but personal address *Dear Mrs. Janoschka*. Vögele (1996: 80) calls these means 'intensifiers' as they strengthen the impact on the user to react. So, the identifiable sender *Thomas Benz*, who is the SWISS' *Head of Marketing Switzerland*, personalizes the e-mail and addresses me exclusively, although hypothesizing about my marital status. At the end of the first part of this e-mail, there is a commonly used polite closing formula, *Yours sincerely*. Animated texts and images, viz. the shopping bag which visualizes the online shop, internal links, such as the index menu, as well as external links (2) indicated by the deictic term *here* are new technologically- and medium-based intensifiers. They offer the user immediate access to a linked website/webpage and provide further information. In this e-mail, hyperlinks are highlighted and marked in blue in a text otherwise written in black. Imperative sentences (1, 2) are typical means of direct (e)-advertising. Here, they repeatedly operate as an indirect invitation to online shopping. The second imperative (2) additionally functions as a strengthening reminder, as it is usually placed at the end of the e-mail.

(1) Come and discover the variety of international brands (...)
(2) Come along with SWISS on a shopping tour*
     [*in blue print, signaling a hyperlink]

Sentence (3) stimulates one's curiosity through the unspecified indication that much more is available in the online shop. The convenience factor of non-stop home shopping (4) is another intensifier in the same way as the key terms *advantage* and *special*

---

3. For instance, at *Amazon.com*, book offers and recommendations are based on the customer's surfing and purchasing behavior.

4. Traditional mailing letters give their readers time to react. To avoid this time lag, advertisers often include a certain time frame during which a special offer is available.

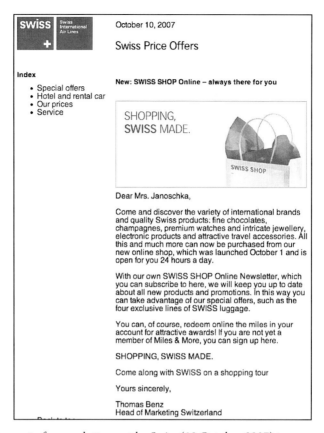

Figure 3. Excerpt of a newsletter sent by Swiss (10 October 2007) to my personal e-mail account

offers (5) are. Both terms create the impression of a kind of exclusivity from which the addressee can profit.

(3)   All this and much more (...)
(4)   (...) is open for *you** 24 hours a day.
(5)   (...) *you** can take *advantage** of our *special offers** (...) exclusive lines of SWISS luggage.
(6)   SHOPPING, SWISS MADE.
      [*my emphasis]

The slogan in (6) is highlighted by capitalization and by its partial repetition on the image: the ambiguous term *SWISS*, which stands for the company's shortened corporate name, is also a national prestige symbol *SWISS made*, foregrounding the company's origin. Capitalization and, at times, special ways of spelling are frequently used as attention getting devices in advertising (e.g., Leech 1966; Janich 2003).

Different forms of personal and possessive pronouns, such as the exclusive *we* and *our,* refer to the company *SWISS,* including the individual sender *Thomas Benz* as part of the company. The e-letter never uses the *I*-form. The only function Benz' name and position serve is to make the letter distinct and more reliable. The frequent use of the personal pronoun *you,* as in (4) and (5), shows the clear focus on the addressee. A linguistic orientation towards the receiver is common in direct (e)-mailings (cf., e.g., Janoschka 2005). This method of addressing the other corresponds to spoken conversation; here, it imitates the address procedure when communicating with another person. Moreover, the e-mail uses additional markers of spoken language, such as simple sentences and a low lexical density, due to the many repetitions (Hughes 1996: 33). This undemanding language style helps the addressee to grasp the message of the e-mail much faster, which could be crucial on the high-speed Internet.

The function of various catchy key terms, for instance, *NEW* and *special offers,* etc., is to speed up a (spontaneous) reaction, making it easier for the addressee to give feedback. Speed-up devices in advertising contribute to its success. It seems apparent that the more time addressees let pass until they plan to respond to an e-mail, the less likely they are to react at all.

As this section makes clear, direct e-advertising uses various linguistic and non-linguistic intensifiers to initiate and accelerate user responses. With this in mind, addressees are clearly at the centre of attention, which is linguistically expressed by features such as the addressee's name and the second person singular pronoun *you.* Although only qualitatively exemplified here, imperative sentences (see Brinker 1997), questions, and spoken language modes are typical of direct advertising communication (e.g., Janoschka 2004, 2005; Vögele 1996; Dürscheid 2006).

3. Weblogs

3.1 Definition and functions

The term 'weblog' was coined by Jorn Barger, one of the first American bloggers, at the end of 1997 to describe the process of

> logging the best stuff I find as I surf, on a daily basis: www.mcs.net/~jorn/html/ weblog.html. This will cover any and everything that interests me, from net culture to politics to literature etc (OED Online 2003).

Weblogs are "a recent addition to the repertoire of computer-mediated communication (CMC) technologies through which people can socialize online" (Herring et al. 2005: 1). Through weblogs, Internet users can reflect and exchange their interests, thoughts and opinions. The reasons why people blog vary from "to express oneself creatively" (52%), to "to document personal experiences and share them with others" (50%), "to stay in touch with friends and family" (37%), "to motivate other people to action" (29%), "to entertain others" (28%), "to influence the way other people think" (27%) and, with a share of 7%, bloggers want to make money from the blog (PEW 2006).[5] In this sense, blogs can be news sources (e.g., BBC News) and/or opinion spreading platforms on various issues. They can be a means of external business communication, i.e. a tool with which a company addresses its target groups and also facilitates direct feedback on advertising campaigns, products, etc. In addition to this, blogs can also be used as an entertaining platform and for social networking purposes (e.g., Łopacińska 2008).

Blog owners, i.e. blog authors, are called 'bloggers'. Their contributions or 'posts' (Figure 4, element 1) must be differentiated from 'comments' made by blog users/writers (Figure 4, element 3). These comments could also be made by the author (Figure 4, element 2) as a reaction to user contributions. Besides active participants, there are also passive users who only read the entries. The post depicted here (element 1) is dated *Wednesday, July 4, 2007* and entitled with the question *Huh?*. In the right margin,

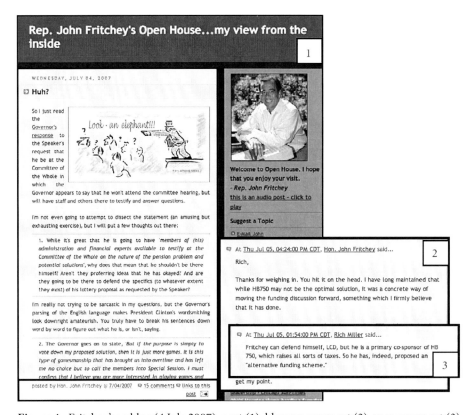

Figure 4. Fritchey's weblog (4 July 2007): post (1), blogger comment (2), user comment (3)

---

5.   Multiple answers were possible.

the blog owner *John Fritchey,* a politician from Illinois, is displayed. Below his photo, there is a list of interactive elements, such as a link to an audio post, an invitation to send an e-mail or visit his website, reports on *Current Illinois Political News,* links to other blogs and the blog archive beginning in August 2005.

Blogs are often linked to other blogs and websites. They can be purely text-based but often include multimedia elements such as images, sound files and video clips or streams. Search engines, such as *Technorati,* provide information on the most frequently searched items in the form of listed weblogs entries.

Bloggers have created diverse content. As such, one can distinguish between different types of blogs or genres: from the first blog types of personal online diaries and journals (see, e.g., Łopacińska 2008) – Justin Hall is considered to be the pioneer of this kind of weblog; he started documenting his life in 1994 (Harmanci 2005) – to a relatively new type, in which the "marketization of discourse" (Fairclough 1993: 143; see also Fairclough 1995)[6] is central, namely advertising blogs, such as corporate weblogs. Other blog types can focus on particular subjects such as travel, news, sport or politics.

Political blogs have proved a powerful tool in political campaigning. As evidenced in the 2008 US presidential campaign, presidential candidates have started actively and successfully to use the Web as an integral campaigning tool. These weblogs could also serve to promote the party's issue agenda. On a more personal level, politicians can simulate a closeness to the visitors of their blog. This might encourage a dialogue between the blogger and the users, which also supports the development of a virtual community around the politician. Moreover, this controlled media product, with little regulation, can help politicians transfer an original idea or opinion to the public much faster and without reliance on other mass media or journalists. Politicians could use the blog to understand and learn something about tendencies and moods, as well as what opinion leaders in the community might think. This characterization of political weblogs reflects what Fairclough (1993: 146) calls the "generation of new hybrid, partly promotional genres." As the following analysis will show, various functions and linguistic elements are involved when identifying this genre, i.e. from self-promotional claims to social practice.

From the user's perspective, participants are in direct contact with the blogging politician. They can comment or ask questions which would not be answered as directly or immediately via other media or information tools. The principle of gatekeeper is, therefore, a relic of ancient times, at least to some extent. Participants' identity can be made explicit or left implicit. This communication tool is open 24 hours a day, so users have unlimited access to it.

---

6.   The marketization of discourse can also refer to "the restructuring of the order of discourse on the model of more central market organizations" (Fairclough 1993: 143), whereby the traditional discourse structures of advertising are applied to services and public institutions, such as universities (see Fairclough 1993, 1995) and politics.

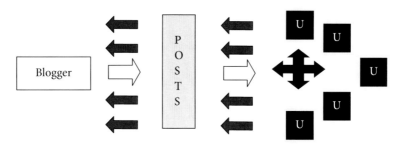

Figure 5. Process of weblog communication

3.2   Process of communication

The process of weblog communication is similar to that of direct advertising with two exceptions: firstly, users (U) can not only reply to the blogger (sender) but can also communicate among themselves, and secondly, the blogger can react immediately to user comments (Figure 5).

In other words, and as the illustration shows, blogging is a "key metaphor for interactivity (...): one-to-one, one-to-many, many-to-many" (Burstein 2005: xxi), in which producer and interpreter roles alternate. The interrelated user communication, visualized by the black cross, is not analyzed in this study.

4.   Data

John Fritchey is an American Democrat (Illinois), a representative of the 11th district. He was born on March 2, 1964 at Barksdale Air Force Base in Bossier City, Louisiana. In 1986, the family man – John and his wife Karen have one daughter – received a B.A. degree in Economics from The University of Michigan and earned a law degree from Northwestern University Chicago in 1989. Seven years later, Fritchey ran for State Representative and was first elected to the Illinois General Assembly at the age of 32. He is not as widely known as some high-ranking politicians, such as Arnold Schwarzenegger, but "the national Democratic Leadership Council has twice named John as one of their '100 Rising Stars to Watch' in the country" (Fritchey.com). The fact that Fritchey is not so well-known makes his weblog more reliable and authentic in terms of authorship, as he does not seem to delegate work on his weblog to others. In addition, for Fritchey, the weblog might be of concrete use because it facilitates an intensive, more personal exchange with his rather manageable target group, enabling him to get his message across and to strengthen the trust between himself and the blog users (cf., e.g., Coenen 2005). In turn, this brings him closer at grass-roots level. Fritchey's blog is definitely a highly-frequented website. It is impossible to state how many users actually contribute because different people are hidden behind the unidentified name *anonymous*. However, I would estimate the number of active users to be in the region of 250.

Fritchey has run his weblog, which is entitled *Rep. John Fritchey's Open House...my view from the inside* (http://johnfritchey.blogspot.com/) since August 2005. The quantitative part of this analysis (Figure 6) adds up to 654 weblog entries, collected in a year-long period from March 2006 to February 2007. The total number of entries is divided into 106 posts and 548 user and blogger comments, which reveals an interactive weblog.

The higher the number of posts, the higher the number of corresponding comments (cf., e.g., May, August, October 2006). For the comparative analysis of weblogs as a means of direct advertising, I have considered only commented posts, for the following reason: commercial e-mails are the first contact medium with the addressee and are thus comparable to posts. With this advertising platform, the politician informs, persuades and presumably also entertains his audience. A political post is, therefore, the counterpart of a commercial e-mail.

Table 1 shows that almost every Fritchey post (82%) has been commented on, i.e. 87 out of 106 posts. For instance, in May 2006, which was a comparatively productive month, Fritchey published 21 posts, of which 19 were commented upon. June (3) and July (4), in contrast, were less prolific but were nevertheless looked at by the blog readership.

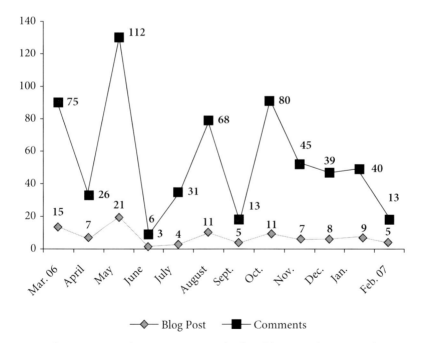

Figure 6. Relation posts and comments in Fritchey's weblog: March 2006 – February 2007

Table 1. Total number of posts in relation to commented posts

	Total posts	Commented posts
Mar 06	15	12
Apr 06	7	6
May 06	21	19
June 06	3	1
July 06	4	4
Aug 06	11	10
Sept 06	5	3
Oct 06	11	9
Nov 06	7	6
Dec 06	8	6
Jan 07	9	7
Feb 07	5	4
Sum	**106**	**87**

For the following linguistic analysis, I have selected only those posts that triggered a comment. More precisely, only the most interactive and hence, most appealing entries, namely posts that received 10 or more comments, are considered. This amounts to 21 commented posts in total. Altogether, they comprise 9.267 words, which is, on average, 441.3 words per post.

For the quantitative examination, I have taken into account only pronouns which are used by or which substitute for Fritchey, such as *I*, i.e. literal quotes or reported speeches that refer to others are not counted. Likewise the pronoun *you*, when it is not directed at blog users, has not been considered.[7] This method of exclusion applies to all linguistic means analyzed in this paper.

5.   Linguistic weapons of the Fritchey blog

The quantitative analysis shows that the most frequently applied linguistic strategies in the 21 of the 87 commented posts are personal and possessive pronouns of a) the first person singular (182) *I, me, my/mine* referring to the blog owner as an individual, as well as b) the third person plural pronouns (34) *we, us, our* in the role of inclusive and exclusive party-related references. In addition to hedges *I think* (16), *I'm not sure* (6), *I believe* (7), *possibly* (1), *maybe* (1) etc., the second largest group, namely some syntactic constructions, such as questions (25), imperatives (10) and conditional constructions, i.e. subjunctives built with *could, would, should, might* (84), are characteristic features of the posts (Figure 7).

---

7.   There is one quoted example in which the term *you* addresses Fritchey.

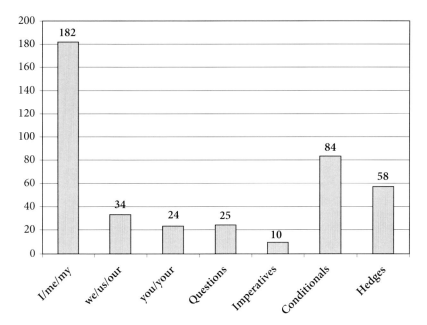

Figure 7. Linguistic means and strategies in 21 Fritchey posts (03/2006 – 02/2007)

The following subsections will treat the linguistic weapons of personal and possessive pronouns (5.1.), questions (5.2.) and imperatives (5.3.) in more detail.

5.1 Author-centric personal and possessive pronouns

Personal and possessive pronouns provide the background for the evaluation of the interactive nature of a text and its focus, i.e. whether it is sender or addressee-orientated. It seems obvious that first and second person pronouns are relevant in these respects. In my corpus, the high number of personal and possessive pronouns (240) reflect the interactive purpose of the posts. In more detail, the high number of *I/me* and *my/mine*, with 182 instances, and the comparably low occurrence of the second person pronoun *you*, with 24 instances, show a strong blogger/writer-orientation. In this matter, the Democrat's posts clearly differ from direct advertising (e)-mailings, which usually center the addressee as a means of initiating response, as previously exemplified by the SWISS newsletter (Figure 3). Moreover, considering the relation between 34 instances of mainly exclusive *we* and the *I*-form, *John Fritchey's* position as an individual becomes apparent. Unlike the *SWISS/Benz* focus (Figure 3), it is not the company or the political party which is spotlighted.

The following quote (7) is part of a post in which Fritchey describes the way in which he experienced the *Election Day* 22nd March 2006, where candidates for governor were elected in the Primary. In regard to content and language use, he communicates on a very personal level, first explaining what he did, namely talking to citizens about the *new ballots*, the fact that voters *don't trust the machines*, the weather situation in Springfield, school organization etc., and then giving information on what the outcome was for the different candidates. Fritchey explicitly updates this post four times by writing in bold, capital letters *UPDATE 6 p.m.*, *UPDATE 7.30 p.m.*, *UPDATE 8.30 p.m.* and the last one *UPDATE 12.30 a.m.*. Both the expected results [*no*] *real surprises* and his discomfort about the slow results *slower than I'd like*, are statements about his personal beliefs and news, giving his personal insights:

> (7)   *I've* talked with a *bunch of folks* around the City and State, and not hearing *any real surprises* thus far. *Results* are coming in *slower than I'd like*, but *we* were informed that that would be the case (March 22, 2006).

The set of interactional elements, such as the colloquialism *bunch of folks*, the ellipsis [*the*] *results*, the contracted forms *I've* and *I'd*, and the inclusive *we*,[8] are tactics of positive politeness (Brown and Levinson 1987). With this speech act, Fritchey creates the impression of everyone sitting in the same boat, placing himself and his addressees in the same position *we*, which is unlike his role of a political representative. This might not be astonishing on election day. Fritchey's communication style is thus very emotional, reflecting engagement and high involvement in this matter. If one considers that Fritchey knows his conversation partners, one could argue that he seeks support from his virtual community and intends to sit out this day together with them.

In the next quote (8), Fritchey also reveals private information. He implicitly refers to his family status as a *father* when he first mentions his *daughter* and secondly uses the 2nd person plural pronoun *our,* which includes his wife.

> (8)   During the course of *trick or treating* with *our daughter* this evening, *I had at least four different neighbors tell me* about how sick they are of the incessant onslaught of *campaign ads* (October 31, 2006).

One could conclude that he used *our* intentionally, if one considers that the second part of the sentence is continued in the *I*-form: *I had (...) four neighbors tell me*. An intact family is a sign of social integrity which, especially in politics, provides a positive image. However, one could interpret this change of perspective, which highlights himself, as a matter of context. The sentence starts with private matters, but finally refers to a public, or at least a non-family related issue, namely *campaign ads*.

Showing Fritchey in his paternal role as a private person is also realized through the reference to an important children's tradition of Halloween *trick or treating*. Fritchey informs readers about his neighbors' attitudes towards campaign ads, giving the statement some emphasis by the flexible number of families *at least four* who complained.

---

8.   In this context it is not clear whether *we* is meant inclusively or exclusively. Interpreted as the latter, it could count as a means of positive politeness strategy.

Another form of direct address Fritchey applies in his post on election day is when he thanks *everyone* (9) who voted without influencing the individual's *you* freedom of choice:

(9)　*To everyone,** who voted, whoever *you** voted for, thank *you** for being part of the process (March 22, 2006).
[*my emphasis]

Placed at the end of this post, this sentence not only functions as a final acknowledgement, but also involves the politician's concern that people make use of their right to vote.

5.2　Opinion providing questions

In the 21 posts, Fritchey uses a total of 25 questions. These can be classified into five headline questions (10–14), 13 questions used in the post to address the blog users and seven questions which are asked by third parties, such as guest bloggers, or are in quotes. In comparison to e-mailings, one could argue that post headlines are equivalent to the reference line in an e-mail header or the form of address in the e-mail. If headlines are composed as questions, they are often posed in the way the sender wants them to be answered. This takes place in the subsequent text. Similar to personal pronouns and directives discussed below, questions also reflect the interactive nature of a text.

　　Headlines are aimed at attracting attention, arousing the readers' interest and persuading them to read the body copy. A traditional categorization of headlines uses a binary grouping of 'nominal headlines' and 'verbal headlines' (e.g., Maurer 1972; Simon-Vanderbergen 1981). This classification has been criticized due to a number of cases in which the application is unclear, such as *Men too old,* and a lack of semantic consideration (e.g., Schneider 2000). Since the interpretation and function of headlines depend on various aspects, such as context meaning and addressee-orientation, a pragmatic point of view will cast a constructive light on my analysis of questions in this weblog. For my corpus, I would like to use the following distinction: a) Questions addressing the reader indirectly through their interest generating competence and b) Questions which address the blog readers directly.

　　Due to the limited information in the form of an adverb of time, as in headline (10), or of a comparative, as in (11), more context is necessary in order to grasp the questions' meaning than in (12), (13) and (14).

(10)　Now? (April 17, 2006)
(11)　Closer? (October 22, 2006)
(12)　Has the Governor Seen the Light? (May 19, 2006)
(13)　What's your Take on the Game? (August 22, 2006)
(14)　Where's the Party (Going)? (January 22, 2007)

The linguistic strategy of providing partial information in headlines, namely only touching on a topic, suggests the prerequisite of reading the whole text in order to disclose the headlines' reference meaning. Only question (13) can be categorized as a direct reader address question, using the pronoun *your*. In this case, *your* could be interpreted as an interactive discourse element of the weblog. All other questions represent news reporting style, viz. questions that talk only indirectly to the reader.

Fritchey continues in this manner when he uses questions in the posts. There are some interrogatives that do not really address someone, as in (15), and others that refer to the blog user directly as in (16).

(15)   What's wrong with this picture? A lot (May 31, 2006).

(16)   Good news you say? It looks that way, but there's a catch (July 31, 2006).

Question (15) gives Fritchey the floor for his explanations. He first exemplifies the problem and then comments on it. Here, the question's function is to emphasize his personal viewpoint. Although there is a personal *you* address, question (16) fulfills the same purpose. It seems that Fritchey is preventing the audience from adopting what he considers to be a misguided opinion or belief. In this case (16), Fritchey approaches a justification for the right interpretation of the facts. In (17), the politician uses a third method of question address when he deliberately employs a quote by someone else in which he himself is addressed:

(17)   John, what are you thinking? Aren't we just getting over clergy sex scandals in IL? And you want to provide them new safe harbor? You actually want to make it legal for girls to notify their clergy rapists rather than parents when they're pregnant – and then bypass the judicial bypass? (April 10, 2006)

Similar to the previous question (16), this quote (17), in which he is addressed by his first name *John,* allows Fritchey to comment directly and to react to the issue raised through another politician's attack. This accusation is strengthened by the personal level of address and the linguistic stress effected through the syntactical position of *you* as in *And you want to provide* (...). Using questions and third party quotes is a means by which bloggers can justify, legitimate and correct statements or opinions that are not in the politicians' interest. As a result, the politician spotlights himself. Quotes are also used in direct e-mailings but less in order to defend one's position and more to strengthen, for instance, sales arguments. Although there are no questions used in the newsletter (Figure 3), this is not representative for direct advertising (cf., e.g., Janoschka 2005). Questions in newsletters have the same functions as in posts, viz. addressing potential customers and providing customized information. Nevertheless, in direct advertising, there seems to be a preference for a more direct language style, namely directives.

5.3   Directives

Directive speech acts aim to cause the hearer or reader to carry out an action straight away. Directives are usually requests, commands or advice (e.g., Searle 1991; see also

Okulska this volume). These imperatives are frequently used in direct advertising (cf. Brinker 1997: 110). With them, advertisers also try to initiate an addressee reaction. *Buy now*, *click here* are concise, explicit commands which either aim to trigger a non-conversational but physical reaction, such as purchasing a product, or a communicative act, e.g., giving feedback. The reason for repetitive use of imperatives, particularly in direct advertising, lies in the need for a fast reaction. The more immediate a reaction is, the less people will spend time weighing up the need for their reaction. In other words, an attractive offer is more likely to be considered if a customer reaction follows quickly. Often, this reaction is enforced through a special time frame in which the offer is available. However, it is self evident that any addressee reaction is triggered by a combination of various factors and not just the use of directives.

In political blogs, no goods but ideologies, thoughts and opinions are sold. Thus, the focal point here is not to influence someone's purchasing behavior but to assure the blogger's position, convince conversation partners, change their attitudes or initiate feedback, etc. As a consequence, these motives are an indirect or direct request to participate in the blog communication. In (18), Fritchey uses the directive as an optional invitation to the blog users to comment on a previously mentioned issue:

(18)   Feel free to comment (October 4, 2006).

In (19), the directive supports Fritchey's point of view when he uses it as a means of clarification or as an excuse (20):

(19)   Let me be clear (March 23, 2006).
(20)   To my friends at my local Starbucks, don't get me wrong, I love you guys (August 30, 2006).

The demand (21) for a reply *tell me* is weakened by the politeness element *please* and makes it even weaker by the adverb *just*.

(21)   *Just please tell me* that somebody in City Council isn't going to try to legislate this (August 30, 2006).

Users are requested to read a quoted article by the imperative sentence (22). It functions as an introductory sentence, which first of all discloses that the subsequent information is a third party's literary property. Moreover, Fritchey reflects his personal opinion when he gives a reason why this article should be read: *interesting thoughts*. Although this is a semantically empty noun phrase to describe the content of a text, it might function as a pragmatic means of creating curiosity and implicating the process of reading the passage.

(22)   Read the rest of the article, it raises some *interesting thoughts* and closes with this: (May 22, 2006).
(23)   You get the idea. *Have at it* (August 22, 2006).

Have at it (23) is a western American colloquial term for 'begin' or 'have a go at it'. It implies that there is something waiting ahead and that one should begin to do whatever is appropriate. In this case, the directive functions as a call to send Fritchey more ideas. The imperative could also imply that the task is very difficult. Then, it is a request to try one's best. Colloquial terms reflect an informal communication style. They are either a sign of in-group language or a strategy that implies being mentally closer to one's followers and acting in concert.

5.4   Other linguistic weapons in the political blog

In addition to directives, imperatives and personal pronouns, there are other linguistic means which reflect a special emphasis: the capitalization of words, such as *I HATE* (March 22, 2006), *BUT, AND* (July 31, 2006), is a graphic accentuation which stresses their meaning. These can be found occasionally. As previously mentioned, Fritchey also makes use of colloquialisms such as *Have at it* (23) and *Who the hell knows?* (March 22, 2006) to convey in-group membership with these positive politeness tactics. Moreover, the Democrat uses sentence initial ellipses to emotionally express his physical and mental strain during the election day *Still too early*, *Just got*, *Looks like* (March 22, 2006). In this special context, they suggest a continuously up-dated blog structure with which Fritchey develops tension and keeps the readers involved. However, ellipses are generally less traceable in Fritchey's blog. Both ellipses and colloquialisms are also spoken mode features. Their usage depends on the functions and communication style they should fulfill in the discourse. Here, they could be interpreted as informal language to signal a similar communication level.

Fritchey exploits the medium's technical capabilities when he linguistically refers and links to multimedia elements, such as a video clip published on *YouTube.com*, *You can see the video here* (August 19, 2006). The deictic term *here* is a hyperlink to http://www.youtube.com/watch?v=drMHtcjOLj0 (accessed January 6, 2008).

All these means ranging from colloquialisms, ellipsis and hyperlinks to graphic elements could also be detected in e-mailings. An informal communication style, however, is less common in the mass advertising discourse. Commercially addressed people are rather anonymous target groups which share some demographic and psychological features. Hence, the communicative distance does not stipulate an in-group style. In a political weblog, some communication partners might be of a known and identifiable identity, such as *Carol Fritchey* (J. Fritchey's cousin; 19 October 2005) and *John Ruberry* (31 August 2006) or are, at least, known by their online names, such as *vikkitikkitavi* (5 December 2005) and *Rob* (28 April 2008) because of their regular involvement. An informal language style is, therefore, more likely. Besides, it is a technique Fritchey uses repeatedly in order to be closer to the community. In (20), for instance, he apologizes for his open-minded way before spreading thoughts about Starbucks employees joining a union when he addresses them with *To my friends* and colloquially tells them *I love you guys*. Of course, this post is not exclusively directed at the Starbucks employees, even if they have been part of his blog community so far. Instead, it seems that he wants to weaken the stringent opinion he has, which is read by his familiar blog readers, with these terms of address.

Similar to informal language, strategies of apologizing for not being able to communicate on a regular basis, might definitely be more common weapons in direct weblog communication than in advertising. As a method of excuse, Fritchey uses a form of indirect apology about why he is repetitively not able (24) to post any news as regularly as the community might have expected him to do:

(24) Once again, my posting has slowed as a result of my busy schedule (...) (May 31, 2006).

(25) I am out of town and had no intention of posting for several days. But then something happened which I couldn't let pass (October 4, 2006).

The explanation used in (25) gives an insight into his personal thinking and emotional state. Fritchey first elucidates that he had not intended to update his blog for several days because he was not in town, but then something had happened which had occupied him in such a way that he had felt the urge to express his worries and to communicate with his audience.

A final strategic linguistic weapon which I would like to touch upon here are the groups of frequently applied conditional sentences and hedges (cf. Figure 7). There are two reasons why I will not discuss them in detail in this paper: first, as markers of politeness strategies, they convey an optional mode of dealing with something, i.e. placing a condition upon the addressee agreement. This is less favorable in action-demanding direct advertising and hence, beside the point of comparison in this paper. Secondly – and this is the more relevant reason – hedges, which are usually categorized as negative politeness strategies for diminishing the impact of a speech act (Brown and Levinson 1987), seem to have another, almost contradictory function in political communication. In (26), Fritchey uses the phrases *I/do not/believe* to strengthen his opinion:

(26) As *I* have previously stated, *while I believe* that there is a *shortage of doctors* in parts of our state, and *while I agree* that malpractice rates are higher than they should be, *I do not believe* that either of these facts were caused by our previously-existing *malpractice laws* (November 21, 2006).

The first reference is a substantiated doubling of the antecedent subordinate clause with which Fritchey confirms what he said before. In the second negative reference, *believe* functions as an opposition marker when Fritchey states that their *malpractice laws* are not to blame for the *shortage of doctors*, etc. The whole interpretation of Fritchey's hedging is nailed down by the repetitive use of *believe*. Repetition is a rhetorical device commonly applied in political discourse. It reveals an author's intention to give a word, phrase or sentence a stronger emphasis. Throughout this paragraph (26), different words are repeated in various places: *while I* (anaphora), *I* and *believe*.

Fritchey gives himself a stronger emphasis through the accentuation of *while I* and his opinion *believe,* but it appears that he does not want to avoid committing himself to the intent of his own words. Hence, in this political weblog, hedging seems to have an emphasizing but not a diminishing function with which the politician intends to strengthen his position. This particular case of 'political hedging' needs special consideration in another analysis.

6.   Summary and conclusion

Although the examples I have chosen are of course only selectively representative of political weblog and e-mailing communication, they seem to reflect some parallels. Both text types reveal a similar communication process and make use of similar linguistic persuasion strategies or, as I have called them, 'linguistic weapons': the audience is addressed by questions and imperative sentences, using typical discourse features, such as first and second person personal and possessive pronouns and different terms of address. However, the frequency and the form of application differ. Although a balanced quantitative comparison between both text types has not been made in this paper, it is clear that the most striking difference relates to the positioning of the sender and receiver. It is the politician *I* who is centered in the posts, whereas in e-mailings the addressee *you* seems to assure a successful communication. The questions used in the political posts are content-establishing constructions and less addressee-focused. In e-mailings, they could serve a similar function, but, in connection with the audience perspective, they should challenge the receiver to respond. Likewise, imperatives should initiate feedback or an action as a result of the conceptualization of the commercial message exchange.

In conclusion, I suggest that political weblogs are highly correlated with direct advertising, but they have another focus. In politics, it is the sender, viz. the politician, who is the advertised brand. In e-mailings, it is the product or service which evokes a need in the customer. The weapon of linguistic persuasion by means of the *I/you*-perspective is, therefore, shifted. This could be additionally explained by the private matters Fritchey includes in his posts, as well as the community approach in the political weblog discourse and his, from time to time, informal language style. Conversation partners are more or less acquainted with each other, not necessarily personally but by their (alias) user names; although in this special field of politics, one could expect most of the Fritchey blog users to share the same political ideology or party and thus know each other. In e-mailings, however, communication is anonymous, even if addressees' purchasing behavior and preferences can be tracked and stored online and then exploited to construct an advertising message with which the addressee feels individually and personally addressed.

The idea presents itself that the weblog, as such, is a weapon which blogging politicians take advantage of: to cultivate one's own weblog is a new, high-speed way of presenting and positioning oneself, gathering first-hand information and finding out what the blogging community really thinks – in other words, boosting the grassroots efforts.

The data analyzed provides a fruitful basis for the following future research: since this weblog is relatively interactive, the exchange between post and user comments, but also between user and blogger comments – as a reaction to the individual user – definitely needs further examination. Moreover, the use and functions of hedges together with conditionals in political weblogs necessitates a more detailed inspection.

References

Brassington, Frances and Pettitt, Stephen. 2005. *Essentials of Marketing*. Harlow: Prentice Hall.

Brinker, Klaus. 1997. *Linguistische Textanalyse*. Berlin: Erich Schmidt Verlag.

Brown, Penelope and Levinson, Stephen C. 1987. *Politeness: Some Universals in Language Usage*. Cambridge: Cambridge University Press.

Burstein, Dan. 2005. "Introduction." In *Blog! How the Newest Media Revolution Is Changing Politics, Business, and Culture*, David Klein and Dan Burstein (eds), xi–xxvi. New York: cds Books.

Coenen, Christopher. 2005."Weblogs als Mittel der Kommunikation zwischen Politik und Bürgern – Neue Chancen für E-Demokratie?" *Kommunikation@ Gesellschaft* 6: 5. Retrieved September 1, 2007 from http://www.soz.uni-frankfurt.de/K.G/B5_2005_Coenen.pdf.

Dürscheid, Christa. 2006. "Werbe-Anschreiben im intermedialen Vergleich." In *Angewandte Textlinguistik. Perspektiven für den Deutsch- und Fremdsprachenunterricht. Europäische Studien zur Textlinguistik 2*, Arne Ziegler and Maximilian Scherner (eds), 141–156. Tübingen: Narr.

Fairclough, Norman. 1993. "Critical discourse analysis and the marketization of public discourse: The universities." *Discourse & Society* 4 (2): 133–168.

—. 1995. *Critical Discourse Analysis: The Critical Study of Language*. London: Longman.

—. 2001. *Language and Power*. Essex: Longman.

Fritchey.com. "About John." Retrieved May 15, 2009 from http://www.fritchey.com/about.html.

Harmanci, Reyhan. "Time to get a life – pioneer blogger Justin Hall bows out at 31." Retrieved December 9, 2007 from http://www.sfgate.com/cgi-bin/article.cgi?file=/c/a/2005/02/20/MNGBKBEJO01.DTL.

Herring, Susan C., Kouper, Inna, Paolillo, John C., Scheidt, Lois Ann, Tyworth, Michael, Welsch, Peter, Wright, Elijah and Yu, Ning. 2005. "Conversation in the blogosphere: An analysis 'from bottom up'." Proceedings of the Thirty-Eight Hawai'i International Conference on System Science (HICSS-38). Los Alamitos: IEEE Press. Retrieved December 11, 2007 from http://www.blogninja.com/hicss05.blogconv.pdf.

Herring, Susan C., Scheidt, Lois Ann, Bonus, Sabrina, and Wright, Elijah. 2004. "Bridging the gap: A genre analysis of weblogs." Proceedings of the 37th Hawai'i International Conference on System Sciences (HICSS-37). Los Alamitos: EEE Computer Society Press. Retrieved January 21, 2005 from http://www.blogninja.com/DDGDD04.doc.

Horsbøl Anders. 2006. "From our plan to my promises: Multimodal shifts in political advertisements." In *Mediating Ideology in Text and Image*, Inger Lassen, Jeanne Strunck and Torben Vestergaard (eds), 149–172. Amsterdam: Benjamins.

Hughes, Rebecca. 1996. *English in Speech and Writing*. London: Routledge.

Maurer, Hanspeter. 1972. *Die Entwicklung der englischen Zeitungsschlagzeile von der Mitte der zwanziger Jahre bis zur Gegenwart*. Bern: Francke.

Janich, Nina. 2003. *Werbesprache. Ein Arbeitsbuch*. Tübingen: Narr.

Janoschka, Anja. 2004. *Web Advertising*. Amsterdam: Benjamins.

—. 2005. "A comparative analysis of direct print mailings and spam." *Lodz Papers in Pragmatics* 1: 91–120.

Leech Geoffrey, N. 1966. *English in Advertising*. London: Longman.

Łopacińska, Zuzanna. 2008. "Dialogicity of Internet blogs." In *Discourse Variation across Communities, Cultures and Times*, Urszula Okulska and Grzegorz Kowalski (eds), 123–154. Warsaw: University of Warsaw.

OED Online. 2003. "Weblog." Retrieved December 13, 2007 from http://dictionary.oed.com/cgi/entry/00319399?single=1&query_type=word&queryword=weblog&first=1&max_to_show=10.

PEW/INTERNET. 2006. "Bloggers." Retrieved November 10, 2007 from http://www.pewinternet.org/pdfs/PIP%20Bloggers%20Report%20July%2019%202006.pdf.

Schneider, Kristina. 2000. "The emergence and development of headlines in English newspapers." In *English Media Texts – Past and Present*, Friedrich Ungerer (ed.), 45–65. Amsterdam: Benjamins.

Searle, John. 1991. "Indirect speech acts." *Pragmatics: A Reader*, Steven Davis (ed.), 265–277. Oxford: Oxford University Press.

Sifry, Micah L. 2005. "Politicians who blog (Let's make a list)." Retrieved August 1, 2007 from http://personaldemocracy.com/node/453.

Simon-Vanderbergen, Anne M. 1981. *The Grammar of Headlines in the Times 1870–1970*. Brussel: AWLSK.

Vögele, Siegfried. 1996. *Dialogmethode. Das Verkaufsgespräch per Brief und Antwortkarte*. Heidelberg: Redline.

CHAPTER 13

The language of political opinion

Discourse, rhetoric and voting behavior

James Moir

1. Introduction

Clarke et al. (2004) have conducted one of the most extensive analyses of British voting patterns from 1964 to 2001 using Gallup opinion poll and British Election Study voting survey data. They argue that the British voting public can be characterized in their recent voting patterns in terms of short-term evaluations of party leaders and their public image and performance, overall party performance, and reactions to political issues of the day. This can be viewed as part of a wider trend towards opinionation, that is, an ideology of *having* opinions on matters, and of wanting to know what the opinion of others is. Of course, opinions being located 'down' at the perceptual-cognitive level appear to leave little room for more wider sociological concerns. Indeed Clarke et al. (2004) suggest that the sociological approach to understanding the British voting behavior in terms of social class characteristics and party allegiance is much weaker than in the past although its salience is very much dependent upon the kinds of questions and surveys used.

This paper takes the work of Clarke et al. (2004) as its starting point given its landmark importance in charting and attempting to explain the nature of British political voting over what can loosely be considered as modern political times. It examines the demise of the time-honored sociological approach in favor of a focus on the 'opinionated' voter. However, this focus is not concerned with attempting to treat opinions as related to some inner psychological state but rather as a discourse located in a historical context, and one in which the mass media have a considerable stake (see Lassen, Strunck and Vestergaard 2006). In effect, this paper argues that there has been a rise, largely promulgated through the media, that voters *should* have opinions about political matters, or indeed the political process itself. This individualizes the political process and reduces it to a matter of intrapsychic cognitions and perceptions. These points are illustrated with reference to the recent departure of Tony Blair as Prime Minister, and the subsequent succession of Gordon Brown.

2. From sociological factors to valence politics

First, it is important to chart the move from the traditional sociological approach to understanding the electorate to the focus on the individual voter charted in the work of Clarke et al. (2004). This traditional approach has three main elements in considering how the British electorate votes in terms of sociological factors: (i) relatively fixed social characteristics, such as social class or region that are associated with long-term socialization processes and which predispose individuals to support one party rather than another; (ii) the outcomes of these socialization processes can be either reinforced or undermined by the individual's social context, for example an individual's employment, the place where he or she lives, and the informal groups to which he or she belongs and; (iii) this amalgam of social characteristics and social contexts produces a distinctive social psychology of voting. During the course of an individual's lifetime and again largely due to socialization, most people tend to develop stable and enduring identification with a political party and this in turn serves to provide them with a means of interpreting political information and to predispose them to vote for the same party in successive elections. Other contingent factors, such as the condition of the economy, specific political issues in vogue at the time, perceptions of party leaders, or national and international events, would cause some people to switch their votes between elections. But, according to this approach to understanding voting patterns in post-war Britain, most people would continue to vote according to their structural positions and their party identifications and this, in turn, would be associated with relative electoral stability. Electoral change and voting patterns could occur in the longer term in this view, but is an evolving process inter-twined with changes in the social structure of Britain.

However, the sociological account of British electoral voting patterns has been challenged. Even early on, Crewe, Sarlvik and Alt (1977) noted a decline in the strength of party identification, despite there being little evidence of an accompanying social structural change that would have produced this apparent decline. It is also the case that more recent work has focused upon the 'loss the heartlands' argument and voter apathy. As Clarke et al. (2004) note, it may well be that the 2001 election turnout decline is associated with a disaffection among Labour supporters because of their party's failure to 'deliver the goods' by improving health care, education, transportation and other vital public services during its first term in office. As Clarke et al. (2004: 4) put it: "In this regard it would appear that voters are more concerned with policy outcomes than they are with policy commitments."

Clarke et al. (2004) note that many electoral analysts in Britain have followed their counterparts in many other advanced democracies and have moved away from models that place 'sociological' factors, such as social location and long-term party attachments as the primary explanatory model. This has been largely replaced by voting models where the principal explanatory variables are leader and party images, issue perceptions, and assessments of economic performance. In particular, there has been a move to focus on the individual at the centre of this process which is rooted in Down's (1957) classic study, *An Economic Theory of Democracy*, in which the act of voting depends on a calculation of the personal costs and benefits of voting. However, Clarke et al. note that they have followed a simple model of 'individual rationality' in this regard, but have recognized that voters' cost–benefit calculations are more indecisive, impressionistic, and sometimes emotionally driven than a straightforward rational choice theory would permit. In doing so, they have maintained their distance from what may be seen as sociological determinism, and, instead, taken a more social psychological approach in terms of what they refer to as 'valence politics.'

A valence model involves two elements (i) party identification in terms of an evaluative 'running tally' of performance and competence; and (ii) short-term reactions that can either be towards contemporary issues or retrospective applied. These elements apply especially where there is a consensus as to what the key political matters are as they affect the electorate. In Britain, it is argued that matters such as a relatively strong economy, affordable quality healthcare and the National Health Service, a good education system, tackling crime, and a defense policy that is fit for purpose in terms of national interest and Britain's role in the world. It is held that political parties and their leaders are therefore judged on how well they match up with the electorate's expectations with regard to these political indicators at a given electoral point. In short, which party relative to the others comes out well in the tally of recent and current evaluations is favored.

Clarke et al. (2004) argue that voters do not necessarily have the resources or the inclination to inform themselves fully about the political choices that are available to them in any given election. It is suggested that as a result, they tend to use judgmental shortcuts that enable them to avoid or reduce the need to constantly update their political knowledge and information. They propose an approach that combines a focus on valence issues with the view that voters use such shortcuts when making their electoral decisions. These judgments, in turn, are arrived at through leadership evaluations and party identification.

The importance of voters' perceptions of party leaders as heuristic devices is explained in terms of their authority and status in speaking for party policy. Political parties themselves are not necessarily homogeneous organizational entities. Parties typically have local, regional, and national organizations that do not always convey a single, unified political message. The stance taken with regard to manifesto commitments at election time is frequently the result of public debate among competing personalities within parties, and often played out in the media spotlight. This can often involve the articulation of different shades of emphasis with regard to policy positions and sometimes displaying very different intellectual traditions. Under this media saturated coverage, it is not always clear to voters what 'the party' actually stands for. However, despite the media's best efforts to sometimes highlight these apparent inconsistencies and divisions it is argued that voters perceive what the party stands for through the voice of its leader. The leader being the main figure and spokesperson for a party is someone whom voters can make judgments about in terms of their character and competence and trustworthiness. He or she is the party's most clearly identified, single individual who, if elected, will take ultimate responsibility for what the government does or fails to do. For many voters then, assessing the leader is a very convenient way of assessing the likely competence of the party in office. However, leader images, particularly televised images, are not the only heuristic that voters use in order to estimate parties' likely performance. As noted above, voters' competence assessments are also informed by their party identifications.

Following Fiorina (1981) and others who have conceptualized partisanship in terms of an individual rationality approach, Clarke et al. (2004) view party identification as a store of accumulated information about political parties. Most commonly the strength of partisan attachments is updated through the voter's assessment of the parties' political and economic performance, and in turn this is used to inform electoral choice. However, in addition to this running tally assessment and a more individualistic cost-benefit judgment it is possible that people consider the group and system-wide benefits that might accrue from their participation in the electoral system. It may well be the case that many voters believe that the legitimacy and maintenance of the political system is dependent upon the citizenry actively participating in the electoral system. The general expectation upon people to vote, and to consider political, social and economic factors as they affect the populace, is taken as providing a broader political calculation. A *valence politics* approach is held to offer a more plausible characterization of the psychology of political participation in Britain over the past forty years. The focus on how judgments about parties' likely performance in office affects electoral choice, how such judgments are the result of the application of cognitive shortcuts, such as leadership images and party identification, and how perceptions of broader group and the democratic system affect citizens' decisions to vote, are all taken as providing a better approach than focusing upon active participation. This is taken as being a more fruitful approach to understanding how people vote that maintains a distance from sociological determinism.

However, it is also possible to trace an increasing trend towards decision-making as being located 'down' at the individualized sphere of personal choice. This perspective has most notably been advocated by Ulrich Beck in terms of a transition in the nature and experience of risk and representing a 'categorical shift' with respect to the individual and society (Beck 1992: 127). In this risk society 'old' collective forms of identity have been replaced by 'new' identifications that are rooted in individual actions. Beck traces this shift back to the 1970s and argues that the Fordist era of production and wealth distribution, in which economic and political interests were bound up with the desired ends of full employment and high standards of welfare and healthcare, ran into problems. Beck reasons that negative outcomes such as rise of mass unemployment, industrial pollution and nuclear hazards effectively created a schism in the institutional structures associated with Fordism and ushered in era preoccupied with the problem of insecurity and risk (Beck 1992: 49). In the risk society perspective citizens are now individually accountable for themselves and their economic opportunities, and of course reflexively related to this is the view that their part in the democratic process is bound up with these individual biographies. Thus Beck notes that the traditional place of family ties and class has given way to secondary agencies and institutions which "stamp the biography of the individual and make that person dependent upon fashions, social policy, economic cycles and markets" (Beck 1992: 131).

3. From cognitive heuristics to opinionation as ideology

Beck's risk society perspective provides a wider ideological background to voter behavior as the outcome of individual opinions but his broad-brush approach is only partially useful. His risk society thesis is not without critique given the broad claims that sometimes gloss over features that indicate some degree of continuity in the social reproduction of Western societies (see, e.g., Mythen 2005). In considering how people respond to the democratic process, what is needed is a consideration of social psychological aspects in terms of how both rational and non-rational evaluations of political parties and their leaders are conditioned by perceptual-cognitive heuristics. The image of the British voter as being swayed by short-term evaluations and political allegiances, especially related to party leader image, certainly seems to resonate with some of the recent press coverage of electoral issues. However, if we cautiously anchor this to Beck's perspective, then opinionation can be considered as ideological, and its increasing prominence in the media has become evident during the latter part of the previous century and up to where we are now.

The sophistication and centrality of opinion polling and its representation in the media is well documented (e.g., Herbst 1998; Lavrakas and Holley 1990; Mancini 1999). Britain, in common with most other countries, has witnessed a growth in the frequency of surveys, particularly those directly commissioned by the media. There has been a phenomenal growth in polling techniques and analyses, particularly in terms of computerized systems. However, notwithstanding the greater degree of sophistication of these polls they have remained rooted in certain key assumptions about the nature of voting psychology. Indeed, it could be argued that these polls have served to promote an ideology of opinionation in which an inner state of mind (i.e. *having* an opinion for) is taken as a warrant for action (i.e. casting a vote in an election). In this way the individual psychology, how someone thinks about a particular issue or political party, is seen as the focus of attention.

Thus *having* a set of opinions is conventionally associated with how people 'think' and the way this relates to their actions. To express an opinion is to possess the quality of having thought about some issue or other, and to demonstrate that an individual *thinks* before they engage in the electoral process. This is the political actor whose actions are reasoned and have some basis which others can understand and assess. Thus expressions of opinions can be considered as related to social processes in terms of an association between how people account for matters and seeing them as psychological entities. In this way a major cultural dualism is maintained: taking people's 'outward' accounts and actions and considering these as representations of what they are like 'inside' as rational agents. However, opinionation can be considered as the outcome of people's engagement within social practices rather than as something they bring to the political process as best sense representations of parties and their politics. The whole notion of opinionation is based upon viewing people as rational agents and derives from accountability within practices rather than as the result of some sort of cognitive processing and exchange of representations.

A perceptual-cognitivist view of opinionation is, of course, the basis of much psychological investigation which trades on the assumption that people are concerned with interacting with one another in order to understand what they are thinking and feeling. This is part of a wider cultural commonplace, an 'inner/outer' dualism, which is integral to a range of social practices. The notion of these two separate realms is therefore a major rhetorical feature that is incorporated into how people interact with one another. It provides a means of trading on notions of 'sense making' as well as the portrayal of people's inner mental states. There is a huge cultural imperative to communicate in an intelligible way and to be able to convey one's 'thoughts' in the form of judgments, reasons, and evaluations as the outcome of some kind of deliberative mental *process*. Seeking opinionative judgments about political parties and their politics implies the lone individual in brining to bear his or her internal mental apparatus to these external matters in a way that involves some mental effort. And once having worked on it there is an outcome – in cognitive processing terms an 'input-process-output' model – in which the outcome is voting behavior.

I want to suggest that this model is orientated to in discourse as part of the social practices that people engage in. Opinionation is something that people orientate to in terms of how they portray their political views and actions. Notice here that orientating to something does not necessarily involve an explicit mention of these psychological terms but rather how people treat each other as if these are germane or at stake. In effect, this orientation is one of a discourse of perceptual-cognitivism as process, as something that is normatively attended to as a means of accomplishing order within social practices, in this case the dynamics of the political engagement.

The nature of this order is founded upon an orientation of people as participating in employing opinionative practices that generate what individuals 'think' about certain political issues and events. In this way these issues and events are placed prior to this operation, as having happened and needing to be communicated, to be 'understood' as the basis for individual voting intentions and behavior. In this communication model people are placed in amongst a realm of political events and occurrences and a realm of mental operations requiring to be brought together. The giving of opinions about these matters is associated with the psychological notion of *perception*, which is in turn related *behavior* through a psychological linkage between the two. This kind of rhetorical construction displays persons as rational agents who reach 'decisions,' *have* opinions, have deliberated matters to some extent, and who can account for how they vote in a way that 'makes sense' to others. It is interesting to note here how even accounts that allude to emotions as the basis for actions may nonetheless be treated as rational in terms of their accountability or intelligibility. We can see why a person might have a certain political opinion given their perception of a given political issue or party leader or performance. This is the basis of opinion polling and of course its representation in the media; people are assumed to want to know what others *think* about the political issues of the day.

4.   Beyond cognitivist assumptions: Academic and everyday practices

As noted above the testing of public opinion through polling typically trades on a 'sense making' rhetoric in which the mind is theorized as a mental system that operates upon an external reality in order to produce a rational account of it. However, the decoupling of cognitive activity from opinionation as a social practice through the use of such polling methods is what makes this activity easier to portray as the outcome of some inner sense-making process. People's views are rendered as individual opinions, evaluations and judgments rather than as an ideological practice. It sustains the view that we make electoral choices via our opinions, and that socio-structural factors are *de facto* ruled out of court. Everything comes down to a matter of individual choice.

Although this kind of voluntarism and model of mind is very much the lifeblood of modern cognitive psychology, it can also be found in less explicit ways within other, more unlikely, realms which accord more theoretical weight to social practice. As Potter and Edwards (2001) point out, the social theorist Pierre Bourdieu may be considered an unlikely advocate of cognitivism but his theorization of *habitus* (e.g. Bourdieu 1977, 1992) trades on an unreflexive 'inner/outer' dichotomy. This presupposes the development of a psychological system in which dispositions associated with membership of social and cultural groups come to generate practices, perceptions, attitudes and opinions. This system is then able to produce 'meaning' (i.e. make sense), store and process it. This in turn can be related to people's partisanship and voting behavior. Now whilst Bourdieu gives more weight to social practice and culture than that of cognitive psychology, he still trades on this 'inner/outer' dualism and the reification of 'mind' as a perceptual system.

More recently there has been a systematic attempt to map out the relationship between cognitive science and social theory along the dimension of 'strong/weak' cognitivism (Strydom 2007). Strong cognitivism can be found in approaches that effectively presuppose mental properties that are associated with findings from the cognitive sciences. These include such aspects as neurophysiological structures and processes as well as informational or cognitive processes that are the subject of interest to both those working in the more natural science areas of ethology and biology and to those involved in the world of artificial intelligence. On the other hand, weak cognitivism utilizes socially derived mental representations such as beliefs, intentions, motives, meanings, reasons, and of course, opinions. The latter is the traditional stock-in-trade of the social sciences, although there have been recent attempts at a rapprochement between this weak form of cognitivism and the stronger version in terms of communicative-discursive approach (Habermas 2003; Eder 2007). Both social theorists acknowledge evolutionary processes, but also stress that human sociality involves having experiences, learning and communicating about the world such that the social world becomes realized.

But whilst academic disciplines such as psychology and sociology trade on this inner mind/outer world dualism it is also, of course, constructed and maintained as noted above in the everyday practice of opinion polling and its representation in the media. There is a common discursive currency of reference to what people think about political matters and how they might or might not be influenced by what other people think about how others think. This can be seen in the amount of media coverage given over to representations of political issues and opinion poll data. Much of this is presented in terms of opinion poll survey, pie charts and other visual techniques. Shifts in public opinion are charted, discussed and assessed. This becomes all the more intensive and frenetic at election time as poll information is updated on an almost daily basis. However, there has been an increasing trend to include polls in the coverage of political stories as a means of displaying public opinion towards 'live' issues and events. This is perhaps part of what can be considered a wider trend of 'lifestyle politics' (Shah et al. 2007), in which people express their politics, not via the ballot box, but through their consumer choices. Political action in this sense is 'down' at the level of direct interaction with others. However, the interplay between the public's interest in party politics and their issue-focused is perhaps less well understood. The explosion in media coverage of political issues through for example dedicated television news channels or interactive websites is a testament to the fact that political news is itself a product that is consumed in an increasingly on-demand fashion. Add to this the personalization or presidentialization of politics (Hazan 1996; Maddens and Fiers 2004; Mughan 1993; Poguntke and Webb 2005) as a feature of media focus in terms of popularity ratings and appears to lend support for a move away from straightforward party political allegiance and a move towards individual opinionation.

5.   Anti-cognitivism, anti-foundationalism and models of personhood and the political process

In order to explore the ideological basis of opinionation it would be unhelpful to start from the assumption that such a dualism exists, that there is a psychological system that operates upon an external political reality in order to produce vies about it. For one thing such an assumption is not necessarily a cultural universal, and for another people themselves do not exclusively make reference to such a dualism in terms of 'sense making' as they discuss political matters. For example, people can and do engage in sociological discourse about such matters in terms of socio-structural factors. However, for the purpose of studying how people make of use this dualism with regard to the generation and maintenance of opinionation there is no need to start from a cognitivist position. The reason for adopting a non-cognitivist approach is that the focus is on how this inner/outer dualism is pressed into service as an ideological practice where opinion giving is something that is viewed as being entirely germane to the electoral process. In other words opinionation is constructed as an almost necessary feature of the voting behavior.

It would also be absurd to begin from a point of doing what is being studied, that is, how the landscape of political reality and mind are associated in order to examine opinions as a generative force. To take these as givens would be to fall back on a perceptual-cognitive model as a foundational assumption instead of examining how this model functions in ideological terms. The analytic pay-off for this is in terms of achieving a means of dealing with its sheer pervasiveness as a means of accomplishing opinionation as a normatively generative discourse in the electoral process. So my starting point is to adopt an analytically agnostic stance with regard to the 'inner mind' and 'external political reality' and instead of adopt an epistemologically relativist, or antifoundationalist, position. This involves examining how versions of such a political reality are produced, principally through the media, and in particular as related to the production of what counts as relevant for the formation of opinionation.

It should also be noted that the position adopted does not require any stipulation of a model of the person or society. In other words, the focus is squarely upon the business of what gets constructed as opinionative persons within society and how this is accomplished as an aspect of a wider discourse about the electoral process. By taking seriously the issue of what gets constructed as political opinions, particularly via the media, then the more traditional approach to the electorate as consisting of individual causal entities is bypassed altogether. By not starting with some pre-defined model of the voter, especially the traditional cognitivist model, in which the issue is one of understanding how people perceive political matters, it is possible to treat opinions and political issues as cultural categories that are traded upon and maintained as an ideology that guides the electoral process.

The significance of such an analytical move is that it allows the focus of study to become how opinionation is not, for most people, some psychological problem to be resolved but rather a practical sociological concern and construction. Much has been written recently about the discursive means by which people construct and orientate towards discursive psychology (e.g. Edwards and Potter 1992; Edwards 1997; Potter 1996, 2003; te Molder and Potter 2005), but there is much less of a discussion as to how 'thinking' agents are constructed in terms of the direction of 'flow' between inner mind and out reality. Presenting political matters as external to the person and requiring to be made sense of in the formation of opinions, or in stressing the 'inner' thought processes that need to be brought to upon these matters as resulting in having an opinion, can be examined. General features of these constructions as 'flows' from the 'external' political world to an inner world of mind and *vice versa* forms the framework of this analysis. In doing so one kind of move involves the use of perceptual rhetoric as a means of constructing political matters, and is associated with a mental world of *knowing, understanding* and *evaluating* matters. The other works in the opposite direction and involves the establishment of a person's state of 'mind', what their opinion actually is, by seeking expressions of this through opinion polls.

Both sets of practices are fundamental to the pervasiveness of how opinionation functions as an ideological practice. Again it is worth re-iterating at this point the focus here is on the construction of political opinions as an accounting practice in terms of a culturally embedded inner/outer dualism. This is accomplished by looking at opinion polling and associated commentary with respect to the transition between Tony Blair and Gordon Brown as British Prime Minister presented on the BBC News website. This was chosen for reasons of accessibility in order to illustrate this discourse of opinionation and because of the recent growth in such on-line material.

6.   Making political matters the subject of opinion

Political matters can be presented as a means of constituting their existence in a particular way with an outcome of trying to make sense of them as a set of cognitive operations. This form of accounting presents the political engagement in terms of 'mental processes' being *required* to operate upon the material that is presented in order to 'make sense' of it and form opinion. In this way the events are placed prior to this operation, as having happened or as being the case and needing to be 'understood' through the opinions of others. This can be seen in the following extracts (1–5) from the BBC news website.

Extract 1 (see Figure 1) charts Blair's popularity rating of his terms as Prime Minister, including election outcomes, against what is presented as key political issues of the day. This provides a means of overviewing Blair's premiership in order to apprehend or grasp the nature of the impact of these events in order to show how opinion of him changed over time. The selection and active constitution of these 'events' is occluded through their reification as 'external' political matters that impacted upon people's internal evaluations. These are presented as *the* issues, or in the valence politics model, those areas where there is consensus on what the issues that matter are. Thus the public perception of Blair is presented as being the fundamental issue that requires to be 'understood' or 'made sense' of in terms reacting to these issues.

Extracts 2 and 3 (see Figure 2 and Figure 3, respectively), in turn, show monthly poll round-ups of the range of issues that are presented as being the subject of opinion polls. In Extract 2 these range from policing in relation to terrorism at one end of the spectrum to voters views on the 2012 London Olympic Games logo. This diverse patterning of what counts as matters of political opinionation is further exemplified in Extract 3 which

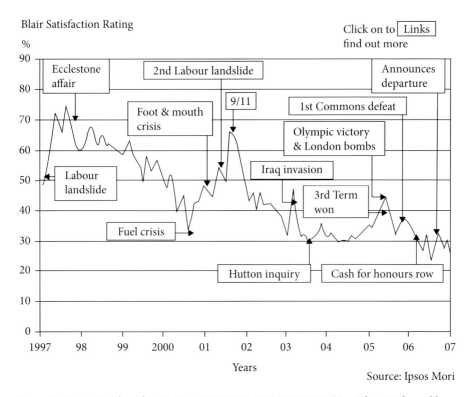

Figure 1. Extract 1: Thursday, 10 May 2007, 07:20 GMT 08:20 UK; *Tony Blair: Highs and lows*

predictably focuses upon voter opinions of Gordon Brown in the early days of his Prime Ministership to the issue of should the Government promote marriage.

One of the key points in the presentation of these polls is the straightforward use of percentages with the accompanying extracted aspect of the question that is taken as being the key issue at stake. Percentages are commonly associated with questionnaire responses and readily understood as means of representing an aggregation of opinions. When combined with the paired down extracts from polling questions or statements (e.g. "new police powers to 'stop and question' anyone they need to", "children brought up by a single parent are more likely to get into trouble than children brought up by married parents"), and the one word evaluative descriptors (e.g. "satisfied," "agree," disapprove"), they can be presented as short cuts into the collective 'thinking' of the public on a range of issues.

This association between the presentation of issues, events and occurrences and mental operations that have been applied to them in terms of perception and the formation of individual opinionation is taken as a driving the electoral process. In this way a perceptual-cognitivist form of accounting is actively maintained as an ideological force in which such matters become the subject of a kind of liberal choice in how they are interpreted and evaluated in terms of an active 'inner' response; the production

> The month opened with government proposals for new police powers to counter the threat of terrorism.
>
> These certainly proved controversial in Parliament and across the media, but Populus/BBC Daily Politics (sampled 6–7 June) appeared to find a very receptive public audience for such measures.
>
> Some 75% of respondents supported "new police powers to 'stop and question' anyone they need to," and 65% agreed the government should put combating terrorism ahead of concerns for civil liberties.
>
> *2012 logo*
> MORI also found that 79% of people had seen the new London Olympics 2012 logo, and among these 68% disapproved of it.
>
> *Blair departure*
> MORI/Observer (sampled 14–20 June) provided their last monthly measure of satisfaction with Tony Blair before his resignation as prime minister: 33% said they were satisfied with him, compared with 60% who expressed dissatisfaction – a net figure of –27%. By comparison, David Cameron's net satisfaction rating was –5% and Sir Menzies Campbell's –12%.

Figure 2. Extract 2: Tuesday, 3 July 2007, 12:13 GMT 13:13 UK; *Poll Watch: June 2007*

of political opinions. It can also be the basis for creating a version of temporality in terms of how the electorate voted on the basis of their opinions. The election result is constructed as being the collective 'opinionative voice of the people' as a judgment on the Government in office.

The motive of electoral advantage, as evidenced in the opinion polls, can become a topic in itself that voters need to attend to. Extract 4 (see Figure 4) shows the media speculation about whether or not Gordon Brown would hold a 'snap' general election. A contrast structure is used to show why this might be the case. At the outset of the article reference is made to asking *anyone* if Gordon Brown would hold a general election and that the answer would invariably be one of *Why would he?* This is *solved* within the piece in terms of the *bounce* he has received in terms of his early performance and by simple virtue of the fact that there has been a change of personnel. However, the main point to note is how the article focuses upon Mr. Brown's machinations regarding calling an election and how this becomes the issue in itself. Mr. Brown is therefore characterized "calculating and planning" with regards to calling an early election thereby taking advantage of a bounce in the opinion polls and being able to claim "it was only right and proper that the British people should have their say on their new prime minister." In this piece, the scenario of overlaying a motive of seeking electoral advantage with a rhetorical veneer of acting in the interest of democracy, is placed upon the "new" Prime Minister. This again, highlights the predictable focus on the party leader and, in a way, implicitly draws upon the notion of the electorate

The month began with an ICM poll for Woodnewton Associates (sampled 1–3 July) asking whether, in the context of climate change, it was a good or bad idea for the government to increase capacity for the number of flights allowed at UK airports.

Some 60% thought it a bad idea whilst 35% thought it a good one.

The month began encouragingly for Gordon Brown with a Populus/BBC Politics Show poll (sampled 4–5 July).

When people were asked whether they preferred to have Tony Blair rather than Gordon Brown "leading the country at this time" (i.e. in the immediate aftermath of the Glasgow/London bomb plots), 60% disagreed compared with 32% who agreed.

Marriage views
Following the final report of the Conservative Social Justice policy group published earlier in the month, two polls tested public attitudes towards marriage and the family.

Populus for the BBC's Daily Politics (sampled 11–12 July) found that 56% disagreed with the statement "children brought up by a single parent are more likely to get into trouble than children brought up by married parents."

And there was a significant gender divide over this: 48% of men disagreed, compared with 64% of women.

ICM for the Sunday Telegraph (sampled 11–13 July) found that the institution of marriage was personally important to 80% of respondents: that 57% thought it was right for government to encourage marriage; and that 70% agreed it was better for parents of children to be married.

Figure 3. Extract 3: Wednesday, 1 August 2007, 09:37 GMT 10:37 UK; *Poll Watch: July 2007*

maintaining a running tally of political performance. It is interesting to note that as events have transpired, speculation over an early election was soon overtaken by encroaching economic issues which resulted in a marked decline in Mr. Brown's poll ratings as Prime Minister, only for these to rise again in the face of his performance over the global banking crisis, and then to fall again in relation to his handling of the MPs expenses scandal.

All these examples indicate the ways in which an inner/outer dualism is maintained as a pervasive discursive cultural common place with regard to the electoral process. Here the individual brings his or her mind to bear upon the world thus preserving intact the notion of the psychological individual. The construction of forming opinions about the issues is taken as a requirement to drive the electoral process, thereby overriding notions of committed political allegiance. Matters of opinion are constantly being presented and updated in order to 'assist' the electorate in their role in the political process. However, perhaps the result of this is not a better informed public but rather a preoccupation with opinionation itself.

> *A few weeks ago when anyone asked whether Gordon Brown would hold a snap election in the autumn the answer was invariably "why would he." Ask the same question today and the answer may very well be "why wouldn't he."*
>
> The "new" prime minister is enjoying a predicted bounce in the polls and is offering what appears to be a popular, more serious and less glitzy approach to leadership and just that period of "intense and compelling activity."
>
> If Britain went to the polls today, a fourth Labour victory with around double the current majority is what the current opinion surveys suggest as the likely outcome.
>
> So, after a good summer holiday during which, knowing Mr Brown, he will never stop calculating and planning, could he return in September and, shortly afterwards, spring a general election?
>
> There are historical examples of prime ministers either going early or waiting, and suffering as a result – Labour's Clem Atlee in 1951 (early) and Jim Callaghan in 1979 (late) and the Tories' Ted Heath in 1974 (early).
>
> But they probably don't offer any real insights – other than how unpredictable this game is – as conditions are always entirely different.
>
> Mr Brown could take advantage of the bounce while being able to claim it was only right and proper that the British people should have their say on their new prime minister. And, let's face it, even if he "bounced" to victory that would not lessen the five-year mandate he would have.
>
> Either way, what Mr Brown almost certainly will not want to do is wait until the last moment, by which time all room for manoeuvre is closed off. The actual deadline for the next election is summer 2010, although recent tradition from both parties suggest the "normal" time for an election would be May 2009. But even that may be leaving it a bit late for Mr Brown, who might well expect to have lost a bit of bounce by then.
>
> So spring next year looks on the face of it to be the best option – but clearly there are arguments for and against all the different dates and the PM knows the virtues of keeping your opponents guessing.

Figure 4. Extract 4: Thursday, 2 August 2007, 09:05 GMT 10:05 UK

7.   Making opinions visible

The 'flow' can be made to move in the other direction, that is, how 'inner' opinions are made invoked and made a visible and relevant feature of political engagement. This typically involves invitations to participate in opinion polls surveys. These are presented as just what people need to do to express their opinions and to know about what other people think. This 'information' is treated as the expression of a mental process with any fluctuations and changes as the result of some sort of social influence process.

Extract 5 (see Figure 5) below is a case in point where a 'perception panel' reacts in real time to a political speech and then can see how others reacted overall, depending on which party they support. Note how the viewer is able to 'see' others' opinions in terms of reactions to the unfolding speech. This provides an interpretation of these opinions based on declared party allegiance and a kind of reflexive engagement with the process of opinionation. This is a case of where making opinions visible is taken as being just what politics is about. This is short term politics taken to a new level: instantaneous reaction to others and their opinions. In all of this there is a danger that reducing political matters down to the level of individual psychological operation, and how it is influenced by 'seeing' that of others, that the *political* in political opinions is in danger of being displaced, and that all we are left with is a focus on opinionation. In other words, what the polls show about what others 'think' becomes privileged over a discussion of the actual political issues themselves.

The Perception Panel measures how you the viewers react to the big conference speeches – in real time! We're the first TV programme in the world to do this, and we want you to get involved: call 0800 666 808 for more details, or read on...

Tuesday September 26th: Tony Blair
We've never had so many calls to the Perception Panel as we did for Tony Blair's final conference speech as Labour Party leader.

Re-built not privatised
First, we looked at how you responded to Mr Blair's comments on the NHS.

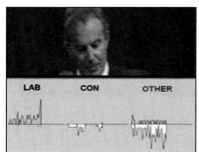

"Let's be clear. Over the past ten years, Britain has invested more in our public services than any comparable nation in the world. From near the bottom in Europe to the average in a decade. 300,000 more workers, treble the money, 25% more pay in real terms and the largest ever hospital programme; that is an NHS being re-built not privatised."

At this point, we saw, unsurprisingly, peaks from Labour supporters, and equally unsurprisingly, a negative reaction from Tories. But among people not aligned with any of the three main parties – which is about 50% of the population – we saw a marked disapproval. This indicated that while Labour's health service plans played well in the hall, they may not be popular among the wider public and among potential voters.

http://news.bbc.co.uk/go/pr/fr/-/1/hi/programmes/the_daily_politics/5382160.stm   Published: 2006/09/26 16:39:39 GMT

Figure 5. Extract 5: *Perception Panel: Tony Blair*

The viewer is given a schematic representation of how others are reacting to Mr. Blair's speech with particular reference to his comments about a "re-built, not privatized" health service. The accompanying text draws attention the "unsurprising" viewer reactions in terms of declared party allegiance thereby reinforcing the view that these people are influenced in their reception of the speech by their predisposed political attitudes and beliefs. However, the commentary goes on to raise the visibility of to the 50% of politically non-aligned viewers who "disapproved" of his comments. The viewers are therefore presented as being a "wider public" and "potential voters" beyond those in the "hall." This serves to construct the unpopularity of this policy issue through consensus of opinion, and it is this visibility of this collective sum of opinions that is presented as newsworthy. Those without a declared political allegiance, and by implication more open-minded on the issue, are given the final 'word' in terms of "disapproval." There is therefore a careful management in this commentary about reception of the speech in terms of aligned versus non-aligned political allegiance and the way in which the latter is privileged over the other as being newsworthy.

8.   Conclusion

The notion of these two separate realms – inner mind and external political matters – that need to be brought together in terms of opinion formation is now a central feature of mediated political engagement. Opinion polling and the presentation of 'the issues' dominate media coverage and are key to the maintenance of opinionation as an ideological practice. The construction of this practice in terms of the inner/outer dualism represents a means of portraying what the electoral process *is* about in terms of a psychological individual who brings his or her mental realm to the vote in terms of opinions as the basis for accountable action. It is a 'single-minded,' opinion driven model of the person that is implicitly presented, and that it is what people 'think' about political matters that is in turn presented as newsworthy. The analyses of the extracts presented in this paper illustrate the extent to which issues are converted in opinions for consumption in an ever more fast-paced and complex means of representation.

It can be argued that rather taking valence politics as a cognitive model involving keeping a running tally on party political performance, the focus ought to be on the neo-liberal discourse of opinionation, of people being expected to be single-minded and *have* views which are influenced by knowing others' views. This discourse taps into zeitgeist of the times, as Beck (1992) would have it; an age of insecurity and risk, of individualism set in relation to appeals to the market-like structures and globalization where these are valued in and of themselves as an ethic for guiding human action. The image of the voter is one of building and maintaining something like a loose-leaf folder of opinions that can be updated, and that informs voting behavior at a given point in time. However, it can be argued that this straightjackets the way people approach such matters in terms of short-term reactions to political issues and does not allow for them to be in several minds about an issue. In other words, it assumes people have fairly clear and consistent views about these discrete issues and plays down partisanship. It is also the case that these judgments are taken as matters of opinion bound up with the 'perception' of how politicians respond to events rather than any sense of commitment to a party political doctrine. Unlike Clarke et al. (2004), who present a valence politics model as being an advance on the sociological approach, it can be argued that a sociological account of political opinionation as an ideological practice is what is required. Rather than taking perceptual-cognitivism as the engine of voting patterns we should consider how the media in implicated in the relentless pursuit of opinionation as a form of social life and the charting of its shifting patterns as the collective focus of attention.

References

Beck, Ulrich. 1992. *Risk Society: Towards a New Modernity.* London: Sage.

Bourdieu, Pierre. 1977. *Outline of a Theory of Practice.* Cambridge: Cambridge University Press.

—. 1992. *Language and Symbolic Power.* Polity Press.

Clarke, Harold, Sanders, David, Stewart, Marianne C. and Whiteley, Paul. 2004. *Political Choice in Britain.* Oxford: Oxford University Press.

Crewe, Ivor, Sarlvik, Bo and Alt, James. 1977. "Partisan dealignment in Britain, 1964–1974." *British Journal of Political Science* 7: 129–190.

Eder, Klaus. 2007. "Cognitive sociology and the theory of communicative action: The role of communication and language in the making of social bond." *European Journal of Social Theory* 10 (3): 389–408.

Edwards, Derek. 1997. *Discourse and Cognition.* London: Sage.

Edwards, Derek and Potter, Jonathan. 1992. *Discursive Psychology.* London: Sage.

Goodwin, Charles. 1995. "Seeing in depth." *Social Studies of Science* 25: 237–274.

Fiorina, Morris. 1981. *Retrospective Voting in American National Elections.* New Have: Yale University Press.

Habermas, Jürgen. 2003. *Truth & Justification.* Cambridge: Polity.

Hazan, Reuven Y. 1996. "Presidential parliamentarism: Direct popular election of the prime minister." *Electoral Studies* 15: 21–38.

Herbst, Susan. 1998. *Reading Public Opinion. How Political Actors View the Democratic Process.* Chicago: Chicago University Press.

Lassen, Inger, Strunck, Jeanne and Vestergaard, Torben (eds). 2006. *Mediating Ideology in Text and Image.* Amsterdam: Benjamins.

Lavrakas, Paul, Holley, Jack and Miller, Peter (eds). 1990. *Polling and Presidential Election Coverage.* Newbury Park, CA: Sage.

Maddens, Bart and Fiers, Steffan. 2004. "The direct PM election and the institutional presidentialisation of parliamentary systems." *Electoral Studies* 23: 769–793.

Mancini, Paulo. 1999. "New frontiers in political professionalism." *Political Communication* 16: 231–246.

Mughan, Anthony. 1993. "Party leader and presidentialism in the 1992 election: A post war per-
    spective." In *British Elections and Parties Yearbook, 1993,* David Denver, Pippa Norris, Colin
    Rallings and David Broughton (eds), 193–204. Hemel, Hempstead: Harvester Wheatsheaf.

Mythen, Gabe. 2005. "Employment, individualization and insecurity: Rethinking the risk soci-
    ety perspective." *The Sociological Review* 53 (1): 130–149.

Poguntke, Thomas and Webb, Paul (eds). 2005. *The Presidentialization of Politics in Democratic
    Societies.* Oxford: Oxford University Press.

Potter, Jonathan. 1996. *Representing Reality: Discourse Rhetoric and Social Construction.*
    London: Sage.

—. 2003. "Discursive psychology: Between method and paradigm." *Discourse & Society* 14 (6):
    783–794.

Potter, Jonathan and Edwards, Derek. 2001. "Sociolinguistics, cognitivism and discursive psy-
    chology." In *Sociolinguistics and Social Theory,* Nicholas Coupland, Srikant Sarangi and
    Christopher N. Candlin (eds), 88–103. Harlow, Essex: Pearson Education.

Shah, Dhavan V., McLeod, Douglas M., Kim, Eunkyung, Lee, Sun Young, Gotlieb, Melissa R.,
    Ho, Shirley S. and Breivik, Hilde. 2007. "Political consumerism: How communication and
    consumption orientations drive 'Lifestyle Politics.'" *The ANNALS of the American Academy
    of Political and Social Science* 611: 217–235.

Strydom, Piet A. 2007. "Cartography of contemporary cognitive social theory." *European Jour-
    nal of Social Theory* 10 (3): 339–356.

te Molder, Hedwig and Potter, Jonathan (eds). 2005. *Conversation & Cognition.* Cambridge:
    Cambridge University Press.

CHAPTER 14

Political communication

Mediated by translation

Christina Schäffner

1. Introduction

As members of cultures and discourse communities, we encounter political discourse nearly every day. Political discourse can be defined in a broad sense as a complex form of human activity. It is realized in a variety of discourse types (or genres), whose discourse organization and textual structure is determined by the respective discursive practices (Chilton and Schäffner 1997). In the context of Critical Discourse Analysis (especially Fairclough 1995), discursive practice refers to the production, circulation and consumption of the discourse. For political communication, some of these discursive practices operate within the internal domain of policy-making and have politicians as both text producers and addressees. Other discursive practices are aimed at the general public and communicate, explain, and justify political decisions. Text producers in such cases can be politicians, political scientists, civil servants, or journalists, with the mass media playing a decisive role in the circulation of the discourse.

Processes of communication and mediation of politics occur within and across genres and discourse types. For example, a Prime Minister's address to the national Parliament may also be transmitted live to the general public via TV or radio. Newspapers may present summary reports on the next day, often accompanied by evaluative commentaries or editorials. Presidents on a state visit to another country often give joint press conferences with the host to international journalists (see also Fraser this volume). These journalists will write (often evaluative) reports about the visit and they may quote – verbatim or indirectly – arguments provided at such a press conference. In such cases, the (re)presentation of one event, or discursive practice (e.g. a Parliamentary debate, a state visit, a press conference) is incorporated within the context of another event, or discursive practice (e.g. a news report, an editorial). In short: political discourse is transferred in processes of recontextualization. In these recontextualization processes, messages and arguments are transformed. In addition to subtle linguistic transformations as adapting a quote to incorporate it in the syntactic structure of a sentence, recontextualization also often involves the "filtering of some meaning potentials of a discourse" (Blackledge 2005: 121), which is reflected in omissions, additions, and reformulations of the initial text in the new context. The two examples below illustrate recontextualization processes:

> Back in March Barack Obama compared the Democratic primary to a "good movie" that has lasted "half an hour too long" (*The Economist*, 17 May 2008, p. 62).
> A battalion of PP members has lined up behind Ms San Gil. They include Ana Botella, the normally discreet wife of Mr Rajoy's predecessor, José María Aznar, [...] "María San Gil is a moral, political and emotional reference point," she said pointedly (*The Economist*, 17 May 2008, p. 53).

The second example reflects recontextualization across linguistic and cultural boundaries, which means that translation has been involved. In this chapter, I will illustrate the role of translation with reference to three discursive practices and discourse types which are typical of political communication, (i) political interviews, (ii) press conferences, and (iii) political speeches. I will argue that translational recontextualization is determined by institutional policies and ideologies. Institutions, such as governments and mass media, enable communication across languages and cultures, they can give privilege to specific information at the expense of other information, but they can also hinder and prohibit information from being circulated. That is, discursive practices are not neutral, and neither is the translational activity as part of such practices, or rather, as constituting its own practice.

2.   Political interview

On 1 June 2007, the then Russian President Putin gave an interview to a selected group of journalists from the G8 countries. One newspaper or magazine from each country had been invited to send one journalist: *Der Spiegel*, a German weekly magazine, and the daily newspapers *The Times* from the United Kingdom, *Le Figaro* from France, *Kommersant* from Russia, *Wall Street Journal* from the USA, *The Globe and Mail* from Canada, *Corriere della Sera* from Italy, and *Nihon Keizai Shimbun* from Japan. The initiative had come from Putin, giving him the opportunity to present his political ideas and arguments to the people in the G8 countries, via their respective media, just a few days before the beginning of the 2007 meeting of the G8 countries, held 6–8 June 2007 in Heiligendamm, Germany. The interview was conducted in Putin's residence, with Putin and the eight journalists sitting around a table (see photos on http://212.248.33.60/p771175/r_1/Putin,_G8/). There was live transmission to another room in the same building where fellow journalists representing the eight papers were able to follow the interview and take notes. Simultaneous interpreting was provided, with the interpreters in all probability working from booths (in the photos, we can see the journalists wearing small headphones).

The whole interview lasted for several hours and included a dinner. The procedures had been discussed and agreed before (e.g. turn allocation). As is to be expected, the various newspapers reported differently about this interview, in terms of content, quantity, focus and layout. In the complex processes of recontextualization, a number of transformations occurred, including transformations from one language into another, which in itself was a complex process, involving recording the interpreters' renderings and translating them in full or selectively for the publication. However, translation is invisible in the texts as published in the mass media. Only *Globe and Mail* mentions translation in its report, saying 'Mr. Putin's remarks, translated from Russian, [...]'. None of the other papers include an explicit reference to the fact that translation and interpreting was involved.

A comparison of the reports in some of the newspapers which were accessible (i.e. the print version of *Der Spiegel*, and the online versions of *Spiegel International*, publishing in English, *The Times, Le Figaro, Kommersant* in the original Russian and in English, *Globe and Mail*) revealed a number of recontextualization strategies. The most obvious difference is the length of the texts. *Information Clearing House*, which presents itself as 'an independent media source' and a 'one person's effort to correct the distorted perceptions provided by commercial media' (http://www.informationclearinghouse.info/who.htm) indicated its text as being a full transcript of the interview. *Kommersant* published a complete transcript all in Russian, presented as a complete stenographic report of the interview. For this paper, only the additional report about the interview has been analyzed. All the other newspapers analyzed have much shorter texts, with the selection of information determined mainly by the national political interests. In *Der Spiegel*, there are a few paragraphs which do not show up in the transcript of *Information Clearing House*, which could either mean that this transcript is in fact not a complete one, or that the German journalists added information which they had got in a previous interview (*Kommersant* refers to another interview that Putin had granted international journalists a few days before). Moreover, the information arrangement is different as well, with the newspaper texts having been made coherent in terms of topic, and with a sense of climax.

The information about the event itself is either found at the very beginning of the text, in a sur-title or in a sub-title, or in a separate box on a page, or in the text itself. This information ranges from a short list of the newspapers present to evaluative comments about the dinner served or Putin's behavior. Some of the texts kept the question-answer format, thus giving the readers the features of the interview genre, whereas others had transformed the initial interview into a report. Table 1 below summarizes these findings.

The actual interviewers, i.e. the journalists, are identified only in *Information Clearing House* and in the *Kommersant* transcript, although not by their own name, but by the name of the newspaper. In most of the newspaper reports, the interviewer is unknown. If the interview format is retained, typically only the labels 'Question' and 'Putin' are used (see also Table 3). In some papers, however, the reader gets the

Table 1. Length, contextualization, genre

	Length	Contextualization	Text presented as interview?
Der Spiegel (German print version) 4 June 2007	2,291 words	Short text on event, printed in a separate box, only countries listed who were represented by journalists	Yes, Question-Answer format
Spiegel International (English, online) 4 June 2007	2,905 words	As above, with short text on event right at the beginning of the text	Yes, Question-Answer format
The Times (online) 4 June 2007	1,804 words	In text itself, including description of building, dinner, procedures and arrangements	No, direct quotes combined with 'he said,' 'Putin argued that' etc.
Le Figaro (online) 4 June 2007	1,461 words	No	Yes, Question-Answer format
Kommersant (online, Russian and English texts are identical) 4 June 2007	1,522 words in the English version	Before main text and in text itself, all journalists listed by name, including description of dinner, procedures, comments on Putin's behavior	No, few direct quotes integrated in report (the complete transcript retains the interview format)
Globe and Mail (online) 4 June 2007	1,896 words	In text itself, including reference to translation	No, direct quotes integrated in report, combined with 'he said,' 'he added'
Corriere della Sera (online) 4 June 2007	1,908 words	Short paragraph at beginning of text	Yes, Question-Answer format
Information Clearing House (online)	19,259 words	No	Yes, Question-Answer format

impression that the interview was granted solely to one newspaper. This is in particular the case for *The Times* and *Le Figaro*, which do not inform their readers of the presence of other journalists, and which have transformed the interview into a report. In both cases, the information provided in the lead conveys this impression, cf.:

> *The Times:* Vladimir Putin tells our correspondent that [...]

This lead is followed by the name of the journalist (Bronwen Maddox).

> *Le Figaro:* Propos recueillis par Fabrice Nodé-Langlois et Pierre Rousselin
> Dans en entretien au Figaro, le président russe réplique [...]

Only for the first question, interviewer and interviewee are identified, using capital letters and bold font:

> **LE FIGARO:** ...
> **Vladimir POUTINE:** ...

In the following parts, Putin's name precedes the answers, but for the questions only bold font is used. The same method, i.e. bold font for the questions, is used by *Corriere della Sera*. Such a strategy of hiding (or misattributing) the interviewer results in the (deliberate?) invisibility of fellow journalists and/or competitor newspapers.

The main titles of the published text, and in particular the sub-titles, reflect what the respective papers have identified as their main focus of the story, as illustrated in Table 2 below. Sur-titles are used only by *Spiegel International* (G-8 Interview with Vladimir Putin) and *Corriere della Sera* (Tensione con gli Usa su armamenti, diritti umani, caso Litvinenko. «Non uso un linguaggio da luna di miele»), the first one just indicating the event, the second one, however, providing content information.

It is mainly the sub-titles (or the lead; van Dijk 1985) which mention the topics that the respective newspapers identified as most relevant to their own country. It is noticeable that several papers use the quote 'I'm a democrat', either in the main title or in the sub-title. This is an extract from an exchange, which most of the papers reproduce extensively, as shown in Table 3 below (font and capital letters as in the original texts).

What is interesting is the way in which the information was selected and presented, in terms of quantity and style of presentation. If we take *Information Clearing House* as – in their own words – providing a complete transcript of the text, we see that Putin's answer has been reduced. The comparison to what happens in North America and Europe has been omitted in *Times Online* and generalized in *The Globe and Mail*. The reference to Gandhi does not show up in *Der Spiegel*. Comparing the German text in *Der Spiegel* to its English translation in *Spiegel International*, we can also see how the knowledge of the readers was taken into account. In the German version, the reference to Chancellor Schroeder has been omitted, since the text producer could rely on his readers knowing who had used these words to characterize Putin ('lupenreiner Demokrat' are the exact words used by Schroeder, rendered into English in the texts analyzed as 'pure, flawless, democrat of the finest sort'). Putin's answer to this question is signaled by '(laughs)' in *International Clearing House* and also in the complete Russian transcript in *Kommersant*. He is then taking up the question and repeating it before coming up with an affirmative answer, which is hedged by 'of course' (in the English version, also in Putin's original reply in Russian). He then asks a rhetorical question, repeats it in a qualified way, and then gives an answer. The impression that is conveyed by these strategies is of Putin engaging in a kind of role play with the journalists, reflecting some amusement. The exaggerations ('tragedy, I'm all alone, the only one of my kind in the whole wide world, no one to talk to' and the reference to Gandhi) contribute to this strategy.

Table 2. Main titles and sub-titles

	Main title	Sub-title
Information Clearing House	Russian President Putin's Interview with G8 Newspaper Journalists	President Vladimir Putin Fields Questions from G8 Member Countries' Newspaper Journalists
Der Spiegel	"Ich bin ein echter Demokrat"	Staatspräsident Wladimir Putin über den Raketenstreit mit den USA, die gefährdete Zusammenarbeit mit Westfirmen bei der Energieerschließung von russischem Erdgas und Demokratiedefizite bei Europäern und Amerikanern
Spiegel International	'I am a True Democrat'	Russian President Vladimir Putin discusses the missile dispute with the United States, the risks of cooperating with Western companies in the production of Russian natural gas and what he describes as democratic deficiencies in the United States and Europe
Times Online	'I'm a pure and absolute democrat. It's a tragedy that I'm the only one.'	Vladimir Putin tells our correspondent that he is Gandhi's true heir and warns against hypocrisy on human rights
Le Figaro	Poutine: "La Russe devra choisir descibles en Europe"	Dans en entretien au Figaro, le président russe réplique au projet américain de système antimissiles en menaçant de pointer ses propres engins sur des cibles en Europe.
Kommersant (English version)	Putin Serves Up a Hot Menu	G8 Journalists Dine with Russian President On Friday, Russian President Vladimir Putin gave an interview to journalists from the countries of the G8. Kommersant special correspondent Andrei Kolesnikov, a participant in the meeting, recounts the dramatic story of Putin's swim in the fraught waters of international media. We'll all just have to wait for the dramatic story of Putin's decision to extend the president's term in office to seven years.
Globe and Mail	Putin threatens to target Europe	He also lashes out at NATO and insists he's world's only true democrat..
Corriere della Sera	Putin: pronto a puntare i missili sull'Europa	Intervista al presidente russo: le manifestazioni represse? Sciocchezze

Table 3. 'I am a democrat'

Information Clearing House	**DER SPIEGEL:** Mr President, former Chancellor Gerhard Schroeder called you a 'pure democrat.' Do you consider yourself such? **VLADIMIR PUTIN:** (laughs) Am I a 'pure democrat'? Of course I am, absolutely. But do you know what the problem is? Not even a problem but a real tragedy? The problem is that I'm all alone, the only one of my kind in the whole wide world. Just look at what's happening in North America, it's simply awful: torture, homeless people, Guantanamo, people detained without trial and investigation. Just look at what's happening in Europe: harsh treatment of demonstrators, rubber bullets and tear gas used first in one capital then in another, demonstrators killed on the streets. That's not even to mention the post-Soviet area. Only the guys in Ukraine still gave hope, but they've completely discredited themselves now and things are moving towards total tyranny there; complete violation of the Constitution and the law and so on. There is no one to talk to since Mahatma Gandhi died.
Der Spiegel	**FRAGE:** Herr Putin, sind Sie ein lupenreiner Demokrat? **Putin:** Ja, natürlich bin ich ein echter Demokrat. Aber es sieht so aus, als gäbe es in der Welt keine Demokraten mehr: In Amerika wird gefoltert, zum Beispiel in Guantanamo, in Europa geht die Polizei mit Gas gegen Demonstranten vor, manchmal sterben sogar Menschen auf der Straße. Wir beachten übrigens ein Moratorium zur Todesstrafe. In anderen G-8-Ländern wird sie sogar häufig vollstreckt.
Spiegel International	**QUESTION:** Mr Putin, are you the "flawless democrat" that former German chancellor Gerhard Schröder once described you to be? **Putin:** Of course I am an absolutely true democrat. The tragedy is that I am alone. There are no such other democrats in the world. The Americans torture at Guantanamo, and in Europe the police use gas against protesters. Sometimes protesters are killed in the streets. We have, incidentally, a moratorium on the death penalty, which is often enforced in other G-8 countries.
Times Online	"Of course, I am a pure and absolute democrat," he said. "But you know what the problem is – not a problem, a real tragedy – that I am alone. There are no such pure democrats in the world. Since Mahatma Gandhi, there has been no one."
Le Figaro	**Gerhard Schroeder vous a qualifié de «pur démocrate». L'êtes-vous vraiment?** Oui, bien sûr! Bien sûr que je suis un pur et absolu démocrate! La tragédie, c'est que je suis le seul pur démocrate au monde. Voyez les États-Unis: des tortures horribles, des sans-abri, Guantanamo. Voyez l'Europe: des manifestations violentes, durement réprimées, Même les Ukrainiens se sont discrédités et vont vers la tyrannie. Depuis la mort de Gandhi, je n'ai personne à qui parler!
Kommersant	But then the editor-in-chief of Der Spiegel asked the Russian president whether he is, as former German chancellor Gerhard Shroeder has said, a democrat of the finest sort. This question was put to Mr. Putin several says [sic] ago at the EU-Russia summit in Samara, and I thought that the president would be miffed about it. Instead, however, we received the answer of the year: "Of course I am a pure and absolute democrat...but the real problem is that after the death of Mahatma Gandhi, there is no one [for me] to talk to."

Globe and Mail	And, when the flaws in Russian democracy were cited, he mentioned the 2000 U.S. presidential elections." Of course, I am a pure and absolute democrat," he said. "The tragedy is that I am alone. I am the only such pure democrat. There are no such other democrats in the world. Let us see what is happening in North America: Just horrible torture. The homeless. Guantanamo. Detentions without normal court proceedings." "After the death of Mahatma Gandhi," he added, with a smile, "I have nobody to talk to."
Corriere della Sera	**Vladimir Vladimirovich, qualcuno chiede che la Russia sia esclusa dal G8 perché la sua democrazia è troppo imperfetta. Cosa risponde?** «È una cosa che non ha senso. Siamo nel G8 perché ci hanno invitati. E per quanto riguarda la nostra democrazia non siamo gli unici ad avere difetti. Con la differenza che gli altri non attraversano un periodo di trasformazioni epocali come noi. Del resto alcune libertà sono garantite da noi meglio che altrove. Per esempio noi non abbiamo la pena di morte e nemmeno i senza casa, Guantánamo, la tortura, la violenza contro i dimostranti».

In most of the reports in the mass media analyzed, the style has changed. As a result, Putin comes across as more authoritative and forceful. In *Le Figaro* and both versions of *Spiegel*, a direct question-answer format is presented, cf.:

> *Le Figaro*:
> Gerhard Schroeder vous a qualifié de «pur démocrate». L'êtes-vous vraiment? (Literally: Gerhrad Schroeder has characterised you as a 'pure democrat.' Are you one indeed?)
> Oui, bien sûr! Bien sûr que je suis un pur et absolu démocrate! (Literally: Yes, of course! Of course I am a pure and absolute democrat! note also the use of exclamation marks)

> *Der Spiegel*:
> **Spiegel**: Herr Putin, sind Sie ein lupenreiner Demokrat? (Literally: Mr Putin, are you a flawless democrat?)
> **Putin:** Ja, natürlich bin ich ein echter Demokrat. (Literally: Yes, of course I am a pure democrat.)

> *Spiegel International*:
> Spiegel: Mr Putin, are you the "flawless democrat" that former German chancellor Gerhard Schröder once described you to be?
> Putin: Of course I am an absolutely true democrat.

The 'of course' here reinforces the affirmative answer. The English version of *Spiegel International* is even more forceful compared to the German one in the sentence that follows this statement:

> Aber es sieht so aus, als gäbe es in der Welt keine Demokraten mehr: (Literally: It looks as if there were no more democrats in the world.) (*Spiegel*)

> The tragedy is that I am alone. There are no such other democrats in the world. (*Spiegel International*)

The German version is somewhat hedged ('als' followed by subjunctive – as if), whereas the English version is presented as a plain fact. The fact that 'tragedy' shows up in the English translation allows for the assumption that the *Spiegel International* translators did not work purely on the basis of the German text alone but had other English texts available as well. Alternatively, the German text might have been shortened further for publication.

Times Online has only the answer ('"Of course, I am a pure and absolute democrat," he said'), but no question; and in *The Globe and Mail*, the answer ('"Of course, I am a pure and absolute democrat," he said') follows a reference to a more generalized issue ('And, when the flaws in Russian democracy were cited, [...]'). *Globe and Mail* is the only paper which adds a metacommunicative comment to give an indication of Putin's attitude in this particular exchange ('[...] he added, with a smile').

Whereas some changes are due to the readers' background knowledge (such as the omission of the reference to Schroeder in *Der Spiegel*), other changes in the syntactic and semantic structure result in a modification of focus and evaluation. Assuming that *International Clearing House* has the complete transcript (which might well be based on the complete Russian stenographic transcript), we see a list of things as happening in North America ('Just look at what's happening in North America, it's simply awful: torture, homeless people, Guantanamo, people detained without trial and investigation.'), with the implication that these are acts which do not fit a democratic society. The same list, although slightly shortened, is used in *Le Figaro* ('Voyez les États-Unis: des tortures horribles, des sans-abri, Guantanamo.') and in *Globe and Mail* ('[...] Just horrible torture. The homeless. Guantanamo. Detentions without normal court proceedings.'). Whereas in *International Clearing House* all examples are evaluated as 'awful', in both *Le Figaro* and *Globe and Mail* only 'torture' is qualified by this evaluative adjective. *Times Online* and *Kommersant* have omitted this whole piece of information, whereas both the German and the English version of *Spiegel* reflect a change of transitivity, cf.:

> In Amerika wird gefoltert, zum Beispiel in Guantanamo, [...] (Literally: There is torture applied in America, for example in Guantanamo [...])
> The Americans torture at Guantanamo, [...]

In the German version, the passive form of the verb for 'torture' is used, which puts emphasis on the action, and the space where this action happens is enlarged ('in America'). In *Spiegel International*, an active sentence is used, thus putting the focus on the agents of torturing ('the Americans'). This image of Putin claiming to be a true democrat and implicitly criticizing Americans for their actions is in stark contrast to the image of a joking and less accusatory Putin as reflected in *International Clearing House* (on translation strategies at *Spiegel International* see Schäffner 2005, in press).

Corriere della Sera gives a somewhat different account: the question itself is not addressed to Putin himself but is of a more general nature (literally: 'It is said that

Russia should be excluded from the G8 since its democracy is imperfect'). In his reply, Putin speaks about Russia (the last sentence literally: 'For example, we do not have the death penalty and not even homeless people, Guantánamo, torture, violence against protesters'), thus setting Russia apart from other, not named, countries.

What this example should have made clear is that media interests and ideologies play a role in how information is selected and presented. Even information that is used by nearly all publications (e.g. Putin's quote about being a democrat) is presented somewhat differently as far as lexical and syntactic details are concerned. The complexity of processes involves transformations from spoken to written (transcription of the interview), from one language into another (in this case, probably even between several languages, if each journalist used their own mother tongue), from full-length text to extract (omissions, additions, restructuring, rearrangement of information), from initial copy to published text tailored for a particular readership (e.g. explanations), and tailored to the journalistic conventions of the various media (e.g. transformation of the interview genre). As a result of these transformations, readers of the respective newspapers get a different impression of the topics discussed in the interview and of the way in which Putin expressed his views. Deletions, rearrangements of information, substitutions and paraphrasing are typical examples of transformations that text producers (i.e. journalists, revisors, editors) make use of in the recontextualization processes (i.e. here: recontextualization from the actual interview to the published text). As Blackledge argues, all such transformations are "dependent on the goals, values and interests of the context into which the discursive practice is being recontextualised" (Blackledge 2005: 122). The role of translation in this complex network of recontextualization processes, however, has so far been underresearched. Analyzing translational recontextualizations and the associated transformations can contribute new insights into the role played by mass media in the representation of politics and politicians across linguistic and cultural boundaries.

As communicative events move along further the political and media chain, they often undergo additional textual transformations. The initial event may move into the background or even disappear altogether from the discourse (cf. also Kovalyova this volume). For example, in a press briefing from the UK Prime Minister's Official Spokesman on 4 June 2007, we see a reference to the article in *The Times*, but not to the original interview event:

> Asked what the Prime Minister's response was to President Putin's words in the Times, the Prime Minister's Official Spokesman (PMOS) replied that the new missile defence system that was being put forward by the US was not aimed at Russia, as had been made clear. [...] (http://www.number-10.gov.uk/output/Page11834.asp)

The Times' text has thus its own identity and serves as a reference point for new textual and discursive chains. Press briefings and press conferences are another discursive event at which translation and interpreting are often relevant, even if not always visible.

3.   Press conference

Political press conferences are part of political discourse (see Fraser this volume), but since they are held for representatives of the media who in turn construct their own discourse following a press conference – a process which again involves recontextualization and transformations – press conferences are also a part of media discourse. In fact, Bhatia characterizes press conferences as "mediatization of political action" (Bhatia 2006: 176).

The example I will use for illustrating the role of translation is the joint press conference by the German Chancellor Angela Merkel and US President George Bush, held in Stralsund, Germany, on 13 July 2006, on the occasion of a visit by Bush to Germany. Initial longer statements by Merkel and Bush, respectively, are followed by questions and answers. The transcripts of the press conference (or: 'press availability' as it is called by the White House) have been made available on the websites of the German government and of the Office of the Press Secretary of the White House, in each case only in German and in English. A comparison of the two versions does not reveal any significant omissions or additions, but a number of changes in terms of style and genre conventions. In the German version, there is no explicit indication of translation or interpreting, whereas the US website provides information in brackets ('as translated') after the first turn by Merkel (font as in original), cf.:

> **BK'IN DR. MERKEL:** Ich freue mich, den amerikanischen Präsidenten heute hier in Stralsund noch einmal herzlich willkommen zu heißen!. [...]
>
> CHANCELLOR MERKEL: (As translated.) Ladies and gentlemen, I am delighted to be able to welcome the President of the United States here in Stralsund yet again. [...]

In some other cases of press availabilities, the White House website has a link to a video recording which makes it possible to state precisely whether simultaneous or consecutive interpreting was used. More recent transcripts on the German government website also indicate explicitly that the transcript of the non-German text is based on simultaneous (or more rarely consecutive) interpreting (as can be seen, for example, in the case of a press conference held by Angela Merkel and Tony Blair on 3 June 2007 in Berlin, http://www.g-8.de/Content/DE/Mitschrift/Pressekonferenzen/ 2007/06/2007-06-03-bk-blair.html). In the case of the 2006 Merkel and Bush press conference, a comparison of the two versions leads to the assumption that consecutive interpreting was used (the media do not usually make a clear difference between translation and interpreting). In the English version, 'Ladies and gentlemen' has been added, as a standard form of address.

There are differences in how the two institutions indicate the two speakers: in both cases, the official titles and capital letters (and bold font in German) are used (BK'IN Dr. MERKEL and P BUSH for the German government, where BK'IN stands for 'Bundeskanzlerin', the female form of Chancellor, and P stands for 'Präsident;' CHANCELLOR MERKEL and PRESIDENT BUSH for the US government website). It is surprising to see that the informal 'Du'-Form ('ich danke dir') was chosen by the interpreter in the first turn by Bush, cf.:

> PRESIDENT BUSH: Chancellor, thank you very much. Thanks for the invitation. This is a beautiful part of the world [...]
> **P BUSH:** Frau Bundeskanzlerin, ich danke dir sehr herzlich für die Einladung. [...]

The informal form signals a close personal relationship between the two politicians, and the interpreter's decision might have been motivated by the previous discourse. Most noticeable are differences in style. More precisely, the German version of President Bush's turns reflects evidence of what may be called stylistic enhancement or style elevation. Just one paragraph will be given for illustration. Whereas the English version reflects features such as false starts (e.g. 'we talked – spent a lot of time'), rephrasing (e.g. 'it was something – an option'), or hedges (e.g. 'you know'), the German version shows features of written text in that it is syntactically well formed, cf.:

> You know, on the Iranian issue, for example, the last time that we were together we talked – spent a lot of time on Iran, and the Chancellor was wondering whether or not the United States would ever come to the table to negotiate with the Iranians. You made that pretty clear to me that you thought it was something – an option we ought to consider, which I did. And I made it clear to the Iranians that if they were to do what they said they would do, which is to stop enrichment in a verifiable fashion, we're more than pleased to come back to the table. [...]
>
> Das tun wir auch, was den Iran betrifft. Bei unserem letzten Treffen haben wir mit dieser Frage sehr viel Zeit verbracht. Dabei wurde die Frage gestellt: Werden sich die Vereinigten Staaten jemals zum Verhandlungstisch begeben? Die Bundeskanzlerin hat mich auch dazu aufgefordert, darüber nachzudenken. Ich habe dann Folgendes gesagt: Wenn die Iraner nachweislich mit der Urananreicherung aufhören, dann werden wir zum Verhandlungstisch zurückkehren. [...]
>
> (Literally: We do so as well concerning Iran. At our last meeting we spent a lot of time on this issue. The question was asked then: Will the United States ever go to the negotiating table? The Chancellor also asked me to think about this. I then said the following: If the Iranians stopped uranium enrichment in a verifiable way, then we will return to the negotiating table.)

We can also notice a change in transitivity here: whereas in the English original, Bush addresses Merkel directly ('You made that pretty clear to me that you thought [...]'), the third person is used in the German version ('Die Bundeskanzlerin hat mich auch dazu aufgefordert [...]'). Moreover, in the English original, the Iranians are presented as the addressees of Bush's proposition ('I made it clear to the Iranians'), whereas in the German version, the addressee is left implicit ('I then said the following'), but could be interpreted as being Merkel due the structure of the paragraph. As a result of these shifts, Bush comes across as less demanding and authoritative in the German version.

Another difference between the German and the US version concerns the way the interaction with the journalist is handled, which, in fact, can be characterized as another example of style elevation. On the German website, German journalists are identified by name (but without any indication of the newspaper they represent), US journalists, however, are hidden behind the label 'Frage' ('question'). The US website uses 'Q' for 'question' throughout, that is, German journalists are not identified by name on the US website, cf.:

> FRAGE SCHARLACK: Frau Bundeskanzlerin, Sie sprachen davon [...]
> Q Chancellor, you spoke about [...]

When it comes to US journalists, the US transcript reflects interaction of an informal nature, with President Bush selecting a journalist to ask a question, and the journalist introducing himself and addressing the two politicians. The German website has omitted these features of interaction, cf.:

> PRESIDENT BUSH: [...] So I appreciate the Chancellor's position on this. Yes, Terry.
> Q Madam Chancellor, Mr. President. Terry Hunt with the AP. Looking ahead to St. Petersburg, I'd like to ask you, [...]
>
> P BUSH [...] Ich schätze die Position der Bundeskanzlerin sehr, was diese Frage betrifft. (Literally: I very much appreciate the Chancellor's position on this issue.)
> FRAGE: Was das G8-Gipfeltreffen in St. Petersburg betrifft, möchte ich folgende Fragen stellen: [...] (Literally: Concerning the G8-summit in St. Petersburg, I'd like to ask the following questions [...])

The use of the first name also reflects some familiarity between the speakers and shows Bush displaying commonality with the journalists. In the following extract, the same informal exchange with the journalist is reflected, with the additional features of interruption and sidetracking, in particular the mixing of sensitive political issues with the trivial discussion of what will be served for dinner (note the addition of the metacommunicative 'laughter'). The German website, again, has omitted all these informal exchanges, cf.:

> PRESIDENT BUSH: [...] President Assad needs to show some leadership towards peace. [...]
> Steve.
> Q Thank you, sir. Just to follow up –
>
> PRESIDENT BUSH: Follow up on?
> Q On both of these. Does it concern you that the Beirut airport has been bombed? And do you see a risk of triggering a wider war?
> And on Iran, they've, so far, refused to respond. Is it now past the deadline, or do they still have more time to respond?

PRESIDENT BUSH: I thought you were going to ask me about the pig.

Q I'm curious about that, too. (Laughter)

PRESIDENT BUSH: The pig? I'll tell you tomorrow after I eat it. The Iranian issue is […]

P BUSH: […] und Präsident Assad muss rechenschaftspflichtig sein, was den Frieden betrifft.

FRAGE: Um bei diesem Thema nachzuhaken: Machen Sie sich Sorgen darüber, dass der Flughafen in Beirut bombardiert worden ist? Gibt es das Risiko, dass es zu zusätzlichem Kriegsgeschehen kommt?

Was den Iran betrifft: Haben Sie jetzt mehr Zeit? Ist die Frist verlängert worden?

P BUSH: Ich dachte, es würde um das Schwein gehen. Aber ich werde morgen sagen, wie mir das Schwein schmeckt, nachdem ich davon gekostet haben werde. Die Iran-Frage […]

(Literally: P Bush: […] President Assad must take on responsibility as concerns peace.

Question: To follow up on this topic. Does it concern you that the Beirut airport has been bombed? Is there the risk of a wider war?

And on Iran: do you have more time now? Has the time to respond been extended?

P BUSH: I thought you were asking about the pig. I will tell you tomorrow how I liked it once I have tasted it. The Iran issue […])

I suspect a typing error occurred in the German transcript: 'Haben Sie jetzt mehr Zeit?' (do you have time now?). 'Sie' with capital initial letter is the formal form of 'you', whereas 'sie' with small initial letter is the plural pronoun 'they'. If you listen to a speaker, the difference is not immediately obvious but requires the context to disambiguate the pronoun. The journalist made it clear in his question that he was speaking about Iranian politicians. The interpreter too meant 'sie' to refer to Iran, as becomes clear in the phrase that follows.

The differences between the two websites in terms of style give different impressions to the readers about the nature of press conferences. Informality, orality and friendly interaction seem to be the expected and accepted characteristic features for the US audience, whereas the producers of the German website seem to value factual information and linguistic correctness. This may explain the textual interventions in terms of grammar and style as well as the omissions we see on the German website. An analysis of some more website transcripts of press conferences has confirmed these findings. German- and English-speaking journalists who use such transcripts for their own reporting about press conferences, may convey different information, bearing in mind that even more transformations may occur in the discursive chain from a transcript of a press conference to an evaluative report in a newspaper. Equally, political analysts or students who wish to do a discourse analysis of press conferences and/or of politicians' discourse at such a discursive event, will inevitably end up with somewhat different findings and images of politicians, depending on the language version they study. Discourse analysts, therefore, cannot ignore the fact that they are dealing with translations, and for their own analyses, the institutional, social, ideological contexts in which translations were produced need to be taken into account as well.

Politicians and journalists engage with translated texts, they react by commenting on, supporting or criticizing statements by other politicians, which is another form of recontextualization. I will illustrate this with the example of a political speech.

4. Political speech

In October 2005, BBC News reported on the British Prime Minister's reaction to a speech by the Iranian President Ahmadinejad as follows:

> Tony Blair has expressed "revulsion" at the Iranian president's assertion that he wanted Israel "wiped off the map" (27 October 2005). (http://news.bbc.co.uk/1/hi/uk_politics/4380306.stm)
>
> In this quote, Blair uses a direct quote from the speech which the Iranian President Mahmoud Ahmadinejad had delivered at a conference, entitled 'The World without Zionism', in Tehran on 26 October 2005. It is particularly this phrase 'wipe off the map' that was repeatedly taken up by politicians and journalists and was commented on. However, the Iranian President delivered his speech in his own Persian language, and there are in fact different English translations of his speech, prepared by different institutions. Table 4 below shows the English versions I have looked at (provided by *Al-Jazeera*, a media network with its headquarter in Doha, Qatar; the daily *New York Times*; the *Middle East Research Institute, MEMRI,* a press monitoring organization located in Washington, DC; and the Iranian Students' News Agency, *ISNA*). The table also shows how the various institutions introduce the speech and comment on the translation, which in some cases is only an extract translation (which in itself is ideologically significant, since the decision about which information to include or to omit is not taken at random).

As can be seen, most of the institutions mention the relevant phrase in the title and/or the lead. In the speech, there are two paragraphs where this phrase becomes relevant. In the first case, Ahmadinejad is quoting Imam Khomeini, and in the second one later in the speech, he refers to the situation in Palestine at that time. What we see in the quotes below is that the translators have used different strategies for rendering the two paragraphs into English, including strategies such as additions in brackets and explanations, cf.:

> *Al-Jazeera:*
> [...] "As the Imam said, Israel must be wiped off the map," said Ahmadinejad, referring to Iran's revolutionary leader Ayat Allah Khomeini. [...]
> Nevertheless, Ahmadinejad said, "There is no doubt that the new wave (of attacks) in Palestine will soon wipe off this disgraceful blot (Israel) from the face of the Islamic world."

Table 4. Titles and lead for Ahmadinejad's speech in translation

	Main title	Lead
Al-Jazeera	Ahmadinejad: Wipe Israel off map	Ahmadinejad addressed students at a conference Iranian President Mahmoud Ahmadinejad has openly called for Israel to be wiped off the map
New York Times	Full Translation of Ahmadinejad's Speech	This is a translation, by Nazila Fathi in The New York Times Tehran bureau, of the October 26 speech by President Mahmoud Ahmadinejad to an Islamic Student Associations conference on "The World Without Zionism." The conference was held in Tehran, at the Interior Ministry. The text of the speech was posted online, in Persian, by the Iranian Student News Agency (www.isnagency.com). Bracketed explanatory material is from Ms. Fathi.
MEMRI	Iranian President at Tehran Conference: 'Very Soon, This Stain of Disgrace [i.e. Israel] Will Be Purged From the Center of the Islamic World – and This is Attainable'	[...] At the conference, Iranian President Mahmoud Ahmadinejad spoke to the representatives [...] The Iranian Students News Agency (ISNA), published the full text of Ahmadinejad's speech. The following is a translation of excerpts from ISNA's report and from the speech
ISNA	Transcript of speech by Iranian President Mahmoud Ahmadinejad at "World Without Zionism" conference in Tehran	Reported by Iranian government-owned news agency ISNA on 26 October 2005 at 13:10 local time (for original Persian text see: ...) Iranian President Mahmoud Ahmadinejad made a keynote speech on Wednesday at the gathering of 4,000 students organized by the Association of Islamic Students Societies. The text follows:

New York Times:

[...] Our dear Imam said that the occupying regime must be wiped off the map and this was a very wise statement. [...]

I have no doubt that the new wave that has started in Palestine, and we witness it in the Islamic world too, will eliminate this disgraceful stain from the Islamic world.

Middle East Media Research Institute (MEMRI):

[...] Imam [Komeini] said: 'This regime that is occupying Qods [Jerusalem] must be eliminated from the pages of history.' This sentence is very wise. [...]

I do not doubt that the new wave which has begun in our dear Palestine and which today we are also witnessing in the Islamic world is a wave of morality which has spread all over the Islamic world. Very soon, this stain of disgrace [i.e. Israel] will be purged from the center of the Islamic world – and this is attainable.

ISNA:

[...] Our dear Imam ordered that the occupying regime in Al-Qods be wiped off the face of the earth. This was a very wise statement. [...]

I have no doubt that the new wave that has started in dear Palestine and which we witness today all over the Islamic world will soon wipe this scourge of shame from the Islamic world. This can be done.

The Iranian President's own website has only a very short summary of the speech, entitled 'Ahmadinejad: Supporters of Israel will face wrath of Islamic ummah.' There is only one reference to the relevant phrase as follows:

> [...] He further expressed his firm belief that the new wave of confrontations generated in Palestine and the growing turmoil in the Islamic world would in no time wipe Israel away. [...]

The additions in brackets can be characterized as translators' (or editors') interventions in that they specify a referent for an evaluative phrase (see 'this disgraceful blot (Israel)' in *Al-Jazeera* and 'this stain of disgrace [i.e. Israel]' in *MEMRI*). As we see from Table 4, some of the media refer to *ISNA* as the source which published the original text which they used for their own translations. These translations, however, differ from the English translation that *ISNA* itself provided. This shows again that in the process of translational recontextualization, transformations occurred which are ideologically relevant.

The particular phrase 'wipe off the map' was subsequently hotly debated, and it was also argued that it had been mistranslated. What has to be acknowledged, however, is that it is this particular phrase that has been cited more often than the other versions. Once a text is in the public domain, it serves as a reference point for other discursive events and forms the basis for political and legal debates, independent of any factual 'truth' or 'accurate' translation. This can be illustrated with a quote from an article by *The Guardian's* columnist Jonathan Steele, the article entitled 'Lost in translation':

> The phrase has been seized on by western and Israeli hawks to re-double suspicions of the Iranian government's intentions, so it is important to get the truth of what he really said. I took my translation – "the regime occupying Jerusalem must vanish from the page of time" – from the indefatigable Professor Juan Cole's website where it has been for several weeks. [...]
> (http://commentisfree.guardian.co.uk/jonathan_steele/2006/06/post_155.html)

A question of interest to a Translation Studies researcher is therefore also: why is one particular translation recontextualized more often than others? Why does it 'survive' in complex chains of discourse? The answers to these questions are not that easy to find, but they are to be analyzed in conjunction with a related question, i.e.: who decides which translation is passed on to politicians and to the media? In the case of the British government, the BBC Monitoring Service is the main provider of translations, and it also conveys information from sources that publish in English, as *Al-Jazeera* does (see Schäffner in press). This explains why in official government texts and speeches, this particular version as provided by the BBC Monitoring Service gets repeated, as can also be seen in the following report about a speech by the current Prime Minister Gordon Brown:

> [...] But in the Knesset it had a special resonance. Members applauded when he moved from Auschwitz to anti-Semitism and then to the threat from Teheran. "It is totally abhorrent for the president of Iran to call for Israel to be wiped off the map of the world," Mr Brown said, reiterating Britain's determination to prevent Iran getting a bomb (*The Economist*, 26 July 2008).

The BBC itself defended its decision to continue using the phrase 'wipe off the map' by referring to the expertise of their translation provider, cf.:

> The BBC's experts at the Monitoring advise "there is no direct translation into English of the Farsi phrase used by Mahmoud Ahmadinejad. Therefore there a number of possible ways of rendering the Farsi original into English. However, in the context of the whole passage we believe our original interpretation is an accurate reflection of the words." (http://www.bbc.co.uk/blogs/theeditors/2007/03/06/index.html)

The Guardian too, shows loyalty to its line of argument in that it corrected its own use of a different translation which had been used in a report about a walkout of some politicians during Ahmadinejad's speech at a 2009 UN conference in Geneva, cf:

> Giving background to this week's controversy over remarks by President Mahmoud Ahmadinejad of Iran, a story mentioned his previous call for Israel to be "wiped off the pages of history." The translation of the statement he made in 2005 [...] had been the subject of dispute. A more literal translation is: "the regime occupying Jerusalem must vanish from the page of time," and this is the translation we should have used (as noted in Corrections and clarifications, 28 July 2007). (*The Guardian*, 23 April 2009, in the section 'Corrections and clarifications')

The phrase 'must vanish from the page of time' is the one which had been justified by Jonathan Steele (see above). The choice of and reliance on a translation provider has thus to be seen in the context of power struggles about opinions, beliefs, and ideologies. (Extracts from) translations which fit the institutional ideology are much more likely to be quoted repeatedly and circulated more widely than those that reflect ideologies which are contradictory to their own ideologies.

In the concluding section, I will comment on what the discipline of Translation Studies can contribute to the analysis of such recontextualization processes.

5. Political discourse and translation studies

The discussion of the examples above should have made clear that translation plays an essential role in international political communication. Political arguments cross linguistic and cultural boundaries as a result of translation, and such cross-lingual and cross-cultural recontextualization processes reflect the institutional conditions in which they are embedded. That is, the textual profiles of translations are determined by the communicative aims and by the institutional policies and ideologies. As we have seen in the case of the political interview, the (amount of) information selected for publication in the respective print media reflects the topics and political issues which are of particular relevance to the country, or more precisely, to the political group(s) which the newspaper is more or less openly lending its voice to. In addition to quantitative differences between the original interview and its published versions, transformations include rearranging information and turning the interview genre into a report about an interview. Whereas adaptations of genre conventions are primarily determined by institutional rules and traditions (e.g., it is the normal procedure for *The Times* to present interviews in a reporting form), rearranging information can be seen as ideologically significant since it allows to give a more prominent position to a specific topic. Even if a full-text translation was submitted, there are processes of revision and editing at work, which in the case of media institutions do not involve professional translators but are carried out by journalists and editors who base their decisions on the values of journalism. The textual transformations performed by journalists as translators as well as by editors can thus also be explained with reference to 'gatekeeping functions' (e.g. Vuorinen 1995). That is, controlling the quantity of the original text, reorganizing its structure, transforming messages (such as changes between active and passive sentence structures), and also supplementing messages (for example by adding contextualizing information) are functions which reflect the importance of ideology in the translational recontextualization processes.

Such gatekeeping functions also operate in the case of press conferences, at a more socio-political level as far as the admission of journalists is concerned, and at a communicative-ideological level in respect of the interaction with journalists. Recontextualization is at work when transcripts of press conferences are made available on government websites. As the example above has shown, a comparison of the German and US-American versions of the same press conference reveals differences in the quantity, the genre, and the linguistic structure of the messages. As a result, the image constructed of the politicians is different, with politicians being presented as more authoritative on the website of the German government due to omissions of small talk and to style enhancements in the transformation of the oral speech into a written text. These amendments to the texts are done by staff in the press office and reflect institutional values and policies.

Another example of message supplementing has been seen in the *New York Times'* text of President Ahmadinejad's speech, where explanations were added in brackets. In this case, however, the translator herself was credited as the agent of these textual interventions. Power is at play here as well, since powerful mass media get quoted by other mass media more often than others. Moreover, only a few international news agencies are the leading providers of news, including translated news, to mass media (cf. Bielsa 2007). In the international chain of discourse, some voices are therefore represented and heard more frequently than others. It is again as a result of such cross-lingual and cross-cultural recontextualization processes, that the English phrase 'wipe off the map' has become the most frequently cited translation of Ahmadinejad's original words. Translations can thus both reflect and contribute to ideological debates and conflicts.

What all these examples have illustrated is that translations are not straightforward and faithful reproductions of their source texts, as often assumed by lay-people. The more traditional view of translation as transfer of meaning, resulting in a target text which is equivalent to its source text, which formed the basis of linguistics-based theories of translation (e.g. Catford 1965; Koller 1979), has been replaced by modern views which understand translation as a purposeful activity (e.g. Vermeer 1996), as norm-governed behavior (Toury 1995), as a socio-political practice (e.g. Venuti 1995), embedded in socio-historical contexts and determined by cultural, ideological, institutional conditions and constraints. Translation Studies has emerged as an independent discipline in its own right, often characterized as an interdiscipline (cf. Snell-Hornby et al. 1992). The ideological dimension of translation, aptly captured in the quote below, has recently seen much more attention (e.g. Calzada Pérez 2002).

> Translation is not simply an act of faithful reproduction but, rather, a deliberate and conscious act of selection, assemblage, structuration and fabrication – and even, in some cases of falsification, refusal of information, counterfeiting, and the creation of secret codes (Tymoczko and Gentzler 2002: xxi).

The textual profiles of translations can thus not be commented on and assessed simply by comparing them to the original source texts to identify 'losses' or 'mistranslations'. An awareness of translating as a social practice means that translation strategies which result in a specific profile of the target text need to be explained with reference to the socio-political conditions in which the translations were produced. In an article analyzing transformations of a text for the Taiwanese press, Sai-Hua and Nakamura (2005) make a difference between translation and transformation, arguing that 'translation' is an inappropriate term to explain recontextualization processes for the press. This line of argument reflects a narrow view of translation as linguistic equivalence between source text and target text. However, since any translation involves transformation, there is no need for keeping the two terms strictly separate when we speak about media translation. Both the social contexts in which translations are produced, including newspaper translation, and all the products themselves, i.e. the target texts, are of interest to a Translation Studies scholar. However, both the processes and the products can only be fully understood if the whole framework of actions surrounding the translators, as well as the policies and ideologies that underlie these actions, are taken into consideration. It is this interest in analyzing the influences of social, cultural, political, and ideological contexts on texts and discourse, which modern Translation Studies shares with Critical Discourse Analysis.

As said at the beginning of this paper, translation affects recontextualization processes across linguistic, cultural, and ideological boundaries, and as such, translation is an integral part of the politics of international relations. The production, distribution, and consumption of translations are discursive practices, determined by socio-political factors in the widest sense. By linking translations (as products) to their social contexts, causes and effects of translations can be discovered (cf. Chesterman 1998). A causal model of translation allows asking questions such as: What causal conditions seem to give rise to particular translation profile features? What effects do given profile features seem to have on readers? Which particular socio-cultural and ideological constraints influence the translation policy in general and the target text production in particular? In this paper, I have mainly illustrated textual profiles and I have tried to explain them with reference to the institutional contexts in which they were produced. What still remains to be done, however, is a more detailed and extensive exploration of the actual translation practices in political settings that result in the textual profiles as illustrated above. For news translation, some insights have already been gained (for example, Bassnett 2004; Bielsa 2007; Bielsa and Bassnett 2008; Holland 2006; Kang 2007), but the translation practices in political institutions are not yet well known. Research questions to be addressed would then, for example, be: What exactly are the translation practices in political institutions (in particular governments, press offices of governments, embassies)? What is their translation policy? Who decides on the selection of texts for translation? Who produces translations of political speeches, documents, press releases, etc.? What influence do these institutional policies and practices have on the dissemination and reception of translated political discourse?

In order to find answers to these questions, the textual analysis will have to be combined with a sociological analysis (cf. Wolf and Fukari 2007). In this way, insights into the respective roles of the actual agents involved in the complex translation processes (translators, editors, staff officers, political advisors, etc) as well as in the power relations can be gained. Translation Studies can thus add a particular perspective to enhancing our understanding of political discourse and political communication across linguistic, cultural, and ideological barriers.

References

Bassnett, Susan. 2004. "Trusting reporters: What exactly did Saddam say?" *The Linguist* 43: 176–178.
Bhatia, Aditi. 2006. "Critical discourse analysis of political press conferences." *Discourse & Society* 17: 173–203.
Bielsa, Esperança. 2007. "Translation in global news agencies." *Target* 19: 135–155.
Bielsa, Esperança and Bassnett, Susan. 2008. *Translation in Global News.* London: Routledge.

Blackledge, Adrian. 2005. *Discourse and Power in a Multilingual World*. Amsterdam/Philadelphia: John Benjamins.

Calzada Pérez, Maria (ed.). 2002. *Apropos of Ideology. Translation Studies on Ideology – Ideologies in Translation Studies*. Manchester: St Jerome.

Catford, John C. 1965. *A Linguistic Theory of Translation*. London: Oxford University Press.

Chesterman, Andrew. 1998. "Causes, translations, effects." *Target* 10: 201–230.

Chilton, Paul and Schäffner, Christina. 1997. "Discourse and politics." In *Discourse Studies: A Multidisciplinary Introduction, Vol. 2: Discourse as Social Interaction*, Teun A. van Dijk (ed.), 206–230. London: Sage.

Fairclough, Norman. 1995. *Critical Discourse Analysis*. London: Longman.

Holland, Robert. 2006. "Language(s) in the global news: Translation, audience design and discourse (mis)representation." *Target* 18: 229–259.

Kang, Ji-Hae. 2007. "Recontextualization of news discourse: A case study of translation of news discourse on North Korea." *The Translator* 13: 219–242.

Koller, Werner. 1979. *Einführung in die Übersetzungswissenschaft*. Heidelberg: Quelle & Meyer.

Sai-Hua, Kuo and Nakamura, Mari. 2005. "Translation or transformation? A case study of language and ideology in the Taiwanese press." *Discourse & Society* 16: 393–417.

Schäffner, Christina. 2005. "Bringing a German voice to English-speaking readers: Spiegel International." *Language and Intercultural Communication* 5: 154–167.

—. In press. "Crosscultural translation and conflicting ideologies." In *Essays on Translation and Cultural Identity: Selected Essays*, Micaela Muñoz-Calvo (ed.).

Snell-Hornby, Mary, Pöchhacker, Franz and Kaindl, Klaus (eds). 1992. *Translation Studies. An Interdiscipline*. Amsterdam and Philadelphia: John Benjamins.

Toury, Gideon. 1995. *Descriptive Translation Studies and Beyond*. Amsterdam: John Benjamins.

Tymoczko, Maria and Gentzler, Edwin (eds). 2002. *Translation and Power*. Amherst: University of Massachusetts Press.

van Dijk, Teun A. 1985. "Structures of news in the press." In *Discourse and Communication: New Approaches to the Analysis of Mass Media Discourse and Communication*, Teun A. van Dijk (ed.), 69–93. Berlin: de Gruyter.

Venuti, Lawrence. 1995. *The Translator's Invisibility*. London: Routledge.

Vermeer, Hans J. 1996. *A Skopos Theory of Translation (Some Arguments for and against)*. Heidelberg: TEXTconTEXT.

Vuorinen, Erkka. 1995. "Source text status and (News) Translation." In *Aspectus varii translationis*, Riita Oittinen and Jukka-Pekka Varonen (eds), 89–102. Tampere: Tampere University.

Wolf, Michaela and Fukardi, Alexandra (eds). 2007. *Constructing a Sociology of Translation*. Amsterdam and Philadelphia: John Benjamins.

Analyzed texts

(1)   Interview with President Putin
      Russian President Putin's interview with G8 newspaper journalist
          Information Clearing House
          http://www.informationclearinghouse.info/article17855.htm   (Retrieved
          12 May 2008).

"Ich bin ein echter Demokrat."
> *Der Spiegel*, 4 June 2007, pp. 116–120
> 'I am a True Democrat' *Spiegel Online*, 4 June 2007,
> http://www.spiegel.de/international/world/0,1518,486345,00.html   (Retrieved 12 May 2008).

'I'm a pure and absolute democrat. It's a tragedy that I'm the only one.'
> *Times Online*, 4 June 2007,
> http://www.timesonline.co.uk/tol/news/world/europe/article1878792.ece?print=yes (Retrieved 12 May 2008).

Poutine: "La Russe devra choisir des cibles en Europe."
> *Le Figaro*, 4 June 2007,
> http://www.lefigaro.fr/international/20070604.FIG000000301_poutine_la_russie_devra_choisir_des_cibles_en_europe.html (Retrieved 12 May 2008).

Putin serves up a hot menu
> *Kommersant*, 4 June 2007,
> http://212.248.33.60/p771175/r_1/Putin,_G8/(Retrieved 12 May 2008)
> Complete transcript of the interview all in Russian (Стенограмма беседы Владимира Путина с журналистами стран G8) http://www.kommersant.ru/articles/2007/putin.html (Retrieved 16 July 2009).

Putin threatens to target Europe
> *Globe and Mail*, 4 June 2007,
> http://www.theglobeandmail.com/servlet/story/RTGAM.20070602.wputin01/BNStory/International?home (Retrieved 12 May 2008).

Putin: pronto a puntare i missili sull'Europa
> *Corriere della Sera*, 4 June 2007,
> http://www.corriere.it/Primo_Piano/Esteri?2007/06_giugno/03/putin_missili_litvinenko.html (Retrieved 10 September 2007).

(2) Press conference Merkel and Bush
Pressekonferenz von Angela Merkel und George W. Bush am 13. Juli 2006 in Stralsund
> http://www.bundesregierung.de/nn_1516/Content/DE/Mitschrift/Pressekonferenzen/2006/07/2006-07-13pressekonferenz-merkel-bush.html (Retrieved 12 May 2008).

President Bush and German Chancellor Merkel participate in press availability
> The White House, Office of the Press Secretary
> http://www.whitehouse.gov/news/releases/2006/07/20060713-4.html (Retrieved 12 May 2008).

(3) Speech by Ahmadinejad
Ahmadinejad: Wipe Israel off map
> *Al-Jazeera*

http://english.aljazeera.net/NR/exeres/15E6BF77-6F91-46EE-A4B5-A3CE0E9957EA.htm (Retrieved 10 September 2007).

Full Translation of Ahmadinejad's Speech
New York Times
http://www.nytimes.com/2005/10/30/weekinreview/30iran.html?ex=1136782800&en=d932ad0feae2cdef&ei=5070 (Retrieved 12 May 2008).

Iranian President at Tehran Conference: 'Very Soon, This Stain of Disgrace [i.e. Israel]
Will Be Purged From the Center of the Islamic World – and This is Attainable'
Middle East Media Research Institute
http://memri.org/bin/articles.cgi?Page=archives&Area=sd&ID=SP101305 (Retrieved 12 May 2008).

Transcript of speech by Iranian President Mahmoud Ahmadinejad at "World Without Zionism" conference in Tehran
ISNA
http://www.iranfocus.com/modules/news/article.php?storyid=4164 (Retrieved 12 May 2008).

Ahmadinejad: Supporters of Israel will face wrath of Islamic ummah
http://www.president.ir/eng/ahmadinejad/cronicnews/1384/08/4/index-e.htm#b3 (Retrieved 12 May 2008).

CHAPTER 15

Media practices in reporting political crises

Natalia Kovalyova

1. Introduction

A recent wave of revolutions in Eastern Europe – both similar to each other and different from events previously placed in that category – could hardly have been missed by the global community. Bulldozer Revolution in Serbia in 2000, the Rose Revolution in Georgia in 2003, the Orange Revolution in Ukraine in 2004, and the Tulip Revolution in Kyrgyzstan in 2005 – together have come to constitute a "second wave of postcommunist electoral revolutions" (Tucker 2005). Their strikingly matching scenarios were a topic of much discussion as the events were unfolding. Apart from being close in time, these mass movements arose against corrupt governments that had been in power since the demise of communist regimes, were centered around elections fraud that ignited mass protests, and led to the resignation of the incumbent president and the installment of the opposition leader in office. And they made headlines across the globe. What turned a tedious contestation of fraudulent vote-count into an attractive story to cover by the world leading newspapers? Was it a new story or a nostalgic rerun of the previously successful grand narrative of the East-West confrontation?

The media have long been viewed not only as a provider of information, entertainment, or companionship but also as a force instrumental in shaping the world for us, which we – for the most part now – experience largely in a mediated rather than a direct form. Noble as these roles are, they do not exhaust the possibilities for the media involvement, nor do they stop us from wondering what sort of a picture shows in the window that is the media, for they do not passively channel the information but actively construct – frame – the picture we see. The unavoidable process of framing lies at the core of many media effects. Framing is both good and bad for those of us who are in the audience. It provides a structure to which further information is added, allowing recognition of the familiar features in the information flow and helping us to make sense of the new content relying on what we already know, that is, for which we have a frame/schema/scenario. Yet, framing also discourages alternative routes of thinking about objects, people, events, phenomena, etc. When the topic is close to home and direct experience with it is possible, the power of the media does not loom as large. It is when remote places to which we lack direct access are in focus that the media's impact upon us grows exponentially. And it is precisely in reports from distant places that the media's claims of "direct, value-free, objective transcription of some absolute external reality" (White 2003: 61) reveal their subjective groundings and that particular viewpoints and value orientations are "made to seem to arise naturally from apparently 'factual' informational content" (White 2006: 66).

In addition to content framing, studies of international news have found that news outlets tend to place a heavy emphasis upon culturally or politically 'proximate' areas (Christensen 2005: 110) while covering other parts of the world relatively sparsely save for natural disasters, conflicts, and similar 'sensations'. Some scholars linked this finding to the workings of the 'news cycle' and criteria of newsworthiness applied by the media when selecting events to cover. Others, like Herman and Chomsky (1988), highlighted the ideological nature of news gathering and reporting and claimed that international news reports in the US support (implicitly or otherwise) the national foreign policy priorities.

Herman and Chomsky's argument finds additional support in news coverage from parts of the world that have recently been through a political transformation. With the end of the Cold War, for instance, reporting from Eastern and Central Europe to the Western public became a framing challenge. The old story of the battle between the super-powers with a clear division of good guys and bad guys, sides and issues, and an unmistakably certainty in one's course of actions has been done away with. Enemies against whom each side defined itself vanished in a matter of days. That void has not been filled entirely although two possible replacements have been tried, namely, a transition to (or a promotion of) democracy and the chaos of early independence days in the newly emerged states. However, a peaceful transition to democracy lacks the drama that compels the audience's attention for a long period of time. The longing for a grand, overarching story that brings many isolated observations together prompts reporters to see events from less than democratic parts of the world as a struggle for democracy although those may not display a sufficient number of features to secure a place in a democratic camp. As Schipani-Aduriz (2007: 93) noted, in the West a widespread opinion has it that "the only choice is between totalitarianism (which is inadmissible) and democracy (as the inevitable option)," a situation in which events are interpreted as fitting a simplistic scenario: "people on the streets and nations breaking free from tyranny to embrace the freedom and democracy emulated from the West with new leaders addressing the crowds" (Schipani-Aduriz 2007: 95). The popular unrest, therefore, is labeled as an expression of people's free will and an indicator of strife for freedom. The problem with a single framework readily available for the interpretation, further points out Schipani-Aduriz (2007: 95), is that "although such master patterns help us sustain thought, they may also take the place of it."

Furthermore, it is important to remember that the media – be they journalists reporting from the field or editors in their offices – operate under a certain set of rules of the profession that guide selection and presentation of the material. As Lance Bennett (1996) notes, these rules are responsible for standardization of content and diminishing diversity of the news, at least when it comes to the US. Exploring journalist practices in covering politics, Bennett (1996) identifies five rules: building the story line upon official viewpoints, tailoring the story towards the conflict among powerful key players, following the trail of power beyond normal institutions, using familiar cultural metaphors, and seeking credible images that have a potential of becoming news icons. Do the media pursue their agenda and follow their practices in all circumstances? Do they operate under the same set of rules while reporting crises and disasters? The part that follows takes these questions to explore the media coverage of one particular political situation.

2.   The 'Orange Revolution': A case in point

The pre-election situation in Ukraine in the fall of 2004 was bound to develop into mass unrest. Previous elections already earned a nickname of Kuchmagate thanks to the corruption of the incumbent and his cabinet. The upcoming 2004 election cycle was expected to be at least as dirty. On October 31, 2004, in the first round of the presidential elections, neither Viktor Yanukovich (the official favorite successor to the outgoing president Leonid Kuchma) nor Viktor Yuschenko (the opposition leader) received more than 50% of the votes necessary to claim an electoral victory. A second round was scheduled on November 21, on which day dramatic changes in turnout figures as well as instances of voter fraud were reported in the regions carried by Yanukovich. The Central Election Commission, nevertheless, declared him the winner, provoking the opposition to call people to the streets of the capital city in protest. Within a few days that followed, Ukrainian Parliament and Ukraine's Supreme Court declared results invalid and ordered another round to be run on December 26, which Yushchenko won and in an orderly fashion was inaugurated a new president of Ukraine.

Technically, the dispute could be solved in a peaceful way only by introducing changes to the nation's constitution. Garnering mass support, the opposition managed to press for changes in the existing body of Ukrainian laws that allowed for a third round of voting to take place. In the months (and now years) after the protesters left Independence Square in Kiev, several political scientists proposed explanations of the events from standpoints of a modular approach (Beissinger 2007), political realignment (Katchanovski 2006), collective action (Tucker 2005), etc., but the name under which they have become popularly known is the 'Orange Revolution'.

This paper takes the case of the political situation in Ukraine in 2004 to examine reporting practices of the Western print media and to probe into creating a 'revolutionary' interpretation of the events. It asks the following questions: Did the events in Ukraine in the fall of 2004 – as they were reported in the media – constitute a revolution? Who (reportedly) were the parties to the revolutionary conflict and what relations between them were reported? What was at stake during the confrontation? Were there any glaring omissions from the 'Orange' story as the world heard it? What did the 'Orange' coverage add to Bennett's repertoire of reporting practices and journalistic norms? Throughout the paper I refer to the events as the Orange Revolution (no quotation marks) and to their discursive construction in the media as the 'Orange Revolution' (quotation marks added). This distinction serves two purposes: to differentiate the accounts from happenings on the ground and to emphasize a strategic move by the media in upholding this particular label.

The analysis uses a collection of 776 news reports on the Orange Revolution that appeared in October – December 2004 in major Western newspapers and news agencies: the *BBC, CNN, Deutsche Welle, The New York Times, Los Angeles Times, The Washington Post, The Times, The Financial Times, Associated Press, Agency France Press*, and *Reuter*. All reports were captured using Lexis-Nexis services observing the following time-frame. It starts three weeks prior the first round of election of October 31, 2004 and ends three weeks after the rerun of December 26, 2004. All stories containing the search keywords *Ukraine* and *elections* were captured. In addition to stories in English, news reports from the *BBC* and *Deutsche Welle* were captured in other languages prominent in the region (Ukrainian, Russian, Polish, and German).

The analysis employs a frame analytical methodology paying a close attention to the language of news reports and focusing on labels, agents, metaphors, analogies, and attributions. Working from a deductive perspective that asks what elements constitute a frame, I follow Entman (1993) suggestions to identify frames by "the presence or absence of certain keywords, stock phrases, stereotyped images, sources of information and sentences that provide thematically reinforcing clusters of facts or judgments" (Entman 1993: 52). Acknowledging the inevitability of framing in journalistic work, the paper engages in uncovering the dominant and subordinate (if any) frames adopted by reporters to make sense out of events. It further traces the rhetorical patterns of information organization in the reports to illuminate upon the degree of adherence towards the five journalistic norms discussed above (relying on official sources, capitalizing on a conflict between key figures, following the power trail, using familiar metaphors, and seeking iconic images).

3.   Revolutionary framing

Like many political concepts (e.g., rights, representation, sovereignty, national interest, public opinion, democracy, citizenship, etc.), revolution enjoys numerous definitions and comes in many types. Some see it as a form of change that is rapid and violent. Samuel Huntington (1968: 264), for instance, thinks of a revolution as a "rapid, fundamental, and violent domestic change in the dominant values and myths of a society, in its political situation, social structure, leadership, and government activity and policies." Jack Goldstone (1991) underlines a component of crisis profound enough to severely cripple the capacity of the government to govern. A widely popular definition of revolution formulated by Theda Skocpol (1979) distinguishes between social revolutions, political revolutions, and rebellions depending on the transformations in a society's class structure that they produce. Trimberger (1978: 2) stresses a violent "takeover of the central state apparatus" and the destruction of the power of the dominant social group of the old regime.

None of these criteria apply to the events unfolding in Ukraine in the fall of 2004. Dubbed as a revolution, they do not quite meet the part of being revolutionary: no structural social changes have occurred or have been triggered, no class grievances were feeding protests, no transformation in the composition of the elites has happened (the new president and his prime minister held the top positions in the government earlier), no state breakdown occurred (although the campaign used the theme of the country's split and secession), no destruction of any social group (let alone the dominant one) has taken place except for removing from office a corrupt clan. All actions taken by Orange 'revolutionaries' were insistently legal actions sought and accomplished through existing institutions (the Supreme Court and the parliament) although a collective action component (supporters called to the streets) was highly visible. Nor does the Orange Revolution meet in full the criteria of being a revolution from the above as outlined by Trimberger (1979). During the election campaign, the leaders of the Orange Revolution did not hold a position in the government; they emphasized non-violent, institutional ways of resolving the conflict over the vote rig; they prevailed by garnering support of the masses (by directly 'going public' if we are to borrow a phrase from Samuel Kernell); no radial ideology was employed to win hearts and minds of the voting public; and finally, no destruction of the political or economic bases was attempted.

Thus, in a very strict sense of a word, the term *revolution* is a misnomer for those events as they do not come with long term consequences, alleviation of common grievances, or structural changes of the social and political makeup of the country. Rather, a 'revolutionary' character of the movement hinges upon its success in overthrowing a political regime (Tucker 2005: 2). Yet, even the 'regime change' is too loaded a term, as it implies changes that run deeper than a mere change of hands at the top can produce.

Events – political, social, or otherwise – do not, unfortunately, speak for themselves and must be woven into some larger storyline from which they take on their meanings. Working through selections and omissions, through emphases and overtones, the mass media frame the events for us, shaping our understanding of the situation, clarifying it or obscuring it even more. How did the world learn about the events in Ukraine? Was the international public shown (and convinced in) their true revolutionary character? Was the picture internally coherent and uncontroversial? Was the verdict of "revolution" ever questioned? Exploring the role played by the international media in the process of making sense out of the Orange Revolution, my analysis departs from the point at which theorizing about revolutions meets a rhetorical approach to public events, a point discovered by Foran (1993: 7), who highlighted the issue of agency and two key vantage points related to it: actors (individuals and coalitions) and the role of ideas, culture, beliefs, values, and/or ideology played in motivating them. In order to answer the question of how the events received the name of a revolution, I will examine elements central to the frame construction: the players, the relations among them (named or implied), the stakes, and the ideas, beliefs, and culturally-informed symbols that informed the players.

4.   Who were the players?

The key players in any elections are, expectedly, voters and candidates (several of them at the start of the electoral season and usually the two rivals later on). In Ukraine 2004, however, a circle of interested parties expanded as the campaign went along. Some publicly announced their preferences in the outcomes of the elections; others resorted to indirect influence and manipulation behind the scenes. The three immediately affected and thus openly pro-active figures on the political arena were the outgoing president Kuchma, the candidate supported by the administration – prime-minister Viktor Yanukovich, and the opposition leader – Viktor Yushchenko. The chances of the two to win were estimated to be very close to each other, and there was no certainty as to who is clearly a better choice for "both were gray; only one was a bit brighter," as one of the top businessmen in Ukraine remarked. Both promised prosperous Ukraine, employed patriotic rhetoric, and fought for their own political, economic, and, some argued, physical survival.

Another cluster of actors prominent in the campaign as well as in the protests were the youth activist organizations, often trained by Western foundations in issue advocacy, basics of political campaigning, public mobilization, and other skills deemed necessary for responsible citizens of a viable democracy (1–2):

(1)   Pora, a student activist group that *staged a march* of at least 10,000 people demanding a fair runoff, has demanded that authorities announce a complete vote count by Tuesday, or else *face protests* (*Los Angeles Times*, 22 November 2004).

(2)   A new organization has appeared – "Pora" – consisting mostly of students, who are ready to risk a lot. On Sunday some of them *threw themselves under the bus [wheels] in order to stop Yanukovich's supporters* with their absentee's ballots in hand to vote at the polling stations away from home (*BBC*, 24 November 2004, translation from Russian is mine – NK).

The activist groups were not always acting in a radical, attention-grabbing fashion illustrated by the quote in above (2). On the contrary, their activism – crucial to the success of mass mobilization – earned them all-around praises. As one scholar put it, "The scale, duration and level of professionalism of the mass protests took political scientists and commentators in Europe and North America completely by surprise" (Copsey 2005: 99) and challenged the "consensus on the behavior of Ukrainian voters" that existed prior to the elections of 2004. Of course, bare enthusiasm could not sustain a 17-day long vigil on the streets of Kiev. As Copsey disclosed, "considerable sums of money" found their way to the protesters and made it easier for them to "provide for food, sanitation, and other needs" (Copsey 2005: 103).

Discussions of material support to the protests inevitably put a spotlight not only on donations but also on sponsors. A persistent thematic thread of international aid to the opposition runs throughout the news coverage and reveals parties with vested interests in the outcomes of the Ukrainian elections that preferred to remain behind the scenes and, often of necessity, beyond the nation's borders (3–4):

(3) *The United States and other western governments* have become deeply involved in the election by helping to finance either the main exit poll, conducted by a consortium of respected Ukrainian polling agencies, and by vigorously urging authorities to conduct an honest vote count (*Los Angeles Times*, 22 November 2004).

(4) No *US money* was send directly to Ukrainian political parties, the officials say. In most cases, it was funneled through organizations like *the Carnegie Foundation* or through *groups aligned with Republicans and Democrats* that organized election training, with *human rights forums* or with *independent news outlets* (*Associated Press*, 10 December 2004).

In addition to sponsoring opinion polls, activist groups, and the alternative media referenced in excerpts (3–4), Western support took other forms as well. President Bush sent a special envoy to Ukraine to "support democracy on the ground" and encouraged countless international observers to ensure that the elections meet international standards.

With the promise of the NATO expansion in the air and given the geopolitical location of Ukraine, it was not hard to predict that another giant player pulling the strings behind the scene would be Russia. In fact, president Putin's visit to Ukraine before the first round of election and a pro-Russian platform of the candidate who had the so-called 'administrative resource' at his disposal hinted at Russian involvement in the campaign as well.

This assortment of players brought the election to a different level: at stake was not so much the future well-being of Ukraine's population nor their present grievances nor the fate of democracy there; rather, Ukraine – once again – turned into a battlefield of competing geopolitical juggernauts. The ghosts of the Cold War were flying around tempting a reporter or two to follow a much trodden path of drawing the line and casting the events into a battle between the former arch-enemies. It comes as no surprise that with geopolitics as an encompassing theme, the elections became detached from their democratic meaning and turned into the elitists' endeavor. Or as *The New York Times* phrased it, "Besides the three men with claims to the Ukrainian presidency … few people in Ukraine have as much at stake" (*The New York Times*, 02 December 2004).

However, elections, even those framed as a game for the powerful, cannot occur without participating population, diverse in their attitudes, political instincts, motivation, and engagement. Protesters, as it turned out, made Yuschenko's most valuable asset. It was the pressure from people on the streets that drove the necessary amendments to the constitution through the legislation and ensured a "peaceful ... resolution of the crisis" (Copsey 2005: 106). Not all protesters were equally enthusiastic, democratically minded, or even altruistic. While some were clearly touched by the 'revolutionary' spirit and attracted to defending the common cause, others found the events extremely entertaining and amusing. News reports did present opinions of the supporters from both camps (as excerpts 5–6 demonstrate) and quoted people from a range of background but their portrayals reflected the imperative of drama and a human interest story, making it difficult to tell the typical from the sensational:

(5) Nadiya Luchko, 56, *a retired engineer* who was at the post-midnight rally said she thought that the most important thing about Yushchenko's apparent victory was that "we won't be ashamed of this *person to represent our country in other countries*" (*Los Angeles Times*, 27 December 2004).

(6) Anatoliy Zaverenya, 43, said he came to Kiev from the eastern city of Luhansk not so much to support Yanukovich as *to defend Ukraine*, "If Yushchenko wins, *Ukraine will be sold to the West, to the US, to Americans*," he said (*Associated Press*, 24 December 2004).

(7) Last Thursday morning, Natalia Dimitruk, *an interpreter for the deaf* on the official state UT-1 television, disregarded the anchor's report on Prime Minister Viktor F Yanukovich's claim of victory and, in her small inset on the screen, began to sign something else altogether. "*The results announced by the Central Electoral Commission are rigged*," she said in the sign language used in the former Soviet states. "Do not believe them" (*The New York Times*, 29 November 2004).

(8) *Expensive cars festooned in orange*; *orange-clad* demonstrators *queuing at McDonald's*; ladies *dressed in fur coats with orange ribbons* – these are all signs that Ukraine's "orange revolution" has enormous support from its newly emerging middle class (*BBC*, 1 December 2004).

Democratic fervor of the masses was somewhat problematic to pinpoint for the news reports. While an incident with the deaf interpreter on the TV (7) may count as an act of civil disobedience, its spread and/or contagious nature becomes questionable when along its side appears a portrayal of Ukrainian emerging middle class (8) parading orange ribbons on their fur coats, helping protesters with housing and food out of hopes for future profits under the banner of market and entrepreneurship. The festive mood around the protesters' tents, concerts and a large screen fitting a music festival venue added to the carnivaleque atmosphere that came in contrast to their slogans which, according to *The New York Times*, read: "We're *for freedom!*" (*The New York Times*, 22 November 2004).

The age of those portrayed in the news makes another curious feature of the 'revolutionary' coverage. Very few people in the news are in their 30s or 40s; the overwhelming majority is either the retirees (in their 60s and 70s) or the students (20s). Where were Ukrainian teachers, doctors, shop-assistants, taxi-drivers, office clerks that they never figured prominently in the news? Although this observation of news

reports' population should not be taken as a conclusive remark on the political behavior of Ukrainian population, it points towards the lack identified earlier: namely, a
peculiar absence from the reports of revolutionary passions sweeping the country.
True, the victory was secured by less than three million votes cast for the opposition
leader (see Table 1). It was hardly a landslide. Yet, why was the drama of the revolution
there? Had anyone converted politically as a result of the 'revolutionary' events? Did
the Orange Revolution help create staunch democrats out of reportedly apathetic
Ukrainians? The answers to such questions could only be speculative as the Western
audience saw an emotionally lukewarm presentation occasionally spiced up by the old
scare of the Soviet Union.

If participants on the ground did not fit the revolutionary suit, they were not described as voters either. Surprisingly absent from the coverage were the accounts of
voter-turnout – a matter of much worry in any modern democracy in the West. In the
'orange' story, widely circulated were the exit poll numbers (about 54% for Yushchenko,
about 10% less for Yanukovich) and the results of both rounds. But how many
Ukrainians went to the polling stations, how many stayed home to watch the events on
the TV, and who exactly made the support base for either candidate were the issues
fallen off the radar screen of the media.

Occasionally, the reports would rhetorically pit one candidate against the other by
quoting derogatory remarks the opposing camps reserved for each other. For instance, in
(9), the label 'band' suggested that Yanukovich's supporters had a criminal background and
evoked a well-publicized biographical fact of the candidate's criminal past. Although the
source of the term was not identified, its mere mention further damaged his reputation:

(9) Although generally peaceful, voting on Sunday was marred by many reports
of irregularities in voter list and some charges that *bands of Yanukovich supporters* were traveling by bus to multiple polling stations to repeatedly cast
absentee ballots *(Los Angeles Times*, 22 November 2004).

Table 1. Summary of the 31 October and 26 December 2004 Ukraine presidential election results

Candidates (nominating parties)	Votes first round	%	Votes rerun	%
Viktor Yushchenko (self-nominated)	11,188,675	39.90	15,115,712	51.99
Viktor Yanukovych (Party of Regions)	11,008,731	39.26	12,848,528	44.20
Oleksandr Moroz (Socialist Party of Ukraine)	1,632,098	5.82		
Petro Symonenko (Communist Party of Ukraine)	1,396,135	4.97		
Nataliya Vitrenko (Progressive Socialist Party of Ukraine)	429,794	1.53		
Source: Central Electoral Commission				

Also, despite the continuous calls from leaders of the oppositions for non-violent activities on the streets of Kiev, a certain amount of emotional stirring was present and made its way into the news reports – primarily through human interest stories (10):

> (10)   As Yushchenko's supporters began filling Independence Square this morning, the atmosphere was *more festive than confrontational.* Among the 7000 or so who turned up was Emilia Veryaovska. "My ancestors fought *for the freedom of Ukraine,* and though I'm 68, *I will fight for Ukraine,* not only for my children but for all Ukrainians to live in a free country," said retired pharmacist as the crowd listened to rock music and periodically chanted Yushchenko's name. "I couldn't help coming here," she added. "The KGB killed members of my family in 1952 and *their blood calls me here*" (*Los Angeles Times,* 22 November 2004).

Personal vendettas like the one referred to in excerpt (10), that has been brooding for the past fifty years and aims against the state that no longer exists, did not take off as a workable frame for the events. An explanation close at hand, and very plausible at that, is a strict control over the revolutionary agenda executed by the opposition camp. The contestation over the vote fraud could not have possibly been allowed to develop into a full-scale confrontation with personal grievances to relieve. A true revolutionary movement could deal with those. Staged mass protests of the Orange Revolution had to be focused on the main goal of the opposition – a victory in the elections. The following section on the stakes in the confrontation will further elaborate on these matters.

5.   What was at stake?

An openly-stated craving of the Ukrainian public for attention from the international community and their hyper-awareness of the significance of the electoral outcomes in geo-political terms surfaced early in the reports and remained highly visible throughout their course. As formulated in and by the media reports, the stakes fit the global geo-political puzzle: whether the country would lean toward the West or towards the East (which equals Russia in those parts). Reports the *BBC*:

> (11)   On the dawn of the elections day, Ukraine finds itself at the center of *unprecedented attention of the international community.* Special statements about events in Ukraine were made by *the European Union,* many prominent *western analysts,* and even *the US presidential candidate John Kerry.* Some of the observers even rate Ukrainian elections as *second in importance to the US after their own presidential campaign. BBC,* 5 October 2004, translation from Russian is mine – NK).

Reporting for the domestic audience, the Western media could be expected to tailor reports to foreground elements that would speak to folks at home. In the case of the Orange Revolution, such tailoring turned the events into a shape odd and familiar at once. The standards of living, reforms, democratic freedoms were the topics that no one seemed to be picking up. Comments from prominent figures and ordinary people interviewed on the street converged on the same point – Ukraine's image and the status on the international arena, as the excerpt (12) below illustrates:

(12)   "When I traveled around and talked to *Europeans*, they used to think that Ukraine doesn't really want democracy and *is not really part of Europe*," said Stepan Chop, a political science student who went to Kiev for the rallies. "Now, no one can say that. We're not different form the Poles, or the Hungarians, or the other who stood up. We think *the world has heard*" (*The Washington Post*, 15 December 2004).

The New York Times (13) captured a similar wish to prove the country's reputation internationally:

(13)   ... I stood among flag-waving demonstrators in Independence Square in Kiev and heard the leader of Ukraine's 'orange revolution', Viktor Yushchenko, triumphantly declare that Ukraine was *a European country*. Not Western, not merely democratic, and obviously not American – European (*The New York Times*, 17 December 2004).

Many wanted to overturn not just an election, but also an impression. This congruency between elites and the masses in understanding the meaning and the mission of the nation was instrumental later on when ordinary citizens were called to the streets to defend the country's image.

Reinforcing this understanding, the inaugural address by Victor Yushchenko would later promise to lead the country into the "mainstream Europe" stating that "we are no longer on the edge of Europe... we are situated in the center of Europe." Was it what the people cast their vote for – which camp to be counted in? Were the days and nights in Independence Square about being called European? Was it (and is it, really) such a close to heart issue for a Ukrainian? Were there any issues closer to home and interests more vital than being labeled 'European'? If there were any, they were re-shaped and re-phrased to follow the suit of geopolitical interests of the elites. Excerpts below (14–16) present a range of issues cited by the members of Ukrainian public interviewed by the media that goes from a wish for a better life to a wish for honest government, to European integration, and to benefits of the free market:

(14)   Local observers say that the Orange revolution has showed that Ukraine' new middle class no longer prepared to put up with *red tape and cronyism*, flourishing during President Leonid Kuchma's regime (*BBC*, 1 December 2004).

(15)   Myron Kostiv, the Iskra [a light bulb factory – NK] board chairman, made no secret of his preference in the election [...] "It is important that *the rule of law* is implemented. It is important *for people and for business*" (*The Washington Post*, 15 December 2004).

(16)   "At stake in the election is whether Ukraine, under Yushchenko, will *break free from Moscow's influence* and set itself on a path to *join the European Union and the NATO,* or will sink back into the orbit of Russia, its *former colonial ruler* (*The Sunday Times,* 26 December 2004).

Suspiciously absent from these reports are alternative views and alternative futures for Ukraine and for its people, most importantly the views from the other, East-leaning camp. Why did the reporters not venture out in the Ukrainian provinces where demonstrators gathered in the streets as well? While there could have been several good reasons to stay at the center of the revolutionary turmoil, a skew towards a single – pro-revolutionary – interpretation of the events is apparent and detrimental to the ideal of an unbiased, balanced coverage.

At a closer examination of news reports, an explanation starts shaping up: they all contain keywords hinting at a god term whose charm is hard, if not altogether impossible, to break. The rule of law and entrepreneurship mentioned in excerpt (15), freedom and independence gestured towards in excerpt (16) are ingredients of a democratic order. An interpretation of popular sentiments as democratic was readily available and hard to argue against. Indeed, the popular mobilization 'conjured' up in Ukraine in 2004 was taken by many as a sign of "profound devotion to the western-style democratic values and procedures" (Narvselius 2007: 29). Unfortunately, the story-line in the reports in my sample did not form a neat account of a democratic growth in Ukraine. Even at the onset of the confrontation between the two camps, democracy rarely figured on top of their priority lists.

6.   What were the frames?

As previous sections have demonstrated, there was plenty of 'building' material to construct several interpretations of the unfolding events. There were multiple parties involved, with agendas sometimes overlapping and suggesting coalitions and joint efforts and sometimes diverging diametrically to the point of breaking common bonds and revealing irreconcilable deeply- felt interests. Their statements contradicted each other regarding scenarios of Ukrainian futures and memories of "national grievances caused by the Soviet regime" (Narvselius 2007: 31).

To understand the direction in which the events were heading was a challenge. To report them to a distant reader in a coherent manner was even more daunting. A lot of commonly available frames worked for an episode or two but did not hold for the rest. For example, the *East-West confrontation,* so often evoked by protesters, was compromised by their insistence that Ukraine is a European, not mere a "western" country and certainly not an American one, as one participant told *The New York Times* (*New York Times* 17 December 2004). If Europe was a "center of gravity," where did that place their sponsors? In these new dimensions, the old polarization of East-West, read

Russia and the US, was a bit of a stretch. A new Russian scare did not collect enough substance to materialize, although – by many accounts – it was looming large. A *liberation frame* assigning Russia a role of a "former colonial ruler," as a reporter from *The Sunday Times* phrased it, also stood on shaky grounds. After all, this was a second, post-communist revolution. Ukraine has been an independent nation for more than a decade. If the revolution was to break off the communist yoke, yearning for the rule of law and the end of corruption, the latter were not of Russia's making (although, undoubtedly, its legacy). *Visionary frames* of the Ukrainian global mission that circulated in the campaign rhetoric of both candidates would not resonate with the international reader, so the press did not pick them up. The *electoral horse-race* did not work as a fall-back option either. The campaign was finished before the events in Ukraine caught the attention of the international media. The US presidential campaign had also come to an end and parallels and analogies that could have enlightened the coverage would, at that point in time, fall flat.

As this brief overview shows, framing possibilities abound but none could sustain itself for a prolonged period of time. Incoming information was fragmented and did not fit the available molds. Confusion, however, was not unique to the Orange Revolution. As Gitlin (2003: 29) observed in the case of Students for a Democratic Society movement in the mid-1960s, "the overall effect of media coverage was blurred and contradictory; there was not a single voice... in short, the media were far from mirror passively reflecting facts found in the real world."

For reporters covering the Orange Revolution, two options were plausible: to introduce an innovate frame/frames or to turn to a default mode of operation. The media preferred a second option. They relied on a safety net of proven professional practices and followed the official line, which in Ukraine 2004 meant telling a *'revolutionary' story*.

The events of the presidential electoral campaign did not promise to develop into anything radical at first, although from the very beginning it was understood that those might not be regular elections. Before the first round of elections, the outgoing president Kuchma registered his determination to see to an orderly development of the campaign. He reportedly said:

(17) *A revolution won't happen.* We will have elections worthy of a European country of the 21st century (*BBC*, 22 November 2004, translation from Ukrainian is mine–NK).

On the same day, the reports of the BBC Russian service stated that:

(18) ...Viktor Yushchenko called to his supporters not to leave Independence Square in Kiev for the night and *to continue the protest* (*BBC*, 22 November 2004, translation from Russian is mine–NK).

Demands for freedom, however, unlike those for the fair vote count, did not last long, but as the rallies did not disperse with time, the situation was pronounced critical for the government who could not ensure fair elections and did not seem to be agreeable to an immediate compromise. Quoting Yushchenko:

> (19)   The *government* has lost control over the political, financial, and economic process in Ukraine, so we will propose the resignation of *Yanukovich's government* (*Los Angeles Times*, 30 November 2004).

With the word of government's inability to control the situation spread around, the road was open to more drastic interpretations of the events and the label of a revolution was ready at hand (24). Reports the *BBC News*:

> (20)   "It is a Ukrainian *bourgeois revolution*," says Olexandr Irvanets, a Ukrainian intellectual and writer. It is *a follow-up to the 'national' revolution* at the end of the 1980s, when Soviet Union collapsed, he says (*BBC*, 1 December 2004).

Yet, this revolution had a surprisingly festive air about it, suggestive more of a political cum public relations campaign than of the uprising of the oppressed classes (21–22):

> (21)   Despite Yushchenko's assertion that the county was on "*the edge of civil war*," the mood among his supports in the streets remain *more festive than fearful* (*Los Angeles Times*, 25 November 2004).
>
> (22)   The lack of violence and *the carnival air* surrounding the rallies have been factor in gaining outside support for Yushchenko's claims and making it difficult for President Leonid Kuchma, Yanukovich's political patron, to crack down, *Western diplomats say* (*The Washington Post*, 9 December 2004).

Notably, throughout the corpus of the reports under analysis, the term 'revolution' never came without quotation marks around it nor without a disclaiming attribute of 'the so-called', although comments secured by the media from an expert in the area – Zbigniew Brzeziński, a National Security advisor to president Carter – suggested an acceptable revolutionary interpretation (23):

> (23)   We see here the mass expression of thirst for change, the explosion of self-awareness that captured significant portions of the Ukrainian society (*BBC*, 2 December 2004, translation from Russian is mine–NK).

Labels employed by the media to describe the Orange Revolution did not remain stable, as the reporters were working out the frame for the occasion. Even after the opposition's supporters took to the street, the media continued experimenting with different descriptors ranging from *the protest* on November 22 to *political rallies* on November 29 (if one followed the *BBC*) and upgrading *political tensions* to a slightly more telling category of a *political rebellion* (if one preferred *The New York Times'* reports) although participants on the grounds used more dramatic definitions:

(24) "You prevented *a coup* against the state!" he [Yuri Lutsenko, a Socialist deputy – NK] roared at the crowds – meaning that the pressure they had applied on the parliament by their presence, had prevented the resolution getting any further than being accepted as a subject for debate (*BBC News*, 30 November 2004).

It took ten days for the media to adopt the term of *revolution* discarding the interim labels. Yet, the *revolutionary frame* did not connect all the dots in the picture: it missed the grievances and class interests that come to a clash producing revolutions, it did not demonstrate the revolutionary spirit swiftly spreading across the nation, and it did not identify new people in the position of power. Soon, the revolution was called off and the revolutionary agitation wore out. As the chronology in above demonstrates, 'revolution' was the frame pushed for by the Ukrainian opposition. Moreover, given the developments in the 'revolutionary' scenario, the opposition was much in need of mass support or at least an impression of such support. Without it, its case in the electoral battle would have been very slim. The reluctance of the media to pick up the 'revolutionary' story and present the elites' conflict in 'revolutionary' colors testifies to their considerate approach to coverage. Yet, I argue here, the very professionalism of the journalists covering the Ukrainian elections of 2004 worked against them. Their practices of indexing the story to the official version led them to fall prey to a skillful manipulation by the opposition campaign management team.

With people called off the streets, reporters kept Ukraine for a while on the frontpage 'normalizing' the political upheaval and its memories, telling stories with a human touch – about young couples met and married on Independence Square, of businessmen feeding the protesters, of prospects of a brighter future, and the like. But 'normal' stories further obscured the grand narrative of popular resistance, removed the exotic air from the events, and put them on an equal footing with other news competing for the audience's attention. With the drama over, the awkward story of the 'Orange Revolution' could not and did not last.

7.   What were the practices?

Our discussion of framing let us to conclude that episodic frames applied by the media to make sense of the Orange Revolution did not add up to a unified all-encompassing interpretation. A revolutionary frame did not have enough elements to sustain itself and would have forced the events to appear 'larger than life'. To navigate conflicting narratives and fragmented discourses, the media resorted to guidelines provided by the norms of professional practice. However, only three out of five guidelines, as those have been specified by Bennett (1996), were followed. The overall interpretation was oriented to the statements by key players (rule 1). With instances of shifting definitions, the story was developed as a conflict between the main characters (rule 2), although a preference was given to the winning (rebellious) party, and less attention was paid to the actions of the pro-government candidate and his supporters. Reports did follow the story beyond the institutional settings and the legal details of the contestation (rule 3), bringing in a human interest element and drama.

Rule 4 could not be followed very closely in the international coverage of the Orange Revolution. Familiar metaphors and analogies were scare to come by and those that were found beckoned back fears of the old enemies from the Cold War times. Yet, Ukraine 2004 was a relatively new territory to tread. Metaphors, analogies, associations, and stereotypes inherited from the Soviet times did not quite explain it. A clear reference point for this new geopolitical entity was not obvious, but absolutely necessary. For a reported event to be evaluated, it must be "typified," reminds us Alexander, in a sense that "it must be explained as a typical and even anticipated example of some thing or category that was known about before" (Alexander 2002: 12). Should one have looked at the fall of the Berlin Wall? The Russian revolution of 1917? An Iranian revolution? The turmoil around elections in Latin America or something else as an anchoring point? None of those historical events made a good exemplar for Ukraine, where mass mobilization took everyone (including Ukrainians themselves) by surprise (Narvselious 2007: 29; Copsey 2005: 99).

Finally, the choice of credible images with a potential of becoming iconic (rule 5) has proven difficult. The most outstanding symbolic element – the color orange – was a weak candidate for a potent icon. In Ukrainian culture (at least until 2004), orange did not trigger any culturally loaded associations. Its political value was even more uncertain.

Thus, the overall approach to the 'Orange Revolution' developed in the direction of a 'stick-to-your-guns' imperative. A political crisis in a distant land and the absence of a readily available interpretive frame for its understanding did not move reporters towards seeking an innovative angle, an improved practice, or an original format. Moreover, actively seeking dramatic moments, the media might have been attracted to the Orange Revolution because the events promised drama, a stir of emotions, and non-trivial plot lines. In a way, the label of a revolution and the frame it revived were too attractive to drop. With the frame in hand, the media went "to seek out crisis" (Raboy and Dagenais 1992) where there was little of it. Dependency on crisis and a perceived threat by normalcy, explain Raboy and Dagenais (1992: 4), lead to the media "paying even more attention to a fabricated crisis than to one that can stake a material claim to reality." And although people on the streets are hard to ignore, one needs to exercise caution not to attribute to them revolutionary feelings or noble motives of protecting and/or defending democracy. What is more, the media preferences for the officially sanctioned view on political events leave interests and motives of the politicians on the other side of the critical probe. As a result, reporters run the risk of falling prey to their own customs, projecting a version of reality that politicians want the broader public to have. As the case under analysis demonstrated, the coverage of the Orange Revolution served as an excellent promotional tool and a mobilization scheme for the opposition, precisely because the media behaved in the way they usually do, following the official word, watching closely the powerful figures, and looking for memorable images.

8. Conclusion

As our analysis has shown, the media did not discover the Orange Revolution. Instead, they were instrumental in making those events appear as something more than protests and rallies. In this sense, the media, reluctantly, helped to put a revolutionary label on the events what could have otherwise been regarded as a contestation of the fraudulent vote-count – not an infrequent occurrence nowadays both in more advanced democracies and in countries that undergo the process of democratization.

The Orange Revolution was called off when the compromise among the elites was reached. Unfortunately, the revolutionary spirit did not carry over into more mundane tasks of re-structuring and re-building of government. It was hard to award the Orange Revolution its name from the very beginning – it did not stem from the clash of class interests, it didn't bring changes in the society, although the power changed hands. It was successful as a movement – and very well organized – with resources that have been accumulated during several years through democracy promotion programs funded by Western organizations. Yet, what it demonstrated was "the longing for revolutions" (Yack 1986), the longing for social transformations, the nostalgia for a lost grand narrative that explains the world, ensures its security, and provides a blueprint for our understanding of the future. It attracted the media by the trappings of such a transformational event. Journalistic practices allowed the Western press to create a believable picture. Bu the same journalistic practices (indexing the official opinion, in particular) compelled the media to keep in circulation the label that was empty of content. As Jeffrey Alexander would have put it, "the means of symbolic production" (Alexander 2002) remained in the hands of politicians. The media followed their lead.

References

Alexander, Jeffrey C. 2002. "On the social construction of moral universals: The 'Holocaust' form war crime to trauma drama." *European Journal of Social Theory* 5 (1): 5–85.

Alexseev, Mikhail and Bennett, W. Lance. 1995. "For whom the gates open: News reporting and government source patterns in the United States, Great Britain, and Russia." *Political Communication* 12: 395–412.

Baysha, Olga and Hallahan, Kirk. 2004. "Media framing of the Ukrainian political crisis 2000–2001." *Journalism Studies* 5 (2): 233–246.

Beissinger, Mark. 2007. "Structure and example in modular political phenomena: The diffusion of Bulldozer/Rose/Orange/Tulip revolutions." *Perspectives on Politics* 5 (2): 259–276.

Bennett, W. Lance. 1996. "An introduction to journalism norms and representations of politics." *Political Communication* 13: 373–384.

Christensen, Christian. 2005. "Pocketbooks or prayer beads? U.S/U.K. newspaper coverage of the 2002 Turkish elections." *The Harvard International Journal of Press/Politics* 10 (1): 109–128.

Copsey, Nathaniel. 2005. "Popular politics and the Ukrainian presidential election of 2004." *Politics* 25 (2): 99–106.

de Vreese, Claes H. 2005. "News framing: Theory and typology." *Information Design Journal + Document Design* 13 (1): 51–62.

Ekström, Mats and Johansson, Bengt. 2006. "Talk scandals." *Media, Culture, & Society* 30 (1): 61–79.

Entman, Robert M. 1991. "Framing U.S. coverage of international news: Contrasts in narratives of the KAL and Iran air incidents." *Journal of Communication* 41 (1): 6–27.

—. 1993. "Framing: Toward clarification of a fractured paradigm." *Journal of Communication* 43: 51–58.

Foran, John. 1993. "Theories of revolution revisited: Towards a fourth generation?" *Sociological Theory* 11: 1–20.

Gamson, William and Wolsfeld, Gadi. 1993. "Movements and media as interacting systems." *Annals of the American Academy of Political and Social Science* 528: 114–125.

Gitlin, Todd. 2003. *The Whole World is Watching: Mass Media in the Making and Unmaking of the New Left* [2nd ed.]. Berkeley, CA: University of California Press.

Goldstone, Jack. 1980. "Theories of revolution: the third generation." *World Politics* 32: 425–453.

—. 1991. "Ideology, cultural frameworks, and the process of revolution." *Theory and Society* 20: 405–53.

—. 2001. "Toward a fourth generation of revolutionary theory." *Annual Review of Political Science 2001*: 139–187.

Goodwin, Jeff. 1994. "Towards a new sociology of revolutions." *Theory and Society* 23: 731–766.

Halliday, Julian, Jansen, Sue Curry and Schneider, James. 1992. "Framing the crisis in Eastern Europe." In *Media, Crisis and Democracy: Mass Communication and the Disruption of Social Order*, Marc Raboy and Bernard Dagenais (eds), 63–78. London, Newbury Park, New Delhi: Sage Publications.

Herman, Edward S. and Noam Chomsky. 1988. *Manufacturing Consent: The Political Economy of the Mass Media*. New York: Pantheon Books.

Huntington, Samuel P. 1968. *Political Order in Changing Societies*. New Haven: Yale University Press.

Katchanovksi, Ivan. "The Orange Revolution? The political realignment and regional division in Ukraine." Paper presented at the 2006 Annual Conference of the Canadian Political Science Association in Toronto.

Narvselius, Eleonora. 2007. "Cultural identifications, political representations and national project(s) on the symbolic arena of the Orange Revolution." *Studies in Ethnicity and Nationalism* 7 (2): 29–55.

Raboy, Marc and Dagenais, Bernard. 1992. "Introduction: Media and the politics of crisis." In *Media, Crisis and Democracy: Mass Communication and the Disruption of Social Order*, Marc Raboy and Bernard Dagenais (eds), 1–15. London, Newbury Park, New Delhi: Sage Publications.

Schipani-Aduriz, Andres. 2007. "Through an orange-colored lens: Western media, constructed imagery, and color revolution." *Democratization* 15 (1): 87–116.

Sewell, William. 1996. "Historical events as transformations of structure: Inventing revolution at the Bastille." *Theory and Society* 25: 841–881.

Skocpol, Theda. 1979. *States and Social Revolutions: A Comparative Analysis of France, Russia, and China*. Cambridge: Cambridge University Press.

Snow, David A., Rochford, E. Burke, Jr., Worden, Steven K. and Benford, Robert D. 1986. "Frame alignment processes, micromobilization, and movement participation." *American Sociological Review* 51: 464–481.

Trimberger, Ellen Key. 1978. *Revolution from Above: Military Bureaucrats and Development in Japan, Turkey, Egypt, and Peru*. New Brunswick, NJ: Transaction Books.

Tuchman, Gaye. 1973. "Making news by doing work: Routinizing the unexpected." *American Journal of Sociology* 79 (10): 110–131.

Tucker, Joshua. 2005. "Enough! Electoral fraud, collective action problems, and the '2nd wave' of post-communist democratic revolutions." Manuscript, Princeton University.

Tullock, Gordon. 1971. "The paradox of revolution." *Public Choice* 11: 89–99.

Watkins, S. Craig. 2001. "Framing protest: News media frames of the million man march." *Critical Studies in Media Communication* 18 (1): 83–101.

White, Peter R. 2003. "News as history: Your daily gossip." In *Re/reading the Past: Critical and Functional Perspectives on Time and Value*, James R. Martin and Ruth Wodak (eds), 61–89. Amsterdam/Philadephia: Johns Benjamins Publishing Company.

—. 2006. "Evaluative semantics and ideological positioning in journalistic discourse: A new framework for analysis." In *Mediating Ideology in Text and Image: Ten Critical Studies*, Inger Lassen, Jeanne Strunck and Torben Vestergaard (eds), 38–67. Amsterdam/Philadelphia: Johns Benjamins Publishing Company.

Yack, Bernard. 1986. *The Longing for Total Revolution: Philosophic Sources of Social Discontent from Rousseau to Marx and Nietzsche*. Princeton, NJ: Princeton University Press.

PART V

Politicizing 'linguistic human rights'

CHAPTER 16

The practice and politics of multilingualism

Adrian Blackledge

1. Introduction

Scholars in linguistic human rights have focused on the rights of indigenous peoples and various dominated groups, including linguistic minorities (Skutnabb-Kangas 2000, 2008; Skutnabb-Kangas and Phillipson 2008). May (2005) argues that a key weakness in much existing scholarship in this area is a tendency to discuss minority language rights in collective, uniform terms, while Blommaert (2005: 391) speaks of the 'fundamental problems' of the linguistic rights paradigm, with its 'deeply idealized notions of language and society'. Like Blommaert, May proposes that more ethnographic accounts are needed to explore the connections between broader principles and actual, multifaceted, language values and use 'on the ground' in complex multilingual contexts (2005: 338). This chapter endeavors to provide one example of an ethnographic-sociolinguistic approach to the issue of language rights.

2. Minority language rights

Wiley (2005: 600), speaking of the USA, argues that "monolingualism is the real linguistic deficiency in this country." The same can be said of the UK, and yet the discourse of politicians and media commentators frequently proposes that monolingualism in English is the natural and desirable state. At the same time, more than 300 languages are spoken in the UK on a daily basis. This raises questions about who controls the circulation of linguistic resources, and which sets of linguistic resources are permissible or legitimate in which settings. That is, it raises questions about who has the right to use their own language, where, when, and how. Joseph (2006: 45) points out that monolingual communities are 'a figment of the imagination', demanding the marginalization or outright ignoring of anyone who speaks something other than the majority language, or speaks the majority language in a way that diverges from the general norm, or both. Shohamy (2006: 173) argues that "monolingualism is a myth detached from reality that must be recognized as such by educational systems." Shohamy adds that educational institutions have often been required to subscribe to the 'ideological aspiration' of monolingual competence.

One of the frequently heard criteria for nation and/or state formation has been commonality of language. Hobsbawm demonstrates that in nineteenth century Europe language was regarded as 'the only adequate indicator of nationality' (1990: 21). However, it is not sufficient to say that speakers of the same language belong to the same nation-state. Billig (1995: 29) argues that the creation of a national hegemony often involves a hegemony of language. A 'common-sense' understanding of the relationship between language and nation ignores the diversity and variety of the language(s) spoken within many states. As Rampton's (1995, 2006) work has made clear, even the notion of a single 'English' language is an over-simplification, as new varieties emerge from different cultural and social contexts. Linguistic resources function differently in different linguistic systems, and this renders the study of language in society complex. However, it is to this complexity that we must attend "if we want to make linguistic rights more than just a trope in political-linguistic discourse" (Blommaert 2005: 403). Pujolar (2007) demonstrates that multilingual practices and skills have had an uneasy fit in the national and linguistic order. Bilingual communities have often been seen as a threat to cultural unification. Heller (1999) argues that the concept of a 'linguistic minority' only makes sense within an ideological framework of nationalism in which language is central to the construction of the nation. She further proposes that "linguistic minorities are created by nationalisms which exclude them" (Heller 1999: 7). At the same time, Moyer and Martin Rojo (2007) point out that migrants are the new social actors challenging the hegemonic linguistic construction of the nation-state from below in different ways. They argue that migrants from different language backgrounds constitute a challenge for traditional nationalist discourses and ideologies in the institutions of multilingual democratic states, as "multilingual reality comes up against national ideologies of monolingualism and homogeneity" (Moyer and Martin Rojo 2007: 156). Blommaert (2005: 411) argues that the notion of 'single' languages attached to single collections of attributes, values and effects is inadequate: "Ethnographically we will always see complex blending, mixing and reallocation processes, in which the differences between 'languages' are altogether just one factor. Inequality has to do with *modes of language use*, not with languages." Blommaert argues that we need to develop an awareness that is not only about the 'language' you speak, but also about *how*, *when*, and *to whom* you speak. Inequality is a matter of voice, not only of language; it is a social issue rather than only a linguistic one.

Debates about language and languages in the UK have become evident in political discourse throughout the first decade of the twenty-first century. Following terrorist attacks on New York and London in 2001 and 2005 respectively, social and political arenas altered. In the first decade of the twenty-first century the British government introduced more Acts of Parliament than ever before to require immigrants and visitors to demonstrate their proficiency in English in order to gain access to certain economic, cultural, and symbolic resources. In this period proficiency in English has come to represent national unity, British (or perhaps English) identity, and social cohesion, while the use of languages other than English has come to be regarded as (or to symbolize) a threat to the security of the state. In 2001, following violence in the streets of northern towns in England, some politicians suggested that there were causal links between social disorder and people failing to learn or speak English (Blackledge 2005). In 2002 the (then) Home Secretary, David Blunkett argued that linguistic minority people should speak English at home amongst their families because "speaking English…helps overcome the schizophrenia which bedevils generational relationships." In the same year the British Government introduced new legislation which extended requirements for applicants for British citizenship to take an English language test to demonstrate their proficiency in English (or Welsh or Scots Gaelic). In 2005 a computer-based version of this test was introduced, also requiring evidence of 'knowledge of life in the UK'. In April 2007 the test was extended as a requirement for applicants for indefinite leave to remain in the U.K. 2007 saw the introduction of a requirement for 'visiting preachers' to demonstrate 'a proper command of English' (at IELTS Level 6), and for welfare claimants to provide evidence that they were learning English. In 2008 the Government proposed a 'pre-entry English requirement' for those applying for visas to join their spouses in the U.K. In the same year the Government reformed its immigration system (Home Office 2008), to include English language tests for those seeking to progress from 'temporary residence' to 'probationary citizenship'. As elsewhere in these discourses, proficiency in English is explicitly linked to 'British values'. Joseph (2006: 33) argues that in such discourses multilingualism feels like a threat to the very foundation of a culture, since the language itself is the principal text in which the culture's mental past and its present coherence are grounded. The English language testing regime which has been so rapidly extended by the British Government acts in the name of cultural and linguistic unification. It is a regime based on the notion that when all are able to demonstrate English language proficiency, we will be able to achieve national unity, and a sense of common belonging. It is also based on the notion that the use and visibility of minority languages other than English threatens this sense of national unity and common belonging. The language testing regime is by no means peculiar to the U.K. Two recent volumes (Extra et al. 2009; Hogan-Brun et al. 2009) amply demonstrate the recent widespread adoption of language testing for citizenship, especially by European governments.

One of the key theoretical paradigms which underpins analysis of reproduction of language ideologies in this chapter is that developed by French sociologist Pierre Bourdieu. For Bourdieu, the social order is produced and reproduced in "an abundance of tangible self-evidences" (2000: 181), which give the illusion of common-sense reality. Dominated groups in society are complicit in their own domination because the power of the dominant group is inscribed in the bodies of the dominated. The inscription of this *habitus*, or way of being, comes about through ongoing acts of recognition and misrecognition in the social arena. The relation between *habitus* and *field* creates the conditions in which existing shared self-evidences are produced and reproduced. In this context 'self-evidences' are those apparently common-sense misrecognitions which constantly construct and reinforce hegemonic ideologies. This process of *symbolic violence*, of production and reproduction of common-sense consensus, occurs in discourses in the media, education, politics, the economy, and the law, to mention only institutional contexts. Language ideologies contribute to the production and reproduction of social difference, constructing some languages and varieties as of greater worth than other languages and varieties. This process can only succeed when, in the "institutionalised circle of collective misrecognition" (Bourdieu 1991: 153), dominant and dominated groups alike accept the greater value of certain languages and varieties. The circle of collective misrecognition comes into being through ideological discourse in contexts which include education, law, politics, economics, media and the academy. In an increasingly globalized environment, the State is not necessarily involved in this process at all levels. However, "the State makes a decisive contribution towards the production and reproduction of the instruments of construction of social reality" (Bourdieu 2000: 175).

Bourdieu's model of the symbolic value of one language or language variety above others rests on his notion that a symbolically dominated group is complicit in the misrecognition, or valorization, of that language or variety. The official language or standard variety becomes the language of hegemonic institutions because the dominant and the subordinated group both misrecognise it as a superior language. For Bourdieu, this misrecognition of the arbitrary nature of the legitimacy of the dominant language (and culture) "contributes towards reproducing existing power relations" (1977: 30). There are striking similarities in the ways ideologies misrecognise differences among linguistic practices in different contexts, often identifying linguistic varieties with 'typical' persons and activities and accounting for the differentiation among them. In these processes the linguistic behaviors of others are simplified and are seen as deriving from speakers' character or moral virtue, rather than from historical accident. The official language, or standard variety, often comes to be misrecognised as having greater moral, aesthetic and/or intellectual worth than contesting languages or varieties. In Bourdieu's terms, those who are not speakers of the official language or standard variety are subject to symbolic domination, as they believe in the legitimacy of that language or variety, and "Symbolic power is misrecognised as (and therefore transformed into) legitimate power" (1991: 170). Bourdieu suggests that we have to be able to identify relations of power in familiar discourses, because symbolic power "is that invisible power which can be exercised only with the complicity of those who do not want to know that they are subject to it or even that they themselves exercise it" (1991: 164). Very often, multilingual societies which apparently tolerate or promote heterogeneity in fact undervalue or appear to ignore the linguistic diversity of their populace. A liberal orientation to equality of opportunity for all may mask an ideological drive towards homogeneity, a drive which potentially marginalizes or excludes those who either refuse, or are unwilling, to conform. Bourdieu argues that where the symbolic value of one language or language variety is privileged above others, the symbolically dominated group is complicit in the misrecognition, or valorization, of that language or variety. When some forms of talk are valued over others, this also entails the valuing of some ideologies or ways of thinking over others. The constructed relation between nation-state and one national language entails a civic culture that is based on particular values and expressed in a particular language (Ricento 2005). One of the most powerful domains in which English is misrecognised as the sole legitimate language is that of education.

3.   Multilingualism

Debates about language cannot be treated as simply 'linguistic' or 'cultural heritage' issues, but are "important political questions that may affect the social and economic position of the social groups of a given territory" (Pujolar 2007: 144). That is, debates about language are often debates about immigration, and about 'pluralist' or 'assimilationist' policy in relation to immigrant groups. In public discourse language often becomes inseparably associated with a territorially bounded identity in a relationship that takes language, territory, and identity to be isomorphic (Freeland and Patrick 2004). One implication of this is that ideally the nation should be monolingual, with adherence to another language often (mis)read as a lack of loyalty to the national identity. However, it is not sufficient to say that speakers of the same language belong to the same nation-state. This common-sense understanding of the relationship between language and nation ignores the diversity and variety of the language(s) spoken within many states. Bourdieu argues that the official language is bound up with the state, both in its genesis and in its social uses: "It is in the process of state formation that the conditions are created for constitution of a unified linguistic market, dominated by the official language" (1991: 45). In order for one language to impose itself as the only legitimate one, the linguistic market has to be unified and the different languages (and dialects) of the people measured practically against the legitimate language. The goal of the state is often integration into a single linguistic community, which is "a product of the political domination that is endlessly reproduced by institutions capable of imposing universal recognition of the dominant language, and the condition for the establishment of relations of linguistic domination" (Bourdieu 1991: 46). This linking of language, literacy, and national identity happens in a number of sites which include language planning, standardization, educational policy, citizenship testing, and language instruction for immigrants (Blackledge 2005; Stevenson 2006). Recent work on language testing for citizenship has demonstrated that in a broad range of national contexts particular languages and language varieties become gatekeeping devices to determine who is permitted to become a member of the community of citizens (Blackledge 2005, 2009a, 2009b; Mar-Molinero 2006; Maryns and Blommaert 2006; Stevenson 2006). Another way that governments may seek to impose national identities is through educational policies that decide which languages are to be employed – and thus legitimized – in the public school system. Recent research has clearly documented the interpenetration of the ideological with the local, in institutional, nationalist, and political dimensions. When a language is symbolically linked to national identity, the bureaucratic nation-state faced with a multilingual population may exhibit 'monolingualising tendencies' (Heller 1995: 374). Heller's (1995, 1999, 2006) study of a Francophone school in Ontario observed tensions between the monolingual ideology of the school, and the language use and ideologies of at least some of its students, and found that some of the students resisted the linguistic ideology of the school. Also, in a school which was concerned with using French to resist the domination of English, students set up their resistance to the school through the very language which was oppressing them.

In many Western countries a dominant ideology is constantly produced and reproduced which positions the majority language (often English) as the only language of communication in institutional and other public contexts. Hornberger (2007: 179) argues that "The one-nation-one-language ideology, the idea that a nation-state should be unified by one common language, has held sway in recent Western history." In this ideology minority languages associated with immigrant groups are, as Bourdieu put it, rejected into indignity (Bourdieu 1998: 46). Minority languages which have historically been associated with particular 'ethnic' identities often continue to be important for particular groups (May 2004), but have little capital in majority-language markets. Very often, multilingual societies which apparently tolerate or promote heterogeneity in fact undervalue or appear to ignore the linguistic diversity of their populace. An apparently liberal orientation to equality of opportunity for all may mask an ideological drive towards homogeneity, a drive which potentially marginalizes or excludes those who either refuse, or are unwilling, to conform.

Gal (2006: 15) argues that in powerful discourse monolingualism is often taken to be the natural state of human life. Furthermore, named languages are taken to be homogeneous, and to be expressions of the distinct spirit of a particular group. In this sense, where linguistic practices conform to certain norms and standards, they are effective in legitimizing political arrangements. However, Gal also points out that in Europe a new elite of multilingual speakers (of, e.g., French, German, and English) sustains a breadth of linguistic repertoires which transcends national boundaries. For such groups ethnolinguistic identity may be only an occasional issue. For multilingual speakers of languages with lower status, however, language issues may still be salient as people attempt to negotiate identities, often from relatively powerless positions. Language ideologies are neither simple nor monolithic, however. Notwithstanding the argument that minority language speakers are subject to the symbolic violence of the dominant language ideology, some speakers who (or whose families) may traditionally have been associated with minority 'ethnic' languages are using language and languages in new ways (Rampton 1995, 1999). While some speakers are either unable to negotiate their identities from inextricably powerless positions, and others in powerful positions have no need to do so, some speakers in modern nation-states are using their linguistic skills to negotiate new subject positions (Blackledge and Pavlenko 2001; Pavlenko and Blackledge 2004). In what Gal (2006: 27) describes as 'self-conscious, anti-standardizing moves', such negotiations may include linguistic practices which reframe previous standard varieties, incorporating, *inter alia*, urban popular cultural forms, minority linguistic forms, hybridities and inventions. Here language practices associated with immigrant groups no longer represent backward-looking traditions, but may be linked to global youth culture and urban sophistication. Languages and language practices are not necessarily equated to national identity (but may be so), and are not necessarily dominated by the standardized variety. Despite powerful ideologies of homogeneity, populations in many countries – especially countries with a history of recent immigration – continue to be heterogeneous in their practices. May (2005: 337) proposes that linguistic identities need not be oppositional, and asks "what exactly is wrong with linguistic complementarity?" May calls for further ethnographic studies which articulate and exemplify broad linguistic principles of language ideological research in complex multilingual contexts. Heller and Duchêne (2007: 11) argue that rather than accepting ideological positions in which there is competition over languages, "perhaps we should be asking instead who benefits and who loses from understanding languages the way we do, what is at stake for whom, and how and why language serves as a terrain for competition."

4. Multilingualism and education

2008 was designated by the United Nations Educational, Scientific and Cultural Organisation (UNESCO) as the International Year of Languages. In announcing this initiative, Koïchiro Matsuura, Director-General of UNESCO, said:

> We must act now as a matter of urgency, by encouraging and developing language policies that enable each linguistic community to use its first language, or mother tongue, as widely and as often as possible, including in education...Only if multilingualism is fully accepted can all languages find their place in our globalized world (UNESCO 2008).

Notwithstanding UNESCO's imperative towards education for multilingualism, the education of multilingual students is frequently oriented towards monolingualism rather than multilingualism.

Cummins (2008a) refers to research (August and Shanahan 2006; Cummins 2001; Genesee et al. 2006) which demonstrates that considerable confidence can be placed in the positive outcomes of bilingual education. May (2008: 28) also summarizes research (Thomas and Collier 2002) which found that "minority language students who receive most of their education in English rather than their first language are more likely to fall behind and drop out of school." Edwards and Pritchard Newcombe (2006: 138) found unambiguous evidence that "the longer children are educated using English and the language of the home, the better the results." A summary by McCarty (2007: 34) of recent research finds that there is unequivocal consensus that: "students who enter school with a primary language other than the national or dominant language perform significantly better on academic tasks when they receive consistent and cumulative academic support in the native/heritage language." Cummins refers to "150 empirical studies carried out during the past 30 or so years that have reported a positive association between additive bilingualism and students' linguistic, cognitive, or academic growth" (2007: 112). Tucker (2008: 48) summarizes his review of studies conducted over the last three decades by saying that research "demonstrates conclusively that cognitive, social, personal, and economic benefits accrue to the individual who has an opportunity to develop a high degree of bilingual proficiency." It therefore appears that, contrary to the common-sense understandings of some politicians and policy-makers, time spent learning in more than one language, or in a minority language, is not wasted curriculum time. On the contrary, Tucker (2008: 41) concludes from his reading of the available literature, and from his own extensive research, that "time spent instructing the child in a familiar language is a wise investment." However, in many educational settings, especially in the developed Western world, opportunities to cultivate multilingualism in schools are lost in the persistent drive towards homogeneity.

Garcia et al. (2006: 14) refer to multilingual schools which "exert educational effort that takes into account and builds further on the diversity of languages and literacy practices that children and youth bring to school." This means going beyond acceptance or tolerance of children's languages, to 'cultivation' of languages through their use for teaching and learning. Garcia (2009: 6) further argues that what distinguishes bilingual education programs is the goal of using two languages "to educate generally, meaningfully, equitably, and for tolerance and appreciation of diversity." She points out that in educating broadly, these programs help students to become global and responsible citizens, and teach them to look across cultures and worlds, beyond cultural borders. Furthermore, they "make schooling meaningful and comprehensible for the millions of children whose home languages are different from the dominant language of school and society" (2009: 7). Garcia concludes that "bilingual education is *the only way* to educate children in the twenty-first century" (2009: 5).

McCarty et al. (2006: 91) suggest that despite the multilingual and multicultural nature of societies such as UK and USA, "education policies and practices often deny that multilingual, multicultural reality, attempting to coerce it into a single, monolingualist and monoculturalist mold." Shohamy (2006: 173) further points out that in most educational contexts in the world, a specific national language, spoken by powerful groups in society, is the only legitimate language in schools. At the same time, the languages of minority groups are viewed as having low status, with no legitimate place in schools. Students who are speakers of these languages are often encouraged to leave them behind as they become proficient in the dominant language. Shohamy (2006: 174) argues that the dominant national language is "viewed in ideological terms as part of a national identity embedded with notions that language is an indicator of loyalty, patriotism, belonging, inclusion, and membership." Furthermore, Shohamy points out, not only is the dominant language privileged above others, but schools accord no legitimacy for multimodalities, for mixing of languages, for hybrid forms, or for non-verbal varieties of expression. Busch and Schick (2007) argue that as educational materials and curricula are usually centrally produced by governments, they become a means of promoting a single unified standard as the national language, and in so doing fail to build on learners' own language resources. These ideological positions are perpetuated and reproduced by national tests that assess standards of the dominant language for all students.

Cummins argues that there is currently massive loss of language resources because young children are given few opportunities to use and become literate in their heritage languages. He refers to the negative and inaccurate messages which children receive in school regarding the status and utility of these languages: "Children understand very quickly that the school is an English-only zone and they often internalize ambivalence and shame in relation to their linguistic and cultural heritage" (2005: 590). Edwards (2004: 116) argues that in England government policy towards the education of bilingual learners has been inconsistent. While there has been official encouragement for teachers to adopt bilingual teaching strategies in the early years of children's schooling, this has been at best a transitional approach, designed as support for young children until they are sufficiently proficient in English to leave their community language behind. There has never been a statutory requirement for teachers to maintain students' minority languages in school. Bilingual children learning English as an additional language are placed in English mainstream school classrooms where their language and learning needs are to be met by a working partnership between the subject teacher and English as an additional language (EAL) teacher (Creese 2005). However, even where English as an additional language support teachers are literate in the languages of their students, they may feel use of a language other than English is inappropriate or embarrassing and therefore mostly use English (Baker 2006).

5.   Complementary schools

In the United States and Canada non-statutory educational settings which teach languages to those with familial and/or ancestral ties are usually termed 'heritage language schools' (Hornberger 2005a). In Australia these institutions are normally called 'community language schools' or 'ethnic schools', while in the UK they have often been referred to as 'supplementary schools'. In the present chapter I adopt the term 'complementary schools' (Martin et al. 2004; Creese et al. 2008), to emphasize the positive *complementary* function of these teaching and learning environments in relation to mainstream schools.

Complementary schooling in the UK is a result of historical processes and attitudes which do not consider the learning and teaching of minority languages and cultures as the state's responsibility (Rassool 2008). Creese and Martin (2006: 1) argue that complementary schooling is "a response to a historically monolingual ideology which ignores the complexity of multilingual England." Li Wei (2006: 78) argues that complementary schools in the UK "were set up in response to the failure of the mainstream education system to meet the needs of ethnic minority children and their communities." He further argues that this fact has been deliberately ignored by a succession of UK governments, which have tried to appropriate complementary schools for their own political and economic agendas. Complementary schools have been marginalized in national UK education policy, and "were seen as a minority concern and were left with ethnic minority communities to deal with themselves" (Li Wei 2006: 78). Creese et al. (2006: 23) argue that Gujarati complementary schools in Leicester provided multilingual children with a safe haven for exploring ethnic and linguistic identities while producing opportunities for performing successful learner identities. The complementary schools were "political and social contexts where particular ideologies dominate and children, adolescents, teachers and parents interact to reproduce and reaffirm or resist and challenge these ideologies" (Creese et al. 2006: 24).

In the context of the United States, Garcia (2005: 604) decries the loss of 'safe spaces' provided in bilingual education programs, but suggests that complementary schools can offer an informal, community-led initiative to prize open a 'crack' in the educational homogenization that surrounds the No Child Left Behind Act, allowing bilingual instruction to continue in the face of monolingualizing ideologies. Garcia concedes that heritage languages in education are good for language minority children who are receiving no mother-tongue support in schools, but "they are a far cry from what we should be doing with the nation's bilingualism and biliteracy potential" (2005: 604). Hornberger (2005b: 606) suggests that it is essential for language educators to "fill up implementational spaces with multilingual educational practices" in the face of restrictive policies. Hornberger (2007: 188) views the rise of what she calls 'the heritage language initiative' as a movement which helps to "solidify, support, and promote longstanding grassroots minority language maintenance and revitalization efforts." May (2008: 23) suggests that heritage language programs "can be regarded as an additive and strong bilingual approach." He notes that increasingly, the majority of students in such programs tend to be second language speakers of the target language, the result of previous patterns of language shift and loss of the heritage language. Kagan and Dillon (2008: 151) point out, however, that the teaching of heritage language learners can be complicated by attitudes these students may encounter in the educational system. For example, teachers may insist on 'pure' or 'standard' forms, and in doing so stigmatize varieties spoken in the students' families. Ricento (2005) argues that advocates for the promotion of heritage languages should consider in what ways they may help promote the *status quo* with regard to the status and utility of languages other than English.

6.   Multilingualism in policy and practice

Despite the evident success of at least some forms of bilingual education, politicians and policy-makers are often resistant to this evidence, and consider that access to the dominant language is both more important than, and oppositional to, the teaching and learning of minority languages. In January 2007 the leader of the Conservative opposition party in the UK, Rt. Hon David Cameron M.P., argued that:

> there's so much bilingual support in the classroom that we're almost encouraging people not to learn English until later, and I think you know that's the extent of the failure of multiculturalism, treating separate communities as distinct...these things just create resentment and suspicion. And they undermine the very thing that should have served as a focus for national unity – our sense of British identity (Cameron 2007).

More recently the leader of the Liberal Democratic Party, Nick Clegg M.P., departed from his party's usually liberal stance on immigration issues to tell BBC Television News (28th April 2008) that "too many languages in the classroom make life difficult for teachers." He said "we all have to make efforts to speak the same language because without the same language you know we can't create a glue that keeps things together," and argued that "we need to make sure that at the earliest stage possible, including in the home, young children are encouraged to learn English, that'll be their passport to real integration into British society." In a speech on the same day Clegg said "there must be a real insistence on promoting English language skills, not simply on exploring language diversity ... because without a common language it's impossible to create a common, shared identity." These voices of senior national politicians propose a common-sense view that the more children are required to use English, the better they will learn in the English education system. In fact the politicians go further, and argue that children should use English at all times in the classroom because not to do so may bring about 'separate communities', and pose a threat to 'national unity' and 'British identity'. As these political arguments become naturalised they make their way into debates about education policy and practice, and may be further accepted as natural. A common-sense view emerges, and appears to be accepted, that the use, teaching, and learning of minority languages in schools in England constitutes not only a threat to children's educational attainment, but a threat to society in general.

We are presented, then, with two apparently opposed ideological positions, one proposing that the use and visibility of minority languages other than English constitutes a threat to social cohesion, security, and national identity, the other arguing on the basis of research evidence that the best way to educate some students is through a bilingual approach which makes use of, and accords status to, minority languages other than English. Somewhere in between, living out their lives, are people who have differential access to sets of linguistic resources. We can only understand what apparently contradictory ideological positions mean if we pay close attention to the attitudes, beliefs, and (especially) practices of these people. In the remainder of this chapter I will consider the attitudes, beliefs and practices of some of the students, parents, administrators, and teachers involved in complementary schools in the UK.

The research reported here was conducted as four interlocking case studies, with two researchers working in two complementary schools in each of four communities. The case studies focused on Gujarati schools in Leicester, Turkish schools in London, Cantonese and Mandarin schools in Manchester, and Bengali schools in Birmingham. The present chapter focuses in particular on the Bengali schools in Birmingham. Complementary schools provide language teaching for young people in a non-statutory setting. Bengali complementary schools in Birmingham are managed and run by local community groups on a voluntary basis, usually in hired or borrowed spaces, with few resources. They cater for children between 4–16 years of age, and operate mainly in the evenings and at weekends. The students' families (parents or grandparents) had migrated from the Sylhet region of Bangladesh. One of the specific aims of the research was to investigate how the linguistic practices of students and teachers in complementary schools are used to negotiate young people's multilingual and multicultural identities. Each case study identified two complementary schools in which to observe, record, and interview participants. After four weeks observing in classrooms, two key participant children were identified in each school. In the Bengali schools the four key participant children were all ten years old. These children were audio-recorded during the classes observed, and also for 30 minutes before coming to the class and after leaving class. Stakeholders in the schools were interviewed, including teachers and administrators, and the key participant children and their parents. In all we collected 192 hours of audio-recorded interactional data, wrote 168 sets of field notes, made 16 hours of video-recordings, and interviewed 66 key stakeholders. A more detailed account of the methods used to collect documentary and home-based data are outlined in Blackledge and Creese (2010), and Creese et al. (2008).

7.   Attitudes to, and beliefs about, languages

The founder and administrator of one of the two schools (Icknield Street School) made a forceful and emotional statement following an interview question about the rationale for teaching Bengali to children in Birmingham:

(1)   *ei bhaashar jonno 1952 te amaar theke dosh haath dure Barkat, Salam maara jaae 1952 te* [because of this language in 1952 ten yards away from me Barkat and Salam were killed in 1952] *I was also a student in year 10. from Sylhet to Dhaka was 230 miles we marched there Sylhet to Dhaka 230 miles with slogans. we want our mother language it is a raashtro bhasha* [state language] *how will I forget about my mother language? my brothers gave their life for this language. I will never forget it while I'm alive*   (administrator interview)

Throughout the chapter I am mindful of Pavlenko's (2007: 176) argument that interview or narrative data can not be treated as 'truth' or 'reality itself'. Rather, in line with Pavlenko, I am "sensitive to the fact that speakers use linguistic and narrative resources to present themselves as particular kinds of individuals" (2007: 177). In this research individual participants often positioned themselves in relation to the 'ethnic, linguistic, and cultural loyalties' (Pavlenko 2007: 177) which they chose to emphasize. For this school administrator the 'mother language' was a vital symbol of the founding of the Bangladeshi nation. More than fifty years earlier he had witnessed the incident in which 'language martyrs' were killed while demonstrating against the imposition of Urdu as the national language by West Pakistan, and these events seem to have informed his view that British-born children of Bangladeshi heritage should learn and maintain the Bengali language. The historic incident which marks the Bangladeshi calendar as 'Ekushey February' continues to be celebrated as a key moment in the collective memory of the Bangladeshi nation, and in the Bangladeshi community in UK (Gard'ner 2004). One of the senior teachers in the same school argued that learning Bengali was associated with maintaining knowledge of Bangladeshi 'roots':

(2)   *We may have become British Bangladeshi or British Indians but we don't have fair skin and we cannot mix with them. We have our own roots and to know about our roots we must know our language*   (teacher interview)

For both of these Bangladeshi-born men, teaching and learning Bengali is an important means of reproducing their 'heritage' in the next generation.

Another teacher, Mr. S, argues that learning Bengali is associated with maintaining knowledge of Bangladeshi 'roots':

(3)   *theek ei bhabe ami mone kori protekta bhasha je je bhasha Jodi aamra British Bangladeshi, British Indian hoe gechi taar poro aamraa shaada chaamraa naa amraa shaadader shaathe mishte paarchi naa. jodio aamraa bidehe aashchi, aamraa oder shaathe mishte paarsi naa. Aamaader nijoshso ektaa root aache, shei root ke jannar jonno protek taa jati taaer nijesho bhaashaa shikha uchith. British holam shetaa thik aache kintu amader root aache she shommondhe jaana taa bhalo, ei janaar jonno mainstream schoole jodi compulsory kora hoe main school gula te taahole bhaalo*

[similarly I think each one of us should learn our language. We may be British Bangladeshi or British Indians but we don't have fair skin and we cannot mix with them. We have our own root and to know about our root we must know our language. It's okay that we are British but we have our roots and it is good to know about it. That is why it will be good if these languages are made compulsory in mainstream school]   (teacher interview)

Here the teacher goes beyond arguing that Bengali should be taught to children and young people in complementary schools, to propose that Bengali, together with other minority languages, should become compulsory in state schools.

Many of the students' parents agreed. The mother of ten-year-old Shazia suggests that learning Bengali offers opportunities to her daughter, and that she would like Bengali to be taught in the mainstream (state) primary school:

(4)   *when they go to high school they have Hindi, Urdu, but in primary school they don't have that option so it would be better if they had it from scratch instead of going to two different places ... it would be nice of they started it from primary school, the Bengali, one or two hours a week would be nice*   (parent interview)

One mother typically told us that it was important that her children should be able to speak Bengali because:

(5)   *Bengali is our mother land, where we come from; really we come from Bangladesh. Even if you are born in this country it doesn't matter, we need to know our mother language first*   (parent interview)

Asked why it was important to learn the language of the 'mother land', she said *you need to know your side of the story, where your parents come from, you've got to know both from this country and the other one*. We heard an explicit rationale from administrators, teachers, and parents that a key aim of the school was for the children to learn Bengali because knowledge of the national language carried features of Bangladeshi/Bengali 'cultural heritage'. Shazia's parents went on to say that they expected her to take GCSE and perhaps A-level Bengali, although they acknowledged that this may not be available in all schools. Shazia's mother, who worked in a local primary school herself, had a positive attitude to the use and teaching of minority languages in schools:

(6)   *We'd appreciate it if they could have it in normal schools like in some schools there is a Bengali teacher – in [another school] when I took my little daughter the teacher was speaking Bengali with the Bengali children. I was sitting in the staff room and hearing her speak Bengali to the children and I was thinking why is she speaking like that, then I found out later on in a parents' workshop that they encourage it, like the Urdu classroom assistant they want to continue the language with children of different backgrounds now they want Somali, she was speaking completely Bengali completely Sylheti dialect she was speaking, but there is no Bangla class and most parents are complaining like children are losing their language. When they start nursery they are young children they pick up the things that come in front of them*   (parent interview)

Here Shazia's mother values the teaching of languages other than English in the primary school, and has noticed that in some schools there is the opportunity for young children to learn through Sylheti. She was aware that *some schools do not allow you to use your own language in the playground because you could be talking about the other person so they say keep it to English*. She argued that if teachers give children the choice to use their home language, the children should do so. Bodrul's mother also argued that bilingualism was a good thing for her children:

(7)   *they speak English, they always speak English, they were born here, their moth-er- tongue is English. That's why I'm thinking that if they understand Bengali and talk in Bengali then they've got used to both languages they know two lan-guages dui taa bhasha bola* [to speak two languages] *I think that's good. Dekhsen naa aamder ei deshe oneke bipodhe pore, oneke aache English jaane naa okhaane Bangali jaanaa thaake okhaane Bengali ta bijhie dilo koto help hoe* [you can see in this country when someone is in difficulty, there are many who don't know English, in those situations if there is someone who knows Bangla then it's a big help.] *Whatever, they learn more*   (parent interview)

Here Bodrul's mother seems to argue that to speak two languages (*dui taa bhasha bola I think that's good*) is a good thing in itself. We heard this argument frequently in inter-views with parents, teachers, and students.

8.   Multilingual practices

Our audio recordings in the homes of the complementary school students revealed how they used a broad range of linguistic resources to create meanings. Aleha, a stu-dent at one of the Bengali schools, used slightly different linguistic resources with her mother and her father. With her mother a typical interaction included Sylheti (the regional variety of north-east Bangladesh) and English. In the excerpt below Aleha and her sister Rumana are about to leave their house and say goodbye to their parents respectfully with the Arabic-derived *salam alaikum*. Mainly English is used by Aleha with her older sister and her mother, while Sylheti is used with her father:

(8)   Aleha: *Rumana, come on. I'm going amma, salam alaikum*
                 [mother, salam alaikum]
                 salam alaikum abba, zaairam aami
                 [salam alaikum father. I'm going]

While *I'm going* is spoken in English to her mother, Aleha uses Sylheti to say the same thing to her father. Notable here is the unmarked and quite usual multilingualism of the interaction: English, Sylheti, and an Arabic-derived phrase enjoy a flexible and non-conflictual co-existence. We recorded many instances of flexible linguistic prac-tice, especially in the homes of students who attended the Bengali schools. This was mainly because we gained more comprehensive access to these households, due to their proximity to the Bengali schools. In the following example Tamim, a ten-year-old boy, is asking his mother whether he is allowed to go on the school camping trip:

(8)   *amma aami camping-e zaaitaam. aafne last year here disoin aamaare disoin-naa. aami camping zaaitaam aafne aamaare disenna*
[mother, I want to go camping you allowed him last year but not me. I want to go camping you didn't allow me last year]
(home audio-recording, Bengali case study)

This is an unremarkable, quite usual example of flexible language practice in the students' family settings, of the sort we heard on each occasion that we audio-recorded the children and young people at home. Such multilingual practice at least partly constitutes the context for our investigation of multilingualism in the institutional setting of the complementary school.

We were also able to record some of the students who attended the Bengali schools reading the Qur'an, with their Qur'anic Arabic tutor. The tutor would come to the students' houses to instruct them. One of the eight-year-old boys we met was practicing to become a Hafiz-e-Qur'an (someone who learns the entire Qur'an by heart). The children appeared to be largely enthusiastic about their Arabic reading of the Qur'an. In the following example the tutor has come to the house of Tamim and Shazia, and the children are reciting Arabic terms along with him:

(9)   Tutor: *qaribun, qareebun, qareeb* {reads along with Shazia, often repeating the same words} *Re- yaa ze- yaa qaa ri- bun*
Shazia: *six times forsi* [I read it six times]
Tutor: *qaf zabar qaa, re zer ri, be pesh bu, nun, qareebun* {spells the Arabic words. This is repeated many times} *laam zabar laa*
Tamim: *Aami khaali ekhtaa mistake khorsi, ekhtaa mistake khorsi Sir* [I made only one mistake, only one mistake sir]
(home audio-recording, Bengali case study)

Here the tutor is teaching the children to learn the words in Arabic by repeating them after him. Tamim uses Qur'anic Arabic, Sylheti and English side-by-side. None of the Arabic words are given a definition or meaning by the tutor. However, Tamim told us that although he was not able to understand as he was reading, the tutor would explain passages, and *after I finish it, I am going to get an English version of the Qur'an so that I can understand every word of it.* Tamim read the verse fluently with little help from his tutor, and demonstrated (in Sylheti and English) his positive attitude to reading Arabic, saying proudly that he had made only one mistake in the passage he had been reading.

Characteristic of the linguistic interactions of the students we audio-recorded in and out of complementary school classrooms was a playfulness and creativity. Students engaged with and accessed a broad range of linguistic resources. Bangladeshi-heritage children watched Hindi films, and were familiar with Hindi songs. They sang along with the songs, and were able to express their preferences and dislikes. In the following example the two sisters Rumana and Aleha are watching a film just before going to Bengali class:

(10) {Rumana sings with the music on TV}

Rumana: *it's a funny movie that. this one, Hera Pheri. really funny, I like this song*

Aleha: *I like* {to baby sister} (3) *talk, talk, say amaar naam Durdana say amaar naam Durdana* [say my name is Durdana]

Durdana: *one khe* [who's there?]

Rumana: *rock your body, rock your body, rock your body, rock your body,* {singing along in Hindi} *tumhare bina* [without you] *chaenna aaye* [there's no peace] *rock your body*

(home audio-recording, Bengali case study)

Here singing along with the Hindi film music (*tumhare bina* etc.) seems to be a usual feature of the children's linguistic world, as they move in and out of English, Sylheti, and Hindi while listening to, participating in, and enjoying the Hindi film. At the same time they engage bilingually with their baby sister Durdana's attempts to speak into the digital recording device.

In Example 11 ten-year-old Tamim uses English to complain about his younger sibling, Naseem. His younger sister Shopna also joins in, using English and Sylheti:

(11) Tamim: *don't man, shut up is that* (.) *you can go upstairs, you can go upstairs do you wanna watch it stop fighting all the time, I love it but don't, don't, don't*

Shopna: *Naseem stop it. don't man etaa khotaa hononsnaani* [why don't you listen?] (home audio-recording, Bengali case study)

In the next moment the door bell rings, and Tamim asks his younger sister Tasmia to open the door:

(12) Tamim: *the man oh furi aaise* [that woman has come] *she has to come back. khulo* [open] *khulo, khulo* [open, open] *Tasmia, don't you* (..) *my hand is stuck like that*

(home audio-recording, Bengali case study)

Tamim has a lot on his hands. He is responsible for looking after his younger brother while his two sisters also get involved. The doorbell rings and he must answer it while making sure his siblings are under control. His language use reflects the domestic scene, with a lot going on and with different siblings making different demands of him. His language expresses the urgency and informality of 'being responsible'. He and his sister, Shopna, use their languages to impose order, to simultaneously discipline and encourage Naseem, to make sure the door is opened, and to deal with a visitor. In the interaction linguistic resources are put to use to manage a domestic scene. Less apparent is the switching of languages, more apparent is a flexible use of linguistic resources. That is, rather than thinking of Tamim's languages as distinct codes delivering different functions, it is more useful to consider the signs at his disposal as a responsible sibling, to cope with the social context at hand.

9. Multilingual school practices

Teachers often told us that in their teaching they kept Bengali separate from English, as the best way to teach the heritage language was to ensure that this language alone was used in the classroom. However, we discovered that Bengali was often used flexibly alongside English. In the following example, typically, Bengali is taught through curriculum content which reminds the students of symbols of national belonging:

(13)   T: *ei. eitaai aamaader jaatio shongeet othobaa national anthem. ekhon aamaader Bangladesher ko-e ektaa jinish aache jaatio bol-e.*
[This, this is our national anthem. now, we have a few things in Bangladesh which are our national symbols.] *jaatio shongeet* [national anthem] *jaatio kobi* [national poet], *jaatio phul* [national flower] *baa jaatio baa national fol* [or national or national fruit] *baa national paakhi* [or national bird] *Bangladesher jaatio fol ki?* [what is the national fruit of Bangladesh?]

Ss: {no response}

T: *water lily, water lily, water lily Bangla, water lily, shapla.*
etaa aamaader jaatio ful [this is our national flower.]
jaatio paakhi (.) doel [national bird (.) doel]
{pauses and addresses researcher} *doel-er Englishtaa ki apa?* [what is the English for doel, apa?]

R: {unsure, hesitates} *dove*

T: *er por-e jaatio kobi, poet, national poet, national poet Kazi Nazrul Islam* [after this national poet, poet, national poet Kazi Nazrul Islam]   (classroom video-recording, Bengali school)

Here the process of teaching Bengali is intimately interwoven with the process of teaching symbolic representations of Bangladesh, as knowledge of the national/cultural symbols, like knowledge of the Bengali language, comes to represent Bengali 'heritage'.

In a similar example, from the other Bengali school in our study, T is the teacher, and is engaged with teaching key moments in the making of Bangladesh as a nation:

T: *Bangladesher teen taa national day aache, jaatio dibosh*
[Bangladesh has three national days, national events] *national day not national anthem*

Shahnaz: *independence day*

T: *etaa Banglae ki bolbe shaadhinota dibosh Ekushey*
February shohid dibosh aage bolo Ekushey February shohid dibosh [in
Bangla it is shaadhinota dibosh 21st February is shohid dibosh first say
21st February is shohid dibosh]

Shahnaz: *ekushey February shohid dibosh*

T: *er pore aashlo shaadhinota dibosh* [after that comes shaadhinotaa dibosh]
independence day, independence day is not Bangla, it is English. Banglae
holo [in Bangla it is] *shaadhinota dibosh*

Shahnaz: *chaabbish-e March* [26th March]

T: *shaadhinota dibosh*

Shahnaz: *chaabbish-e March* [26th March]

T: *lastly nine months we fought against Pakistani collaborator*

Shahnaz: *language day*

T: *language day holo ekushey February. Chaabbish March independence day.*
Sholoi December, after nine months bijoy dibosh [victory day] *Pakistani occu-*
pied army ke aamraa surrender korchi [we made the occupied forces of Pakistan surrender their arms] *Al Badr against our independence war ke aamraa*
chutaaisi [we chased them out] *How many national days in Bangladesh?*

Shahnaz: *three*

T: *Bangladesher jaatio dibosh koiti?* [how many national days in Bangladesh?]

Shahnaz: *teen ti* [three]

T: *Shaadhinota dibosh ebong bijoy dibosh chilo 1971. Bhasha dibosh chilo*
1952. Aar bhaasha dibosh kon din chilo 52. Tokhon amraa choto [inde-
pendence day and victory day was in 1971. Language day was in 1952.
Language day was 52 when we were young] *Inshaallah eta every day jodi*
aamraa every day discuss kori taahole bhaalo [by the grace of God it is
good if we discuss this every day]

(classroom video-recording, Bengali school)

Curriculum content here is strongly nationalistic, and appears to have the aim of in-
stilling in the young language learners an understanding of key dates and events in the
making of the Bangladeshi nation. The ten-year-old student seems to have some pre-
existing knowledge of the historical context, and is prepared to volunteer this. For example she offers the date of Bangladeshi independence from West Pakistan, and is
confidently able to do so in Bengali. The teacher moves comfortably between Bengali
and English within and between sentences, and in his final statement uses the common
Islamic expression *Inshallah*, derived from Arabic, and also in Bengali and English.
The young student tends to respond in English when the teacher asks a question in

English, and in Bengali when the teacher asks a question in Bengali. Language teaching here invents for the young students a sense of national belonging which is firmly rooted in narratives of collective memory. The teachers' stories of poignant martyrdoms and heroic victories, remembered as 'our own', serve the purpose of reproducing the national memory and imagination (Anderson 1983).

However, the students were not always as accepting of the teaching of language, heritage and nationalism in the complementary schools. In Example 15 the students are not convinced that they should have to speak Bengali in class:

(15)   T: *Bangla-e maato etaa Bangla class* [speak in Bangla this is Bangla class]
       khaali English maato to etaa Bangla class khene [if you speak in English
       only then why is this the Bangla class?]
    S1: *miss you can choose*
    S2: *I know English*
    S1: *why?*
    T: *because tumi Bangali* [because you are Bengali]
    S2: *my aunty chose it. she speaks English all the time.*

(classroom audio-recording, Bengali school)

S2 argues that since her aunt (also of Bangladeshi heritage) chooses to speak English rather than Bengali, a precedent has been set.

Those who spoke 'Sylheti' were often criticized by 'more educated' people who spoke 'Bengali'. They were characterized by the administrator of one of the schools as members of the 'scheduled', or 'untouchable' caste: people without rights or resources in the Indian sub-continent:

(16)   *publicraa ki dibe amar aapne especially bujhben amader desher je shob lok
       aashche ora kon category lok aashchilo, mostly from scheduled caste, gorib,
       dukhi krishokra aashchilo. oder maa baba o lekha pora interested naa oder chele
       meye raa o pora lekha interested naa. oraa baidhitamolok schoole jete hoe pri-
       mary schoole sholo bochor porjonto jete hoe, ei jonne schoole jaai.*
       [what will the public contribute? you [the researcher] especially will under-
       stand what type of people came from our country. they belonged to the cate-
       gory of scheduled caste, they are the poor, the deprived, farmers. their parents
       were not interested in education nor are the children interested. they go to
       school because it's compulsory]   (administrator interview, Bengali school)

Here the Sylheti speakers are referred to as the 'scheduled caste'. Regarded as the least educated group in society, with no resources of any kind, they are considered to be the lowest of the low. Here linguistic features are viewed as reflecting and expressing broader social images of people. One of the teachers argued that children should learn Bengali for '*moral reasons*'. Here linguistic features that index the social group appear to be iconic representations of them, as if a linguistic feature depicted or displayed a social group's inherent nature or essence. Bourdieu and Darbel (1991: 112) argue that some more powerful groups provide 'an essentialist representation of the division of their society into barbarians and civilized people'. Here the fact of speaking 'Sylheti', rather than 'Bengali', appeared to index the Sylheti group in particularly negative terms, despite the relative similarities between the 'Bengali' and 'Sylheti' sets of linguistic resources. Here, as elsewhere in this study, linguistic hierarchies were not confined to relations between 'English' and the minority language, but also existed in nuanced ways between the minority languages of particular communities.

10. Discussion: The politics and practice of multilingualism

What can we say, then, about politics, multilingualism, and minority language rights? The detailed ethnographic study reported here offered complex messages. It was evident from our recordings in the homes of our participants that multilingualism was the usual, uncontested, and unmarked means of communication in the family setting. It was also clear that the poorly-funded, grassroots movement to teach minority languages other than English in borrowed spaces, with meager resources, was at least partly a response to state education provision which favored monolingualism, and failed to guarantee children the opportunity to be educated in or through their heritage/community language. We frequently heard strongly-stated arguments that the Bengali language was associated with 'cultural heritage', 'nationalism', and 'being Bengali'. In these informal classrooms Bangladeshi-heritage people claim the right to pass on to the next generation their language and culture. However, this is not a straightforward process. Language, like heritage and nationalism, changes as it travels. It is not a bounded, enumerable entity which can be packaged and offered as a gift in the assumption that when it is unwrapped it will be the same as it was. Rather, like heritage and nationalism, it is a process, a site of negotiation, an exchange, something haggled over and bartered for. The administrator who so eloquently narrated his dramatic story of marching to Dhaka to defend his language claimed the right to pass on the Bengali language to the next generation. However, the students enrolled in the Bengali classes are young people born and raised in a multicultural urban neighborhood where English is their strongest language, and where they access linguistic resources which circulate at both local and global levels. These are young people who habitually incorporate in their linguistic portfolio features of global capital such as Bollywood film, hip-hop, rap, and *bhangra* music, together with the language of the latest DVD releases, computer- and video-games, and new web-based resources. This is not to say that they are always in opposition to the linguistic and 'cultural' resources on offer in their complementary schools. In fact at times they are very much involved in their learning, proud of their multilingualism, and of their heritage. But they do not fully accept a version of multilingualism which is based on long-distance or out-of-place nationalisms or heritages, or one based on the separation of languages. Rather, they play with their rich linguistic assets, taking from their teachers what they need, and using language on their own terms. Of course every interaction is different, and sometimes these negotiations result in teachers having things their way instead. There is almost always a sense of ambiguity, or at the very least a sense of students and teachers (and for that matter parents and friends) investing in language as authentic heritage, at the same time as re-making and reinventing it for the transnational setting in which they find themselves. This is where our ongoing debate lies: at the interstices of nation, heritage, global movement, and new communication, where it is as important to claim the right to the language of global popular culture as to learn the language of family and heritage. For the students the right to access linguistic resources was a site of negotiation. As the mother of ten-year-old Tamim told us: *oraa to shokhole capture korte paarteche* [they seem to be able to grasp it all]. The right claimed by the young people we met in this ethnographic research project was the right to be multilingual in a world dominated by monolingual ideology.

References

Anderson, Benedict. 1983. *Imagined Communities*. London: Verso.

August, Diane and Shanahan, Timothy (eds). 2006. *Developing Literacy in Second-language Learners*. Mahwah, NJ: Erlbaum.

Baker, Colin. 2006. *Foundations of Bilingual Education and Bilingualism*. Clevedon: Multilingual Matters.

Billig, Michael. 1995. *Banal Nationalism*. Sage: London.

Blackledge, Adrian. 2005. *Discourse and Power in a Multilingual World*. Amsterdam: John Benjamins.

—. 2009a. "Being English, speaking English: Extension to English language testing legislation and the future of multicultural Britain." In *Testing Regimes: Critical Perspectives on Language, Migration and Citizenship in Europe*, Patrick Stevenson, Clare Mar-Molinero and Gabrielle Hogan-Brun (eds), 83–108. Amsterdam: John Benjamins.

—. 2009b. "Language, migration, and citizenship in the United Kingdom." In *Cross-national Perspectives on Language, Migration and Citizenship*. Guus Extra, Massimiliano Spotti and Piet Van Avermaet (eds), 66–86. London: Continuum.

Blackledge, Adrian and Creese, Angela. 2010. *Multilingualism. A Critical Perspective*. London: Continuum.

Blackledge, Adrian and Pavlenko, Aneta. 2001. "Negotiation of identities in multilingual contexts." *International Journal of Bilingualism* 5 (3): 243–259.

Blommaert, Jan. 2005. "Situating language rights: English and Swahili in Tanzania revisited." *Journal of Sociolinguistics* 9 (3): 390–417.

Bourdieu, Pierre. 1977. *Outline of a Theory of Practice*. Cambridge: Cambridge University Press.

—. 1991. *Language and Symbolic Power*. Cambridge: Polity Press.

—. 1998. *Practical Reason*. London: Polity Press.

—. 2000. *Pascalian Meditations*. Cambridge: Polity Press.

Bourdieu, Pierre and Darbel, Alain. 1991. *The Love of Art. European Museums and their Public*. London, Polity Press.

Busch, Brigitta and Schick, Jurgen. 2007. "Educational materials reflecting heteroglossia: Disinventing ethnolinguistic differences in Bosnia-Herzegovina." In *Disinventing and Reconstituting Languages*, Makoni, Sinfree and Alastair Pennycook (eds), 216–232. Clevedon: Multilingual Matters.

Cameron, David. 2007. "Bringing down the barriers to cohesion." Speech, 29th January 2007, Birmingham.

Creese, Angela. 2005. *Teacher Collaboration and Talk in Multilingual Classrooms*. Clevedon: Multilingual Matters.

Creese, Angela and Martin, Peter. 2006. 'Interaction in complementary school contexts: Developing identities of choice – An introduction." *Language and Education* 20 (1): 1–4.

Creese, Angela, Baraç, Taskin, Bhatt, Arvind, Blackledge, Adrian, Hamid, Shahela, Wei, Li, Lytra, Vally, Martin, Peter, Wu, Chao-Jung and Yağcıoğlu-Ali, Dilek. 2008. *Investigating Multilingualism in Complementary Schools in Four Communities*. Final Report. RES-000–23-1180. University of Birmingham.

Creese, Angela, Bhatt, Arvind, Bhojani, Nirmala and Martin, Peter. 2006. "Multicultural, heritage and learner identities in complementary schools." *Language and Education* 20 (1): 23–44.

Cummins, Jim. 2001. *Negotiating Identities: Education for Empowerment in a Diverse Society* [2nd ed.]. Los Angeles, CA.: California Association for Bilingual Education.

—. 2005. "A proposal for action: Strategies for recognizing heritage language competence as a learning resource within the mainstream classroom." *The Modern Language Journal* 89: 585–592.

—. 2007. "Language interactions in the classroom: From coercive to collaborative relations of power." In *Bilingual Education: An Introductory Reader*, Ofelia Garcia and Colin Baker (eds), 108–136. Clevedon: Multilingual Matters.

—. 2008. "Introduction." In *Encyclopedia of Language and Education, Vol. 5: Bilingual Education*, Jim Cummins and Nancy Hornberger (eds), xiii-xxiii. Science + Business Media LLC: Springer.

Edwards, Viv. 2004. *Multilingualism in the English-speaking World: Pedigree of Nations*. Oxford: Wiley Blackwell.

Edwards, Viv and Pritchard Newcombe, Lynda. 2006. "Back to basics: Marketing the benefits of bilingualism to parents." In *Imagining Multilingual Schools. Languages in Education and Globalization*. Ofelia Garcia, Tove Skutnabb-Kangas and Maria Torres-Guzman (eds), 137–149. Clevedon: Multilingual Matters.

Extra, Guus, Massimiliano Spotti and Van Avermaet, Piet (eds). 2009. *Language Testing, Migration and Citizenship: Cross-national Perspectives*. London: Continuum.

Freeland, Jane and Patrick, Donna. 2004. "Language rights and language survival. Sociolinguistic and sociocultural perspectives." In *Language Rights and Language Survival*, Jane Freeland and Donna Patrick (eds), 35–53. Manchester: St. Jerome.

Gal, Susan. 2006. "Migration, minorities and multilingualism: Language ideologies in Europe." In *Language Ideologies, Policies and Practices. Language and the Future of Europe*, Clare Mar-Molinero and Patrick Stevenson (eds), 13–27. Basingstoke: Palgrave Macmillan.

Garcia, Ofelia. 2005. "Positioning heritage languages in the United States." *The Modern Language Journal* 89 (IV): 601–605.

—. 2009. *Bilingual Education in the 21st Century: A Global Perspective*. Oxford: Wiley-Blackwell.

Garcia, Ofelia, Skutnabb-Kangas, Tove and Torres-Guzman, Maria. 2006. "Weaving spaces and (de)constructing ways for multilingual schools: The actual and the imagined." In *Imagining Multilingual Schools. Languages in Education and Globalization*. Ofelia Garcia, Tove Skutnabb-Kangas and Maria Torres-Guzman (eds), 3–50. Clevedon: Multilingual Matters.

Gard'ner, James Maitland. 2004. "Heritage protection and social inclusion: A case study from the Bangladeshi community of East London." *International Journal of Heritage Studies* 10 (1): 75–92.

Heller, Monica. 1995. "Language choice, social institutions and symbolic domination." *Language in Society* 24: 373–405.

—. 1999. *Linguistic Minorities and Modernity. A Sociolinguistic Ethnography.* London/New York: Longman.

—. 2006. *Linguistic Minorities and Modernity* [2nd ed.]. London: Continuum.

Heller, Monica and Duchêne, Alexandre. 2007. "Discourses of endangerment: Sociolinguistics, globalization, and social order." In *Discourses of Endangerment. Ideology and Interests in the Defence of Languages*, Alexandre Duchêne and Monica Heller (eds), 1–13. London: Continuum.

Hobsbawm, Eric. 1990. *Nations and Nationalism Since 1780: Programme, Myth, Reality.* Cambridge: Cambridge University Press.

Hogan-Brun, Gabrielle, Mar-Molinero, Clare and Stevenson, Patrick (eds). 2009. *Discourses on Language and Integration: Critical Perspectives on Language Testing Regimes in Europe.* Amsterdam: John Benjamins.

Hornberger, Nancy. 2005a. 'Heritage/community language education: US and Australian perspectives." *The International Journal of Bilingual Education and Bilingualism* 8 (2&3): 101–108.

—. 2005b. "Opening and filling up implementational and ideological spaces in heritage language education." *The Modern Language Journal* 89: 605–609.

—. 2007. "Biliteracy, transnationalism, multimodality, and identity:
Trajectories across time and space." *Linguistics and Education* 18: 325–334.

Joseph, John. 2006. *Language and Politics.* Edinburgh: Edinburgh University Press.

Kagan, Olga and Dillon, Kathleen. 2008. "Issues in heritage language learning in the United States." In *Encyclopedia of Language and Education, Vol. 4: Second and Foreign Language Education* [2nd ed.], Nelleke van Deusen-Scholl and Nancy H. Hornberger (eds), 143–156. Springer Science + Business Media LLC.

Mar-Molinero, Clare. 2006. "The European linguistic legacy in a global era: Linguistic imperialism, Spanish and the *Instituto Cervantes.*" In *Language Ideologies, Policies and Practices: Language and the Future of Europe*, Clare Mar-Molinero and Patrick Stevenson (eds), 76–90. London: Palgrave.

Martin, Peter, Creese, Angela, Bhatt, Arvind and Bhojan,i Nirmala. 2004. *Final Report on Complementary Schools and their Communities in Leicester.* Leicester: University of Leicester/ University of Birmingham.

Maryns, Katryn and Blommaert, Jan. 2006. "Conducting dissonance: Codeswitching and differential access to contexts in the Belgian asylum process." In *Language Ideologies, Policies and Practices: Language and the Future of Europe*, Clare Mar-Molinero and Patrick Stevenson (eds), 177–190. London: Palgrave.

May, Stephen. 2004. "Rethinking linguistic human rights. Answering questions of identity, essentialism and mobility." In *Language Rights and Language Survival*, Jane Freeland and Donna Patrick (eds), 35–54. Manchester: St Jerome.

—. 2005. "Language rights: Moving the debate forward." *Journal of Sociolinguistics* 9 (3): 319–347.

—. 2008. "Language education, pluralism, and citizenship." In *Language Policy and Political Issues in Education. Encyclopedia of Language and Education, Vol. 1* [2nd ed.], Stephen May and Nancy Hornberger (eds), 15–30. New York: Springer.

McCarty, Teresa. 2007. "Revitalising indigenous education in homogenizing times." In *Bilingual Education: An Introductory Reader*, Ofelia Garcia and Colin Baker (eds), 33–49. Clevedon: Multilingual Matters.

McCarty, Teresa, Romero, Mary Eunice and Zepeda, Ofelia. 2006. "Reimagining multilingual America: Lessons from Native American youth." In *Imagining Multilingual Schools. Languages in Education and Globalization*, Ofelia Garcia, Tove Skutnabb-Kangas and Maria Torres-Guzman (eds), 91–110. Clevedon: Multilingual Matters.

Moyer, Melissa and Luis, Martin Rojo. 2007. "Language, migration and citizenship: New challenges in the regulation of bilingualism." In *Bilingualism: A Social Approach*, Monika Heller (ed.), 137–160. Basingstoke: Palgrave.

Pavlenko, Aneta. 2007. "Autobiographic narratives as data in applied linguistics." *Applied Linguistics* 28: 163–188.

Pavlenko, Aneta and Blackledge, Adrian. 2004. "New theoretical approaches to the study of negotiation of identities in multilingual contexts." In *Negotiation of Identities in Multilingual Contexts*, Aneta Pavlenko and Adrian Blackledge (eds), 1–33. Clevedon: Multilingual Matters.

Pujolar, Joan. 2007. "Bilingualism and the nation-state in the post-national era." In *Bilingualism: A Social Approach*. Monica Heller (ed.), 71–95. Basingstoke: Palgrave.

Rampton, Ben. 1995. *Crossing: Language and Ethnicity Among Adolescents*. London: Longman.

—. 2006. *Language in Late Modernity*. Cambridge: Cambridge University Press.

Rassool, Naz. 2008. "Language policy and education in Britain." In *Encyclopedia of Language and Education, Vol. 1: Language Policy and Political Issues in Education* [2nd ed.], Stephen May and Nancy H. Hornberger (eds), 267–284. Springer Science + Business Media LLC.

Ricento, Thomas. 2005. "Problems with the 'language-as-resource' discourse in the promotion of heritage languages in the U.S.A." Journal of Sociolinguistics 9 (3): 348–368.

Shohamy, Elana. 2006. "Imagined multilingual schools: How come we don't deliver?" In *Imagining Multilingual Schools. Languages in Education and Globalization*. Ofelia Garcia, Tove Skutnabb-Kangas and Maria Torres-Guzman (eds), 171–183. Clevedon: Multilingual Matters.

Skutnabb-Kangas, Tove. 2000. *Linguistic Genocide in Education – or Worldwide Diversity and Human Rights?* Mahwah, NJ: Lawrence Erlbaum.

—. 2008. "Language rights and bilingual education." In *Encyclopedia of Language and Education, Vol. 5: Bilingual Education* [2nd ed.], Jim Cummins and Nancy H. Hornberger (eds), 117–131. Springer Science + Business Media LLC.

Skutnabb-Kangas, Tove and Phillipson, Robert. 2008. "A human rights perspective on language ecology." In *Encyclopedia of Language and Education, Vol. 9: Ecology of Language* [2nd ed.], Angela Creese, Peter Martin and Nancy. H. Hornberger (eds), 3–13. Springer Science + Business Media LLC.

Stevenson, Patrick. 2006. "'National' languages in transnational contexts: Language, migration and citizenship in Europe." In *Language Ideologies, Policies and Practices: Language and the Future of Europe*, Clare Mar-Molinero and Patrick Stevenson (eds), 147–161. London: Palgrave.

Thomas, Wayne and Collier, Virginia 2002, *A national study of school effectiveness for language minority students' long-term academic achievement*, Center for Research on Education, Diversity and Excellence (CREDE), Santa Cruz.

Tucker, G. Richard. 2008. "Learning other languages: The case for promoting bilingualism within our educational system." In *Heritage Language Education. A New Field Emerging*, Donna Brinton, Olga Kagan and Susan Bauckus (eds), 39–52. London: Routledge.

UNESCO. 2008. "Message from Mr Matsuura, Director-General of UNESCO, on the celebration of 2008, International Year of Languages." Retrieved July 31, 2008 from http://portal.

unesco.org/culture/en/ev.php-URL_ID=35559&URL_DO=DO_TOPIC&URL_SEC-
TION=201.html

Wei, Li. 2006. "Complementary schools, past, present and future." *Language and Education* 20
(1): 76–83.

Wiley, Terry. 2005. "Discontinuities in heritage and community language education: Challenges
for educational language policies." *The International Journal of Bilingual Education and Bilingualism* 8 (2&3): 222–229.

CHAPTER 17

Multilingual development in Germany in the crossfire of ideology and politics*

Carol W. Pfaff

1. Introduction

Germany has seen massive changes in its demography as a result of economic and political transitions of the second half of the 20th and beginning of the 21st centuries which have vastly increased the numbers of immigrants entering and staying in the country. These population movements have affected the superficial linguistic landscape, increasing societal and individual multilingualism on a large scale with the continuous addition of new languages. In turn, language and the expression of language ideologies have come to the forefront of political, academic and popular discussions. Increasingly the formulation of and arguments about social policies have been couched in terms of language. Since Blommaert's (1999) work on the historiography of language ideology, a number of works such as Kymlicka and Norman (2000), Kymlicka and Patten (2004), Mar-Molinero and Stevenson (2006), Castiglione and Longman (2007) have focused on putting the study of language policies into the changing sociopolitical context. A further line of research has been that of critical discourse analysis which focuses on close analyses of texts of policies and policy debates to illuminate the underlying ideologies, as in the publications of Wodak and her associates, for example in studies of discursive construction of national identity in Wodak et al. (1999/2008). Recent work on language policy in Germany (e.g., Piller 2001; Stevenson 2006; Schroeder 2007; Maas 2008) combines both historical contextualization and the analysis of political, academic and popular discourses.

---

*   Thanks are due to Urszula Okulska and Piotr Cap for their organization and hospitality at the conference on Political Linguistics in Warsaw in September 2007, where this paper was originally presented, and for their subsequent suggestions for improvements. In addition, I am indebted to the reviewers from John Benjamins, especially for the suggestion pointing to recent CDA work. I am grateful to Stefan Hollstein and Karin Schmidt for assistance with gathering materials for this paper, to Patrick Stevenson for recent information, and to Meral Dollnick, Tiner Özcelik, Christoph Schroeder and Bernd Bohse for discussion of institutions and ideologies in the Berlin educational and Turkish/German communities. All errors of fact or interpretation are my own.

My goal in this paper is to comment on the current situation in Germany to exemplify the role of language and language policies as instruments of social policies. I present specific policies and practices concerning German and languages other than German which have been proposed and implemented to come to terms with the increasingly heterogeneous population and linguistic diversity. In addition, I examine some examples of the official and popular discourse which reflect the ideologies that underlie these policies and practices. I will show that two countervailing ideologies are evident in these policy developments: on the one hand, the symbolic equation of language and nation, and on the other hand, instrumental/educational conceptions of language proficiency to empower members of minority groups, and majority groups as well. Both of these ideologies have been invoked to support German-only policies and also to support multilingualism involving European and immigrant languages.

The paper is organized as follows. Sections two and three provide the background to the present discussion. Section two focuses on some relevant ideological statements on language at international, European and national levels. Section three provides an overview of the changing demographic situation in Germany. The following sections turn to the actual policies in Germany and how they have been implemented in practice, focusing on national developments and particular instances in Berlin. Section four is devoted to policies and practices focused on proficiency in German, including the increasingly important gate-keeping role of language assessment for adults as well as children. Section five looks at developments in German and European policies aimed at fostering languages other than the national languages, reviewing the changing rationales and provisions for education in both minority languages and languages of high international prestige. Section six presents some final remarks about the current state of affairs and perspectives for the future.

2   Overt policies toward linguistic minorities

This section sets the stage for the examination of the countervailing ideological arguments in some international, European and national language policy statements on linguistic rights of minorities and on the symbolic and practical status of the German language in particular. These policies pertain to language rights, requirements for immigration (and naturalization), language proficiency for educational and professional opportunities, and to support for multilingualism for professional mobility and for the preservation of the social and ethnic identities of minority populations.

2.1   International policies

The discourse on linguistic rights of immigrants and their children in Germany frequently refers to the UN Universal Declaration of Human Rights (1948), which in

Article 2 sets out a very general statement of non-discrimination including language, as well as to the UN Convention on the Rights of the Child (1989), in which several sections apply to language rights: §8 to preserve identity; §13 to assure freedom of expression; and most explicitly §30 to assure the possibility of educational development of cultural identity, language and values.

The UN Declaration on the Rights of Persons Belonging to National or Ethnic, Religious and Linguistic Minorities adopted in 1992 refers specifically to language in Article 2 and Article 4:

Article 2   1.   Persons belonging to national or ethnic, religious and *linguistic minorities* (hereinafter referred to as persons belonging to minorities) have the right to enjoy their own culture, to profess and practice their own religion, *and to use their own language, in private and in public, freely and without interference or any form of discrimination.* [...]

Article 4   2.   States shall take measures to create favourable conditions to enable persons belonging to minorities to express their characteristics and to develop their culture, *language*, religion, traditions and customs, except where specific practices are in violation of national law and contrary to international standards.

3.   States should take appropriate measures so that, wherever possible, persons belonging to minorities have *adequate opportunities to learn their mother tongue or to have instruction in their mother tongue.*

4.   States should, where appropriate, *take measures in the field of education, in order to encourage the knowledge of the history, traditions, language and culture of the minorities* existing within their territory. Persons belonging to minorities should have adequate opportunities to gain knowledge of the society as a whole.

Although these declarations were primarily symbolic statements with few binding practical consequences, they have been important and are often cited in connection with the formulation or reformulation of policies. The actual implementation of policies supporting mother tongue rights has been uneven in practice. See Extra and Yağmur (2004) for a review of mother tongue use and educational support in six European cities, including Hamburg, and my discussion of Reich and Hienz de Albentiis' (1998) survey of community and public mother tongue programs in Germany (Pfaff 2003). Borde and Albrecht (2007) discuss mother tongue services for adults and Hottmann (2008) focuses on services for both adults and children in Berlin.

2.2   European policies

Most discussions on European language policy relate either to the choice of official and working languages of the European Union or to provisions for the regional and minority languages spoken by indigenous populations of the member states. These issues are discussed in papers in the collection edited by Castiglione and Longman (2007) but are not treated here.

Policies directed at the possibility of free labor migration between EU member states, while not pertaining to language *per se*, have clear implications for language learning and teaching, as is explicit in the Barcelona statement of 2002, which sets the goal that all EU citizens should be able to speak two other languages in addition to their own. After the creation of the Multilingualism portfolio in January 2007, the newly appointed commissioner, Leonard Orban, in his speech "Multilingualism and Competitiveness" (Brussels, July 5, 2007), emphasized the contribution of multilingualism to business and advocated language training within companies. The Language Policy Division of the Council of Europe has supported fostering plurilingualism through education (Fleming 2007), and the position paper for the European Commission (Maalouf et al. 2008) motivates inclusion of immigrant languages as a means of defusing fundamentalist separatist ideologies in the migrant populations. Ramifications of European policies in Germany are discussed in 5.

2.3   National policies

Language policies in Europe (as in many other countries) are still strongly influenced by the notion that nations are, or ideally should be, monolingual (Blommaert and Verschueren 1998). Although national monolingualism has never been the case in Europe, as pointed out by Gal (2006), the ideal and ideology persist and continue to have enormous influence. Germany is no exception here as seen in the debate which has raged in recent political discussion about whether German should be explicitly recognized as the national language. Although German is specified as the *Amtssprache* ('language of official business') in several regulations, the German Constitution (*Grundgesetz* 'basic law'), established in 1949, does not have an explicit statement of national language. Language is mentioned only in Article 3, paragraph 3 on non-discrimination of gender, national origin, race, country of origin, ethnicity or language. Recently this lack of constitutional anchoring of German as the national language has been the subject of debate, connected with arguments about the symbolic importance of such a statement, similar to the discussions starting in the 1980s about Official English in the USA.

In 2005, the *Verein der deutschen Sprache* (VDS) ('Association of the German Language'), a group dedicated to the protection of the German language in various ways, called for the constitution to be amended to explicitly name German as the national language, as it is in the constitutions of Austria and Lichtenstein, and as one of the national languages of Switzerland. German Bundestagspräsident, Norbert Lammert (CDU), also called for this change in the *Grundgesetz* (*Westdeutsche Zeitung*, February 13, 2007).

In 2007, there was an extensive and heated exchange of views published on the VDS Forum *Klartext Sprachenpolitik: Deutsch ins Grundgesetz* ('Plain text language policy: German in the Basic Law') on whether the change would be symbolic only or would have practical consequences. Views expressed range from the extreme opinion that German is symbolically essential, as it is the embodiment of German culture, to the opinion that specifying the German language in the constitution would establish it as a duty rather than a right, raising questions about whether this would restrict the rights of regional minorities such as Danes and Sorbs to use their languages, or whether university lectures could be held in languages other than German, and whether immigrant minority language speakers would be permitted to have interpreters in court. The discussion also touched on a local issue, to be examined further below (in 4.2.2.), whether pupils with migrant background should be allowed to speak in their ethnic languages in the schoolyard during breaks.

In addition to the symbolic issue and such practical language rights, concrete language policies at the federal and state levels have been important in the changing regulations about requirements for immigrants and with respect to naturalization, immigration and residence permits. The most significant change has been to replace the doctrine of citizenship based on ancestry (*jus sanguinis*) which was in place until 2000 to allow for the possibility of naturalization of non-German migrants, which however has not (yet) proceeded to citizenship based on birth (*jus solis*). Maas (2008: 234–236) discusses the historical and political reasons for the very late introduction of this change in Germany in contrast to other European countries. This change has resulted in a central role for proficiency in the German language in the developing policies for immigration (*Zuwanderung*) and for naturalization (*Einbürgerung*), as discussed by Stevenson and Schanze (2009) and in 4.1. below. The importance of these policies must be understood in the context of actual demographic changes and their consequences for German society.

3. Demography and distribution of linguistic minorities in Germany

While Germany has not traditionally been regarded (or regarded itself) as a country of immigration, this picture has changed as a result of several waves of immigration into the country since 1950. According to the statistics of the Ministry for the Interior (*Bundesministerium des Innern*, 2005/2008), the proportion of foreigners has risen from 1% in 1950 to almost 9% in 2007.

The source of immigration since the 1950s has differed over time. The first major wave originated in the recruitment of foreign workers (*Gastarbeiter*) from Mediterranean countries, especially Turkey, between 1955 and 1973. After the end of the period of recruitment, immigration came from family members joining workers who immigrated previously. After 1985, there were two main sources of immigration: asylum seekers and ethnic German repatriates returning from Eastern Europe and the other countries of the (former) Soviet Union (*Aussiedler*). A further source of immigration comes from students and workers from within the expanding European Union. Recently, workers with high technical skills, many from Asian countries, have contributed significantly to the immigration. Table 1, shows the figures for immigration from those countries with more than 1,000 immigrants in 2007.

As shown in Table 1, Turkey has continued to be the country of origin of a large number of new immigrants, and recent controversial language requirements for immigration are implicitly aimed at curbing Turkish and other non-European immigration, particularly of spouses of current residents. In fact, the rate of immigration has been declining, but it is unclear whether this can be partially attributed to more stringent language requirements since 2007 as discussed in 4.1.

Figures based on citizenship do not fully represent the extent of linguistic diversity. On the one hand, the immigrants to Germany may come from linguistic minorities within their countries of origin, as in the case of Kurdish speakers from Turkey, Iran, Iraq and Syria.[1] Nor is German citizenship necessarily a good representation of linguistic diversity in the case of the *Aussiedler* who automatically became German citizens whether or not they spoke German at the time of immigration. Further, naturalized German citizens and their children are not necessarily dominant (or in some cases even very fluent) in German. Lately, the term 'persons with migrant background' (*mit Migrationshintergrund*) has become current to refer both to foreign nationals and to naturalized German citizens, as well as to their children and grandchildren born in Germany.

Table 1. Immigration to Germany in 2007 (countries with more than 1000 immigrants Source: Statistisches Bundesamt, Wiesbaden 2008 (Table 14, pp. 98–109)

Country	Total immigrants
Poland	74, 910
Turkey	22,478
Bulgaria	12,885
Russian Federation	12,790
China	12,746
Italy	12,669
Serbia & Montenegro	10,800
India	8,444
Iraq	6,049
Greece	5,311
Bosnia & Herzegovina	4,650
Vietnam	3,734
Afghanistan	1,377

1.   Since Kurds are classified as citizens of various countries, their number can only be estimated. See Ammann (2000) *Kurdistan Kultur und Hilfsverein* (http:www.kkh-ev.de) and a report in the *Tagesspiegel*, 1 July 2008 (www.tagesspiegel.de/berlin/Roj-TV;art270,2563206).

The annual Microcensus survey conducted in 2005[2] focused on characteristics of residents with migrant background who account for almost 20% of the total population, as shown in Figure 1. Table 2 presents the estimated actual population calculated by Woellert et al. (2009) in their interpretation of the significance of the Microcensus results for successful integration.

Within Germany, the population with migrant background is not evenly distributed but concentrated in the federal states which belonged to West Germany before

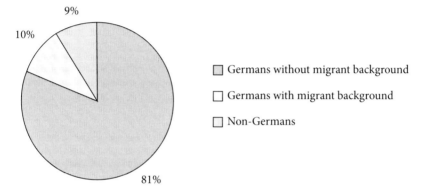

9%

10%

81%

☐ Germans without migrant background

☐ Germans with migrant background

☐ Non-Germans

Figure 1. Demography: German population. Microcensus of Germany 2005

Table 2. Population of Germany in 2005 by area of origin: estimates from the Microcensus 2005 Source: Woellert et al. (2009: 26–27)

Origin*	Estimated population	Percent of total	Percent under age 15	Percent over age 64
Aussiedler	3,962,000	4.7%	17.7%	14.2%
Turkey	2,812,000	3.4%	27.7%	3.5%
EU except Southern Europe	1,907,000	2.3%	17.6%	9.9%
EU Southern Europe	1,527,000	1.8%	19.6%	6.7%
Former Yugoslavia	1,146,000	1.4%	20.6%	5.1%
Far East	734,000	0.9%	25.6%	1.9%
Near East	542,000	0.6%	28.6%	3.1%
Africa	502,000	0.6%	27.5%	2.2%
native Germans	67,682,000	81.0%	12.0%	21.8%

*Categories for the place of origin are those used in Woellert et al. (2009), and they reflect a mixture of geographical, political and ethnic designations

---

2. The Microcensus of 2005 was based on a sample of 800,000 households, 1% of the total (Woellert et al. 2009: 11).

reunification. Even though some *Aussiedler* and re-migrants from Eastern Europe were resettled in the 'new federal states' in former East Germany, the proportion of non-Germans in the new federal states is much lower than in the old federal states of West Germany. Within the federal states the non-German population is concentrated in cities, within cities – in certain districts, and within districts – in certain neighborhoods.

3.1   Linguistic and educational consequences of concentration of non-Germans

As shown in Table 2, the population with migration background is unevenly distributed by age as well as geographically. Given the immigration and natural increase of the populations with and without migrant background, the current and future population of children and adolescents with migrant background is even more sharply skewed toward high proportions of pre-school, school age and young adults entering the job market. The report of the "Working groups on integration" (2008) points out that almost one third of the children under 5 in Germany have an immigrant background. A recent survey of Berlin reports that 40% of children and adolescents under 18 have a migrant background, which reaches 60% in the districts Mitte, Neukölln and Friedrichshain-Kreuzberg (*Tagesspiegel*, July 1, 2008). The situation is even more extreme in certain neighborhoods, where in some schools the percentage of pupils with migrant background is over 90%. For example, the Herbert Hoover School in Wedding had 95.1% non-German language background in 2007, and the Robert Koch School in Kreuzberg had 91% non-German language background in 2006 (97% grades 7–10, 85% grades 11–13). These two schools, which have similar ethnic compositions, have developed different language policies, as will be discussed in 4.4.2.

As Schroeder (2007) points out, in the diglossic verbal repertoire of migrants in Germany, the formal and informal varieties are frequently based on different languages, German in formal and school settings, the ethnic languages in informal domains. Many adults in such neighborhoods lack standard, or colloquial, or even minimally proficient German. This has been argued to be one of the major difficulties in their integration. Children growing up in these environments are exposed to German less frequently, and the varieties of German are often non-standard; thus they often lack proficiency in the expected varieties of German at school entry. For many, lack of expected proficiency levels persists, resulting in their assignment to secondary schools of different types, e.g., Hauptschule rather than Gymnasium,[3] which has consequences for access to university. Pupils with non-German background drop out of school or leave with a lower degree of completion than German children, as shown by the figures for

---

3.   *Hauptschulabschluss* – after the 9th grade; qualified to continue education at Realschule or to begin vocational training (apprenticeship). *Erweiterte Hauptschulabschluss* – after the 10th grade; qualified to continue education at Gymnasium or begin vocational training. *Realschulabschluss* – after the 10th grade; opportunity to go on to courses of education at upper secondary level that lead to the *Abitur*, the necessary qualification for admission to university after the 12th or 13th grade.

Berlin school leavers for the school years 1994/1995, 2000/2001 and 2006/2007, which reflect this disparity. As shown in Table 3, the educational outcome for non-Germans has improved in several respects during this period; the proportion of non-Germans who leave school without any diploma has declined consistently, and the proportion of those who attain the Abitur qualifying them for university entrance has risen, but they are still severely underrepresented compared to those with German citizenship.

An independent measure of the discrepancy between the educational success of pupils with and without migrant background was also provided by the results of the international PISA and IGLU[4] tests of 15–year olds and 4th graders, respectively, in which Germany ranked very low, causing a shock to all who had believed the German educational system to be very good. Analysis of the results in terms of migrant vs. non-migrant background revealed further that Germany was among the most disparate, as reflected in the title of the *Spiegel* article "Weltspitze bei Benachteilungung von Migranten" ('World leader in disadvantage of migrants') (*Spiegel*, December 4, 2007). This discrepancy led to scrutiny of the German school system, resulting in recently proposed or implemented reform, most notably combining Hauptschule and Realschule, and assuring that all school types contain options which permit pupils to attain the Abitur. Since school policy is regulated by the individual Federal States, it is noteworthy that these reforms are not uniform across all of Germany, but reflect regional and political differences.[5]

Table 3. Secondary school leavers in Berlin: type of diploma for all pupils and non-Germans Source: Statistisches Landesamt, Berlin

Type of Diploma	1994/1995		2000/2001		2006/2007	
	all pupils	non-German	all pupils	non-German	all pupils	non-German
no diploma	10.9%	29.5%	11.7%	26.6%	10.4%	22.1%
Hauptschule	6.8%	9.9%	6.7%	10.1%	7.6%	11.8%
extended Hauptschule	14.5%	22.1%	14.0%	21.4%	15.3%	24.8%
Realschule	37.0%	27.3%	36.0%	28.0%	28.8%	25.9%
Gymnasium-level Abitur	30.8%	11.3%	31.5%	13.9%	38.0%	15.3%

4. PISA = Program for International Student Assessment, IGLU ('PIRLS') = *Internationale Grundschul-Lese-Untersuchung* ('Progress in International Reading Literacy Study').

5. In Berlin the Senat passed the reform February 10, 2009 in which a two-tiered system is to be implemented starting in the school year 2010/11 and completed by the school year 2013/14 (*dpa-Dossier Kulturpolitik* 30/20.07.2009). In the former East German States, the two-tiered solution has been (re)instated. The former West German states, such as Bremen, Hamburg and other with liberal governments, have adopted the two-tiered reform, while others, such as Bavaria, Hessen, Lower Saxony and others with conservative governments, retain the three-tiered system. An overview can be found at http://bildungsklick.de/a/69207/schulstruktur-stand-und-debatte-in-den-laendern.

In addition to proposals to reform the school system, there have also been investigations attempting to identify the socioeconomic factors which might account for the disparities. Analyses of the PISA results are presented in Baumert et al. (2003) and Stanat (2003). Entorf and Minoiu (2004) compare the linguistic, social and educational background of migrant pupils in Germany to that of migrant pupils in other European and non-European countries with high proportions of migrants. They conclude that home language is the decisive factor, as evidenced by their finding that reading proficiency scores of migrant students improve substantially when the language spoken at home is the national language rather than a foreign language (2004: 5). Although this finding is based on correlations in a cross-sectional rather than longitudinal comparison, their formulation reinforces the ideology that minority languages are detrimental. This view of the causes of the disproportionately low academic achievement of children with migrant background has contributed to increasing focus on German for migrants and their children, discussed in the next section.

4.   Focus on German language proficiency

Policies and programs which focus on the German language are primarily motivated by two ideologies: firstly, the perceived importance of a common language for integration of the migrant population into the wider German society and, secondly, the importance of mastery of German for the educational achievement and future access to a wider range of academic and occupational options. In recent years language proficiency has come to play an increasingly important gate-keeping role in overt immigration, naturalization and integration policies directed toward adults and to children and adolescents, as discussed in the following sections.

4.1   German proficiency requirements for adults

4.1.1   *Immigration*
In 2007, the Minister of the Interior tabled a proposal for reform of the *Zuwanderungsgesetz* ('immigration law') which, among other provisions, required prospective immigrants, particularly spouses of current residents, to prove proficiency in German *before* being allowed to enter. Crucially, and controversially, this law contained an exclusion clause, so that the requirement was waived for citizens of many countries. The relevant provisions of the law are as follows:

> *German proficiency requirement for immigration of spouse*
> *August 19, 2007: Reform of §30 of the Immigration Act of 2004*
>> *Dem Ehegatten eines Ausländers ist eine Aufenthaltserlaubnis zu erteilen, wenn ...*

> *2. der Ehegatte sich **zumindest auf einfache Art in deutscher Sprache ver-**
> **ständigen kann** ...*
>
> *Satz 1 Nr. 2 ist für die Erteilung der Aufenthaltserlaubnis unbeachtlich, wenn ...*
> *4. der Ausländer **wegen seiner Staatsangehörigkeit** auch für einen*
> *Aufenthalt, der kein Kurzaufenthalt ist, visumfrei in das Bundesgebiet*
> *einreisen und sich darin aufhalten darf.*
>
> 'A residence permit shall be granted to the spouse of a foreign national if ...
> 2. the spouse is *able to communicate in the German language at least in a*
> *simple manner* ...
>
> Paragraph 1 No. 2 shall not affect the granting of the residence permit if...
> 4. *on the basis of his nationality*, the foreign national can enter and remain
> in the Federal Republic without a visa even for a longer period.'

This proposal was intensely debated in a hearing to which representatives of international, ethnic and academic organizations were invited and position papers were submitted by Amnesty International and other human rights organizations. Critics of the proposal claimed that it violated human rights of the potential immigrants from countries where it would be difficult or impossible to acquire German proficiency before their arrival, and further that it was unfairly formulated since, in addition to spouses from Schengen countries who have visa-free entry, according to §41, spouses from certain other countries, including Australia, Israel, Japan, Canada, the Korean Republic, New Zealand and the USA, were exceptions who did not have to prove knowledge of German. Despite the fact that a number of representatives voted against passage of the revised law with these changes, it was passed by the Bundestag July 6, 2007. This ruling was judged to be constitutional on December 19, 2007.[6]

It is clear that the regulations and debates on language policies for adult potential immigrants, citizens and persons of non-German background, despite their apparent practical focus, are clearly not implemented consistently on the basis of actual language proficiency. As Stevenson (2006: 158) points out with respect to the debates on integration, "If a particular degree of linguistic proficiency is essential for integration, why does this apply only to some migrants and not to others? Either it is, as official discourses appear to insist, a fundamental principle or it is not." As Stevenson also suggests, it appears that the actual target is not language proficiency but other ascribed (or feared) aspects of the potential immigrants or citizens, their religious or political affiliation, which is perceived as a potential threat to the nation, particularly after terrorist attacks in the early 21st century.

---

6.   For links to position papers and arguments, see the website of the Flüchtlingsrat-Berlin, December 2007, On the rationale for the judgment, see the website of the Domestic Policy Speaker of the CDU, Hans-Peter Uhl, http://www.uhl-csu.de/cm/upload/4_0808–Uhl-Ehegattennachzug.pdf.

According to the answer given in the Bundestag to the question posed by the Left party, the effect of this law was to reduce the immigration of spouses from Turkey by 70% in 2008.[7] One effect of the new ruling was to increase the number of language courses in Turkey, for instance the Goethe Institute program in Izmir, discussed by Kösem (2009).

4.1.2   Naturalization

Due to political and socio-historical circumstances discussed by Maas (2008), Germany's shift from a definition of citizenship only in terms of ancestry (*jus sanguinis*) to permit naturalization came late. Since the revision of criteria for naturalization introduced in 2000, German language proficiency has come to be a significant part of the requirements, reflecting the ideology of language as an essential characteristic of national belonging, as pointed out by Piller (2001: 272f). The wording of the requirement, however, is couched in practical terms, as seen in the formulation by the *Bundesministerium des Inneren* (Ministry of the Interior):

> *Ausreichende Kenntnisse der deutschen Sprache liegen vor, wenn [...] mit ihm ein seinem Alter und Bildungsstand entsprechendes Gespräch geführt werden kann.*
> 'Sufficient knowledge of the German language is present if [...] a conversation that is appropriate to his age and educational level can be conducted with him' [Piller's translation].

Piller makes two points embodied in the phrase *ausreichende Kenntnisse in der deutschen Sprache*: firstly, that in these conversations the burden of the conversation rests on the applicant, while "the power to impose reception" is under the control of the German naturalization officer. Secondly, she points out that the practice assumes that any (monolingual) native speaker can judge the proficiency of a second language speaker. Similar points are made by Maas (2008: 237–239, 252) in his discussion of this and similar formulations.

Standards for assessment of language proficiency were under the jurisdiction of the individual federal states, varied according to the prevailing political view and were more or less restrictive. They could involve grammatical correctness and literacy. However, in conjunction with efforts to harmonize regulations across the European Union, subsequent revision in August 2007 specified that proficiency in the German language established as attainment of the level B1 of the European Reference Framework for Languages. This framework is characterized by its reliance on communicative proficiencies rather than on grammatical correctness or literacy, although literacy is essential to be able to read the questions about citizenship and life in Germany posted on the internet. The B1 competencies are shown below:

> *B1 "Threshold" Competencies*
> *Common European Framework of Reference for Languages*

---

7.   For effects on immigration of spouses from Turkey, see http://www.jurblog. de/2008/03/25auswirkungen-der-neuen-sprachanforderungern-beim-ehegattenhachzug-starker-rueckgang-bei-erteilung -von-via-aus-der-tuerkei/.

Can understand the main points of clear standard input on familiar matters regularly encountered in work, school, leisure, etc.

Can deal with most situations likely to arise whilst travelling in an area where the language is spoken.

Can produce simple connected text on topics which are familiar or of personal interest.

Can describe experiences and events, dreams, hopes &ambitions and briefly give reasons and explanations for opinions and plans.

These B1 competencies are still vague and, as stated, may be of questionable relevance for many prospective citizens. For instance, how likely is clear standard input in oral encounters in daily life? Clearly, many everyday interactions take place with speakers of nonstandard (regional or ethnic) varieties, possibly even including 'foreigner talk'. Nonetheless, insofar as these European Reference Framework standards are aimed at the prospective citizens' ability to engage in everyday communication, they represent a step forward from informal evaluation of language proficiency by government office workers who may react unfavorably to grammatical shibboleths. Work on tests for the integration courses discussed in the next section has led to more precise definitions of these competencies.

4.1.3   *Integration*

In Germany until recently, little thought or planning was addressed to the language development of the immigrants, as it was assumed that the second generation children who grew up in Germany would naturally have acquired German. But it became clear that, for many, this was not the case in view of their difficulties in primary school and their severe over-representation in the lowest secondary school type and their high dropout rates and high rate of unemployment, often attributed to insufficient proficiency in German. Awareness of this as a social problem became acute when the shocking findings of the poor performance of pupils with migration background on the PISA tests were announced, as discussed in 3.1. above. These findings for children and adolescents, as well as the concerns raised by continuing immigration of spouses and by conditions for naturalization discussed in the previous sections, directed public and institutional attention to the causes of this perceived lack of integration and to the search for remedies.

Van Parijs (2007: 242f), echoing frequently voiced views, suggests that "... for three distinct reasons ... the mechanisms of linguistic integration, essential for facilitating the implementation of the territoriality principle, are losing their grip." First, the spread of satellite and cable TV considerably reduces the exposure of immigrants of all ages and their children, grandchildren, etc., to the local language. Second, he claims, knowledge of English, introduced through the educational system and in the surrounding environment is a factor. Third, in countries, such as Germany, with a well developed welfare state, it is possible for a significant proportion of the immigrant population of working age to live for long periods without entering a work community. The outcome is that the work sphere is less effective than earlier and elsewhere in providing immigrants with both the opportunity and the motivations to learn the local language. This position distributes the responsibility for failed integration to the state, to technology, as well as to lack of will of the minority group members.

The extent to which these factors really hold true for the local communities is unclear[8] but it is widely believed that such factors are significant. It was decided that measures should be taken to foster the acquisition and development of German language skills of adult immigrants.

In January 2005, the German government initiated the *Integrationskurs* ('integration course') for adults. This course is obligatory for new arrivals and for unemployed residents of 5 years or more without adequate knowledge of German or otherwise deemed in need of integration.[9] The course is predominantly devoted to German language instruction, initially 600 hours, with the goal of attainment of the B1 level of the European Reference Framework for Languages, as now required for naturalization, plus 30 hours of civic 'orientation' in historical, legal and cultural aspects of German life.

Both positive and negative sanctions were proposed: for successful completion of the course, participants were rewarded with a residence permit and with reduction of the number of years of residence (from 8 to 7) necessary for naturalization. Those who failed to attend could be refused extension of their residence permits, and recipients of unemployment compensation could be penalized 10% of the amount (press release of the Ministry of the Interior, January 17, 2007). The imposition of negative sanctions was controversial, considered by some to constitute an infraction of immigrants' human rights and was widely discussed in the media and debated in parliament. In addition the effectiveness of the program was questioned.

An evaluation of the *Integrationskurs* by the Ramboll Management Consultants commissioned by the Ministry of the Interior, based on interviews with institutions and participants, was published in 2006. At this point, 250,000 participants had attended 16,850 courses at 1,800 institutions, but only 45% of the participants had passed the final exam at level B1. Many of the participants, especially those who were illiterate at the outset of the course, did not even take the final examination. Completion of the course, while regarded by the participants and teachers as contributing positively to social integration, had little effect in reducing unemployment among the participants. As far as the sanctions are concerned, the commission concluded that these had not

---

8.   The survey by Boos-Nüning and Karakaşoğlu (2005) of women from several of the main immigrant groups includes the use of ethnic languages and German, however, the analysis of degree of integration by ethnic group and residence based on data from the Microcensus survey by Woellert et al. (2009) does not, since the Microcensus survey did not include relevant data on language.

9.   According to the information of the Bundesamt for Migration and Refugees (2009), a person can be judged especially in need of integration if they have custody of a child and cannot speak simple German.

been used consistently, partly because attendance was often not reported, partly because the measures were not regarded as likely to be effective. The commission recommended that the sanctions be more consistently applied (Emminghaus et al. 2006).[10]

New regulations were passed by the Ministry of the Interior in November 2007. The position that language is the prerequisite for integration was maintained, as was the view that the *Integrationskurs* was effective in facilitating this. However, certain changes were ordered to come into effect since January 1, 2009. These included making the course duration flexible, to allow for 430–1200 hours of instruction, with up to 900 hours of language instruction for those with special needs. In addition, testing was to be obligatory, using a new test with scaled measurement of A2-B1 achievement levels according to the European Reference Framework for Languages. Sanctions as such are not explicitly mentioned in the new law, which apparently still allows for refusal of an extension of the residence permit of a person who does not attend or who does not pass the test (Ministry of the Interior, November 27, 2007). A new language test for the *Zertifikat Deutsch* ('Certificate in German') specifically designed for migrants has now been prepared by the Goethe Institute and *TELC GmbH* ('The European Language Certificate Ltd.'). This test, coordinated with a program of instruction, and containing much more specific criteria for oral and written proficiencies appropriate for A2 and B1 levels, began to be implemented in 2009.[11]

In sum, we see that for policies affecting adult migrants from initial immigration through naturalization to residence permits, language proficiency in German has become paramount in determining eligibility. Although the arguments are couched in terms of instrumental and practical terms, the fact that these provisions are applied selectively to migrants from certain ethnic backgrounds considered problematic makes it apparent that language proficiency is being used as a politically acceptable means to implement ethnic or national screening. Nevertheless, the effect that language courses especially designed for adult migrants can be seen as a positive by-product of the focus on language proficiency.

---

10. An updated report by the Bundesamt für Migration und Flüchtlinge on the changes and outcomes of the *Integrationskurs* is available at http://www.bamf.de/cln_092/SharedDocs/Anlagen/DE/Integration/Publikationen/Integrationskurse/Integrationskursbilanz-2008,templateId =raw,property=publicationFile.pdf/Integrationskursbilanz-2008.pdf. A further project investigating the effect of the *Integrationskurs* is currently in progress. This project, carried out by the *MARPLAN Forschungsgesellschaft mbH* ('MARPLAN Research Group'), evaluates participants at the beginning and end of the *Integrationskurs*, as well as after one year, with a control group of non-participants evaluated in 2008 and 2009. http://www.bamf.de/cln_101/nn_444062/SharedDocs/Projekte/DE/Migration/Forschung/Integration/laufende/forschung-integrationsverlauf-Integrationsteilnehmer.html.

11. See http://www.goethe.de/lhr/pro/daz/dfz/dtz_Pruefungshandbuch.pdf. The tests and results of initial implementation were presented at a conference in September 2009 in Berlin, which also included international discussants on the rationale and ideologies underlying language testing for citizenship in European and other countries.

4.2   German proficiency requirements for migrant children and youth

Turning now to policies directed at children and youth with migrant background, we find that focus on their development of proficiency in German is equally strong, but grounded more plausibly in educational necessity. As discussed in an earlier paper (Pfaff 2003: 199–203), the current focus is on German at the expense of children's ethnic mother tongues. This view has become even more intense in the last years, as seen in the report published by the work group on integration (May 20, 2008), which indicated that more emphasis on German proficiency is needed, particularly to facilitate transitions from preschool to school for young children and from school to work for adolescents.[12]

4.2.1   *Language screening at school entry*

Short 'screening tests,' such as 'Deutsch Plus' or 'Fit in Deutsch,' are supposedly designed to identify children at risk of educational failure due to insufficient command of German at school entry, although, as Schroeder (2007) points out, there is as yet little evidence about what language skills are actually necessary at school entry. Many different tests were developed and have been widely employed in the federal states of former West Germany. Despite much criticism of such tests in psychometric and theoretical terms (Ehlich et al. 2005), application of these tests continues. In 2006, 25,000 4-year olds in Berlin were tested with Fit in Deutsch with the result that a quarter of all children were assessed as needing language remediation, while the proportion of children with migrant background was assessed as 67%. Similarly, such tests were to be given to all 4-year olds in North Rhein-Westfalia (NRW). The Minister for Family and Integration, Armin Laschet (CDU), supported this policy, saying that these tests represent a core aspect of the integration policy (efms Migration Report, February 2007).

In practice, these screening policies hinge on the measurement of proficiency in German, and as for adults, discussion centered on ascertaining the relevant linguistic standards and designing appropriate instruments used to assess proficiency. Two positions have been taken: one reflects a traditional focus on vocabulary and grammatical correctness in the standard variety, the other a focus on functional and pragmatic abilities in everyday interactions.[13] Assessment of language proficiency at school entry remained important and tests proliferated. In its evaluation of various available tests, the *FörMig* program (*Förderung von Kindern und Jugendlichen mit Migrationhintergrund* ('Support for children and adolescents with migrant background') decided that it was

---

12.   See http://www.bamf.de/cln_092/SharedDocs/Anlagen/DE/Integration/Publikationen/Integrationsprogramm/ErgebnBericht__SprachBildung....pdf.

13.   The SISMIK Screening, developed at the *Staatsinstitut für Frühpädagogik* in Munich (Ulich and Mayr 2003), took a much broader view of preschool language abilities. It involved several days of observation of preschoolers in spontaneous natural interactions and semi-structured elicitation situations. However, according to Christa Kieferle (p.c. June 2008), the interactive and communicative aspects of the screening have been eliminated, and only the grammatical tests continue to be regularly used in Munich.

appropriate to use multiple tests and screening procedures to assess proficiency and monitor progress rather than fixing on a particular test (see Lengvel et al. 2009).

4.2.2 *Language practices in secondary schools*

In addition to language testing, policies at the local level have been directed toward the informal language practices of the pupils. The two Berlin secondary schools mentioned above, which have high proportions of pupils with migrant background, developed very different language policies. The Robert Koch School in Kreuzberg implements a policy of tolerance toward language use in the school, and is one of the few offering Turkish as a second foreign language from the 7th through 13th grade. In contrast, in February 2005, the Herbert Hoover School in Wedding adopted an explicit German-only policy, establishing that German is the only language to be used, not only in the classroom but at any time anywhere on the premises. As a result of their having instituted this policy, the German National Foundation awarded the Herbert Hoover School the National Prize in 2006. Article 3 of the *Hausordnung* ('house rules') of the school specifies:

> *Die Schulsprache unserer Schule ist Deutsch, die Amtssprache der Bundesrepublik Deutschland. Jeder Schüler ist verpflichtet, sich im Geltungsbereich der Hausordnung nur in dieser Sprache zu verständigen.*
>
> 'The school language of our school is German, the administrative language of the Federal Republic of Germany. Every pupil is required to communicate in this language within the jurisdiction of these regulations.'

This school policy provoked much controversy in Berlin and was discussed in the popular press not only in Germany but in other countries where there are similar issues of immigration and language, as well as by expert commentators on language policy (e.g., Maas 2008; Stevenson and Schanze 2009).

An examination of some of the statements by the principal of the school at the time, Jutta Steinkamp, as well as some of the pupils, is revealing of the ideologies and assumptions underlying this policy.[14] Steinkamp claimed that it was a matter of politeness to pupils of different native languages that they should not be or feel they were excluded on the playground. The pupil representative also endorsed the policy on the grounds that proficiency in German was essential for future occupational success (*Spiegel*, January 23, 2006). The *Magazin für politische Bildung* ('Magazine for Political Education') presents the principal's view that most of the 370 pupils spoke no German

---

14.   It is noteworthy that the beliefs expressed by Ms. Steinkamp do not correspond to information from a study of language practices of Turkish pupils in Germany and France, where it was clear from responses to an extensive questionnaire on secondary school pupils' language practices at home and outside that the majority of secondary school pupils in both communities used a considerable amount of German (or French) within their families (with siblings and, in many cases, with parents or even grandparents) as well as with peers in afterschool activities (Akıncı and Pfaff 2008). See also Neumann and Reich (2009) for discussion of the acquisition of Turkish by monolinguals and bilinguals.

at home as a rationale for their need to speak as much German as possible while at school. In the English language edition of *Deutsche Welle* (August 16, 2007) the following statements by the principal were reported:

> "Steinkamp said an external commission of experts has just said the introduction of the measure has improved discipline and academic standards. And the idea is being taken up by other schools at both home and abroad."
> "We had a lot of aggression. And pupils I talked to, they said: well, there are quite a lot of misunderstandings and there are the different languages, we don't understand them, perhaps it was an aggressive word, I don't know and so our pupils started to fight with each other..."
> "The teachers do not have to enforce the ban with sanctions, she adds, because most pupils have accepted the rule by now. At home, nine out of ten of her students don't speak German. Turkish, Polish or Russian are more common."
> "School is the only occasion where they speak German. I mean it's natural that in their communities, in their families they speak in their mother tongue. So they have to practise it here. Where else? Where else could they do it?"

As far as the opinion of pupils is concerned, the *Deutsche Welle* article reported one said, "It's good for our future. In every job, we have to talk in German" – a clear example of Blommaert's (1999: 7) characterization of the role of the public institutions such as schools in (re)producing ideologies.

Opponents including principals and teachers at many other Berlin schools and elsewhere reacted against the Hoover School directive, as did several Berlin politicians with Turkish background. Özcan Mutlu of the Green Party acknowledged that it was appropriate to use German exclusively in the classroom, but sharply criticized the German-only policy on the playground as an infringement of Article 3 of the German constitution, which guarantees non-discrimination. Safter Çınar, speaker of the Turkish Association and of the Turkish parents' association, expresses support for both German and the first language:

> *Wir haben keine nationalistischen Scheuklappen. Im Gegenteil. Zur Integration in eine multikulturelle Gesellschaft gehören auch Mehrsprachigkeit und die selbstbewusste Beherrschung der Muttersprache* (*Tagesspiegel*, June 22, 2007).
> 'We do not have nationalistic blinders. On the contrary. Multilingualism and the self-aware competence in the mother tongue are essential parts of integration in a multicultural society.'

The decisive role of language proficiency in German in fostering social integration of Turks and Germans has also been questioned by Özçelik (2006). Her empirical sociolinguistic investigation of 12–15-year-old second generation Turkish boys at a variety of different school types in Berlin found that they had mainly intra-ethnic friendships, independent of their linguistic proficiency in German.

Meanwhile, the Herbert Hoover School has moved to accommodate minority languages to a certain extent. Although the German-only policy is still officially in effect, the *Tagesspiegel* reported that on the basis of interest on the part of its pupils, the school began offering Turkish instruction after school in the 9th and 10th grades (*Tagesspiegel*, February 27, 2007), though as of August 2009, this program is not mentioned on their homepage. In the following section, I turn to the policies which, like this new direction for the Herbert Hoover School, focus on incorporating instruction in languages other than German, including those of migrant minorities, into their regular programs.

5.   Focus on multilingualism/plurilingualism

The term *multilingualism* has been used to characterize both societies and individuals. Recently, two terms have been distinguished by the Council of Europe (2008):

–   *Multilingualism* refers to the presence in a geographical area, large or small, of more than one 'variety of language', i.e. the mode of speaking of a social group whether it is formally recognised as a language or not; in such an area individuals may be monolingual, speaking only their own variety.

–   *Plurilingualism* refers to the repertoire of varieties of language which many individuals use, and is therefore the opposite of monolingualism; it includes the language variety referred to as 'mother tongue' or 'first language' and any number of other languages or varieties. Thus in multilingual areas some individuals are monolingual and some are plurilingual.

In these terms Germany is both multilingual and plurilingual. It is multilingual on the basis of encompassing social groups which use different languages: the majority language German; regional minority languages, such as Danish and Sorbian; migrant minority languages, such as Turkish and Serbian, which are the national languages of countries that are not (as yet) part of the EU; or minority languages, such as Arabic or Farsi, which are national languages of countries unlikely to become EU members. There are also speakers in communities where languages or varieties from EU countries are spoken, such as English or French or Polish. It is also plurilingual in that individuals from all such communities may (and often do) use more than one language.

This section focuses on how the educational system has come to terms with the multilingualism and plurilingualism of migrant minority children and adolescents in their first languages and in German, and how these pupils and others from the 'mainstream' German population are to be facilitated in becoming plurilingual, particularly in languages deemed essential or useful in the current global economy and culture, both within and outside the borders of the European Union. As the German term *Mehrsprachigkeit* has generally been used for both multilingualism and plurilingualism in educational contexts, and since the actual pupil populations belong to overlapping types, in the following discussion I will continue to use the term 'multilingualism' – the more customary term.

As noted above, international declarations have supported the right to education in the mother tongue with the goal of migrant children's well-being and cultural integration in their ethnic communities. In Germany, implementation of this has historically been left largely up to the communities themselves, with some support from the federal states which offered room and occasional financial support for teaching such classes (Pfaff 1981). However, as documented by Reich and de Albentiis (1998) in their survey of mother tongue education in the former West German federal states, the number of courses and participants has declined (Pfaff 2003).

However, recent policy appears to be changing toward increased focus on languages other than German, this time with the focus not so much on the integration and well-being of migrant children in their own communities (or, with an eye to their possible return to their countries of origin), but looking ahead to their integration into the German economy, to improved social integration in the wider socially diverse community and, finally, to increased economic and educational mobility within and beyond the European Union. An overview of instructional programs as of 2001 in each of the German federal states is provided in the brochure *Mehrsprachigkeit an deutschen Schulen ein Länderüberblick* ('Multilingualism at German schools: An overview of the federal states,' 2001). This document details both programs aimed at remedial German instruction, discussed above, as well as programs for instruction in languages other than German for children who speak those languages as L1 and for the majority of German children.

5.1   Europaschulen

An important innovation reflecting the changed rationale for mother tongue education to the promotion of minority and majority multilingual competence has been the establishment and proliferation of two-way bilingual education programs in a number of languages. Several German cities have private schools which offer bilingual immersion programs. In addition, several have instituted public schools with immersion or partial immersion programs in a number of languages. The Berlin model, the *Staatliche Europaschulen Berlin* ('State European Schools in Berlin') (SESB), is unique in Germany in the number of different language pairs represented and in the fact that, in addition to primary level, they were conceived as continuing through secondary level as well, leading to the Abitur. These schools, founded on the assumption that highly proficient multilingualism is highly advantageous, are intended to prepare pupils for occupations and study internationally, and to serve as a bridge between Western and Central Europe. At the same time, with their bicultural approach, where pupils with different background learn with and from each other, they intend to make a significant contribution to combating prejudice and discrimination.

The SESB began in 1992 with 160 first grade pupils in programs with the three language pairs: German/English, German/French and German/Russian, the languages of the former occupying forces. It now encompasses nine language pairs, including those spoken by immigrant populations in Berlin: Spanish, Italian, Portuguese, Greek, Turkish and Polish, shown in Table 4. By 2008 the SESB program has grown to 6,000 pupils at 18 primary and 12 secondary schools. The first classes of pupils in the initial programs have now graduated, and additional schools are planned. Table 4 shows the year the schools were established, beginning at primary level, the type of secondary schools established and the percentage of pupils at each secondary school who are classified as having a non-German home language.

Although the SESB model was originally conceived for pupil populations of equal numbers of German L1 and partner language L1, in practice the proportions of German and non-German home language pupils may differ greatly from this ideal. The disparities reflect both the popularity and prestige of the western European international languages English and French and of Spanish and Italian, which have high proportions of German L1 pupils, as opposed to the Turkish and Greek programs, which have much higher proportions of pupils with the ethnic L1 as home language.[15] It is noteworthy that pupils at the 6th and 8th grades in both the English-German schools, where the number of non-German home language speakers is low, and at the Turkish-German schools, where the number of non-German home language speakers is high, won prizes in 2008/2009 for essays written in their partner languages on the topic "The country of

Table 4. Dual language immersion programs in the *Staatliche Europaschulen Berlin* (SESB)

Language	Year established	Secondary school type Percent of pupils with non-German home language in school year 2008/09		
		Realschule	Gesamtschule	Gymnasium
English	1992/93	50.6%	–	24.2%
French	1992/93	–	–	19.1%
Russian	1992/93	–	56.0%	–
Spanish	1994/95	–	–	34.9%
Italian	1994/95	72.4%	–	38.4%
Turkish	1995/96	–	80.6%	–
modern Greek	1995/96	82.9%	–	66.7%
Portuguese	1997/98	–	12.5%	66.7%
Polish	1997/98	–	49.4%	–

15.   Determination of home language is not always obvious. The figures in Table 4 are taken from the website showing profiles of each secondary school for each language pair. http://www.berlin.de/sen/bildung/schulverzeichnis_und_portraets/anwendung/schuelerschaft.aspx?view=ndh. The Greek and Portuguese gymnasium programs share the same school site; the same proportion for non-German home language is reported for both programs in the.SESB schools.

my partner language/The country of my first language" (Zinke 2009).[16] Clearly, this assigned topic fits well into the ideology of multilingualism, espoused for Europe.

5.2   Turkish as language of instruction

In addition to the Turkish-German *Europaschulen*, another group of bilingual literacy programs for Turkish/German has been developed in Berlin. These programs in Turkish-German biliteracy (*zweisprachige Alphabetisierung*) began in 1980–1986 as an experimental program (*Modellversuch*) in Kreuzberg, spread to other schools and districts, and have been supported by the Berlin Senate since 1987. Nehr and Karajoli (1995) present results of a longitudinal study of several variants of the bilingual literacy program in 1989–1991 which indicate that, as in bilingual education programs elsewhere, the positive results do not become evident immediately, but they bring significant gains particularly for pupils in mixed Turkish-German classes. In the school year 1999/2000, the program was extended upward to include the 5th and 6th grades, and extended downward to the preschool, which for the first time provided Turkish instruction for the German children as well as those with Turkish background. The extension of its programs has been advocated by the teachers union (*Gewerkschaft Erziehung und Wissenschaft*) as well as the Turkish parents' organization (*Türkischer Elternverein*) (Harnisch and Nehr 1998). After hearings on its effectiveness in 2001, the Berlin Senate approved requests for further support of this program, which has been recognized by the Europarat as a model for bilingual education of language minorities with low social prestige in Europe. However, due in part to lack of funding for evaluation research, the effectiveness of this program has not yet been fully documented, and the number of participating schools has fallen.

Support for Turkish and other first languages of pupils with migration background has grown in recent years. Several schools now offer several of these languages as foreign languages for credit as a second foreign language after English or French, and others offer special courses aimed at preparation of youth with migrant background for job market in which those languages would be useful. In Berlin, 13 foreign languages are currently offered in the public schools as a first, second or third foreign language: English, French, Spanish, Italian, Portuguese, Russian, Polish, Modern Greek, Turkish, Japanese, Chinese, as well as classical Greek and Latin. Eight secondary schools currently offer Turkish as a second foreign language.[17]

In February 2008, the controversy about Turkish as a language of instruction became heated after the visit of the Turkish Prime Minister, Recep Tayyip Erdoğan, in February 2008. During his visit to Berlin, on February 8, 2008, Prime Minister Erdoğan

---

16. Press release Berlin education: http://www.berlin.de/landespressestelle/archiv/2009/05/26/1286/index.html.

17. See   http://www.berlin.de/imperia/md/content/sen-bildung/besondere_paedagogische_konzepte/sprachen_lernen/fremdsprachen_berliner_schule.pdf.

and Chancellor Merkel participated in a discussion with a group of Turkish and German pupils gathered at the German chancellery. In his comments there, Erdoğan called for Turkish-medium schools in Germany to be staffed by teachers from Turkey, saying that ability to speak the first language was necessary to facilitate acquisition of better German. Among those attending this event were pupils from the 12th grade class at the Robert Koch School, where I am currently conducting an investigation of language development in their first, second and foreign languages (Pfaff 2009). In group discussions about the meeting with Erdoğan and Merkel, the pupils did not favor all-Turkish schools in Germany. One remarked that they already had Turkish schools, referring to the high proportion of Turkish-speaking pupils at schools such as theirs where Turkish as a second foreign language is also an option.

Other German politicians and representatives of business and trade organizations, as well as Kenan Kolat, head of the Turkish community in Germany, all rejected the idea of all-Turkish schools as proposed by Erdoğan. Several, however, supported Turkish as a second foreign language. These included the SPD representative for integration, as well as Ute Vogt and Barbara Dorn, of the *Bundesvereinigung der Deutschen Arbeitgeberverbände* and the *Deutsche Industrie- und Handelskammer* (DIHK) respectively. The option to include Turkish as a second foreign language would fit well into the framework of the multiple 'personal adoptive languages' proposal outlined by Orban (2007) and with the Council of Europe (2008) and European Commission focus on fostering plurilingualism, as discussed in the next section.

5.3   European views on multilingualism and plurilingualism

As with the discussions within Germany, statements and developing policies for Europe reflect both instrumental and integrative aspects of multilingualism. The Council of Europe recently published two reports in 2008, one on language and integration of adult immigrants and one on language education policies for children, youth and continuing education. These are reviews and discussions of specific policies in several European countries, mentioned here for the sake of completeness but not discussed in detail.[18] The European Commission, in contrast, has taken a more general approach to gathering the opinions of public and non-governmental organizations and interest groups.

The European Commission Report, "A rewarding challenge. How the multiplicity of languages could strengthen Europe,"[19] written by the French-Lebanese author Amin Maalouf, and based on meetings and discussions with writers, academics and directors of language academies in several European countries in 2007, suggests that if

---

18.   See Little (2008) "The linguistic integration of adult minorities" (www.coe.int/lang) and the Council of Europe *Language Education Policy 2008* (http://www.coe.int/t/dg4/linguistic/Division_EN.asp).

19.   See   http://www.euractiv.com/en/culture/eu-multilingualism-strategy-focus-language-learning/article-170364.

immigrants could maintain their languages and pass them on to their children, they would have less need to express their identity in religious fanaticism. This passage represents a new departure in the ideology called on in support of mother tongue education and, as such, warrants quotation at some length:

> Immigration is occupying an ever bigger place in the political, economic, social and intellectual life of our continent. We could say in this regard what we said on the subject of European diversity in general, i.e. that it is simultaneously a source of enrichment but also a source of tension, and that a wise policy is one which while recognising the full complexity of the issue would endeavour to make the utmost of the advantages and play down the drawbacks. We feel that the approach we are proposing to manage linguistic diversity could contribute significantly to this twofold objective.
>
> For immigrants, the *personal adoptive language* should in the normal run of events be that of the country in which they have chosen to live. A thorough knowledge of the national language and the culture it carries with it is essential if they are to integrate into the host society and play their part in economic, social, intellectual, artistic and political life. For immigrants to Europe, it is also a factor of adhesion to Europe in general, its Community project, its cultural heritage and its fundamental values.
>
> In parallel with this and, we might say, in reciprocal fashion, it is vital for the countries of Europe to understand how important it is for every immigrant or person originating from immigration, to maintain knowledge of their own language of origin. A young person who loses the language of his ancestors also loses the ability to communicate effortlessly with his parents and that is a factor of social dysfunctioning which can lead to violence. Excessive assertion of identity often stems from a feeling of guilt in relation to one's culture of origin, a guilt which is sometimes expressed by exacerbated religion-based reactions. To describe it differently, the immigrant or a person whose origins lie in immigration and is able to speak his mother tongue and would be able to teach it to his children, knowing that his language and culture of origin are respected in the host society, would have less of a need to assuage his thirst for identity in another way. To allow migrants, European and non-European alike, to gain access easily to their language of origin and allow them to maintain what we could term their linguistic and cultural dignity, to us once again seems a powerful antidote against fanaticism. A sense of belonging, in the religious and linguistic sense, is patently one of the most powerful components of identity. But the two facets function differently and sometimes vie with one another. Belonging in the religious sense is exclusive, belonging in the linguistic sense is not (Maalouf et al. 2008: 20).

In September 2008, the European Commission adopted the Communication "Multilingualism: An asset for Europe and a shared commitment,"[20] which resulted in a call

---

20. 1 COM(2008)566 (http://ec.europa.eu/education/languages/news/news2853_en.htm).

for expressions of interest in a Civil Society Platform to promote multilingualism. The purpose of the call was "to give organisations from the culture, non-formal and informal education and learning and other sectors of the civil society and the media, the opportunity to express interest in participating in a structured dialogue with the European Commission." The proposed Civil Society Platform should concentrate its work on the three main objectives of the 2008 Communication: to raise awareness of the value and opportunities of the EU's linguistic diversity; to encourage the removal of barriers to intercultural dialogue and social inclusion; and to achieve the Barcelona objective to communicate in two foreign languages. The platform is intended for *non-governmental* organizations of civil society and the media, and representatives of public institutions, whether national, regional or local, will be offered other channels to express their views. The platform will provide recommendations for an EU language conference in 2011 (action 9.4. of the Communication).

6. Final remarks:
Multiple messages on the path to a multilingual and plurilingual Germany

Language policy issues continue to be a significant part of the discussion about much wider social issues concerning immigration, naturalization and integration of recent migrants into the majority population in Germany. However, there is no single ideology or line of policy planning. Policies focused on German proficiency as well as those focused on multilingualism are debated both in terms of desired practical outcomes and the important symbolic role of language and personal identification, whether with the nation or with the ethnic group. Both turn on arguments that language is essential, albeit in two different senses.

That the German language is essential in the sense of being necessary in practice is acknowledged by all; what remains controversial is the extent to which the level of proficiency in German should be decisive in permitting or preventing access to residence permits and social support or to certain educational and occupational options. As we have seen, the application of the laws is not uniform for all immigrants, suggesting that language proficiency is not the underlying issue, but rather a convenient, apparently objective instrument of social and political policies to control options for immigrants and their families. After much criticism of the vague language in which the required skills have been couched, there have been steps taken to professionalize the assessment of language proficiency, specifying the skills at the European Reference Framework A1 level, required for spousal immigration, or the A2 or B1, required to achieve the *Start Deutsch 2* (A2) or *Zertifikat Deutsch* (B1) levels to complete the integration course successfully. Although the integration course still consists primarily of language instruction, the imbalance of language to cultural learning may be mitigated by the reorganization of the language courses to focus on areas of life in Germany where adult migrants frequently have contact with Germans in dealing with educational issues of their children or with contacts with employers, government officials or health services. However it is not yet clear whether attainment of these levels of proficiency in German will actually give a significant boost to social integration for the participants.

As far as language at schools is concerned, we have seen that schools can function as instruments of reproduction of ideologies. This is true for German-only ideology, as at the Herbert Hoover School, where linguistic minority pupils are led to internalize (or at least articulate on some occasions) the view that German-only policies are appropriate everywhere on the school grounds. It is also true for the multilingual and plurilingual ideologies, as at the *Europaschulen*, where pupils are encouraged to write essays on their own multinational identities in the language other than their declared mother tongue. Here the value of maintaining migrant minority languages for the personal and cultural identification of the children of migrants is acknowledged in addition to the potential instrumental value of multilingualism in the minority languages in their future roles in European and global economies. Fears that such support will decrease integration are voiced, but at present they are outweighed by the advantages of added competencies. Further it has been suggested that political recognition and support for their languages could actually function to defuse the perceived religious, cultural and political divisions. Such arguments in support of minority languages of course also refer to essentialist views of language and culture, this time from the point of view of the ethnic minorities rather than the national majority.

Looking at the language of the various policy statements and laws themselves and at the public discourse about these policies along the lines suggested by de Cillia and Wodak (2007) provides further insight into the current political positions. We see that even while the bulk of the overt arguments rely on instrumental views, the underlying essentialist ideologies of language and nation, and language and culture occasionally come to the fore. We find instances of overt reference to essentialist identification of the German language as an index of identification with Germany, taking use of the language as a signal of 'integration,' whereas the place of diglossia as a legitimate pattern for migrants is rarely acknowledged. The arguments themselves frequently rely on stereotypes about the daily life of the minority populations, which is visible, for instance, in the assertion that (many) migrant children, particularly those with Turkish background, have no contact with German before entering preschool programs. These assumptions are not well supported by the available empirical studies, however, survey data need to be supplemented by further (ethnographic) research. Finally, the linguistic realizations within the discourse, particularly in the popular press, frequently employ metaphoric expressions, such as *Parallelgesellschaften* ('parallel societies'), which, again, emphasize the supposedly self-chosen encapsulation of the ethnic groups within the native German society, in effect blaming the victim. Here too, further analysis of the regulations, as well as of official and popular debates about them, readily available online, would be worthwhile projects for future research.

In general, although it appears that language policy discussions are more balanced at present than they have been in some time, it remains to be seen whether the European

Commission initiative to involve non-official institutions and groups in the serious discussion of public policies and practices will have positive results, as is to be hoped, and that widespread dissemination of these discussions will contribute to more enlightenment on advantages of individual plurilingualism in multilingual societies such as Germany.

References

Akıncı, Mehmet-Ali and Pfaff, Carol W. 2008. "Language choice, cultural and literacy practices of Turkish bilingual adolescents in France and in Germany." Paper presented at AILA Congress. Essen.

Amman, Brigit. 2000. *Kurden in Europa. Ethnizität und Diaspora*. Münster: Lit Verlag.

Baumert, Jürgen, Trautwein, Ulrich and Artelt, Cordula. 2003. "Schulumwelten – institutionelle Bedingungen des Lehrens und Lernens." In *PISA 2000: Ein differenzierter Blick auf die Länder der Bundesrepublik Deutschland*, Jürgen Baumert, Cordula Artelt, Eckhard Klieme, Michael Neubrand, Manfred Prenzel, Ulrich Schiefele, Wolfgang Schneider, Klaus Tillmann and Manfred Weiss (eds), 261–331. Opladen: Leske and Budrich.

Berlin Senatsverwaltung für Bildung, Jugend und Sport. 2002. *Rahmenplan für Unterricht und Erziehung in der Berliner Schule. Deutsch als Zweitsprache für Schüler und Schülerinnen im Alter von 6 bis 15 Jahren unterschiedlicher Niveaustufen in allen Schularten*. [Framework for instruction and education in Berlin Schools: German as second language for pupils from 6–15 years old at various levels in all school types]. Retrieved June 20, 2009 from http://www.berlin.de/rubrik/politik-und-verwaltung/senatsverwaltungen/.

Berlin Senat für Bildung Wissenschaft und Forschung. 2008. "Deutsch als Zweitsprache (DaZ)." [German as a second language]. Retrieved June 20, 2009 from http://www.berlin.de/sen/bildung/foerderung/schueler_nichtdeutscher_herkunftssprache/daz.html.

Berlin Senat für Bildung Wissenschaft und Forschung. 2008. *Blickpunkt Schule Schuljahr 2007/2008*. Retrieved June 20, 2009 from http://www.berlin.de/sen/bildung/foerderung/schueler_nichtdeutscher_herkunftssprache/daz.html.

Blommaert, Jan (ed.). 1999. *Language Ideological Debates*. Berlin: Mouton De Gruyter.

Blommaert, Jan and Verschueren, Jef. 1998. "The role of language in European nationalist ideologies." In *Language Ideologies. Practice and Theory*, Bambi Schieffelin, Kathryn A. Woolard and Paul V. Kroskrity (eds), 189–210. Oxford: Oxford University Press.

Boos-Nünning, Ursula and Karakaşoğlu, Yasemin. 2005 *Viele Welten leben. Lebenssituation und -orientierungen von Mädchen mit griechischem, italienischem, jugoslawischem, türkischem und Aussiedlerhintergund in Deutschland*. Münster: Waxmann.

Borde, Theda and Albrecht, Niels-Jens (eds). 2007. *Innovative Konzepte für Integration und Partizipation. Bedarfsanalyse zur interkulturellen Kommunikation in Institutionen und für Modelle neuer Arbeitsfelder*. Frankfurt: IKO-Verlag für Interkulturelle Kommunikation.

Bericht der Beauftragten der Bundesregierung für Migration, Flüchtlinge und Integration über die Lage der Ausländerinnen und Ausländer in Deutschland (Dezember 2007). Retrieved June 20, 2009 from http://www.fluechtlingsinfo-berlin.de/fr/zuwg/Lagebericht_2007.pdf.

Bundesministerium des Innern. 2005/2008. "The development of migration since 1950." [updated: February 2008]. Retrieved June 20, 2009 from http://www.zuwanderung.de/english/1_statistik.html.

Bundesamt für Migration und Flüchtlinge. "Sprachliche Bildung für Menschen mit Migrationshintergrund in Deutschland" [Language education for persons with migrant background]. Retrieved May 20, 2008 from http://www.bamf.de/cln_092/SharedDocs/Anlagen/DE/Integration/Publikationen/Integrationsprogramm/ErgebnBericht__SprachBildung,templateId=raw,property=publicationFile.pdf/ErgebnBericht_SprachBildung.pdf.

Bundesamt für Migration und Flüchtlinge. [Research in progress on the course of integration with participants in the Integrationskurs]. Retrieved May 20, 2008 from http://www.bamf.de/cln_101/nn_444062/SharedDocs/Projekte/DE/Migration/Forschung/Integration/laufende/forschung-integrationsverlauf-Integrationsteilnehmer.html.

Bundesministerium des Innern. Pressemitteilung vom 17. Januar 07 [press release on Integrationskurs]. Retrieved May 20, 2008 from http://www.bmi.bund.de/cln_012/nn_122688/Internet/Content/Nachrichten/Pressemitteilungen/2007/01/Bericht__Evaluation__Integrationskurse.html.

Bundesministerium des Innern 2007. Neufassung der Integrationskursverordnung [Revision of regulation of the Integration Course]. Retrieved May 20, 2008 from http://www.aufenthaltstitel.de/stichwort/integrationskurs.html.

Bundesministerium des Innern 2008. Pressemitteilung zum Einbürgerungstest [press release on naturalization test]. Retrieved June 30, 2009 from http://www.bmi.bund.de/cln_028/nn_122688/Internet/Content/Nachrichten/Pressemitteilungen/2008/07/Fragenkatalog__Einbuergerungstest.html.

Castiglione, Dario and Longman, Chris (eds). 2007. *The Language Question in Europe and Diverse Societies. Political, Legal and Social Perspectives.* Oxford and Portland, OR: Hart Publishing.

Çınar, Safter. 2007. Interview: Wir fühlen uns diskriminiert. Der Sprecher des Türkischen Bundes Berlin Çınar zur Deutschpflicht an Schulen. In *Tagesspiegel*, June 22, 2007.

Council of Europe. *Language Education Policy 2008.* Retrieved June 30, 2009 from http://www.coe.int/t/dg4/linguistic/Division_EN.asp.

de Cillia, Rudolf and Wodak, Ruth. 2007. "Katastrophe und Wiedergeburt Zur diskursiven Konstruktion gemeinsamer Geschichte im Österreich des Jahres." In *Diskurse und Texte. Festschrift für Konrad Ehlich zum 65. Geburtstag*, Angelika Redder (ed.), 117–128. Tübingen: Stauffenburg Verlag.

Ehlich, Konrad (ed.). 2005. *Anforderungen an Verfahren der regelmäßigen Sprachstandsfeststellung als Grundlage für die frühe und individuelle Förderung von Kindern mit und ohne Migrationshintergrund.* Bonn/Berlin: BMBF.

Ehlich, Konrad, Montanari, Elke and Hila, Anna. 2007. "Recherche und Dokumentation hinsichtlich der Sprachbedarfe von Teilnehmenden an Integrationskursen *DaZ* – InDaZ – im Rahmen des Projektes des *Goethe-Instituts* zur Erstellung eines Rahmencurriculums für Integrationskurse." Retrieved June 30, 2009 from http://www.goethe.de/mmo/priv/3689940-STANDARD.pdf.

Entorf, Horst and Minoiu, Nicoleta. 2005. "What a difference immigration policy makes: A comparison of PISA scores in Europe and traditional countries of immigration." *German Economic Review* 6 (3): 355–376.

Emminghaus, Christoph and Stern, Tobias. 2006. "Evaluation der Integrationskurse nach dem Zuwanderungsgesetz Abschlussbericht und Gutachten über Verbesserungspotenziale bei der Umsetzung der Integrationskurse." Berlin: Bundesministerium für Inneres.

Extra, Guus and van Avermaet, Piet (eds). 2009. *Language Testing, Migration and Citizenship.* London: Continuum.

Extra, Guus and Yağmur, Kutlay. 2004. *Urban Multilingualism in Europe: Immigrant Minority Languages at Home and School*. Clevedon: Multilingual Matters.

Gal, Susan. 2006. "Migration, minorities and multilingualism: Language ideologies in Europe." In *Language Ideologies, Policies and Practices. Language and the Future of Europe*, Clare Mar-Molinero and Patrick Stevenson (eds), 13–27. Palgrave Macmillan.

Harnisch, Ulrike and Nehr, Monika. 1998. "Zweisprachige Alphabetisierung und Erziehung in Berlin." In *Pfade durch Babylon. Konzepte und Beispiele für den Umgang mit sprachlicher Vielfalt in Schule und Gesellschaft*, Katharina Kuhs and Wolfgang Steinig (eds), 103–114. Freiburg im Breisgau: Fillibach Verlag.

Hille, Peter. 2007. "Controversial school language ban appears to be working." *Deutsche Welle* August 16, 2007.

Hottmann, Lucy. 2008. "Turkish language provision in Berlin." M.A. dissertation, Faculty of Humanities. Manchester University.

Kalter, Frank. 2006. "Auf der Suche nach einer Erklärung für die spezifischen Arbeitsmarktnachteile Jugendlicher türkischer Herkunft. Zugleich eine Replik auf den Beitrag von Holger Seibert und Heike Solga: 'Gleiche Chancen dank einer abgeschlossenen Ausbildung?'" [In Search of an explanation for the specific labor market disadvantages of second generation Turkish migrant children Simultaneously a comment on the contribution of Holger Seibert and Heike Solga]. *Zeitschrift für Soziologie* 35 (2): 110–131.

Kösem, Nuray. 2009. "Unterricht mit lernungewohnten Teilnehmern." Paper presented at the XI Türkischer Internationaler Germanistik Kongress, Izmir.

Kymlicka, Will and Norman, Wayne. 2000. "Citizenship in culturally diverse societies: Issues, contexts, concepts." In *Citizenship in Diverse Societies*, Will Kymlicka and Wayne Norman (eds), 1–41. Oxford: Oxford University Press.

Kymlicka, Will and Patten, Alan. (eds). 2004. *Language Rights and Political Theory*. Oxford: Oxford University Press.

Lengyel, Drorit, Reich, Hans H., Roth, Hans-Joachim and Döll, Marion (eds). 2009. *Von der Sprachdiagnose zur Sprachförderung*. FÖRMIG Edition, Bd. 5. Münster: Waxmann.

Maas, Utz. 2008. *Sprache und Sprachen in der Migrationsgesellschaft*. Osnabrück: Universitätsverlag Osnabrück.

Neumann, Ursula and Reich, Hans H. (eds). 2009. *Erwerb des Türkischen in einsprachigen und mehrsprachigen Situationen*. FÖRMIG Edition, Bd. 6. Münster: Waxmann.

Özçelik, Tiner. 2006. Zum Zusammenhang von Deutschkenntnissen und Kontaktbeziehungen zu Deutschen am Beispiel der Türken zweiter Generation in Berlin. Unpublished Master's thesis, Freie Universität Berlin.

Orban, Leonard. 2007. "Multilingualism and competitiveness." Speech of the European Commissioner for Multilingualism. July 5, 2007. Retrieved June 30, 2009 from http://europa.eu/rapid/pressReleasesAction.do?reference=SPEECH/07/472&format=HTML&aged=0&language=EN&guiLanguage=en.

Perlmann-Balme, Michaela, Plassmann, Sibylle and Zeidler, Beate. 2009. Deutsch-Test für Zuwanderer A2–B1. Prüfungsziele-Testbeschreibung. [German Test for immigrants A2–B1. Objectives and Test Description]. Retrieved July 31, 2009 from http://www.goethe.de/lhr/pro/daz/dfz/dtz_Pruefungshandbuch.pdf.

Pfaff, Carol W. 1981. "Sociolinguistic problems of immigrants: Foreign workers and their children in Germany." *Language in Society* 10: 155–188.

—. 1993. "Turkish language development in Germany." In *Immigrant Languages in Europe*, Guus Extra and Ludo Verhoeven (eds), 119–146. Clevedon: Multilingual Matters.

—. 2000. "Bilingual verbal repertoires represented in the speech of Turkish/Danish and Turkish/German bilingual children in the Køge and Kita projects." In *Det er Conversation 801 Değil mi?. Perspectives on the Bilingualism of Turkish Speaking Children and Adolescents in North Western Europe.* Anne Holmen and Normann Jørgensen (eds), 195–229. Køge Series K7. Copenhagen: Royal Danish School of Educational Studies.

—. 2003. "Ideological and political framing of bilingual development: Reflections on studies of Turkish/German in Berlin." In *Multilingualism in Global and Local Perspectives*, Kenneth Hyltenstam and Kari Fraurud (eds), 191–219. Stockholm: Centre for Research on Bilingualism and Rinkeby Institute of Multilingual Research.

—. 2009. "Parallel assessment of oral and written text production of multilinguals: Methodological and analytic issues." In *Empirische Befunde zu DaZ-Erwerb und Sprachförderung*, Bernt Ahrenholz (ed.), 213–233. Freiburg im Breisgau: Fillibach.

Pfaff, Carol and Akıncı, Mehmet-Ali. 2008. "Die Sprachkompetenz bilingualer Schüler türkischer Herkunft in Frankreich und Deutschland" [The linguistic competence of bilingual pupils with Turkish background in France and Germany]. DAAD-PROCOPE; EGIDE-PCH grant "#D06 28214, Jan 2007-Dec 2008.

Piller, Ingrid. 2001. "Naturalization language testing and its basis in ideologies of national identity and citizenship." *International Journal of Bilingualism* 5 (3): 259–277.

Reich, Hans H. and Hienz de Albentiis, Milena. 1998. "Der Herkunfts-sprachenunterricht. Erlaßlage und statistische Entwicklung in den alten Bundesländern." *Deutsch lernen* 1: 3–45.

Seibert, Holger and Solga, Heike. 2005. "Gleiche Chancen dank einer abgeschlossenen Ausbildung?" *Zeitschrift für Soziologie* 5: 30–44.

Senatsverwaltung für Bildung, Wissenschaft und Forschung 2007. Fremdsprachen in der Berliner Schule. Fremdsprachenwahl in der Grundschule und in den weiterführenden Schulen. Retrieved June 30, 2009 from http://www.berlin.de/imperia/md/content/sen-bildung/besondere_paedagogische_konzepte/sprachen_lernen/fremdsprachen_berliner_schule.pdf.

Stanat, Petra. 2003. "Schulleistungen von Jugendlichen mit Migrationshintergrund: Differenzierung deskriptiver Befunde aus PISA und PISA-E" [Learning outcomes of students from immigrant families: A differentiated look at descriptive findings from PISA and PISA-E]. In *PISA 2000: Ein differenzierter Blick auf die Länder der Bundesrepublik Deutschland*, Jürgen Baumert, Cordula Artelt, Eckhard Klieme, Michael Neubrand, Manfred Prenzel, Ulrich Schiefele, Wolfgang Schneider, Klaus Tillmann and Manfred Weiss (eds), 243–260. Opladen: Leske and Budrich.

Statistisches Bundesamt 2008. Bevölkerung und Erwerbstätigkeit. Einbürgerungen [Population and employment: Naturalization]. Retrieved June 30, 2009 from http://www.stern.de/politik/deutschland/zuwanderung-sprachtest-schreckt-offenbar-von-einbuergerung-ab-662401.html.

Stevenson, Patrick. 2006. "'National' languages in transnational contexts: Language, migration and citizenship in Europe." In *Language Ideologies, Policies and Practices. Language and the Future of Europe*, Clare Mar-Molinero and Patrick Stevenson (eds), 147–161. Palgrave Macmillan.

Stevenson, Patrick and Schanze, Livia. 2009. "Language, migration and citizenship in Germany: Discourses on integration and belonging." In *Language Testing, Migration and Citizenship. Cross-National Perspectives on Integration Regimes*, Guus Extra, Massimiliano Spotti and Piet van Avermaet (eds), 16–38. London: Continuum Books.

Der Tagesspiegel 2008. "Bevölkerung: Statistik." Retrieved June 30, 2009 from http://www.tagesspiegel.de/berlin/Bevoelkerung-Statistik;art270,2563138.

Ulich, Michaela and Mayr, Toni. 2003. *SISMiK. Sprachverhalten und Interesse an Sprache bei Migrantenkindern in Kindertageseinrichtungen*. Verlag Herder: Freiburg i.Br.

Van Parijs, Philippe. 2007. "Europe's linguistic challenge." In *The Language Question in Europe and Diverse Societies. Political, Legal and Social Perspectives*, Dario Castiglione and Chris Longman (eds), 217–253. Oxford and Portland, OR: Hart Publishing.

Verein der deutschen Sprache. 2007. Forum. Sprachenpolitik: Deutsch ins Grundgesetz. Retrieved June 30, 2009 from http://www.vds-ev.de/forum/viewtopic.php?TopicID=2407 &page=4.

Woellert, Franziska, Kröhnert, Steffen, Sippel, Lilli and Klingholz, Reiner. 2009. *Ungenutzte Potential. Zur Lage der Integration in Deutschland*. Berlin: Berlin-Institut für Bevölkerung und Entwicklung.

Wodak, Ruth, de Cillia, Rudolf, Reisigl, Martin and Liebhart, Karin. 2008. *The Discursive Construction of National Identity* [2nd ed.]. Edinburgh: Edinburgh University Press.

Zinke, Claudia. 2009. "Schüler der Staatlichen Europaschule Berlin sind fitr für Europa" Press release Berlin education. Retrieved September 30, 2009 from http://www.berlin.de/lande-spressestelle/archiv/2009/05/26/1286/index.html.

CHAPTER 18

Against the assimilationist tide

Nurturing Puerto Rican children's bilingual, bicultural, and academic development in preschool

Bruce Johnson-Beykont and Zeynep F. Beykont

1. Introduction

Language minority students continue to be the fastest growing portion of the general student population in the United States. The number of language minority students in K-12 has increased from 3.8 million in 1979 to 10.8 million in 2007, and now they constitute 20% of the total enrolment (NCES, 2009). This trend is especially prevalent for the preschool years where depending on the state one in every three to five children is a language minority (Collins and Ribeiro 2004).

The U.S. has failed to respond to the linguistic and educational needs of its diverse student population. Puerto Rican students in particular achieve at the lowest levels compared to all other language groups (Coleman 1981; Del Valle 1998; Dobles and Segarra 1998; Gibson and Ogbu 1991; Nieto 1998, 2000b). From the time they enter schools, disproportionate numbers of Puerto Rican children fall behind academically, are placed in special needs classes, are retained, and leave school without a high school diploma (ASPIRA 1993; Baratz-Snowden et al. 1988; Masso 2003; National Center for Education Statistics 1995; Nieto 1998, 2000b; Walsh 1990, 2000).[1] Conversely, they are underrepresented in gifted and talented programs and in advanced classes (New York Board of Education 1997; Nieto 1998, 2000b). This persistent picture of negative school experiences has been documented repeatedly for the past five decades.

In the public and scholarly discourse, varied arguments have been forwarded to account for Puerto Rican students' low school achievement (see Beykont 1994; Gibson 1991; Nieto 1998, 2000b; Wong Fillmore and Valadez 1986; Zentella 1997 for reviews). The low school achievement is attributed to these children's supposed inadequate intellectual, cognitive, and linguistic abilities and to their families' scarce economic resources. Bilingualism, code-switching behavior, and use of nonstandard varieties of Spanish in the

---

1. In some Northeastern districts, compared to a 14% dropout rate for whites, the dropout rate for Puerto Ricans reaches 80–90% (President's Advisory Commission, 1996).

community are seen to cause children's mental confusion and a lack of proficiency in both Spanish and English. Attributions are also made to the low educational backgrounds of the families, educationally unstimulating home contexts, and a mismatch between the learning and thinking style at home and in schools. Each of these explanations places the blame on the Puerto Rican community and on children for failing in the U.S. public school system designed by and for white, middle class native English speakers.

In this chapter, we report on a Spanish-English enrichment bilingual preschool program that is being designed specifically for Puerto Rican children in the U.S. In general, enrichment bilingual preschool programs are characterized by substantial and prolonged use of Spanish and English (Beykont 1997a; Christian 1994; Lindholm 1990; Lindholm-Leary 2001, 2005). Native-English and native-Spanish speaking children are taught basic vocabulary and preliteracy skills and early concepts of math and science bilingually. The teachers are bilingual, and so are the instructional materials. The curriculum builds on what children know to teach the knowledge base valued in U.S. schools. These programs aim to develop children's bilingualism, inculcate pride in their cultural identities, and prepare children for the academic challenges of U.S. elementary schools.

We were invited to act as consultants to La Casa de los Niños, a bilingual preschool located within a predominantly Puerto Rican low-income housing project in a Northeastern U.S. city. Everyone residing in this community is bilingual to varied degrees, except for the elderly and new arrivals from Puerto Rico, who tend to be monolingual Spanish speakers. Generally, adults use either Spanish only or both English and Spanish when speaking with their children or other adults at home. Children, on the other hand, tend to use either English only or both English and Spanish when speaking with their siblings and peers and Spanish only or both English and Spanish when speaking with their parents and other adults in the community. While both English and Spanish can be heard in children's homes and on the streets of the housing project, usually Spanish is the language used for church and other important civic events, such as marriages and graduation ceremonies, as well as national celebrations, such as Puerto Rican Independence Day.

Most preschoolers attending La Casa were born in the U.S. and live in low-income households with one or two adults, the majority of whom were born outside the U.S (Johnson-Beykont and Beykont 1998).[2] La Casa parents have completed an average of 9 years of formal education with a range of 6–18 years. Children can be enrolled in La Casa when they reach 2 years and 9 months; they graduate when they are 5 or 6 years old, and enter kindergarten classes in local public schools. The preschool has three classrooms, each serving a different age group: three-, four-, and five-year-olds. Each classroom has Spanish-dominant and English-dominant children who are bilingual to varied degrees. Teachers, assistant teachers, administrative staff and classroom volunteers are also bilingual to varied degrees.

La Casa was established in the 1970s as a result of organizing efforts of the Puerto Rican community. It had experienced years of success and had been a source of

---

2.   Parents receive government subsidies that help low-income families pay for preschool.

community pride as one of the first model bilingual preschools, but had recently lost its focus and direction. Administrators, active parents, and teachers wished to take a critical look at the strengths and weaknesses of the existing preschool program and to make changes so that it would better serve the children and the families in the community. In one-on-one interviews, a primary concern of the parents involved in La Casa was that the existing preschool program was not providing sufficient support for the children's bilingual skills. Many associated Spanish proficiency with the children's cultural identity: "She comes from two Hispanic parents. It is good to know their cultural backgrounds.", "They must know what identifies us.", "We are Hispanics, maintaining our language is a principle." Some parents also underscored the importance of Spanish-English bilingualism in the children's future schooling, and job prospects: "If I decide to move to Puerto Rico she can read and write or if I decide to stay here she can read and write." Others noted that bilingual children will "...have more opportunity in the future" and that "when they grow up they can take advantage of being bilingual and know both languages equally." Both parents and school personnel were concerned that, throughout their years at La Casa, the children were shifting to use increasingly more English. While adults were fully committed to developing the children's language skills in both English and Spanish the question was how best to achieve the goal of full bilingualism.

In the interviews, La Casa parents also emphasized that the preschool should do more to nurture the children's bicultural identity. They wanted La Casa to help the children develop a heartfelt pride and deep-rooted comfort in their Puerto Rican identity and the Spanish-speaking culture, and from that secure foundation, they thought, the children could be helped to reach out to, understand, and join with the English-speaking mainstream culture. Teaching through two languages was seen as a vital part of developing the children's bicultural identity. The participants also underscored the importance of teaching both the U.S. and Puerto Rican cultures. Reasons for teaching Puerto Rican culture connected to family roots, the parents' birthplace, and the child's identity: "We live here and belong to the Hispanic race.", "It's important to me that my child knows his/her country and mine." Others expressed a desire for their children to understand "who they are and where they come from so they won't forget their roots." Learning about the mainstream U.S. culture was believed necessary because these children "live in a country that is not theirs and the culture that is different," and "it is where they are being raised, so it is important to learn the culture."

Another concern of the parents was that the children at La Casa were not being adequately prepared for the academic challenges of elementary schools. Some parents thought that the children at La Casa "spent too little time in studies" and "need more reading skills" and "less time playing." Both the parents and center staff suggested that "the curriculum needs more work" and wanted to improve the teaching of early reading, writing, and math skills. There was confusion, however, and often conflicting ideas about how the goal of preparing children for the academic challenges of elementary schools could be best achieved.

In this chapter, we first describe the sociopolitical context in which La Casa's Spanish-English enrichment bilingual preschool program operates. The theoretical framework that informed our work at this child-care center is then examined in relation to two essential program components, namely classroom language use and curriculum. The final part of the paper draws lessons from the experiences at La Casa and highlights the importance of developing a theory-based bilingual program.

2.   The sociopolitical context of the program

The U.S. maintains an assimilationist orientation toward its linguistically and culturally diverse population (Alba and Nee 2005; Beykont 1994, 1996; Donahue 1995; Gonzalez 1975; Navarro 1985; Ovando and McLaren 2000; Paulston 1974; Ruiz 1984). Historically, nation building has rested on the absorption of language groups into the U.S. English-speaking mainstream and the severance of connections to home culture and language because the maintenance of native languages can be divisive (see Beykont 1994, 2002b; Crawford 1991, 1998 for reviews). Standard English is the prestige language of the country, the language of higher education and economic opportunity, and the one at the top of the country's clear language hierarchy (Fishman 1966, 1991; Macedo 1993, 2000). Language groups are enticed to learn the prestige language based on a false promise that, once they gain proficiency, they will have access to the same power, privileges, and opportunities that native speakers of Standard English enjoy (Beykont 2000, 2002a; Macedo 2000; Navarro 1985).

The prevalent assimilationist orientation toward diversity in the U.S. has been translated into school language policies and programs characterized by an exclusive or predominant use of English as the language of instruction and a one-way school/community relationship, where only language groups not the schools are expected to learn, change, and adapt (Beykont 1994, 1997a; Ruiz 1984). The assimilationist policies and programs work on the pedagogical assumption that the more children are exposed to instructional use of the English language, the faster they will learn English (see Beykont 1994, 1996 and Cummins 1981, 1989, 2000 for reviews). When students' native languages are used for instructional purposes, their use is temporary. Ultimately, the goal of the assimilationist school language policies is children's acquisition of academic skills in English only. The maintenance and continued development of academic skills in the students' native languages is not valued or at least not supported in schools.

With schools as English-only or English-mostly environments, children quickly replace their respective native languages with English and find themselves unable to communicate with their grandparents, relatives, and sometimes even with their parents (Beykont 2000; Fishman 1991, 2001; Garcia 2001; Nettle and Romaine 2000; Souza 2000; Wong Fillmore 1991). In fact, school language policies can be seen as a critical reason for the shift and rapid loss of languages in the U.S. over the last century (Beykont, 2002b; Crawford 1991; Gonzalez 1975; Wong Fillmore 2000). The general pattern has been that language groups lose their native languages within two or three generations or even faster (Veltman 1983, 2000). Home to over 300 language groups, the U.S. ironically prides itself on being a monolingual English country.

The pattern of language maintenance and shift observed in the Puerto Rican community is strikingly different from that of many other language groups that transitioned into English monolingualism within a couple of generations (Zentella 1997, 2005). Spanish maintenance is still prevalent and valued in the Puerto Rican community, despite the assimilationist pressures. Many factors contribute to this unique sociolinguistic situation. Puerto Rico is a colony of the U.S., and historically language has played an important role in Puerto Rico's relationship with the colonizer (Beykont 1994; Nieto 1998, 2000b; Reyes 2000; Walsh 1990; Zentella 1997, 2005). Since the U.S. seized the island in 1898, the U.S. government has attempted persistently to impose English on Puerto Ricans on the island both as a language of education and official business. Puerto Ricans living in the U.S., similar to all other language groups, are also pressured to switch to English monolingualism rapidly. Against the assimilationist forces, Spanish is the glue that binds Puerto Ricans residing in the U.S. and on the island, and marks a refutation of the U.S. hegemony. The maintenance of Spanish is a vital means of cultural survival against the colonizing power of the English-speaking culture both in the U.S. and in Puerto Rico.

Another reason for this unique pattern of Spanish maintenance in the community is the U.S. citizenship and traveling rights granted to Puerto Ricans. For a variety of reasons, including employment, families freely travel back and forth between the predominantly English-speaking culture of the U.S. and the Spanish-speaking culture of Puerto Rico (Cafferty and Rivera-Martinez 1981; Coleman 1981; Santiago Santiago 1986). Every time they move, families cross language and cultural boundaries (Clachar 1997; Nieto 2000b; Reyes 2000; Zavala 2000). This model of 'circulatory migration' has nurtured strong ties to Puerto Rico and the Spanish language, reinforced Spanish and English use, and has helped the community maintain their bilingualism.

For children, geographic mobility means struggling to succeed in two school cultures: one with a primary mission to promote academic skills in English (in the U.S.) and the other to promote academic skills in Spanish (in Puerto Rico). In the U.S., Puerto Rican children tend to live in low-income inner-city neighborhoods, and attend segregated, under-funded, and overcrowded public schools (Beykont 1994; Dobles and Segarro 1998; Laosa 2000; Zentella 1997, 2005). They have little support in adjusting to the school context because teachers, administrators, school personnel, and historical figures in the curriculum seldom look like, speak like, or represent their home cultures (Beykont 1994, 2000; Nieto 1998, 2000b; Walsh 1990, 2000). Puerto Ricans experience discrimination because of their accents, dialects, and lack of proficiency in Standard English and Standard Spanish and are treated as linguistically, culturally, and racially different others (Cafferty and Rivera-Martinez 1981; Nieto 1998, 2000b; Reyes 2000). Generally, Spanish skills of Puerto Rican children erode during elementary and secondary school years only to be reclaimed when they begin to assume adult roles and parental responsibilities in the community (Zentella 1997, 2005).

Since the late 1990's Puerto Rican students' school experiences have also been adversely affected by the 'English Only' movement, which aims to legislate English as the official language of the U.S., and to discontinue public services in minority languages including native language instruction in schools and translation services in courts (Beykont 2000, 2002b; Crawford 1997, 2000). Warning against the politically divisive potential of immigrant languages, leaders of the movement have convinced the voters in 26 states across the U.S. that bilingual services and native language supports in schools should be banned. For example, in California, the English Only law reduces school services for language minority students to one year in a structured immersion program.[3] While mixing children of different age and grade levels for educational purposes is allowed, using students' native languages for instructional purposes is strictly prohibited. In fact, parents can sue teachers who use any language other than English in classrooms.

As the bilingual programs are being phased out in the English-only states, a majority of Puerto Rican students are in mainstream classrooms or structured immersion programs (Laosa 2000; U.S. Department of Education 2002). In either case, their access to school activities and social circles is limited until they gain English fluency. If Puerto Rican students are placed into mainstream classrooms, they discover quickly that the educational, cultural, and linguistic value of Spanish is low in the U.S. schools and that Standard English is the only power language, while other languages, dialects, and accents are stigmatized (Beykont 1994, 2000, 2002a; Macedo 2000). In mainstream classrooms Puerto Rican students meet teachers most of whom do not have Spanish skills and the professional preparation to assess and address the unique academic and linguistic needs of bilingual students (Maxwell-Jolly and Gándara 2002; Nieto 2000a; Wong Fillmore and Snow 2000). A large number of these students end up placed into special education classrooms because their natural difficulties in learning through a second language are mistaken for learning disabilities (Stefanakis 2000).

If Puerto Rican students are placed in a structured immersion program, they are more likely to have teachers who are trained to teach second language learners, even though their teachers may not understand or speak Spanish (Maxwell-Jolly and Gándara 2002). Once again, the primary purpose of structured immersion programs is to promote monolingualism in English and prepare students for placement into mainstream classrooms in one year. Often the program is relegated to a basement both physically (many programs designed specifically for language minority students in the U.S. are segregated from the rest of the school) and politically (these programs are known as remedial programs, and are stigmatized and devalued by the larger school community) (Nieto 1998, 2000a).

---

3.   The law does not apply to students who are in enrichment/two-way bilingual programs in which native English and native Spanish speaking students are integrated for bilingual instruction.

How to prepare Puerto Rican children for the harsh reality of the U.S. elementary schools? How to develop their language skills in both Spanish and English? How to inculcate a healthy identification with their cultural heritage so that they can meet the mainstream culture from a position of strength? How to build a solid academic foundation for success in elementary schools? These were the questions that have concerned the community, and motivated our theory-based intervention at La Casa. In the following, we focus on two aspects of the program that went through revision, namely classroom language use and the curriculum.

3. Classroom language use

Our approach to classroom language use at La Casa was guided by Cummins' theoretical framework that postulates a close relationship between children's first and second language skills (Baker 2001; Bialystok and Cummins 1991; Cummins 1981, 1986, 2000). Cummins distinguishes the language used in everyday conversations, i.e., context-embedded language skills, from the language that is demanded in formal educational settings, i.e., context-reduced academic language skills. Children's context-embedded language use is supported by many paralinguistic cues, such as gestures and intonation, as well as by shared knowledge and setting. Context-reduced language use, on the other hand, relies almost exclusively on language cues, and it does not assume a shared background knowledge or setting when communicating new information and therefore constitutes a more demanding communicative task for children.

Cummins' linguistic interdependence hypothesis predicts that context-reduced language skills are cross-lingual (Cummins 1981, 1986, 1991, 2000). Provided children have enough exposure and motivation to learn the second language, the instructional use of the native language does not inhibit but rather enhances a child's acquisition of academic language skills in the second language. Those who have highly developed context-reduced language skills in their native language tend to develop highly developed context-reduced language skills in their second language. Explaining his interdependence hypothesis and common underlying proficiency notion, Cummins (1989) maintains that

> in a Spanish-English bilingual program, Spanish instruction that develops Spanish reading and writing skills is not just developing *Spanish* skills, it is also developing a deeper conceptual and linguistic proficiency that is strongly related to the development of literacy in the majority language (English). In other words, although surface aspects of different languages are clearly separate, there is an underlying cognitive/academic proficiency, which is common across languages. This common underlying proficiency makes possible the transfer of cognitive/ academic or literacy-related skills across languages (Cummins 1989: 44).

International research and local experience suggest that this transfer from one language to another does not occur readily (Abu-Rabia 2001, 2004; Berriz 2000; Beykont

1993, 1997a; Diaz, Moll and Mehan 1986; Freeman 1996; Gonzalez 1996; Kwong 2000; Moll, Diaz, Estrada and Lopes 1992; Roller 1988; Wong Fillmore and Valadez 1986). When children have exposure to native speakers of the target language, they can practice and develop a good command of everyday (context-embedded) use of a second language in two to three years. Developing context-reduced academic language skills, on the other hand, may take five to seven years in bilingual programs (Cummins 1981; Collier 1992, 1995; Hakuta 2000; Lopez and Greenfield 2004; Thomas and Collier 1997). There are several conditions that nurture the language transfer. Children need to be in a high quality program, such as an enrichment bilingual program, that (a) builds on their first language, and provides sustained support to both languages for a long period of time (Collier 1992, 1995; Cummins 1981, 2000; Lanauze and Snow 1989; Snow 1991); (b) provides frequent classroom opportunities for children to produce language with peers and adults (Cazden, Snow and Heise-Baigorria 1990; Dickinson and Snow 1987; Dickinson and Tabors 1991; Garcia 1993; Swain 1985, 1995, 1996); and (c) elicits context-reduced academic language skills in both languages (Cummins 1981, 2000; Diaz, Moll and Mehan 1986; Gee 2002; Dickinson and Snow 1987; Dickinson and Tabors 1991; Moll, et al. 1992a, 1992b; Verhoeven 1987, 1994, 2007).

First, children need to be supported in a bilingual program that builds upon their native language skills and provides support for both the first and second languages through prolonged bilingual instruction (Beykont 1994; Collier 1992, 1995; Cummins 1981, 2000; Lanauze and Snow 1989; Snow 1991). The unique sociolinguistic context in which the enrichment bilingual preschool program at La Casa is implemented does not permit the identification of the children's native or second language. Each child in this community uses, and is exposed to, both English and Spanish to varied degrees in their daily lives, and can at best be identified as English- or Spanish-dominant. Each of the three classrooms at La Casa had both Spanish- and English-dominant children. Equal classroom time needed to be allocated to both of these languages in order to build on the children's context-embedded oral communication skills. The staff decided that a bilingual program model in which children spend 50% of time in Spanish and 50% in English would be the most coherent approach to teaching through two languages at this preschool. This decision also affords adequate exposure to academic uses in both languages and allows each child to develop a foundation in his/her dominant language, which can be transferred to the non-dominant language.

La Casa teachers had to carefully plan and purposefully use language across the curriculum in order to ensure that equal time is spent on English and Spanish, and provide sufficient language input in a child's nondominant language (Krashen 1982, 1985, 1996). Teachers discontinued their use of the concurrent translation approach, in which all information is translated from one language to another regularly, so that children comprehend classroom activities and readings. Previous research and practical experience have shown that a concurrent translation approach leads to children tuning out teachers when their nondominant language is used and tuning in again for explanations given in their dominant language (Baker 2001; Legarreta 1977, 1979;

Pena-Hughes and Solis 1980; Wong Fillmore and Valadez 1986). Teachers have decided to adopt an 'alternate day approach' instead; they started conducting all classroom activities in one language each school day, e.g., in Spanish on Monday, English on Tuesday, Spanish on Wednesday, and so on. Children are encouraged to use the classroom language of the day but are allowed to use either language for asking clarifying questions, during group discussions, or in peer interactions. In order to model mature uses of both languages, and give maximum exposure to natural and classroom uses of both English and Spanish, teachers only use the designated language of the day. We expect that, in the communicative context of a preschool classroom, children can comprehend meaning and follow instructions in their nondominant language by interpreting the general purpose of an activity. Teacher cues, such as a teacher's demonstration or gestures, showing of an object or a picture, and varied language accommodations, such as a teacher's adjustment of his or her language use to the level of understanding of the child, also help children to comprehend instruction in their nondominant language (Baker 2001; McLaughlin 1985; Wong Fillmore and Valadez 1986).

A second condition for the successful transfer of academic language skills from the native language to the second is a language-rich classroom setting (Cazden, Snow and Heise-Baigorria 1990; Dickinson and Snow 1987; Dickinson and Tabors 1991; Garcia 1993; Swain 1985, 1995, 1996). In a language-rich classroom setting, children have exposure to the varied uses of Spanish and English, and many opportunities to produce language, negotiate meaning, and practice their newly emerging language skills with peers and adults. In each classroom at La Casa, there are many language role models and conversation partners, including English- and Spanish-dominant peers, a bilingual teacher, and a bilingual teaching assistant. La Casa classroom activities needed to be reorganized in order to capitalize on all the language resources. The challenge was to avoid excessive reliance on whole-group activities in which teachers do most of the talking and prompt children only for factual information and short answers to their questions (Garcia 1993; Kagan 1986; Mehan 1979). In whole-group activities, children have little opportunity to participate in extended talk or to use "complex language functions that reflect higher order cognitive processes" (Garcia 1993: 85). Small group activities allow children to solicit assistance from peers, and engage each other in discussions of content, clarification, and comprehension of the material, and in the use of complex academic language (Baker 2001; Diaz, Moll and Mehan 1986; Cohen 1984, 1986; Jacob 1984; McGroarty 1989). For example, peer activities that involve or encourage pretending the use of literacy, in the form of creating shopping lists, writing prescriptions at the pretend pharmacy, and inventing recipes in the kitchen corner, have been found to promote children's preliteracy skills and vocabulary development. Teachers can expand peer talk by participating in play alongside children or by observing and interjecting comments and questions that both introduce and elicit academic vocabulary and discourse patterns ("I am sorry, I only understand English. Can you use your English to tell me what is on the menu today?").

Teachers at La Casa have realized that they needed to strike a better balance between teacher-led whole group activities and one-on-one or small group activities. Instead of always reading stories to the entire group, teachers now frequently read and discuss a story with a small group of children, while others are involved in different activities. One-on-one or small group reading with an adult is also made possible by recruiting volunteers into the classrooms. A college-educated past-parent comes to read to the children in Spanish, and a native-English speaking teenage volunteer reads to them in English. Through these varied means, children at La Casa spend more time in small groups that invite children's extended talk and negotiation of meaning. We expected that more frequent reliance on one-on-one and small group activities would provide a more active language learning context for the transfer of skills (from dominant to non-dominant language and vice versa) because children would have an opportunity to receive more language input and produce more language in conversations with peers and adults.

A third condition for the positive transfer of skills from one language to the other is purposeful teaching aimed to develop children's context-reduced language skills, the "underlying cognitive/academic proficiency which is common across languages" (Cummins 1989: 44). In an active bilingual classroom context, children readily develop everyday fluency in both languages. However, children's acquisition of context-reduced academic language skills, print knowledge, and vocabulary takes a long time and concentrated effort (Cummins 1981, 2000; Diaz, Moll and Mehan 1986; Gee 2002; Dickinson and Snow 1987; Dickinson and Tabors 1991; Moll et al. 1992a, 1992b; Verhoeven 1987, 1994, 2007). At La Casa, teachers have recognized the need to place greater emphasis on academic language use, and to deliberately reinforce context-reduced language skills across the curriculum throughout the day. The teachers now plan each day's activities in order to provide more opportunities for the children to learn the uses of academic language "in ways that are expected in mainstream classrooms" (Jipson 1991: 127). A conscious professional development, focus on language and collaborative team planning sessions have allowed the center staff to see that throughout each school day there are many opportunities to teach language. In addition to organized activity times, teachers can also utilize routine times, such as lunch, snack, as well as clean up time, and special events, such as field trips and holiday celebrations, to reinforce the children's academic language skills.

At La Casa, the children's print knowledge and appreciation for varied functions of print was nurtured by reequipping the dramatic play area with print materials, such as telephone books, food recipes, shopping lists, menus from local restaurants, and ingredient lists cut from food/cereal boxes. In the dramatic play area children naturally speak and hear both English and Spanish as they play and talk with peers. With the financial help of a local bank, La Casa's book collection was expanded with developmentally and culturally appropriate Spanish and English storybooks. Teachers started spending more classroom time reading and rereading the storybooks to children employing methods that are commonly used during reading in U.S. elementary

schools, such as engaging in lengthy discussions of a story and asking students to anticipate what will happen next. As mentioned above, the daily presence of classroom
volunteers permits one-on-one or small group reading and the children's greater participation in recall and discussion of stories. The children have also the opportunity to
practice their emerging context-reduced language skills during the sharing time each
day, when they describe home, family, and community events to their peers and to
teachers; during art activities, when they talk about what they are drawing; and during
free play, when they discuss colors and shapes of blocks and stories embedded in what
they are building.

School wide curriculum themes, such as "World of Nature" and "Nutrition and
Our Bodies", create opportunities for children to acquire many related vocabulary
words and concepts via classroom activities, discussions, stories, and songs. Snacks,
lunch breaks, and cooking activities are ideal times to reinforce these newly acquired
vocabulary words, for example, through using names of fruits, vegetables, and other
food items common in Puerto Rico and the U.S., or discussion of their nutritional
value. The children's comprehension of sound-letter correspondence is strengthened
as teachers write new words on large sheets of paper and post them in the house corner
or cooking area. We expected that the sustained focus on language and literacy experiences, coupled with changes in the curriculum described below, would contribute to
the children's bilingual/bicultural development as well as their academic preparation
for U.S. schools.

4. Curriculum

A constructivist framework provided the theoretical backbone for our curriculum renewal work at La Casa. Constructivist theory emphasizes the active role of children in
building their understanding of the world through interaction with objects in their
immediate environment (Flavell 1985; Piaget 1967) and in social interaction with
more knowledgeable others and peers (Cole and Cole 1989; Gallimore and Tharp
1990; Vygotsky 1978; Wertsch 1985). In order to support the children's identity development and prepare them for the challenges of elementary schools, our efforts focused
on assuring that La Casa's program was developmentally and culturally appropriate. A
developmentally appropriate curriculum is responsive to the stages and phases of children's development across the cognitive, physical, social, and emotional domains. It is
also sensitive to local conditions and cultural values as well as individual children's
needs and interests (NAEYC 1997; NAEYC and NAECS/SDE 1992). A culturally appropriate curriculum incorporates children's families, languages, values, and home
cultures into classrooms in a respectful, comprehensive, and authentic manner
(Bowman 1992; Derman-Sparks 1992; Derman-Sparks and ABC Task Force 1989;
Quintero 1998). There is growing consensus in the field that "culture and language are
critical components of children's development, [and that classroom] practices cannot

be developmentally appropriate unless they are responsive to cultural and linguistic diversity" (NAEYC 1997: 4).

We discussed with teachers the implications of a constructivist framework for how 3- to 5-year-old children learn, and how teachers can support their learning. Initially at La Casa we found an over-reliance on the use of pencil-and-paper seat work and, after discussion with administrators and teachers, changes were instituted towards greater emphasis in the curriculum on providing children of all ages with numerous opportunities for hands-on learning and small group activities. For example, instead of having children count by rote memorization the numbers from one to twenty and repeat the number words after a teacher holds up a flash card, La Casa's teachers began to emphasize games and activities in which children handle concrete objects in ways that naturally teach the meaning of numbers and the usefulness of counting. Counting the number of children in one's small group on one's fingers, and then going to the kitchen to get the required number of milk glasses; or building a block tower as tall as one's friend, counting the number of blocks used, and then writing a number symbol that represents the number on a wall chart, are more meaningful activities. Teachers continue to have children practice counting to 20, and pencil-and-paper seat work is utilized in the oldest group so that children are familiar with the format before they enter kindergarten, but La Casa's children are also gaining a deeper understanding of the number concepts and the everyday uses of math in play-based activities.

The constructivist framework has also led to a redesign of some parts of La Casa classrooms so that more learning materials are placed in child-accessible locations in activity centers that provide children rich opportunities for discovery and application of new concepts and emerging skills (Dodge and Colker 1998; Hohmann and Weikart 2002; NAEYC 1997; Quintero 1998). We expected that children would feel more comfortable to explore and learn in activity centers that include familiar objects. For example, the play food in the dramatic play corner of each classroom now includes many items common to the kitchens in the children's actual homes (e.g. empty boxes of arroz con pollo mix and tins of imported Puerto Rican coffee) and the walls are decorated with photos from home, authentic shopping lists written in Spanish and in English from Puerto Rican kitchens, and bilingual menus from local restaurants. Similarly, the dress-up clothes collection used for make-believe play includes clothing that would be found in Puerto Rico (e.g. colorful lightweight clothes) and clothing that children would find familiar from its use in the La Casa community (e.g. boots and heavy hats for protection against the winter snow). Throughout the day, children are engaged with a varied assortment of culturally relevant hands-on learning materials and activities.

Teachers in constructivist classrooms, in addition to being designers of effective environments that children explore on their own, are also guides for children's learning and organizers of group experiences in which children practice new skills with the support of their peers, teachers, and other adults. Correcting an over reliance on teacher-led whole-group activities, daily schedules in La Casa classrooms needed to be reorganized to allow for a variety of groupings: one-on-one interactions between adult and child, adults working with small groups of children, and peer activities. Volunteers from the community are now utilized to offer more frequent one-on-one and small group activities led by adults. In addition to providing more individualized attention to children, the presence of positive adult role models from the La Casa community also helps to nurture the development of the children's identity. Derman-Sparks (1992) notes:

> By two years of age, children have already embarked on their lifelong task of figuring out "who I am".... Since racism makes the task of constructing a knowledgeable, confident self and group identity much more difficult for children of color, nurturing each child's positive identity and appreciation of other members of his ethnic group constitutes a primary goal of the curriculum (Derman-Sparks 1992: 125).

Another aspect of our curriculum renewal required discussion and planning of what exactly children should learn in preschool. We led a three-month group study that involved the center director and head teachers in crafting an explicit set of learning goals and activities. The center staff first reviewed both the formal and informal goals that had guided their prior teaching, examined some of the most widely used early childhood curriculum texts, investigated the expectations of local kindergarten classrooms, and then sat together in meetings twice each week to design a set of learning goals that would fit their particular children and context. Particular emphasis was placed on selecting materials, activities, and themes that strengthen the children's sense of cultural identity. For example, in addition to U.S. holidays and celebrations, La Casa has incorporated Puerto Rican national holidays, celebrations, and traditions into its curriculum for many years. Puerto Rican Independence Day has always been celebrated, as have the birthdays of famous patriots. The staff's goal setting and review of the curriculum highlighted the importance of these center traditions for preserving and building the children's self-concept and cultural knowledge, and encouraged teachers into purposeful planning of further activities of this kind.

La Casa's staff settled on the curriculum framework suggested by Dodge and Colker (1998) as a basis from which to build their own set of developmentally and culturally appropriate curricular goals. Conceptualizing development integrally across all domains, Dodge and Colker (1998) delineate the areas of self-esteem, positive attitude toward school, and cooperative pro-social behavior within the domain of socio-emotional development; learning skills, problem-solving skills, logical thinking, concepts and information, representational thinking, and language and pre-literacy skills in the cognitive domain; and gross motor skills, fine motor skills, and the use of senses in the physical domain. La Casa's staff carefully selected goals in all these areas; their curriculum now is clearly focused on the development of the whole child.

Varied daily activities woven into thematic units provide opportunities for simultaneous development across the domains. For example, one activity within one curricular theme, "The Homes We Live In", can address children's physical, cognitive, social, and emotional development simultaneously. In the block area, children may construct replicas of the floor plan of their homes or build models of the high rise apartment where they live. This block activity fosters physical development by eliciting fine motor movements, improving eye-hand coordination, and increasing dexterity. With practice, children build ever more intricate block constructions to represent their homes and neighborhoods. The activity also naturally stimulates cognitive development as children playfully explore fundamental concepts such as shape, color, size, weight, balance, and quantity. Classifying blocks by shape and color, sorting them by size or weight, utilizing a particular pattern (e.g., big, small, big, small) to build a wall, comparing relative heights of block constructions, and examining what happens to quantity when blocks are added or taken away – these activities provide the foundation of basic knowledge and skills upon which later mathematical and scientific thinking will be constructed. In addition, identity development is enhanced as discussions – resulting from child initiation or teacher-directed guidance – focus on home, family, and community. Social skills are enhanced as classmates work side-by-side, share, and resolve conflicts. Language skills develop as children hear and produce language, give and receive feedback, and negotiate meaning. La Casa's classrooms have always contained blocks, but teachers now utilize the block activities differently. The process of setting clear goals and instituting a theory-based curriculum has provided the teachers with a framework for understanding the rich developmental possibilities of hands-on play-based block activities.

In addition to our curriculum renewal efforts, a key aspect of our plan to prepare La Casa's children for success in public schools was to nurture parents' roles as partners with teachers in support of children's learning. The consultants, director, and teachers agreed that our efforts to devise a new set of goals and curriculum should be widely publicized and carefully explained to parents and families. In general, La Casa's teachers had utilized informal chats during morning drop-off and afternoon pick-up times and semiannual parent-teacher conferences to communicate with families concerning La Casa's philosophy, children's progress, and the daily activities at school. A decision was made to supplement daily informal conversations with parents by special meetings so that teachers themselves could introduce and discuss their revised classroom goals and activities and proudly present achievements. As Bowman (1992) has noted:

> Interpretation of the school's agenda to parents is as important as - perhaps more important than - many of the other tasks at which teachers spend their time. Only if parents and teachers can collaborate are children free to learn from both (Bowman 1992: 136).

Parental expectations concerning teaching and learning in preschool had to be directly addressed in these meetings. For example, many parents wanted to see preschool activities that looked like 'school' and felt reassured when they saw children completing pencil-and-paper worksheets, reciting the alphabet, and responding in chorus to flash cards. Yet, teachers were moving to de-emphasize the excessive use of these practices and to emphasize more play-based, hands-on activities. Similarly, many parents applauded teacher-led whole group activities in which children sat quietly and all appeared orderly-these activities probably reminded them of their own school experiences. Yet, teachers were changing their classroom practices to create more opportunities for children to work in small groups and often noisier and less orderly peer activities because these settings allow greater opportunity for children to learn and develop language skills by talking about what they do. At the same time children's development of age-appropriate self-control and cooperative pro-social behavior continues to be reinforced at La Casa. For example, as preschoolers move from one age group to the next, teachers focus increasingly on turn-taking and on extending the children's capacity for delaying gratification, attention-span, and self-control to sit and focus on stories read in larger groups. These aspects of social and emotional development are behavioral expectations essential for success in local elementary schools.

Along with discussions in meetings, teachers invited parents to spend more time in classrooms. This gives parents a chance to familiarize themselves with the new curriculum content and activities, and to observe the hands-on, constructivist approach to learning. Parents in turn offer their expertise and knowledge of varied themes (Moll, Diaz, Estrada and Lopes 1992). For example, the "Making Music" and "Community Helpers" themes feature many parents and family members. These volunteers actively support the teachers' work in the classroom by, for example, showing the children how to play a variety of musical instruments, teaching Spanish and English songs, and talking about their jobs.

La Casa's parents are also encouraged to support the children's academic preparation by reading to them. The center staff have developed a lending library of Spanish and English children's books that families borrow and take home to read with children. The director and teachers carefully selected developmentally and culturally appropriate book titles, and funding was donated by a local bank to purchase the first set of books, protective carrying bags, and a cabinet for storage at the center. Two parents volunteered to oversee the distribution of the books and to keep track of loans and returns. The parents appreciate and make regular use of La Casa's lending library. Currently the center director is fundraising to purchase a collection of educational toys and videos so that families may also borrow these materials for use at home.

Ceremonies that underscore the importance of education and successful completion of educational milestones within the community also bring parents together in support of children's education. For example, the center has a tradition of marking the June graduation of children in the five-year-old group and celebrating their readiness for kindergarten. Preparations begin weeks in advance: a stage is erected in the central plaza of the housing project, songs are rehearsed by each classroom for public presentation, family members contribute home-cooked food for the event, graduating children are fitted for caps and gowns, bilingual diplomas are printed, children help to prepare invitations for community leaders and of course all family members, and during the graduation ceremony as each child's name is called, diplomas are distributed by La Casa's director. The joy and pride evident in parents' and community members' faces is reflected in the bearing and outlook of these five-year olds – the graduates have accomplished something important and they are headed off to elementary school with the support of family and community.

While the graduation day is viewed as an important symbolic event at La Casa, the staff want parents to continue their engagement and to be active advocates for their children once they graduate from the preschool. La Casa offers counseling and informational meetings to parents and all community members about the public schools. Parents are informed about bilingual laws and their rights to request bilingual classroom placements for their children and to obtain information on schools offering programs in the language of their choice. The center director is also developing institutional relationships between the child care center and the local schools. For example, the director and teachers visit nearby schools to meet with kindergarten teachers, and children from La Casa's oldest group take tours of these schools. In addition, local teachers and school officials have been invited to community meetings at La Casa where they explain their schools' goals, curricula and procedures to be followed for the kindergarten registration. Developing these relationships places La Casa, as an institution, in a better position to intervene in the future with schools on behalf of its graduates and to bolster families' individual advocacy efforts.

5.   Discussion

Puerto Rican children in the U.S. face an urgent situation. Decades of achievement and dropout data point to an alarming picture of academic performance of Puerto Rican children in public schools. In this chapter we have described a community-based effort to alter the general pattern of Puerto Rican academic failure by designing a preschool program that specifically addresses their children's needs. The community members in this low-income housing project had long believed that the early childhood years are essential for long-term school success and established La Casa de los Niños three decades ago. Yet, the initial organic relationship between the community and preschool had eroded over time, and the existing program was no longer adequately supporting the children's bilingual skills, cultural identity, and academic preparation.

A theory-based intervention at La Casa illuminated the connections across the areas of concern and permitted teachers to address them in a systematic manner. Changes in classroom language policy aimed at fostering children's bilingual skills also promote bicultural and academic development and vice versa. A 50-50 language model and an alternate day approach to bilingual instruction supports Spanish-dominant and English-dominant children's academic proficiency in their dominant language (Legarreta 1977; 1979). Children's academic proficiency in the dominant language can be transferred to the nondominant language in programs offering extensive and prolonged support for both languages and systematic teaching of decontextualized language skills (Cummins 1981, 1986, 1989, 2000; Lanauze and Snow 1989). Furthermore, equal recognition and reinforcement of Spanish and English in the classroom communicates equal status of both languages. In these 'additive' educational contexts children can gain English and Spanish skills without the threat of losing one or the

other language and feel secure to identify with both cultures without the fear of sever-
ing connection with either (Lambert 1981; Cummins 1986, 2000; Navarro 1985; Ruiz
1984). Language programs with an additive orientation have been empirically documented to promote bilingual and bicultural development of language minority children in varied settings including Ireland, Scotland, Wales, Canada, New Zealand, and
Australia (Beykont 1997b, 2008; Cazden, Snow and Heise-Baigorria 1990; Cummins
1989, 2000; Clyne 1991, 2005; García, Skutnabb-Kangas and Torres-Guzmán 2006;
Hornberger 1998; Fishman 1991; Hatoss and Shelly 2009; May 2001; McCarty 2002;
Skutnabb-Kangas 1981; Spolsky 2002).

The new curriculum at La Casa builds on Puerto Rican children's strengths, i.e.
what they know, what they can do, what they have, what they are interested in, and
what they are curious about. Teachers capitalize on children's varied language skills
and knowledge base by reorganizing classrooms to permit participation in academically challenging activities in small group, large group, and individual play settings. A
shift away from sole reliance on paper-and-pencil activities allows children to follow
their natural curiosity, pursue their varied interests, and construct new understandings in hands-on activities in learning centers. The use of culturally familiar materials
and language helps children learn unfamiliar content (Baker 2001; Brisk 2006, 2008;
Clarke 1997; Nielsen and Beykont 1997). The knowledge base of parents and community members enriches the program when they act as curricular resources, e.g., by
bringing their skills and experience to bear on school wide themes, and reading with
their children at home and in school (Ada 1995, 1997; Delgado-Gaitan 1990; Hornberger 1990; Moll 1992; Moll and Diaz 1985; Moll et al. 1992a, 1992b).

The process of change at La Casa was unique in many ways. Typically, policy and
program changes are handed down by administrators or outside consultants. At La
Casa, due to the director's commitment to a community-based process, all teachers
and parents were involved in the needs assessment and goal setting phase (Johnson-
Beykont, in prep.). Staff then critically examined program strengths and weaknesses
and made decisions that led to modifications in classroom language use and curriculum. This participatory approach has increased the likelihood that the new program at
La Casa is culturally appropriate and responsive to the local context and children. An
inclusive process, though time consuming, has created a shared sense of ownership for
the changes and the collective will to carry through with the center's ambitious plans.

While attending preschool, La Casa's children are protected from some of the most
virulently derogatory and assimilationist influences rampant in U.S. society. When
they meet the mainstream full force in the primary schools outside the tightly-knit
housing project community, the children of La Casa will be abruptly confronted by a
wave of culturally demeaning messages. They will quickly learn that Standard English
is the language of power and the Spanish language and Puerto Rican culture are devalued in the U.S. schools. Even if children attend bilingual programs, these placements
will be temporary. A powerful array of forces push children to stop using Spanish and
thereby break an intimate connection with their culture. The full promise of bilingual

programs cannot be realized when assimilationist school language policies and elementary and secondary programs undermine Puerto Rican children's cultural, linguistic, and academic strengths, and strip them of their cultural and linguistic resources.

U.S. schools generally work best for middle-class white students who speak standard English at home and in their immediate communities. These children have long benefited from education in preschools and elementary and high schools that offer classroom pedagogy that is culturally responsive to middle class whites and reinforces their strengths – their cultural knowledge, home language and discourse styles, as well as home culture (see Garcia 1993 and 2001 for reviews). All children deserve an educationally supportive environment to realize their full potential. That is what the staff and parents have tried to create at La Casa-an educational program designed to support the language and identity development of Puerto Rican children.

The La Casa example presents a model of self-directed community action to protect and extend the cultural and linguistic resources of Puerto Rican children in an enrichment bilingual preschool program. Efforts such as those instituted at La Casa may help to forestall language shift and to imbue children with a stronger sense of pride in their cultural heritage before they enter mainstream elementary schools. A three-year preschool program, however, is much less than what Puerto Rican children need. Additional community-based programs that promote success in school and sustain connection to home languages and culture are necessary to guide young people throughout the elementary and secondary school years. Recognizing this issue, the La Casa staff and neighborhood activists are developing plans to revitalize the community's after-school, weekend, and summer programs for schoolage children and teens. These programs will offer ongoing academic and bilingual language support within an additive framework that builds on children's knowledge base, language skills, and pride in Puerto Rican culture. With success in its preschool efforts, La Casa has a solid base from which to grow these new programs with the trust and active support of the parents and community members.

Children who live near La Casa de los Niños and in many other language minority communities in the U.S. and around the world face an urgent situation. Too many of our young confront a societal ethos that demeans their bilingualism, their culture, and their families. They will need pride in their language and culture, strong ties to the community, a solid academic base, and ongoing academic and language support for bilingual proficiency to weather the storm and resist the assimilationist tide. Preschools are certainly not the sole answer. All schools must change to better meet the needs of diverse student populations. Changes in schools will only come through political struggle to make schooling more responsive to all children and communities, and to alter negative societal attitudes toward bilingualism and multiculturalism. These are long-term solutions, yet there is an urgency that faces us. La Casa's enrichment bilingual preschool program is an example of what one community is attempting.

References

Abu-Rabia, Salim. 2001. "Testing the interdependence hypothesis among native adult bilingual Russian-English students." *Journal of PsycholinguisticResearch* 30(4): 437–455.

—. 2004. "Reading ability in Ethiopian learners of Hebrew: How important is phonemic awareness? *Language, Culture and Curriculum* 17(3): 196–202.

Ada, Alma Flor. 1995. "Fostering the home-school connection." In *Reclaiming Our Voices: Bilingual Education, Critical Pedagogy and Praxis*, J. Frederickson (ed.). Ontario, CA: California Association for Bilingual Education. Retrieved July 31, 2009 from www.osi.hu/iep/minorities/resbook1/Fostering.htm.

Ada, Alma Flor. 1997. "Mother-tongue literacy as a bridge between home and school cultures." In *The Power of Two Languages: Literacy and Biliteracy for Spanish Speaking Students*, Josefina Villamil Tinajero and Alma Flor Ada (eds), 209–219. New York: MacMillan/McGraw-Hill.

Alba, Richard and Nee, Victor. 2005. "Rethinking assimilation theory for a new era of immigration." In *The New Immigration: An Interdisciplinary Reader*, Marcelo Suarez-Orozco, Carola Suarez-Orozco and Desiree Qin-Hilliard (eds), 35–66. Denver, Colorado: OLIN e-pub.

ASPIRA Institute for Policy Research. 1993. *Facing the Facts: The State of Hispanic Education*. Washington, DC: ASPIRA.

Baker, Colin. 2001. *Foundations of Bilingual Education and Bilingualism* [3rd ed.]. Clevedon, UK: Multilingual Matters.

Baratz-Snowden, Joan, Rock, Donald A., Pollack, Judith and Wilder, Gita Z. 1988. *Parent Preference Study*. Final Report. ERIC Clearinghouse. ED320444.

Berriz, Berta R. 2000. "Raising children's cultural voices: Strategies for developing literacy in two languages." In *Lifting Every Voice: Politics and Pedagogy of Bilingualism*, Zeynep F. Beykont (ed.), 71–94. Cambridge: Harvard Education Pub.

Beykont, Zeynep F. 1993. "The choice of language policies and programs: A comparative view." *Special Studies in Comparative Education* 31: 125–190.

—. 1994. *Academic Progress of a Nondominant Group: Education of Puerto Rican Children in New York City's Late-Exit Bilingual Programs*. Doctoral dissertation submitted to Harvard University: Cambridge, MA.

—. 1996. *Language Based Oppression in Educational Organizations*. Final Report submitted to the Community Fellows Program, MIT: Cambridge, MA.

—. 1997a. "Refocusing school language policy discussions." In *International Handbook of Education and Development: Preparing Schools, Students, and Nations for the Twenty-first Century*, William K. Cummings and Noel F. McGinn (eds), 263–282. New York: Pergamon.

—. 1997b. "School-language policy decisions for nondominant language groups." In *Quality Education for All: Community-Oriented Approaches*, H. Dean Nielsen and William K. Cummings (eds), 79–122. New York: Garland.

— (ed.). 2000. *Lifting Every Voice: Pedagogy and Politics of Bilingualism*. Cambridge, MA: Harvard Education Pub.

— (ed.). 2002a. *The Power of Culture: Teaching Across Language Difference*. Cambridge, MA: Harvard Education Pub.

—. 2002b. "English-only language policies in the United States." *Proceedings of the World Congress on Language Policies*. LINGUAPAX, UNESCO: Barcelona, Spain. Retrieved June 30, 2008 from http://www.linguapax.org/congres/taller/taller1/Beykont.html.

—. 2008. "Heritage language maintenance in an English-dominant context: A study of Turkish youth in Victoria." Paper presented at Heritage Language Learner Conference, December 6–9, Cape Town University, South Africa.

Bialystok, Ellen and Cummins, Jim. 1991. "Language, cognition, and education of bilingual children." In *Language Processing in Bilingual Children*, Ellen Bialystok (ed.), 222–232. Cambridge: Cambridge University Press.

Brisk, Maria. 2006. *Bilingual Education: From Compensatory to Quality Schooling* [2nd ed.]. Mahwah, N.J.: Lawrence Erlbaum Associates.

—. 2008. *Inclusive Pedagogy for English Language Learners: A Handbook of Research-Informed Practices*. New York: Lawrence Erlbaum Associates.

Bowman, Barbara T. 1992. "Reaching potentials of minority children through developmentally and culturally appropriate programs." In *Reaching Potentials: Appropriate Curriculum and Assessment for Young Children, Vol. 1*, Sue Bredekamp and Teresa Rosegrant (eds), 128–138. Washington, DC: National Association for the Education of Young Children.

Cafferty, Pastora San Juan and Rivera-Martinez, Carmen. 1981. *The Politics of Language: The Dilemma of Bilingual Education for Puerto Ricans*. Boulder, CO: West View Press.

Cazden, Courtney, Snow, Catherine E. and Heise-Baigorria, Cornelia. 1990. *Language Planning in Preschool Education with Annotated Bibliography*. Report prepared at request of Consultative Group on Early Childhood Care & Development, UNICEF.

Christian, Donna. 1994. "Two way bilingual education: Students learning through two languages." *The National Center for Research on Cultural Diversity and Second Language Learning, Educational Practice Report, 12*. Washington, D. C.: Center for Applied Linguistics.

Clachar, Arlene. 1997. "Students' reflections on the social, political, and ideological role of English in Puerto Rico." *Hispanic Journal of Behavioral Sciences* 19 (4): 461–478.

Clarke, Pamela. 1997. "School curriculum in the periphery: The case of South India." In *Quality Education for All: Community-Oriented Approaches*, H. Dean Nielsen and William K. Cummings (eds), 123–138. New York: Garland.

Clyne, Michael. 1991. *Community Languages: The Australian Experience*. Cambridge: Cambridge University Press.

—. 2005. *Australia's Language Potential*. Sydney: University of New South Wales Press.

Cohen, Elizabeth G. 1984. "Talking and working together." In *The Social Context of Instruction: Group Organization and Group Processes*, Penelope L. Peterson, Louise C. Wilkinson and Maureen Hallinan (eds), 171–187. New York: Academic Press.

—. 1986. *Designing Group Work: Strategies for the Heterogenous Classroom*. New York: Teachers College Press.

Cole, Michael and Cole, Sheila R. 1989. *The Development of Children*. New York: Scientific American Books.

Coleman, James S. 1981. "Foreword." In *The Politics of Language: The Dilemma of Bilingual Education for Puerto Ricans*, Pastora San Juan Cafferty and Carmen Rivera-Martinez (eds), 1–11. Boulder, CO: Westview Press.

Collier, Virginia P. 1992. "A synthesis of studies examining long-term language minority student data on academic achievement." *Bilingual Research Journal* 16 (1 & 2): 187–212.

—. 1995. *Acquiring a Second Language for School*. Washington, DC: National Clearinghouse for Bilingual Education.

Collins, Ray and Ribeiro, Rose. 2004. "Toward an early care and education agenda for Hispanic children." *Early Childhood Research and Practice* 6 (2). Retrieved http://ecrp.uiuc.edu/v6n2/collins.html.

Crawford, James. 1991. *Bilingual Education: History, Politics, Theory and Practice.* NJ: Bilingual Education Services, Inc.

—. 1997. *The Official English Question.* Retrieved June 30, 2008 from http://ourworld.compuserve.com/homepages/jWCRAWFORD/question.htm.

—. 1998. "Language politics in the U.S.A.: The paradox of bilingual education." *Social Justice* 25 (3): 1–13.

—. 2000. *At War with Diversity: U.S. Language Policy in an Age of Anxiety.* Multilingual Matters: Clevedon.

Cummins, Jim. 1981. "The role of primary language development in promoting educational success for language minority students." In *Schooling and Language Minority Students: A Theoretical Framework,* California State Department of Education (ed.), 3–49. Sacramento: California State Department of Education, Office of Bilingual Bicultural Education.

—. 1986. "Empowering minority students: A framework for intervention." *Harvard Educational Review* 56: 18–36.

—. 1989. *Empowering Minority Students.* Sacramento, CA: California Association for Bilingual Education.

—. 1991. "Interdependence of first- and second-language proficiency in bilingual children." In *Language Processing in Bilingual Children,* Ellen Bialystok (ed.), 70–89. Cambridge: Cambridge University Press.

—. 2000. *Language, Power and Pedagogy: Bilingual Children in the Crossfire.* Clevedon, UK: Multilingual Matters.

Delgado-Gaitan, Concha. 1990. *Literacy for Empowerment: The Role of Parents in Children's Education.* New York: Falmer Press.

Del Valle, Sandra. 1998. Bilingual education for Puerto Ricans in New York City: From hope to compromise." In *Harvard Educational Review,* Ricardo Dobles and José Antonio Segarra (eds), 68 (2): 193–217.

Derman-Sparks, Louise. 1992. "Reaching potentials through antibias, multicultural curriculum." In *Reaching Potentials: Appropriate Curriculum and Assessment for Young Children, Vol. 1,* Sue Bredekamp and Teresa Rosegrant (eds), 114–127. Washington, DC: NAEYC.

Derman-Sparks, Louise. 1989. *Anti-bias Curriculum: Tools For Empowering Young Children.* Washington, DC: NAEYC.

Diaz, Stephen, Moll, Luis C. and Mehan, Hugh. 1986. "Sociocultural resources in instruction: A context-specific approach." In *Beyond Language: Social and Cultural Factors in Schooling Language Minority Students,* Shirley Heath (ed.), 187–230. Los Angeles: Evaluation, Dissemination and Assessment Center, California State University.

Dickinson, David K. and Snow, Catherine E. 1987. "Interrelationships among prereading and oral language skills in kindergartners from two social classes." *Research on Childhood Education Quarterly* 2: 1–25.

Dickinson, David K. and Tabors, Patton O. 1991. "Early literacy: Linkages between home, school, and literacy achievement at age five." *Journal of Research in Childhood Education* 6: 30–46.

Dobles, Ricardo and Segarro, José Antonio (eds). 1998. "Introduction." *Harvard Educational Review* 68 (2): vii-xv.

Dodge, Diane. T. and Colker, Laura J. 1998. *The Creative Curriculum for Early Childhood* [3rd ed.]. Washington, DC: Teaching Strategies.

Dolson, David P. and Mayer, Jan. 1992. "Longitudinal study of three program models for language-minority students: A critical examination of reported findings." *Bilingual Research Journal* 16 (1 & 2): 105–157.

Donahue, Thomas S. 1995. "American language policy and compensatory opinion." In *Power and Inequality in Language Education*, James W. Tollefson (ed.), 112–141. Cambridge, UK: Cambridge University Press.

Fishman, Joshua A. 1966. *Language Loyalty in the U.S.: The Maintenance and Perpetuation of Non-English Mother Tongues by American Ethnic and Religious Groups*. The Hague, The Netherlands: Mouton & Co.

—. 1991. *Reversing Language Shift: Theoretical and Empirical Foundations of Assistance to Threatened Languages*. Clevedon, UK: Multilingual Matters.

— (ed.). 2001. *Can Threatened Languages be Saved? Reversing Language Shift, Revisited: A 21st Century Perspective*. Clevedon, UK: Multilingual Matters.

Flavell, John H. 1985. *Cognitive Development* [2nd ed.]. Englewood Cliffs, NJ: Prentice Hall.

Freeman, Rebecca D. 1996. "Dual-language planning at Oyster bilingual school: 'It's much more than language.'" *TESOL Quarterly* 30: 557–582.

Gallimore, Ronald and Tharp, Roland. 1990. "Teaching mind in society: Teaching, schooling, and literate discourse." In *Vygotsky and Education: Instructional Implications and Applications of Sociohistorical Psychology*, Luis Moll (ed.), 175–205. Cambridge, England: Cambridge University Press.

Garcia, Eugene E. 1993. "Language, culture, and education." Review of Research in Education 19: 51–98.

—. 2001. *Hispanics Education in the United States: Raíces y alas*. Lanham, ML: Rowman & Littlefield Publishers, Inc.

García, Ofelia, Skutnabb-Kangas, Tobe and Torres-Guzmán, Maria (eds). 2006. *Imagining Multilingual Schools: Languages in Education and Globalization*. Clevedon: Multilingual Matters.

Gee, James P. 2002. "Literacies, identities and discourses." In *Developing Advanced Literacy in First and Second Languages: Meaning with Power*, Mary J. Schleppegrell and M. Cecilia Colombi (eds), 159–175. Mahwah, NJ: Lawrence Erlbaum.

Gibson, Margaret A. 1991. "Minorities and schooling: Some implications." In *Minority Status and Schooling: A Comparative Study of Immigrant and Involuntary Minorities*, Margaret A. Gibson and John Ogbu (eds), 44–62. New York: Garland.

Gibson, Margaret A. and Ogbu, John (eds). 1991. *Minority Status and Schooling: A Comparative Study of Immigrant and Involuntary Minorities*. New York: Garland.

Gonzalez, Andrew. 1996. "Evaluating bilingual education in the Philippines: Towards a multidimensional model of evaluation in language planning." In *Readings in Philippine Sociolinguistics* [2nd ed.], Maria Lourdes S. Bautista (ed.), 327–340. Manila: De La Salle University Press.

Gonzalez, Josué M. 1975. "Coming of age in bilingual/bicultural education: A historical perspective." *Inequality in Education* 19: 5–17.

Hakuta, Kenji. 2000. "How long does it take English learners to attain proficiency." *University of California Linguistic Minority Research Institute. Policy Reports*. Retrieved June 30, 2008 from http://repositories.cdlib.org/lmri/pr/hakuta.

Hatoss, Aniko and Tulloch, Shelly. 2009. "Language maintenance and identity among Sudanese-Australian refugee-background youth." *Journal of Multicultural and Multilingual Development* 30 (2): 127–144.

Hornberger, Nancy. 1998. "Language policy, language education, language rights: Indigenous, immigrant, and international." *Language in Society* 27: 439–458.

—. 1990. "Creating successful learning contexts for bilingual literacy." *Teachers College Record* 92 (2): 212–229.

Hohmann, Mary and Weikart, David P. 2002. *Educating Young Children: Active Learning Practices for Preschool and Child Care Programs* [2nd ed.]. Ypsilanti, MI: High/Scope Press.

Jacob, Evelyn. 1984. "Learning literacy through play: Puerto Rican kindergarten children." In *Awakening To Literacy,* Hillel Goelman, Antoinette A. Oberg and Frank Smith (eds), 73–86. Exeter, NH: Heinemann Educational Books.

Jipson, Janice. 1991. "Developmentally appropriate practice: culture, curriculum, connections." *Early-Education-and-Development* 2 (2): 120-136.

Johnson-Beykont, Bruce. forthcoming. "A participatory approach to program renewal: Experiences in a community-based bilingual preschool."

Johnson-Beykont, Bruce and Beykont, Zeynep F. 1998. Formative Evaluation Study of a Bilingual Community-based Preschool Program: Final Report. Unpublished report.

Kagan, Spencer. 1986. "Cooperative learning and sociocultural factors in schooling." In *Beyond Language: Social and Cultural Factors in Schooling Language Minority Students,* Shirley Heath (ed.), 231–285. Los Angeles: Evaluation, Dissemination and Assessment Center, California State University.

Krashen, Stephen D. 1982. *Principles and Practice in Second Language Acquisition.* Oxford, England: Pergamon Press.

—. 1985. *The Input Hypothesis: Issues and Implications.* New York: Longman Press.

—. 1996. *Under Attack: The Case against Bilingual Education.* Culver City, California: Language Education Associates.

Kwong, Katy M. 2000. "Bilingualism equals access: The case of Chinese high school students." In *Lifting Every Voice: Politics and Pedagogy of Bilingualism*, Zeynep F. Beykont (ed.), 43–53. Cambridge, MA: Harvard Education Pub.

Lambert, William E. 1981. "Bilingualism: Its nature and significance." *Bilingual Education Series 10.* Washington, D.C.: The Center for Applied Linguistics.

Lanauze, Milagros E. and Snow, Catherine E. 1989. "The relation between first and second-language writing skills." *Linguistics and Education* 1: 323–339.

Laosa, Luis. 2000. "Nonlanguage characteristics of instructional services for language-minority students." *NCBE Resource Collection Series 20.* Washington, D.C.: The George Washington University.

Legarreta, Dorothy. 1977. "Language choice in bilingual classrooms." *TESOL Quarterly* 11 (1): 9–16.

—. 1979. "The effects of program models on language acquisition by Spanish speaking children." *TESOL Quarterly* 13 (4): 521–534

Lindholm, Kathryn. 1990. "Bilingual immersion education: Criteria for program development." In *Bilingual Education: Issues and Strategies*, Amado M. Padilla, Halford H. Fairchild and Concepción M. Valdez (eds), 91–105. Newbury Park, CA: Corwin Press.

Lindholm-Leary, Kathryn J. 2001. *Dual Language Education.* Clevedon, UK: Multilingual Matters.

—. 2005. "The rich promise of two-way immersion." *Educational Leadership* 62 (4): 56–59.

López, Lisa M. and Greenfield, Daryl B. 2004. "The cross-language transfer of phonological skills of Hispanic head start children." *Bilingual Research Journal* 28: 1–8.

Macedo, Donaldo. 1993. "Literacy for stupidification: The pedagogy of big lies." *Harvard Educational Review* 63(2): 183–207.

—. 2000. "Decolonizing English only: The democratic power of bilingualism." In *Lifting Every Voice: Pedagogy and Politics of Bilingualism*, Zeynep F. Beykont (ed.), 21–42. Cambridge, MA: Harvard Education Pub.

Masso, James. 2003. *Teaching and Learning in a Multicultural Classroom.* South Melbourne: James Nicholas Pub.

Maxwell-Jolly, Julie and Gándara, Patricia. 2002. "A quest for quality: Providing qualified teachers for California's English learners." In *The Power of Culture: Teaching Across Language Difference*, Zeynep F. Beykont (ed.), 43–70. Cambridge: Harvard Education Pub.

May, Stephen. 2001. *Language and Minority Rights*. London: Longman.

McGroarty, Mary. 1989. "The benefits of cooperative learning arrangements in second language instruction." *NABE Journal* 13 (2): 127–143.

McLaughlin, Barry. 1985. *Second Language Acquisition in Childhood, Vol. 2: School-age Children* [2nd ed.]. Hillsdale, NJ: Lawrence Erlbaum.

Mehan, Hugh. 1979. *Learning Lessons*. Cambridge: Harvard University Press.

Moll, Luis C. 1992. "Bilingual classroom studies and community analysis: Some recent trends." *Educational Researcher* 21 (2): 20–24.

Moll, Luis C. and Diaz, Stephen. 1985. "Ethnographic pedagogy: Promoting effective bilingual instruction." In *Advances in Bilingual Education Research*, Eugene E. Garcia and Raymond V. Padilla (eds), 127–149. Tucson: The University of Arizona Press.

Moll, Luis C., Diaz, Stephen, Estrada, Elette and Lopes, Lawrence M. 1992a. "Making contexts: The social construction of lessons in two languages." In *Cross Cultural Literacy*, Marietta Saravia-Shore and Steven F. Arvizu (eds), 339–366. New York, London: Garland.

Moll, Luis C., Amanti, Cathy, Neff, Deborah and Gonzalez, Norma. 1992b. "Funds of knowledge for teaching: Using a qualitative approach to connect homes and classrooms." *Theory into Practice* XXXI (2): 132–141.

National Association for the Education of Young Children (NAEYC). 1997. "NAEYC position statement: Developmentally appropriate practice in early childhood programs serving children from birth through age 8." In *Developmentally Appropriate Practice in Early Childhood Programs* [revised ed.], Sue Bredekamp and Carol Copple (eds), 3–30. Washington, DC: NAEYC.

National Association for the Education of Young Children and National Association of Early Childhood Specialists in State Departments of Education (NAEYC). 1992. "Guidelines for appropriate curriculum content and assessment in programs serving children ages 3 through 8." In *Reaching Potentials: Appropriate Curriculum and Assessment for Young Children, Vol. 1.*, Sue Bredekamp and Teresa Rosegrant (eds), 9–27. Washington, D.C.: NAEYC & NAECS/SDE.

NCES National Center for Education Statistics (NCES). 1995. *The Educational Progress of Hispanic Students*. Washington, D.C.: United States Department of Education, Office of Educational Research and Improvement.

National Center for Education Statistics (NCES). 2009. *Participation in Education: Elementary/ Secondary Education*. Retrieved September 30, 2009 from http://nces.ed.gov/programs/coe/2009/section1/indicators08.asp.

Navarro, Richard A. 1985. "The problems of language, education and society: Who decides?" In *Advances in Bilingual Education Research*, Eugene E. Garcia and Raymond V. Padilla (eds), 289–313. Tucson: The University of Arizona Press.

Nettle, Daniel and Romaine, Suzanne. 2000. *Vanishing Voices: The Extinction of the World's Languages*. Oxford: Oxford University Press.

New York Board of Education. 1997. *Programs Serving Gifted And Talented Students in New York City Public Scho54ols, 1995–1996*. New York: NY.

Nielsen, Dean H. and Beykont, Zeynep F. 1997. "Reaching the periphery: Toward a community-oriented approach." In *Quality Education for All: Community Oriented Approaches*, H. Dean Nielsen and William K. Cummings (eds), 247–267. New York: Garland.

Nieto, Sonia. 1998. "Fact and fiction: Stories of Puerto Ricans in U.S. schools." *Harvard Educational Review* 68(2): 133–163.

—. 2000a. "Bringing bilingual education out of the basement and other imperatives for teacher education." In *Lifting Every Voice: Politics and Pedagogy of Bilingualism*, Zeynep F. Beykont (ed.), 187–207. Cambridge: Harvard Education Pub.

—. 2000b. "Puerto Rican students in U.S. schools: A brief history." In *Puerto Rican Students in U.S. Schools*, Sonia Nieto (ed.), 5–38. New York: Routledge.

Ovando, Carlos J. and McLaren, Peter (eds). 2000. *The Politics of Multiculturalism and Bilingual Education: Students and Teachers Caught in the Cross Fire*. Boston: McGraw-Hill.

Paulston, Christina B. 1974. *Implications of Language Learning Theory for Language Planning: Concerns in Bilingual Education*. Arlington, VA: Center for Applied Linguistics.

Pena-Hughes, Eva and Solis, Juan. 1980. *ABC's*. McAllen, Texas: McAllen Independent School District.

President's Advisory Commission on Educational Excellence for Hispanic Americans (1996). *Our Nation on the Fault Line: Hispanic American Education*. Washington, D.C.: U.S. Government Printing Office.

Piaget, Jean. 1967. *Six Psychological Studies*. New York: Random House.

Quintero, Elizabeth. 1998. "Developmentally appropriate practice: Rethinking the preschool curriculum with Latino families." In *Educating Latino students: A Guide to Successful Practice*, Maria L. Gonzalez, Ana Huerta-Macias and Josefina V. Tinajero (eds), 63–86. Lancaster, PA: Technomic Pub.

Reyes, Xaé Alicia. 2000. "Return migrant students: Yankee go home?" In *Puerto Rican Students in U.S. Schools*, Sonia Nieto (ed.), 39–68. New York: Routledge.

Roller, Cathy M. 1988. "Transfer of cognitive academic competence and L2 reading in a rural Zimbabwean primary school." *TESOL Quarterly* 22 (2): 303-318.

Ruiz, Richard. 1984. "Orientations in language planning." *NABE Journal* 8 (2): 15-34.

Santiago Santiago, Isaura. 1986. "Aspira v. Board of Education revisited." *American Journal of Education* 95 (1): 149–199.

Saville-Troike, Muriel. 1978. *A Guide to Culture in the Classroom*. Rosslyn, VA: National Clearinghouse for Bilingual Education.

Snow, Catherine E. 1991. "The theoretical basis for relationships between language and literacy in development." *Journal of Research in Childhood Education* 6 (1): 5–10.

Souza, Heloisa. 2000. "Language loss and language gain in the Brazilian community: The role of schools and families." In *Lifting Every Voice: Politics and Pedagogy of Bilingualism*, Zeynep F. Beykont (ed.), 7–20. Cambridge: Harvard Education Pub.

Stefanakis, Evangeline H. 2000. "Teachers' judgments do count: Assessing bilingual students." In *Lifting Every Voice: Politics and Pedagogy of Bilingualism*, Zeynep F. Beykont (ed.), 139–160. Cambridge: Harvard Education Pub.

Spolsky, Bernard. 2002. "Prospects for the survival of the Navajo language: A reconsideration." *Anthropology and Education Quarterly* 33(2): 139–162.

Swain, Merill. 1985. "Communicative competence: Some roles of comprehensible input and comprehensible output in its development." In *Input in Second Language Acquisition*, Susan M. Gass and Carolyn Madden (eds), 235–256. Rowley, MA: Newbury House.

—. 1995. "Three functions of output in second language learning." In *Principle and Practice in Applied Linguistics*, Guy Cook and Barbara Seidlhofer (eds), 125–144. Oxford: Oxford University Press.

—. 1996. "Discovering successful second language teaching strategies and practices: From programme evaluation to classroom experimentation." *Journal of Multilingual and Multicultural Development* 17(2): 89–105.

Thomas, Wayne P. and Collier, Virginia P. 1997. *School Effectiveness for Language Minority Students*. Washington, D.C.: National Clearinghouse for Bilingual Education.

U.S. Department of Education. 2002. *The Growing Numbers of Limited English Proficient Students 1992/1993–2002/2003*. Washington, D.C.: Office of English Language Acquisition, Language Enhancement and Academic Achievement for Limited English Proficient Students (OELA).

Veltman, Calvin J. 1983. *Language Shift in the US*. The Hague: Mouton.

—. 2000. "The American linguistic mosaic: Understanding language shift in the United States." In *New Immigrants in the United States: Readings for Second Language Educators*, Sandra L. McKay and Sau-Ling C. Wong (eds), 58–93. Cambridge, UK: Cambridge University Press.

Verhoeven, Ludo. T. (1987). Literacy in a second language context: Teaching immigrant children to read, *Educational Review* 39 (3): 245–261.

—. 1994. "Transfer in bilingual development: The linguistic interdependence hypothesis revisited." *Language Learning* 44 (3): 379–415.

—. 2007. "Early bilingualism, language transfer, and phonological awareness." *Applied Psycholinguistics* 28 (3): 425–439.

Vygotsky, Lev S. 1978. *Mind in Society*. Cambridge, MA: Harvard University Press.

Walsh, Catherine E. 1990. *Pedagogy and the Struggle for Voice: Issues of Language, Power, and Schooling for Puerto Ricans*. Westport, Connecticut: Bergin& Garvey.

—. 2000. "The struggle of 'imagined communities' in school: identification, survival, and belonging for Puerto Ricans." In *Puerto Rican Students in U.S. Schools*, Sonia Nieto (ed.), 97–114. New York: Routledge.

Werstch, James. 1985. *Vygotsky and the Social Formation of the Mind*. Cambridge, MA: Harvard University Press.

Wong Fillmore, Lily. 1991. "When learning a second language means losing the first." *Early Childhood Research Quarterly* 6: 323–346.

—. 2000. "Loss of family languages: Should educators be concerned?" *Theory into Practice* 39 (4): 203–210.

Wong Fillmore, Lily and Snow, Catherine, E. 2000. What *Teachers Need to Know about Language*. Retrieved June 30, 2008 from http://www.cal.org/ericcll/teachers/teachers.pdf.

Wong Fillmore, Lily and Valadez, Concepcion. 1986. "Teaching bilingual learners." In *Handbook of Research on Teaching* [3rd ed.], Merlin C. Wittock (ed.), 648–685. New York: Macmillan.

Zavala, Maria V. 2000. "Puerto Rican identity: What's language got to do with it?" In *Puerto Rican Students in U.S. Schools*, S. Nieto (ed.), 115–136. New York: Routledge.

Zentella, Ana C. 1997. *Growing up Bilingual*. Oxford, England: Basil Blackwell.

—. 2005. *Language and Literacy in Latino Families and Communities*. New York: Teachers' College Press.

CHAPTER 19

How language affects two components of racial prejudice?

A socio-psychological approach to linguistic relativism

Michał Bilewicz* and Agnieszka Bocheńska

1. Introduction

The impact of language on human cognition has become an important problem both for psychologists and for linguists. According to the hypothesis of linguistic relativity, language constrains human cognition (Whorf 1956; Gumperz and Levinson 1996; Stapel and Semin 2007). Thus, users of different languages have different cognitive systems and, in consequence, perceive the same objects in different ways. In the times of increased trans-national mobility the problem of cognitive consequences of these processes seems socially relevant and remains still unresolved. This necessitates research by social psychologists, sociologists and linguists into attitudes, cognitions and emotions of foreign language learners, who adapt to foreign cultures via the acquisition and use of these languages. The linguistic relativity hypothesis provides a unique theoretical framework for such studies.

2. The linguistic relativity hypothesis

The linguistic relativity hypothesis makes two main claims: (1) languages, especially those of different language families, differ in important ways from one another and (2) the structure and lexicon of our language shapes the way we conceptualize and perceive reality. These two claims, taken together, form the basis of the relativist standpoint: human perceptions of the world are constrained by different spoken languages, or as Whorf puts it, "We dissect nature along lines laid down by our native languages.

* This research was supported by the Polish Ministry of Science and Higher Education Grant N N106 0886 33 "Psychological Threat and Intergroup Relations" (director: Mirosław Kofta). Correspondence should be addressed to bilewicz@psych.uw.edu.pl.

The categories and types that we isolate from the world of phenomena we do not find there because they stare every observer in the face; on the contrary, the world is presented in a kaleidoscopic flux of impressions which has to be organized by our minds – and this means largely by the linguistic systems in our minds" (1956: 213).

The linguistic relativity hypothesis has stirred up much discussion among linguists (see Gumperz and Levinson 1996), however it has not attracted much attention of social psychologists, who should be even more interested in verifying its claims (for some recent exceptions see Stapel and Semin 2007; Holtgraves and Kashima 2008). Until now there have been no attempts to discuss the question of linguistic relativism in relation to the most important phenomena of political psychology: prejudice, discrimination, stereotyping, racism and xenophobia. The present paper discusses an issue that seems untouched by social psychologists: the impact of language on the cognitive and affective component of prejudice. Studying bilinguals who accommodate to their second language with their cognitive structure gives a unique opportunity to discuss the most important phenomena of linguistic relativity.

3.   Bilingualism, code-switching and its context

Researchers give several definitions of bilingualism. According to the classic approach, bilingualism is "native-like control of two languages" (Bloomfield 1935: 56). A more precise definition has been proposed by Macnamara (1966), who understands bilingualism as possession of at least one of the language skills (listening, speaking, reading and writing) in a second language, even if such skills are minimally developed.

Language acquisition seems to be impossible without acquisition of the culture transmitted by this language. Therefore, acquisition of two languages (L1 and L2) by bilingual subjects means being somehow affected by two different cultures (Scheu 2000). Linguistic groups vary in terms of distinctive traits such as ethnic vivacity and, what follows from it, linguistic spontaneity. It means that in situations of conflict they act like distinct entities (Bourhis and Giles 1977). Users of L1 and L2 belong in consequence not only to two different linguistic, but also social groups. They can take different attitudes towards these two groups, and often treat speakers of L1 as an in-group and speakers of L2 as an out-group. Code-switching from L1 to L2 (or vice versa) in interaction with out-group members can express changing attitudes towards these out-group members.

Code-switching is considered a specific kind of language variation within bilingual discourse. As code-switching we understand the use of different languages or language varieties within a single conversation or written text. It is a characteristic of bilingual speech. Researchers have found out that bilinguals switch codes for different purposes. Generally, it is possible to distinguish linguistic and social motivations for code-switching, the latter expressing the individual's social and cultural identity (Scheu 2000) or the nature of intergroup relations and tensions. Research on the social dimension of code-switching has been done with the use of three theoretical frameworks, including (1) interpretive sociolinguistics (Gumperz 1982), perceiving code-switching as a common feature of bilinguals' speech repertoire – in its view, code-switching acquires its social meaning through the norms of interpretation shared by the community; (2) the markedness model by Myers-Scotton (1993), describing certain code choices marked for certain situations and configurations of speakers; and (3) Speech Accommodation Theory (SAT) (Bourhis and Giles 1977), distinguishing specific types of interaction between members of different groups.

4. Accommodation to the second language

According to SAT, bilinguals shift their speech patterns and accommodate them to the out-group when interacting with the out-group members in the out-group's language (Bourhis and Giles 1977). Accommodation can be caused by the need to improve the quality of communication, the need for social approval, or the need to identify with the speaker. Generally, accommodation makes the cultural exchange easier.

There is a tenable amount of work suggesting that accommodation occurs when people respond to questionnaires in their second language. Bilinguals in Hong Kong, for example, have been observed to respond in a more Westernized way on the Dogmatism Scale in English than in Chinese (Earle 1969). A similar effect has been obtained in the Twenty Statements Test that compared English to Chinese (Trafimow et al. 1997). Another study performed in Hong-Kong (Bond 1983) demonstrated that participants responding to a value questionnaire in their native language (Chinese) noticed a greater difference between a typical Chinese inhabitant of Hong-Kong and a typical Westerner than when they responded to the same questionnaire in their second language (English). On the other hand, Bond and Yang (1982) observed an opposite tendency in Hong-Kong bilinguals who were subjected to two language versions of the Rokeach Value Survey. For some questionnaire items their answers to the English version differed from those to the Chinese version in that they were skewed more to the 'Western' direction (cross-cultural accommodation), and for others – more to the Chinese direction (ethnic affirmation). Having analyzed the meaning of these items for the participants, Bond and Yang (1982) found out that when a value was perceived as important, the cross-cultural accommodation did not occur.

The results of studies of linguistic accommodation suggest that there is a general tendency to switch cognitions, attitudes and values when shifting to other languages – even when completing a questionnaire. These findings may support the linguistic relativity concept. At the same time some values are not subject to such accommodation processes, thus switching to other language does not necessarily mean full cross-cultural accommodation. This leads to an important question in the field of political psychology: Do people accommodate to the culture of high political correctness after switching to its language?

5.   Prejudice: Cognition and emotion

Since the seminal work of Gordon Allport, *The Nature of Prejudice* (1954), psychologists have distinguished two forms, or two components, of prejudice. According to Allport, "An adequate definition of prejudice contains two essential ingredients. There must be an attitude of favor or disfavor; and it must be related to overgeneralized belief. Prejudiced statements sometimes express attitudinal factor, sometimes the belief factor" (1954: 13). The first component includes affective reaction to an object of prejudice, while the second is a cognitive schema, or a stereotype.

In more recent research in social and political psychology, the two concepts are even more separated. Social-cognition experiments prove that in such phenomena as stereotyping and prejudice, cognitive processes are clearly separable from affective orientations toward an out-group (Ashmore and Del-Boca 1981; Brewer and Kramer 1985). Stangor, Sullivan and Ford (1991) compared the impact of stereotypical beliefs about and of affective responses to national, ethnic, and religious groups on preferred social distance and attitudes toward out-groups. In two studies, emotional responses to the target groups were found to be a more consistent and stronger predictor of attitudes and social distance than were social stereotypes. What is more, the authors report very low correlation between the cognitive and affective components of prejudice (between $r = 0.13$ and $r = 0.26$), which stresses the importance to distinguish affective and cognitive components of stereotyping. These findings are well grounded on the neurophysiological nature of psychological processes: emotions seem to arise from a functionally separate system that is functionally independent from the system of reasoning and intellectual functioning. Emotional processes are unintentional, implicit and processed in different areas of the human brain than cognitive processes (LeDoux 1996). In attitude research, implicit and explicit processes are also separated: Greenwald and Banaji (1995), for example, have stressed the importance to distinguish explicit and implicit indices of attitudes. The explicit measures of attitudes function in a conscious mode, while the implicit measures operate in an unconscious fashion, and represent affective states.

There are several approaches to the study of the affective component of prejudice: survey researchers typically use 'feeling thermometer' techniques (Sidanius, Pratto and Bobo 1996), while other attitude researchers prefer open-ended questions to tap the affective ingredient of a stereotype (Esses, Haddock and Zanna 1993). In the 1990s psychologists reported that Europeans do not feel positive emotions when thinking about immigrants, and this is a part of a larger phenomenon of 'subtle prejudice' (Pettigrew and Meertens 1995). Gaertner and Dovidio (1986) suggest that emotional aversion, as an uncontrolled component of prejudice, is responsible for the lack of helping behavior toward black people.

There have also been many attempts in psychological literature to tap the cognitive component of prejudice. The most inspiring include the notion of 'symbolic racism' – a belief that black people violate American values (Sears 1988), or 'modern prejudice' – denoting opposition to affirmative actions (McConahay 1986). There are also more extreme forms of such beliefs observable in people's conviction that others lack some

essential human qualities and values (Struch and Schwartz 1989). Such dehumanization justifies aggression towards members of a stereotyped group.

6. Accommodating prejudice?

Taking into consideration the psychological reasons for the distinction between the
affective and cognitive processes underlying prejudice, of the two components of this
phenomenon, the cognitive one (i.e. stereotypical beliefs), can be said to undergo linguistic accommodation. Critical discourse analysis demonstrates that certain cultures
(e.g., Spain) have developed elitist racist discursive norms that are maintained by the
education, political practices and everyday linguistic discrimination of immigrants
(van Dijk 2005), while some other cultures do not evince such discursive norms. It can
thus be hypothesized that by switching to a different language people conform to the
discursive norms of that language, no matter whether they are politically correct or
not. What follows from it is that switching to a language of high vs. low political correctness may also lead people to express their prejudice at different levels of discursive
explicitness. The desire to appear politically correct makes them suppress their preju-
diciary attitudes, and show greater support for the values of tolerance. Van Boven
(2000), for instance, has shown that mechanisms of pluralistic ignorance elevate the
level of support for political correctness: people who overestimate the number of politically correct peers show a higher level of political correctness. Thus, when they
perceive the language they speak as having high standards of political correctness, they
become more politically correct themselves. Crandall, Eshleman and O'Brien (2002)
suggest that when people report the motivation to suppress prejudice, they are in fact
reporting the pressure to change their attitudes to conform to the norm of a prevailing
group. In their study participants closely adhered to group norms when expressing
prejudice, evaluating scenarios of discrimination, and reacting to hostile jokes.

   Switching into a 'politically correct language' makes affective and cognitive prejudice
operate in different ways. More specifically, affective prejudice, which is unaware, implicit and uncontrolled, does not decline when participants switch to a language of high
political correctness. Franco and Maass (1999), for instance, find out that implicit and
explicit measures of prejudice are positively correlated only for an out-group that was not
protected by norms of political correctness (religious fundamentalists), while for a group
normatively protected (Jews) there was a negative relation between the two forms of
prejudice: the more the participants expressed a negative attitude at the implicit level, the
less they expressed explicit prejudice. Dambrun and Guimond (2004) suggest that people with automatic negative affect try to over-compensate their automatic negativity.
They present themselves in a more favorable manner by positive judgments about the
out-group that is normatively protected by standards of political correctness.

   The comparison of the Polish and French languages seems very interesting in this
respect. We suspect the Polish language to allow a higher level of openness in expressing

prejudiced attitudes because of the way the values and judgments are expressed in this language. For example, what Zarzycka (2006) observes in selected titles of the Polish press is that the attitudes of Poles towards black people as reflected in texts on immigrant ethnic minorities from 1989–2003 were to a great extent negative. In her view, many expressions and lexemes of this discourse were influenced by traditional anti-black stereotypes. By contrast, Grzmil-Tylutki (2000) suggests that in French discourse the process of valuation is more implicit and subtle. Polish discourse, on the other hand, is thought to express values and judgments in a more explicit way. Finally, differences in how the two cultures under scrutiny (and hence also their languages) communicate ethnicity-oriented bias are also reported, for instance, in the Anti-Defamation League surveys (see, e.g., ADL 2007) and by Heitmeyer and Zick (2007).

On the basis of these observations, we hypothesize that Polish-French bilingual students who are asked to complete an attitude questionnaire in the French language will accommodate the degree of explicitness in communicating their stereotypical beliefs (cognitive component of prejudice), but they will not be able to accommodate their gut-level reactions (emotional component of prejudice). This hypothesis was tested in the study presented below.

7.   Method

7.1   Participants

56 high school students aged between 15 and 19 participated in the research (42 females, 12 males, 2 undeclared). All of them attended a bilingual Polish-French high school in Warsaw. Polish was their mother-tongue, however all of them had considerably long training in French ($M = 4.96$ years). Each week they speak ($M = 7.38$ hours) and read ($M = 3.41$ hours) French. 17.9% of them declared to 'think in French' very often, 17.9% – often, and 32.1% – from time to time. They voluntarily participated in the study.

7.2   Procedure

Participants were randomly assigned to one of two conditions. In the first condition they were given a questionnaire in their native language (Polish), while in the second condition they received a questionnaire in their second language (French). Both questionnaires included measures of cognitive and affective components of prejudice.

7.3   Measures

Cognitive prejudice. The measure of cognitive prejudice was adopted from Struch and Schwartz's (1989) research on dehumanization. Participants were asked to what extent they agree that three characteristics related to distinctively human values could be attributed to black people. These included:

- *considerateness and compassion for others,*
- *concern for the welfare of all of the society members,*
- *raising their children to be humane.*

Participants indicated their answers on a scale ranging from 1 (*not at all*) to 5 (*extremely*). The overall *attribution of humanity* score was computed using the average of the three items (Cronbach alpha = .54). This measure indicated the cognitive component of prejudice, as it captured the participants' beliefs and opinions about black people.

Affective prejudice. The measure of affective prejudice was adopted from Pettigrew and Meertens' (1995) subtle prejudice measure. Participants were asked how often they feel certain positive emotions towards black people, including:

- *sympathy,*
- *admiration,*
- *confidence,*
- *respect.*

Using a four-point scale (from *never* to *very often*) participants rated four positive emotions that they feel toward black people. The mean score was used as an overall score of *positive emotions* towards black people (Cronbach alpha = .86). Relevant research (Pettigrew and Meertens 1995) suggests that the lack of positive emotions toward out-group members is a typical expression of subtle affective prejudice.

7.4 Results

The analysis of variance included one between subjects factor (linguistic version of a questionnaire: Polish vs. French) and one within subjects factor (two negative indicators of prejudice: humanity ascription to black people vs. positive emotions towards black people). ANOVA indicated no main effect for the linguistic version of a questionnaire on the two indicators of prejudice taken together, $F(1,54) = .48, p = .90$. However, there was a significant interaction of the linguistic version of the questionnaire and the two forms of prejudice, $F(1,54) = 8.92, p < .005$. The planned comparisons approach has allowed to statistically determine the direction of this interaction. The statistically significant effect could be observed only on the cognitive part of prejudice: participants who were asked to complete the questionnaire in French ascribed significantly more humanity to black people ($M = 3.52$) than those who completed the questionnaire in Polish ($M = 3.18$), $F(1,54) = 4.16, p < .05$. There was no statistically significant effect on positive emotions, but there was a marginal effect: participants who completed the questionnaire in French felt less positive emotions toward black people ($M = 2.79$) than those who declared these emotions in their own language ($M = 3.15$), $F(1,54) = 3.70, p = .06$.

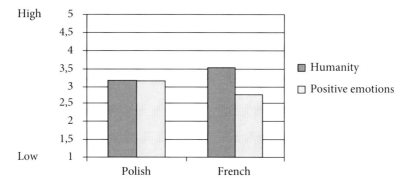

Figure 1. Humanity ascription to black people and positive affect towards black people as a function of the linguistic version of the questionnaire (Polish vs. French)

8.   Discussion

The experiment presented above is the first attempt to study the accommodation of prejudice. We have selected two languages – Polish and French, differing in the degree of openness in expressing personal opinion on matters that may potentially elicit prejudice-marked responses. It has been assumed that the Polish participants who were asked to speak or write French will accommodate to more restrictive norms of political correctness in that their views about black people will change after switching to the language used. We asked participants to declare their opinions about black people's humanity, i.e. they provided answers to the question: to what extent black people share cultural values specific for human beings (cf. also Struch and Schwartz 1989). As we predicted, students who completed the questionnaire in French ascribed significantly more humanity to black people, thus they accommodated to the norms of political correctness typical of the French language.

Such an observation seems to support the linguistic relativity hypothesis: people tend to change their intergroup cognition after switching to a different language. This cognitive switch may be intentional, and language users may be aware of the norms existing in a given language. This does not however falsify the concept of linguistic relativity, but only restricts its range to intentional cognitive processes.

The strong claim of the linguistic relativity hypothesis would predict that it is also implicit and unintentional psychological processes that change when participants switch to a different language. The most uncontrollable of them are emotional processes, which in the present project have been tested in a group of bilingual students who were asked about their feelings toward black people. This measure, used previously by Pettigrew and Meertens (1995), taps the level of unintentional and subtle prejudice, i.e. the lack of positive emotions toward a racial out-group. When applied to the two groups studied, the test has conveyed results that are nearly unaffected by the questionnaire's language in that they do not reveal significant differences between the respondents who provided their answers in French and those who provided their answers in their native language, Polish. However, within the marginal difference effect that could be observed, the participants who responded to the questionnaire in French turned out slightly more prejudiced on this measure: they declared marginally less positive emotions toward black people than those who responded in Polish. This may suggest that the process of linguistic accommodation is based on the suppression of stereotypical beliefs, which leads to the activation of unintentional emotional prejudice.

The problems with self-regulation of prejudice are well known in social psychology. Suppressing stereotypes makes stereotypical knowledge more accessible (Macrae et al. 1994). What is more, people who try to suppress their stereotype during intergroup contact more rely on stereotypes in their perception of an out-group member than those who are not asked to suppress their stereotype (Macrae et al. 1996). Thus, the suppression of a cognitive stereotype makes emotional, uncontrolled prejudice more probable.

This knowledge sheds some light on the results of our study. While speaking in the French language, the informants examined were trying to suppress their stereotypical beliefs, which in turn led to greater expression of uncontrolled prejudiced emotions. Such an effect allows to argue tentatively that linguistic accommodation is only a form of cognitive suppression, activating negative emotions. However, to what extent this is true should further be verified by means of indirect techniques, such as, e.g., the Implicit Association Test (see Greenwald and Banaji 1995).

To sum up, the linguistic relativity hypothesis, in view of which perceptions of the world are constrained by different spoken languages, remains an interesting field of psychological investigation. It raises many questions about awareness of these linguistic constraints of perception. Psychological studies of bilinguals show that people intentionally accommodate to the language they speak, but their prejudice-related gut reactions seem to be unaffected by the language spoken, as they function beyond the level of consciousness and intentionality.

References

ADL. 2007. "Attitudes toward Jews and the Middle East in five European countries." Retrieved May 31, 2007 from http://www.adl.org/on11.03.2008.

Allport, Gordon W. 1954. *The Nature or Prejudice*. Cambridge, MA: Addison Wesley.

Ashmore, Richard D. and Del Boca, Frances K. 1981. "Conceptual approaches to stereotypes and stereotyping." In *Cognitive Processes in Stereotyping and Intergroup Behavior*, David Hamilton (ed.), 37–81. Hillsdale, NJ.: Erlbaum Publishers.

Bloomfield, Leonard. 1935. *Language*. New York: Holt Reinhart and Winston.

Bond, Michael. 1983. "How language variation affects inter-cultural differentiation of values by Hong Kong bilinguals." *Journal of Language and Social Psychology* 2: 57–66.

Bond, Michael, Yang, Kuo-Shu. 1982. "The variable impact of questionnaire language on Chinese bilinguals from Hong Kong." *Journal of Cross-Cultural Psychology* 13: 169–185.

Bourhis, Richard Y. and Giles, Howard. 1977. "The language of intergroup distinctiveness." In *Language, Ethnicity and Intergroup Relations*, Howard Giles (ed.), 119–135. London: Academic Press.

Brewer, Marilynn B. and Kramer, Roderick M. 1985. "The psychology of inter-group attitudes and behavior." *Annual Review of Psychology* 36: 219–43.

Crandall, Christian S., Eshleman, Amy and O'Brien, Laurie. 2002. "Social norms and the expression and suppression of prejudice: The struggle for internalization." *Journal of Personality and Social Psychology* 82: 359–378.

Dambrun, Michaell and Guimond, Serge. 2004. "Implicit and explicit measures of prejudice and stereotyping: Do they assess the same underlying knowledge structure?" *European Journal of Social Psychology* 34: 663–676

Devine, Patricia G. 1989. "Stereotypes and prejudice: The automatic and controlled components." *Journal of Personality and Social Psychology* 56: 5–18.

Earle, Margaret J. 1969. "A cross-cultural and cross-language comparison of dogmatism scores." *Journal of Social Psychology* 79: 19–24.

Esses, Victoria M., Haddock, Geoff and Zanna, Mark P. 1993. "Values, stereotypes, and emotions as determinants of intergroup attitudes." In *Affect, Cognition, and Stereotyping: Intergroup Processes in Group Perception*, Diane M. Mackie and David L. Hamilton (eds), 137–166. San Diego, CA: Academic.

Franco, Francesca M. and Maass, Anne. 1999. "Intentional control over prejudice: When the choice of the measure matters." *European Journal of Social Psychology* 29: 469–477.

Gaertner, Samuel L. and Dovidio, Jack F. 1986. "The aversive form of racism." In *Prejudice, Discrimination, and Racism,* Jack F. Dovidio and Samuel L. Gaertner (eds), 61–89. Orlando, FL: Academic Press.

Greenwald, Anthony G. and Banaji, Mahzarin R. 1995. "Implicit social cognition: Attitudes, self-esteem, and stereotypes." *Psychological Review* 102: 4–27.

Grzmil-Tylutki, Halina. 2000. *Francuski i polski dyskurs ekologiczny w perspektywie aksjologicznej [French and Polish Ecological Discourse from the Axiological Perspective].* Kraków: Wydawnictwo Uniwersytetu Jagiellońskiego.

Gumperz, John J. 1982. *Discourse Strategies.* Cambridge: Cambridge University.

Gumperz, John J. and Levinson Stephen C. (eds). 1996. *Rethinking Linguistic Relativity.* Cambridge, MA: Cambridge University Press.

Heitmeyer, Wilhelm and Zick, Andreas. 2007. "Group-focused enmity in Europe." Paper presented at EFC DMIIG-Meeting, Turin, March 2007.

Holtgraves, Thomas. M. and Kashima, Yoshisa. 2008. "Language, meaning, and social cognition." *Personality and Social Psychology Review* 12: 73–94.

LeDoux, John. 1996. *The Emotional Brain.* New York: Simon & Schuster.

Macnamara, John. 1966. *Bilingualism and Primary Education.* Edinburgh: Edinburgh University Press.

Macrae, Colin N., Bodenhausen, Galen V., Milne, Alan B. and Jetten, Jolanda. 1994. "Out of mind but back in sight: Stereotypes on the rebound." Journal of Personality and Social Psychology 67: 808–817.

Macrae, Colin N., Bodenhausen, Galen V., Milne, Alan B. and Wheeler, Victoria. 1996. "On resisting the temptation for simplification: Counterintentional effects of stereotype suppression on social memory.",*Social Cognition* 14: 1–20.

McConahay, John B. 1986. "Modern racism, ambivalence, and the modern racism scale." In *Prejudice, Discrimination, and Racism*, Jack F. Dovidio and Samuel L. Gaertner (eds), 91–125. Orlando, FL: Academic Press.

Myers-Scotton, Carol. 1993. *Social Motivations for Codeswitching*. Oxford: Oxford University Press.

Pettigrew, Thomas F. and Meertens, Roel W. 1995. "Subtle and blatant prejudice in western Europe." European Journal of Social Psychology 25 (1): 57–75.

Pierson, Herbert D.and Bond, Michael H. 1982. "How do Chinese bilinguals respond to variations of interviewer language and ethnicity?" *Journal of Language and Social Psychology* 1: 123–139.

Scheu, Dagmar U. 2000. "Cultural constraints in biliguals' codeswitching." *International Journal of Intercultural Relations* 24: 131–150.

Sears, David O. 1988. "Symbolic racism." In *Eliminating Racism: Profiles in Controversy*, Phyllis A. Katz and Dalmas A. Taylor (eds), 53–84. New York: Plenum.

Sidanius, Jim, Pratto, Felicia and Bobo, Lawrence. 1996. "Racism, conservatism, affirmative action and intellectual sophistication: A matter of principled conservatism or group dominance?" *Journal of Personality and Social Psychology* 67: 998–1011.

Stangor, Charles, Sullivan, Linda A., Ford, Thomas E. 1991. "Affective and cognitive determinants of prejudice" *Social Cognition* 9: 359–380.

Stapel, Diederik A. and Semin, Gun R. 2007. "The magic spell of language: Linguistic categories and their perceptual consequences" Journal of Personality and Social Psychology 93: 34–48.

Struch, Naomi and Schwartz, Shalom H. 1989. "Intergroup aggression: Its predictors and distinctness from in-group bias" *Journal of Personality and Social Psychology* 56 (3): 364–373.

Trafimow, David, Silverman, Ellen S., Fan, Ryth M. and Law, Josephine S. F. 1997. "The effects of language and priming on the relative accessibility of the private self and the collective self." Journal of Cross-Cultural Psychology 28: 107–123.

Van Boven, Leaf. 2000. "Pluralistic ignorance and political correctness: The case of affirmative action." *Political Psychology* 21: 267–288.

van Dijk, Teun A. 2005. *Racism and Discourse in Spain and Latin America*. Amsterdam: Benjamins.

Whorf, Benjamin Lee. 1956. *Language, Thought And Reality: Selected Writings of Benjamin Lee Whorf*. Cambridge, MA.: The MIT Press.

Zarzycka, Grażyna. 2006. *Dyskurs prasowy o cudzoziemcach [Press Discourse on Foreigners]*. Łódź: Wydawnictwo Uniwersytetu Łódzkiego.

PART VI

Conclusion

CHAPTER 20

Exploring 'political communication(s)'

Contexts, procedures and outlook

Urszula Okulska and Piotr Cap

1.   'Language of politics' and (or) 'politics of language': A reflection

The aim of this volume was to respond, descriptively, typologically and methodologically, to the diversity of research territories and practices in Political Linguistics (PL),
by collecting, testing, organizing and expanding them through coherent Analysis of
Political Discourse (APD). In putting together what we believe constitutes an authoritative, state-of-the-art picture of this approach, we took into account the existing liberalism in deeming a given piece of discourse 'political'. As we remarked in Chapter 1,
APD has come to define virtually any procedure of analyzing language and language
matters in political, public and other social contexts that entail implementing/execut-
ing power for and gaining/manifesting superiority through furthering interactants'
communicative goals. This means that, nowadays, APD is an enterprise which accommodates such apparently diverse practices as giving a parliamentary speech by a president of a state, writing an online blog by a media commentator, or carrying out administrative procedures through language in the European Union.

Instead of engaging in a polemic on the quality and quantity of empirical data in
PL that ought to be considered 'political', we proposed a structure whose goal was to,
(i), give coherence to the field inasmuch as such a coherence can be attempted to date,
(ii), suggest (more) research in the directions which seem the most promising in the
way of systematizing the PL stage further on through combining and developing its
conceptual and methodological tools into the apparatus of APD. To that end we included papers applying top-down and bottom-up methods of analysis, synchronic and
diachronic viewpoints, critical and theoretical arguments, qualitative and quantitative
procedures, etc. The papers dealt with a wealth of contemporary as well as historical
discourses occurring in different geopolitical settings. In this way, a vast scene was set
for grouping the particular instances of political discourse into categories reflecting
the current division of labor among the PL analysts.

In proposing these categories we followed, essentially, a well-trodden path: the
distinction between the *language of politics* (traditionally the language of political

activities and of politicians acting in their political capacity; esp. papers in Parts II-IV) and the *politics of language* (policies concerning languages; esp. papers in Part V). This distinction, however apparently the most workable to date, is not without faults, and evidence is as close as the current volume. There is, first of all, no clear dividing line between the two domains as regards their ontological vis-à-vis performative composition. It might be tempting to see, say, an analysis of conceptual metaphor belong *exclusively* to the language of politics, just because it is a stable part of the rhetorical arsenal of a politician, potentially available for labeling different entities on the political stage (viz. the Skinner/Squillacote chapter in this volume). Yet the same conceptual metaphor, when treated performatively rather than merely ontologically, starts encroaching onto the other territory, the politics of language. Consider, for instance, the chapter by Pfaff (this volume), where, at one point, metaphor is considered one of language realizations of policy-making about languages. The metaphor case is an example of the possible convergence of studies into what is rhetorically available for a political actor to accomplish his/her goals, and what the actual process of accomplishing these goals says about language constructs involved in it. Books or even papers which try to accommodate both, can possibly be located on either side, the language of politics/the politics of language, only due to differences in their emphasis.

There are, in fact, more problems with the distinction, which involve the hybridization of communicative genres (features of one genre – e.g., a presidential inaugural – get incorporated into another), the blending of generic styles, recontextualization of the original discourse, etc. They all may cause some parts of the data investigated (and thus the analysis itself) to belong to the 'language' domain and some to the 'politics' domain. We do not have space here to elaborate on these instances; in our view, they mostly reiterate the problem signaled in the conceptual metaphor case above and do little in the way of revisiting the division or showing how it could be used as a feasible basis for providing PL with a more coherent research agenda for the future. The current task is, indeed, to make the most of the language of politics/politics of language distinction, refine it for, possibly, some more precise sub-typologies, and find ways in which it could yield controlling category or categories of description, with their own tools of analysis. All of this, of course, with the awareness of the limitations suggested.

While there might be, conceivably, a number of methods to further utilize the linguistic-political interface as it is accounted for in PL studies today, the structure of the present volume signposts at least one such avenue, which will be tentatively explored below.

The papers included in our collection under the 'language of politics' umbrella have shown, despite the thematic and theoretical heterogeneity, a potential to build up a hierarchical sequence. Within this sequence, research in conceptualization and labeling (Part II), and studies in pragmalinguistic ways in which conceptualizations are realized and imposed upon the political scene (Part III), get subsumed under the uppermost category of mediatization (Part IV). Analysis of mediatized communication draws upon the cognitive and pragmalinguistic input, to verify its rhetorical effectiveness in accessing the maximal range of recipients through different channels of transmission. In fact, as suggested in the structure of this volume, it is not only methodologically superior within the 'language of politics' domain; it also makes a direct contact with research in the 'politics of language', since most of the latter relies for success on the media communication of policies. Altogether, studies in mediatized communication emerge as the most potent and consequential enterprise in systematizing the PL scene at its bottom level. They appear to play a crucial role in judging, eventually, which of the particular language acts and constructs are capable of exerting large-scale political and social impact, and which do not stand the test of mediatization and should perhaps be brushed aside in analysis.

What follows in the next section is a list of points to consider, collectively, as a tentative premise for postulating that mediatized communication be a cornerstone research area in the development of APD further on. It includes points of different theoretical status and analytic caliber and is by no means exhaustive. Its objective is to indicate some of the characteristics of 'political communication' (viewed through the lens of APD, i.e., with emphasis placed also on 'political', viz. power-linked, aspects of public/institutional communication in general) in and through all sorts of media which endorse the importance of its analysis as expressed in the above postulate.

2. The media outlook

a. Apparently, most of the data that APD deals with belong to mediatized politics, in its both power-enacting and institutional shape (cf. Tenscher 1998; Fetzer and Lauerbach 2007; Triandafyllidou et al. 2009). The pervasiveness of mediatized political communication has gone much beyond the area of scholarly investigation; it is safe to say that, nowadays, political discourse in the media is for most people the only way in which they ever encounter politics (cf. Fetzer and Lauerbach 2007). As a result, we are faced with a plethora of data that reflect different degrees of institutionalization and thus can be grouped into genres and subgenres generating or attracting specific methods of analysis (some of them going beyond the linguistic and inviting issues of multimodality). For instance, mediatized political communication can be categorized according to its referential characteristics – it can involve the discourse of political agents in the media, the discourse of journalists with politicians in the media, the discourse of journalists about politics, political agents and political institutions in the media, the mediatized discourse of street folk enquired by journalists to voice political opinions, and perhaps more. Each of these discourses undergoes a different degree of mediatization and reformulation of the political message (relatively little in the case of a political debate televised live and in entirety, but potentially huge in the case of a journalist collecting 'vox pops' to present a selection of opinions, followed by his or her own commentary). To study what exactly determines a given degree of reformulation and how the different levels complement as well as interact with each other (one can imagine situations in which one kind of discourse embeds another – consider a journalist quoting popular opinions while interviewing a politician) is thus a methodologically viable undertaking. It is such, not only typologically, but also in terms of the appropriation of feasible analytic procedures (macro- and micro-sociological, ethnomethodological, ethnographic). Let alone, of course, the specific benefits that come from studying the 'lowest level', the mediatized discourse of ordinary people approached for political opinions. As Fiske (1996) or Fetzer and Weizman (2006) admit, the discourse analytic research in audience reception of and reaction to political messages is still a rather neglected area. The wealth and diversity of the data available from mediatized politics allow all this and conceivably more: a comparative perspective. The study of the discursive practices and strategies whereby culturally homogeneous versus culturally heterogeneous discourses are constructed can enrich "phenomenology of media language [that] would have as its task the job of investigating the connections between media, language and the world" (cf. Scannell 1998: 263).

b.   Any communicative act, be it a promise, a denial, an apology, etc., can be, potentially, mediatized for increased 'political' (viz. social) impact (in which case we tend to talk of a 'public promise', 'public denial' and so on). This applies to all acts of 'political communication' (in its broadest sense – see Chapter 1), whether subsumed under the 'language of politics' or the 'politics of language' umbrella. However, not all of these acts (or actually, the language constructs involved in their lexical composition) show exactly the same capacity of affecting the target audience. The application of some language constructs (figurative language, thesis-antithesis patterns, assertion-based sequences; cf. e.g. Cap 2008) may go a long way towards obtaining large-scale social effects, while the use of others may turn disappointing in this respect. As a consequence, mediatization, which naturally exposes political-linguistic tools of communication to continual verification by the mass recipient (which is then a promisingly objective sort of verification) can be seen as a way to extract those constructs which are worth further attention of APD analysts and for which adequate methods of analysis should be appropriated or developed. The resulting studies in the kind, range and strength of social impact of broadly 'political' messages should make even tighter the bond between the theoretical apparatuses of PL/APD and CDA, the connection we wrote about in Chapter 1. And as far as a review of and elaboration on the language of politics/politics of language distinction is concerned, it would be quite interesting to see which of the two involves more powerful and more universally appealing constructs – if there is any such dominance in the first place.

c.   Mediatized communication seems to essentialize one of the most distinctive features of APD in general, its reflective-interpretative 'bi-directionality'. As we indicated in Chapter 1, APD does more than just reflect events which occur in the world; it interprets these events and formulates understandings, thereby contributing to the constitution of a new reality. Studies in mediatized communication make this characteristic extremely salient. They access large quantities of data (viz. point a. above), investigate them at multiple levels of reformulation, and thus yield a comprehensive range of interpretations for the evolution of the new sociopolitical and institutional arrangements (cf. Fairclough 1998). In that sense, they inscribe in the inherent *constructivism* of discourse research (cf. Fetzer and Lauerbach 2007; Triandafyllidou et al. 2009), which starts from the 'static' analysis of social structures (reflected in language), but culminates in the 'dynamic' analysis of social processes, i.e. the methods (applied through language) the members of a social group use to rearrange these structures and the institutions that endorse or legitimate them. This involves both the 'language of politics' and the 'politics of language' strands, though it would take a much desired study to determine whatever each of them has to offer in the way of accounting for the social structures as they are and interpreting them with a view to provoking a social change. Tentatively, a dominance could be postulated on the 'politics of language' side, which exhibits the emphasis upon political acting (concerning language policies) through language, rather than (the conceptual grounding of) language tools available to a politician. Of course, such a postulate involves some simplification, since the language tools are not only 'available for use'; they can be and are actually used in the 'political acting'. Altogether then, it seems that further research in the reflective-interpretative 'bi-directionality' of mediatized communication and 'political discourse' in general could make some instances of the 'language of politics' and 'politics of language' merge in analysis.

d.   Finally, we must not ignore the ethical dimension. If APD can ever live up to the critical scholarship aspiration to safeguard (or restore) the integrity of sociopolitical behavior (recall the closing of Chapter 1), then the greatest contribution should come from studies in mediatized communication. Most research in mediatized public discourse involves looking at the many institutional and social levels through which a 'political' message passes, to reach the destination recipient (cf. point a. above). The length and complexity of the mediatization channels make it the case that the possibility of distortion and miscommunication (whether intended or accidental) is huge and if that happens, the impact extends over a vast audience. It is thus a responsibility of media language analysts to pinpoint and describe such situations, so the 'political' communicators get the sense they are monitored, while the audience develop rhetorical sensitivity to be able to trace down the instances in which message distortion (or manipulation) is at play.

The rationale for such an undertaking lies in the observation that *traditional* political communication occurring in and through the media has been falling short "of the democratic ideal according to which free, objective and scrupulous media inform the public on political decisions and issues, at the same time controlling the actors in the political sphere by insisting on the transparency of the political process and on the justification of its decisions to the public" (Fetzer and Lauerbach 2007: 6). This ideal has been put in jeopardy by a number of trends: the oversimplification of the states of affairs following time constraints and other production pressures, the trivialization of the broadcasting caused by commercial demands, the growing symbiosis of the media and the political class whereby politicians exchange the often unreliable or misleading information for publicity, and so on (cf. Cameron 2003). Each of these trends is certainly worth analyzing from the linguistic-political and political-linguistic perspective alike; contrary to the c. point above, here it is hard to come up with an immediate idea where exactly one would find more of the explanatory power. On a more constructive note, however, one could foresee tangible benefits from a diachronic bent of such an analysis, since the tendencies mentioned are due to the rapid technological and social progress and the evolution of the relationship between the media, political actors, their audience, as well as the world of commerce. Speaking of which, the rapidity of the technological progress affecting the access range of the politics performed in and through the media is in itself yet another reason to consider studies in mediatized communication a priority in the APD agenda.

***

The proposal to consider research in mediatized communication a cornerstone territory of APD must not be read as colliding with, indeed, the inherent richness and diversity of this approach, which are, in the long run, nothing but methodologically productive. Even if more and more research avenues are proposed for channeling the empirical focus, selecting the most promising analytic tools and working out methods that could be used more universally across the entire PL discipline, they will still need to rely for their plausibility on the vast quantities of data, extracted from multiple thematic domains in diverse geopolitical settings. The language of politics/politics of language distinction is of help; while far from ideal, it not only provides a basic structure to account for the thematic differences on both sides, but also gives a sense of the differences in emphasis that APD practitioners put on the 'linguistic' and the 'political' component. The language of politics strand has its emphasis on language, its conceptual basis and functional characteristics that are deployed in acts of 'political communication'. To the extra methodological benefit, the cognitive-pragmatic interface underlying construction and performance of the language of politics allows hierarchical analysis, which contributes to the allocation of descriptive tools (based in cognitive linguistics, pragmatics, sociolinguistics, corpus studies, etc.) to the specific levels. Needless to say, such an analysis may result in uncovering a controlling category (e.g. mediatized communication) functioning as the ultimate verification device for language constructs and their social and political efficacy (viz. b. above).

The politics of language strand has its emphasis on 'politics', but the studies in policy-making *about* languages provide, however often indirectly, insights in how the particular policies are enacted *through* language. The fact that, in such studies, the 'linguistic' analysis remains somewhat 'in the background' or 'follows from' the issues of policy-making (which we saw in Part V contending against the monolingual norms in education) prevents any methodological hierarchization of the language of politics type. Nonetheless, the description of the language forms and functions involved in the 'politics of language' is a natural complementation of the accounts produced at the other end. Once we make the two strands work together within (and for) the vast, representative and continually developing PL/APD area (viz. mediatized communication), we should receive from both a truly comprehensive instruction in what mental concepts and lexical constructs are the most prevalent and powerful in 'political discourse' in general, thus deserving a thorough scrutiny by APD practitioners.

References

Cameron, Deborah. 2003. "Globalizing 'communication.'" In *New Media Language*, Jean Aitchison and Diana M. Lewis (eds), 27–35. London: Routledge.

Cap, Piotr. 2008. *Legitimisation in Political Discourse: A Cross-Disciplinary Perspective on the Modern US War Rhetoric* [2nd revised ed.]. Newcastle: Cambridge Scholars Publishing.

Fairclough, Norman. 1998. "Political discourse in the media: An analytical framework." In *Approaches to Media Discourse*, Allan Bell and Peter Garrett (eds), 142–162. Oxford: Blackwell.

Fetzer, Anita and Lauerbach, Gerda E. (eds). 2007. *Political Discourse in the Media*. Amsterdam: Benjamins.

Fetzer, Anita and Weizman, Elda. 2006. "Political discourse as mediated and public discourse." *Journal of Pragmatics* 38 (2): 143–153.

Fiske, John. 1996. *Media Matters. Race and Gender in U.S. Politics*. Minneapolis: University of Minnesota Press.

Scannell, Paddy. 1998. "Media-language-world." In *Approaches to Media Discourse*, Allan Bell and Peter Garrett (eds), 252–267. Oxford: Blackwell.

Tenscher, Jens. 1998. "Politik fuer das Fernsehen – Politik im Fernsehen – Theorien, Trends und Perspektiven." In *Politikvermittlung und Demokratie in der Mediengesellschaft*, Ulrich Sarcinelli (ed.), 184–208. Bonn: Bundeszentrale fuer politische Bildung.

Triandafyllidou, Anna, Wodak, Ruth and Krzyżanowski, Michał (eds). 2009. *The European Public Sphere and the Media. Europe in Crisis*. Basingstoke: Palgrave Macmillan.

Contributors

Andreas Musolff (andreas.musolff@durham.ac.uk) is Professor of German at Durham University. He has published widely on the history of political discourse, metaphor theory and the history of pragmatics. His monographs include *Metaphor and Political Discourse* (2004), *Mirror Images of Europe* (2000) and *Krieg gegen die Öffentlichkeit. Terrorismus und politischer Sprachgebrauch* (1996). He has co-edited *Metaphor and Discourse* (2009), *Discourses of Intercultural Identity in Britain, Germany and Eastern Europe* (Special Issue of the *Journal of Multilingual & Multicultural Development*, 2004) and *Attitudes towards Europe. Language in the Unification Process* (2001). He is a member of the Executive Committee of the Societas Linguistica Europaea and of the editorial boards of *Journal of Germanic Studies, German as a Foreign Language, Aptum, Zeitschrift für Sprachkritik und Sprachkultur*.

Daniel Skinner (danskinner@gmail.com) (Ph.D., City University of New York) is Assistant Professor of Political Science at Capital University, Columbus, OH. His research and teaching interests include political theory, rhetoric, medical humanities, feminist theory and health care policy. He is currently developing a book manuscript that examines the development of the concept of 'medical necessity' in the United States. Daniel Skinner has recently completed a book chapter entitled "The Poetics of American Circumcision on the Margins of Medical Necessity", in: *Understanding Emerging Epidemics: Social and Political Approaches*, Ananya Mukherjea (ed.) (2010, Emerald Insight Press, UK).

Rosa Squillacote is a student at University of California Berkeley School of Law. Her current research concerns the intersections of criminal justice, poverty and human rights law.

Jan Chovanec (chovanec@phil.muni.cz) is Assistant Professor in the Department of English and American Studies at the Faculty of Arts, Masaryk University in Brno, Czech Republic. He has published in linguistic journals (*Discourse & Communication*) and volumes (*The Linguistics of Football; Language and the Law: International Outlooks*). He teaches classes in media discourse, language and law, and sociolinguistics. His research interests include the interactive nature of discourse in media contexts, the representation of social actors, face and politeness in interpersonal interactions, and word play. He has recently focused on dialogism and the language of live text commentary. He is the editor-in-chief of the journal *Brno Studies in English*.

Katarzyna Molek-Kozakowska (molekk@uni.opole.pl) Ph.D., is Assistant Professor at Institute of English Studies, Opole University. She specializes in linguistics, discourse analysis and cultural/media studies. She has published a dozen articles on mass-mediated political discourse, and presented papers on such issues as metaphor, personalization and persuasion in American media. She has recently been interested in the methodology of qualitative research and critical media literacy. Recent publications include: "Descriptive and interpretative methods in Critical Discourse Analysis" (2008, Olsztyn UP), "Theory and practice of media education: A case for critical media literacy" (2009, Opole UP), "Metaphor as a rhetorical device in the U.S. interventionist discourse" (2009, Kolegium Karkonoskie), and "Time compression in the evolution of meaning of political labels *liberal* and *conservative* in the context of ideological struggle in the U.S." (2009, Opole UP).

Ibrahim A. El-Hussari (ihousari@lau.edu.lb) is Professor of English and Cultural Studies at the School of Arts and Sciences, Department of Humanities, Lebanese American University, Beirut, Lebanon. He earned two doctorates, one in American Literature from the University of Kensington, California, USA (1990), and the other in Applied Linguistics from the University of Leicester, United Kingdom (2001). His main field of interest and research is discourse analysis, political linguistics, comparative literature, and cultural studies. He has participated in many international conferences on a variety of topics, including conflict-resolution strategies. He has been writing extensively on language and linguistics, culture, comparative literature, and translation. So far, he has published six academic books on a variety of topics, seventeen story-books under Juvenile and Young Adults' Literature, and twelve articles in peer-reviewed international journals. His last two books include *The Quest for Meaning in William Faulkner's "The Sound and the Fury": A Study in Narrative Discourse* (2008) and *Cultural Awareness Between Theory and Practice: A Case Study* (2009).

Piotr Cap (strus_pl@yahoo.com) is Professor at Institute of English, University of Łódź, where he holds the Chair of Pragmatics. He specializes in linguistic pragmatics, discourse analysis, political linguistics, media and business communication. A Fulbright Fellow at the University of California, Berkeley and Boston University, he has been invited to research and teach at several American and European universities, including Birmingham University, the University of Munich and Antwerp University. He has authored and edited 11 books (including 4 monographs) and some 70 research papers (with Palgrave Macmillan, Elsevier Science, Max Niemeyer, Peter Lang Verlag, Cambridge Scholars Publishing). He is Managing Editor of the *International Review of Pragmatics* (Leiden/Boston: Brill) and member of editorial advisory boards of other pragmatics and discourse related journals, including *Pragmatics: The Quarterly of the International Pragmatics Association*. During the past 15 years, he has given over 70 papers (including plenaries) at international conferences and congresses.

Tony Bastow (tonybastow@hotmail.com) holds a Ph.D. in corpus linguistics from the University of Birmingham, UK. He has a particular interest in the application of corpus methodology to discourse and rhetoric in written texts, and has published a number of articles in this area. He has given conference papers in several countries, including Ireland, Sweden, Spain, Poland and Russia. He is currently a lecturer in English Language and Linguistics at the Class School of Education, University of East London.

Elena Magistro (e.magistro@rhul.ac.uk) has a background in translation from the University of Bologna, holds an M.A. in Linguistics from York University, and she is currently completing her postgraduate studies at the Department of Italian of the University of London Royal Holloway. Her research interests include pragmatics, politeness, contrastive rhetoric, translation and multilingualism in the institutions of the European Union. Her major publications include: (in collaboration with Dr. Giuditta Caliendo) "The human face of the European Union: A critical study" (*CADAAD Journal*, 2009), "Promoting the European identity: Politeness strategies in the discourse of the European Union" (*CADAAD Journal*, 2007) and "The multilingual classroom: New rhetorical frontiers in L2 writing?" (*The College Quarterly*, 2007). She is currently investigating the relationship between politeness and the discourse of the European Union.

Urszula Okulska (u.okulska@uw.edu.pl) is Assistant Professor at Institute of Applied Linguisitics, University of Warsaw. Her research interests include sociolinguistics (contemporary and historical), pragmatics, historical linguistics, text linguistics, discourse analysis and corpus linguistics. She has published the monograph *Gender and the formation of Modern Standard English* (Peter Lang, 2006), and co-edited volumes on global English from a European perspective (Peter Lang, 2004), metalinguistic discourse (Peter Lang, 2006), corpora in English-Polish contrastive linguistics (Universitas, 2006), discourse variation in communities, cultures and times (University of Warsaw, 2008), as well as on age in language and culture (Mouton de Gruyter, 2010). The topics of her publications are additionally related to synchronic and diachronic aspects of language change, development of English specialized genres, professional/institutional communication, speech/discourse communities and the applicability of language corpora to sociolinguistic, discourse-pragmatic and ethnolinguistic research.

Bruce Fraser (bfraser@bu.edu) is Professor of Linguistics and Education at Boston University. After graduating from MIT and working for a number of years in syntax, he turned his attention to the area of semantics and pragmatics, where his writing includes work on politeness, metaphor, idioms, speech acts, apologizing, and threatening. Most recently, his work has focused on the area of discourse markers (e.g., *but, however, so, then, furthermore, and*) and connectors of discourse that typically signal a relationship between two adjacent segments. In a series of papers beginning in 1990, he has set forth a theory of discourse markers, which defines this functional class, and distinguishes them from other particles and similar lexical formatives. He has characterized both the class of contrastive discourse markers (e.g., *but, however, nevertheless, on the contrary, instead,…*) and the class of implicative discourse markers (*so, thus, then, therefore, as a result,…*), and examined them in considerable detail. In addition, he has focused on several specific discourse markers, for example *but*, and is currently conducting research to examine the extent to which the primary discourse markers in different languages are used with the same functions and in the same pragmatic domains.

Anja Janoschka (anja.janoschka@hslu.ch) holds a post-doctoral post within the Communication and Marketing Department at Lucerne University of Applied Sciences. She has a doctoral degree in English linguistics with a specialization in (new) media communication and pragmatics from the University of Zurich, and is the author of the book *Web Advertising*. Anja Janoschka has done interdisciplinary research on advertising and marketing strategies, intercultural discourse and political and business communication, such as corporate weblogs, personalized communication, direct advertising discourse and integrated communication. Her previous career as a consultant in an international advertising agency allows her to combine practical knowledge with a scientific perspective.

James Moir (j.moir@abertay.ac.uk), Ph.D., is a senior lecturer in sociology at the University of Abertay Dundee, Scotland, U.K., with a research interest in the application of discourse analysis across a wide range of socio-psychological topics. This has involved the study of discourses of occupational identities, doctor—patient interactions and shared decision-making, the discursive construction of tourism as visual experience, Western discourse surrounding death and dying, and (in this volume) the role of the media in promoting a discourse of opinionation with respect to political issues. Dr. Moir is currently a Senior Associate of the U.K. Higher Education Academy's Centre for Sociology, Anthropology and Politics (C-SAP), and is now conducting a project on the inter-related discursive constructions of personal development planning, graduate attributes and citizenship within higher education.

Christina Schaeffner (C.Schaeffner@aston.ac.uk) is Professor of Translation Studies at Aston University, Birmingham, UK. She has a Ph.D. from Leipzig University, Germany. At Aston, she has been teaching undergraduate and postgraduate courses in translation studies, interpreting, and text analysis, and has supervised Ph.D. students in these areas. Her main research areas are translation studies, political discourse analysis, metaphor research (esp. in political texts and from a translational perspective), and translation didactics. She was a member of the EMT expert group set up by the Directorate General for Translation (DGT) of the European Commission, whose main task is to make specific proposals with a view to implementing a European Master's in Translation (EMT) throughout the European Union. Her recent publications include: "Political discourse and translation", in: Li Wei and Vivian Cook (eds.) *Contemporary Applied Linguistics. Language for the Real World* (Continuum), "Does translation hinder integration?", *Forum* (2009), and "Doctoral training programmes: Research skills for the discipline or career management skills?", in: Gyde Hansen, Andrew Chesterman and Heidrun Gerzymisch-Arbogast (eds.) *Efforts and Models in Interpreting and Translation Research* (Benjamins, 2009).

Natalia Kovalyova (nvk@mail.utexas.edu), Ph.D., University of Texas at Austin, studies discourse, power, and persuasion in a variety of contexts from presidential rhetoric to everyday talk. Her special interests lie in the area of Eastern European politics and the media, as well as the evolution of their relationship. She has presented on this topic at numerous international conferences. Her most recent research focuses on the emergent public sphere and the oscillations between democracy and authoritarianism in post-communist societies. In her capacity as Research Assistant at the Annette Strauss Institute for Civic Participation, Dr. Kovalyova has worked on civic education projects in Texas.

Adrian Blackledge (a.j.blackledge@bham.ac.uk) is Professor of Bilingualism in the School of Education, University of Birmingham. His research interests include the politics of multilingualism, linguistic ethnography, education of linguistic minority students, negotiation of identities in multilingual contexts, and language testing, citizenship, and immigration. His publications include *Multilingualism, A Critical Perspective* (with Angela Creese, 2010, Continuum), *Discourse and Power in a Multilingual World* (2005, John Benjamins), *Negotiation of Identities in Multilingual Contexts* (with Aneta Pavlenko, 2004, Multilingual Matters), *Multilingualism, Second Language Learning and Gender* (2001, Mouton de Gruyter; co-edited with Aneta Pavlenko, Ingrid Piller, and Marya Teutsch-Dwyer), and *Literacy, Power, and Social Justice* (2001, Trentham Books).

Carol W. Pfaff (jfkilxpf@zedat.fu-berlin.de) has recently retired as Professor of Linguistics at Freie Universität Berlin in the Department of North American Studies (1977-2009), and earlier worked in the USA at the California State University, Fresno, and the University of Texas at Austin. Her work focuses on language development and use of minority languages by children and adults in comparative sociopolitical contexts. She is the editor of the volume *First and Second Language Acquisition Processes* in the series of the *European-North American Cross-Linguistic Second Language Research*, and was Fellow in Residence in a research group on bilingualism at the Netherlands Institute for Advanced Studies in 1995/1996. In the last several years, she has focused on the study of trilingual language development in a bi-national German/French research project on later language development of children and adolescents with Turkish migrant background. She is currently working on the book *Language Ideologies, Language Practices and Language Development: Studies of Turkish/German Bilingual Children in Berlin*.

Bruce Johnson-Beykont (bjb_istanbul@yahoo.com) is Assistant Professor in the Department of Primary Education at Bogazici University in Istanbul, Turkey. He has worked in the U.S. and internationally as a consultant in the area of early childhood curriculum, teacher professional development, and educational reform. Dr. Johnson-Beykont began in the early childhood field as a classroom teacher of young children and later served as an educational administrator. He received a doctorate in Administration, Planning and Social Policy from the Harvard Graduate School of

Education. His current research interests include the socio-cultural construction of child-rearing and schooling practices, effective models of professional development for in-service and pre-service teachers, and teaching as reflective practice.

Zeynep F. Beykont (beykont@post.harvard.edu) received a doctoral degree in Human Development and Psychology from the Harvard Graduate School of Education. Her research centers on policies, programs, and practices that support the language, identity, and academic development of immigrant and ethnic minority youth. Dr. Beykont has published on issues of equity, access, and excellence in the education of diverse populations. Her edited volumes include: *Lifting Every Voice: Pedagogy and Politics of Bilingualism* (Cambridge: Harvard Education Press, 2000), *The Power of Culture: Teaching across Language Difference* (Cambridge: Harvard Education Press, 2002), and *International Perspectives on Youth Conflict and Development* (New York: Oxford University Press, 2006, with Daiute, Nucci, and Higson-Smith).

Michał Bilewicz (michalbilewicz@gmail.com) is Assistant Professor at Faculty of Psychology, University of Warsaw, where he coordinates the Center for Research on Prejudice. Previously he was a DAAD Post-Doctoral Researcher at Friedrich-Schiller-University in Jena (Germany) and Fulbright Visiting Scholar at the New School for Social Research (USA). Michał Bilewicz specializes in the social psychology of inter-group relations. His main research interests include past-related moral emotions (collective guilt, regret, shame), processes of dehumanization, communication on an inter-group level (content of inter-group contact), and issues related to social identity (complex identities, structure of identification, threatened identities). He has published in *Group Processes & Intergroup Relations*, *Journal of Applied Social Psychology* and *Cities*.

Agnieszka Bocheńska (bohem@poczta.onet.pl) is a student of psychology and French studies at University of Warsaw. Her research interests involve topics related to bilingualism, prejudice, inter-group relations, and to the impact of linguistic factors on these relations.

Index

In the series *Discourse Approaches to Politics, Society and Culture* the following titles have been published thus far or are scheduled for publication:

9   RICHARDSON, John E.: (Mis)Representing Islam. The racism and rhetoric of British broadsheet newspapers. 2004. xxiii, 262 pp.

8   MARTIN, J.R. and Ruth WODAK (eds.): Re/reading the past. Critical and functional perspectives on time and value. 2003. vi, 277 pp.

7   ENSINK, Titus and Christoph SAUER (eds.): The Art of Commemoration. Fifty years after the Warsaw Uprising. 2003. xii, 246 pp.

6   DUNNE, Michele Durocher: Democracy in Contemporary Egyptian Political Discourse. 2003. xii, 179 pp.

5   THIESMEYER, Lynn (ed.): Discourse and Silencing. Representation and the language of displacement. 2003. x, 316 pp.

4   CHILTON, Paul and Christina SCHÄFFNER (eds.): Politics as Text and Talk. Analytic approaches to political discourse. 2002. x, 246 pp.

3   CHNG, Huang Hoon: Separate and Unequal. Judicial rhetoric and women's rights. 2002. viii, 157 pp.

2   LITOSSELITI, Lia and Jane SUNDERLAND (eds.): Gender Identity and Discourse Analysis. 2002. viii, 336 pp.

1   GELBER, Katharine: Speaking Back. The free speech versus hate speech debate. 2002. xiv, 177 pp.